BEHAVIORISM:
A CONCEPTUAL RECONSTRUCTION

G. E. Zuriff

BEHAVIORISM:
A Conceptual Reconstruction

COLUMBIA UNIVERSITY PRESS
NEW YORK 1985

Library of Congress Cataloging in Publication Data

Zuriff, G. E. (Gerald E.)
Behaviorism: a conceptual reconstruction.

Bibliography: p.
Includes index.
1. Behaviorism (Psychology) 2. Behaviorism (Psychology)—Philosophy. 3. Behaviorism (Psychology)—History. I. Title.
BF199.Z88 1985 150.19'43 84-12657
ISBN 0-231-05912-4 (alk. paper)
ISBN 0-231-05913-2 (pbk.)

Columbia University Press
New York Guildford, Surrey

Printed in the United States of America

Clothbound editions of Columbia University Press Books are Smyth-sewn and printed on permanent and durable acid-free paper

Book design by Ken Venezio

To My Friends
with a little help from whom I get by

Contents

Preface

This book has been brewing since 1962. As an undergraduate philosophy major at Columbia that year, I decided to learn something about psychology. But the introductory psychology course I took, the notorious one developed by Keller and Schoenfeld, could have been better entitled "An Introduction to Operant Conditioning," because that is what psychology was at Columbia in those days.

Unlike most of my classmates, who grumbled about the narrowness of the course, I found myself intrigued by the behaviorist approach to the mind. My reading of Skinner's *Science and Human Behavior* affected me profoundly, and I chose philosophy of psychology to be my field as it has been ever since. Columbia was a particularly good place to begin, with behaviorism as an aggressive and lively ideology in the psychology department and a renewed interest in the study of mind in the philosophy department.

The next logical step seemed to be Harvard to work with Skinner. By the time I arrived at Harvard, Skinner was retired from active laboratory research, and most of my contact was with Dick Herrnstein. Dick had somehow acquired the quaint notion that psychologists should devote themselves to discovering the laws of behavior rather than fighting the ideological battles of behaviorism. If you nagged him enough, he could talk philosophy of science as well as anyone, but for the most part, my four years in his lab were spent learning how to do good science. Eventually I emerged with several completed experiments in operant conditioning, a couple of publications, a thesis, and a Ph.D.

Concurrent with my work in the lab, I managed to establish some contact with Fred Skinner and to learn about the exciting issues he was pursuing. I also took advantage of the offerings of the Harvard philosophers, including Van Quine and later, Hilary Putnam and Nelson Goodman.

In 1968 I assumed my current position in the Department of Psychology at Wheaton College. Wheaton's liberal attitudes toward research and its supportive collegial atmosphere allowed me the two years of floundering it took to define my intellectual goals. Also at this time, the founding of the journal *Behaviorism* by Willard Day finally provided a ready outlet for my writing which, because of its philosophical orientation, did not find a welcome reception from other journals.

During my first sabbatical, spent in Berkeley, California, I conceived the idea for this book. Upon my return to Wheaton in 1975, I began developing an outline and bibliography. Research began in earnest in 1977. I spent the next four years ensconced in the Psychology Research Library at Harvard University, reading everything written about and by behaviorists. I am indebted to Miss Annelise Katz, Librarian, for her assistance and snacks during that trying period. Bleary-eyed and enriched by hundreds of note cards, I began the actual writing of the book in 1980.

My writing accelerated during the academic year 1981–1982, my second sabbatical, granted and financed by Wheaton College. I was also generously supported by a National Endowment for the Humanities Fellowship for College Teachers. My thanks also to the Department of Psychology and Social Relations at Harvard University which provided me with an office, intellectual stimulation, friendships, and a position as Visiting Scholar that year. Funds to cover the costs of manuscript preparation were provided by a grant from the Mellon Foundation and small grants from the Committee on Faculty Research at Wheaton College.

Portions of the first draft, completed in November, 1982, were read by a number of colleagues: Jim Blight, Dick Herrnstein, Pere Juliá, Drazen Prelec, Howie Rachlin, Fred Skinner, Larry Smith, Mark Snyderman, and Gladys Topkis. My thanks to all of them for their comments and suggestions. A special commendation to Barry Schwartz who was the first person, other than possibly myself, to read the entire manuscript and whose critique was particularly helpful. Incorporating the suggestions of these readers, I completed the final draft in August, 1983. Any deficiencies in the final product are solely the responsibility of these readers, either for not noting the problems or for not persuading me to make the necessary changes.

I am grateful to a number of people who were instrumental in preparing the manuscript: Nancy Shepardson and her staff for much of the early typing, Sue Taylor for her wizardry at word processing, and Leslie Bialler for his skilled editorial pencil. Maggie Vaughan, assisted by her bottle of extra-strength Tylenol, prepared the entire bibliography, a herculean task, performed with dedication and care. My special appreciation goes to Susan Koscielniak and Columbia University Press for their wisdom and courage in deciding to publish this book at a time when other university presses would not even consider a book that is scholarly, behavioristic, and philosophical. I hope Columbia makes a lot of money on it.

On the personal side, I thank Ken Prager and Elizabeth Van Ranst for their continued encouragement and Peggy Rosenthal who got me to stop researching and start writing. Finally, I want to share the joy of this accomplishment with my parents whose love and support were always there for me. They struggled so that I could have the opportunities denied them. The result is a book they do not fully understand but which they fully appreciate.

GERALD ZURIFF

March 12, 1984
Cambridge, Massachusetts

תושלב׳ע

CHAPTER 1

General Overview

Behaviorism is the conceptual framework underlying a particular science of behavior rather than that science itself. This framework consists of a philosophy of science, a philosophy of mind, an empirical background theory, and an ideology. My goal is to present a conceptual reconstruction of behaviorism, beginning with a few fundamental premises and then examining their logical development. In following a logical rather than a chronological order, such a reconstruction differs from a history of behaviorism. Yet, the reconstruction will take into account ideas proposed throughout the history of behaviorism.

Because it is fruitless to look for necessary and sufficient conditions to identify behaviorist ideas, I shall portray a loose family resemblance which characterizes the variety of positions that constitute behaviorism. I shall include both philosophical behaviorism and behavior therapy as members of the behaviorist conceptual family.

In this reconstruction of behaviorism, the fundamental premise is that psychology is a natural science. Two corollaries are that psychology is to be empirically based and that it is to be objective. To a large extent, the reconstruction of behaviorism is the elaboration of what it means for psychology to be empirical and objective.

After dominating American psychology for nearly a half century, behaviorism today finds itself on the defensive. New and competing approaches to psychology have arisen in the wake of advances in psycholinguistics, cognitive science, and philosophy. A reformulation of behaviorism is called for—one that takes into account these critical challenges. Some of them may be integrated into behaviorist thought to create a more sophisticated and viable behaviorism. Others must be either discarded if found wanting or conceded as damaging refutations of aspects of behaviorism.

BEHAVIORISM'S "ISM"

Behaviorism is not the science of behavior developed by behaviorists since the turn of the century. It is, rather, the conceptual framework underlying that science. The science itself, at times called "praxiology," "behavioristics," and "anthroponomy," consists of the findings, principles, laws, and theories formulated through the study of behavior.[1] Behavior*ism,* on the other hand, represents the assumptions, values, and presuppositions implicit in this science.[2]

To articulate the implicit conceptual framework of behaviorism requires a special methodology. For the most part, behaviorists are, and have been, dedicated scientists whose foremost concern is their experimental research and theorizing. Relatively little of their writings is devoted to the explication of the philosophy underlying their research. This was especially true during the decades when American experimental psychology was synonymous with behaviorist psychology, and behaviorism was taken for granted. Therefore, the unearthing of behaviorism is an inductive task. First, an entire corpus of behaviorist research must be scrutinized to find its characteristic features. Then it is necessary to determine the sorts of presuppositions that must underlie the research in order for it to have manifested these features.

Although behaviorism is an integrated framework, it is possible to discern four components. First, behaviorism is a philosophy of science. Before any empirical findings, behaviorism dictates canons concerning what sorts of psychological questions are worth pursuing and what methods are acceptable in searching for answers. Similarly, behaviorist doctrines define what kinds of concepts are acceptable and what form a psychological theory should take. Behaviorism also advocates certain criteria for the adequacy of a scientific explanation. Thus, behaviorism provides a strict framework in which behaviorist scientific activity takes place, thereby determining, *a priori,* important characteristics of the resulting behavioral science.

Second, behaviorism is also a philosophy of mind with certain assumptions about human nature as well as about the essential workings of the mind. This philosophy of mind is interdependent with behaviorist philosophy of science; each justifies the other. Given the assumptions of the behaviorist philosophy of mind, the kinds of methods, theories, and explanations favored by behaviorist philosophy of science appear most appropriate. Conversely, the behaviorist philosophy of science supports its philosophy of mind. A science restricted to a limited set of methods and explanations will tend to confirm a particular conception of mind.[3]

Third, although the emphasis in the present work will be on the conceptual, inextricably interwoven in the fabric of behaviorism are several important empirical assumptions. These very general empirical hypotheses constitute a background theory for behavioral theories that may otherwise differ considerably from one another. These empirical presuppositions consist of a few basic assumptions about behavior and its relationship to the environment and also a set of beliefs about the relative effectiveness of various methods in scientific research and theorizing. The interdependence between behaviorist philosophy of science and philosophy of mind extends to this empirical background theory.

Fourth, behaviorism also represents a certain set of values. It recommends goals for behavioral science and suggests standards for evaluating scientific activity. Values are even more salient with respect to applied behavioral science in which behaviorism promotes applications congruent with particular social aims. Behaviorism must therefore be seen as an ideology as well as a philosophy of psychology. Philosophy and ideology are tightly integrated in behaviorism, and one cannot be fully understood without the other.

These four interdependent components comprise the conceptual framework of behaviorism.[4] A major goal of this book is to explicate this framework. It will not, therefore, be concerned with presenting particular theories of learning or specific methods of behavior modification, except in so far as they illustrate conceptual points.

CONCEPTUAL RECONSTRUCTION

There are several ways in which this goal can be achieved. One might begin by inspecting the best of contemporary behavioral research and constructing a philosophy to characterize and guide it. Although this approach may generate a sound philosophy, it is not true to *behaviorism*. First, it ignores the history of behaviorism over the past seventy years. More important, it misses the diversity of behaviorism. Although behaviorism is a "school" of psychology, it encompasses a variety of philosophical positions, many of which still stand as powerful and interesting approaches to psychology.[5] Thus, by ignoring the past, *de novo* philosophizing adopts the term "behaviorism" only by expropriation while losing the conceptual substance of the term.

A second method of explicating behaviorism is by analyzing its development since its inception and describing the changes in its fundamental ideas over successive periods.[6] Such a historical reconstruction would be true to both the history and diversity of behaviorism. However, this approach has its own disadvantages: it creates difficulties in the analysis of individual conceptual issues, many of which cut across historical periods. A chronological approach misses the abstract continuity that transcends historical demarcations. Furthermore, in a historical reconstruction the emphasis is often on particular figures rather than conceptual themes. Interest shifts to the intellectual development of prominent individuals, the influences acting on them, the consistency of their thought, and the correct interpretation of their writings. Conceptual issues are easily lost in the welter of these historical questions.

This book adopts a third approach, that of conceptual reconstruction. The entire scope of behaviorism, roughly 1910 to the present, is considered, and the reconstruction is organized around conceptual issues rather than historical periods or important individuals. The conceptual framework of behaviorism is elaborated as a logical rather than as a chronological development. It begins with a few fundamental premises, but because the implications of these basic underlying assumptions can be developed in more than one way, the reconstructed conceptual framework is organized more like a branching tree diagram than like an extended linear system. Each node of the tree represents a conceptual choice point, often created by a criticism of behaviorism or by the application of behaviorist analysis to a new question. Each branch growing from a node symbolizes a different behaviorist conceptual decision in response to the choice point. Thus, from an initial set of simple premises, an elaborate, rich, and complex network develops, with branches leading to nodes, and nodes generating further branches. The branching tree image emphasizes that behaviorism is a family of conceptual positions rather than a homogeneous school of psychology.

The justification for this conceptual reconstruction lies in its success in making intelligible the scientific activities of a large number of behavioral psychologists. By explicating the conceptual framework underlying an enormous corpus of research and theory, it imposes a coherence on an important but diverse body of American psychology. Most important, in reconstructing behaviorism in an abstract and coherent way, it exposes both strengths and weaknesses, leading to the formulation of a sound behaviorism to meet the challenges of contemporary psychology and philosophy.

A conceptual reconstruction differs from a history of behaviorism in several respects. First, chronology is not respected, and chronological anomalies abound. For example, a criticism of behaviorism raised in 1970 may be adequately answered by a behaviorist idea appearing in 1920. Second, there is no concern for preserving consistency in the thought of individual behaviorists. As practical scientists, behaviorists are not usually overly concerned with philosophical nuances, nor are they averse to changing their views. Therefore, their pronouncements often reveal ambiguities, contradictions, and gradual changes. Third, the importance of an idea in a conceptual reconstruction may not correspond to its historical significance. Often a position that functions critically within a conceptual reconstruction may have been proposed by someone who had little influence on other behaviorists. Fourth, in a conceptual reconstruction, ideas are examined independent of their original context. Conceptual positions maintained to justify a particular research program or proposed as a defense against a specific criticism are examined in isolation and related to issues they were never intended to address.

THE BEHAVIORIST DIALOGUE

A convenient fiction for understanding the practice of conceptual reconstruction is the "behaviorist dialogue." In an imaginary forum, all behaviorists as well as all their expositors, commentators, and critics, from the beginnings of the movement to the present, are gathered to discuss the major conceptual questions of psychology regardless of whether their lives, in fact, overlapped. Early behaviorists respond to questions which may not have been raised until after their deaths. Behaviorists with no following whatsoever speak with as much right as the most illustrious founders of behaviorist systems. Also present are thinkers whose ideas are highly relevant to the task of conceptual reconstruction although they do not discuss behaviorism directly.

Why include the early behaviorists in the dialogue? To be sure, the science of behavior has made significant strides over the past seventy years, and the behavioral scientists of 1920 have very little of interest to say to their counterparts of today concerning behavioral theory. However, on the conceptual level, behaviorism (and psychology in general) has not shown similar progress. The fundamental questions concerning the nature of psychology have not been answered, nor is it obvious that progress is being made. Instead, certain recurrent themes are discussed, debated into a numbing stillness, and dropped unsettled, only to reappear years later in a different guise and under a new terminology. Therefore, the behaviorist of 1920 may have much of relevance to say to the modern psychologist formulating a conceptual framework for psychology. Indeed, early behaviorist writings often are more explicit on the reasons behind a particular position than later works, which may adhere to a behaviorist tenet out of a sense of loyalty to a school even though the original reasons have long been forgotten or may no longer be valid.

As moderator of the dialogue, I structure the discussion, choosing the issues to be examined and developing their logical implications. As interpreter of the dialogue, I make the discussion accessible to the modern reader. Much of early behaviorist writings appears in an idiom foreign to contemporary ears, and I translate the early terminology and style into the language of today. When necessary I also extrapolate from a behaviorist's position on one issue to the topic under discussion.

As evaluator and arbiter of the dialogue, I attempt the task of constructing a behaviorism that is sound by contemporary standards. Not all the positions articulated in the behaviorist dialogue can be accepted as valid. Some have internal flaws while others are discredited by recent research which has refuted aspects of their empirical background theory. Yet others have not adequately met objections raised by their critics, including other behaviorists. My goal is to prune the behaviorist tree diagram of these weak positions and to note those paths through the diagram which I believe are critically sound.

Although there is more than one valid path through the behaviorist tree diagram, none of them is complete. Behaviorism has not responded fully to the many objections raised to challenge it. In some cases behaviorists have simply been unaware of the challenges. In others, there has not been sufficient time for assimilating and meeting the challenge. As yet, a sound modern behaviorism has not been fully developed. However, I believe that a sound behaviorism generally consistent with the valid positions of traditional behaviorism can be developed. My fourth role, therefore, in addition to moderator, interpreter, and arbiter, is that of active participant in the behaviorist dialogue, filling the conceptual gaps or, at least, pointing in the direction of solutions. More often than not, pointing is all that is possible because the resolution of a conceptual issue often depends on facts as yet unknown or on questions of values and personal preference.

WHO IS A BEHAVIORIST?

A conceptual reconstruction presupposes that behaviorist ideas can be identified before the characterization of behaviorism. But how can we decide whom to admit to the behaviorist dialogue without first knowing the results of that dialogue? Ideally what is needed is a set of necessary and sufficient conditions for an idea to qualify as behavioristic. However, given the diversity of behaviorist views, no such conditions exist.[7] The intellectual commitments shared by all behaviorists are so broad that they are held also by most nonbehaviorist and even antibehaviorist schools of experimental psychology. Conversely, although it is possible to formulate a particular behaviorist position that is clearly distinct from every nonbehaviorist psychology, this position would not accurately describe the views of a large number of behaviorists.[8]

A more fruitful approach is suggested by Wittgenstein's concept of "family resemblance."[9] In looking at a photograph of a large family, one may note that although not every family member has the same nose, or eyes, or mouth, there is a similarity of features that constitutes the family resemblance. Each family member shares the resemblance even though there is no one feature that characterizes each and every member. Some members show the family "look" very strongly; others, so weakly that they appear as belonging to the family only in the context of the photograph.

So too behaviorists can be viewed as sharing a family resemblance. Although they cannot be identified by a strict set of necessary and sufficient properties, they can be recognized by their common family resemblance: a set of overlapping features, some related by ties of similarity and some by historical association. Some of these features are more important and relevant than others for defining behaviorism. An idea may be said to be a "central" family trait of behaviorism if: (1) it is shared by a large number of behaviorists, and (2) it appears early in the *logical* (not chronological) development of the behaviorist tree diagram and therefore plays a major role in determining the nature of subsequent choice points and branching positions. A position without these characteristics may be said to be "peripheral." Many peripheral positions lie on the border between behaviorism and another school, often resembling the latter more than the former.

To recognize the family resemblance the equivalent of a family photograph is needed.[10] The portrait of behaviorism as drawn by its critics cannot be used for this purpose since the result would be merely a picture of a group of scowling strawmen. Nor should the photograph include everyone who has ever claimed to be a behaviorist; self-identification as a behaviorist is not a sufficient condition for inclusion in the behaviorist family.[11] Conversely, rejection of behaviorism is not a sufficient condition for exclusion. Major behaviorists have on occasion dissociated themselves from the label "behaviorist" to distinguish their positions from those of their behaviorist colleagues while maintaining theories that, in retrospect, are clearly behavioristic.[12] In addition, critics of one version of behaviorism have occasionally espoused points of view congruent with other versions. Thus, an idea historically presented as "antibehaviorist" may find its way into the behaviorist family.

Even without any clear-cut criteria for identifying members of the behaviorist family, a small number of psychologists are universally recognized as behaviorists. Among the early behaviorists this group includes J. B. Watson (1878–1958), the founder and popularizer of the movement, and A. P. Weiss (1879–1931), a vigorous early champion of behaviorism. As behaviorism developed from a programmatic philosophy of psychology into a conceptual basis for well-developed psychological theories, "neobehaviorists" appeared with competing theories of behavior. Prominent among these are E. R. Guthrie (1886–1959), E. C. Tolman (1886–1959), C. L. Hull (1884–1952), K. W. Spence (1907–1967), and B. F. Skinner (1904–).

From an examination of the works of this small prototype group, a family resemblance emerges. If additional ideas which share the resemblance are added, the structure is slightly altered, thereby allowing for the incorporation of still other ideas. Eventually a broad behaviorist conceptual family develops, and that resulting family resemblance is characterized in this book. This final characterization of behaviorism may not coincide perfectly with initial intuitions. For example, the theories of Tolman, one of the original "prototype" behaviorists, appear on the periphery of the behaviorist conceptual family as finally characterized, rather than at its center.

Philosophers and Clinicians

Two groups of behaviorists deserve special mention. First is a group of philosophers whose approach to psychology is closely related to that of behaviorist psychologists. Some of them developed a philosophy of mind in which mental concepts are to be understood in terms of observable behavior rather than private consciousness. Because this philosophy of mind, known as "analytic behaviorism," is congenial to psychological behaviorism, some behaviorist psychologists borrow from analytic behaviorists, such as Ryle and Wittgenstein, in formulating their conceptual positions.[13]

Other philosophical behaviorists were more concerned with philosophy of science. These philosophers, known as "logical behaviorists," include logical positivists such as Carnap and Hempel.[14] They attempted to develop canons to ensure the empiricalness and meaningfulness of scientific statements. Because these concerns are shared by behaviorist psychologists, many behaviorists show the influence of logical behaviorism, especially during the period when American philosophy of science was dominated by logical positivism.

Philosophical behaviorists perceived no important alliance with psychological behaviorism because they identified it with Watson's early brand of behaviorism. However, later and more sophisticated versions of behaviorism have much in common with philosophical behaviorism. For this reason, the various versions of philosophical behaviorism are here included in the behaviorist conceptual family.

A second group of behaviorists meriting special attention consists of behavior therapists. In fact, today the term "behaviorist" is often identified with behavior modification in the mind of the general public. In its beginnings, behavior therapy, or behavior modification, grew out of behaviorist science. The early therapy techniques were closely related, in name if not in fact, to the methods, findings, and theories of behaviorist learning theory. Similarly, the philosophy of science underlying early behavior therapy had much in common with that of behaviorist experimental psychology. As behavior therapy developed, however, its techniques, methods, and philosophy became increasingly diverse. Today some of the many versions of behavior therapy continue to share a strong family resemblance with behaviorism while others belong only on the periphery of the behaviorist family and have only the most tenuous ties with behaviorism.[15] Therefore, in the present reconstruction of behaviorism, some ideas associated with behavior therapy are presented as behaviorist positions and others are considered criticisms of behaviorism.

PSYCHOLOGY IS A SCIENCE

The first premise in the conceptual reconstruction of behaviorism—the opening statement of the behaviorist dialogue—can be found in the first sentence of Watson's famous article "Psychology as the Behaviorist Views It," the formal beginning of behaviorism:

> Psychology as the behaviorist views it is a purely objective experimental branch of natural science. Its theoretical goal is . . . prediction and control. . . . (1913a, p. 158)

The premise is clearly enunciated: Psychology is a natural science.[16] All the remaining conceptual reconstruction of behaviorism is essentially an elaboration of what it means for psychology to be a natural science.

In describing psychology as a "branch of natural science," the passage implies some sort of unity among the various sciences. Although the sciences may differ from one another in their subject matter and their special techniques, they have a commonality that makes it possible to see the various sciences as "branches" of natural science. Thus, behaviorism sees a continuity among the sciences, and between psychology and the other biological sciences in particular.

The passage also associates science with prediction and control. One way of interpreting this is that behaviorists are suggesting a useful goal for their science. A stronger interpretation is that prediction and control are proposed as the defining characteristics of their science, or even of science in general. That is, an activity is judged as "scientific" to the extent that it contributes to the prediction and control of phenomena.

The last sentence of the quoted passage reads in full: "Its theoretical goal is the prediction and control *of behavior.*" I omitted "of behavior" because the belief that behavior is the subject matter of psychology occurs later in the conceptual reconstruction. From the mere premise that psychology is a science, it does not follow that behavior is the only possible subject matter. Such a conclusion follows from the initial premise only in conjunction with several other corollaries, two of which are especially noteworthy.

The first is that science, and psychology in particular, must be empirically based.[17] This corollary is developed in great detail in the course of the conceptual reconstruction. For now, the corollary can be interpreted in very general terms. The empiricalness of psychology will be taken to mean that the fundamental facts of psychology are to be derived through the senses, preferably through careful perception, and ideally through experimentally controlled observation. The corollary of empiricalness excludes the kinds of knowledge derived from nonempirical sources such as mystical revelation, empathy, intuition, religious dogma, innate ideas, and authority.

The second corollary is that science, and psychology in particular, must be objective.[18] The meaning of objectivity for behaviorism, like the meaning of empiricalness, is apparent only in the context of the full reconstruction of behaviorism. At this point, objectivity will be taken to mean simply that psychology should be independent of the individual prejudices, tastes, and private opinions of the scientist. Statements of findings and theories should therefore be as precise and unambiguous as possible so they are not subject to diverse individual interpretations.

Many of the methods excluded by the empiricalness criterion, such as empathy and intuition, are also excluded by the objectivity criterion. Methods sanctioned by the former are generally also acceptable by the latter. Results of empirical methods are objective in that they are open to anyone's observation and do not depend on the subjective belief of an individual scientist. Nevertheless, objectivity and empiricalness are not the same. For example, as is discussed in the next chapter, introspection, as a method for acquiring knowledge about the mind, has been considered by some to be empirical and yet nonobjective. The two corollaries will therefore be kept distinct. Together the two support Watson's view of psychology as a "purely objective experimental branch of natural science."

SYNOPSIS

To a striking degree, the conceptual reconstruction of behaviorism is the elaboration of the fundamental premise that psychology is a branch of natural science given the two corollaries of empiricalness and objectivity. Part I (chapters 2–5) discusses how this premise and its corollaries develop into behaviorist views on the structure of science. Behaviorist science is founded on observation, and chapter 2 shows how the canons of objectivity and empiricalness dictate what types of observation are acceptable by behaviorist standards and why introspection is rejected. Chapter 3 examines behaviorist views on how observations are to be transformed into data reports that retain empiricalness and objectivity. In chapters 4 and 5, behaviorist notions about the nature of psychological theory are explored, concentrating on the question of what sorts of theory can guide research and at the same time maintain empirical links and objectivity.

Part II (chapters 6–8) looks at the major behaviorist assumptions about the nature of behavior, that is, behaviorism's background theory. Chapter 6 discusses various meanings of "stimulus-response psychology" and rejects nearly all of them in favor of a very broad definition compatible with behaviorist premises. Chapter 7 defends this broad conception of stimulus-response psychology against two major objections: (1) the contention that behavior is organized by purposive principles incompatible with the principles of stimulus-response psychology and (2) the psycholinguistic challenge that the organization of verbal behavior cannot be accounted for by stimulus-response principles. Chapter 8 discusses how stimulus-response psychology, broadly conceived, approaches complex psychological processes and defends this approach against the objections raised by cognitivism.

Part III (chapters 9–12) is concerned with behaviorist attempts to deal with mental concepts in a scientific way. Chapter 9 explains why behaviorism rejects the concept of a self and how this concept can be replaced in behaviorist theory. Chapters 10 and 11 review behaviorist treatments of mentalistic language when it is used to describe others (chapter 10) or when it is used to talk about one's own mind (chapter 11). Finally, chapter 12 presents a behaviorist theory of knowledge loosely derived from behaviorist psychology. This psychologically based epistemology closely links behaviorism to the intellectual traditions of positivism and pragmatism. The thesis that behaviorism can be understood as a psychological pragmatic positivism is then used to characterize the behaviorist conceptual family resemblance and to make intelligible fundamental behaviorist assumptions about science, empiricalness, and objectivity.

PART I

THE SCIENCE

CHAPTER 2

Observation: The Case Against Introspection

For behaviorism, psychology is to be based on scientific observation, but introspective observation of the phenomenal world is not acceptable. Behaviorists offer a variety of objections to introspection; one is that introspection is especially prone to error and distortion. However, proponents of introspection reply that it can be as objective as any other kind of observation when carried out properly. A second objection is that introspection's subject matter, consciousness, is not objective. This criticism, however, is not decisive because it is based on unsupported metaphysical notions of objectivity.

Another objection is that introspective observations are private and unverifiable. One reply to this objection is that introspective observations can be verified indirectly. However, this reply can be rejected because introspective observations logically do not lend themselves to indirect verification in the way other kinds of observations do. A second reply is to deny the private-public distinction and argue either that all observation, including introspection, is public, or that all observation, including observation of the physical environment, is ultimately private.

A fourth objection is that introspective reports do not achieve intersubjective agreement. The distinction between subjective and objective is thus replaced by the distinction between subjective and intersubjective. Introspection's lack of intersubjectivity may be an empirical contingent fact, or it might be a necessary truth based on the logical impossibility of a private language. A fifth objection is based on a theory of how verbal reports of private events are learned and maintained. This theory suggests that such reports are unreliable.

The joint criteria of objectivity and empiricalness discussed in the preceding chapter are intended to exclude psychological methods such as intuition, empathy, anthropomorphism, and psychoanalytic interpretation as means of data collection.[1] How then is the mind to be studied? One traditional answer to this question is that one can, through a kind of inward observation known as "introspection," acquire knowledge about one's own mind. Proponents of introspection maintain that one has better and more direct access to one's own mind than to objects in the environment.[2] In contrast to the senses, which often deceive, direct introspective knowledge is more likely to be veridical.[3]

Behaviorism, however, rejects introspection as a method of observation for a variety of reasons.[4] Thus, the first node in the behaviorist conceptual tree diagram is the rejection of introspection, and the branches leading from this node are the various reasons for this rejection. This chapter will examine and evaluate each of these branches, and in so doing, will clarify behaviorist conceptions of empiricalness and scientific objectivity.

OBJECTION 1: IT DOES NOT WORK

One common criticism of introspection is that it is internally flawed and does not achieve what it claims. For example, it is often noted that, as Freud demonstrated, much of what is of psychological significance is either unconscious or else distorted by the defense mechanisms. Therefore, introspection is neither a revealing nor an objective method.[5] It is also argued that introspection is really "retrospection" because the introspector is actually reporting from error-prone memory, not current direct experience.[6] A third objection is that introspection is an unreliable method because introspectors are often inconsistent and vague in their reports.[7] Because of these internal weaknesses, it appears that introspection does not qualify as an objective method.

Reply

Proponents of introspection do not find these criticisms overwhelming. They argue that any method of observation is subject to distortion and error. They maintain that objectivity lies in the care with which an observation is carried out, and introspection can be implemented with as much care as any other method. Introspectors may be highly trained, the introspections may be conducted under rigorously controlled circumstances, and the procedures used may be specified precisely.[8] Thus, if behaviorists argue that introspection is not objective, they must mean "objective" in some sense other than unbiased and unprejudiced by personal taste.[9]

OBJECTION 2: ITS CONTENTS ARE NOT OBJECTIVE

Perhaps a more compelling objection to introspection is the behaviorist allegation that its subject matter is not objective. Normal scientific observation has as its object the physical universe, while introspection studies the impalpable mental world. The physical universe is objective in that it possesses spatial location external to the mind, is independent of the observer's state, and is relatively stable and enduring. In contrast, the phenomenal world of consciousness exists only within the mind, possesses no spatial location, depends on the state of the observer, is ever changing, and is ephemeral.[10] Hence it is a subjective world, and its observation, through introspection, is perforce a subjective technique.[11]

This objection coincides with two fundamental behaviorist attitudes. The first is the general behaviorist suspicion of consciousness. For many behaviorists, consciousness, as some nonphysical substance, is to be rejected as a residue from earlier unscientific mystical belief in spirit or soul.[12] Second, as mentioned in the preceding chapter, an important behaviorist family trait is the attitude that psychology should be continuous with the rest of science. According to this attitude, all science, including psychology, has the same subject matter, namely the material universe; the various sciences differ only in their area of specialization. For psychology the domain is the behavior of organisms. However, if the object of introspection is nonmaterial consciousness, then the domain of psychology differs radically from that of the other sciences, and the behaviorist hope for the unity of science must be abandoned.[13]

Reply

However, this objection is not decisive. First, the object of introspection need not be construed as consciousness. First-person reports about feelings and sensations are interpreted by many behaviorists and nonbehaviorists alike a reports about physical events occurring within the body.[14] Thus, introspection may be viewed as an empirical method for observing objects and events that are just as physical as overt behavior. The only major difference between introspection and observation of behavior is that the former observes events within the skin and makes use of the intereoceptive sensory system while the latter observes phenomena on the outside of the skin through the extereoceptive system.[15]

Even if the object of introspection is taken to be consciousness, the behaviorist objection faces a second difficulty: It is based on unsupported metaphysical theses. First, it asserts that consciousness is ontologically suspect but offers in support what appear to be circular arguments: Consciousness is not objective; therefore, introspection, the method of observing it, is invalid; therefore, consciousness, known only through introspection is not an objective topic of inquiry.[16] If the ontological inferiority of consciousness is to support the rejection of introspection, then this inferiority must be argued independently of the validity of introspection. Second, the comparison between consciousness and an external objective physical world independent of human experience is based on the unsupported metaphysical thesis that such a world exists.[17] The introspectionist is not inclined to grant the behaviorist metaphysical theses, for to do so is to exclude phenomenal experience from the purview of science.[18]

Two Sciences with Two Subject Matters

One possible resolution of this disagreement between introspectionists and those behaviorists who reject consciousness as a possible subject matter is for psychology to subdivide into two sciences. One would be the science of behavior, the other the science of experience.[19] For the behaviorist, the science of experience would be discontinuous with the other sciences because its subject matter and its method of introspection are unique. However, if experience can be studied scientifically and introspection is the only appropriate method, then the unity of science is a small sacrifice to make in order to acquire important scientific knowledge.

Furthermore, according to many introspectionists, unity of science does not have to be abandoned even if a science of experience is pursued. They contend that the unity of science derives from the fact that ultimately all science deals with the private experience of the individual observer. The only distinction between a science of experience and the others is to be found in the attitude of the observer, not in the subject matter.[20] In the science of experience, private experience is studied from the perspective of its being dependent upon the observer while in the other sciences that same subject matter, private experience, is investigated from the perspective of its being independent of the observer.[21] Whether this difference in perspective is nevertheless sufficient to undermine the unity of science depends largely on what are seen as the fundamental hallmarks of science.

OBJECTION 3: IT IS PRIVATE

For many behaviorists, an important hallmark of science is its public nature. A scientific observation is available to all, at least in principle, so in a sense, observations can be shared.[22] As Guthrie (1950) expresses it:

> What appeals to me as the outstanding aim and requirement of science [is] its public character—its foundation in human communication, not merely in the private experience of individuals. When Whitehead says theory must agree with experience, the only test of that agreement and the ultimate meaning of that agreement is its shareable character. Scientific observations must be repeatable by others. (p. 99)

In contrast, an introspection is private and can be carried out only by the one whose experience is being observed. Because the data are not directly available to anyone else, they are not publicly shared. While an animal's speed can be observed and measured by many experimenters, the intensity of a pain can be directly observed by only one introspector. Hebb (1958) is quite explicit:

> *Public*, or *objective evidence* is defined as evidence which might be obtained equally well by any of a number of observers: in most cases, evidence which two or more observers can record at the same time. *Private*, or *subjective*, or *introspective evidence* concerns events within the observer himself, and by nature of things available to that one observer only. (p. 4)

If "subjective" is equated with "private" and "objective" is identified with "public," then introspection does not qualify as an objective method of observation.[23] A science based on introspection is, therefore, not possible.

Verifiability

That introspections are private results in an important consequence: Reports of introspective observation cannot possibly be verified by other observers. There is no way for another observer to check the accuracy of the report since only one person has access to the data. In contrast, with public data, verification is always a possibility, at least in principle. The reports of an observer can be checked by others, and the observation thereby gains in credibility. "Objective" can therefore be identified with "verifiable" as well as "public." Observations which cannot be verified, even in principle, depend solely on trust in the one observer for acceptance, and therefore may be said to lack objectivity. Therefore, introspection can be rejected as unverifiable as well as private.[24]

It should be noted that there are really two types of verification, both of which introspection lacks. First, there is the kind of verification that occurs when several observers examine the same event simultaneously. In the second kind of verification, replication, the observations are successive rather than simultaneous. In either case, verification is achieved when the observation reports coincide. Both kinds of verification are possible with observations of behavior. With introspection neither kind is. Observers cannot simultaneously or successively observe the same private experience. Although several people may be experiencing pain, they are not experiencing the *same* pain. Pains, as experiences, are inherently private. Therefore, the congruence of reports among the experiencers of pain or over successive experiences of pain does not verify the report of any one of them. Each is a report of a numerically different experience.

Thus, the impossibility of verification by either simultaneous observation or successive replication is ultimately a logical consequence of the private nature of introspection. If science is to deal exclusively with verifiable and therefore public data, then introspective observation is not a method for obtaining scientific data. This is not to say that private data do not exist or that they cannot be known but only that as far as science is concerned, such data are unacceptable.[25] As de Laguna (1919b) states it:

Behaviorism, as a scientific theory, and not a metaphysical doctrine, is not concerned with the question whether or not there be conscious processes which are hidden from all but one. Its contention is merely that if there be such processes they can not by the very nature of the case be objects of scientific study. For it is an essential condition of scientific investigation of any phenomenon that observations made by one individual shall be verifiable by others. (p. 297)

Psychological introspection is then to be distinguished from ordinary "objective" observation just because it is the observation of that which is essentially private and incommunicable. (p. 299)

Prima facie, the exclusion from science of data which cannot be verified by others makes good intuitive sense.[26] Objectivity in science would seem to demand that data not be accepted solely on the basis of claims by a single observer. Data must be subject to scrutiny by others who can check, confirm, or disconfirm them. If objectivity does not lie in the ontological nature of what is observed, it can at least be found in the guarantee that what is accepted as an observation does not rely on the unverifiable judgment of a single individual.

Reply 1: Indirect Verification

This objection to introspective observation assumes that observation reports can be verified only by shared or replicated observation. However, in practice, there are many other kinds of verification. Consider Jones who testifies that he saw Smith at Park Square at noon on Monday. Assume there are no other witnesses. By hypothesis, then, Jones' report is based on an observation by only one observer. Yet Jones' report is not unverifiable. There may be many bits of evidence to support or contradict his observation, and these pieces of evidence have an important bearing on the likelihood that Jones is accurate. For example, suppose Smith's fingerprints and a button from Smith's jacket are found at Park Square. Or, another witness might report that he saw Smith headed in the direction of Park Square at 11:45 A.M. on Monday. Moreover, character witnesses might testify that Jones is a man of good moral character, a keen observer, and has no motive to lie about Smith. More and more facts could be added to this account until the point is reached at which Jones' observation report is accepted as supported beyond a reasonable doubt. Of course, it cannot be shown that *no* doubt is possible, but even in the case where many observers share a public observation and agree in their reports, there is also still room for unreasonable doubt if a skeptic demands. Thus, Jones' testimony is an example in which an observation by a single observer is verifiable even in the absence of shared observation and replication.

By analogy, a supporter of introspection could argue, although introspective observations are carried out only by a single observer, the resulting observational reports can be indirectly verified.[27] Jones' report that he is experiencing feelings of hunger might be tested by observing whether he eats food when it is offered. Further evidence might come from information about how long Jones has gone without food. Moreover, Jones may be known to be an honest individual with no reason to lie about his hunger. Eventually, enough evidence might be adduced to confirm (or disconfirm) Jones' introspective observation beyond a reasonable doubt even though only Jones can observe his own feelings of hunger. Therefore, argues the introspectionist, introspective observation meets scientific standards of objectivity.

The Rejection of Indirect Verification. This introspectionist reply is based on an analogy between indirect confirmation in cases of observations which logically can be public but which in fact are not (e.g., Jones' observation of Smith) and observations which logically cannot be public (e.g., Jones' introspection of his feelings of hunger). However, a central disanalogy between the two calls into question the introspectionist claim to scientific respectability. The two differ fundamentally with regard to the relationship between the evidence and the report it supports. With public observations this relationship is based on empirically determined regularities which are themselves established by public observations. Thus, for example, the finding of Smith's fingerprints is evidence supporting Jones' report because of empirically observed correlations between fingerprints and a person's location. These correlations are publicly observable and verifiable. With private introspections, however, the relationship between public evidence and private observation is different. In order for Jones' publicly observable eating behavior (or indeed any kind of publicly observable event) to serve as evidence to support his report of hunger, it is necessary to establish a correlation between the two. However, to accomplish this, observation of the two is required. Hunger, rather than mere reports of hunger, must be observed and correlated with behavior. However, by hypothesis, hunger can be observed only by private observation, and the validity of such observation is precisely the question at issue.

Thus, the introspectionist reply begs the question: Introspective observation is claimed to be an objectively valid method because introspective reports can be indirectly verified, but introspective reports can be indirectly verified only if introspective observation is assumed to be a valid method. Similarly, Jones' accuracy can be known only by examining the correlation between his reports and the objects of his reports. However, only the former are publicly observable. To be sure, it can be shown that Jones is a trained and accurate observer of publicly available events. But to infer from this that Jones is also to be trusted in his private observations is again to beg the question and to assume the essential similarity between public and private observation.

This disanalogy between public and private with respect to indirect verification of observational reports derives from a logically more basic difference.

With publicly observable data, although there are many instances in which only one observer has access to the observation, logically, the observation is open to many. Therefore, correlations can be established by publicly verified observations, so that on those occasions when only one observer is available, the observational report can be indirectly verified by publicly observable evidence. However, with introspection, the observations are logically private. Therefore, correlations between the observations and publicly observable events cannot be established, and publicly observable events cannot be used for indirect verification of the introspective report.

Reply 2: Denial of the Public-Private Distinction

The behaviorist objection to introspective observation on the grounds that it is private and therefore unverifiable is predicated on the distinction between private and public. However, this distinction is itself open to criticism. Consider a paradigm case of public observation. Ten trained psychologists observe a rat, and all ten report that the rat has pressed a lever. Contrast this with ten sociologists who simultaneously touch a hot stove, and all ten report pain. Only the former case is conceptualized as an instance of public observation: All ten psychologists are considered to be observing the same things, the same movements of the same rat. The latter case is conceptualized as private observation: Each participant is viewed as experiencing only a separate individual pain. While there is only one public rat in the former case, there are ten separate private pains in the latter. However, it is not obvious why this is so.

All Observations Are Public. We say that the ten psychologists hear the same clicking sound of the depressed lever, feel the same furriness of the rat, and see its white color; why then do we not say that the sociologists feel the same pain of the hot stove? Is it not simply the behaviorist metaphysical bias which asserts that only the external physical world is real and therefore shareable while the phenomenal world is only in the mind and therefore private?[28] If this metaphysical bias in favor of the physical is rejected, then phenomenal reports are seen to be verifiable. An introspector's report of a painful sensation when touching a hot stove can be verified by having others experience that sensation.[29] Thus the private-public distinction at the base of the behaviorist objection to introspective data can itself be rejected by introspectionists who argue that introspective data are public.

However, this argument against the public-private distinction raises serious problems for the supporters of introspective data. Assume that an introspector A reports sensation S occurs under conditions C but that other introspectors report that S does not occur under conditions C. If it is maintained that introspective data are public, then the report of A has been disconfirmed, and the conclusion is that A did not observe sensation S. In practice, however, introspective studies do not generally draw such conclusions. Instead it is assumed that because of individual differences, introspectors may provide different reports even under the same circumstances. Hence, the divergent report is not disconfirmed and is assumed rather to reflect an individual difference. Thus, undermining the public-private distinction by construing all observation as public conflicts with the actual practice of introspective research.[30]

All Observations Are Private. Alternatively, the introspectionist can deny the distinction by arguing that all observation is private. Return to the ten psychologists observing the rat: Why do we say that all observe the "same" rat? Why do we not say that each is observing only a private experience of the rat? Indeed, from the optics of the situation it is known that each has a different perspective of the rat, and in that sense does not see the same thing. Furthermore, physiology tells us that the psychologists are responding to the effects of ten different sets of light rays impinging on ten different systems of visual receptors. Why not conclude that there are ten percepts of the rat just as there are ten pains?

Taking the argument a step further, an introspectionist can claim that all observation is based on private experience. Knowledge of the external world is in reality an inference from the immediate but private percept with which the observer is in direct contact. All observation is thus private observation, and the public-private distinction of the behaviorist therefore fails. Contrary to behaviorist claims, science does involve, and indeed ultimately depends on, the private experience of the scientist.[31] Verification is not via shared public experience but rather through the congruence of private experiences. Thus one scientist can verify the reports of another only because private percepts as reported by the first scientist agree with the private percepts of the second.

In response to this argument that all observation is ultimately private, behaviorists present various counterarguments. One is simply to deny the premise that, strictly speaking, observation is never of external physical objects but is rather of private experience. Many behaviorists adhere to a realist position and maintain that, contrary to introspectionism, the external world is directly observed and known.[32] Some behaviorists label the introspectionist premise the "Copy Theory" because it posits that the organism must first create internally a copy of the external world before it can come to know the external world. Objections to the Copy Theory emphasize its incoherence: it cannot satisfactorily account for how the organism constructs the copy or how the copy is observed once it is somehow constructed.[33] Yet other behaviorists argue that the very notion of observation of private experience is a conceptual error. The concept of observation is logically tied to the paradigmatic case in which physical objects are observed. Whether or not private occurrences are involved in these paradigmatic cases is irrelevant. Extension of the concept to private experience is a category mistake because the logic of the concept does not apply.[34]

OBJECTION 4: IT DOES NOT ACHIEVE INTERSUBJECTIVE AGREEMENT

Another behaviorist response to the claim that all observation is ultimately private is to grant the claim but to substitute a methodological distinction for the original public-private distinction. Some behaviorists distinguish between the world of immediate experience and the world constructed out of it. It is the latter world that is selected as the subject matter of science.[35] Tolman (1935) draws the distinction in these terms:

> Immediate experience, as initially given . . . is an initial, common matrix out of which both physics and psychology are evolved. . . . Physics does not present another real behind that of immediate experience. Nor does psychology, as such, study this real of immediate experience in a more firsthand way than does physics. Physics is a set of logical constructs. . . . Psychology is . . . but another such set of logical constructs . . . . There is still left . . . in my universe a dichotomy, but it is a dichotomy not between physical entities, and mental entities, but between both of these as mere logical constructs, on the one hand, and immediate experience as the actually given, rich, qualified, diffuse, matrix from which both sciences are evolved, on the other. (pp. 359–360)

This distinction corresponds closely to the introspectionist distinction between "mediate" (or constructed) and "immediate" experience. However, whereas the introspectionists founded a science on reports of immediate experience, behaviorists who accept the distinction argue that in selecting a data base for a scientific psychology, only reports about mediate experience are acceptable. Their justification for this claim is methodological. Behaviorists reason that science is ultimately a social enterprise, and its success is heavily dependent on communication and cooperation within a community of scientists. A key element in fostering this cooperation is the choice of a data base that affords the greatest possible degree of agreement and communication among observers. If scientists cannot communicate and agree about their basic observations, there is little hope for scientific progress.

Thus, intersubjective agreement and communication are critical criteria in selecting a data base.[36] Reports about the physical world meet these criteria. Observers, for example, tend to agree and communicate easily over whether a rat has pressed a lever. In contrast, reports about phenomenal experience do not meet the test of intersubjective agreement and communication, even under controlled conditions. Spence (1957) develops the argument this way:

> I would propose to accept as the criterion for the selection of this basic [descriptive] vocabulary of psychology the methodological requirement that its terms designate a class of observations (items or aspects of experiential data) that display the highest possible degree of intersubjective consistency. By degree of intersubjective consis-

tency is meant the extent to which there is agreement among observers concerning a particular observable datum. . . . Such objective data or *public* experiences are to be contrasted with the subjective data or *private* experiences that are obtained by the kind of observation that psychologists call introspection or self-observation. These latter experiences . . . do not satisfactorily meet the criterion of intersubjective observational consistency. (pp. 99–100)

Thus, introspective data can be rejected on purely methodological grounds. No metaphysical considerations enter because the critical agreement is among observational reports and not between report and reality.[37] Public-private becomes intersubjective-subjective.

This Failure as an Empirical Fact

Opinion is divided as to why phenomenal reports fail to meet the criteria of intersubjective agreement and communication. Some have argued that this failure is a contingent empirical finding rather than a logical necessity.[38] It is therefore subject to empirical disconfirmation. Indeed, an introspectionist might well argue that there is not much evidence to support the conclusion that introspection has failed and behaviorist forms of observation have succeeded in meeting standards of intersubjective agreement. Certainly no careful comparative study has been performed to determine the exact degree of intersubjective agreement achieved by various forms of observation.

Moreover, such a study is not even possible unless the concept of "intersubjective agreement" is more precisely defined. What degree is necessary? How is agreement to be measured? Who exactly are the observers who must "agree"?[39] If a random selection of the adult population is meant, then surely the study would not find the expected results. Many observations in the natural sciences are so complex and require so much training (e.g., observations of a microscope slide) that the agreement likely to be achieved among randomly selected observers will be quite small. On the other hand, if the observers are highly trained and have a good deal of experience in the science, then not only will agreement be high among natural scientists, but agreement is also likely to be high among highly trained and experienced introspectors.[40] Thus, the empirical hypothesis that introspective observation has failed to achieve intersubjective agreement is far from being empirically confirmed and should not deter the introspectionist from pursuing a science of phenomenal experience.

This Failure as Logical Fact

On the other hand, the failure to achieve intersubjective agreement might be a logically necessary truth rather than an empirical hypothesis. In a purely phenomenal science, introspective reports refer exclusively to aspects of the introspector's private experience rather than to aspects of the publicly observable world. Indeed, an introspector who does refer to the publicly observable world is committing what is termed the "stimulus error." Therefore, the introspector's observational reports are formulated in a private language, i.e., one which refers exclusively to private experience. However, it is not clear whether a private language is logically possible.[41]

The argument against private language hinges on the logical fact that for a term "Y" to refer to X, there must be a notion of what an X is and when it recurs. With natural languages, there is a general consensus among a community about what an X is, and therefore, the term "Y" conveys meaning to the members of that community. However, with a private language there are no criteria for what an X is and when it can be said to recur. The introspector is the sole judge of when an event is to be considered an X. The introspector's report "Y" conveys no meaning to a listener because the listener does not know in what respect the event now occurring is the same as the event occurring when the introspector last said "Y" or next says "Y." The events are the "same" only in so far as the introspector thinks they are the same. Therefore, the introspector cannot logically be mistaken in reporting "Y." But if mistakes are not logically possible, then correct identification is also not logically possible. Therefore, there is no concept of what an X is or when it recurs, and the term "Y" does not refer. It follows that a private language is not a language at all.

The argument can be restated in psychological terms. Imagine that a pigeon's response has been rewarded in the presence of a particular stimulus, S. Next a sequence of stimuli is presented to the pigeon. If an observer has seen the first stimulus, S, but does not see any of the later stimuli, what can the observer infer about the stimulus currently displayed to the pigeon given that the pigeon is responding? There are an infinite number of ways in which the pigeon might be generalizing from the original stimulus S to the present stimulus. They might be of a similar color, size, shape, distance, or any of an infinite number of attributes. Indeed they may have nothing more in common than that they are both presentations.

In fact, whatever set of stimuli the pigeon responds to can always be found to have *some* property in common just because *any* set of objects can be found to have something in common. Therefore, any response is correct in the sense that the stimulus responded to will be the same as S in *some* respect. Clearly an observer can infer nothing about the current stimulus from the pigeon's response. Just as the pigeon's identification response conveys no information about the stimuli to an observer of the response, in the same way the introspector's response "Y" conveys no information to a listener about the introspector's phenomenal world. To be sure, the listener can infer that the introspector's current experience is the "same" as the experience the introspector had at the last report "Y," but in the absence of any criterion of sameness, this inference says nothing.

Thus if a private language is logically impossible then an intersubjective science of the private phenomenal world is also impossible. The behaviorist conclusion, therefore, is that although all empirical knowledge derives ultimately from the private experiential matrix of the individual scientist, the constructed public world, rather than that matrix, is the subject matter of science, and hence of psychology. Only study of the former can achieve the intersubjective agreement and communication required by science.

Private Language and the Experiential Matrix

It is important to interpret carefully what is being asserted by those behaviorists who maintain that individual experience is the matrix out of which all observations proceed. This position is certainly not a dualism of mind and matter. Instead, to state that all observations are ultimately private is in a sense to state a truism. For a subject to observe or know the external world, it is necessary for that subject to interact with the object of observation. The set of events constituting this interaction, M, can be conceived in many ways. For example, M can be conceptualized as the set of physiological events occurring when energy from the object impinges on the subject's sense receptors. Alternately, M can be viewed as the mental processes occurring when the object produces sensations in the subject's mind.

Under either interpretation, M can be conceptualized as "private" in the sense that the interaction of subject A with object X is to be designated M_{AX} and is not to be considered identical to the interaction M_{BX} of subject B with the same object X. Therefore, it follows that knowledge or observation of an object can always be said to be "mediated by a private process." However, this conclusion does not state an empirical finding but rather can be interpreted as a stipulation or recommendation on how talk about observation ought to be carried on. Nor does it entail anything about the ontological status of this private process. Therefore, a behaviorist who acknowledges that all observations are mediated by "private experience" does not thereby necessarily postulate a phenomenal world ontologically distinct from the material world.[42]

Nor does the decision to talk about private experience M_{AX} entail that A's talk about the object X is really talk about the private event M_{AX}. In learning to talk about X, the learner, L, as well as the teacher, T, representing the language community, interact with X. Therefore, by the stipulation stated above, it can be said that both M_{LX} and M_{TX} occur. The teacher's task is to train L to say "Y," the term used to designate X, only when it is appropriate, e.g., only when X is present. Training is successful, and L becomes a member of the language community (for the word "Y," at least) when L says "Y" only on those occasions when T agrees—i.e., when T also would have said "Y." Note that successful learning is determined solely by the agreement between L's use of the term "Y" and the community's use of the term as represented by T. Agreement between M_{TX} and M_{LX} is not a condition for membership in a language community. All that is necessary is that the events M_{TX} produce in T the tendency to say "Y," and that the events M_{LX} produce in L the tendency to say "Y." M_{LX} and M_{TX} may differ in any number of respects. Furthermore, L and T will tend to agree in their identification of novel instances of X.[43] Intersubjective agreement is thus built into the learning of talk about the external world even though knowledge of this external world may be said to be mediated by private processes.

Intersubjective verification is built in the same way. Assume that A reports "Y." By the stipulation above, if A observed X then M_{AX} occurred. To verify A's report, B can either share the observation simultaneously or replicate it. If M_{BX} does occur then B will report "Y," thereby verifying A's report. Note again that neither verification nor disconfirmation in any way involves a comparison of M_{AX} and M_{BX}. The critical comparison is between reports, not between private processes. Congruence between private processes is irrelevant, and they drop out of the verification procedure just as Wittgenstein's beetle is canceled out.[44]

Nor does the external object X enter into any comparisons, either with private processes or with reports. Indeed, the "external world" can also be entirely dropped from the argument, except as a label for certain kinds of reports. Some behaviorists suggest, for example, that humans learn to discriminate between their dreams, images, and hallucinations and their perceptions of the real world on the basis of intersubjective agreement.[45] The behaviorist argument then reduces to the methodological principle that only reports achieving intersubjective agreement are scientifically acceptable, and such reports may be called "reports about the external world."

Everyday Private Language

The conclusion that a private language is not possible seems to fly in the face of everyday life, in which people talk to one another about private inner happenings such as pains, emotions, and thoughts. Although this talk is not always precise, it does seem to achieve some degree of mutual understanding, intersubjective agreement, and verification. To explain these facts, behaviorists argue that such talk is learned and maintained by links, perhaps highly indirect, between the inner happenings and observables in the public domain. The nature of this linkage (discussed in chapter 11) is described in various ways.[46] Tolman, for example, speaks of a "behavior analogue" on the basis of which talk about one's emotions is learned.[47] Skinner describes the observables as the "discriminative stimuli" used by the verbal community to set up contingencies of reinforcement in teaching verbal responses to private events.[48] Wittgenstein conceptualizes the observable events and behaviors as "criteria" for the use of a phenomenal term.[49] The linkage is crucial, and in its absence, as in a hypothetical purely phenomenal language, communication is not possible.[50]

Between the extremes of the purely phenomenal language with no links to observables and the language of the natural sciences with strong links to observables there lies a continuum of terms with varying degrees of linkage. Terms on this continuum will also differ, therefore, in the degree to which they can achieve intersubjective agreement, communication, and verification when used. Terms at the end of the continuum approaching the purely phenomenal vocabulary would be expected to achieve little success in these respects while the opposite would be true at the other end. Much of the controversy in evaluating classical introspectionism is related to the fact that the terms used in classical introspectionism come from a wide range within this continuum. To the extent that introspectionist terms approach the purely phenomenal, problems arise, while research using terms more closely linked to stimulus conditions and observable behaviors will show more promise.[51]

OBJECTION 5: IT IS UNRELIABLE

In contrasting his "radical behaviorism" with the more conventional "methodological behaviorism" Skinner (1974) says:

> Methodological behaviorism and some versions of logical positivism ruled private events out of bounds because there could be no public agreement about their validity. Introspection could not be accepted as a scientific practice. . . . Radical behaviorism, however, takes a different line. . . . [It] does not insist upon truth by agreement and can therefore consider events taking place in the private world within the skin. It does not call these events unobservable, and it does not dismiss them as subjective. (p. 16)

Skinner thus rejects intersubjective agreement as a criterion for objectivity. He argues that social consensus about a statement does not guarantee the truth of that statement. Furthermore, Skinner observes, the truth by agreement doctrine prevents consideration of private events within psychology because intersubjective agreement is confined to public events according to that doctrine. Thus in rejecting the truth by agreement philosophy Skinner claims to broaden the scope of scientific psychology to include the study of private events.[52]

Skinner also suggests how a verbal community can train speakers to respond discriminatively to private stimuli. Skinner theorizes that in teaching verbal responses to private stimuli, the verbal community makes use of public stimuli tied to the private stimulation.[53] The verbal responses constituting the language of first-person reports are thus not a purely phenomenal vocabulary—they must have some tie, however tenuous, to public stimuli. It is therefore possible for a verbal community to train its members to speak about private stimuli.

Having rejected intersubjective agreement and verifiability as criteria for the acceptance of observation reports, Skinner seems to open the way for first-person reports of private stimuli to qualify as observation reports. However, Skinner does not take this final step. As explained in chapter 11, Skinner's theory implies that the connection between a private event and a verbal response will not usually be a reliable one. He therefore does not trust first-person reports of private events and does not use them as observation reports. His reasons for rejecting introspection are thus based, in part, on an unproven empirical hypothesis and constitute a fifth behaviorist objection to introspection. (Skinner's other reasons for ignoring introspection are discussed in chapter 11.) In practice, then, Skinner does agree with the behaviorist exclusion of introspection from scientific methods of observation.

Some behaviorists follow Skinner's lead but without his cautious attitude. Given Skinner's theory of how verbal responses to private stimuli can be learned, some behaviorists admit first-person reports of private events as full-fledged and significant sources of scientific data. Although these behaviorists still emphasize the importance of observing behavior, they also accept introspection as a valid method for observing private data.[54] Their position, however, must be located at the periphery of the behaviorist conceptual family. The central behaviorist position is the rejection of introspection as a method of scientific observation for the various reasons reviewed above.

CONCLUSION

Behaviorism rejects introspection as a method of scientific observation on a number of grounds. Those based on the nature of the contents of introspection (e.g., that they are subjective or private) do not stand up to close analysis. On the other hand, objections based on the nature of the method itself fare better. First, there is the methodological objection that introspection fails to achieve intersubjective agreement. Second is the empirically based objection that introspective reports are necessarily unreliable because of the way they are supposedly learned and maintained. These two objections demonstrate two features of behaviorist conceptions of objectivity: (1) Objectivity is closely associated with intersubjective agreement and communication; and (2) standards of objectivity depend, in part, on the findings and theories of the science of behavior.

CHAPTER 3

The Behavioral Data Language

In selecting a domain for psychology, behaviorism distinguishes between behavior and physiology. A priori *attempts to draw this distinction having failed, an empirical or theoretical definition of behavior emerging from a science of behavior is probably the most useful. The distinction is important for molar behaviorism which argues, mostly on tactical grounds, for an autonomous science of behavior independent of physiology.*

For a science of behavior to develop, observation must generate descriptive reports, couched in the categories of language and perception. Some epistemologists conclude that all observation is dictated by theory. Nevertheless, it seems that the degree to which an observation is contaminated by theory varies, depending on the observation. On this continuum between the purely observational and the purely inferential, intersubjective agreement can be used as a convenient measure, with objectivity increasing with increasing intersubjective agreement.

In constructing a behavioral data language, some behaviorists insist that only physical descriptions be used. However, this insistence is not only impractical; it is also based on false intuitions about the ontological superiority of physical properties. Psychology must be free to use properties it finds effective as long as they are intersubjectively identifiable.

Most behaviorists prefer to exclude from the behavioral data language any descriptions expressed in: action language, the intensional mode, purposive terms, or molar categories. In practice, this preference is often violated. The reasons both for the preferences and for the violations are varied, and they further clarify behaviorist notions of empiricalness and objectivity.

Functional definitions of stimulus and response are derived from empirical findings. They often specify properties that are psychological—i.e., derived from psychological experiments and not used by the other sciences. Despite appearances to the contrary, a functional approach is not circular, nor does it contaminate the behavioral data language with theory.

Having rejected introspection, behaviorism is restricted to observations of the natural world. The next major node in the behaviorist conceptual tree diagram is the selection from that world of a domain for psychology. Although all behaviorists agree that behavior is the domain of psychology, they disagree on what constitutes behavior, and their various notions of behavior form the branches leading from this second node.

Once a domain is defined, the next major node forms around the question of how observations of this domain are to be reported, since observations alone are an inadequate basis for a science. They must be described, and descriptions require a language. Behaviorists insist that the descriptive language of psychology must meet their standards of objectivity and empiricalness, and they propose various methods to ensure this.[1] These proposals constitute the branches arising from the third major node. This chapter will examine and evaluate these various behaviorist conceptions of behavior and scientific description.

BEHAVIOR AND PHYSIOLOGY

The Behavioral Superfice

In defining behavior as the domain of psychology, a serious problem arises in distinguishing between behavior and physiological events. Despite numerous behaviorist attempts to define this boundary, or "behavioral superfice" in Bentley's phrase,[2] it remains elusive. Even the distinction between what is inside the body and what is outside is not helpful, for the skin is not an important border in defining the behavioral superfice. As discussed in the next chapter, behaviorists commonly speak of "covert" behavior, "neural responses," and "private stimuli." Although located inside the body, these events are included within the domain of behavior. Similarly, the popular behaviorist definition of behavior in terms of "muscle contraction and glandular secretion" refers to events normally inside the body. Attempts to differentiate psychology as the study of the organism as a whole in contrast to physiology as the study of parts of the organism also fail because psychologists often study isolated responses (e.g., the eye blink) and physiologists frequently investigate systems (e.g., reproduction) that involve large-scale and coordinated mechanisms.[3]

A priori definitions of this sort are inevitably inadequate because they attempt to carve out a scientific domain before it is known which phenomena are usefully investigated by a particular methodology, relevant to a particular scientific interest, or covered by a particular scientific theory. A more promising approach is to propose *a posteriori* definitions dependent on actual developments within a science of behavior. Such definitions change along with the science.

Early behaviorist experiments concentrated on behaviors, such as maze running, eye blinks, and lever pressing, which on the basis of antecedent research seemed to be good prospects for further investigation. These prototype experiments comprise initial paradigms for the domain of behaviorist science, and they constitute a primitive definition of "behavior." With advances in behavioral research, laws are discovered which govern not only the paradigm behaviors but a wider range of phenomena as well. This range then determines a scientific domain, with "behavior" defined as whatever conforms to these laws.[4] Thus emerges an empirical definition of the behaviorist domain. At a more advanced stage, laws are organized by comprehensive psychological theories, and the terms of the science are extended to whatever phenomena are covered by a theory.[5] Conceivably, this theoretical definition of the behavioral domain may even exclude phenomena initially thought to be paradigmatic behavior. Thus, the domain of the behavioral science, and the distinction between the behavioral and the physiological in particular, cannot be precisely defined *a priori* but rather must evolve in a dialectic within the science itself.

Molar Behaviorism

Not all behaviorists wish to exclude physiological events from the domain of psychology. To the majority who do, however, a common objection is that such a restricted domain is not scientifically legitimate. It is often argued that behavior is just an outward manifestation of biological events occurring within the organism and that behavior is in reality just a subdomain of a neurophysiological science.[6]

Behaviorists who reject this criticism argue that an autonomous science of behavior independent of physiology is not only possible but also desirable.[7] This position, known as "molar behaviorism," can be interpreted as both a prescription about what the subject matter of psychology should be and an empirical hypothesis about the outcome of the proposed program. As the latter, molar behaviorism hypothesizes that lawfulness can be found at the behavioral level without appeal to physiological events inside the body. Without such lawfulness a molar behaviorist science would not be possible.

As a prescription, molar behaviorism asserts also that an autonomous science of behavior is desirable. Such claims rest on assumptions concerning the purposes and goals of science.[8] Within the behaviorist family, the commonly shared belief is that the goals of scientific psychology are the prediction and control of behavior, as mentioned in chapter 1. If the hypothesis that lawfulness exists at the behavioral level is confirmed, then these twin goals are attainable by an autonomous science of behavior. Descriptions of the current environment in conjunction with laws stating how behavior is a function of the environment yield predictions of behavior. Conversely, behavioral laws may be used to determine how the environment must be changed in order to modify behavior in a desired direction, thereby mediating the control of behavior.

In opposition to molar behaviorism it is argued that inclusion of reports about physiology in psychology's data base can improve prediction and control. Knowledge of the physiological causes of behavior might increase the precision of prediction, and direct physiological manipulation, rather than environmental change, might be the most effective method for modifying behavior. In rejecting this line of reasoning, molar behaviorists note that, in fact, present knowledge of physiology is insufficient for either the prediction or control of behavior. In contrast, currently available behavioral laws have already proven useful for these purposes. Second, they argue that lawfulness cannot be created by knowledge of the physiological mechanisms mediating that lawfulness. Lawfulness between behavior and the environment either exists or it does not, and lawfulness in the intermediate steps does not change that fact.[9] Third, even if knowledge of physiology improved prediction and control of behavior, in practice, the relevant physiological events are usually inaccessible. It is normally far simpler to observe or manipulate the environment in order to predict or control behavior than to observe or modify events in the nervous system, especially when large numbers of people are affected by the same environment.[10]

Besides these practical arguments, a distrust of the role of physiology in psychology also underlies behaviorist support for molar behaviorism. Many behaviorists fear that a concern with physiology tends to divert attention away from behavior, the major interest of psychology, and away from the environment, the ultimate cause of behavior.[11] Some behaviorists also see the threat of mind-body dualism lurking in physiological psychology.[12] They argue that physiological psychology often finds a proximate cause for events of interest but then leaves this proximate cause unexplained, giving the impression that it is brought about by an agent or act of will hidden in the recesses of the central nervous system. In contrast, a molar science of behavior, by showing that behavior is caused by the environment, excludes unscientific causes of this sort.

The arguments supporting molar behaviorism clearly show that its choice of behavior in relation to the environment as its sole data must be viewed in part as a tactical decision. It is based on an assessment of what course of action shows the most promise for achieving the scientific prediction and control of behavior, given our present state of knowledge. As our knowledge grows with the development of the two sciences, it is possible that this assessment will change.[13] In this respect the exclusion of physiological observations from the molar behaviorist data base contrasts with the exclusion of introspective observations. The rejection of the latter, as discussed in the preceding chapter, is in some cases based on epistemological considerations rather than tactical ones, and is therefore not in all cases relative to the contemporary state of scientific knowledge.

In restricting the domain of psychology to behavior and its relationship to the environment, molar behaviorism does not entirely exclude physiology from the science of behavior. For one thing, physiology may play a theoretical role. As is discussed in the next chapter, many behaviorists contend that hypothetical constructs denoting physiological processes must be included in a psychological theory intended to organize and explain molar behavioral laws. Second, some behaviorists who support an autonomous behavioral science nevertheless propose that this science will eventually be reduced to a more fundamental science of physiology.[14] This will occur when the postulates of a completed science of behavior are demonstrated to be the theorems of the reducing science. Promoting a reduction of this sort is congruent with behaviorist aspirations toward the unity of science. It also supports the case for molar behaviorism since the reduction is possible only after the molar behavioral science is completed.[15] Third, a behaviorist may use physiological findings and theory as heuristics for suggesting hypotheses concerning behavior. This heuristic function usually proves reciprocal, since behavioral laws and theory may prove equally useful for guiding physiological research.[16]

FROM SENSORY STIMULATION TO SCIENTIFIC REPORT

Definitions of behavior demarcate a scientific domain; they do not create a data base. The latter is reserved for the human scientist in interaction with the natural world. Characterizing this interaction is an epistemological problem not yet satisfactorily resolved. Obviously the mere arrival at a sensory receptor of energy from an object is only a necessary but not a sufficient condition for a scientific empirical observation.

In analyzing the concept of observation, the behaviorist science has the advantage that the process of observation falls within its domain. Not only does observation provide a data base for psychology, it is itself also a subject for investigation by that science.[17] According to many behaviorists, observation is a kind of behavior. Although no movements are necessarily associated with an act of observation, it still falls within the rubric of "behavior" under some empirical or theoretical definitions.[18] Some behaviorists, for example, suggest that observation is a learned skill, acquired by the same principles as are other forms of complex behavior.[19] Others maintain that observation involves a covert perceptual response governed by the same laws that describe overt behavior.[20]

The occurrence of an observation does not in itself contribute to the data base. First the observation must be transformed into a data report, and it is this report, in some linguistic form, that enters the data base. To be sure, an individual may acquire considerable knowledge through observation without ever verbalizing it. However, for this knowledge to constitute a science, verbalization of some form is necessary. Science is a social enterprise characterized by verbal statements of laws and theories.[21]

Just as an observation cannot be defined simply as a reaction to sensory stimulation, so a report cannot be defined as a vocal reaction to stimulation even though that vocal reaction imparts knowledge about that stimulation. The melting of an ice cube is not a report about the temperature, nor is an infant's cry a report of its discomfort although in both cases there is a reliable correlation between an event and its known cause. These events may, however, function as indicants, or measuring instruments, for some unobserved cause. Whether or not they are indicants and instruments depends on whether someone uses them for these purposes. Thus, something is an indicant or instrument, in addition to being a mere series of causally related events, depending on its role in human activity.

A verbal response is a report, in addition to being a mere indicant when it plays a rather more complicated role in human social interactions.[22] Both speaker and listener are part of a language community whose members communicate in a number of ways, one of which is reporting. Skinner's theory of verbal behavior suggests one way to conceptualize these social interactions. He theorizes that the verbal community shapes and reinforces verbal reports (i.e., "tacts") because these reports reinforce members of the verbal community by extending their contact with the environment.[23] As discussed in chapter 7, contingencies of reinforcement are used by some behaviorists for a behavioral interpretation of purpose. Therefore, in contrast to reflexive cries and melting ice cubes, true reports may be said to be verbal responses which occur for the purpose of imparting knowledge.

Categories

It would appear, *prima facie,* that the objectivity of an observational report can be determined in a fairly straightforward manner. It should depend simply on how closely the report corresponds to what is observed. But measuring this correspondence requires a comparison between a report and the world reported about. This conception, however, is misleading. Reports are in the form of statements, but the world is not propositionalized. Words and sentences cannot be compared with the universe to measure the degree of correspondence. There are criteria for assessing the degree of correspondence between two descriptions but not between a description and the world.[24] Therefore, objectivity must be determined by comparisons among descriptions rather than between a description and the world.

Verbal descriptions capture the world by classifying stimulation from the world into the categories of language. A language with a different word for each and every stimulation would neither communicate usefully nor could it be learned. Natural languages note recurrences of stimulation by using the same descriptions to report them. In one sense, however, stimulation never recurs. One stimulation is never strictly identical to another if for no reason other than that they differ in either temporal or spatial location. Therefore, language categories carry identity criteria that indicate which properties to note and which to ignore in classifying two stimulations in the same category as a recurrence. These criteria are human products, either as deliberate creations or as the results of natural human tendencies to transfer and generalize previous learning. Consequently, there is no unique description or set of descriptions inherent in nature. The universe can be classified in an infinite number of ways, none of which is the only true one. The choice of a classification system is a human choice and therefore subject to human goals and interests.[25]

It is not only observational reports that are dependent on a system of categories; so are the observations themselves. What a stimulation is perceived as depends heavily on the observer's previous experience. This previous experience, as summarized by perceptual variables such as set, expectation, and memory, has been amply experimentally demonstrated to influence perception, even in the apparently simple case of signal detection. Thus, observation as well as observational reports are conceptual in nature, and the belief in observational purity, unaffected by the perceiver's contribution, is a false hope.

Observation Versus Theory

Although observations and observational reports are relative to a set of concepts, this does not in itself undermine the behaviorist search for empirical objectivity. The implication is that more than one set of observational reports can accurately describe a scientific subject matter, but given human flexibility in creating and interchanging concepts, this fact should pose no problem. Observations and observational reports can still be empirical and objective.

However, some epistemologists cast doubt on this conclusion. They argue that the concepts operating in everyday perception can be viewed as a primitive theoretical system. As science develops, this primitive system is gradually replaced by more formal scientific theory. Since the concepts of perception are thus supplied by theory, observation is, in a sense, dictated by theory. Therefore, there are no theory-independent facts by which to test a theory. Since all observation is theory-laden, a comprehensive theory, or world view, cannot be overthrown by disconfirming observations. In particular, there is no rational way to decide between two rival theories, since each determines only observations compatible with itself, and there are no neutral facts by which to evaluate the competing claims.[26]

This thesis denying the distinction between the theoretical and the observational seems to doom behaviorist attempts to establish a science which is both objective and empirical. The thesis implies on the one hand that no datum is purely empirical, since all observation is contaminated by theory, and on the other hand that no data-gathering method is objective, since all observations are dependent on the particular theoretical views of the observer.

For the most part, behaviorists ignore the thesis and continue to collect data they consider objective and empirical. Those who do acknowledge the thesis often argue that it is exaggerated. Although theory may influence observation, this effect, they claim, can be overcome by careful scientific methods.[27] Two rival theorists, for example, can agree as to whether a rat turned right or left without letting their competing theories dictate their observations. Indeed it is difficult to evaluate the thesis on this point. To demonstrate instances in which observation is theory-laden or that rival theories are incommensurate it is necessary to use either theory-neutral facts, which the thesis denies, or the theory-laden facts of yet another paradigm theory.[28] Moreover, if the thesis is itself a paradigm theory, then it, too, will dictate observations of scientific activity confirmatory of itself.

Although the arguments for the thesis are therefore not conclusive, its antithesis, namely that there is a sharp and clear distinction between the observational and the theoretical, is equally difficult to defend. Because perception and report are necessarily conceptual, observation cannot be entirely independent of knowledge and belief. However, it should be possible to establish a continuum based on the degree to which knowledge and belief contribute to the data report. Surely there is a difference between the report "Smith ran five miles" and the report "Smith unconsciously attempted to impress his friends with his running" as descriptions of the same event. Although each report may involve inference and interpretation, clearly they are of a greater degree in the latter.

No known metric for precise measurement along this continuum currently exists. However, in practice, many behaviorists tend, in effect, to use intersubjective agreement as a convenient index. Descriptions which command universal assent from observers can be regarded at one end of the continuum while those generating much disagreement are at the other.[29] Somewhere between the two extremes, a degree of disagreement occurs at which point the description is said to be inferential, interpretive, or theoretical, rather than observational. The location of this point must be imprecise because, as noted, intersubjective agreement has never been precisely defined or measured. Nor is there any consensus on the degree of intersubjective agreement required for a description to qualify as an observation. Nevertheless, the fact that there is only an imprecise border on a continuum rather than two discontinuous sharply defined classes does not imply that there is no distinction between observation and theory. No point sharply differentiates when day becomes night either, yet the distinction between night and day is as clear as the difference between night and day.[30]

Supporters of the thesis denying the distinction between theory and observation might reply that intersubjective agreement is not a valid measure of observational purity since it may indicate merely the degree to which observers share the same theoretical paradigm. If this is the case, then intersubjectivity and behaviorist objectivity may indeed be relative to the scientific paradigm shared by behaviorists. Only within this paradigm can intersubjective agreement be used to distinguish the objective and empirical observation from the subjective and inferential interpretation. However, because evaluation of the thesis is so difficult this relativity need not necessarily be conceded. On the other hand, if the thesis is true, then the relativity of objectivity and empiricalness to a paradigm is still not particularly damaging to behaviorism. Relativity is necessarily true, according to the thesis, for all of science, not just psychology, and the science of behavior can proceed as normal science.

CRITERIA FOR THE BEHAVIORAL DATA LANGUAGE

The problem therefore confronting the behaviorist is to characterize the kind of reports which optimize both intersubjective agreement and scientific usefulness. This latter criterion is important because, as shown below, those descriptions with maximum intersubjective agreement are too narrow to be of use to the science. Therefore, it is likely that the characterization of acceptable data reports will change as the science develops and notions of usefulness change. The body of acceptable data reports constitutes the data base of the science and, in characterizing these reports, the behaviorist may be said to define a "behavioral data language." This latter phrase is used rather than the more common "observational language" in order not to suggest that it is based on a clear-cut distinction between observation and theory.

Physical Description

One way behaviorists define the behavioral data language is to restrict it to *physical* descriptions of behavior and the environment. "Physical description," however, can mean a number of things. It can mean descriptions mentioning only those predicates used by the physical sciences. In this case, responses could be described as movements of bodily parts from one set of coordinates in space to another. Similarly, stimuli could be described in terms of measurements of energy either arriving at the sensory receptor (the "proximal stimulus") or actually stimulating activity in a receptor (the "effective stimulus").[31]

A somewhat broader definition of "physical description" includes not only the properties of physical science but also relational properties defined in terms of the former.[32] Relational properties create no problems because, in one sense, all physical properties are relational. When an object is described as "7 centimeters," its length is being specified relative to a standard unit of length.

The "decibel" as a unit of sound intensity is a good example because it is explicitly defined as a ratio. Moreover, which properties are considered relational is itself relative to what is taken as basic or absolute. For example, if density is assumed as an absolute property then mass can be regarded as a relationship between density and volume. Thus, relational properties defined by psychology are just as "physical" as those used in physics. This conclusion, however, has no bearing on the question of whether relational properties actually function as discriminative stimuli for organisms.[33] The present point is only that descriptions of relational properties, such as "being the larger of two squares," seem to be suitable candidates for the behavioral data language.

Objection 1: It is Impractical. Although a number of behaviorists pay lip-service to the ideal of a data language consisting solely of physical descriptions of this sort, in fact, no behaviorist has ever carried out this program.[34] First, the complexity of describing even the simplest response (e.g., a smile) in this way is overwhelming. Second, the technological problems in continually measuring all the energies at sensory receptors appear practically insurmountable. Moreover, to determine the energy arriving at a recessed receptor like the retina or the energy effectively stimulating a receptor requires observation inside the body.[35] Thus, a behavioral data language restricted to the predicates used in the physical sciences is of no practical value.

One partial solution is to relax the requirement for descriptions of stimuli at the receptor and allow descriptions of objects in the environment (i.e., the "distal" or "potential" stimulus) without concern for how their energies impinge on the sensory receptor.[36] This waiver helps somewhat, but the problem is not solved entirely. Many distal stimuli are also extremely difficult to describe with the properties of physics. For example, many behaviors (e.g., smiling) are distal stimuli for other nearby organisms. If they cannot be physically described as responses, they also cannot be physically described as stimuli.

Objection 2: Objective ≠ Physical. Despite the impracticality of restricting the behavioral data language to the predicates of the physical sciences, some behaviorists still insist that the language of the physical sciences is the ideal for psychology. They feel that the properties discovered by the other natural sciences are the most fundamental and objective descriptions of nature. They claim that in reporting an object as "3 inches" a more objective description is given than when it is reported as a "wide smile." Objects or events reported by the latter description differ in a variety of ways, and the attribution of the description seems to be primarily a matter of human subjective judgment. The property "3 inches," however, appears to be an objective property of a class of objects all of which share an absolutely identical feature, not subject to human judgment. This line of reasoning is congruent with the traditional theory of identical elements which maintains that objects are similar or are classified together because they possess identical elements in common.[37] Thus, some behaviorists contend, the properties of physics denote phenomena sharing inherent identical elements of nature while other classificatory schemes rely on subjective judgments.

The fallacy of this line of reasoning becomes apparent when one questions the nature of the element that all three-inch objects have in common.[38] Of course they share the property "3 inches," but by the same token, all wide smiles share the property "wide smile." True, wide smiles differ from one to another, but so do three-inch objects. Consider a three-inch-deep pond, a three-inch distance between two points in a vacuum, and a sphere with a three-inch circumference. A possible reply might be that the element all these three-inch objects have in common is that they yield identical results when identical measuring operations are applied to them. However, in what sense are the measuring operations or the results "identical"? Consider how one measures the depth of a pond in comparison to how one measures the circumference of a sphere. Measurement of objects by use of a measuring rod, for example, involves a variety of movements, depending on the size, shape, orientation, and composition of the object, among other factors. In what way are all these measuring activities "identical"?

Even the basic property of number presents similar problems. Three days, three tables, three sentences, and three theories are all identical in number, but how are the counting procedures the "same" in each case? Similar questions arise concerning the results of the operations. If the scientist orally reports the result by saying "Three inches," is this the identical result as the written record "three inches" or "3 in." or someone else saying "Three inches" with a different voice? There is a further complication: an operation is a measurement only under the proper conditions. Extreme temperatures, the presence of magnetic fields, electrical disturbances, etc. may disqualify the operations from constituting a measurement. Because there are an indefinite number of ways in which conditions are not proper, it is not possible to state explicitly all the operations necessary for a measurement, nor are the operations necessary to create standard conditions the same in every case.

It seems clear from these considerations that the operations by which objects are known to have a physical property, even one as basic as "3 inches," form a *class* of operations sharing no common element other than they are measuring operations properly carried out. The rules for class membership cannot be explicated and depend ultimately on human judgment. It follows that there is no "identical" measuring operation or result to serve as the identical element shared by all three-inch objects. The only identical element for all three-inch objects is that they are three inches, just as being a wide smile is the identical element for all wide smiles. Just as humans develop tacit knowledge as to when an activity is a proper measuring operation, so they learn to recognize when facial movements are wide smiles.

The above considerations refute the views of those behaviorists who contend that the properties used in physics are inherent in nature and therefore objective. As argued earlier, there are many classificatory systems for categorizing the world, and those of the natural sciences are only a small subset. The properties attributed to nature are always relative to identity criteria created by humans. Criteria for all properties, including those of physics, depend ultimately on human pattern recognition.[39] In no sense does one particular set of properties, rather than another, describe nature "as it really is."

An Alternative: Intersubjective Agreement. Not all properties are equally useful for science, however, since not all properties are equally recognizable or specifiable. Some properties are poorly defined, and training in discriminating them cannot be highly successful. Therefore, intersubjective agreement in identifying them is not great, and their usefulness for science is minimal. Thus, instead of attributing objectivity to only those properties thought to be inherent in nature, a more pragmatic criterion can be substituted. Predicates can be judged as objective and admitted to the behavioral data language on the basis of the degree of intersubjective agreement they achieve. The properties used by the physical sciences are often identifiable by simple pointer readings for which discrimination training can be rather precise. Hence, the recognizability of these properties, as measured by intersubjective agreement, is extremely high.[40] Yet, as argued above, a data language limited to these predicates is too narrow for psychology.

A behvioral science must therefore make use of a broader range of properties, including those which achieve a high degree of intersubjective agreement in their application but are not the standard properties of the other sciences.[41] The degree of intersubjective agreement required for a predicate to qualify for the behavioral data language is not a settled question. Nor are there rules for formulating descriptions which meet such a qualification. It appears that the acceptability of particular properties must be judged on a case-by-case basis, at least for the present. In the final analysis, the objectivity of the science depends ultimately on sound human scientific judgment in these decisions.

An Initial Formulation

It is clear from these considerations that the boundary of the behavioral data language is neither sharply defined nor permanent. Whether or not a report is an "objective" description and whether or not it is "observational" are more a matter of its position on a *continuum* than of its possession of certain all-or-none features, and intersubjective agreement proves to be an important axis of these continua. Because behaviorists differ as to the exact location of that boundary, it may be impossible to define a precise border without appealing to arbitrary standards. Nevertheless, a number of behaviorists suggest rules which provide a general characterization. A convenient reference point is the set of guidelines advanced by MacCorquodale and Meehl (1954) whose formulation is influential, representative, and instructive.[42] For the construction of a data language they suggest:

> We begin with the complete stream of activity as it runs off in the time sequence, the rich, raw, unclassified *flux* of behavior. Any arbitrary *interval* of the flux can be demarcated by time-points and examined for the presence of certain properties. The operational specification of a *descriptive property* of an interval permits the use of words referring to the animal's visible anatomy, the descriptive words of the physical thing-language, and special words which we define explicitly in terms of these. Observation-sentences are formulated in these words, and must not involve even implicit reference to any other interval of the flux. . . .
>
> Non-extensional connectives such as "in order that . . ." . . . are clearly forbidden as going beyond the descriptive properties of the interval. (pp. 220–221)

This formulation is helpful in conceptualizing a number of issues related to the composition of the behavioral data language.

Action Language

One of these issues is whether descriptions of behavior as actions are permitted in the behavioral data language. The concept of an action is best elucidated by examples distinguishing action language from action-neutral language. Consider the difference between the description "The rat pressed the lever down" (action language) and "The movement of the rat's limbs caused a deflection of the lever" (action-neutral language); or "The rat moved its paw from A to B" (action) versus "The rat's paw moved from A to B" (action-neutral).[43] It is difficult to specify precisely what distinguishes the two kinds of descriptions, but at least one difference is that the action description implies that the behavior is brought about by an agent.[44] Whereas the action description says that the rat produced the deflection, the action-neutral description leaves open the possibility that the rat's body caused the deflection by being dropped onto the lever, or by undergoing a convulsion.

It would seem that action language violates behaviorist canons for the behavioral data language. First, it appears that action language breaches MacCorquodale and Meehl's stricture that observation sentences not involve "implicit reference to any other intervals of the flux." To determine if a person's bodily movement is an action rather than, say, a tic, muscle spasm, or conditioned reflex, it is often necessary to know or infer something about the provenance of that movement. In describing a movement as an action, one is therefore implicitly saying something about the context of that movement.[45]

On the continuum discussed above, action language thus seems to fall too far in the "interpretive" range for behaviorist comfort. Second, to describe a movement as an action is to apply the conceptual scheme of agency to the description of behavior, and this seems undesirable for a number of reasons. As explained in chapter 9, the concept of the agent bears certain connotations, such as the notion of free will, which are contrary to fundamental behaviorist views of behavior.[46]

Nevertheless, in practice, most behaviorists use action language almost exclusively in describing behavior.[47] Action-neutral descriptions of behavior are difficult to formulate, and action language is therefore used for convenience. There is a tradeoff between observational purity and usefulness. Also, it can be argued that the criteria for describing a movement as an action are objective and observable, and therefore, action language is merely a higher-order description of what is observed.[48] Indeed, some have argued that these higher-order descriptions are so basic that normally we *see* behavior as actions rather than as movements, and further interpretation is unnecessary.[49]

Intensional Descriptions

Another issue that arises in the construction of a behavioral data language is whether to include intensional language. Intensionality is a concept that has been understood in many ways.[50] It may refer to true descriptions of behavior, which mention objects which do not necessarily exist. For example, "The rat searches for food" or "The rat expects food" are intensional in this sense, since they may be true even if the food does not exist. Descriptions of this sort are referentially opaque in that terms with identical reference cannot necessarily be substituted for one another. For example, if Bill is Mary's father, but Tom does not know this, then "Mary's father" cannot be substituted for "Bill" in the sentence "Tom is expecting Bill to arrive."

Intensional descriptions may include those which attribute a propositional attitude to a person even though that person may have not emitted any verbal behavior. For example, "Tom hopes it will rain," attributes the proposition "It will rain" to Tom although he may not have stated it explicitly. Or intensional descriptions may refer to descriptions of behavior and the environment in terms of their meaning for the subject rather than in terms independent of the subject's perceptions and beliefs about the world.[51]

With some notable exceptions, behaviorists generally reject intensional language for inclusion in the behavioral data language.[52] For one thing, the intensional mode of discourse is not used by any other science. Therefore, the use of intensional language would undermine the behaviorist pursuit of the unity of science. Furthermore, if the intensional mode is not reducible to extensional discourse, then psychology is irreducible to some more basic science.[53] Second, intensional language entails ideas antithetical to behaviorist doctrines. Since the objects of propositional attitudes do not necessarily exist, they are often said to "inexist" in the mind, as Brentano expresses it. Similarly, intensional descriptions of organisms imply consciousness. To say that something is "hoping," "believing," or "expecting" implies that it is conscious. Thus, intensionality would inject mind and consciousness where behaviorists try to eliminate them.

A third objection to intensionality in the data language is that it presupposes as basic properties of behavior certain qualities which behaviorists prefer to explain rather than assume as given.[54] By taking "The rat searches for the food" as a fundamental description of behavior, the intensional mode already assumes a kind of intelligence and adaptiveness that ought to be explained by behavioral theories beginning with fewer presuppositions. Similarly, the process by which stimuli and responses acquire meaning for the subject or by which subjects adopt beliefs and expectations ought to be explained by the behavioral science and not presupposed by incorporating intensional language into observational reports. The rejection of intensional language for the behavioral data language does not imply that intensional descriptions are illegitimate or have no place in a science of behavior. They certainly have their use in everyday speech, and within the behavioral science they may be incorporated either in the theoretical language (chapter 4) or given a behavioral interpretation (chapter 10).

Perhaps the most incisive objection to the inclusion of intensional language in the behavioral data language is that the intensional mode involves far too much interpretation and too little observation. At that end of the continuum, it fails to achieve intersubjective agreement and is anthropomorphic and projective. Quine (1960) expresses his doubts about intensionality in these terms:

> The underlying methodology of the idioms of propositional attitude contrasts strikingly with the spirit of objective science at is most representative. . . . In indirect quotation we project ourselves into what, from his remarks and other indications, we imagine the speaker's state of mind to have been, and then we say what, in our language, is natural and relevant for us in the state thus feigned. An indirect quotation we can usually expect to rate only as better or worse, more or less faithful, and we cannot hope for a strict standard of more or less; what is involved is evaluation, relative to special purposes, of an essentially dramatic act. . . . In the strictest scientific spirit . . . the essentially dramatic idiom of propositional attitudes will find no place. (pp. 218–219)

Moreover, as Quine notes, the attribution of propositional attitudes also encounters problems arising from the indeterminacy of translation thesis according to which the attribution of a proposition, through translation or indirect quotation, is relative to a nonunique system of analytic hypotheses.[55] This indeterminacy adds further imprecision to intensional descriptions, thereby reducing their suitability for the behavioral data language.

Although in principle behaviorists avoid using intensional discourse in the data language, in practice, intensional language occasionally appears in behaviorist descriptions. Indeed, some critics argue that such instances are not mere oversights on the part of behaviorists but that intensional descriptions are absolutely necessary for understanding behavior.[56] In contrast to most behaviorists, Tolman agrees with this contention and makes extensive use of intensionality. He speaks of experimental subjects, including rats, as "propositionalizing" and imputing descriptions to stimuli.[57] He also represents knowledge in the form of beliefs, expectations, and cognitions. However, it is not clear whether Tolman intends these descriptions to be part of the behavioral data language or whether these intensional attributions are intervening variables (see next chapter).[58]

Movement Versus Achievement

Descriptions of behavior within the behavioral data language are traditionally classified as either reports of movements or reports of achievement.[59] In the former, behavior is described as a movement, or set of movements, independent of what effects these movements have. For example, "The rat's front paws moved to the right" is a movement-description. In contrast, "The rat depressed the lever," by specifying only the effect of the behavior, is an achievement-description. Just as the movement-description does not indicate how the movements affect the environment, so the achievement-description does not specify which movements brought about the achievement. A rat can depress a lever in many ways, and the achievement-description does not report which one actually occurred.

This movement-versus-achievement distinction does not bear close scrutiny. In order to report that a movement has occurred, it is necessary to detect that movement. Often this detection is performed by a recording instrument. For example, a device detects when saliva is secreted or when an eyelid has closed. In this case, the movement is said to have occurred only when behavior has a particular effect on the recording instrument. Moreover, there is more than one way in which this effect can be brought about. Thus, the movement-description reduces to an achievement-description. In situations in which there is no formal recording instrument, the human observer must detect the movement. However, in this case, the human observer is functioning as a detection instrument. The observer, too, detects the movement only when it has a certain effect on the perceptual system, and this effect can be brought about in a variety of ways. In either case, movement-description reduces to achievement-description.[60]

This analysis conceptualizes a human observer as a detection or recognition instrument and is helpful in resolving problems raised above with regard to properties that cannot usefully be defined by the dimensions used by the physical sciences. These properties can be said to be defined by the reaction of the human recognition instrument.[61] Some properties, useful to the behavioral data language, cannot be specified by the properties of physics and are wholly dependent on human pattern recognition. This fact partly justifies the practice of describing stimuli in "perceptual" terms, that is, in terms of how they appear to the experimenter rather than by their physical parameters.[62] Two lights, for example, might be described as "red and blue" and "of equal brightness" rather than as being of a particular wavelength and intensity. When the human observer is conceptualized as a recognition instrument, then intersubjective agreement, both within and across observers, can be understood as a measure of the reliability of this instrument, and the importance of intersubjective agreement can be more readily appreciated.

Purposive Language

Yet another problem arising in choosing a behavioral data language is whether or not to include purposive descriptions of behavior. Although most behaviorists reject purposive language, others disagree. They argue that a description of behavior as movement or even as achievement is inadequate. Behavior, they claim, has descriptive properties beyond those of movements and achievements because behavior has purpose.[63] As Tolman (1932), the leading exponent for these "purposive behaviorists," asserts:

> Granting . . . that behavior . . . has descriptive properties of its own, we must next ask just what . . . these identifying properties are. The first . . . answer to this question is . . . that behavior . . . always seems to have the character of getting-to or getting-from a specific goal-object, or goal-situation. The complete identification of any single behavior-act requires . . . a reference first to some particular goal-object . . . which that act is getting to, or . . . getting from, or both. (p. 10)

It is obvious that a description of behavior as mere movement lacks any mention of the purpose of the behavior. Even an achievement-description fails to depict the purposive qualities of behavior. On the one hand, not all achievements are purposes. A rat, for example may inadvertently depress a lever by backing into it while escaping an electric shock or by emitting an unconditioned reflex. In either case the achievement-response of lever deflection has occurred but not the purposive act of deflecting a lever. On the other hand, behavior can be purposive without achievement. A rat may run through a maze for the purpose of getting the food at the end although it does not achieve this goal. It may not even achieve the effect "approaching the food" because its route through the maze may increase its distance from the food or because there is no food in the goal box. Hence, although achievement-descriptions are somewhat teleological in that they involve effects rather than means, they are not fully purposive.

Behaviorist opposition to purposive behaviorism arises on two counts. First, many behaviorists, while possibly agreeing that behavior manifests purposiveness, deny that this characteristic must be taken as a fundamental descriptive property of behavior. Instead, they maintain, the purposive qualities of behavior can be explained as the result of more basic properties of behavior described as movements or achievements (see chapter 7). Purposive behaviorists, however, contend that purposive qualities of behavior are "emergent" and belong among the basic descriptive properties of behavior.[64]

This doctrine of "emergence" is not clearly explicated by purposive behaviorists, and it is therefore difficult to assess their claim. Some of the ambiguity of the position is apparent in Tolman (1932):

> "Emergent" behavior phenomena are *correlated* with physiological phenomena of muscle and gland and sense organ. But descriptively they are different from the latter. Whether they are or are not ultimately in some metaphysical sense completely reducible to the latter we are not here attempting to say. (footnote, p. 7, emphasis added)

If in stressing the emergent nature of purpose the doctrine merely asserts that purposive properties do not appear among the descriptive properties of movements, or achievements, then surely it is correct. However, this fact has no bearing on whether or not purposiveness is *explainable* by a theory at some simpler level of descriptive analysis. On the other hand, if the doctrine asserts *a priori* that purposiveness as an emergent is not explainable at a more molecular behavioral level then the doctrine appears premature.[65] Perhaps purposive behaviorism is best viewed then as the empirical hypothesis that lawfulness, and therefore prediction and control, can most clearly be found within data described purposively rather than as movements or achievements.

A second source of behaviorist criticism of purposive behaviorism is that purposive descriptions are highly interpretive and therefore do not achieve the degree of intersubjective consensus desirable for the behavioral data language.[66] To this criticism, a purposive behaviorist can reply that it is only with the everyday concepts of purpose that disagreement is common. Scientifically defined purposive concepts can be objectively attributed on the basis of objective criteria, and intersubjective agreement can be maintained. Two objective criteria suggested for purpose are "persistence until" and "docility."[67] The former is demonstrated when an organism continues to have the same goal object despite variations in behavior caused by obstacles or changes in the location of the goal and when its behavior ceases when the goal object is removed entirely. "Docility" refers to the demonstration of learning relative to a particular goal. That is,

> Wherever a response is ready (a) to break out into trial and error and (b) to select . . . the more efficient of such trials and errors with respect to getting that end—such a response expresses and defines something which, for convenience, we name as a purpose. Wherever such a set of facts appears . . . there we have objectively manifested and defined that which is conveniently called a purpose. (Tolman, 1932, p. 14)

By these objective criteria, Tolman believes, purposes can be identified with a high degree of intersubjective agreement.

This reply on the part of the purposive behaviorist is not entirely convincing. First, it is not obvious that the required observations for attributing purposiveness can be performed without presupposing purposiveness. For example, can constancy of the goal-object despite variations in intervening obstacles (i.e., "persistence until") be demonstrated without assuming knowledge of the goal-object? Second, the objective criteria for purpose comprise a series of experiments on the basis of which purpose can be attributed. Without the evidence of these experiments, the attribution of purpose is only a hypothesis about the possible results of the required experiments. Therefore, a report in purposive terms of an observation of a single instance of behavior transcends the observation and enters the realm of inference.[68] It violates MacCorquodale and Meehl's condition that observation sentences not involve "implicit references to any other intervals of the flux." Hence, purposive language, even with objective application criteria, does not appear to be a good candidate for the behavioral data language.

Descriptive Level

Descriptions also differ in descriptive level, or degree of "molarity."[69] A particular instance of arm and finger movements might be describable as "writing a name," "signing a check," or "buying a house," each of which is an accurate description of the act. Similarly, a part of the environment might simultaneously be "a table," "a piece of furniture," or "a birthday gift." The descriptions differ as to the context in which they embed the behavior. "Signing a check" embeds the movement in a context that includes social institutions, such as money and banks, while "writing a name" does not.[70]

For this reason some behaviorists oppose the use of molar description in the behavioral data language since it goes beyond the properties of the interval being observed. It involves more interpretation than the simpler, more molecular description. Furthermore, it is claimed, molecular description in terms of a series of movements or muscle contractions conserves much of the information lost in molar description.

In reply to this objection to molar description it should be noted that molecular description also loses information. It is not clear that the description "buying a house" can be derived from a description of the person's movements. For this derivation it is necessary to include a description of the social institutions, and such a description at a molecular level of movements is impossible. Therefore, a molecular description loses crucial information and may in fact fail to capture what the person is doing.[71]

Like the other features of descriptions discussed above, molarity is a dimension rather than an all-or-none quality. Usually the more molar the description, the greater its social significance. It is more important to know that a man is robbing a bank than that he is raising his arm, even though he may be robbing the bank by raising his arm. On the other hand, the more molar the description, the greater the context behavior is embedded in and the more room for misinterpretation. There is likely to be more intersubjective agreement over whether a man winked his eye than over whether he was trying to attract attention, even though it may be true that he was trying to attract attention by winking his eye.[72] Also, lawfulness might be more readily found with more molar units of behavior. Thus, in selecting a descriptive level for the behavioral data language, there is often a trade-off between social significance and lawfulness on the one hand, and intersubjective agreement on the other. Once again, good scientific judgment is called for.

FUNCTIONAL DEFINITION

Behaviorist standards of objectivity and empiricalness determine necessary but not sufficient conditions for inclusion in the behavior data language. Selection often depends on empirical findings. One typical behaviorist strategy is to select predicates which categorize behavior and the environment into classes experimentally found to be lawfully related. This "functional" approach can be illustrated by a schematic example. An experimenter begins with an initial class of behaviors defined by some set of features. Certain aspects of this response class (e.g., its frequency of occurrence) are found to be functionally related to certain aspects of the environment. By judicious variation of the environment and careful observation of the behavior, the experimenter can delineate a class of environmental events covered by the functional relationship. This class is a "functional stimulus class."

In exploring the limits of the functional relationship, the experimenter may find that the functional stimulus class controls a class of behavior not perfectly congruent with the initial class of behaviors. The experimenter then delineates the class of behaviors empirically found to be under the functional control of the functional stimulus class, thus determining a "functional response class." Experimental study of the functional response class may suggest adjustments in the membership of the functional stimulus class which, in turn, may suggest further modifications of the functional response class. This process of titration eventually distills functional stimulus and response classes that optimize the lawfulness between behavior and environment. This point is often judged by "smoothness of curves" or "simplicity." The actual process of functional definition does not necessarily follow the steps of this idealized illustration. The only critical feature is that stimulus and response classes are defined on the basis of what is empirically found to be functionally related.[73]

Circularity

Definitions of this sort appear hopelessly circular. Stimulus is what controls response, and response is what is controlled by stimulus.[74] The circularity, however, is more apparent than real. There is indeed a kind of circularity, or better, a reciprocity, in the *process* of functional definition. Adjustment in the definition of a functional stimulus class may cause a corresponding adjustment of a functional stimulus class, and vice versa. This circularity, however, is a "virtuous" rather than a vicious cycle, with each cycle tightening the functional correlation. If the experimenter's intuitions prove valid, the cycles spiral inward, and later adjustments are near zero. If the cycles do not, then they serve notice that the experimenter is on the wrong track.

There is also a benign circularity in definition. Stimulus is defined in terms of response, and response in terms of stimulus. However, this circularity, too, is not troublesome. Relationships must always be defined this way. The central definition is that of the "functional relation," and "stimulus" and "response" are defined in pairs as the *relata* of this relationship. It also follows that the statement "Responses are functionally related to stimuli" is indeed a tautology when referring to functional responses and stimuli.

Nevertheless, the functional approach is far from vacuous. Demonstrating that a particular functional stimulus or response class is not the null set has serious empirical significance. That certain specified bits of behavior form a functional response class in relation to certain specified aspects of the environment forming the associated functional stimulus class is not a tautology. To escape the tautology, however, it is necessary that the functional stimulus and response classes be specified independent of one another. If the response is specified as "whatever is controlled by the functional stimulus," and the stimulus is specified as "whatever is responsible for the functional response," then the formulation is again enmeshed in circularity.

Thus, the functional approach must consist of two logically distinct processes. One, the *selection* process, consists of the delineation of response and stimulus classes. This is the titration procedure, described above, by which the members of the two classes are selected so as to maximize orderliness in the data. In this selection process, stimulus and response classes are related by a reciprocity in which members are selected for one class on the basis of their effects on members of the other class, and vice versa.

The other process is that of *specification:* Once functional classes are selected, it is necessary to specify them. In this process, at least one of the classes must be specified independently of the other. This implies that when a functional response class is specified as an achievement class (e.g., "any body movement that deflects the lever"), and a stimulus (e.g., "lever") is mentioned in the specification, that stimulus term must be defined by its ordinary dictionary meaning rather than by a functional definition.

Specification

The independent specification of a functional class poses a number of problems. Often the stimulus and response classes yielded by the functional selection process do not correspond to classes defined by a property used by science. For example, the functional stimulus class controlling the verbal response "Same loudness as the comparison tone" consists of tones of various frequencies and intensities which have no physical parameter in common. Their sole identity derives from the fact that they are judged by human listeners to be of equal loudness. To be sure, the locus of all points representing these tones can be described by an "equal loudness contour" on a graph with intensity and frequency as the two axes. Yet, this locus does not correspond to any acoustical property of sound typically of interest to physics.

Often a name is given to the property exemplified by a functional class that does not correspond to a property used by other sciences. In this example, the members of the class may be said to share the "same loudness." Because functional classes of this sort are selected on the basis of the behavior of an organism rather than the effects on a more typical measuring instrument, the property is often called "psychological."[75] Note that the property is "psychological" only because of the selection criteria for class membership, and not because of its ontological status or because it is "non-physical." In fact, equal loudness contours can be specified solely in terms of the obviously physical parameters of frequency and intensity.

Other functional classes, or psychological properties, cannot so readily be specified by the properties of natural science. More often than not, the members selected for a functional class have no commonalities specifiable by basic scientific properties. This is, of course, the very problem encountered above in relation to the construction of the behavioral data language: Many properties of interest to psychology are not those used by the other sciences. Therefore, the considerations discussed above are relevant to the present problem.

Relational properties acceptable for the behavioral data language are also suitable for the specification of a functional class. It is, however, an empirical question whether a relational property, in fact, characterizes any functional stimulus class. The controversy surrounding the phenomena of transposition can be viewed as a debate concerning this question.[76] In any case, as argued above, the use of relational properties in no way compromises the objectivity of behavioral language.

On the other hand, specifications using properties which are neither those of the physical sciences nor relations among them raise the difficulties discussed above. Properties of this sort are often necessary and useful, and behaviorists must use them when they are called for. Once again intersubjective agreement in using them to identify a class is an important criterion for their acceptability. If they can be specified precisely enough to mediate the prediction and control of behavior, then their use can be justified. Acceptability depends ultimately on scientific judgment in a case-by-case consideration of proposed functional class specifications.[77]

Functional Classes for Verbal Behavior

A special problem arises in specifying functional stimuli for verbal behavior. Often a verbal response is under the control of a highly abstract and subtle property of the environment. In many of these cases, the best and perhaps the only way to specify the functional stimulus class is by using a description in the same form as the verbal response under examination.[78] For example, suppose a subject emits the verbal response "twice as many." Assume further that it is found that the subject emits this verbal response only when presented with two groups of objects and one group has twice as many elements as the other. In specifying this functional stimulus class it will be necessary to use the term "twice as many" although this is the form of the verbal response being considered.

Does this create a vicious circularity? Not necessarily. It is possible that although the form of the response emitted by the subject is the same as that emitted by the experimenter in specifying the stimulus, the two may not belong to the same functional response class. The experimenter's response may relate to the environment and to other behaviors in ways that are different from those of the subject's response. This difference in function is reflected in the logical distinction, to be discussed in chapter 11, between the "object language" of the subject and the "pragmatic meta-language" of the experimenter.

The situation is inescapable. The subject's verbal response R_1 is explained, in part, by specifying a functional stimulus. This specification is itself a verbal response, R_2, emitted by the experimenter. Therefore, R_2 can also be explained, by a second experimenter, starting with its functional discriminative stimulus as specified by R_3. If the experimenters are careful in their discriminations and descriptions, then R_2 and R_3 will be identical, or at least synonymous. Eventually the supply of synonyms will be exhausted as R_3 is explained by R_4, and so on.

There is no need, however, to enter this infinite series. R_j is adequately explained by using R_{j+1}, and the explanation is not vitiated by the fact that that R_{j+1} can also be explained. *Every* explanation is in the form of behavior which can be explained although it need not be. On the other hand, the practice of using the response-to-be-explained in specifying the stimulus can be misused. Asserting that X is the functional stimulus for the verbal response "X" can come to serve as a substitute for the careful specification of functional stimuli. Therefore, wherever possible, the practice is to be avoided.

Intensionality

A functional approach offers the opportunity to reintroduce aspects of intensionality into the behavioral science. In functional terms, the stimulus for a particular response is not necessarily a momentary energy of specific physical dimensions arriving at the receptors. The functional class of environmental events, all of which leave behavior invariant, is ordinarily best specified as complex objects or situations which have meaning and may not correspond to specific physical dimensions immediately affecting the organism. As Holt says, the stimulus "recedes."[79] This receded functional stimulus, because it is selected by the subject's behavior rather than by *a priori* properties, is, in a sense, an "intensional" stimulus.[80] Similarly, specification of the functional response will rarely be possible in terms of bodily movements. Instead, the specification will be a more molar description of a set of behaviors that covary and hence have functional "meaning" for the subject.[81] Functional stimuli and responses differ, however, from traditional intensional objects in that the former are to be specified using extensional predicates and they are conceived as classes whose members exist in the world rather than inexist in the mind.

What Is Learned

The use of functional definitions reintroduces the question, discussed above, as to whether observation is necessarily contaminated by theory. A description of a bit of behavior in functional terms seems to be dictated by a theory or hypothesis about how that behavior is related to a class of stimuli. The question of what is learned illustrates the point.

When an instance of behavior occurs, there are multiple ways of describing, or categorizing it. For example, the behavior of a rat in a maze at a particular moment might equally well be described as:

R_1 = turning right
R_2 = turning south
R_3 = turning toward the light
R_4 = a description of a particular group of effector movements.

Assume that this instance of behavior occurs under circumstances (e.g., reinforcement, contiguity) which produce learning. As a result there will be a change in some class of behaviors.

It is a matter of considerable debate among behaviorists as to the exact nature of this class. The four descriptions of behavior listed above not only report the behavior, they also categorize it into four different classes which are not fully coextensive. Under certain circumstances, the behavior of turning right is not the behavior of turning south, nor is it always equivalent to a certain group of effector movements. The controversy over what is learned concerns the question of which description of the instance of behavior also accurately characterizes the class of behaviors altered by learning.[82] Thus the debate can be understood as a disagreement over the definition of the functional response class.

Each theory of what is learned is partly supported by experiments in which the various proposed functional classes do not overlap so it can be determined which class is the learned one.[83] From experiments of this sort along with other theoretical considerations, a theory of what is learned emerges. If descriptive data reports are dictated by theory in this way, then the behavioral data language seems seriously contaminated by theory.

A closer examination, however, reveals that observational reports are not compromised in a functional approach. Note that each of the four descriptions listed above meets the standards of objectivity and empiricalness discussed earlier. Observers, regardless of their theoretical orientations, would reach a high degree of intersubjective agreement over the applicability of any one of these descriptions to a particular instance of behavior. As a report of a particular instance of behavior, each is independent of any theory of learning. Confusion occurs because the description of the instance of behavior is also the description of a class of behaviors. What *is* dictated by theory is the *selection* of one from these acceptable, objective, and learning-theory-independent descriptions of a datum.[84] The theory determines into which of four possible classes the response is most *usefully* categorized.

Theory determines this selection because it suggests which descriptions yield the greatest simplicity and orderliness in the science. Consider an example. Suppose that experimental research indicates the functional response class for learning is best described by description R_1 (i.e., turning right). A generalization about learning can then be simply stated: When R_1 occurs under conditions a, b, c, . . . (e.g., reinforcement, contiguity), then response class R_1 is altered in ways x, y, z, . . . (e.g., increases in frequency). If, however, description R_2 (i.e., turning south) is used for the behavioral data language, then the generalization grows more complicated. It is not true that when R_2 occurs under learning conditions that the response class R_2 is learned. Therefore, additional statements are necessary. These statements might be in the form of rules on transforming a R_2 description into a R_1 description, or alternately, they may take the form of a complex disjunction of many more specific laws.

Use of the appropriate descriptions in the behavioral data language thus simplifies generalizations, and it does the same for higher level behavioral laws and theories.[85] Experimental findings and theory thus help in the *choice* of the most useful observational description for an instance of behavior, but they do not undermine its descriptive or observational nature.

CONCLUSION

Behaviorist conceptions of empiricalness and objectivity in observation carry over to behaviorist views on the behavioral data language. However, the attempt to insure objectivity and empiricalness by restricting the behavioral data language to physical descriptions fails for a number of reasons. This rejection of a purely physical language opens the way for psychological properties, especially those distilled by a functional approach to behavioral analysis. Functional properties must still be objective, and one way to measure their objectivity is through the intersubjective agreement they achieve.

Intersubjective agreement is also a criterion for judging other candidates for acceptance into the behavioral data language. Descriptions that are inferential, intensional, purposive, molar, or in action language are suspect, partly because of this criterion. Because these qualities, as well as the degree of intersubjective agreement that they achieve, vary and are not all-or-none, many decisions about acceptability into the behavioral data language are not clear-cut and often depend on a context of tradeoffs between intersubjective agreement and other desirable qualities.

CHAPTER 4

Theoretical Concepts

Behaviorism admits a variety of theoretical concepts into the science of behavior. These concepts differ in how closely they are linked to the behavioral data language. Transformations within the behavioral data language are securely linked and pose no problem. State, dispositional, and operationally defined concepts, however, provide only partial definitions since they are indeterminate and, in the case of the first two, open as well. In practice, even operationally defined concepts are also open.

Intervening variables tie together a set of interrelated independent variables with a set of interrelated dependent variables. Behaviorists differ as to whether the benefits of intervening variables outweigh their dangers. This debate centers on the tactical issue of whether concepts facilitate or inhibit research and explanation rather than on the philosophical respectability of intervening variables.

A similar debate arises over the admission of hypothetical constructs, theoretical concepts which explicitly refer to unobserved entities. Proponents argue that hypothetical constructs are necessary if the science of behavior is to be reducible, explanatory, and fertile. Opponents see these constructs as diluting the objective and empirical nature of the science. Although none of these arguments is conclusive and many depend on individual intuitions about how research is best performed, most behaviorists do incorporate hypothetical constructs in their theories. Nevertheless, they implicitly impose restrictions on the postulated features of these constructs so that the dangers are reduced.

For the reasons discussed in the preceding chapter, the boundaries of the behavioral data language are not sharply defined. Yet, wherever they are drawn, the study of behavior must exceed them to establish a science. It must transcend the immediate momentary observation to impose or discover coherence in its subject matter. Therefore, concepts must be introduced which do not qualify as terms in the behavioral data language.

This requirement, however, raises serious problems for the behaviorist program. By tying the behavioral data language to observation and intersubjective agreement, behaviorists ensure that terms within this language meet the twin criteria of empiricalness and objectivity. To introduce terms outside this language is to risk including subjective and speculative notions. Therefore, behaviorists insist that theoretical concepts be linked securely to the behavioral data language. They disagree, however, on the nature of this linkage, differing on how loose a linkage is permissible.[1] This issue forms the next major node of the behaviorist conceptual tree diagram.

FIRST-ORDER CONCEPTS

Transformations Within the Behavioral Data Language

Many theoretical concepts are unproblematic because they represent mere transformations within the behavioral data language. "Rate of response" is an example of a concept which integrates over multiple observations but is not the equivalent of the set of them. Similarly, the "average number of subjects turning right," when not a whole number, represents a datum that cannot possibly be observed.

Because none of these concepts refers to any entity or process existing in some unobserved realm and because they can all be defined solely by terms within the behavioral data language, they pose no methodological problems.[2] Indeed, by some definitions of the behavioral data language, these concepts are included in it. Under the other definitions, their unproblematic nature and their proximity to the data language should admit them to what might be labeled the "extended behavioral data language."

States and Dispositions

In the simplest case, behavioral laws permit the inference of statements about responses from statements about the external environment. The form of such laws would be: "Given stimuli a, b, c, . . . then responses x, y, z, . . ." It is clear from elementary considerations about behavior, however, that laws of this form are inadequate. More often than not, the response is not uniquely determined by external environmental conditions alone. Consider a few simple examples: a dog's response when food is placed before it depends on whether it is hungry; a female rat's response to a male rat depends on its estrous cycle; whether a tap to the knee elicits a jerk depends on the subject's health. In all these illustrations, the response depends on factors other than an external stimulus. These factors are "states" of the organism and include its age, health, species, hunger, wakefulness, and emotion.

A state then is a variable determining which stimulus-response laws are in effect.[3] The functions served by state variables can be demonstrated by an idealized model. Assume a universe consisting of only one organism, A, only two stimuli, S_1 and S_2, and only two responses, R_1 and R_2. Suppose it is found that at times S_1 produces R_1, but on other occasions it produces R_2. Likewise it is found that S_2 occasionally produces R_1 and at other times it produces R_2. At first glance, no lawfulness is apparent. However, assume further that it is found that A's response to a stimulus depends on its state, T(A), which can take on two possible values, $T_1(A)$ or $T_2(A)$. Lawfulness might be introduced as follows:

$$T_1(A):\ S_1 \longrightarrow R_1$$
$$T_1(A):\ S_2 \longrightarrow R_2$$
$$T_2(A):\ S_1 \longrightarrow R_2$$
$$T_2(A):\ S_2 \longrightarrow R_1$$

Laws of this form are common. Often T is referred to as the "parameter" for the equation relating stimulus and response. Note, however, that the term considered the parameter is merely a matter of convention, and there is nothing inherently "parametric" about a state. A stimulus, too, can function as a parameter in the above model:

$$S_1:\ T_1(A) \longrightarrow R_1$$
$$S_1:\ T_2(A) \longrightarrow R_2$$
$$S_2:\ T_1(A) \longrightarrow R_2$$
$$S_2:\ T_2(A) \longrightarrow R_1$$

State variables thus serve the function of restoring lawfulness to stimulus-response connections when a simple one-to-one correspondence between stimulus and response is lacking.[4]

States are not observable in the same way as stimuli and responses. For example, the dog is thought of as hungry even when no food-related stimuli or responses are present. Thus an organism may be reported to be in state T at a particular time even though nothing observed at that time indicates the state. Hence, terms denoting states do not qualify for the behavioral data language.

A common approach to states is to admit them to the science but to define them solely by terms in the behavioral data language. The organism is said to be in the state if and only if certain stimuli produce certain responses. In the model above this can be formulated:

$$T_1(A) \text{ iff } [(S_1 \longrightarrow R_1) \text{ or } (S_2 \longrightarrow R_2)]$$

That is, A is in state T_1 if and only if either S_1 produces R_1, or S_2 produces R_2. The definition contains only stimulus and response terms from the behavioral data language.

Understood this way, states are dispositions, concepts commonly used in both science and everyday speech.[5] To say that an object is soluble, for example, is not to say that it is in the process of dissolving, but that when placed in water it will dissolve. In general, to attribute a disposition to a object is to state that under certain conditions, called "test conditions," certain outcomes will result. Thus states (e.g., hunger) can be construed as dispositions in which the stimuli are the test conditions (e.g., food), and the responses are the outcomes (e.g., eating).

Note that for both dispositions and states, the conditional is assumed to hold only when certain other conditions obtain: the soluble substance is not expected to dissolve if the water is frozen. These other conditions are covered by the *ceteris paribus* clause implicitly included in the definition of a dispositional term, although these conditions cannot be exhaustively listed. Since both test conditions (stimuli) and outcomes (responses) are public and observable, the attribution of a state meets behaviorist criteria of objectivity and empiricalness.

Operationally Defined Concepts

A methodological procedure ensuring that all introduced concepts possess a similar linkage to observations is offered by operationism. Bridgman (1927) suggests that a concept be identified with the operations used to measure it:

> To find the length of an object, we have to perform certain physical operations. The concept of length is therefore fixed when the operations by which length is measured are fixed: that is, the concept of length involves as much as and nothing more than a set of operations; *the concept is synonymous with the corresponding set of operations*. (p. 5)

In adapting operational principles to psychology Stevens (1939) asserts:

> A term denotes something only when there are concrete criteria for its applicability; and a proposition has empirical meaning only when the criteria of its truth or falsity consist of concrete operations which can be performed upon demand. . . . When we attempt to reduce complex operations to simpler and simpler ones, we find in the end that discrimination, or differential response, is the fundamental operation. (p. 228)

Operationist principles are neatly congruent with behaviorist aspirations. If it is stipulated that operations must be publicly observable (i.e., introspection is excluded), repeatable, and specified precisely enough for others to carry them out, then there will be intersubjective agreement and verifiability for the operations, their results, and consequently the application of the concept.[6] As a prescription, operationism stipulates that concepts be introduced only by operational definitions—i.e., in terms of operations used to measure the concept. As a test, operationism states that concepts that cannot be given an operational definition are scientifically unacceptable.

For application in behaviorist psychology, operationism requires certain modifications. In Bridgman's original formulation, operationism concerns the relationship between concept and measurement in physics. As compared with physics, psychology has developed very few concepts which can be measured in any precise way. Therefore, operational definitions in psychology often give only the operations used to detect and apply the concept. For example, the concept "having a sensation of red" may be operationally defined by the operations used to set up a perceptual experiment in which the subject reports "I see red." Here the operations define when the concept "having a sensation of red" may be applied to the subject but do not include measuring operations.[7] By this broadening of operationism, behaviorists extend the use of operationist methodology to concepts as yet unquantified, thereby ensuring that a larger range of concepts meet behaviorist standards of acceptability.

Although in principle operationism seems straightforward, in practice its application is not without ambiguity. One source of indeterminateness is the sense in which the concept is "synonymous with" the operations. Taken literally this is unintelligible.[8] It would mean, for instance, that "distance" *means* "the operation of choosing a standard unit, the operation of marking off a rod with these units, the operation of placing the rod next to an object, etc."

A more acceptable interpretation of operationism would be that the concept (e.g., distance) is defined as the result of a set of specified operations (e.g., measurement with a ruler). In particular, to say that a certain object, A, possesses a property, T, at a particular value, N (e.g., "The distance to the table is 90 cm") is to specify the results ("pointer readings") of those operations. Thus,

$$[T(A) = N] \quad \text{iff} \quad [(\text{operations on } A) \longrightarrow N]$$

When T is a property which is not measurable, then N represents a two-valued function indicating whether or not A possesses T.

Formulated in this way, operationally defined concepts are dispositions. The operations are equivalent to the test conditions, and the results of the operations are equivalent to the test outcomes.[9] What operationism adds to the analysis of dispositions is the principle that *all* concepts are dispositional, even ones like weight and distance.

Partial Definitions

States, dispositions, and operationally defined concepts appear, therefore, to have a common logical form:

$$T(A) \quad \text{iff} \quad [S(A) \longrightarrow R]$$

A serious problem with all three types of concepts is that the definition is in the form of a conditional: "$S(A) \longrightarrow R$." By truth functional logic, a conditional is true if the antecedent of the conditional is false. Therefore, T(A) is true if S(A) is false. For example, any rock not placed in water is soluble by this kind of definition of a disposition.[10] Therefore, Carnap suggests an alternate formulation:

$$S(A) \longrightarrow [R \text{ iff } T(A)]$$

This says that if the test condition is in effect, then an object may be said to have the disposition if and only if the required outcome occurs. In the example, "soluble" would be defined as follows: If an object is placed in water then that object may be said to be soluble if and only if it dissolves. Under this formulation the rock not in water ceases to be a problem, for it does not satisfy the definition. Carnap calls his formula a "bilateral reduction sentence," and he recommends its use for introducing dispositional terms.[11]

Bilateral reduction sentences have logical properties with important implications for introducing terms into behaviorist psychology. First, the state or disposition T is defined only if S(A) obtains, and the application of the concept is therefore indeterminate for all those instances in which S(A) does not obtain. This area of indeterminacy leaves open the possibility that test conditions other than S(A) can be used when S(A) does not obtain. Thus a second characteristic of introduction by bilateral reduction sentences is that it is "open" in the sense that further bilateral reduction sentences—i.e., test conditions and outcomes for the disposition—can be added as they are discovered, thereby reducing the area of indeterminacy.

As additional bilateral reduction sentences accrue, the result is what Carnap calls a "reductive chain" in the form:

$$\begin{array}{l} S_1(A) \longrightarrow [R_1 \text{ iff } T(A)] \\ S_2(A) \longrightarrow [R_2 \text{ iff } T(A)] \\ S_3(A) \longrightarrow [R_3 \text{ iff } T(A)] \\ \quad\quad\quad\vdots \\ S_n(A) \longrightarrow [R_n \text{ iff } T(A)] \end{array}$$

where S_i represents a test condition, and R_i represents the associated outcome. Indeed, most dispositions in everyday speech are manifest in more than one way. For example, to say that Jones knows algebra is to attribute to him an ability to do many things. Moreover, the attribution is open in that other manifestations may be added as, say, he learns to use a computer and can therefore demonstrate his knowledge of algebra in new ways. This open nature of dispositional concepts permits them to play an integrative role in concept formation.

The open texture of reductive chains and their indeterminacy mean that the reductive chain provides only a "partial" definition of a dispositional term.[12] The reductive chain is therefore neither an explicit operational definition of the term nor a "translation" of the term into the behavioral data language. Acceptance of dispositional terms into the behaviorist science thus means the admission of concepts tied to the behavioral data language by a link weaker than explicit definition.

Partial Definitions and Operational Definitions

Operational definitions are also indeterminate since they assign no value when the operation is not in effect. However, in contrast to reductive chains, operational definitions are meant to be closed definitions. A concept is defined by only one operation, and different operations define different concepts. If a particular concept is defined by a certain measuring operation, and a second operation is discovered that apparently measures the concept as well, strict operationism demands that the second operation be considered as defining a second concept rather than as an alternate measure of the first. Thus, strict operational definitions do not share the open texture of Carnap's reductive chains and therefore cannot function in concept formation as reductive chains do.[13]

Behaviorists treat this issue in several ways. The heroic response is to sacrifice the integrative role of concepts in favor of the protection offered by strict operationism. This decision means that for each operation, a separate set of empirical laws is required to relate a concept to other variables. Strict operationism demands that a law relating two nonoperationalized variables, X, which can be measured in *m* ways, and Y, which can by measured in *n* ways, must be construed not as a single general law but as $m \times n$ separate laws. Furthermore, according to strict operationism, the *m* methods thought to measure X, cannot be viewed as different ways of disclosing the same magnitude. Instead, each method defines a different variable. The resulting *m* variables are then considered to be related by empirical laws over an observed range rather than by the fact that they all reveal some common aspect of nature.[14] Although such a conservative approach creates a science less vulnerable to the need for major revision with new discoveries, it clearly pays a price in loss of simplicity and integration.[15] If the convergence of concepts and laws is a prerequisite and consequence of theory development then operationism may shield science only by inhibiting its growth.

Other behaviorists, unwilling to sacrifice either integration or caution, try to fuse the two. This feat is accomplished by suggesting a method for integrating operations into a single concept. According to this approach, concepts are initially to be defined by only one operation. If continued experimental research reveals that two operations consistently yield the same results, then the two operations may be considered as measuring and defining the same concept.[16] Additional operations can be added to the concept by the same means, as further research warrants. This approach is appealing because it appears to retain the virtues of operationism without sacrificing theoretical convergence. However, this approach raises difficulties of its own.

First, the suggested method for integrating operations undermines the very rationale for Bridgman's operationism. Relativity theory had shown that physics was led to a crisis by the assumption that its basic concepts, such as time and space, can be measured in various ways all revealing the same underlying physical property. This assumption had to be abandoned with the discovery that the equivalence of different measurement procedures breaks down at the extremes of the range and that measurement is dependent on the conditions of the observation. Operationism is intended as a replacement. Thus, the behaviorist suggestion that two operations may be said to measure and define the same concept if they yield the same results is in effect to make the inductive leap that operationism was meant to forbid.[17] The observed congruence of two measurement operations over a restricted range and under a limited set of circumstances does not permit the identification of the two, according to the strict operational approach.

A second problem with the behaviorist suggestion arises in determining when the two operations give the same results. If initially each measurement operation defines a distinct concept, then a third operation is needed to define the concept of "sameness of results."[18] However, the nature of this third operation is never precisely specified. This problem is especially acute when there is little overlap in area of application for the two operations. For example, the method of triangulation is commonly used to measure extraterrestial distances where there is no possibility for a comparison with distance as measured by a rod. Although the problem of defining the third operation may not prove to be insurmountable, it has yet to be resolved in ways that are consistent both with operationism and with the exigencies of concept formation in scientific theory.

Underlying these questions about operationism and concept formation is a more fundamental problem in operationism. Operationists have not successfully provided criteria for the individuation of operations.[19] That is, there is no formal way of determining whether or not two activities represent the same operation. In Bridgman's classic example, measuring distance by use of a rod is not the same operation as measurement by use of light rays; therefore they define two concepts. But what about the operation of measuring with a ruler marked in meters compared with one marked in feet? Are Smith's movements in using a ruler the same operation as Jones'? Is measuring with a rod in the morning the same operation as measuring in the evening? There are an infinite number of ways in which any two activities are similar and different. Without a criterion of individuation, there is no way to decide when to ignore the differences and classify the two activities as the same operation and when to ignore the similarities and consider the two as defining different concepts.

In practice it is only *a posteriori* that such distinctions are drawn. Only after it is known that temperature affects length is measurement at extreme temperatures considered to be a different operation from measurement at middle-range temperatures. It cannot be known in advance which similarities and differences are to be selected or ignored in defining operations. If the initial intuition is incorrect in that certain ignored differences are found to be important and the class is too broad, then the resulting empirical laws and correlations will not have the same simplicity and orderliness as a classification which distinguishes on the basis of those differences. Conversely, if the concept is defined too narrowly—i.e., important similarities are ignored—then the resulting laws will display redundancy. Expansion of the classification results in the convergence of many laws into fewer but more general ones.[20] There are no formal rules for constructing categories that maximize both simplicity and comprehensiveness.[21] Therefore, operationism is not an algorithm for concept formation.[22]

From these considerations it follows that although an operational definition may be formulated at any given stage, it is subject to revision in so far as its criteria for individuation of operations are vulnerable to change. Viewed this way, operational definitions acquire the open-textured quality of reductive chains. The only major difference is that with the reductive chain, the concept is viewed as open at all stages, and new reduction sentences are merely added to the existing scheme. From the operationist point of view, the concept is given a fixed closed definition, and every revision of individuation criteria is viewed as introducing a new concept, albeit with the same name.[23] Whether concept development is visualized as the gradual evolution of a single concept or as series of discrete substitutions of improved concepts for less useful ones of the same name seems to be more a matter of taste rather than fundamental epistemological principle. Thus the differences between concepts introduced by reductive chains and those operationally defined all but vanish.[24]

INTERVENING VARIABLES

Dispositional concepts and operationally defined concepts share important logical features with the "intervening variable," a type of concept introduced by Tolman which plays a central role in behaviorist matatheory.[25] Tolman (1938a) describes his use of the intervening variable in this way:

> A theory, as I shall conceive it, is a set of "intervening variables." These to-be-inserted intervening variables are 'constructs,' which we . . . evolve as a useful way of breaking down into more manageable form the original complete [empirical] function. . . . And I have conceived a set of . . . functions to connect these intervening variables severally to the independent variables, on the one hand, and a function . . . to combine them together and connect them to the final dependent variable, on the other. (p. 9)

An intervening variable thus represents a relationship between a set of interrelated independent variables and a set of interrelated dependent variables.

When behavioral measures covary, this correlation can be named and conceptualized as a common factor among all the measures. For example, a rat's rate of lever pressing for water, its toleration for quinine in its drinking water, and the amount it drinks when provided with free access to water are three behavioral measures which tend to covary. This covariation can be said to represent an intervening variable, termed "thirst," reflected by each of the three behavioral measures.

The intervening variable is also securely linked to the independent variables. It is, as behaviorists often describe it, "anchored on both sides."[26] To be anchored on the other side, the state must be shown to correlate with a set of interrelated independent variables. Thus, for example, the number of hours the rat is deprived of water, the amount of salt in its diet, and the temperature of its cage correlate, in that each one affects behavior in similar ways. Therefore, it can be said that these independent variables all affect a common state called "thirst." Anchored on both sides, the intervening variable represents the relationship between a set of dependent variables, which covary as a function of each of a set of independent variables, and a set of independent variables each of which produces the same covariation in the set of dependent variables.

Ideally the anchoring on the two sides should be quantitative and given by defining equations. In practice this kind of definition is rarely achieved, but a model of the ideal introduction of an intervening variable in the simplest case helps to illustrate its conceptual status. At the minimum, the introduction of an intervening variable, T, requires two independent variables, I_1 and I_2, two dependent variables, D_1 and D_2, and four empirically derived equations. In an initial experiment, often termed the "defining experiment," the relationship between D_1 and I_1 is determined while all other relevant variables are held constant.[27] From the defining experiment:

(1) $$D_1 = F(I_1)$$

The intervening variable T is introduced by stipulation either in terms of D_1 or I_1. It is of no importance which is chosen since the choice of one logically entails the relationship of T to the other. Thus:

(2) $T = G(D_1)$ by stipulation, therefore
(3) $T = G(F(I_1))$ by the stipulation in conjunction with equation (1).

Equations (2) and (3) define T in terms of dependent and independent variables and thus securely anchor the intervening variable on both sides. Three more empirical relationships between dependent and independent variables must be determined. Since there are two dependent and two independent variables, there are four different sequences in which this can be carried out. Because all four achieve the same purpose, only one will be illustrated.

In a second experiment, the relationship between D_1 and I_2 is determined:

(4) $$D_1 = H(I_2)$$

By the inductive logic of the intervening variable, it is assumed that values of D_1 when produced by changes in I_2 reflect T in the same way as those produced by changes in I_1. Therefore from equations (2) and (4):

(5) $$T = G(H(I_2))$$

In a third experiment, the relationship of D_2 to I_1 is determined:

(6) $$D_2 = K(I_1)$$

By the inductive logic of the intervening variable it is assumed that D_2 also reflects T. From equation (3) it follows that:

(7) $$I_1 = F^\star(G^\star(T))$$

Where $F^\star$ and $G^\star$ are the inverse functions of F and G, respectively; i.e., for any function, P, there is an inverse function, $P^\star$, such that for all x, $P^\star(P(x)) = x$. Therefore, from the assumptions of the intervening variable and equations (6) and (7):

(8) $$D_2 = K(F^\star(G^\star(T)))$$
$$= K(F^\star(G^\star(G(H(I_2))))) \text{ from equation (5)}$$
(9) $$= K(F^\star(H(I_2))).$$

Equation (9) is the key equation for the intervening variable. It is an empirical law relating an empirically defined dependent variable D_2 to an empirically defined independent variable I_2. However, this law is derived by inductive logic, prior to empirical observation, from three empirically derived equations and the assumptions of the intervening variable. The derivation of equation (9) can thus be viewed as a prediction prior to the fourth experiment, or as an explanation of equation (9) if it is indeed found to be the result of the fourth experiment. In either case, the derivation makes use of T. If the results of the fourth experiment conform to equation (9) then the assumptions gain in degree of confirmation, and the intervening variable T proves to be a useful concept.

Additional variables can be added to the intervening variable by the same methods. A dependent variable is added by first empirically determining its relationship to an independent variable already known to belong to T. From this result, the assumed relationship of this dependent variable to T may be deduced [cf. equations (6) and (8)]. From this, the relationship of the dependent variable to another independent variable in T may be deduced [cf. equation (9)]. If the deduction is confirmed by experiment, then the candidate is accepted into the intervening variable; if not, it is excluded. A similar technique can be used for testing independent variables for prospective membership in T. Thus the intervening variable is an open concept in that additional variables may be added with new discoveries.[28]

As equations (2) and (3) indicate, intervening variables are defined by both dependent and independent variables. To say that the value of an intervening variable T for an organism has the value N is therefore to say something about the behavior of that organism. However, it is not necessarily to say something about its current behavior. The value of the thirst-intervening-variable for a particular rat as measured by the independent variables may be very high, for example, but behaviors associated with the intervening variable may be absent because other factors interfere. Without available water, the dependent variable amount-drunk cannot be measured. Thus, the value of an intervening variable is reflected in behavior only under appropriate circumstances. Therefore, to say that $T=N$ for an organism is to say that under circumstances C_1 dependent variable D_1 will have value x, under circumstances C_2 dependent variable D_2 will have value y, and so forth throughout the class of dependent variables in T.

When viewed in this way, the intervening variable resembles dispositional concepts and operationally defined concepts discussed above.[29] The circumstances under which an intervening variable is reflected in behavior are equivalent to the test conditions under which a disposition is manifest and the defining operations for an operationally defined concept. Note that it is the circumstances, C_n, and *not* the independent variables, that are equivalent to the test conditions. Similarly, the values of the dependent variables for the intervening variable are the equivalent of the manifest outcomes for the disposition and the results of the measuring operations for the operationally defined concept.

On the other hand, intervening variables differ in significant ways from dispositional and operationally defined concepts. In contrast with strictly operationally defined concepts, intervening variables are open.[30] An intervening variable is realized by a progressively increasing number of behavioral dependent variables while a strictly operationally defined concept is defined by only one operation. Nevertheless, operational definitions serve an important role within the formulation of an intervening variable because each of the variables included in the intervening variable can be operationally defined.

Intervening variables also differ from dispositional concepts. As equation (3) indicates, intervening variables are defined from the stimulus side (i.e., independent variables). Although response measures occur only under appropriate circumstances, the independent variables can be measured and assigned a determinate value even when the circumstances are not appropriate for observing the behavioral measures. For example, a rat may be said to be thirsty although it is not currently under test conditions for the intervening variable of thirst because the intervening variable is also defined in terms of independent variables, such as hours of water deprivation, room temperature, and salt in diet, which can be measured. Therefore, a well formulated intervening variable, unlike a dispositional concept, is determinate even when test conditions do not prevail, and it is not introduced by reductive chains.[31]

THE INTERPRETATION OF DEFINED CONCEPTS

They Are Mere Labels

A common behaviorist interpretation of theoretical concepts is that they are merely labels for observed relationships between behavior and the environment. Most important, they do not stand for entities, events, or processes occurring in an unobserved realm in an organism's body or mind. They are temporally locatable, in that relationships may hold over limited intervals of time, but like all relational concepts, they possess no spatial location.

Although abstract concepts are admitted into behaviorist science, they are not to be reified,[32] or assigned a causal role.[33] An intervening variable "intervenes" only in the sense that the term representing the intervening variable in a behavioral law may be placed in a position intermediate between the dependent and the independent variables. Thus from equations (1) and (2) it may be stated that:

$$D_1 = G^*(T) = F(I_1)$$

and for example, that drinking is a function of thirst, and thirst, in turn, is a function of deprivation of water. However, intervening variables are not to be conceived as events or processes occurring after an environmental event and before a behavioral event.

They Are Eliminable

This view of concepts leads quite naturally to a second, more radical, opinion among behaviorists. If concepts are truly nothing more than names of observed relationships, then why not eliminate them altogether and deal directly with those observed relationships? A well defined concept is easily eliminable, and a vaguely formulated one does not belong in a science anyway. If a disposition is attributed on the basis of some observable property, then the behavior should be explained as a function of that observable property rather than the disposition.[34] If the disposition is ascribed on the basis of the behavior to be explained (e.g., eating is explained as due to hunger which is inferred from the eating behavior) then the concept is circular, and the explanation spurious.

Intervening variables can be eliminated in a similar manner. If an intervening variable is defined by equations of the form of equations (2) and (3), then wherever T appears, it may be replaced by either $G(D_1)$ or $G(F(I_1))$.[35] Therefore, equation (9) derived with the help of T may be derived as well without it:

(10) $I_1 = F^\star(D_1)$ from equation (1)
(11) $D_2 = K(F^\star(D_1))$ from equations (6) and (10).

From equations (4) and (11), equation (9) can be derived:

$$D_2 = K(F^\star(H(I_2)))$$

without using T.

They Are Undesirable

Not only are concepts eliminable, but, opponents argue, their elimination is also desirable. Many behaviorists fear that although a well formulated intervening variable or dispositional concept may be logically impeccable, in practice, the introduction of concepts inevitably leads to misuse. Such concepts, they claim, tend to be hypostatized and are easily regarded as symbolizing unobserved events. All too often, T comes to be viewed as an unobserved inner state of the organism—either a physiological one, or worse, from a behaviorist perspective, a mental one. Mentalism thus follows in the wake of these concepts, especially when they are identified with states known only through introspection.[36]

Besides the dangers of misinterpretation of well formulated concepts, there is the further risk, according to these critics, that once concepts are admissible, poorly formulated ones will be developed.[37] This is likely to occur when an intervening variable is not securely anchored on the stimulus (i.e., independent variable) side. In this case, the intervening variable is the equivalent of a dispositional concept. The peril here is that behavior will be explained as brought on by the disposition, but the disposition itself is left unexplained, with no attempt to link the disposition with its causes in the external environment. Thus behavior is explained by a concept inferred from behavior itself. Although such correlations within behavior may be occasionally useful, they are more likely to inhibit the search for the environmental causal antecedents of both the behavior and the correlations. Because these environmental antecedents are directly manipulable while dispositions are not, their discovery is far more important for the practical control of behavior.[38]

The situation is worse when the concept is anchored on neither side. In this case the concept is often invented *ad hoc* to explain a behavior. Not only are such explanations illegitimate, but they are also misleading. On the one hand, experimental research is diverted from the true causes of behavior and is directed toward the understanding of the inner processes and entities rather than at changing the independent external variables which truly control behavior. Moreover, because the concept is not securely anchored to measurable observations, it is often assigned dimensions different from those used in the other sciences, thereby isolating psychology from the rest of science.

Thus the introduction of dispositional concepts and intervening variables is believed by some behaviorists to lead to several eventualities which are at variance with fundamental behaviorist doctrine. At the same time, however, it is important to note that these arguments are directed at the practical *consequences* of introducing certain concepts into behaviorist psychology rather than at the concepts themselves. Properly formulated dispositional concepts and intervening variables are not logically suspect. The arguments in favor of their elimination involve the possible misinterpretation of the concepts or the introduction of improperly formulated ones. Therefore, the case against dispositional concepts and intervening variables may be said to be a "strategic" one rather than a "philosophical" one.

The Case for Concepts

1. They Mediate Causality. Proponents of concepts argue that the alleged dangers are exaggerated and that concepts offer certain important benefits that ought not to be forfeited.[39] One function served by intervening variables is that they bridge the temporal gap between dependent and independent variables. Very often considerable time may pass between the occurrence of an independent variable such as the reinforcement of a response and the behavior (e.g., the later occurrence of that response) which is a function of that variable. The introduction of an intervening variable, such as habit strength, serves as a contemporaneous summary of the organism's previous history and thus serves to mediate the time interval.[40] When the behavior finally does occur it may be said to be caused by the immediately preceding state, T, rather than by an independent variable in the past.

Although this is a common justification for the introduction of an intervening variable, there are two major problems with it. First, if an intervening variable is truly just a mathematical term fully defined by the equations in which it appears, then it cannot serve as a causal event distinct from the defining variables.[41] Second, the justification assumes that all causality is of the type typified by one billiard ball striking a second one. However, as Hume definitively argued, causal necessity is not observably present even in this case. Yet the requirement that a case always be temporally and spatially contiguous with its effect, sometimes called the "bead theory of causality,"[42] assumes causal necessity.

Some behaviorists therefore adopt a functional view of causality.[43] Functional relations are substituted for causal ones, and "x is a function of y" replaces "x is caused by y." This approach to causality thus avoids any implication that unobserved causal necessity intervenes between cause and effect. It also obviates the need for the contemporaneous occurrence of cause and effect. Therefore, behavior may be said to be a function of an event in the remote past, and there is no need for an intervening variable to mediate. This statement is not meant to deny that physiological events intervene between the two occurrences. Indeed, it is undeniable that such events do occur. The point is that these physiological events do not have to be referred to in order to state a functional relationship between behavior and the environment, and a molar behaviorism, therefore, does not have to sacrifice such relationships.[44]

2. They Simplify. A second justification for the use of intervening variables is that they simplify the formal expression of behavioral laws. Assume that an intervening relates n dependent variables to m independent variables. Without the intervening variable, if each dependent variable is related to each independent variable, $m \times n$ equations are required. With the introduction of the intervening variable T, m equations are required to express T as a function of each independent variable, and n equations for T as a function of each dependent variable, for a total of $m+n$ equations. Hence, for m or $n \geq 2$ and the other ≥ 3, the use of T decreases the number of equations necessary. The savings are only in formal expression. There is no reduction of the number of empirical experiments necessary to establish the behavioral laws, for a variable cannot be assumed to belong to the intervening variable unless it is experimentally proven to be.[45]

In reply to this claim, it can be argued that each dependent variable can be expressed in one equation as a joint function of all the independent variables. In this case, only n long equations are required to express the empirical content of the experimentally determined laws, and this is fewer than the $n+1$ equations necessary to express each of the dependent variables as a function of T (n equations) as well as T as a joint function of all the independent variables.

However, even here, proponents of the intervening variable argue that it serves an important role. They claim that the long equation relating a dependent variable to all the independent variables is so complex that it cannot be dealt with effectively. By subdividing the long equation into smaller groups of independent variables and identifying each group with an intervening variable, the entire equation becomes more intelligible and therefore manageable.[46] Relationships that would otherwise be missed are clarified in an equation judiciously simplified by a chain of intervening variables. To be sure, nothing in the simplified equation using a chain of intervening variables is not captured by the long equations. The simplified equation has only a heuristic advantage over the long equations, not a logical one.

3. They Facilitate Inductive Systematization. By systematizing various empirically determined relationships, an intervening variable facilitates predictions and suggests new experiments. This is a third reason why some behaviorists favor intervening variables. An important instance of this inductive systematization is to be found schematized in equations (1) through (9). This schema is, in effect, an algorithm for suggesting an experiment and predicting its results. Although, as shown above, this same derivation can logically be carried out without T, through equations (10) and (11), it is not as likely that in fact it will be carried out. Without T, equation (11) has no rationale. There is no reason to expect D_2 and D_1 to covary as suggested by equation (11). The introduction of T along with the associated intuitions that T is a function of I_1 and I_2 and that T is reflected by both D_1 and D_2 provide a rationale and motive for the derivation. As the number of variables increases and more than one intervening variable is introduced between dependent and independent variables, the derivation becomes more complex and T becomes a more important heuristic. Hence, T introduces a degree of inductive systematization that would be lost in its absence.[47]

Thus the three arguments in favor of the intervening variable, like the arguments against it, are strategic rather than philosophical. Neither side claims that intervening variables are logically indispensible. The point of contention revolves around the predicted consequences of their use. Proponents assert that such concepts possess heuristic value to facilitate research while opponents aver that concepts encourage abuses which impede scientific progress. Evidence relevant to this disagreement might be found in a historical study of the actual consequences of the use of intervening variables or from a psychology, yet to be achieved, which accounts for scientific thought.

Conventionalism

The justifications offered for the use of intervening variables emphasize their utility and lead quite naturally to a conventionalist view of theoretical terms and theory.[48] Intervening variables are valued because they provide a shorthand summary of observed relationships, mediate the derivation of predictions, and make complex equations more manageable. To be sure, intervening variables must be valid in that they must accurately summarize observations, mediate confirmed predictions, and correctly subdivide complex equations. However, because they do not symbolize events or entities, it is a matter of human choice as to how they are formulated, and in this sense they are conventions. Note, for example, the stipulative nature of equation (2), defining T.[49] Consequently, there is no unique set of valid intervening variables, just as there is no unique true summary of observations. For this reason, intervening variables are selected not merely for their validity but more for their convenience, degree of economy, and effectiveness.

From this conventionalist point of view, it also follows that intervening variables have no unique representation, just as there is no unique shorthand. Mathematical equations are a common method of representation but not the only one. Intervening variables can also be symbolized by diagrams, concrete mechanical models, flow charts, or electrical fields. For example, Tolman's intervening variables are often symbolized by spatial representations.[50] However, these fields are not intended to represent the subject's phenomenological field, nor are they maps of the subject's physical field. Instead, they are economical, and, for Tolman, convenient ways to represent the interaction of the variables affecting behavior and to derive spatial vectors representing the subject's response.

Opposed to a conventionalist interpretation of intervening variables and dispositional concepts is the realist view which argues, on philosophical grounds, that these concepts must be more than mere conventions. If behavior shows the interrelationships symbolized by the concept then there must be something about the organism by virtue of which those interrelationships are true. This "something" then is the true referent of the dispositional concept or the intervening variable.[51] Furthermore, this "something" can play a causal role in behavior. If a disposition or intervening variable is an event distinct from the observable variables, then it can truly "intervene" in the sense that it is a state caused by the independent variables, and it, in turn, can cause behavior.[52]

HYPOTHETICAL CONSTRUCTS

A realist perspective leads quite naturally to the introduction of concepts explicitly intended to refer to unobserved events within the organism. It is helpful to distinguish formally between these concepts and those which are viewed as a mere summary of observed relationships, and MacCorquodale and Meehl (1948) provide the required differentiation. They term the latter kind of concept an "intervening variable," and the former a "hypothetical construct."[53] They define the intervening variable as

> simply a quantity obtained by a specified manipulation of the values of empirical variables: it will involve no hypothesis as to the existence of nonobserved entities or the occurrence of unobserved processes; it will contain, in its complete statement for all purposes of theory and prediction, no words which are not definable either explicitly or by reduction sentences in terms of the empirical variables; and the validity of empirical laws involving only observables will constitute both the necessary and sufficient conditions for the validity of the laws involving these intervening variables. (p. 103)

In contrast, hypothetical constructs are defined as

> concepts which do *not* meet the requirements for intervening variables in the strict sense. That is to say, these constructs involve terms which are not wholly reducible

to empirical terms; they refer to processes or entities that are not directly observed (although they need not be in principle unobservable); the mathematical expression of them cannot be formed simply by a suitable grouping of terms in direct empirical equation; and the truth of the empirical laws involved is a necessary but not a sufficient condition for the truth of these conceptions. (p. 104)

The admission of hypothetical constructs into the science of behavior is a matter of controversy within behaviorist thought. It is obvious why this is so. Hypothetical constructs pose a far greater challenge to behaviorist ideals of empiricalness and objectivity than do intervening variables. Hypothetical constructs are associated with "existence propositions" which assign "surplus meaning" over and above observed correlations. Admission of hypothetical constructs thus means the inclusion of concepts referring to unobservables.

1. They Are Used by Other Sciences

Proponents of hypothetical constructs argue that science, in fact, does not limit itself exclusively to intervening variables. Physics has introduced a vast array of theoretical terms such as "electron" and "neutron" which refer to unobserved events and entities beyond the observations from which their existence is inferred. Modern physics could not have progressed without the introduction of these hypothetical constructs.[54] Therefore, a methodological decision to disallow constructs of this sort in psychology is not reflective of scientific method and might put psychology at a severe disadvantage.

Empiricists impressed by the success of physics construct a metatheoretical model of how such theoretical terms derive empirical significance although they refer to unobservables.[55] According to this model, a theory is an axiomatized uninterpreted calculus. Theoretical terms are introduced by postulates within the theory that provide only an implicit definition of the theoretical terms by stating how they are related to the other terms of the theory.[56] The theory, as a whole, is given empirical significance by a set of "correspondence rules" which connect certain terms of the theory to empirical observations. These correspondence rules may take, among others, the form of operational definitions or reduction sentences. However, only some of the terms of the theory are included in the correspondence rules. Other terms, not given definition by the correspondence rules, are theoretical and have only implicit definitions. They acquire empirical significance only by their role in the entire set of postulates connected at various points to empirical observations by the correspondence rules.

In response to this argument it can be claimed that there are cogent reasons why psychology should not follow the example of physics. First, psychological theory is nowhere near axiomatization. Therefore any model for the introduction of theoretical terms which assumes an axiomatized theory is inapplicable to psychology. Second, as compared to psychology, physics is a far more mature and well developed science. Theoretical concepts are more highly quantified, postulates are more explicit, and theoretical deductions are stricter, so testing of theories is more rigorous. Therefore, the dangers associated with the introduction of theoretical concepts are much less severe in physics than in psychology. Third, unlike physics, psychology must contend with the fact that researchers bring to their theorizing a wealth of prescientific concepts about human action derived from everyday speech, intuition, and their own phenomenology. Inevitably, these subjective and mentalistic notions influence the formulation of theoretical concepts in psychology. Therefore, hypothetical constructs are more vulnerable to misuse in psychology than in physics.[57]

These arguments as to why psychology should not imitate physics are not without irony. A central thrust behind the behaviorist movement is the attempt to transform psychology into a science. Physics, in particular, is upheld as the model psychology should emulate. However, as physics progressed, its associated philosophy of science evolved; but psychology, not blessed with corresponding progress, did not share in this development.[58] Ironically, behaviorist philosophy of science is often defended by appeal to differences between psychology and physics.

2. They Cannot Be Avoided in Practice

A second argument against the limitation of psychology to intervening variables and operationally defined concepts is that in practice psychologists do not treat any concept as if it were one of those two kinds. Suppose, for example, that IQ is operationally defined as what is measured by a particular test, and the intervening variable of hunger is measured by rate of lever pressing for food. Suppose further that after the behavioral measures are recorded, it is discovered that the subjects in both experiments were ill. Under these circumstances, it is commonly concluded that the behavior was not a true measure of the concept. However, if the concept is in fact defined solely in terms of the behavior, then whatever behavior is recorded is, by definition, a measure of the concept. There should be no rationale for saying when the behavior is or is not a "true" measure of the concept. To deny that the behavior is a measure of the concept entails that the concept is something other than what is measured by the behavior. In practice, therefore, it appears that intervening variables and operationally defined concepts are treated as if they are hypothetical constructs.[59]

This argument does not seem conclusive. Operational definitions as well as definitions of intervening variables include implicit *ceteris paribus* clauses to indicate that the outcome or response measure defines the concept only under normal circumstances. Amount eaten is not assumed to measure hunger if the rat's mouth is sewn shut. It is assumed that interfering factors may occur which prevent an outcome or behavioral measure from defining the concept. Thus, when a behavioral outcome is not taken as a true measure of IQ or hunger, this is not because those intervening variables exist as entities over and above the measurements, but because the measurements were not performed under standard conditions.

The interfering factors which preclude conditions from being standard cannot be exhaustively listed, not only because they cannot all be anticipated *a priori*, but also because they are infinite in number. Therefore, some intuitive understanding of the concept is necessary to determine when a factor is an interfering one. Nevertheless, this intuitive grasp of the concept does not entail that an unobservable underlies the concept and is referred to in determining when an outcome is or is not a true measure of the concept. Normally, the intuition results from experience with the observed correlations and the correct unproblematic application of the concept. In fact, all concepts, whether dispositional or not, involve an intuitive understanding which cannot be exhaustively captured by a listing of rules of usage. To know an object is red or triangular also involves knowledge about normal conditions and interfering factors, knowlege which cannot be fully explicated.[60]

3. They Are Important for Reduction

Yet a third argument in favor of hypothetical constructs is that they bridge the gap between psychology and physiology.[61] Hypothetical constructs tend to be characterized in physiological terms. They, therefore can serve a heuristic function in suggesting to physiologists the kind of mechanisms to look for. At some point, the hypothetical constructs of psychology can be identified with the mechanisms discovered by physiology, and the theoretical reduction of psychology to physiology will be accomplished. By combining behavioral as well as physiological features, the hypothetical construct facilitates this reduction. If continuity with the other sciences is a goal of behaviorist psychology then theoretical reduction of psychology to physiology via hypothetical constructs is one way to accomplish this. Intervening variables are unlikely to be helpful in this regard. Because of their conventional nature, intervening variables can be defined and redefined arbitrarily, while physiological mechanisms seem to be matters of fact, not convention.

This argument in support of hypothetical constructs presupposes several questionable assumptions. First, it is not clear that hypothetical constructs are more efficacious for theoretical reduction than intervening variables. With a hypothetical construct, the possibility of attributing invalid properties is ever present. In contrast, a well formulated intervening variable, in not exceeding observations, is more likely to correspond to a physiological constuct than a hypothetical construct with incorrect features.[62] Futhermore, the argument assumes that the subdivision of an entire organism into physiological systems is a given rather than the consequence of human conceptualization. When the skull is opened, the parts of the brain do not appear already labeled with borders neatly laid out. Neural "mechanisms" are created on the basis of a number of considerations, including functional ties as well as anatomical connections. Therefore, physiological mechanisms are conventional in the same sense intervening variables are: both initially are human creations, but both must prove their worth.

Second, the argument assumes that theoretical reduction is the best method for assuring continuity between psychology and the other sciences. Yet, one of the contentions of molar behaviorism is that the legitimacy of a behavioral psychology does not rest on the possibility of its reduction to physiology. To the contrary, the aims of molar behaviorism are best achieved by a purely behavioral psychology, independent of physiology, which is effective for the prediction and control of behavior and is unencumbered by premature speculation about physiology. Continuity with the rest of science can be accomplished by a commonality of methods and underlying assumptions.[63]

4. They Are Necessary for Explaining Behavior

A fourth objection to theories limited to intervening variables and operationally defined concepts is that such theories are not truly explanatory. Because theories of this type refrain from making statements about events internal to the behaving organism, they are often derogatorily referred to as "black-box" theories. At best, it is often argued, black-box theories provide behavioral laws relating input (stimuli) to output (responses), but they do not *explain* these lawful relationships. Only by reference to events inside the black-box, i.e., hypothetical constructs, can behavior be explained.[64]

This objection to black-box theories makes certain tacit assumptions about the nature of explanation that need to be examined. If by "explanation" the nomological-deductive pattern is meant, then clearly black-box theories are explanatory. Particular instances of behavior are explained by deducing statements describing them from general behavioral laws in conjunction with statements about initial conditions. Instead, the objection may be that the behavioral laws used in black-box deductive explanations are simply descriptive of observed regularities rather than explanatory. They are stated as givens rather than as the results of the internal events mediating them.

It is true, as this argument notes, that black-box theories must have a few fundamental behavioral laws from which other laws and statements about particular responses are deduced. These fundamental laws are indeed "primitive" in the sense that they themselves are not deduced from other laws. However, the argument is mistaken in its implicit belief that the situation could be otherwise. As Hume clearly showed, causal laws are not logically necessary. Therefore even explanations referring to hypothetical constructs ultimately appeal to fundamental laws, whether experimental or theoretical, which are primitive in the same sense that the fundamental behavioral laws are.

A proponent of hypothetical constructs might still argue that theories incorporating hypothetical constructs are superior because primitive behavioral laws can be deduced from such theories. Thus these theories explain what is left unexplained in black-box theories. In response to this argument it should be noted that it is always the case that the fundamental laws of one science are possibly the derived theorems of another more fundamental science. This holds as well for theories incorporating physiological hypothetical constructs. Nevertheless, just because a science is possibly reducible to another science, this is no reason to deny that the science is explanatory. If this were the case, then no science, other than the most fundamental one, is explanatory, including physiological pychology.

It appears that the claim that the black-box theories are not explanatory is false when deductive explanation is meant. However, "explanation" may be used in other senses. Often a deductive explanation does not provide the hearer with an intuitive understanding, and consequently the explanation is not epistemically satisfying. Thus, "explanation" may mean "to provide a satisfactory understanding." Those who object to black-box theories are often saying, in effect, that although such theories explain in one sense, they fail to provide understanding. In contrast, theories appealing to physiological mechanisms are said to meet the hearer's epistemic needs and provide an intuitive grasp of the explicandum.[65] Thus, objections to black-box theories often reflect a preference for a certain kind of explanation. Therefore, the explanatory adequacy of black-box theories depends on individual differences over what constitutes subjectively satisfying understanding.

5. They Are Heuristics

A fifth and extremely common objection to a black-box science is that it would be excessively "narrow," thereby impeding scientific progress.[66] Numerous examples in the history of science can be adduced to demonstrate how unobservables were hypothesized to explain certain observations, and then later these hypothetical constructs were found, through direct observation, to have many of the hypothesized properties ascribed to them. Genes, molecules, bacteria, and distant stars are typical examples. In this way the hypothetical construct guides and integrates research. Although the properties assigned to the construct are inferred from observation, they transcend the observations to provide the construct's surplus meaning. This surplus meaning enables the theory to integrate diverse observations which otherwise would not appear to be related. Moreover, from statements about the hypothesized properties, other statements are deduced which have observational implications. These, in turn, suggest experiments which tend either to confirm or disconfirm the statements about the construct. Thus the attempt to characterize fully the theoretical construct and to test this characterization organizes and directs research.[67]

The Case Against Hypothetical Constructs

These arguments in favor of the inclusion of hypothetical constructs appear to be strategic ones, just as are the arguments in favor of intervening variables. The strategic arguments—that psychology should emulate physics, that hypothetical constructs facilitate theoretical reduction, that they provide more satisfactory understanding, or that they are heuristically fertile—reduce to the common theme that the introduction of hypothetical constructs will enhance the progress of psychology, not that they are logically necessary. Similarly, the case against hypothetical constructs is based largely on strategic considerations. In addition to all the objections to intervening variables reviewed above, it is feared that the use of hypothetical constructs will encourage unwarranted speculation, resulting in premature "physiologizing" and the creation of theoretical "fictions."

Hypothetical constructs seem less open to experimental tests because properties can be attributed to them *ad hoc* to accommodate any experimental result, and they therefore appear to provide only spurious explanations. Furthermore, if they are not logically required, then their introduction violates the principle of parsimony by unnecesarily complicating a theory. Theorizing devoted to determining the properties of the hypothetical construct further diverts attention toward inner mechanisms not readily manipulated and away from the environmental factors responsible for both behavior and its physiological mediators. Again, the argument is strategic, not philosophical.[68]

Some behaviorists argue, furthermore, that hypothetical constructs are always dispensable. Constructs are said to intervene between independent and dependent variables. If this relationship is lawful, then the insertion of the construct does not add to the law and is unnecessary. Similarly, if the construct is lawfully related to the independent variable, and the dependent variable is lawfully related to the construct, then again, the dependent variable is lawfully related to the independent variable, and the construct is useless. If, on the other hand, there is no lawfulness, the construct cannot create it. In either case, the construct is dispensable, generating the behaviorist "paradox of theorizing."[69]

Hypothetical Constructs in Behaviorist Theories

In the absence of decisive arguments for or against the use of hypothetical constructs, the decision to introduce them into behaviorist science is left to the strategic intuition of the individual theorist. In point of fact and contrary to the popular image, the majority of behaviorist theories include hypothetical constructs among their theoretical terms. Although there are a vast number of such constructs to be found throughout behaviorist theories, they can, for the most part, be classified into four broad categories.

One category can be characterized as consisting of covert responses. These are conceptualized as similar in all essentials to observable responses except that they are small in scale or else located inside the body. This class includes the subvocal speech and visceral responses Watson and others use to explain thought and emotion.[70] Hull's anticipatory goal reaction, Spence's emotional responses, and Mowrer's "hope" and "fear" form another subclass.[71] Internal perceptual responses, including the "coding response," are also of this type.[72] Finally, one very large subclass of the covert response cateogry is the "mediating response." This covert response has been assigned manifold functions within behaviorist theories, ranging from the mediation of generalization in the absence of physical similarity to the acquisition of meaning in verbal behavior.[73]

Covert stimuli form a second broad category of hypothetical constructs. These are hypothesized to arise from at least three possible sources. First, certain stimuli are caused by various physiological processes within the body. Deprivation of food, for example, leads to physiological changes which constitute potential stimuli for behavior. Or these stimuli may be caused by overt behavior in the form of proprioceptive stimulation arising from muscles and tendons, such as the movement-produced stimuli of Guthrie's theory.[74] Third, covert stimuli may be the result of covert responses, as in the stimulus consequences of Hull's pure stimulus acts or anticipatory goal reaction, which may in turn elicit overt behavior.[75]

A third set of hypothetical constructs consists of long-term physiological mechanism thought to underlie behavioral states or dispositions. State variables pose a problem for those behaviorists who prefer to conceive of responses and stimuli as brief and momentary events because states are long lasting and continuous. However, tonus and postural reflexes provide a model to resolve this difficulty. Therefore, a number of dispositional concepts, including attention, determining tendencies, anticipatory set, attitude, and readiness, are interpreted as states of muscle tonus, postural reflexes, or their conceptual offspring, the "motor set."[76]

The fourth category of hypothetical construct differs significantly from the others. In this category belong overt stimuli and responses which are not hidden inside the organism and are therefore not unobservable in the same sense as internal events are. Nevertheless, these events are hypothetical in that they are postulated although not actually observed, identified, or recorded. Consider, for example, a competing-response theory of extinction. According to this theory, an unreinforced response stops occuring because incompatible responses are conditioned and interfere with it. These competing responses are hypothesized in order to explain an observed decrease in a particular response, but the competing responses are not actually identified.[77]

Characteristics of Hypothetical Constructs in Behaviorist Theories

Although no restrictions are logically imposed on the postulated properties of the hypothetical construct, they nevertheless generally conform to four conditions. First, the properties assigned to the hypothetical construct do not differ substantially from those of observed stimuli and responses. They are conceived as material rather than mental and as obeying the same laws as overt stimuli and responses, with the possible exception that constants in the equations may differ somewhat because of the reduced size of covert forms.[78] Second, hypothetical constructs are commonly located peripherally, in the muscles and glands, rather than in the central nervous system.[79] Third, hypothetical constructs are typically thought to operate under the functional control of environmental variables, that is, their activities are not "autonomous."[80] Fourth, although this condition is rarely achieved, it is preferable that the hypothetical construct be linked by a functional relationship to an observable environmental variable, or an observable behavioral variable, or, ideally, to both. This linkage is different from the intervening variable. With the hypothetical construct, the linkage relates three distinct entities, and the hypothetical construct has a meaning and existence beyond that provided by the functional relationship.

These four conditions combine neatly in a common example of a hypothetical construct. It is hypothesized to begin as an overt muscular response, acquired through the normal laws of learning as a function of external variables. It gradually regresses in magnitude until it is unobservable. In its reduced state it yet remains a response, still muscular, and still under the functional control of environment variables.[81]

These four conditions help to guard against behaviorist fears of unwarranted speculation and the introduction of "fictions." The first condition assures that no properties will be attributed to the construct that are not properties of observables. The second and third conditions allay behaviorist qualms about the taint of mentalism. Behaviorists often argue that because so little is known about the central nervous system, it serves as the last refuge of the soul in psychology. Processes hypothetically located there often have qualities of free will, agency, and the mental.[82] Therefore, by locating covert events in the periphery and keeping them under the functional control of the environment, behaviorists prevent the contamination of their constructs by mentalism. The fourth condition, in conjunction with the first, helps to ensure that the theory in which the hypothetical constructs are embedded is rigorously testable. Unconfirmed postulates can be discarded along with their hypothetical constructs. Thus although behaviorist hypothetical constructs are inferred rather than observed, they are closely related to observables by short lines of inference, thus retaining their empiricalness and objectivity.

CHAPTER 5

Theorizing

Behaviorist theorizing occurs in many forms. At the two extremes are the hypothetico-deductivism of Hull and the descriptivism of Skinner.

The status of Hullian theoretical concepts is somewhat ambiguous. Some are clearly hypothetical constructs. Others appear to be intervening variables but operate as hypothetical constructs.

Hull's hypothetico-deductive method is not like deductive systems in logic and mathematics. Instead, his postulates define concepts as hypothesized quantitative functions of empirically defined variables, and they state hypotheses as to how these concepts combine to determine behavioral variables.

The purpose of a theory, according to Hull, is to mediate the deduction of theorems about observable behavior. Theorems are experimentally tested and either add confirmation to a theory or force its revision. Theory develops through this process of deduction, test, and revision. Explanation is achieved when the description of a phenomenon is deduced as a theorem from a theory.

Skinner's theoretical concepts consist of intervening variables, such as drive, and private events, consisting of covert stimuli and responses. Although the status of the latter is not clear, they are best viewed as hypothetical constructs.

Skinner objects to theories on the grounds that they inhibit fruitful research. Instead, he advocates a descriptivism with an emphasis on discovering orderliness in behavioral data. Theory, for Skinner, consists of economical descriptions of functional relations which subsume a number of behavioral regularities.

Both Hullian and Skinnerian meta-theory are open to criticisms from a nonlinear model of the development of science. This model questions behaviorist assumptions about the continuity of theory development and the relationship of theory to data.

Despite behaviorist attempts to link concepts to the behavioral data language, the relationship of concepts to observation is underdetermined. This linkage is ultimately psychological. Within this context, behaviorist meta-theory can be viewed as a decision to specify concepts precisely enough for scientists to learn to achieve intersubjective agreement, prediction, and control while using them.

Observed regularities in behavior eventually give rise to empirical generalizations, which, in turn, lead to the formulation of scientific laws. Although these generalizations and laws are helpful in achieving the behaviorist goals of prediction and control of behavior, these twin goals are reached even more effectively through the creation of a theoretical system. Such a system mediates prediction and control of a variety of behaviors in a wide variety of situations, and it integrates a broad range of seemingly unrelated phenomena and laws under relatively few basic principles. Thus, a comprehensive and integrative theory uncovers coherence within the domain of the behavioral science and thereby facilitates explanation and understanding.

Behaviorists create theories in a number of ways, each of which represents a branch from the next node considered within the behaviorist conceptual tree diagram. Two of the most influential methods of theorizing are those of Hull and Skinner. The theories of these two are illustrative, not only because their methods are widely followed, but also because they represent two extremes within behaviorism. Between the hypothetico-deductivism of Hull and the descriptivism of Skinner lies a range in which the theories of a large number of behaviorists fall. Because they sit at the extremes, the meta-theories of Hull and Skinner provide relatively clear case studies for the conceptual issues to be examined in this chapter.

HULLIAN THEORIZING

Hull's Constructs

Hullian constructs pose special problems for interpretation. In certain cases, including the anticipatory goal reaction, r_g, it is clear that a hypothetical construct is intended.[1] However, for many of his major constructs, including habit strength, $_SH_R$, and drive, D, the logical status is not as obvious. On the one hand, he explicitly claims that all his constructs are intervening variables as conceptualized by Tolman.[2] On the other hand, when he discusses these constructs, they do not sound like mere convenient groupings of mathematical terms with no independent existences.[3] For example in discussing $_SH_R$ he states:

> It is important to note that habit strength cannot be determined by direct observation, since it exists as an organization as yet largely unknown, hidden within the complex structure of the nervous system. This means [it] can be determined, i.e., can be observed and measured, only indirectly. (1943b, p. 102)

Some of Hull's expositors claim that these statements are merely supplementary physiological speculations, heuristically helpful in the process of theorizing, but not part of the theory *per se*.[4] Indeed, at one point Hull says of a statement of this sort that it is a "kind of background" and "not properly a part of the present system."[5] According to this interpretation, the real theory and the meaning of its theoretical terms consists solely of the quantitative statements supplied by the postulates. Other commentators, on the other hand, maintain that all statements about a theoretical construct contribute to its meaning and must be included in the theory.[6]

Although there is no clear-cut way to determine when a statement is part of the theory and when it is merely supplemental background, one possible criterion is its role in mediating deductions from the theory. Certainly if a statement is necessary for a deduction claimed by the theory, then it is part of the theory. With this criterion in mind, consider the construct S_D, the hypothesized drive stimulus, introduced by Postulate 6: "Associated with every drive (D) is a characteristic drive stimulus (S_D) whose intensity is an increasing montonic function of the drive in question" (Hull, 1943b, p. 253). Using the S_D concept, Hull derives predictions of performance at various levels of drive. Some of these predictions are mediated by the laws of stimulus generalization (Postulate 5). However, the laws of generalization do not apply to S_D unless it is attributed the physical properties of a stimulus.[7] Thus, S_D operates within the theory like a hypothetical construct rather than a purely conceptual intervening variable. It appears, therefore, that no general statement can be made concerning the logical status of Hullian constructs, and each one must be examined separately.[8]

Hull's Postulational Method

Ambiguities arise also in interpreting the logical structure of Hullian theory. On the one hand, Hull, in his early "miniature systems," announces that the systems of Newton and Euclid—with their definitions, axioms, postulates, and theorems—are the models for his own theorizing. His early theories, in fact, are formally presented according to that scheme.[9] It therefore appears that Hullian theory consists of an uninterpreted axiomatized calculus given empirical meaning only through coordination at certain points with experimental variables by a set of correspondence rules.[10] Since not every theoretical term is associated with a correspondence rule, some terms receive only implicit definition and therefore function as hypothetical constructs rather than intervening variables. This impression is further compounded by the fact that Hull divides his term into "defined" and "undefined" and includes his theoretical terms among the latter.[11]

On the other hand, a close examination of Hullian theory reveals that while the form of an axiomatized system is maintained, the theory does not operate as one. First, the postulates define theoretical concepts in terms of experimental variables, and the theory is therefore not an uninterpreted calculus in need of correspondence rules. For example, Postulate 3 of one miniature system (Hull, 1937) states:

A characteristic stimulus-reaction . . . always marks reinforcing states of affairs. . . . The particular stimulus-response combination marking the reinforcing state of affairs in the case of specific drives is determined empirically. (p. 16)

and "reinforcing state of affairs" has already been defined in Definition 1.

Second, by "undefined term" Hull does not refer to terms given only implicit meaning by the theoretical context. He is simply noting the fact that since terms are defined with other terms, at some point definitions are either circular or some terms are simply left formally undefined. It is a matter of convention which terms are chosen to remain formally undefined and to be introduced either by ostension or through ordinary language with its pre-scientific meanings.[12] Hull occasionally leaves his theoretical terms as undefined because he finds it cumbersome to try to provide them with formal definitions. Otherwise the theoretical concepts are introduced by postulates which state equations defining the concept as a mathematical function of experimental variables.

Thus Hull's "hypothetical-deductive" technique cannot be understood in the same sense as it is used in logic and mathematics. His postulates seem to serve a different purpose. Hull begins with a small number of empirical findings—response rate as a function of number of reinforced trials, for example. Although number of reinforced trials is the only variable manipulated, it is obvious that the response rate is a function of a number of variables presumably kept constant (e.g., drive, delay of reinforcement) as well as some which are unknown. It is possible to speculate on how all these variables enter into the equation determining response rate. However, this "long equation" stating response rate as a function of every relevant variable would be unwieldy for suggesting further experimentation. Instead, Hull divides up the long equation into smaller groupings, each of which defines a new quantity such as habit strength and inhibition. Therefore, one role of the postulates is to define these new concepts as an hypothesized quantitative function of empirically defined variables. The second role is to hypothesize how these theoretical variables combine to determine the behavioral variables.[13]

The concept is thus anchored on both sides, and the postulate set therefore consists essentially of definitions and hypothesized empirical relationships. Why then call them "postulates"? Hull gives three reasons. He identifies "postulated" with "hypothesized" and argues that his statements are hypothesized in the sense that his guesses have not yet been proved valid. Second, he argues that since none of his postulates have been shown to be underivable from the others, it is only a supposition that each is a postulate rather than a theorem.[14] Third, he notes that since the postulates define each intervening variable in terms of only a limited subgrouping of all the variables responsible for behavior, predictions about behavior can be made only by combining the various postulates to deduce the behavioral outcome. Consequently, it is a theorem deduced from a set of postulates which is tested, and not any single postulate.[15] Therefore, a postulate is a "postulate" in the sense that it cannot be *directly* tested and so always remains hypothetical.

Role of Hullian Theory

For Hull and his followers the main purpose of a theory is the deduction of theorems about observables. These theorems can be experimentally tested, and if the results conform to the theorem, then the theory gains in its degree of confirmation and the confidence with which it is maintained. Lack of observed congruence with a theorem calls for revision of the theory.

By this process of test and revision, a theory is gradually developed that generates increasingly greater numbers of valid theorems. Therefore, a theory mediating a large number of testable theorems is preferable to one which mediates fewer, because the possibilities of test and revision are greater with the former.[16] Since theorems are statements about future behavior as well as assertions about how the environment determines behavior, they play a critical role in the prediction and control of behavior.

Theory furthermore mediates the explanation of behavior. When a behavior occurs, a description of it may be stated as a theorem. If this theorem is deducible from the theory, then the behavior is explained. This identification of explanation (and prediction) with logical deduction from a theory is congruent with the general behaviorist understanding of objectivity in science. If explanations or predictions are offered on the basis of intuition or empathy, then there is much room for disagreement and controversy. In contrast, logical deductions from clearly stated postulates are more certain to command universal assent.[17] Thus, objectivity in explanation and theory construction, just as with observation, is closely identified with intersubjective agreement among scientists.

Besides mediating prediction, control, and explanation, theories also organize and direct research. The initial postulates are framed so as to conform to the current data on an *ad hoc* basis. Once formulated, however, the system generates theorems about experiments not yet performed, thereby suggesting further research. Furthermore, by simplifying the "long equation," intervening variables help clarify important relationships which may then be experimentally investigated. Thus the Hullian postulates are a source of hypotheses to guide a research program.[18]

SKINNERIAN THEORIZING

Skinner's Constructs

The concepts within Skinner's theory fall into two categories. The first consists of a set of intervening variables, including "reflex reserve," "drive," and "emotion." Each is anchored to both dependent and independent variables and summarizes the changes in the functional relationships between them produced by certain operations. For example, an operation like food deprivation will change the relationship between a schedule of food reinforcement and response rate. To summarize the correlated changes, the concept "drive" is introduced. However, because of the objections to intervening variables discussed in the preceding chapter, Skinner eventually eliminates nearly all of them from his theoretical system.[19]

The second category of Skinnerian constructs consists of "private events." These are covert stimuli and responses which play a fairly prominent role in Skinner's interpretation of behavior. They are attributed the properties of overt stimuli and response, and they are assumed to occur under the functional control of the external environment. Skinner adds that they are not involved in the causation of behavior but are instead "collateral byproducts" of the environmental variables responsible for both covert and overt events.[20] Strictly speaking, however, since in Skinner's interpretation covert events can function as discriminative stimuli, reinforcing stimuli, and punishing stimuli for overt behavior, they clearly do play a causal role.[21] Nevertheless, they do not play as important a role as has traditionally been thought or as might be supposed on the basis of introspection.

From these considerations, it seems that Skinner's private events qualify as hypothetical constructs which generally meet the behaviorist strictures described in chapter 4. Problems arise because an essential feature of a hypothetical construct is that it is inferred rather than observed. However, as discussed in chapter 2, in rejecting intersubjective agreement as a criterion for scientific observation, Skinner opens the way for the acceptance of private observation. This may mean that a verbal response ("tact") to a private stimulus can count as an observation. Therefore, private events may be said to be observed rather than inferred. In this case private events are not hypothetical constructs, and their descriptions are part of the behavioral data language.

On the other hand, Skinner often speaks of private events as inferred.[22] Furthermore, there are good reasons why private events ought to be considered inferred. First, if behaviorist psychology is to be the "psychology of the other one," in Meyer's felicitous phrase,[23] then even if the subject may be said to be observing the private event, the experimenter, representing the science, must be said to infer the private event.

Second, Skinner's statement that private events are the discriminative stimuli for certain verbal responses is, at present, no more than a hypothesis. No proof is currently available to show that any verbal responses enter into causal relationships with private events as required by the hypothesis, or that these private events are stimuli and responses conforming to the same laws as their overt counterparts. Therefore, private stimuli and responses are inferences. Even the subject's verbal responses provide no observational evidence for the hypothesis since they are in the form "I have a toothache" rather than "Stimulus X is occurring in me."[24] Furthermore, many covert events, such as the autoclitics Skinner hypothesizes to be involved in editing speech, are not observed even in the sense of acting as stimuli for verbal reports.[25] For these several reasons it seems appropriate to judge Skinner's private events as inferred and therefore as hypothetical constructs.

Skinner on Theory

Because Skinner objects to both intervening variables and hypothetical constructs, it is not surprising that he objects to theories containing theoretical concepts. Moreover, Skinner also claims that psychological theories in general are neither necessary nor desirable. By "theory" he means

> any explanation of an observed fact which appeals to events taking place somewhere else, at some other level of observation, described in different terms, and measured, if at all, in different dimensions. (1950, p. 193)

This definition is intended to include physiological and mental constructs, as well as inferred explanatory events.

It is not clear whether Skinner's own hypotheses about private events escape this definition. To be sure, private events are described in the same terms as overt behavior and measured in the same dimensions.[26] But whether private events are "events taking place somewhere else, at some other level of observation" is not obvious. They are "somewhere else" in that they are on the other side of the skin from overt behavior, and they must be observed by means other than those used to observe overt behavior.

Nor is it obvious whether Skinner's definition of "theory" covers statements about intervening variables. A well formulated intervening variable is defined by a set of observable variables. It is not a distinct event located elsewhere but is rather a shorthand for observed relationships.[27] To be sure, it is sometimes measured in its own dimensions, such as "habs" for the Hullian $_SH_R$, but these new dimensions are merely transformations of old units, just as "ergs" is merely a transformation of dynes and centimeters.

Whatever the range covered by Skinner's definition of "theory," he argues that theory has a detrimental influence on the development of psychology. He is particularly concerned with the methods, especially hypothetico-deductive techniques, prescribed for the scientist to follow in formulating theory. He admits that at certain points in the history of science and for certain subject matters, these methods may be appropriate, but not for psychology whose subject matter, behavior, shows lawfulness at the level of observables.[28] According to Skinner, scientists who are taught to use these methods exclusively are limited in their ability to do science. For them, theorizing is conceived as a mysterious cognitive activity, and excessive attention is paid to it rather than to behavior.[29] Such scientists will be motivated by the attempt to test theorems of the theory rather than the search for lawfulness in behavior.[30] Their research will be useful only so long as the theory remains in vogue. Once the theory is rejected, the research becomes meaningless.[31]

Theory, he claims, also interferes with the search for lawfulness when it is used as a substitute for that search. When behavior appears to lack orderliness, theorists often invent theoretical processes postulated to show the orderliness apparently absent instead of determining and controlling the variables responsible for the behavior. Orderliness is thus relegated to the theoretical postulates rather than uncovered in the behavior.[32] These postulates are never directly tested as are the theorems deduced from a conjunction of postulates. Consequently, a postulate can never become a fact.[33] On the other hand, if the proper attention is paid to the variables controlling behavior and an appropriate behavioral unit is chosen, orderliness appears directly in the behavior and the postulated theoretical processes become superfluous.[34]

Evaluation of Skinner's Claims

Skinner's objections to the introduction of intervening variables and hypothetical constructs were discusssed in the preceding chapter. With regard to theory construction, Skinner's own research achievements and those of his followers demonstrate that a research program can proceed and even flourish with a minimum of theoretical concepts and in the absence of hypothetico-deductive methods. Theories, in Skinner's sense, are not *necessary*.

That they are also *undesirable* is more difficult to prove.[35] While it is true that Hull's system failed to achieve the theory he envisioned, its heuristic value continues as it and its lineal descendants continued to serve as a source of concepts and experimental hypotheses. Furthermore, it is not clear that the failure of the Hullian system can be attributed to the hypothetico-deductive method.[36] Perhaps the same method on a smaller scale and with more conservative inferences in formulating postulates might meet with more success. Finally, while it is true that some research generated by Hullian theory is no longer useful, much of it stands on its own, and has in some cases been incorporated into other systems, including those of Skinner's followers.[37] Assuming that Hullians used valid experimental procedures, their data are valid. Whether they are also relevant depends on the current standards of relevance. Not every instance of orderliness in behavior found by a Skinnerian will prove to be useful either.

The force of Skinner's second complaint, that postulates cannot become facts, is unclear for several reasons.[38] First, Hull freely admits that his postulates are not open to direct confirmation, but this is not a source of embarrassment for him. The purpose of the postulates is to mediate deductions, not to describe facts. Thus, Skinner's complaint is at base really a restatement of his objection to the hypothetico-deductive methodology. Furthermore, it is not even clear that Hull's postulates cannot be directly tested. Since Hull's postulates are a set of assumed empirical laws rather than an axiomatized uninterpreted calculus, there are ways to test them directly.[39]

Skinner is correct in his third charge that at times psychologists have substituted orderly postulates in place of the search for orderliness in behavior. However, this may show merely that any method may be abused rather than that abuse is an inevitable consequence of a particular method. The search for orderliness in behavior and the avoidance of explanatory fictions may also be abused, as when the results of an experiment are presented in the form of reams of uninterpreted cumulative records.[40]

Skinner's Descriptivism

In place of the kinds of theories he objects to, Skinner offers an alternative, the "experimental analysis of behavior."[41] In this approach, research is guided not by the attempt to test theorems but by the search for orderliness in behavior. This search is based on the scientist's intuition and hunches rather than on the rules of "scientific method." Experimental research is directed toward controlling the subject matter, thereby discovering and demonstrating lawfulness. This lawfulness is stated in empirical functional relationships between behavioral and environmental variables and expressed in concepts chosen for their usefulness in effectively capturing the orderliness in the data. Thus, concepts emerge from the experimental program rather than from *a priori* derivations.[42] Skinner's functional definitions of stimulus and response are examples of this method at work (see chapter 3).

Theory, in the acceptable sense, evolves in the attempt to present the collection of empirical fact in a formal and economical way. A formulation using a minimal number of terms to represent a large number of experimental facts is a theory.[43] As the theory develops, it integrates more facts in increasingly more economical formulations. Theoretical concepts thus merely collate observations and do not refer to nonbehavioral processes. A Skinnerian theory is, therefore, a simple, comprehensive, and abstract description of a corpus of data.[44]

A Skinnerian theory is to be evaluated by its effectiveness in enabling scientists to operate successfully on their subject matter. Since theories are selected by criteria of "effectiveness," "success," and "expediency" for the scientist, the development of theory is closely tied to the psychology of the scientist. For this reason, Skinner emphasizes the importance of a science of science, that is, an empirical study of the behavior of the scientist, to develop empirically founded canons of scientific methodology.[45] Presumably, the scientist is reinforced by the discovery of lawfulness as well as the prediction and control of behavior, so that theories which facilitate these achievements will be chosen. In the long run, contingencies of human survival come to influence the behavior of the scientist, and these will come to exert some control over the development of scientific theory and practice.[46]

Although Skinnerians tend to emphasize their differences with the Hullian scientific method, there are many commonalities. These, as well as the experimental analysis of behavior, are illustrated in Skinner's classic treatment of schedules of reinforcement. Skinner shows that many of the effects of schedules of reinforcement can be understood as the result of conditions prevailing at the time of reinforcement.[47] Presumably, this formulation is an admissible theory in Skinner's sense in that it is an empirical statement which economically describes and integrates a wide array of behavioral findings. This theory explains various experimental results because the results can be deduced from the theory. In this sense, Skinnerian and Hullian explanations are alike in that both explain by theoretical deductions, although the forms of the two theories are, of course, quite different.[48]

Second, Skinner's theory suggests further experiments to test the theory. Many of Skinner's experiments consist of manipulations of the conditions prevailing at the time of reinforcement to see if the effects of the schedule change according to what is expected from the theory. Thus, for both Skinner and Hull, a theory provides suggestions for further experiment. For Skinner a suggestion is useful for gaining greater control over behavior, while for Hull its benefit is as a theorem to test a postulate.

A NONLINEAR MODEL

In both the Hullian and Skinnerian approaches, theory development is seen as a continuous linear process. For Hull, a theory develops as its theorems are experimentally tested. Experimental observations then suggest how the postulates are to be adjusted to accommodate the data. For Skinner, theory develops as the variables controlling behavior are isolated and experimentally explored. Observed functional relations are then systematized in an economical and efficient formulation that gradually comes to subsume an increasingly comprehensive body of data. Thus, in both views, theory development is an evolving process reflecting the interaction of theory and observation.

This linear model, however, is open to two objections.[49] First, this model assumes that observation is independent of theory. Observations are thought to constitute a separate body of facts which test or are subsumed by a theory. However, if observation is theory-dependent then the linear model is flawed. Theory dictates to some extent what the observations are.[50] Thus the congruence of fact and theory does not necessarily represent a gradual convergence of theory with the independent subject matter it is to describe and explain. Instead, the congruence is partly the result of a theory's determining what is taken as a fact. Major shifts in theory occur not because observation fails to correspond to theory but rather because a rival theory, with its own notions of fact and observation, overthrows the old theory in a "scientific revolution." Thus, theory development is a discontinuous process of discrete jumps.

Second, the linear model of theory development assumes a clear-cut relationship between theory and data. Experimental results are supposed to dictate adjustments or expansion of the theory in specifiable ways. However, in practice, the relationship between observation and theory is rarely well determined. For one thing, an experimental result is never related to only one statement of the theory. Instead, the whole theory is tested by an experiment, or alternately, the whole theory subsumes the experimental results.[51] Therefore, it is not clear which statements of a theory are implicated by a particular observation. Furthermore, every experiment also involves a "background theory," that is, certain beliefs about the experimental apparatus as well as the instruments used for observation. Therefore, an experimental result may implicate the background theory as well as the theory in question.

Thus, observations do not clearly dictate theory development. In some cases an observation may lead a theorist to adjust a theory in ways that prove fruitful, and the modified theory predicts and explains a more comprehensive array of facts. In other cases, an observation may lead a theorist to a purely *ad hoc* adjustment in the theory to accommodate the data. The adjustment does not flow organically from the theory; its sole purpose is to save the theory in the face of contradictory evidence.

In yet other cases, a negative finding may be regarded as an anomaly and have no impact at all on the theory. Supporters of the theory may judge that it is premature to try to accommodate the anomaly immediately and that it should be addressed at a later time. Or else, supporters of the theory may doubt the authenticity of the anomaly. Thus, it is possible to maintain a theory despite adverse evidence by a series of *ad hoc* adjustments or by ignoring the negative data.[52] Even a theory universally acknowledged to have been refuted may be held onto because of its heuristic benefits. Thus, a theory is abandoned, on this view, only with the arrival of a competing theory which accommodates the data better than the old one and is a more powerful heuristic. Scientific progress is therefore the result of revolutions which represent discontinuities in theory development.

Reply

The first criticism of the behaviorist linear model of theory development is based on the thesis which denies the distinction between theory and observation. As discussed in chapter 3, this thesis is itself not firmly established. For the most part, behaviorists deny its relevance to their own research. Furthermore, even if the thesis is valid, it is not particularly damaging to behaviorist meta-theory. It simply asserts that a science of behavior is like any other normal science. Each tests its theories by observation, and each draws a distinction between theory and observation that is relative to a paradigm. Within this paradigm, theory development is reasonably continuous.

The second criticism is somewhat off the mark. It assumes that behaviorists claim to have a strict algorithm dictating how observations generate changes in theory. This, however, is generally not the case. Most behaviorists recognize that, in practice, the revision of a theory in the light of experimental results is a creative act of the theorist. This is especially true for Skinnerian meta-theory in which great emphasis is placed upon the intuitive hunches of the scientist.[53]

At a more fundamental level, both criticisms from the nonlinear model are misguided. The linear and nonlinear models are not incompatible; they are simply on different levels of logical discourse. The nonlinear model conceptualizes scientific progress as a succession of scientific paradigms, each containing its own ideas about observation, theory, and theory development. It is thus the paradigm that dictates how normal science is to be carried out, not the nonlinear model. The behaviorist linear model is properly regarded at the level of a scientific paradigm legislating how normal science is to be implemented. As such it is not incompatible with the nonlinear model which is a theory *about* paradigms and is therefore on a more abstract level.

CONCLUSION: THEORY, STRATEGY, AND VALUES

In the philosophy of science reconstructed in part I, behaviorist science begins with observations reported in the behavioral data language. Although behaviorists agree that this language alone is insufficient to operate as a science, they are divided over how to supplement that language to create a true science. The tension stems from the conflict between the impulse to strengthen behavioral theory by expanding the kinds of theoretical concepts admitted and the desire to protect the empiricalness and objectivity that are the rationale of behaviorism.

Operationally defined concepts are readily accepted because they are very closely linked to the behavioral data language, the guarantor of empiricalness and objectivity. Dispositional concepts, introduced by reductive chains, are also met by little resistance although the acceptance of such partially defined concepts means dropping the requirements of strict operational definition. Well formulated intervening variables are defined by the stimulus as well as the response side and are therefore fully determinate, although open, concepts. Nevertheless, the introduction of intervening variables generates much opposition, based mostly on fears that intervening variables will be misused, permitting the introduction of subjective and nonempirical concepts. Disputes over intervening variables, therefore, are basically disagreements over strategy.

Opposition to the introduction of hypothetical constructs is even greater than that to intervening variables. Because these concepts are loosely linked to the behavioral data language there is more opportunity for misuse. Nevertheless, most behaviorist theories admit such concepts although with tacit restrictions.

Finally, there is disagreement over how theoretical constructs are to be interrelated to formulate a theory. The extremes of this controversy are Hullian hypothetico-deductivism and Skinnerian descriptivism. This disagreement is not merely a dispute over the formal expression of a theory. It is more a controversy over the role of theory in the explanation of behavior and in the organization of experimental research. Again, the disagreement is one over strategy. Opponents of descriptive theories claim that such theories lack heuristic value while opponents of hypothetico-deductive theories argue that these obstruct and misdirect research.

Contrary to appearances, the question as to which types of theories and theoretical concepts are most fruitful and strategically the best is not entirely an empirical issue. Questions of "fruitfulness," "heuristic value," and "progress" are all relative to human goals and purposes. If there were agreement on goals and purposes, then perhaps the fruitfulness of a theory could be measured, and questions of strategy would have an empirical answer. However, in the absence of agreement of this sort, controversies over what is the "best strategy" are partly disagreements over values.[54]

Even for behaviorists, among whom there is general concensus that the goals of psychology are the prediction and control of behavior, criteria cannot be formulated in a universally agreed way. First, there is no common opinion on what is meant by the "behavior" to be predicted and controlled.[55] Second, there are sharp disagreements over measures of predictiveness and control. Is predictiveness to be measured purely by number of predictions or should the range of behaviors predicted and the number of species included be considered as well, and given how much weight? Is the prediction and control of human behavior the ultimate goal, or are all species created equal in the eyes of psychology? Is control to be measured by number of behaviors controlled or are socially important behaviors to carry special weight? Is the precise prediction and control of a few behaviors in a few species preferable to the less precise prediction and control of many behaviors among many species? All these questions involve values and are therefore not necessarily subject to resolution by scientific means.[56]

On the other hand, it *is* an empirical question as to what scientists actually do in developing psychological theory. Of course, Skinner is correct that scientists will pursue whatever they find to be most effective, but without a clear definition of "effectiveness," this prediction remains a truism. Skinner may even be correct that in the long run, contingencies of human survival will control the behavior of scientists. In the short term, however, scientists will adopt whatever they individually find most rewarding. To some extent the ability to predict and control behavior is a critical reward for the scientist. However, in an immature science like psychology, where the association between the individual scientist's research and the ultimate goals of the science may be remote, other "irrelevant" rewards exert powerful control over the scientist's behavior. Social rewards in the form of prestige for adhering to a fashionable theory, grant money, admiration, and academic tenure, determine the development of psychological theory to a large, although unknown, extent. The success of a scientific paradigm is not always decided on rational grounds.[57]

It is not clear what role is played in the determination of a scientist's behavior by *a priori* prescriptions as to how science "ought" to proceed. Often these philosophical pronouncements follow the success of a theory. Philosophers formulate a *post hoc* formal reconstruction of what is often a successful case of informal theorizing. The formal reconstruction is then raised as the model to be followed by future theory. However, by the time the nature of this reconstruction is somewhat clarified by debate within the philosophical community, scientists are working on the next theory, which may not fit the former model. Philosophy of science is in a continuous attempt to catch up to science, and is in this sense an epiphenomenon of science, affected by science but having little impact in return.[58]

In any event, psychology contains too few successful theories to serve as models, and no successful models which have been logically reconstructed. Extrapolations from other sciences or from the history of psychology itself, even assuming the evidence is unambiguous, are not decisive, for psychology can always be distinguished from the other sciences, and the present can always be distinguished from the past. Opinions about the best strategy for psychological theory will remain, hunches for the foreseeable future—informed hunches and necessary hunches, to be sure, but hunches nevertheless.

Whither Objectivity and Empiricalness?

Behaviorist doctrine holds that the empiricalness and objectivity of theoretical concepts are to be achieved by linking these concepts to the behavioral data language. However, as this linkage becomes more remote, empiricalness and objectivity are jeopardized. Hypothetical constructs, having the most tenuous ties, are the most at risk. Behaviorist restrictions on the nature of these constructs help to ensure that hypotheses containing them are at least testable. Even with these restrictions, however, the anchoring of these constructs in the behavioral data language is indirect. One model of the nature of this anchoring is that of correspondence rules. However, correspondence rules are not entirely satisfactory. First, psychological theories are not axiomatized in the way required by the correspondence rule model.[59] Second, the notion of correspondence rules is itself open to a number of objections.[60] This leaves the anchoring of hypothetical constructs in doubt.

Intervening variables are well anchored in the ideal but not in practice. Tolman, the originator of the intervening variable, abandons their use, claiming that all useful concepts have surplus meaning beyond the defining equations.[61] One of the few groups of well formulated pure intervening variables in psychology, Skinner's concepts of drive, emotion, and reflex reserve, are eliminated by their creator, precisely on the grounds that having no surplus meaning they can be eliminated. Although Hull maintains his intervening variables to the end, it has been repeatedly shown that they are not anchored on both sides as he intends.[62] Thus in practice, the anchoring of intervening variables is also left in doubt.

Although operationally defined concepts seem more securely anchored, the linkage is not without its own ambiguity. Several operationists recognize that the defining operations are themselves in need of operational definitions.[63] To escape an infinite regress, operationists have suggested three possible resolutions. First, the regress can end when the listener and speaker achieve agreement on what the concept refers to. Second, the regress may end by using the fundamental operation of pointing at the concept's referent. Third, discrimination training, involving reward for response to examples of the concept, can teach the listener to differentiate the referent of the concept.

The problem with the latter two solutions is that they assume that pointing and discrimination training logically determine a unique concept. However, as Wittgenstein repeatedly shows, neither does.[64] Why is it that pointing is assumed to operate in the direction of shoulder to finger and not the opposite? In pointing at a table, how is it known whether "table," "wood," "heavy," or "table top" is intended? Furthermore, no finite number of exemplars used in a discrimination training uniquely determines a rule for the concept. It is possible to choose further instances of the concept in mutually contradictory ways, each of which will be consistent with the finite number of examples initially shown as instances of the concept. Similarly, it is always possible to follow a given rule in mutually contradictory ways, each of which is consistent with the rule.

Identification of concepts is thus logically underdetermined by explicit rules and training with exemplars. How is it then that in fact humans do share concepts and are able to communicate effectively? Wittgenstein's answer is that although training and explicit rules logically underdetermine concepts, psychologically they do not. Because of human nature, when people are given rules or training for using a concept, they tend to "go on" in the same way to apply the concept. Therefore, the concepts of individual members of a language community are congruent with one another and communication is possible. The infinite regress is avoided because human agreement is in fact achieved.

If a concept cannot be logically tied uniquely to its instances in the world, must the behaviorist abandon empiricalness and objectivity as impossible goals? Not necessarily. Because of the nature of the human mind, training and rules do tend to tie a concept to the world in a unique way. However, this does not mean that all concepts are therefore equally well tied. Clearly, if humans are given only one examplar, they are less likely to apply the concept in the same way than if they are given numerous exemplars. Similarly, a set of vaguely specified rules is less likely to lead humans to apply the concept identically as compared to a set of clearly specified rules.

Given this irreducible underdetermination, behaviorists attempt to specify concepts by rules and training in such a way that humans will be likely to apply the concept in a common and useful way. The more precision in specifying a concept, the greater the likelihood of achieving this goal. That it is in fact achieved can be known only by induction from the degree of agreement and success achieved by users of the concept. Thus, intersubjective agreement plays a critical role in the formulation of behaviorist views of concept formation just as it does in behaviorist standards of observation. This is to be expected since observation, as opposed to mere sensory stimulation, involves concepts.[65]

Although behaviorist concepts are thus not linked to the behavioral data language in the ways that behaviorists assume as ideal, they are nevertheless not necessarily lacking in objectivity. Good behaviorist theories provide exemplars of theoretical concepts by applying the concepts to prototype experiments. These provide examples of how theoretical concepts such as "expectation," "habit strength," and "contingency of reinforcement," are applied. Students taught with these exemplars are, in effect, receiving discrimination training in applying a concept.[66] They also receive equations, demonstrations, verbal definitions, and other statements intended to link the concepts to the world.[67] The success of the training and the rules is determined by how well students and colleagues are able to achieve agreement, prediction, and control in using the concepts.[68] Not only is this achievement a measure of success for the training and rules, but it is also a measure of the concept's objectivity.

As a demand for precise rules and rigorous training, behaviorism is open to the challenge that it may over-regulate the use of concepts, develop rigidity, and thereby stifle human creativity and imagination. Perhaps there is a tradeoff between precision and over-regulation. In this case, behaviorism can be characterized by what it considers to be a fair tradeoff. Behaviorists are more impressed with the dangers of unbridled speculation in the history of psychology then they are with the inhibiting effect of precision. Ironically, then, behaviorist insistence on rigor, precision, and objectivity is based ultimately on intuition.

PART II

BEHAVIOR

CHAPTER 6

S-R

Behaviorism is closely associated with S-R psychology. According to one interpretation of S-R, the S-R reflex thesis, all behavior can be analyzed into discrete stereotyped movements, each of which is elicited by an immediately preceding discrete impinging of energy on a sensory receptor.

No important behaviorist theories actually conform to this simple reflexological model. Typically they include principles of learning, internal stimuli, integration, and coordination, which violate the conditions of the model. The inclusion of mediation, especially the habit-family hierarchy, in many behaviorist theories further undermines the model.

All that remains of the original S-R reflex thesis is the assertion that behavior consists of responses, each caused by antecedent stimuli. Even this weakened version of the thesis is contradicted by the concept of the operant, which is emitted rather than elicited. An even weaker version is: All behavior is functionally related to environmental independent variables. Interbehaviorists object to this version and argue that behavior and the environment reciprocally determine one another.

According to a second interpretation of S-R, the S-R learning thesis, learning consists of the association of stimuli and responses. This contrasts with S-S theories, which assert that learning is the acquisition of knowledge. A major problem with S-S theories is in bridging the gap between knowledge and behavior. Often this is accomplished by intuition rather than objective deduction. In S-R theories it is accomplished by including a response term in the primitive learning operation.

The claim that the S-R learning thesis is "narrow" ignores the complexity of major S-R learning theories and functional definition. A second objection to the S-R learning thesis is that learning can occur without a response. In reply, S-R theorists try to show that such learning is derivable from learning operations that do involve a response.

Given the behaviorist philosophy explicated in part I, a science of behavior can develop in many ways as substantive content fills the conceptual framework. In fact, however, behaviorism is closely associated with a particular approach, known as "S-R psychology."[1] The meaning of this phrase constitutes the next major node to be considered in the behaviorist tree diagram. Behaviorists interpret S-R psychology in a variety of ways, each of which suggests a different background theory of behavior. This chapter will examine and evaluate the different forms of S-R psychology with the aim of uncovering these assumptions about the nature of behavior.

In its most general and least controversial sense, "S-R" merely defines a subject matter. It symbolizes a psychology whose object of inquiry consists of behavior, with a "response" as the unit (thereby providing the "R"), in relation to the environment, with a "stimulus" as the unit (providing the "S").[2] In this benign sense, "S-R psychology" bears no empirical content and is roughly coextensive with any science consistent with behaviorist philosophical commitments. The background theory consists merely of the hypothesis that a subject matter thus defined will demonstrate lawfulness relevant to the goals of prediction and control. In addition to this very general definition, S-R psychology can also be interpreted as resting on various empirical principles. Two of the most important of these will here be termed the "S-R reflex thesis" and the "S-R learning thesis," and each will be examined separately.

THE S-R REFLEX THESIS

Succinctly stated, the S-R reflex thesis asserts that all behavior is reflexive in nature, that is, all behavior consists of responses *elicited* by stimuli. "S-R" is, therefore, to be understood as S————————→R. Unfortunately, the terms "reflex" and "elicit" are themselves given to diverse interpretation. To elucidate these concepts it will prove helpful to abstract a "core model" which captures the essential notions. This core model is artificial in that few, if any, behaviorists actually subscribe to it. However, the conceptual extensions and logical development of this model do correspond to various behaviorist theories. Therefore, an examination of this core model and its vicissitudes reveals the assumptions of the S-R reflex thesis.

Reflexology

At least three meanings for the word "reflex" can be distinguished.[3] First, it may refer to the causal relationship between a stimulus and a response mediated by the physiological structure known as the "reflex arc."[4] The stimulus consists of mechanical or electrical energy applied to a receptor, the response is the activity of a limb or gland, and the causal relationship is known as "elicitation." In this sense, a "reflex" is defined by a physiological structure, and the laws governing the reflex are a matter for empirical investigation.

According to a second meaning, the physiology mediating the relationship is irrelevant, and a reflex is defined as any stimulus-response pair which obeys a particular set of laws.[5] These laws relate certain characteristics of the response, such as its latency, threshold, and magnitude, to certain dimensions of the stimulus, such as its intensity and frequency. If these laws accurately describe the relationship between a stimulus and a response, then they may be said to constitute a reflex, and the stimulus is said to "elicit" the response.

Under a third definition, reflex refers to any behavior caused by, and therefore lawfully related to, an antecedent sensory event.[6] Because this definition is independent of the empirical laws governing the causal relationship and the physiology mediating it, more behavior is subsumed than is covered by the two preceding definitions. On the other hand, the concept is not so inclusive as to prove useless because of certain restrictions generally imposed by S-R theorists.

Typically, the stimulus is conceived of as the discrete and relatively brief impinging of energy on a sensory receptor. It also shares temporal contiguity with the response, that is, it "immediately" precedes the response, or at least the latency between stimulus and response is relatively brief. With respect to behavior, the response is to be given a movement-description and defined by its topography. It is said to be "stereotyped" in that it always consists of an invariant movement. In addition, it is conceived of as discrete, brief, and simple. Complex behavior is assumed to be the result of combinations of reflexes.

The most important conditions for the reflex under this definition involve the elicitation relationship between stimulus and response. This relationship is said to be "invariable," in the sense that the stimulus always elicits the same response. Thus a particular stimulus is a sufficient condition for a particular response. Moreover, given the thesis that all behavior is reflexive, a particular stimulus (or any one of a limited number of stimuli) is also a necessary condition for a particular response, thus ruling out the possibility of "spontaneous behavior."[7]

The S-R reflex thesis supplies one solution to the problem of response definition. Prior to any empirical findings, an analysis of behavior can partition behavior into segments of any size, and the selection of a unit of analysis is an open choice. The S-R reflex thesis suggests an obvious candidate for the analytic unit. Behavior can be divided into reflexes, with a response defined as the segment of behavior elicited by a stimulus. The study of behavior is thus the study of reflexes, or "reflexology."[8]

This analysis of behavior into reflexes takes two forms. In the first, a complex action is segmented into a combination of reflexes.[9] They may occur over time, in succession, and over space, as several reflexes occur simultaneously at different locations on the organism. In the second, a skill or action is reduced to a class of reflexes, one of which occurs each time the skill or action is instantiated. For example, the way a rat presses a lever may differ each time, and is therefore not a single stereotyped reflex. Yet the action may be analyzed as a class of reflexes, each of which produces a deflection of the lever. Presumably, the movements differ from one lever press to another because the stimulus differs from one occasion to the other. On any given occasion, though, the lever press consists of a fixed movement as an invariable reaction to a particular stimulus.[10]

Preliminary Extensions of the Model

This simple reflexological model is an artificial abstraction in that no behaviorist adopts this view of behavior. A close approximation to this model is represented by Kuo who contends that:

> Every individual reaction is called forth by a specific stimulus; it cannot be directed or determined by anything else. . . . Every bit of movement of the rat in the maze is determined by the specific nature of the factors in the stimulus pattern (1928, p. 419)

> Behavior is not inherited, nor is it acquired. It is a passive and forced movement mechanically and solely determined by the structural pattern of the organism and the nature of the environmental forces. (1929a, p. 197)

Yet, a close reading of Kuo reveals that even his position does not entirely conform to the simple model.

The major problem with the simple model is that in portraying all behavior as responses to eliciting stimuli, it implies that the structure of behavior corresponds to the structure of the environment. Behavior can do no more than mirror the sequential organization of external events. Yet behavior demonstrates qualities of adaptiveness, fluidity, and purposiveness which are not mere reflections of the environment. Clearly the basic model must be extended to account for the full range of properties exhibited by behavior.

Learning. One very common extension is to incorporate principles by which environmental events that do not elicit a particular movement can acquire this capacity. Assume S_1 is the only stimulus which elicits a specific response, R. In most behaviorist theories S_2 can come to elicit R through some form of association with S_1, usually temporal contiguity. Classical conditioning, as developed by Pavlov, is one such principle of association for S-R theories.[11] Through the association of S_1, S_2, and R, the formerly neutral stimulus S_2 acquires the capacity to elicit R. The acquired relationship $S_2 \longrightarrow R$ is known as a "conditioned reflex."

Adding learning principles to the simple model alters one of its fundamental characteristics. Although S_1 is a sufficient condition for R, it is no longer a necessary condition. Virtually any stimulus can come to elicit R through conditioning. Behavior may still mirror the environment, but the nature of this correspondence is now dependent on the organism's conditioning history.

Internal Stimuli. A second common extension of the basic model is to expand the concept of the stimulus to include events occurring inside the organism. One important class of internal stimuli are proprioceptive stimuli produced by muscle movements. These stimulate proprioceptive receptors within the muscles and tendons, and through conditioning can come to elicit responses. In a sequence of responses known as the "serial response," the proprioceptive stimulus produced by each response elicits the next response. With repeated occurrences of the serial response, conditioning is strengthened, and the behavior sequence is integrated into a response unit. Thus a sequence of responses initially elicited by a sequence of environmental stimuli can, as a result of conditioning, occur as a serial response without the support of those external stimuli. The necessary stimuli are supplied by the behavior itself, and the organism achieves a degree of independence from the environment.[12]

A second class of internal stimuli are those arising as a result of motivational states. Drives such as hunger and thirst are thought to produce characteristic "persisting stimuli" which stimulate internal receptors as long as the drives remain in force.[13] Because these persisting stimuli endure for long periods of time, behavior can exhibit a degree of coherence lacking in the simple view of behavior as a series of discrete reactions to fluctuating momentary stimulations. Furthermore, since these persisting stimuli are related to biological needs, they link behavior to the adaptation of the organism.

Integration and Coordination. In the simple model, a reflex is conceived of as an isolated unit, independent of other reflexes. In fact, reflexes rarely occur in isolation or independently. Rather they may occur simultaneously and may modify, facilitate, or inhibit one another. Observed behavior is really the result of the integration of many reflexes.[14] Even relatively simple movements cannot occur without the coordinated relaxation and contraction of a large number of muscle groups, each representing a different reflex. Furthermore, the occurrence of a reflex may also facilitate or inhibit other responses by lowering or raising their thresholds. Groups of responses whose thresholds have been lowered are said to be in a state of "motor readiness" in that they are "set" to occur.[15]

Thus, behavior is a resultant yielded by multiple forces. Therefore, the invariability of the simple model must be dropped. The consequence of a stimulus is not fixed: the reaction depends on the state of readiness of the response, as well as the other responses and stimuli occurring in the spatial and temporal vicinity. In order to calculate the behavioral resultant it is necessary to consider each reflex separately and then combine them, just as in order to calculate the velocity of a ball rolling down an incline one might analyze into individual vectors the forces acting on it. Therefore, the isolated reflex is an artificial conceptual tool which rarely, if ever, is observed, just as the vectors acting on the ball are not observed in isolation.[16] Adding integration and coordination of reflexes to the basic model thus means that the analysis of behavior cannot consist of the simple partition of behavior into successively and simultaneously occurring independent reflexes. Instead, only the results of an interaction are observed in the data rather than the individual "reflex vectors," which are the basic analytic units.

An important implication is that the observed behavior, as a resultant of many reflexes, may exhibit properties not possessed by any individual reflex.[17] For example, individual reflexes consist of movements to momentary stimulus energies at the receptor, but observed behavior may prove to be best described as a lawful reaction to enduring environmental objects specified by their intrinsic properties (the "receded stimulus") rather than by energy at the subject's receptor. Similarly, integrated behavior, termed a "specific response," is most usefully described as an act rather than as a set of movements.[18]

These considerations suggest the need for composition rules stating how reflexes are to be synthesized into behavior. The phenomena of integration and coordination imply that these composition laws cannot assume the form of simple additive concatenation. Clearly, composition laws of greater complexity are required.[19] If, however, composition laws prove unusable or nonexistent, as Gestalt psychologists argue, then behavior is a true emergent, and psychology cannot be identified with reflexology.

Mediation

The above preliminary modifications of the basic reflexological model partially liberate behavior from its total dependence on the environment. Mediation further extends this process by locating more causes of behavior within the organism. Mediators are behavioral events, either stimuli or responses, occurring inside the organism.[20] Usually they are themselves instigated by external stimuli, but once initiated, they may continue on their own, very much like a serial response. They typically terminate as a stimulus for an overt response. Thus, they "mediate" between an environmental stimulus and an overt response. The observed overt response is therefore not a reaction to the observed environmental stimulus but is rather a reaction to a chain of mediating events initiated by the external stimulus and determined largely by the organism's learning history. Behavior is thereby further freed from its subordination to current momentary stimuli.

As unobserved postulated processes, mediators are hypothetical constructs, and behaviorists tend to conceptualize them according to the principles discussed in chapter 4. That is, mediators are generally postulated as (1) conforming to the behavioral laws governing overt stimuli and responses, (2) peripheral, (3) under the functional control of external variables, (4) lawfully linked to observed dependent and independent variables, and (5) possibly overt at one time before regressing to the covert level. To the extent that these principles are violated, mediators acquire functional autonomy.[21]

Habit-Family Hierarchy. One particularly important mediator is the anticipatory goal reaction, r_g, as developed by Hull and his followers. This r_g is a part of the overt goal reaction—i.e., the response to a stimulus, such as food, which reduces persistent stimuli, such as those arising from hunger. Because of the principles of the goal gradient hypothesis and the process of "short-circuiting," r_g moves forward in the sequence of responses leading to the goal reaction. Eventually it may occur very early in this sequence and through conditioning may come to elicit each of the members of this behavioral chain. Since there is more than one sequence leading to the goal reaction, r_g can come to elicit a set of behavioral sequences, or "habit-family," each of which is initiated by the same external situation and terminated by the same goal reaction. Because the members of the habit-family have different conditioning histories, they are not equally strong. They therefore form a "hierarchy," with the strongest (and most probable) at the top.[22]

The Hullian r_g generally conforms to the behaviorist principles for hypothetical constructs outlined above. Hull postulates that r_g is governed by the laws of the conditioned response as determined through careful experimentation with overt responses such as the eye blink. Nevertheless, the r_g and the habit-family hierarchy are extremely powerful explanatory concepts in accounting for characteristics of behavior not consistent with the simple S-R reflex model. For example, the goal gradient hypothesis, and the short circuiting process that follows from it, help account for the smoothness and efficiency of behavior. Also, transfer of learning across diverse stimulus situations can be explained as a result of mediation by a common r_g.

Similarly, the plasticity of behavior, the fact that organisms are not limited to one response in a situation but can use diverse means to achieve a particular goal, is also accounted for by the habit-family. When confronted with a stimulus, an organism emits the response sequence at the top of its habit-family hierarchy. If this sequence does not achieve the goal, it will be weakened by extinction. Eventually, it will be weaker than the sequence initially below it in the hierarchy. Therefore, this second sequence occurs until it either achieves the goal or is replaced by yet another member of the habit-family hierarchy. In this way, behavior shows a flexibility unaccounted for in the simple S-R model.

In its movement through a behavioral sequence and its mediation of learning throughout a hierarchy, the r_g adds an important dynamic element in the relationship between stimulus and response. Both the persisting stimuli and the ubiquitous r_g serve to integrate behavior and to organize it adaptively around drives and goals. Behavior acquires a coherence and structure missing in the simple S-R model. Although Hull thus uses the principles of the conditioned response to explain behavior, he does not suppose that behavior consists of a series of conditioned stimuli followed by conditioned responses.[23]

The Emitted Operant

Extensions of the basic model leave very little of the original S-R reflex thesis. All that remains is the assertion that behavior consists of responses, each caused by antecedent events acting on the senses, internal or external.[24] Stimuli "elicit" only in the sense that they are causally related to responses.

Skinner's concept of the operant dispenses with even this last vestige of the S-R reflex formula. The operant is a response, functionally defined, which is emitted rather than elicited.[25] Although the emission of an operant always has an antecedent cause, this cause is not necessarily a sensory stimulation. In fact, the antecedent causes may be primarily phylogenic and physiological. Of more importance are the *consequences* of the past emissions of members of the operant class. Some consequences, known as "reinforcements," strengthen the operant and increase the likelihood of its emission. The conditions of reinforcement, known as the "contingencies," are therefore the most important determinant of the operant's occurrence.

Discriminative Stimuli. Among the contingencies, one critical factor is the "discriminative stimulus," or S^D, which sets the occasion for a response to be followed by a reinforcement. Although the S^D is an antecedent stimulus, it differs from the eliciting stimulus of the simple reflexological model.[26] Skinner (1938) expresses the difference in these terms:

> The discriminative stimulus has a very different status from that of the eliciting stimulus. It is less likely to be regarded as a spur or goad and is perhaps best described as "setting the occasion" for a response. Whether or not the response is to occur does not depend upon the discriminative stimulus, once it is present, but upon other factors. . . .
>
> Strictly speaking we should refer to a discriminated operant as "occurring in the presence of" rather than "elicited as a response *to*" S^D. (p. 241)

This distinction between eliciting stimulus and discriminative stimulus requires further clarification. Both are antecedent causes, even in Skinner's sense of causation as functional relation.[27] The difference, therefore, must be found in the type of functional relation. If the term "elicit" is restricted to functional relationships of the type exemplified by the Pavlovian conditioned and unconditioned responses, then the discriminative stimulus cannot be said to elicit. On the other hand if "elicit" is used in the more general sense of causally related, then S^D may be said to elicit a response. Nevertheless, Skinner prefers to withhold the term "elicit" from discriminative stimuli because it has certain connotations related to the simple reflexological model.[28] He argues:

It is neither plausible nor expedient to conceive of the organism as a complicated jack-in-the-box with a long list of tricks, each of which may be evoked by pressing the proper button. The greater part of the behavior of the intact organism is not under this sort of stimulus control. The environment affects the organism in many ways which are not conveniently classed as "stimuli," and even in the field of stimulation only a small part of the forces acting upon the organism elicit responses in the invariable manner of reflex action. (1953a, pp. 49–50)

In drawing this distinction and eliminating the antecedent eliciting stimulus from the field of operant behavior, Skinner rejects a fundamental premise of the S-R reflex thesis.[29]

Reinforcement. Along with the discriminative stimulus, the other important feature of the contingency is the reinforcement. The occurrence of a reinforcement following the emission of a member of an operant class is one of the independent variables determining the later occurrence of other members of that class. Therefore, reinforcement is an antecedent cause of responding. However, the sense in which reinforcement is an antecedent cause is quite different from the antecedent cause of the simple S-R reflex thesis.[30] In the latter, a one-to-one relationship holds between response and stimulus: each response is elicited by a particular preceding stimulus, and fairly close temporal contiguity is necessary. With the operant, in contrast, the reinforcement for a response, R_1, need not immediately precede the next response, R_2, although that reinforcement is an antecedent cause of R_2. Second, the causal effect of a reinforcement is not to produce a single response but rather to increase the probability that an operant response will be emitted, as expressed by an increase in the rate of emission of the response. Reinforcement is therefore responsible for a rate change rather than the elicitation of an individual response.

Theories of reinforcement further illustrate how the concepts of stimulus and response within the operant paradigm differ from those of the reflexological model. These theories generally adopt a functional approach and attempt to find properties of the reinforcing stimulus and the operant response which yield simple, orderly, and basic laws from which a range of behavioral phenomena can be deduced. These functional laws relate some property of behavior, the dependent variable, to some property of reinforcement, the independent variable.[31] The properties selected by these theories characterize stimulus and response in ways that clearly differentiate them from the stimulus and response of simple reflexology.

Typically, they select relative measures of behavior, such as relative response rate and relative time allocation, as dependent variables. Similarly, the independent variables chosen are relative measures such as relative rate of reinforcement. These properties of the reinforcing stimulus and the controlled response are relational, functionally determined, abstract, and integrated over large intervals of time.[32] They contrast sharply with the properties of reflexological events which are momentary, independent, contiguous, discrete, and measured in units of energy.

Interbehaviorism

The foregoing attempt to define the precise empirical content of the S-R reflex thesis consistent with behaviorist theories demonstrates that this thesis is nearly devoid of content. Very few, if any, of the premises examined can be attributed to all, or even most, of the theories included in "S-R psychology." The inclusion of learning, internal stimuli, integration, and mediation in behaviorist theories virtually undermines the S-R thesis. A particular stimulus is neither a necessary nor a sufficient condition for a response. The relationship between stimulus and response is therefore not invariant. Responses are not stereotyped, and stimuli are neither discrete nor simple. Furthermore, response classes defined in terms of achievement do not mention movements.[33] All that remains of the S-R reflex thesis that is consistent with the theories included in S-R psychology is the assertion that all behavior is a dependent variable causally or functionally related to environmental independent variables.

Although this formulation seems innocuous, it has two controversial implications. The first, that no behavior is independent of environmental control, is discussed in chapter 9. The second implication, or perhaps connotation, is that the environment can be defined independently of behavior so that the causal or functional relationship is all unidirectional, from environment to behavior.

Those who reject this second implication argue that the aspects of the environment determining behavior are themselves affected by behavior, and the environment is therefore not a static independent force outside behavior.[34] For example, Kantor (1970) asserts:

> The assumption of a stimulus being merely an object or condition which generates or reinforces a response is untenable. . . .
>
> Stimuli are taken to be prior independent entities or energies that bring about an effect which succeeds it in time. . . .
>
> It is inappropriate to borrow the terms "independent" and "dependent" variables from the mathematicians and then load them with priority and posteriority, causality and effectuality. (p. 106)

Instead, Kantor proposes to study "interbehavior," the interactions of the stimulus and response *functions* forming the psychological situation.[35] Kantor's formula is thus S⟷R rather than S⟶R. In a similar vein Bandura (1974) argues against depicting

> the environment as an autonomous force that automatically shapes and controls behavior. Environments have causes as do behaviors. For the most part, the environ-

ment is only a potentiality until actualized and fashioned by appropriate actions. . . .
By their actions, people play an active role in producing the reinforcing contingencies that impinge upon them. Thus, behavior partly creates the environment, and the environment influences the behavior in a reciprocal fashion. (p. 866)

Although Bandura intends his statement as an attack on theories of operant behavior, the kind of reciprocal determination he describes is recognized on many levels by operant theories. Skinner, for example, extensively discusses what he terms "precurrent behavior," by which humans alter the variables that control their own behavior. One class of precurrent behavior consists of learned responses which have the effect of changing environmental variables so that an undesired response does not occur or a desired response does.[36] This type of self-control is exemplified when one removes cigarettes from one's visual environment so they will not serve as discriminative stimuli for the undesired response of smoking. Intellectual self-management is another example of a precurrent response that alters the environment so that one's own problem-solving behavior is strengthened.[37] Yet another example is countercontrol, in which one emits responses which change the behavior of another person who controls variables that determine one's own behavior.[38] In all these cases, behavior is a function of variables which are themselves a function of behavior.

Theories of reinforcement also explicitly acknowledge the reciprocal determination of behavior and environment. To be sure, it is possible to describe contingencies of reinforcement in ways that make them independent of behavior. For example, a fixed-ratio 10 schedule of reinforcement (FR 10) presents a reinforcement following every tenth response, and this contingency is independent of the behavior that actually occurs. Furthermore, it has been found that behavior is lawfully related to contingencies expressed in this way. However, these lawful relations are not readily related to one another, and the scientific result is a mere listing of schedules of reinforcement, each associated with specific behavioral results.

This is the situation theories of reinforcement are designed to remedy. They select some property of reinforcement, P, possessed by a variety of schedules, which is hypothesized to control behavior. They commonly select a P whose value depends on the behavior generated by the schedule.[39] For example, if P is the rate of reinforcement, then under a FR 10 schedule, P depends on the rate of response generated by that schedule. Such properties will be termed "*dependent* environmental variables," to indicate their dependence on behavior, and will be symbolized as P_D.

Because many reinforcement theories make use of P_D variables, they contain laws of two forms. First are laws, known as "feedback functions," which express P_D as a function of behavior.[40] Second there are "behavior-dependent laws," which state how behavior is a function of P_D. These two sets of laws establish a behavior-environment feedback system in which features of behavior and critical features of reinforcement reciprocally determine one another.[41]

Given (1) the feedback functions for a particular P_D and a particular schedule of reinforcement, and (2) the behavior-dependent laws of a particular theory, it is possible to derive a third kind of law, to be termed a "behavior-independent law." Laws of this type state how behavior is a function of properties of reinforcement which are independent of behavior.[42] Thus these behavior-independent laws are equivalent to the listing of schedules and their behavioral consequence as described above, except that the behavioral phenomena are shown to be logical derivations from a few simple and fundamental laws. Thus, these theories exemplify Skinnerian theorizing as described in chapter 5. The simple and fundamental laws that constitute the essentials of these theories are the behavior-dependent laws. Feedback functions are mere formal *a priori* descriptions of the contingencies, and behavior-independent laws are mere derivations. Hence, these choice theories centrally recognize the reciprocal determination of behavior and environment that Bandura advocates.[43]

Field Theory. S-R psychology is often characterized, especially by Gestalt psychologists, through a contrast between it and field theories.[44] However, the preceding examination of behaviorist theories reveals that they show many features of field theories. First, the variables of which behavior is said to be a function are thought to interact with one another.[45] This interaction is governed by the laws of psychology rather than by the laws of physics. Moreover, the interactions depend on the history of the individual organism. Second, as the discussion of reciprocal determination indicates, the values of these interacting factors are themselves often functions of behavior. Thus the picture emerging from several major behaviorist theories is of behavior affected by a group of interacting psychological forces dependent, in part, on the organism itself, and this portrait captures the essential features of field theory.[46]

Despite these similarities with field theory, behaviorist theories tend to differ from other psychological field theories. Field theories can be characterized by three sets of variables. First are the environmental variables. Second are the variables resulting from the interaction of these environmental variables among themselves and with behavior. Finally, a third set of variables are the behavioral measures. Gestalt field theories generally concentrate on the second set of variables and tend to be vague on how this set is related to the environment and to behavior. In many cases, the second set of variables is inferred from the third set, the behavioral measures. In this case, the derived behavioral laws are known as "R-R laws" to indicate that one behavior, R, is being related to, or predicted from, variables inferred from other behavior, R.[47]

In contrast, behaviorist theories place a premium on functional relationships found to hold between the third set, the behavioral measures, and the first set, the environmental variables. Behavior-independent laws of this sort can be determined, despite the field characteristics of behavior, by the use of feedback functions and composition laws. For reasons to be discussed in chapter 9, many behaviorists believe that behavior has not been adequately explained unless laws of this type have been discovered. Because these laws relate behavior to the environment, they are "S-R laws," as opposed to R-R laws; and S-R psychology, in this sense, can be characterized by the type of laws it seeks.[48] Under this definition, S-R psychology is not incompatible with the existence and fundamental importance of behavior-dependent laws and the field properties of behavior.

THE S-R LEARNING THESIS

One way of defining S-R psychology is to identify it with the S-R reflex thesis. As shown above, the S-R reflex thesis consistent with behaviorist psychology states that behavior is determined by the environment. In its interbehaviorist version it states that behavior and the environment reciprocally determine one another. A second definition of S-R psychology identifies it with another empirical hypothesis, the S-R learning thesis. This states that learning, the change in behavior due to experience, consists of the association of stimuli and responses.

Critics of the S-R learning thesis argue that learning should be described instead as the acquisition of knowledge to guide behavior. This cognitive view of learning would be acceptable by behaviorist standards if "knowledge" could be shorn of its connotations of consciousness and viewed as a theoretical concept mediating between the environment and behavior.[49] With laws relating knowledge to environmental variables on the one hand, and laws relating knowledge to behavioral measures on the other, the prediction and control of behavior would be possible.

In practice, however, attempts to construct a theory using knowledge as a construct do not meet these behaviorist criteria. A cognitive theory is not useful unless it specifies the relationship between knowledge and behavior, but it is precisely in this respect that theories of this type are weak. Much of the opposition to these theories stems from this failure to deduce determinate behavioral consequences from theoretical constructs. A consideration of two theories, cognitive maps and modeling, illustrates the point.

Cognitive Maps

In distinguishing his theory from S-R psychology, Tolman (1948) describes the latter in this way:

There is a school of animal psychologists which believes that the maze behavior of rats is a matter of mere simple stimulus-response connections. Learning, according to them consists in the strengthening of some of these connections and in the weakening of others. According to this "stimulus-response" school the rat in progressing down the maze is helplessly responding to a succession of external stimuli. (p. 189)

In contrast to this S-R theory, Tolman maintains that

in the course of learning something like a field map of the environment gets established in the rat's brain. . . .

the incoming impulses are usually worked over and elaborated in the central control room into a tentative, cognitive-like map of the environment. And it is this tentative map, indicating routes and paths and environmental relationships, which finally determines what responses, if any, the animal will finally release. (p. 192)

Because Tolman holds that learning consists of the acquisition of information about how environmental stimuli are related to one another, or "what leads to what," rather than the connection of responses to stimuli, his theory and similar ones are known as "S-S theories."[50]

The major difficulty of an S-S type theory is in getting from S-S associations to behavior. To use Tolman's metaphor, the problem is to describe how the "cognitive-like map" is read by the subject and then used to determine action. Short of inserting a homunculus to study the map and direct behavior, there is little in Tolman's cognitive map theory to bridge the gap between cognitions and response.[51] As Guthrie aptly puts it, the "rat is left buried in thought," and never makes it through the maze.[52]

In practice, Tolman does, in fact, derive predictions of behavior from his theory. However, these derivations are based on intuition rather than on rigorous deductions of the type demanded by behaviorist canons of objectivity.[53] Implicit in Tolman's derivations is the assumption that the rat is a rational creature and, given its knowledge of S-S associations, will behave appropriately. For example, in explaining the results of a latent learning experiment, Tolman (1948) says:

As long as the animals were not getting any food at the end of the maze they continued to take their time. . . . Once, however, they knew they were to get food, they demonstrated that during the preceding non-rewarded trials they had learned where many of the blinds were. They had been building up a "map," and could utilize the latter as soon as they were motivated to do so. (pp. 194–195)

This derivation is possible only because of the tacit premise that a hungry rat will use its knowledge of the location of food to reduce its entrances into blind alleys. This may seem a reasonable assumption but only because it presupposes reasonableness on the part of the rat. Intuition is therefore needed to decide what a reasonable rat will do, and the explanation is, as Tolman admits, anthropomorphic.[54]

In order to deduce statements about behavior in a rigorous fashion from a psychological theory, it is necessary that a term referring to behavior appear in the theory. This "response-term" might be incorporated into a postulate, or correspondence rule, or empirical law, but it must occur somewhere if the theory is to be predictive of behavior.[55] Without a response-term, the theory cannot entail determinate deductions conerning behavior but must rely on intuition and standards of appropriateness.

The S-R learning thesis solves this problem very simply. The response-term is included in the primitive learning operations postulated by the theory. A "learning operation" is a set of events resulting in a change in behavior called "learning." A learning operation is "primitive" if a theory presents it as a given rather than deriving it from some more basic behavioral principle. Paradigms of classical and operant conditioning are examples of primitive learning operations in that they specify the temporal configuration of a set of events which result in learning, but they are, in most theories, not derived from other conditioning principles. In specifying primitive learning operations, S-R theories include a response as one of the events that must stand in a particular temporal relation with other events in order for learning to occur. The response appearing in the primitive learning operation is then the response appearing in statements about behavior deduced from this theory. The gap between the theory and behavior is easily bridged, and the deduction of behavior is determinate.

Modeling

The S-R solution to the problem of the response-term is not the only one. An alternative is suggested by theories of observational learning, in which learning can occur in the absence of a response through the mere observation of events. Modeling, a type of observational learning, resolves the problem of the response-term by including it in the stimuli observed. A subject learns a response merely by observing another organism (i.e., the "model') perform the response under certain specified conditions.[56] According to Bandura (1977a), a prominent proponent of modeling:

> Behavior is learned symbolically through central processing of response information before it is performed. By observing a model of the desired behavior, an individual forms an idea of how response components must be combined and sequenced to produce the new behavior. In other words, people guide their actions by prior notions rather than by relying on outcomes to tell them what they must do. Observational learning without performance is amply documented in modeling studies using a nonresponse acquisition procedure. (p. 35)

The response-term in modeling theory is thus the *model's* response rather than the learner's. Because the learning operation takes place without a response on the part of the learner, theories of observational learning, such as modeling, are said to differ from S-R theories of learning.

Modeling theories appear to successfully link cognitive constructs to behavior. Nevertheless, even with a modeling theory as sophisticated as Bandura's, implicit intuitions about the reasonableness of the behaving organism intrude into derivations from the theory. Bandura frequently speaks of his cognitive construct, coded information, as "guiding" rather than determining behavior, once again opening a schism between the construct and behavior.[57] Just as with Tolman's "map," a "guide" is something that may or may not be used; and when it is used, it serves its function only when it is used appropriately. The problem is concretely illustrated when Bandura (1977a) states:

> With humans, indices of learning exist that are independent of performance. To measure whether humans have learned a maze by observing successful models, one need only ask them to describe the correct pattern of right and left turns. In addition to verbal indices, formation of representations can be assessed by measures of recognition and understanding not requiring motor reproduction. (pp. 35–36)

In this passage, Bandura implies that a person who observes a model's response not only learns that response, but can also engage in other new behaviors, such as verbal reports, recognition, and understanding. But how does this follow from the theory? Determinate deductions about behavior are for the modeled response only. Deductions about verbal reports and recognition are derivable from the theory only by intuition: Any reasonable person who knows what the model did should also be able to say what the model did, recognize it, and understand it. Although Bandura calls these activities "indices of learning . . . that are independent of performance," they are behaviors, nonetheless, and they are derived from the theory only through the subjective methods of intuition.[58]

The S-S Learning Construct

Yet another device for linking S-S constructs to behavior is to structure the behavioral theory so that the response-term appears somewhere other than in the learning principles. Since no response-terms occur in the learning postulate, the theory may be interpreted to say that learning is a matter of S-S associations, and in this sense, the theory is not an S-R theory. Learning is connected to behavior by including a response-term in a separate statement such as a performance or activation principle.[59] This approach makes the difference between S-S and S-R theories uninteresting. Both theories make the same predictions, and the only difference between them is in their internal logic.[60] Although this difference bears no empirical implications, some theorists claim, nevertheless, that the different logical structures of the two types of theory serve different heuristic functions in guiding research and further theorizing.[61]

One way to infuse empirical import into the differences between the two types of theory is to give them each physiological interpretations. If the learning process is viewed as a hypothetical construct with physiological properties then the dispute between S-S and S-R learning theories may involve matters of fact. For example, one issue is whether learning involves only changes in the relationship among afferent processes (S-S) or whether efferent processes are affected also (S-R). These hypotheses are tested by physiological manipulations which either bypass or eliminate one set of processes or the other during learning.[62]

Objections to S-R Learning

One common criticism of the S-R learning thesis is that it is excessively "narrow." It is alleged that S-R theories reduce all knowledge to the connection of specific movements to specific stimuli although human learning through experience is more comprehensive and abstract than that.[63] This objection might be appropriate for the simple reflexological model discussed above. However, it misses the mark when directed at more complex behaviorist learning theories. For one thing, the response-term of an S-R theory need not be a specific movement. As shown in chapter 3, most behaviorist theories use response classes that are functionally defined. Therefore, the response acquired through a learning operation can be as general and abstract as the data require it to be. Similar considerations apply to stimulus classes functionally defined.

Second, most S-R learning theories include principles of stimulus generalization and response induction so that changes occurring in a response class due to a learning operation can transfer to a range of similar stimuli and responses. Third, S-R theories do not assume that all learning occurs through primitive learning operations. For example, many learning operations can involve mediation and habit-family hierarchies as secondary learning principles derived from the primitive postulates. These secondary learning principles permit learning phenomena of much greater complexity than that produced by the primitive learning operations.[64]

Observational Learning. A second class of objections to the S-R learning thesis stems from findings in which learning occurs even though the learned response does not occur during the learning operation. Findings of this sort come from animal experiments involving insight, latent learning, place learning, and sensory preconditioning.[65] Similarly, observations of everyday life indicate that human adults are capable of learning as a result of a learning operation involving none of the responses learned. For example, one may acquire knowledge by reading a book and then use this knowledge months later by acting in certain ways. These new ways of acting were, in some sense, acquired as a result of reading, but they did not have to occur and be conditioned during the time of reading.

S-R theorists respond to these attacks in a variety of ways. One method is to postulate that responses do occur during such apparently responseless learning operations but that the responses are covert and therefore unobserved.[66] A second approach is to show that the responseless learning operations are secondary learning operations derivable from primitive learning principles which do involve responses. Hull, for example, deduces the results of experiments in latent learning, place learning, and insight as derivations from his more basic learning postulates involving the learning of S-R connections.[67]

In the realm of everyday human behavior, Gewirtz attempts to show that learning through modeling is not a primitive responseless learning operation but is rather a secondary learning principle derivable from S-R operations.[68] The differences between the views of Gewirtz and those of Bandura are illustrative of the contrasts between S-R and S-S learning theories, and an examination of these differences is highly instructive.[69]

Bandura differentiates two basic kinds of learning: learning by response consequence and learning through modeling.[70] Only the former involves a response on the part of the learner, while the latter is an instance of learning by observation. In contrast, Gewirtz argues that learning through modeling is an instance of operant behavior. The behavior of the model plus the reinforcing consequence of that behavior (for the model) function as a complex discriminative stimulus for the learner. When the learner then emits a response that matches that of the model, a reinforcing consequence often follows also. Therefore, through operant conditioning (involving a response), the subject learns to emit the response *match-the-behavior-of-the model* to instances of the discriminative stimulus *a-model-emitting-a-reinforced-behavior*. Note that the terms of the contingency are rather abstract functional classes. The functional response *match-the-behavior-of-a-model* consists of highly diverse movements. Similarly, the functional discriminative stimulus *a-model-emitting-a-reinforced-behavior* encompasses a variety of environmental events.

Bandura also recognizes abstract response classes in his principle of "abstract modeling," in which "observers extract the common attributes exemplified in diverse modeled responses and formulate rules for generating behavior with similar structural characteristics."[71] The major difference between Bandura and Gewirtz reduces to the question of whether learning through modeling can be conceptualized as, or derived from, learning by response consequences—i.e., operant conditioning. Because Gewirtz's operant explanation of modeling can be generalized to all observational learning, the contrast between his theory and that of Bandura illuminates the characteristics of S-R theories of learning.

Disentangling the Issues

It is clear from the preceding discussion that the debate between S-R and S-S theories of learning is a tangle of several empirical and conceptual issues. Separating them helps clarify the debate:

1. Does a theory of behavior require a response-term? This seems to be a conceptual question, and if the goal of a theory is determinate deductions of statements about behavior, then the answer is "yes." In this sense every behavioral theory should be an S-R theory.

2. Does this response-term have to appear in the theory's principles of learning, or can it appear elsewhere in the theory? This, too, seems to be a conceptual question, and the answer is "It's up to the theorist." At this point it is not known how the logical location of the response-term in a theoretical network bears on the adequacy of the theory. An S-R theory with respect to this issue is one that includes the response-term in its learning principles.

3. When a learning operation occurs, are its effects restricted to afferent processes or are efferent processs involved also? This is an empirical question about neurophysiology. An S-R theory with respect to this question is one which asserts that learning does involve efferent processes.

4. Can learning occur as a result of an event not involving the occurrence of the acquired response? This is also an empirical question. From a number of animal experiments as well as everyday experience, it appears that learning through mere observation does occur. With regard to this question, an S-R theory is one that denies learning of this sort is possible.[72]

5. If observational learning is possible, is it a primitive principle or is it derivable from principles which do include the occurrence of a response as critical to the learning operation? This question is quasi-empirical because it involves not only matters of fact but also the ingenuity of theorists in formulating comprehensive principles that encompass many forms of learning. An S-R theory with respect to this issue claims that the phenomena of observational learning, such as latent learning and modeling, are derivable from learning principles involving response events.

CONCLUSION

One interpretation of S-R psychology identifies it with the S-R reflex thesis. In its strict form, this identification is invalid simply because major behaviorist theories do not view behavior as consisting of responses elicited by stimuli. One alternative is to disassociate behaviorism from S-R psychology. The other is to liberalize the S-R reflex thesis to cover behaviorist psychology. Following the latter route, the S-R reflex thesis emerges as the assertion that behavior is determined by the environment (or that behavior and the environment reciprocally determine one another). This liberalized version of the thesis will be discussed at length in chapter 9.

A second interpretation of S-R psychology identifies it with the S-R learning thesis. This thesis is, itself, subject to five different interpretations. Under only one of these (the first) does the thesis follow directly from the conceptual framework of behaviorism reconstructed in Part I. An S-S learning theory consistent with that framework is certainly possible. Therefore, behaviorist resistence to S-S theories is strategic rather than philosophical. S-S theories focus on what the organism knows. Once knowledge enters as a theoretical concept, it is very easy for the theoretician to let intuition replace scientific deduction. Behaviorists fear that S-S theories tend to rely on intuition and anthropomorphism, thereby forfeiting scientific objectivity. Therefore, behaviorists generally eschew S-S theories in favor of the S-R learning thesis.

Although behaviorism is closely identified with S-R psychology, it is clear from this chapter that the latter has been given nearly as many diverse interpretations as the former. Perhaps this matching of ambiguities is as it should be. Problems arise, however when S-R psychology is discussed (or, more usually, attacked) under one interpretation, but the discussion is assumed to apply to all theories subsumed by S-R psychology under other interpretations.

CHAPTER 7

The Organization of Behavior

Critics of behaviorism maintain that the organization of behavior cannot be explained without reference to purpose. Although behaviorists object to teleological explanations, they admit that behavior manifests purposive features such as persistence and flexibility. They attempt to explain these features by theories which do not refer to purpose as a final cause or conscious content.

According to one such theory, purpose is a state variable that changes the relationship between stimuli and responses. In a second theory, purposive qualities result from the conditioning of responses to persisting stimuli arising from various motivational states. Reinforcement theories of purpose explain the purposive qualities of behavior as due to previous contingencies of reinforcement rather than future rewards.

In state variable theories of purpose, intention is identified with a readiness to respond. In mediational theories, it can be identified with the anticipatory goal reaction or with implicit trial and error. In yet other theories, it is related to the verbal control of behavior.

Chomsky claims that the organization of verbal behavior cannot be adequately explained without reference to a generative grammar. His claim that verbal behavior is not under the control of behavioral variables is either a justified rejection of the simple reflexological model or a premature and unsupported speculation. His rejection of finite state grammars refutes the simple reflexological model but not major S-R theories which incorporate state variables, functional response classes, response hierarchies, mediation, and autoclitics, all of which differ from left-right sequencing.

Chomsky's competence model, the generative grammar, can be interpreted as a structural description of functional stimulus and response classes. As such, it is an intervening variable and does not describe processes within the organism. Nor is it more deep, more abstract, or more hidden than other theoretical concepts. If it is interpreted as a hypothetical construct, then it is a poorly defined one.

His argument that the discovery of a competence model takes priority over a performance model is not decisive. In fact, structural and functional analyses can proceed concurrently.

As a nativist, Chomsky assumes complex primitive structural descriptions. He therefore can assume simple primitive learning operations and strong constraints on the acquisition of knowledge. In contrast, behaviorist empiricists assume simple primitive structural descriptions. They therefore require complex secondary learning operations and assume greater variability in the acquisition of behavior.

Many critics of behaviorism argue that S-R psychology as characterized in the preceding chapter is inadequate to account for the organization of behavior.[1] They claim that principles beyond those encompassed by S-R psychology must be appealed to in order to explain the ordered sequence of behavior over time. One such principle of organization is purpose, and a second is generative grammar. I shall examine these two powerful objections to S-R psychology with the aim of clarifying behaviorist views on the organization of behavior.

PURPOSIVISM

A persistent criticism of behaviorist psychology is that it ignores purpose as a determinant of behavioral organization.[2] It is argued, for example, that the behavior of a rat running through a maze is not fully explained by antecedent conditions alone and that the rat's purpose in running, namely to obtain the food in the goal box, must be included in any adequate explanation. McDougall (1926), a vigorous proponent of purposivism in psychology, summarizes the case:

> The behaviorist pretends that each movement displayed is a reflex reaction to some sense-stimulus. . . . But all the successive movements have a meaning . . . for us, and are intelligible to us as a behavior, only when we regard them as incidents of one process of striving. (p. 282)

> You cannot describe intelligibly and adequately the behavior of animals without using language which implies that the animals do not merely respond to stimuli, but that they seek goals and appreciate the several factors of a complex situation in their relations to one another and to the goals they seek. (p. 287)

This issue of purposivism arises in two forms. First is what can be termed "descriptive purposivism," or the claim that behavior cannot be adequately *described* without the use of purposive categories (see chapter 3). "Explanatory purposivism," to be discussed here, is the assertion that behavior, however it is described, is *explained* best (or perhaps only) by purposive principles.

Behaviorist Objections to Teleological Explanation

Behaviorists, for the most part, reject explanatory purposivism because of a number of objections to teleological explanations.[3] Two of these objections are similar to the criticisms of descriptive purposivism. The first is that statements about purpose do not meet behaviorist standards of objectivity. Often an organism's purpose is not obvious, nor is it clear at what point on the evolutionary scale organisms begin to behave with purpose. Humans, of course, can explicitly state their goals and intentions, but for the reasons discussed in chapter 11, behaviorists do not regard first-person reports of this type as entirely reliable. Furthermore, verbal reports do not solve the problem for nonverbal organisms or for adult humans from whom reports are not available. In all these cases, intuition and interpretation must be relied upon to determine goals and purposes, and the attribution of intentions to animals smacks of anthropomorphism.[4] Intersubjective agreement tends to be lower the greater the role of interpretation and intuition, and purposive explanatory principles cannot, therefore, be objectively applied.[5]

The problem is exacerbated if the goals and means must be intensionally characterized.[6] Consider a rat trained to run a maze for food, but on one trial the food is removed from the goal box. The behavior of this rat, now running to an empty box, can be given a teleological explanation even though the behavior cannot, in fact, achieve the goal. Eating the now-absent food is still the rat's intended goal. Conversely, even with food in the goal box, a hungry rat will not run a maze if it has not learned that food has been placed in the goal box. Thus, the existence of a goal and a means is neither necessary nor sufficient for an organism to behave purposively. In addition, it is necessary that the organism *believe* that the goal exists and that a particular behavior is a means to the goal.[7] Thus, teleological explanations may have to be stated in terms of intended, perceived, or believed means and goals, and this requirement adds another layer of interpretation and subjectivity to the application of purposive explanations. Indeterminacy is further compounded because of the interdependency of beliefs and purposes in interpreting the behavior of another organism. What an animal is thought to believe determines, in part, what the animal's purposes are perceived to be, and vice versa.

A second behaviorist objection to both descriptive and explanatory purposivism is that they presuppose what behaviorists would prefer to derive from more fundamental principles. Explanations of behavior in terms of goals, intentions, and purposes assume a degree of intelligence on the part of the organism. If this intelligence can itself be accounted for by principles which do not assume intelligent or teleological operations, then a more basic explanation has been achieved.[8] Less is presupposed, and this basic set of principles may explain not only purposive behavior, but also those aspects of behavior which are not adaptive.

In addition to these two defects shared by both descriptive and explanatory purposivism are those specific to the latter. Explanations of behavior in terms of purposes appear to treat goals as final causes. If the eating of the food is one of the factors explaining the maze running of the rat, then it seems that the usual temporal relations between cause and effect are reversed.[9] The eating of the food is appealed to in explaining the prior running of the maze. This kind of explanatory principle threatens to reintroduce entelechy, or worse, a kind of animistic thinking that is the antithesis of scientific explanation.[10]

To avoid these undesirable implications, a teleological approach can assert that it is the *prior* intention, or having of a purpose, which is the cause of the behavior, rather than the subsequently achieved goal. This solution, however, appears to place the causes of behavior in the mental contents of the mind where they are inaccessible to behaviorist methods of observation and suggests a dualism of mind and body.[11] Moreover, it anthropomorphically attributes prior intentions and conscious purposes to lower animals.

Yet another objection to teleological explanations is that they are not sufficiently determinate.[12] Mechanistic explanations of behavior, it is argued, yield highly specific predictions of behavior while teleological explanations can only suggest in general terms what behaviors are likely to occur. Furthermore, teleological explanations predict only that certain purposes will be achieved, but they are usually silent on the specific behaviors that will occur, since a given purpose can be achieved in a variety of ways.

This last objection cannot be raised by all behaviorists, however. For one thing, not all behaviorist theories generate predictions of specific behaviors. Some provide only probabilities of behaviors. Others specify responses only in highly molar terms. Second, as explained in chapter 3, most behaviorist theories use achievement-descriptions to define response classes. Only an environmental consequence is specified and not the specific movements producing this effect.

Behaviorist Theories of Purpose

Despite these behaviorist objections to teleological explanation, behavior indisputably displays purposive characteristics. Behavior is goal-directed, it shows persistence in the face of obstacles, and it is flexible in assuming a variety of means to achieve a particular end.[13] These qualities must be accounted for by behavioral theory. The behaviorist conceptual strategy in this case is to provide explanations of these purposive properties of behavior by formulating theoretical sketches free of the objectionable features of explanatory purposivism reviewed above.[14]

Purpose as a State Variable. One behaviorist view of purpose is that it is neither a response nor a stimulus but rather a state of the organism determining the relationship between the two. As discussed in chapter 4, state variables are theoretical concepts mediating among observable variables. Purpose can be conceived as either a hypothetical construct referring to neuromuscular states (variously known as "determining tendencies," "motor sets," or "motor attitudes") or as a purely conceptual intervening variable ("readiness," "behavioral disposition"). As the former, the purposive state is assumed to be the result of changes in the resistances or thresholds of specific sets of reflexes due to the kind of integration and coordination of reflex variables discussed in the preceding chapter. As the latter, purpose refers to observed changes in the likelihood of specific sets of responses under certain conditions.

In either case, the purposive properties of behavior are explained as the result of a state variable which increases the probability of a certain class of responses.[15] For example, a rat deprived of food will undergo a change in a state variable that will increase the likelihood of three kinds of responses: (1) consummatory responses (eating) instinctively linked to the state, (2) responses which the rat in the past has learned will lead to eating, and (3) responses which the rat currently learns bring it closer to eating. Goal-directedness appears because the purpose-state-variable both increases the occurrence of responses which produce certain results and permits the learning of only those S-R connections leading to these same results. This learning under the selective direction of a purpose-state-variable can also be used to explain the plasticity of purposive behavior. When an obstacle is encountered, those S-R connections which result in the gradual overcoming of the obstacle are learned and maintained. Furthermore, behavior is persistent because the purpose-state-variable remains in effect until the goal is achieved.

Although state-variable theories of purpose appear to account for a number of the purposive aspects of behavior, they are not entirely satisfactory because they are excessively vague on several major points. First, they have little to say about how the purpose-state-variable is related to environmental independent variables. Second, the theories are not specific about how the state variable selectively strengthens only those behaviors relevant to the purpose or how it selects only the appropriate S-R associations for learning. This selective functioning of the state variable, although couched in S-R terminology, borders on assuming intelligence and final causation in the state's operation, the very features of teleological explanation found unacceptable by most behaviorists.

Purpose and Maintaining Stimuli. Some of the vagueness of state-variable theories is eliminated by conditioning theories with more precise learning principles. Some conditioning theories postulate drive stimuli. In the case of hunger or thirst, for example, deprivation is thought to cause physiological disturbances (in the stomach, mouth, or bloodstream, perhaps) which function as internal stimuli. Drive stimuli for other motives can be acquired through learning. Guthrie, for example, assumes that any conditioned habit when interfered with produces a drive stimulus, termed "excitement," which persists until the habit is able to continue unimpeded. Others assume that acquired motives are learned through a process by which the drive stimuli of basic homeostatic needs come to be associated with the conditioned motives.

Thus, depending on the particular theory, environmental events (or in some cases, hormonal or maturational events) produce internal stimuli, often called "maintaining stimuli," which persist until a goal-response occurs to eliminate them. Once the goal-response eliminates the drive stimulus, no other responses can become associated with the drive stimulus. Therefore, the association conditioned between the drive stimulus and the goal response is both consistent and preserved. This implies that each time an organism is motivated, the drive stimuli activated will elicit goal-responses.[16]

Since there may be a variety of responses which eliminate the drive stimulus, the latter may become associated with a number of responses, including complex serial responses. Different goal-responses will contine to be emitted until the drive stimulus disappears, and behavior therefore shows persistence. New goal-responses that succeed in eliminating the drive stimulus will be learned, and behavior shows "docility," or the ability to learn new means to achieve an end. Thus, the postulation of stimuli associated with motives suggests how several purposive aspects of behavior can be explained without appeal to final causes.

Reinforcement. The most common behaviorist interpretation of purpose involves reinforcement.[17] Theories of reinforcement abound, but they all share the empirical observation that behavior is affected by its consequences. When a response is followed by a positive reinforcement, it increases in its likelihood of future occurrence. When the response later recurs, a purposive explanation is that the response occurs in order to achieve the *future* reinforcement. In contrast, a conditioning explanation is that the response occurs because of the *previous* reinforcement of that response. Skinner (1974) illustrates the point with an example:

> Seeking or looking for something seems to have a particularly strong orientation toward the future. We learn to look for an object when we acquire behavior which commonly has the consequence of discovering it. Thus, to look for a match is to look in a manner previously reinforced by finding matches. To seek help is to act in ways which have in the past led to help. (p. 57)

Purposive behavior is organized not by future goals, but by past consequences. Final causes are replaced by antecedent relationships among responses and stimuli. As Hull (1935a) concludes:

> *Thus the organism through the mere process of conditioning will come to strive for states of affairs which are positively reinforcing.*

On this assumption, states of affairs which organisms will strive to attain are reinforcing agents, not because they will evoke striving, but they evoke striving now because at some time in the past they were potent reinforcing agents, thereby joining stimuli and responses . . . which constitute the striving. (p. 822)

To the extent that behavior occurs because of prior reinforcing consequences it will appear to be goal directed. The persistence of behavior can be explained by the strengthening effect of intermittent reinforcement shown to maintain behavior over long periods even though it rarely achieves reinforcements. Because all responses followed by a reinforcer are strengthened, an organism may possess a large repertoire of responses which lead to a particular reinforcement, and this repertoire accounts for the flexibility of behavior. Response induction and additional conditioning by reinforcement adds to this repertoire, thereby explaining the plasticity of behavior.

Although reinforcement principles avoid the objectionable features of teleological explanation, they are nevertheless barely a step away from the latter. There is no consensus on what constitutes the essence of a teleological explanation, but according to one common formulation, the assertion that in environment E, organism S emits behavior B for the sake of goal G, is equivalent to:

1. In E, B tends to bring about G.
2. B occurs in E because it tends to bring about G.[18]

In this formulation, the critical feature of teleological explanation is its reference to the consequences of B while nonteleological explanations mention only antecedents of B.

This formulation makes use of the phrase "tends to bring about." However, as shown above, it is not sufficient merely that such a relationship exists. It is also necessary that S know about it. S can acquire this knowledge through previous experience. Therefore, the formulation can be emended:

1. In E, B *has brought about* G in S's past.
2. B occurs in E because *it has brought about* G in S's past.

This revised formulation is equivalent to a reinforcement explanation where G is the reinforcement, B is the reinforced response, and E is the discriminative stimulus. Reinforcement principles are thus quite nearly teleological without the objectionable features of purposive explanation.

This revised formulation also deals with some of the problems of intensionality in purposive behavior. For example, the fact that organisms often strive for goals that do not exist (e.g., the rat running the maze from which food has been removed) poses no problem, since the explanation makes reference only to past consequences, not future ones. Furthermore, since reinforcement theories nearly always use functional definitions of stimulus and response classes, E, B, and G cannot be specified *a priori*. The behavior B strengthened by reinforcement is a class whose membership can be determined only empirically by observing which responses in fact increase in frequency. Some of the responses strengthened and therefore included in the functional response class may be responses which do not, in fact, produce the reinforcement. Similarly, the discriminative stimulus E must be functionally specified and may include class members such that B does not achieve G in their presence. This dependence of stimulus and response specification on how S's behavior is affected captures the essence of the claim that goal and means in purposive behavior must be intensionally described. It has the additional advantage that functional specifications are based on empirical observations of transfer experiments and not on S's verbal reports nor on intuition about S's intentions.

Intentions

One problem with these behaviorist explanations of purpose is that they seem to be lacking the processes of anticipation, foreknowledge, and intention which play a critical role in purposive behavior. Humans not only behave purposefully, as behaviorist theories predict, but they also know what they are about to do and why, and they may even plan for it. How do these phenomena fit into behaviorist accounts of purposive behavior?

The Purpose-State-Variable. Under a state-variable interpretation of purpose, the purpose-state-variable predisposes the organism for a particular set of responses. The organism, therefore, may be said to be "prepared," or "ready" for that behavior even before it is emitted. This readiness can be viewed as the foreknowledge or anticipation of their own behavior that organisms have when they behave purposefully. Furthermore, the strengthened responses may be prepared in a sequence along the lines of the serial response discussed in the preceding chapter. Thus, the purpose-state may mirror the sequence of behavior eventually emitted and thereby constitute the behavioral counterpart of a "plan" or "intention."

Anticipatory Goal Reactions. Another common behaviorist strategy is to identify anticipation with an antecedent stimulus related to a goal, or reinforcement, through previous conditioning. The Hullian anticipatory goal reaction, discussed in the preceding chapter, is a good illustration. Since the anticipatory goal reaction r_g is a detachable component of the goal reaction (consummatory response), its relationship to the goal is straightforward. Through the principles of the goal gradient hypothesis and the process of "short-circuiting," r_g moves forward in the sequence of responses leading to the goal. Thus, as the organism runs through a series of responses, it emits supplementary anticipatory responses appropriate to the consuming of the goal it has not yet achieved and may be said to be "anticipating" the goal. If, in addition, the organism can discriminate r_g, perhaps verbally, then the organism may be said to have "foreknowledge" of its purposes.[19]

Because the r_g comes, through conditioning, to elicit each of the various members of a behavioral sequence, expectations, in the form of anticipatory goal reactions, serve to integrate response sequences and to organize behavior around goals. In addition, the habit-family hierarchy that develops out of r_g helps to explain the fact that organisms have multiple means for achieving a goal and will flexibly switch methods when an attempted means is blocked (see chapter 6). Thus, behavior under the antecedent control of anticipatory goal reactions not only shows the marks of purposiveness but also can manifest the foreknowledge, expectations, and intentions of human action.[20]

Mediational Chains. Another way of incorporating intention into a behaviorist account is through the postulation of mediating processes. It is assumed that a sequence of overt responses can occur in covert, or incipient, form, as well. Therefore, an organism at a choice point need not repeatedly emit various overt behaviors until one finally produces a goal stimulus. Instead, the organism emits covert sequences of responses in a form of "implicit trial-and-error." Some of these implicit sequences end in covert stimuli related to past goals. The stimuli may be detachable components of goal reactions such as the Hullian r_g, or Mowrer's "hope."[21] Or the stimuli may be covert forms of responses strengthened by purpose-state-variables. In either case, an implicit response sequence resulting in covert goal-related stimuli then serves as a stimulus to elicit the entire response sequence in *overt* form. The "successful" covert sequence precedes and thereby anticipates the overt sequence and may therefore be said to constitute the organism's plan, intention, and foreknowledge of its own actions and purposes.[22]

In this way the organism is conceptualized as "scanning" various response alternatives available to it by emitting them implicitly. Of these alternatives, the one emitted overtly is the one leading to a particular implicit state or to the highest value of that state. This state, whether it be thought of as Mowrer's hope, Hull's r_g, or in some other form, can be postulated to operate with regard to overt behavior as well. The beginnings of overt behavior sequences are tentatively emitted in the form of overt orienting response, or what is called "vicarious trial and error." These tentative responses may arouse mediating events, such as r_g or hope, which, in turn, further strengthen the continuation of the response sequence.[23] In Mowrer's (1960b) version:

> If, in one situation, an organism makes some distinctive response and experiences a particular pattern of "feedback" and is then either rewarded or punished, and if, in later moving toward this situation the organism "anticipates" being in the situation, i.e., makes some part of the response previously made . . . therein, then this response and its correlated stimuli will call out either hope or fear, and the organism's progress toward the situation in question will be adaptively speeded or slowed. . . .

By thus appropriately responding *at a distance* . . . the subject is said to show *foresight*. (pp. 65–66)

Theories of this sort are illustrative of the interdependence of stimulus and response in S-R theories, in contrast to the simple reflexological model presented in the preceding chapter. Through feedback loops, behavior affects the stimulus configuration by eliciting internal stimuli. Thus, these theories suggest a point of merger between behaviorist S-R theories and cybernetic theories.[24] In both types of theory, a particular output (response) is conceptualized as under the control of a feedback signal (hope, fear, s_g magnitude) which is to be maximized, minimized, or matched to a reference signal by a continuous adjustment of the output. S-R theories may thus use cybernetic principles to explain performance but rely on conditioning theories to explain how the feedback mechanisms develop initially, as well as the origin of the reference signal.[25]

Although mediation has some of the properties of intention, the two cannot be equated. For one thing, the implicit trial-and-error, or thinking, is itself purposeful, goal-directed, and intentional. If purposeful behavior must always be preceded by covert behavioral sequences, then the interpretation runs the risk of an infinite regress in explaining purposeful thought.[26] Second, mediational theories encounter difficulties with the process of scanning alternatives. The organism cannot scan all possible response alternatives because they are limitless. Furthermore, some alternatives are discarded not because they have not in the past led to rewards but because they cannot be carried out as a result of present obstacles. How do present external interfering factors affect internal implicit responses? While these problems are not, in principle, insurmountable, they do underscore the difficulty of capturing the concept of purpose in mediational terms.

Verbal Control of Behavior. Yet another important factor in incorporating intention into behavioral theory is verbal mediation. Behaviorists propose a variety of theories to explain how verbal responses acquire a directive role in organizing nonverbal behavior. For example, a verbal response can be conceived as a type of anticipatory goal reaction. Through some process of conditioning, children learn to name the goals they achieve. Because this verbal label is a detachable component of the reaction, it can move forward in the behavioral sequence, thereby forming a verbal r_g.[27] Eventually humans reach the point at which they can react to a problem by verbalizing a course of action rather than actually carrying it out. The verbal chain that leads to a verbal solution functions as a stimulus to elicit the sequence of named nonverbal behavior.[28] In overt form, such verbalizations are statements of intention.

For those interpretations of purpose emphasizing the organism's history of reinforcement, verbalizations of intention are related to that history. According to Skinner, the verbal community trains its members to discriminate verbally, or to "tact," the contingencies of reinforcement controlling their behavior. These reports are statements about what a person is doing and why, that is, they are statements of intention. As is explained in chapter 11, the discriminative stimuli for these verbal responses may be the environmental independent variables responsible for the behavior, or the behavior itself, or even private events within the organism that are functionally related to the environmental independent variables.

In some cases, the verbal response may function as a stimulus controlling subsequent behavior.[29] For example, a statement of intention in the form of a promise or a resolution may serve as a stimulus to strengthen the behavior intended. In many cases, however, the verbal response may be a mere epiphenomenon of the nonverbal behavior described by the verbal response. If the nonverbal behavior is fully determined by the environmental independent variables, then the verbal response is a mere discrimination of a causal relationship rather than a cause. The verbal response would then be only a collateral byproduct of the same environmental variables that are the true causes of the behavior.[30]

Verbal responses play a more robust causal role when they are in the form of a rule of conduct. Rules are most often acquired by social instruction, as when one receives the travel directions "Make a left after the second traffic light." Or one may construct rules of one's own to distill the effects of previous experience. Both the construction and the following of rules are behavior, and presumably they arise because they proved reinforcing in the history of the community and of the individual. Once these behaviors are acquired, a rule in whatever form—written, spoken by another, said to oneself subvocally—can function as a discriminative stimulus controlling subsequent behavior. Behavior under the functional control of the rule stimulus is called "rule-governed behavior."[31]

Clearly, not all behavior is rule governed in this sense. The behavior of nonverbal animals and children is often purposive, but obviously it is not under the control of verbal discriminative stimuli. Even in the verbal human adult, not all behavior is rule governed. Consider the behavior of following a rule. A person reads, recites, or hears a rule and then follows it. Does the person have to follow yet a second set of rules in order to follow the first set? If no, then the first-order rule following is not rule governed. If yes, then the question can be repeated for the second-order rule following behavior. An infinite regress and the impossibility of all action are avoided only by admitting a level of behavior which is not rule governed, but is rather shaped directly by environmental contingencies without the mediation of verbal stimuli.[32] To be sure, contingency-shaped behavior of this sort often shows regularities describable by rules. In this case, however, the rules exist in the verbal descriptions given by an observer, but not as causal factors in the behavior under observation.

Because so much of human behavior is under verbal control, it is common to view prior verbal control as necessary for intentional action. When the source of verbal control is not obvious or is absent, it is tempting to assume that the antecedent act of intention is hidden in the recesses of consciousness. This conclusion, however, is erroneous. Just as not all behavior is rule governed, so not all intentional behavior is preceded by a verbal statement of intention. Therefore, it is a mistake to extrapolate from prototype cases of human intentional action which include verbal responses to all cases of intentional action.[33]

The control of behavior by verbal stimuli establishes another connection between intensionality and functional classes.[34] There is an obvious and direct link between the terms of a verbal stimulus controlling behavior and the nature of the functional stimulus and response classes appropriate for that behavior. For example, the behavior of a traveler following the rule "Turn right" may be identical to that of a traveler following the rule "Approach the house." However, their behaviors may differ markedly if a detour is required. Thus, when behavior is under verbal control, the manner in which an organism verbalizes rules or contingencies is a good indication of what the important functional classes are.[35] This is a behaviorist analog to the intensionalist claim that action should be understood in terms of how it is perceived by the actor.

GENERATIVE GRAMMAR

The second major objection to be examined in this chapter arises in the field of psycholinguistics. This critique of behaviorism, formulated most vigorously by Chomsky and his followers, questions whether behaviorist principles and assumptions are adequate to account for verbal behavior, or, by extension, for any higher mental process.[36] The challenge from psycholinguistics encompasses at least five issues.

Creativity in Language

The first claim to be considered challenges the fundamental behaviorist assumption that all behavior, and verbal behavior in particular, can be understood as a dependent variable functionally related to environmental variables. Chomsky argues that human speech shows creativity and innovation and is therefore independent of previous conditioning and current stimulation.[37] In Chomsky's (1972) own words:

> The normal use of language is innovative, in the sense that much of what we say . . . is entirely new, not a repetition of anything that we have heard before and not even similar in pattern. . . . But the normal use of language is not only innovative and

potentially infinite in scope, but also free from the control of detectable stimuli, either external or internal. It is because of this freedom from stimulus control that language can serve as an instrument of thought and self-expression. (pp. 11–12)

Chomsky's claim is open to several interpretations. In its strongest version, it may be taken as a denial that human verbal behavior is lawfully (or causally) related to antecedent conditions. As such, Chomsky's argument poses a challenge not only to behaviorism, but also to all scientific approaches which seek to explain phenomena in terms of antecedent causes. Perhaps, then, this interpretation of Chomsky's claim is too strong. Yet, Chomsky's writings do little to discourage it. For example:

It is an interesting question whether the functioning and evolution of human mentality can be accommodated within the framework of physical explanation, as presently conceived, or whether there are new principles, now unknown, that must be invoked, perhaps principles that emerge only at higher levels of organization than can now be submitted to physical investigation. (Chomsky, 1972, p. 98)

A weaker interpretation of Chomsky's claim is that human verbal behavior is independent of *behavioral* antecedents. That is, although speech may have causes, it is, nevertheless, not functionally related to variables such as reinforcement, discriminative stimuli, drive, and previous associations. This interpretation undermines molar behaviorism while leaving general scientific methods intact. Although under this interpretation Chomsky's assertion is an interesting speculation, it is obviously premature. Little or no evidence currently exists to support the hypothesis, and the conceptual arguments in its favor are, at best, inconclusive, as will be shown below. Furthermore, to demonstrate the truth of Chomsky's speculation would be to prove a null hypothesis (i.e., *no* behavioral variables exert functional control over verbal behavior).

Yet a third interpretation of Chomsky's claim is the rather weak assertion that the simple reflexological model, discussed and rejected in the preceding chapter, is inadequate to account for verbal behavior. Chomsky can be understood to be denying that speech consists of a series of reflex movements each elicited by an immediate punctate sensory stimulation. Indeed, in criticizing behavioral science Chomsky (1972) complains that:

The theory of learning has limited itself to a narrow and surely inadequate concept of what is learned—namely a system of stimulus-response connections, a network of associations, a repertoire of behavioral items, a habit hierarchy, or a system of dispositions to respond in a particular way under specifiable stimulus conditions. (p. 72)

If Chomsky's attack is directed at the simple reflexological model, then according to the arguments discussed in the preceding chapter, his claim is both correct and acceptable to most behaviorists.[38]

Chomsky's objection is, nevertheless, of importance to behaviorists, for in his formal argument against specific class of reflexological models, he clarifies their weaknesses, and it is not obvious whether behaviorist extensions of the simple models meet his objections. Chomsky's attack on these simple models, or what he calls "finite state grammars," is the second issue in the psycholinguistic challenge.

Finite State Grammars

Consider a simple reflexological model such as the "serial response" discussed in the previous chapter: R_a elicits R_b, R_b elicits R_c, and so on. A response sequence begins with an initial response and runs to a terminal response, with each intermediate response determined by an immediately preceding event. This principle of behavioral organization is known as "left-right sequencing," a "Markov process," or a "finite state grammar." Applied to language, this principle means that a sentence is produced as each word emitted generates the next word in the sequence until the sentence is completed.[39]

It is evident that left-right sequencing is inadequate to explain the organization of behavior.[40] For one thing, the feedback latency from R_a needed to elicit R_b is too long to mediate the rapid sequences of behavior that occur in many skilled activities.[41] Second, behavior often shows sequential dependencies which exceed those between a response and its immediately preceding state. For example, in the double-alternation maze, animals learn to make one response the first time they encounter a stimulus and a different response the second time they encounter it. Similarly, in the verbal response "The men whom you saw yesterday are now here" the emission of "are" rather than "is" is determined by the use of the plural "men" which does not immediately precede "are." Moreover, the emission of "whom" rather than "who" is determined by the phrase "you saw" which *follows* "whom."[42]

The case against Markov processes as an organizing principle in behavior is most effectively articulated by Lashley.[43] In reviewing the arguments with respect to the organization of verbal behavior, Lashley (1951) concludes:

> From such considerations, it is certain that any theory of grammatical form which ascribes it to direct associative linkage of the words of the sentence overlooks the essential structure of speech. The individual items of the temporal series do not in themselves have a temporal "valence" in their associative connections with other elements. The order is imposed by some other agent. This is true not only of language, but of all skilled movements or successions of movement. (p. 116)

From a purely formalistic set of considerations, Chomsky (1957) reaches a related conclusion:

> In short, the approach to the analysis of grammaticalness suggested here in terms of a finite state Markov process that produces sentences from left to right, appears to

lead to a dead end. . . . If a grammar of this type produces all English sentences, it will produce many non-sentences as well. If it produces only English sentences . . . there will be an infinite number of . . . sentences . . . which it simply will not produce. (p. 24)

These problems for reflexology raised by the facts of serial order in behavior are similar to those posed by the purposive features of behavior. In both cases, behavior is said to have a structure that is more than the mere stringing together of a chain of responses. Behavior displays a coherence that is greater than the concatenation of successive movements. In both cases, behavior is said to depend on what is to come as well as what has been. Just as goals appear to guide the behavior leading to them, so the syntax and meaning of a sentence seem to determine the order of words from which the sentence is constructed. Because of these similarities between the two issues, behaviorist treatments of purpose are relevant to the problem of serial order in behavior. In both cases the proposed solutions are necessarily mere sketches rather than completed theories. Six S-R alternatives to finite state grammars will be reviewed.

State Variables. The state variable, used to explain certain purposive properties of behavior, can also play a role in accounting for the sequencing of behavior. When a state variable, such as a determining tendency, motor set, or behavioral readiness, assumes a high value, then a class of responses is *simultaneously* strengthened. This contrasts with a Markov process in which responses occur only in succession. The simultaneous strengthening of a set of responses permits the interaction of responses before their emission.[44] Therefore, responses overtly emitted late in a sequence can affect responses emitted earlier. Lashley (1951), the critic of simple S-R models, adopts a type of state-variable approach to the problem of serial order:

From such considerations it seems to follow that syntax is not inherent in the words employed or in the idea to be expressed. It is a generalized pattern imposed upon the specific acts as they occur. . . . There are indications that, prior to the internal or overt enunciation of the sentence, an aggregate of word units is partially activated or readied. (p. 119)

This readiness functions as a generalized schema of action that exists prior to a behavioral sequence and determines the order of response emission.

Functional Response Classes. Functional response classes defined in achievement terms suggest a second solution. They do not specify the movements by which achievements are effected. To say, for example, that a lever press will occur is to say nothing about the order of movements which constitute that lever press. The order of these movements may differ from lever press to lever press depending on the organism's position and orientation. It follows that the movements constituting the response—i.e., the internal structure of the response—are not necessarily organized by left-right sequencing. What is true of the lever press is also the case for verbal behavior. Sentences with a variety of word orders may be included in a response class. Thus, even if functional responses occur in left-right sequences, the internal structure of each response may be determined by other principles.[45]

Response Hierarchies. The notion that an achievement-defined response has its own internal structure entails a concept of response hierarchies.[46] Each member of a functional response class F consists of a series of behaviors leading to a certain common achievement. The components of this series and their order may differ since members of F have only end achievements in common. The components of the series may, in turn, be given either a movement-definition or an achievement-definition. For example, if a functional response class is defined as building a house, then members of the class will include all the ways in which this achievement can be accomplished. One member might consist of the series draw plans, buy materials, clear land, etc., in which the elements of the series are themselves assigned achievement-definitions rather than movement-definitions. Therefore each element is also a class of diverse movements. "Draw plans," can be accomplished in a variety of ways, and each of these can further be described in either movement or achievement terms.

This process can be continued indefinitely, with each level of description representing a *class* of events at the next lower level. The order of responses at one level of the hierarchy does not uniquely determine the order of behavior at lower levels. Functional laws involving highly molar functional response classes, therefore, place few constraints on the order of movements actually observed in any instantiation of the law. The observed movements are not necessarily organized by a left-right sequence.

When the functional response class "build house" is strengthened, many behaviors covary in strength. Included in this set is the series draw plans, buy materials, clear land, etc. All of these are *simultaneously* strengthened in a manner akin to Lashley's action schema. They can interact with one another prior to overt emission. Thus, the nature of the strengthened (but not yet emitted) buying-of-materials-response can be modified by the concurrently strengthened (but not yet emitted) clear-the-land-response, even though clearing the land *follows* buying the materials in the overtly emitted response sequence. Under this conception of functional organization, behavior is clearly not governed by left-right sequencing or Markov processes.

Mediation. The role of mediators in organizing observed behavior is limited only by the restrictions placed on the nature of the mediators. If mediating processes are assigned the same properties as overt behavior, then if the latter is assumed to be governed by left-right sequencing, so is the former. As restrictions on mediating processes are lifted, the principles of behavioral organization are changed. If mediation is conceived of as executing the implicit trial-and-error, scanning, and transformations discussed above, then behavioral organization acquires a great deal more flexibility. The speaker may be hypothesized to scan entire sentences prior to emission and to select the grammatical ones. Or given that the entire sentence is available to the speaker prior to emission, it can be transformed so that early parts are made grammatically consistent with later ones.[47]

Frames. The major weakness of left-right sequencing is that dependencies are limited to those between a response and its immediately preceding stimulus. In most behavioral sequences, however, many dependencies span large gaps, especially in language where sentences can be embedded within sentences, thereby separating dependent verbal responses. One behavioral concept that is a partial solution to this problem is the open frame, a kind of discontinuous response.

Suppose that a person has frequently heard sentences in the form of "If X then Y," where X and Y are propositions. This person can acquire a verbal response of the abstract form "If ____, then ____" where the blanks are filled with further verbal behavior. The dependency is between "then" and "if" and not between "then" and whatever happens to precede it in the filled blank. The open frame is a type of relational response, a pattern filled with different verbal material on different occasions. For example, consider the frame "The (plural noun) who (plural verb) (noun) are ____." An instance of this frame would be "The men who built the house are here." Note in this case that because of the frame structure, the plural "are" agrees with the plural "men" rather than the singular "house" that immediately precedes it. Thus the open frame is an improvement over simple left-right sequencing.[48]

The open frame is also relevant to Chomsky's claim that verbal behavior is independent of prior conditioning. One kind of evidence offered in support of this claim is that children often emit sentences or phrases that they have never heard before. One reply to this is that the novel sentence is a combination of learned verbal responses with a learned frame to form a new sentence. For example, a child who has heard "the man's hat," "the man's book," "the man's coat," may acquire the open frame "the man's ____." Upon learning the word "shoes," the child may say "the man's shoes," seemingly an innovation created without previous learning but actually a combination of two types of learning. Thus, the open frame organizes behavior by imposing a schema into which verbal behavior is filled. This schema, or pattern, can be quite abstract, and the degree of abstractness is limited only by the limits of human pattern learning and recognition.

Autoclitics. Yet another solution to the problem of serial order in behavior is suggested by Skinner in this theory of the autoclitic, a verbal response which is a function of other verbal behavior.[49] For example, in the verbal response "I believe it is raining," the phrase "I believe" may be autoclitic in that it is under the stimulus control of an aspect of the verbal response "it is raining," namely its weak strength. Thus, "I believe" is a tact of the low strength of the verbal response which follows it. Therefore, something indicative of the strength of "it's raining" must be available prior to its emission so that "I believe" can tact this level of strength.

Autoclitics also establish the grammar of speech. Suppose a speaker is confronted with two objects: a brown hat and a green book. Assume, therefore, that the tacts "book," "brown," "green," and "hat" are strengthened. The emission of these four does not create a sentence, but the utterance of "The book is green" does qualify. In this latter case, the "is" adds predication through its function as an autoclitic tacting an aspect of the verbal responses "green" and "book," namely that they have the same object as their discriminative stimulus. Note, again, that for "is" to tact this relationship the verbal response "green" must be available in some form prior to its emission so its relationship to "book" can be tacted.

Not all autoclitics are words. As an operant, an autoclitic can be merely an aspect of another response when it can be shown that this aspect is under the independent functional control of behavioral variables. In particular, the order of a series of responses can be considered an independent operant response class. This has important implications for the serial order of verbal responses. As explained above, the autoclitic "is" functions as a tact of a relationship between the verbal responses "book" and "green" (i.e. that they have the same object as discriminative stimulus). But just as "is" can tact this relationship, so can the order of a sequence of words. Thus, for example, the particular order "the green book" tacts the relationship between the verbal responses "green" and "book," i.e., that they have the same object serving as discriminative stimulus.

For the ordering autoclitic to tact aspects of other verbal responses, they must be available in some form before their ordered emission. One way to view this is to assume that the initial verbal behavior, before the addition of autoclitic responses, is strengthened by certain environmental variables. All this initial, or primary, verbal behavior must be simultaneously present so that aspects of it, including relationships within it, can be discriminated by autoclitic responses. The additional processes of composition and self-editing further affect the primary verbal behavior prior to overt emission.[50] When verbal behavior is finally emitted, it occurs in an order determined by the properties and relationships obtaining among strengthened verbal operants concurrently available before emission.

This conception is in sharp contrast to left-to-right sequencing and shares certain similarities with Lashley's suggestion of an aggregate of word units partially activated, or primed, before patterning and emission. With the addition of the autoclitic, the organization of behavior is no longer conceived as governed by a Markov process. Verbal behavior is subject to principles that give it coherence, in that the emission of a verbal response is dependent not only on what immediately precedes it but also on what follows it as well as its relationship to the entire utterance and to the environment, both past and present.[51]

Competence

Although the six behaviorist principles of organization described above differ from a finite grammar, Chomsky rejects them nevertheless. Instead, he contends, the phenomena of language can be understood adequately only by a theory of the form he advocates, a form which, he further maintains, exceeds the conceptual limits of behaviorist psychology. This contention is a third issue in the psycholinguistic challenge to behaviorism.

According to Chomsky, a theory of language must consist of two independent components. The first, a competence model, represents what a speaker (or listener) knows about language and is capable of demonstrating while the second, a theory of performance, explains how the competence of the speaker-listener is realized in actual episodes of speaking and understanding. Chomsky's chief interest is in the former, the theory of competence. His belief in the importance of a competence model and its incompatibility with S-R psychology is summarized in the following passage:

> If we are ever to understand how language is used or acquired, then we must abstract for separate and independent study a cognitive system, a system of knowledge and belief, that develops in early childhood and that interacts with many other factors to determine the kinds of behavior that we observe . . . we must isolate and study the system of *linguistic competence* that underlies behavior but that is not realized in any direct or simple way in behavior. And this system of linguistic competence is qualitatively different from anything that can be described in terms of . . . the concepts of S-R psychology. (Chomsky, 1972, p. 4)

For Chomsky, a competence model is expressed in the form of a grammar:

> A grammar of a language purports to be a description of the ideal speaker-hearer's intrinsic competence. If the grammar is . . . perfectly explicit . . . we may call it a *generative grammar*. A fully adequate grammar must assign to each of an infinite range of sentences a structural description indicating how this sentence is understood by the ideal speaker-hearer. (1965, pp. 4–5)

> By a generative grammar I mean simply a system of rules that in some explicit and well-defined way assigns structural descriptions to sentences. (1965, p. 8)

This conception of a theory of language appears to conflict with behaviorist assumptions in two important ways. First, the competence model, or what a speaker-listener knows, is expressed as a system of rules. In contrast, the S-R learning thesis represents what is learned as a stimulus-response connection or as a behavioral repertoire of responses of varying strengths.[52] Psycholinguists support Chomsky's claim with an example. They argue that if a child learns "Today I walk, yesterday I walk*ed*," "Today I carry, yesterday I car*ried*," and so forth, then on a S-R account the child will know only the responses actually learned. According to a competence model, they contend, the child will have learned a rule and will be competent to apply it to untrained new cases. Thus, when the child learns "Today I play," the verbal response "Yesterday I play*ed*" will be forthcoming without further training. They conclude, therefore, that rules, rather than responses or S-R links, are what is acquired and known.

Chomsky claims a second major difference distinguishes his approach from that of S-R psychology: the latter studies only behavior while he examines the reality underlying behavior. Because actual behavior is the resultant of two interacting factors—competence and performance—it does not directly reflect competence. Competence, therefore, is not immediately observed in verbal behavior but must be inferred. It represents a speaker-listener's *potential* for producing sentences which is infinite, while the speaker-listener's actual output must, of course, be finite. In contrast, S-R theories, according to Chomsky, are interested only in actually observed behavior. As Chomsky (1965) asserts:

> The problem for the linguist, as well as for the child learning the language, is to determine from the data of performance the underlying system of rules that has been mastered by the speaker-hearer and that he puts to use in actual performance. Hence, in the technical sense, linguistic theory is mentalistic, since it is concerned with discovering a mental reality underlying actual behavior. Observed use of language or hypothesized dispositions to responses, habits, and so on, may provide evidence as to the nature of this mental reality, but surely cannot constitute the actual subject matter of linguistics, if this is to be a serious discipline. (p. 4)

This alleged difference between the behaviorist's limitation to behavior and Chomsky's concern with the underlying reality is also expressed in Chomsky's distinction between "surface" and "deep" structure. Chomsky shows that a generative grammar is greatly simplified and many problems are avoided if it includes rules known as "grammatical transformations." A rule of this type operates on a given string with a given constituent structure and converts it into a new string with a new derived constituent structure.[53] The structure resulting from the application of a grammatical transformation can be called a "surface structure," and the structure upon which the transformation is performed is the "deep structure."[54] From this distinction Chomsky (1972) concludes:

Knowledge of a language involves the ability to assign deep and surface structures to an infinite range of sentences, to relate these structures appropriately, and to assign a semantic interpretation and a phonetic interpretation to the paired deep and surface structures. . . .

then a person who knows a specific language has control of a grammar that *generates* (that is, characterizes) the infinite set of potential deep structures, maps them onto associated surface structures, and determines the semantic and phonetic interpretations of these abstract objects. (p. 30)

While the surface structure is closely related to the organization of verbal behavior actually emitted, the deep structure is not present in observed behavior in any direct way. Therefore, an adequate generative grammar must make reference to unobserved abstract structures. The implications for behaviorist psychology are summarized by Chomsky (1972):

It is clear . . . that the surface structure is often misleading and uninformative and that our knowledge of language involves properties of a much more abstract nature, not indicated directly in the surface structure. Furthermore, even . . . artificially simple examples . . . show how hopeless it would be to try to account for linguistic competence in terms of "habits," "disposition," "knowing how," and other concepts associated with the study of behavior, as this study has been circumscribed, quite without warrant, in recent years. (pp. 37–38)

Thus, in contrasting his position with behaviorism, Chomsky contends that the explanatory principles necessary for language must deal with the abstract, the deep, and the unobservable.

In many ways, Chomsky's distinction between competence and performance is not unlike the traditional behaviorist distinction between learning and performance, exemplified by Hull's distinction between habit strength, $_SH_R$, and reaction potential, $_SE_R$.[55] Like competence, $_SH_R$ represents what the organism has learned while $_SE_R$ represents the resultant of all the factors interacting with $_SH_R$ (e.g., motivation) to produce behavior. The learning construct, whether it be Hull's $_SH_R$ or Tolman's cognitive map, never appears directly in behavior because it must interact with other factors in yielding observed behavior. In this sense, the learning construct of S-R theories may also be said to "underlie behavior." Furthermore, the values of behavior determined partially by the learning construct are potentially infinite, since the behavior actually produced by a particular state of learning depends on the values assumed by the other variables in the equation determining behavior, and in theory, these can take on an infinite range of values.

Competence as Structural Description. In describing what a speaker has learned, a generative grammar is also like a set of functional descriptions of stimulus and response classes.[56] As outlined in chapter 3, determining functional classes is an empirical problem. For example, a functional response class can be determined by delineating the class of behaviors that change as the result of a learning operation. Once a functional class, F, is empirically determined, it is necessary to specify the class with a description, D_F.

If a generative grammar is interpreted as a D_F, then several interesting implications follow. First, D_F is a mere description of a class of behaviors or stimuli. It does not suggest how the class is formed, nor why the learning operation affects this particular class. In this sense, a D_F in the form of a grammar refers solely to structure, and not to a process.[57] Second, F, as described by D_F, will contain members that do not actually occur in observed behavior. That is, certain behaviors may be strengthened by a learning operation, but they are not emitted because the other variables do not assume the values needed for their emission. Similarly, not all the stimuli in a functional stimulus class will actually be encountered by the organism. Thus D_F describes a class that is potentially infinite, just as a generative grammar D_F characterizes a potentially infinite set of sentences.

Third, in nearly all behaviorist S-R theories, D_F is not a description of the particular movements and specific stimuli that occurred during the learning operation. Obtained functional classes, or what is learned, are specifiable only by much more abstract descriptions.[58] Therefore, the charge, mentioned above, that S-R theories imply that the child learns only the particular responses occurring during conditioning is unwarranted. The functional class learned is broader and must be empirically determined. Characterizing the class remains a problem to which D_F is the solution. The functional response class acquired by the child who is taught "Today I walk, yesterday I walk*ed*," "Today I carry, yesteray I carri*ed*," is not limited to these two verbal responses. It includes all responses strengthened by this learning operation.[59]

As argued in chapter 3, no *a priori* constraints need by applied to the form of D_F, nor is there a unique D_F for any functional class.[60] Psychologists are free to use any mode of expression to formulate a D_F, including mathematical equations, geometric models, pattern recognition computer programs, or verbal descriptions.[61] What is important is that a D_F be effective, enabling a psychologist to determine definitely whether a behavior or stimulus is or is not a member of F. It serves its function when it acts as a stimulus in controlling the behavior of the psychologist in selecting members of F. It is thus a rule governing the behavior of the scientist in the sense described above.

In the ideal case, D_F can be given in mathematical form. Suppose that as the result of a learning operation, behavior comes under the control of a class of circular stimuli, regardless of their size. Alternately, assume that the behavior acquired is that of moving a limb in a circular fashion. In either case the functional class F, stimulus or response, has a structural description, D_F, of the form $X^2 + Y^2 = N$, the equation for a circle in some geometric coordinate system. Note first that this, or any equation, can also be expressed as a rule for determining if a particular event is a member of F: "Measure X for each point on the locus, square this quantity, then sum it with the square of Y, etc." Second, equations contain operations, such as multiplication, division, and integration, which transform quantities. Third, some of the quantities in the equation are not directly expressed in the data examined. Anyone measuring the simple properties of the circular stimulus or response, such as their circumference or diameter, would find nothing directly corresponding to X^2, yet those "deep" quantities must be considered in determining whether the stimulus or response is a member of F.

Although D_F thus consists of rules, operations, and quantities not directly expressed in the data, it is, nevertheless, nothing more than a structural description of a stimulus or response class. The rules, operations, and indirectly expressed quantities refer to the activities of anyone making use of the equation. They are not descriptions of causal processes or activities with the organism whose responses or controlling stimuli are given by D_F.[62] Indeed, the D_F could be constructed in a different format, with different operations, rules, and deep quantities, and still prove to be an adequate description of F. The only requirement for D_F is that it enable its user to recognize members of F.

It is conceivable that the optimal way to formulate a D_F for verbal behavior is a generative grammar of the sort advocated by Chomsky. That is, it may prove to be the case that frames and other such devices are inadequate to describe the functional classes found and that a D_F must incorporate transformational rules. This would mean, for example, that if in some learning operation, be it reinforcement or mere exposure to speech, a child learns verbal response V_1, then to characterize the functional class the child has learned, a transformational gammar is necessary. The dimensions of similarity between V_1 and a response V_2, emitted by the child at some later time as a result of the earlier learning operation, would be characterized by the transformational generative grammar. Then Chomsky (1965) would be correct in extolling

> the speaker's ability to produce and understand instantly new sentences that are not similar to those previously heard in any physically defined sense or in terms of any notion of frames or classes of elements, nor associated with those previously heard by conditioning, nor obtainable from them by any sort of "generalization" known to psychology or philosophy. (pp. 57–58)

and the fact that

> much of what we say . . . is entirely new, not a repetition of anything that we have heard before and not even similar in pattern—in any useful sense of the terms "similar" and "pattern"—to sentences or discourse that we have heard in the past. (1972, p. 12)

However, whereas Chomsky concludes from this that S-R theory would therefore have to be abandoned, an alternate conclusion is that the concept of D_F would therefore have to be expanded to include a transformational grammar.[63] The grammar would define the dimensions of similarity and generalization.

This latter conclusion is, in fact, not such a radical step for behaviorist psychology. Early debates over what is learned and the phenomenon of transposition demonstrate quite clearly that even in simple animal learning, D_F requires a rather abstract form. Whether D_F needs grammatical transformations is an open matter, but even if they are needed, admitting them requires no major concessions on the part of most S-R theories. D_F, after all, is nothing more than a description, and the question about grammatical transformation is merely a question about what descriptive apparatus is needed for a good specification of stimulus and response classes. The dimensions of generalization and the notions of similarity and pattern are not limited to the properties found useful in physics.[64]

If generative grammar is interpreted as a kind of D_F then it can be viewed as a calculation device used by a scientist to characterize and select members of functional classes. As such, it is an intervening variable (discussed in chapter 4) although not a well defined one (for reasons presented below). It is not unique since more than one device can serve the same purpose, although some devices meet the criteria of simplicity, comprehensiveness, and fruitfulness better than others. The rules, operations, and deep quantities of the grammar are properties of D_F, not processes in the organism.[65] It is therefore quite misleading to say, as does Chomsky, that aspects of the grammar, including its rules, structures, and operations are "constructed," "manipulated," "internalized," "mastered," "developed," "devised," "assigned," "controlled," learned, known, and followed by the speaker.[66] All of these locutions must be viewed as picturesque but confusing ways of saying that the grammar is an accurate description of speaker's functional classes.[67]

That these expressions are misleading and harmful to clear understanding is amply demonstrated by the controversy between Braine and Bever, Fodor, and Weksel.[68] Braine suggests that grammatical structure is learned by "contextual generalization" in which a child learns the position of a unit in a sequence. Thus, Braine is proposing that the pattern characterizing D_F for this kind of learning is a type of frame. Bever et al. reject Braine's proposal and argue that grammatical transformations are required for an adequate structural description.

This debate is an interesting disagreement over what sort of descriptive apparatus is needed for D_F. However, the disagreement degenerates when questions about descriptions are misunderstood as questions about psychological processes. Thus, Bever et al. (1965a), noting that with grammatical transformations there are "underlying structures" (i.e., prior to the transformation), and that "underlying order is never reflected in an actual sentence" (p. 476) conclude:

Hence if the child who learns English learns the rules governing syntax, it follows that he *must learn to manipulate underlying structures, for which his verbal environment provides him with no explicit models*. It is evident that contextual generalization, simply because it *is* a variety of generalization, cannot account for such learning. (p. 476)

From this they draw an even stronger inference:

As the empirical basis for assuming an abstract underlying structure in language becomes broader and the explanatory power of that assumption becomes deeper, *we recommend to all psychologists that they seriously question the adequacy of any theory of learning that cannot account for the fact that such structures are acquired*. (1965b, p. 500)

Apparently Bever et al. believe that if a formula is required for an economical description of some aspect of the behavior of an organism, then that formula is: (1) learned by the organism, and (2) manipulated by the organism in producing its behavior. But surely this does not follow.

Competence as Hypothetical Construct. A generative grammar can also be construed as a hypothetical construct (chapter 4) rather than an intervening variable. Although as a D_F, a generative grammar is not unique, it is possible to choose one specific grammar on various theoretical grounds, and to postulate that it is a description of events within the organism. This is the way Katz (1964/1967) interprets Chomsky:

The basic point of Chomsky's criticisms is that the failure of a taxonomic theory . . . is due to the failure of such theories to concern themselves with mental capacities, events, and processes. . . .

The aim of theory construction in linguistics is taken to be the formulation of a theory that reveals the structure of [a] mechanism and explains the facts of linguistic communication by showing them to be behavioral consequences of the operation of a mechanism with just the structure that the formulated theory attributes to it. (p. 76)

This mechanism is, according to the mentalist linguist, a brain mechanism, a component of a neural system. (p. 77)

The hypothesized mechanism must be capable of affecting the articulatory system of a speaker so as to produce an utterance. (p. 83)

There are two problems with this realistic interpretation of Chomsky's competence model. For one thing, Chomsky (1965) disavows it:[69]

To avoid what has been a continuing misunderstanding, it is perhaps worth while to reiterate that a generative grammar is not a model for a speaker or hearer. . . . When we say that a sentence has certain derivation with respect to a particular generative grammar, we say nothing about how the speaker or hearer might proceed, in some practical or efficient way, to construct such a derivation. . . . this generative grammar does not, in itself, prescribe the character or functioning of a perceptual model or a model of speech production. (p. 9)

A second problem is that as a theoretical concept, either an intervening variable or hypothetical construct, the generative grammar manifests several deficiencies, at least from a behaviorist perspective. Of these, the most serious is that the competence model is tied very loosely to objective observations. Little attention is devoted to the environmental conditions responsible for the creation of the functional class or the neural mechanism. Nor is the generative grammar carefully linked to verbal behavior. Instead, it is designed to describe and explain aspects of language intuited by the linguist. It is the linguist who judges which sentences are grammatical and which sentences are related despite their superficial differences. The generative grammar is thus more concerned with the intuitions of the linguist rather than with verbal behavior of speakers.[70] Because of these deficiencies, the generative grammar is open to all the behaviorist criticisms of theoretical concepts reviewed in chapter 4.

Summary: Competence and S-R Psychology. If the generative grammar is understood as a structural description of functional classes, then it falls within the domain of the traditional problem of what is learned.[71] Chomsky's contribution then is the suggestion that this structural description may be more abstract than previously suspected and may need to include transformational rules. If so, then Chomsky's proposal is an interesting development within S-R psychology. His talk about the speaker-listener's "internalizing," "constructing," and "manipulating" aspects of this structural description must be interpreted as dramatic metaphor. In essence, he recommends a particular intervening variable, and although there are serious objections to its usefulness (discussed below), it is a theoretical concept that fits within the broad concept of S-R psychology developed in the preceding chapter. Chomsky's comptence model deals with the "reality underlying behavior" no more than does any other useful theoretical concept.

If the generative grammar is understood as a description of internal processes reponsible for verbal behavior, then it is a kind of hypothetical construct. Hypothetical constructs are common in behaviorist theories. Hence, there is no reason to conclude that there is an incompatibility between theories of competence and behaviorist psychology merely because the postulated processes of a generative grammar are not observable. Nevertheless, generative grammars generally fail to meet any of the behaviorist tactical criteria for theoretical concepts discussed in chapter 4, and are therefore unacceptable in a behaviorist science on strategic grounds.[72] Given these irreconcilable differences over what is "good" science, it seems gratuitous for the generative grammarian to insist that an internal grammar-hypothetical-construct *"must"* be postulated. As long as this postulation is in the realm of theory rather than data, the grammarian's "must" is without force in the absence of agreed upon standards for scientific strategy.[73]

The Priority of a Competence Model

These differences in scientific strategy are responsible for a fourth issue in the psycholinguistic challenge to behaviorism. Whereas the behaviorist places the greatest emphasis on the study of behavior as a function of environmental variables, Chomsky (1972) asserts:

It is not at all obvious that the study of learning should proceed directly to the investigation of factors that control behavior. . . . It is first necessary to determine the significant characterisitcs of [the] behavioral repertoire. . . . A meaningful study of learning can proceed only after this preliminary task has been carried out and has led to a reasonably well-confirmed theory of underlying competence—in the case of language, to the formulation of the generative grammar that underlies the observed use of language. (p. 73)

This insistence on the priority of the competence model leads Chomsky (1975) to negate entirely the usefulness of the behaviorist enterprise:

No doubt what the organism does depends in part on its experience, but it seems to me entirely hopeless to investigate directly the relation between experience and action. . . .

An attempt . . . to study directly the relation of behavior to past and current experience is doomed to triviality and scientific insignificance. (pp. 16–17)

Chomsky's emphasis on a structural rather than a functional approach to language has a certain commonsense appeal. It seems reasonable that one must know what it is that is learned before one can seriously study the process of learning. However, an equally commonsensical case can be argued for the opposite viewpoint: Before one can specify what is learned one must know what learning is.

Indeed, support for the latter view can be found in the logic of experiments to determine what is learned. In these experiments, an organism is first exposed to some learning operation (e.g., reinforcement, association) and is then tested to delineate the scope of changes in behavior. A characterization of these changes constitutes what is learned. However, without some notion of a learning operation and ways to test for change, this type of experiment cannot be carried out. Principles of behavioral change, relating responses to the environment, are thus presupposed and therefore deserve attention.

Chomsky appears to avoid this requirement for a link between structural and functional principles. His structural analysis seems to proceed in the absence of any concern with "performance" data—i.e., instances of verbal behavior. The waiver, however, is only apparent. In fact, Chomsky's structural principles are connected to, and indeed derived from, behavior. But the behavior is not that of the everyday speaker. Rather, it is the behavior of the linguist in constructing sentences and intuitively judging their grammaticalness and interrelationships.[74] This behavior is very poorly understood and is of greater logical complexity than the behavior of the everyday speaker-listener. A good case could therefore be made for concluding that the *structuralist's* program, beginning with such data, is "entirely hopeless" and "doomed to triviality and scientific insignificance."

In behaviorist practice, structural and functional analyses usually proceed concurrently. In a Hullian type of research program, behavior as a function of environmental variables is studied directly. The resulting relationships are then analyzed, according to the principles discussed in chapter 5, into various constructs, each of which is "anchored" both to behavior and to the environmental variables. Some of these constructs (e.g., $_SH_R$) are related to what is learned, or competence, while others (e.g., D) are performance variables. Likewise, in a Skinnerian research program, structural principles arise directly from an experimental analysis of behavior in relation to the environment. Through the titration procedure discussed in chapters 3 and 5, experimental variables are manipulated until "smooth curves" result. These optimal functional relationships then determine structure in that they specify functional units for the operant response, the discriminative stimulus, and the reinforcement.[75] Thus, although Chomsky's structural approach is one way to begin the study of verbal behavior, it is not the only approach possible, nor is it the only sensible one.

Behaviorist reservations about a purely structural approach to verbal behavior are the same as the behaviorist objections to theoretical concepts reviewed in chapter 4. One bears repeating. In focusing on structure, many psycholinguists have been diverted from their primary data—verbal behavior.[76] They have become increasingly distant from the antecedent conditions ultimately responsible for verbal behavior. Skinner (1974) suggests a diagnosis:

> Structuralism has been strongly encouraged in linguistics because verbal behavior often seems to have an independent status. . . . because we can report it easily. . . .
>
> The availability of verbal behavior in this apparently objective form has caused a great deal of trouble. By dividing such records into words and sentences without regard to the conditions under which the behavior was emitted, we neglect the meaning for the speaker or writer, and almost half the field of verbal behavior therefore escapes attention. Worse still, bits of recorded speech are moved about to compose new "sentences," which are then analyzed. (pp. 97–98)

In short, the contribution of a purely structural approach toward our understanding of verbal behavior is questionable.

The Innateness Hypothesis

The fifth issue dividing behaviorists and many psycholinguists is a subspecies of the nature-nurture controversy that has plagued psychology since its beginnings. Behaviorists, with their empiricist predilections, tend to assume that complex behavior is acquired through learning unless proven otherwise while many psycholinguists adopt nativist views and more readily hypothesize that complex behavior is due to innate factors. Chomsky (1965) argues:

The empiricist effort to show how the assumptions about a language-acquisition device can be *reduced to a conceptual minimum* is quite misplaced. (p. 58)

It seems reasonable to suppose that a child cannot help constructing a particular sort of transformational grammar . . . any more than he can control his perception of solid objects. . . . Thus it may well be that the general features of language structure reflect, not so much the course of one's experience, but rather the general character of one's capacity to acquire knowledge—in the traditional sense, one's innate ideas and innate principles. (p. 59)

Although the nature-nurture debate is often portrayed in the starkest terms, it is obvious that the positions cannot be sharply divided. No nativist denies that experience has some effect on behavior, and even the most ardent empiricist must admit innate factors. A learning theory requires at least one primitive learning principle which specifies a learning operation and its results but which is not derived from more basic principles.[77] The primitive learning principle is thus unlearned, but without it, no learning can take place. Similarly, a primitive D_F (i.e., the structural description of the results of a primitive learning operation) specifies the dimensions of primitive induction and generalization which are also unlearned but presupposed by all learning.[78] Thus, the difference between nativist and empiricist is a matter of degree,[79] and it can, in part, be characterized by three questions involving learning operations.

Complexity of Primitive Structural Description. The changes in behavior produced by a primitive learning operation are specified by a primitive structural description, or D_F. When D_F is in the form of a set of rules, nativists prefer to say that the organism has "knowledge" of these rules, and, in the case of a primitive D_F, "innate knowledge." As noted above, however, this ascription of knowledge amounts to nothing more than the assertion that D_F is an accurate structural description. It does not imply that the organism has conscious knowledge of the rules, refers to the rules, or is guided by the rules.[80]

Empiricists tend to assume that primitive D_F's are simple in form, ideally a specification of a simple property of physics. Generalization across physical dimensions is erroneously assumed to involve less innate knowledge. When a D_F proves to be extremely complex, as in verbal behavior, empiricists tend to assume that it is not a primitive D_F but is rather the result of a derived, or secondary, learning operation, and in this sense is learned.[81] Nativists, in contrast, readily accept complex D_F's, and when one is discovered, nativists tend to assume that it is primitive and therefore innately given.

Complexity of Learning Operations. Since empiricists assume simple primitive D_F's, they must assume a complex secondary learning operation to explain a complex D_F. Thus, for example, confronted with a complex D_F in language acquisition, an empiricist appeals to acquired mediation, or to the previous conditioning of learning sets, or to special contingencies of reinforcement to explain generalization across the complex dimensions of the D_F. In contrast, the nativist assumes complex primitive D_F's so that the learning operation responsible for a complex D_F can therefore be quite simple. The nativist, for example, can hypothesize that a functional class specified by a D_F in the form of a set of grammatical rules of great complexity can be formed by the mere exposure of a child to a small number of spoken sentences. On the other hand, the empiricist would tend to argue that what appears to be "mere exposure" is really the result of a very complex conditioning history.[82]

Variability among Structural Descriptions. For the empiricist, a complex D_F is the derived result of a complex history of learning operations. The D_F's actually observed for a specific organism are therefore the result of that organism's particular conditioning history and current environmental contingencies. Hence empiricists tend to believe that there is a great deal of flexibility in the form of D_F and that given the appropriate conditioning history an organism will show behavior describable by any one of a large variety of possible D_F's.[83] Uniformity of D_F's across individuals and across behaviors must be the result of uniformities in conditioning histories and environments. For the nativist, however, there is little flexibility in the form of a D_F. Complex D_F's are primitive and therefore innately given. Uniformities across individuals and across cultures are the result of the innate constraints on possible D_F's. In the case of verbal behavior, these abstract innate principles comprise a "universal grammar" which characterizes D_F's in all natural languages. If universals can be found to encompass both verbal and nonverbal behavior then they would represent the fundamental organizing principles of the mind.

Thus nativism is both a thesis about what is known innately and a hypothesis about what comes to be known. In assuming rich and complex innate knowledge (primitive D_F's) nativism places strong constraints on what tends to be learned through experience. Empiricism, with its assumption of simple D_F's, leaves learning relatively unrestricted. Behaviorism leans strongly toward the empiricist position, while psycholinguistics currently tends to favor nativism. Although the three questions dividing nativists and empiricists are all empirical, there is little hope of an easy resolution. All the methodological pitfalls that have always bedeviled research on the nature-nurture question cannot be expected to be less intractable with respect to verbal behavior.

CONCLUSION

The adaptation of the organism to its environment is a central concern of behaviorism. Behaviorists are therefore strongly interested in the purposive features of behavior. The major issue dividing them from purposivists is whether these features must be explained by teleological principles. This chapter reviewed a number of theoretical sketches which attempt to account for purpose and intention without appealing to purpose as a final cause or a conscious content. To be sure, none of these sketches has as yet entirely succeeded in this enterprise, but this is simply because there is, as yet, no complete theory of behavior. For their part, purposivists offer no conclusive proofs that the attempt must, in principle, necessarily fail.

On the other hand, many psycholinguists believe that Chomsky has proved that S-R psychology cannot account for verbal behavior. However, a review of his arguments indicates that none of his objections is conclusive. Some await the outcome of empirical investigation. These include his claims that verbal behavior is not controlled by behavioral variables and that considerable knowledge of language is innate.

Although his refutation of finite grammars is valid, it has little relevance for the behaviorist theories reviewed in this chapter which are not based on left-right sequencing principles of organization. Whether or not these theoretical sketches will eventually account for verbal behavior is also not yet known. It they do fail, then other principles will have to be incorporated into behavioral theories. It might prove necessary to include a transformational grammar, but this step does not necessarily violate behaviorist standards. A generative grammar can be interpreted as a structural description of functional stimulus and response classes.

Thus while Chomsky's theory may force a development within S-R psychology, it does not refute it, or, at least, a sophisticated version of it. The abstract philosophical commitments of behaviorism as reconstructed in this book are not to be equated with particular theories of learning. Rather they form a conceptual framework within which development and increased sophistication are possible. It is broad enough to benefit from the insights of rival theories and to integrate them within its own scheme.

CHAPTER 8

Complex Processes

Behaviorists interpret thinking in a variety of ways. Under one interpretation, thought is construed as an intervening variable. As such it is not to be identified with specific episodes such as verbal responses. Under a second interpretation, thinking is a hypothetical construct consisting of mediational processes such as implicit trial and error or covert verbal behavior. Under a third interpretation, thinking consists of precurrent behavior which changes environmental variables so that subsequent problem solving behavior is more likely to occur.

Cognitivism argues that these behaviorist attempts to account for thinking are inadequate. It claims that an adequate theory must postulate internal representations and transformations. However, a consideration of three kinds of findings held as evidence for these internal events shows their postulation is not necessary. In each case behavior can be explained as a function of the environment, given that complex functions are permitted and that a history of interaction with an organism is accepted as a property of an environment.

Cognitivism's insistence on information-processing constructs stems from its internalism which requires temporal contiguity and identity functions in causality and reference to changes in the organism in an explanation. Behaviorism's rejection of information-processing constructs stems from its claim that these constructs divert attention away from behavior, the environment, and the long conditioning history responsible for the construct. Behaviorists also object to the intensionality of information-processing constructs.

The conceptual framework of S-R psychology described in the preceding chapters is associated with a research program concerned primarily with the relatively simple behavior of lower organisms. It is assumed either that the elementary principles discovered at the simple level can be synthesized to explain complex behavior, or that the elementary principles will serve a heuristic function in the eventual study of complex human behavior, which may require a different set of principles.[1] I shall examine various behaviorist attempts to extend the S-R framework to the complexities of human behavior, including thinking and other forms of cognitive activity. At the the same time, this chapter will also confront the challenge from cognitivist psychology which claims that these behaviorist theories are necessarily inadequate.

BEHAVIORIST INTERPRETATIONS OF THOUGHT

Thought as Intervening Variable

The study of human thought is fraught with difficulties, not the least of which is the fact that the term "think" is used in a number of ways.[2] In one of its important senses, "think" refers to a disposition rather than an activity or behavior.[3] For example, in asserting that "Jones thinks that democracy is the best form of government," we do not mean to attribute a particular behavior to Jones or to aver that he is currently engaged in any specific action. Instead, we are asserting that he is disposed to act in a variety of ways, depending on the circumstances.

In their dispositional uses, cognitive terms are closely related to intervening variables (chapter 4). Indeed, Tolman's approach to complex behavior is to incorporate a number of cognitive concepts, including "expectation," "hypothesis," and "cognition," into his behavioral theory in the form of intervening variables, each defined by a set of relationships between a class of environmental independent variables and a class of behavioral dependent variables.[4]

Episodes and Intervening Variables. Under the intervening-variable construal, a thought, or belief, is a concept representing a set of relationships, not a particular event or episode. Consider, for example, the intervening variable of thirst described in chapter 4. A rat's drinking water may represent one of the dependent variables in the thirst-intervening-variable. Yet we would not say that the rat's drinking is the occurrence of the rat's thirst. The thirst is an enduring state, not a response. Instead, the drinking, as one variable in the thirst-intervening-variable, may be said to "manifest" the thirst. Similarly, as an intervening variable, a thought cannot be identified with a particular event or behavioral episode. This fact has two important implications.

First, thought cannot be identified with particular instances of verbal behavior. Verbal behavior, in the form of avowals of thought and beliefs, is usually taken as the most significant dependent variable in the thought-intervening-variable. Nevertheless, if thought is interpreted as an intervening variable, an organism can be said to have a thought, or belief, even in the absence of episodes of verbal behavior. Therefore, the occurrence of verbal behavior is not a necessary condition for a thought.

Nor is the occurrence of verbal behavior a sufficient condition for the existence of thought. The verbal behavior in question must occur under the proper test conditions (chapter 4) and must be related to the independent variables of the thought-intervening-variable in the ways required. Thus, for example, suppose Jones says "Facism is the best form of government" because he has been requested to read this sentence from a book. His verbal response is not a member of the class of dependent variables in the thought-intervening-variable because it is not related to the other variables in the ways required. He therefore cannot be said to think that facism is the best form of government. Thus, contrary to the impression of a number of their critics, behaviorists need not hold that believing or thinking X is equivalent to saying X.

A second important implication of the intervening-variable construal of thought is that it is not logically possible to reward or punish a thought.[5] As a disposition, a thought is not a behavioral event which can be reinforced or punished. Of course, it is possible to reward or punish an instance of one of the dependent variables in the thought-intervening-variable. Indeed, a number of behavior therapy techniques attempt to change thoughts by establishing contingencies of reward or punishment to accomplish precisely this effect.[6] These procedures reward or punish not thoughts but rather occurrences of particular members of the class of behavioral dependent variables belonging to the thought-intervening-variable. Typically these members are verbal and often covert. When successful, these treatments result in changes in virtually the entire class of dependent variables which manifest the thought, including those not directly treated. Hence the relationship between the class of dependent variables and the class of environmental independent variables is changed, and the patient's thought, or belief, may therefore be said to have been changed.

Cognitive Behavior Modification. The relationship between intervening variables and episodes is also important for understanding the controversy between advocates of cognitive behavior modification and supporters of more traditional forms of behavior therapy.[7] Behavior therapists claim to modify directly undesired behavior by manipulating the environmental variables of which it is a function. In opposition to behavior therapy, cognitive behavior modification claims that therapy techniques produce behavior change by changing the client's cognitions. Mahoney (1977c) summarizes the position:

> One of the basic contentions of a cognitive approach to psychotherapy . . . is the dual assertion that (a) deficient or maladaptive cognitive processes are partly responsible for aberrant affect and behavior, and that (b) alteration of cognitive processes is a prerequisite for (or facilitator of) therapeutic improvement. (p. 10)

For example, if Jones is afraid of snakes, his phobia is due in part to his thoughts and beliefs about snakes, and these thoughts and beliefs must be modified if he is to be cured of his fear.

Some of the issues dividing cognitive behavior modification and behavior therapy are empirical in nature. One such disagreement involves the selection of a dependent variable for use in effective treatment. Behavior therapists tend to use techniques in which the target behavior, e.g., Jones approaching a snake, occurs during treatment, often in imagination only. Some practitioners of cognitive therapy deny that this is a necessary condition for successful treatment. The disagreement is thus analogous to the debate between S-R and S-S theorists as to whether a response can be learned if it does not occur during a learning operation (chapter 6). Nevertheless, many cognitive behavior modification theorists admit that techniques in which the target behavior does occur may be the most effective. Still, they maintain that these procedures work by changing cognitions.

Other issues dividing behavior therapy and cognitive behavior modification involve a conceptual confusion masquerading as an empirical question. If thoughts and beliefs are dispositional concepts, or intervening variables, then there is no empirical sense to the debate over whether therapeutic techniques work directly on behavior or whether they affect behavior only via cognitive processes. For Jones to be cured, his behavior with respect to snakes must be modified in a variety of ways. The class of behaviors modified in successful therapy is virtually coextensive with the class of dependent variables belonging to the thought-intervening-variable associated with Jones' beliefs about snakes. Therefore, to cure Jones by modifying his repertoire of behavior with respect to snakes, including his verbal behavior, is *ipso facto* to change his beliefs. Conversely, if thoughts and beliefs are intervening variables, then to change Jones' thoughts and beliefs is *ipso facto* to change his behavior in a variety of ways.[8]

Conceptual muddles arise, moreover, when a decision to give a realist interpretation to a disposition is presented as if it were an empirical discovery. For example, Bandura (1977a) in his ongoing debate with behavior therapy asserts:

> In the social learning view, psychological changes, regardless of the method used to achieve them, derive from a common mechanism. . . . change is mediated through cognitive processes. . . .
>
> Psychological procedures, whatever their form, alter expectations of personal efficacy. (p. 79)

Expectancies are defined as follows:

> An outcome expectancy is defined as a person's estimate that a given behavior will lead to certain outcomes. An efficacy expectation is the conviction that one can successfully execute the behavior required to produce the outcomes. (1977b, p. 193)

Bandura's cognitivist thesis is that these efficacy expectations are a major determinant of behavior and that behavior therapy changes behavior through its intervening effects on efficacy expectations. His evidence consists of studies showing correlations between changes in efficacy expectations, defined by the subject's estimates, and changes in the ability to approach feared objects. Now, in their everyday meanings, convictions and expectations are dispositional concepts. They are reflected in a variety of covarying behaviors, including verbal behavior. What Bandura has done is to single out one behavior, namely verbal estimates of personal efficacy, and to treat it as if it were a direct measure of a "central cognitive mechanism" causally responsible for all the other changes in behavior. Bandura thus transforms an expectation, or belief, from a disposition into an internal mechanism by the use of the subject's estimates.

In contrast, for the reasons discussed in chapter 11, most behaviorists object to treating verbal reports in this fashion. Therefore, they prefer to view the verbal report as merely one of a class of correlated behaviors, no one of which causes any other. This class of responses is the behavioral side of an intervening variable and is causally related to a class of environmental independent variables.

Thus, the question as to whether desensitization affects behavior directly or only through its effects on efficacy expectations is not an empirical question. It depends on whether or not one prefers a realist interpretation of dispositional concepts, and this preference, in turn, is related to the conceptual issues discussed in chapters 4, 9, and 12.

Control by Abstract Properties. Behavior is also said to be thoughtful, in a dispositional sense, when it is organized in functional response classes or controlled by functional stimulus classes which are describable in very abstract and complex terms (chapter 3).[9] Humans are capable of responding to extremely subtle and abstract features of the environment, and much intelligent behavior is the exercise of this capacity. Examples include the ability of a musician to respond appropriately to a musical score, and a physician to make a diagnosis following a medical examination. In all these cases, it is possible for the person to respond immediately without having to engage in any further behavior, whether overt or covert, because of previous training in discriminating abstract, complex, and subtle features of environmental stimuli.[10] Similarly, on the response side, it is possible that through training, functional response units are formed which are describable only by very abstract and complex features.[11]

When behavior comes to be controlled by abstract functional stimuli, the person may be said to have "insight."[12] Similarly, when behavior is organized into abstract functional responses, the person may be said to have developed a "response strategy." In either case, under an intervening-variable interpretation these cognitive terms can be viewed as higher-order descriptions of the relationships between abstract aspects of behavior and the environment, and not as cognitive processes over and above the observed relationships.

Cognition and Behavior. Because virtually all changes in behavior, even the most elementary, involve classes of behavior and classes of environmental events, it is nearly always possible to find systematic relationships among these classes and to construct an intervening variable. Therefore, nearly any behavior change can be conceptualized in cognitive terms. Consider a simple case of operant conditioning. A rat presses a lever, a pellet of food is delivered, and the rat then presses the lever at an increased rate. Although powers of ratiocination are not usually attributed to rats, it is nevertheless possible to interpret the rat's behavior with cognitive intervening variables because the changes in behavior due to operant conditioning are widespread, and the independent variables are numerous. The rat may be said to increase its rate of lever pressing because it "knows it can get food," "expects to get food," "forms the hypothesis that bar pressing will get it food," or "has the insight that bar pressing leads to food."[13]

Since, as shown in chapter 4, intervening variables are logically dispensable, cognitive concepts of this sort are not necessary for a science of behavior. One question dividing cognitivists and behaviorists is whether these concepts are desirable. Cognitivists insist that cognitive concepts are important for understanding behavior while behaviorists, for the most part, find these concepts unacceptable.

Many of the behaviorist objections to cognitive concepts are founded on the general behaviorist opposition to theoretical concepts reviewed in chapter 4. Objections to cognitive constructs, in particular, center on the claim that these constructs are not properly linked to behavior or to the environment. Behaviorists argue that cognitive concepts are inferred from the very behavior they are used to explain, and therefore spuriously explain only by renaming.[14] A sudden drop in an error curve, for example, is explained as due to insight when the only evidence for the insight is the drop in the curve.[15] In a similar vein, behaviorists contend that cognitive concepts are not securely linked to behavioral dependent variables, and therefore do not permit the determinate deduction of statements about behavior.[16] This problem in getting from knowledge to behavior parallels the objection raised in opposition to S-S psychology as discussed in chapter 6.

Thought as Hypothetical Construct

Under a second interpretation, thought is a hypothetical construct postulated to consist of covert events occurring within the body. They intermediate between the environment and overt behavior, so as to improve the organism's adaptation to its world.

Covert Mediators. Some behaviorists interpret thought as consisting of covert chains of internal responses.[17] These covert activities have no immediate effect on the environment; their sole function is to serve as stimuli for an eventual overt instrumental response. Hence, they are, in Hull's terminology, "pure stimulus acts."[18] The mediating response, or r_m, is an example, as is Hull's anticipatory goal reaction. As discussed in chapter 7, covert activities of this sort are used to explain behavior which shows foresight, meaning, conceptualization, and other aspects of thought. In general, these inner events function as the behaviorist counterpart of the "ideas" in mentalistic epistemology.

Covert behavioral events are typically conceived of as conditioned responses to external stimuli, and they may therefore come to function in the organism's behavior as substitutes for those external stimuli.[19] In Hull's (1930b) version:

> It may be said that through the operation of a variety of principles and circumstances, the world in a very important sense has stamped the pattern of its action upon a physical object [i.e., the organism]. The imprint has been made in such a way that a functional parallel of this action segment of the physical world has become part of the organism. Henceforth the organism will carry about continuously a kind of replica of the world segment. In this very intimate and biologically significant sense the organism may be said to know the world. (p. 514)

Because mediating behavioral events can thus function as symbolic substitutes for the external world, they have much in common with the "internal representations" postulated by the neomentalist theories discussed below.[20]

As discussed in chapter 4, behaviorists tend to restrict the properties of their hypothetical constructs in certain respects. Covert events are assumed to conform to the behavioral laws governing overt stimuli and responses and to be lawfully linked to observable dependent and independent variables. They thus operate under the functional control of external variables. To the extent that these conditions are violated by a theory, mediators acquire functional autonomy. Mediators not under the control of environmental stimuli and obeying laws different from those of observable behavior hardly deserve to be called "stimuli" and "responses." Long interacting chains of mediators of this sort have only very tenuous ties to the concept of behavior. Mediational processes which have lost their behavioral moorings can be assigned functions isomorphic to the information-processing operations of automata theory, even though they continue to be called "stimuli" and "responses." Thus, as mediational theory drifts away from the paradigm of observable behavior it merges with neomentalism.[21]

Covert Trial and Error. In some mediational theories, thinking is conceived as a covert form of trial and error.[22] When an organism is initially confronted with a problem, it emits a variety of responses until one finally eliminates the obstacle. As explained in chapter 7, the organism eventually learns to emit these responses covertly, that is, to "think" before acting on a problem. Covert responses are assumed to require less effort than overt behavior and to be emitted in an abbreviated form. Therefore, this covert trial and error is more efficient than its overt counterpart. Furthermore, it is hypothesized that the real-world results of the covert trials are somehow covertly represented in the organism, who then overtly emits that response leading to the solution. The organism is thus conceived as "scanning" its available response alternatives along with their consequences and then emitting the one with the highest valued outcome.

Covert Verbal Behavior. In another interpretation of thinking, the covert activity mediating between environment and overt behavior is verbal, or at least gestural.[23] Because words are both symbolic and easily manipulable, covert speech can serve many functions. Words can represent the external world by describing it. In covert trial and error, response alternatives and outcomes can be verbally symbolized. Furthermore, reasoning and logic, which are verbal in nature, can be incorporated into covert talking.

Criticisms of this identification of thought with subvocal speech are legion. In essence they attempt to show that subvocal speech is neither a necessary nor a sufficient condition for thinking. To show the latter, critics note that a person—or a parrot for that matter—can emit a sentence, either overtly or covertly, without understanding it, and this verbal behavior is not a thought.[24] To demonstrate the converse, that is, thought without verbal behavior, critics point to nonverbal organisms, such as infants and lower animals or even adult humans injected with curare, who can think although they cannot speak, vocally or subvocally.[25] Further evidence against the theory comes from instances in which people report they have a thought they cannot put into words or that they think before they speak. In both these cases there is thought without verbal behavior. That the same thought can be expressed in different verbal forms similarly indicates that a thought cannot be equated with a particular verbal response.[26] Also, there are thoughts in the form of nonverbal visual images.[27] All these criticisms indicate that although subvocal verbal behavior may play some role in thinking, the simple equation of thought and speech is not viable.

Thought as Precurrent Behavior

In another approach to complex behavior, thinking is identified with any behavior, covert or overt, which plays a role in solving a problem. Skinner (1968) describes this kind of behavior in these terms:

Certain kinds of behavior traditionally identified with thinking must . . . be analyzed and taught as such. Some parts of our behavior alter and improve the effectiveness of other parts in what may be called intellectual self-management. Faced with a situation in which no effective behavior is available (in which we cannot emit a response which is likely to be reinforced), we behave in ways which make effective behavior possible (we improve our chances of reinforcement). In doing so, technically speaking, we execute a "precurrent" response which changes either our environment or ourselves in such a way that "consummatory" behavior occurs. (pp. 120–121)

Thus, when faced with an obstacle to further behavior, e.g., a car that will not start, people emit a variety of precurrent responses. They may, for example, read a manual on automobile mechanics, recite rules they have learned concerning what to do when the car will not start, or look under the hood of the car. In each of these examples, they provide themselves with supplementary stimuli likely to evoke further behavior which will solve the problem.

They thus modify the environmental independent variables of which their own behavior is a function, and may therefore be said to engage in "intellectual self-management."[28] Note that the precurrent behavior comprising this intellectual self-management may be covert or overt. People may recite rules aloud or say them subvocally. They may look at a diagram in a car manual or they may recall an image.

Precurrent behavior is relevant to thought only when thinking is conceived of as an activity. In its dispositional sense, thought can exist in the absence of precurrent responses. Also, thought can refer to the arriving at a solution rather than the activity leading to the solution. One "thinks" of the answer. In this latter sense, the thinking occurs instantaneously without any supplementary behavior.[29] Precurrent behavior is relevant to this sense of thinking only in that precurrent behavior may precede and facilitate the instantaneous arriving at a solution. Hence, intellectual self-management is not a necessary condition for thinking in all the senses of that term.

The important question is whether precurrent behavior is a sufficient condition for thought; whether behavior itself ever deserves the designation "thinking." Suppose, for example, in the illustration above, the car owner slams the hood in disgust, and this action somehow exposes the defective engine part so that the person can now fix the car. Surely, the behavior of slamming the hood, although it changes the environment so that later behavior will be reinforced, is not thought. We are tempted to conclude that thought is something that lies behind the behavior and cannot be the behavior itself.

As this example shows, not every behavior which leads ultimately to a reinforcement is a precurrent response of intellectual self-management. Instead, it is the context which determines whether a response exemplifies intellectual self-management and therefore thinking. One important aspect of that context is the conditioning history of the response. Precurrent responses are those acquired because, in the past, similar responses were ultimately reinforced by a problem solution. In the terminology of operant conditioning, a problem is the discriminative stimulus for the precurrent response, and the solution to the problem is the reinforcement at the end of the behavioral chain of which the precurrent response is a link. Given the behaviorist interpretation of purpose in terms of reinforcement (chapter 7), this formulation of precurrent behavior can be transformed into purposive language: Precurrent behavior is behavior which occurs for the purpose of solving a problem. It is identified by its role in the adaptation of the organism to its environment.[30]

Therefore, slamming the hood of the car in disgust is not thinking because the action does not have the required history of reinforcement. The response does not occur because it previously resulted in a solution to a problem. Conversely, a previously conditioned precurrent response may, on a particular occasion, not produce a solution, yet it is still a case of thinking because of its history. Thinking behavior, whether overt or covert, is thus distinguished from other behavior, not by any immaterial substance underlying the behavior, but by its behavioral context.

Similarly, an event or object is a symbol and medium of thought because of its history and function within the control of behavior. Resemblance to the object symbolized is neither a necessary nor a sufficient condition for something to be a symbol. A few marks on a sheet, unintelligible to anyone else, can serve as a symbol of an engine to someone engaged in problem solving if the marks control subsequent behavior in ways analogous to how the engine itself would control that behavior. Conversely, a realistic photograph of the engine is not a symbol of the engine if it plays no role in behavior. Similarly, the stating or reading of a rule, equation, formula, or a warning is not precurrent behavior if it does not control subsequent behavior in the required way. What distinguishes the car owner's recitation of the rules for starting a car from that of a parrot is that only in the former case does the recitation provide stimuli which evoke problem solving behavior. An object or event is thus a symbol, or vehicle of thought, because of the role it plays in controlling subsequent behavior, and it acquires this role because of the conditioning history of the thinker. Without this role, the very same object or event is "dead" and meaningless. It is brought to life not by underlying immaterial thoughts but by its behavioral context.

The importance of behavioral context means that a behavior cannot be identified as thinking on the basis of its form alone and that thinking is not limited to any particular type of behavior.[31] This leads some to conclude that thought must exist in some mental realm apart from behavior. To the contrary, the present analysis suggests that what makes a behavior thinking is not its conscious accompaniments but rather its conditioning history and the type of control it exerts on other behavior. This view is expressed by Skinner (1957a) in a section entitled "Thought as Behavior":[32]

> The simplest and most satisfactory view is that thought is simply *behavior*—verbal or nonverbal, covert or overt. It is not some mysterious process responsible for behavior but the very behavior itself in all the complexity of its controlling relations, with respect to both man the behaver and the environment in which he lives. . . .
> So conceived, thought is . . . action itself, subject to analysis with the concepts and techniques of the natural sciences, and ultimately to be accounted for in terms of controlling variables. (p. 449)

THE COGNITIVIST CHALLENGE

The Information-Processing Paradigm

In general, behaviorists prefer to explain complex behavior in terms of either observables or unobservables assigned the properties of overt stimuli and responses. A version of the cognitive approach, known as the "information-processing paradigm," argues that behavior cannot be adequately understood at the behavioral level.[33] According to this paradigm, it is necessary to postulate internal activities of a nonbehavioral sort. These events are functionally characterized in the abstract terms of information-processing operations and automata theory. This abstract characterization can be realized in a variety of ways, including the operation of an electronic computer or the nervous system of an adult human. Because the events functionally characterized are the internal causes of behavior and can be identified with the intentions, beliefs, and thoughts of the organism, they can be said to be "mental." Because they represent the ways the organism processes its knowledge of the world, they may be said to be "cognitive."[34] Despite the mentalism, no dualism is implied. The abstract characterization can be realized in purely physical form as in the material states of a computer or the neurophysiology of an organism. Hence, the approach is known as "neomentalistic."[35]

Cognitivists within the information-processing approach do not view their differences with behaviorists as a mere disagreement over preferences in theoretical constructs. Many appear to believe that it is *necessary* to postulate the kinds of information-processing operations assumed in their theories. In particular, they contend that at least two internal cognitive processes "*must*" be postulated by any satisfactory theory of behavior.

Internal Representations and Transformations

The first of these is the "internal representation." Neomentalists argue that behavior is not a response to the objective external world but is rather dependent on the organism's internal representation of the world, a representation which is not in precise correspondence with the external world.[36] Attneave (1974), for example, asserts bluntly:

> The statement that the world as we know it is a representation is . . . a truism—there is really no way it can be wrong. . . . We can say in the first place, then, that knowing necessarily involves representation. (p. 493)

Neisser (1967) is similarly confident:

> We have no direct, *immediate* access to the world, nor to any of its properties. . . . Whatever we know of reality has been *mediated*, not only by the organs of sense but by complex systems which interpret and reinterpret sensory information. (p. 3)

Fodor, Bever, and Garrett (1974) summarize the position:

> Mentalists are committed to the view that the behavior of an organism is contingent upon its internal states—in particular, upon the character of its subjective representation of the environment. (p. 506)

The second cognitive process which "must" be postulated is the set of operations, or transformations, which process information reaching the organism. Neisser (1967) explains:

> As used here, the term "cognition" refers to all the processes by which the sensory input is transformed, reduced, elaborated, stored, recovered, and used. . . .
>
> The basic reason for studying cognitive processes has become as clear as the reason for studying anything else: because they are there. Our knowledge of the world *must* be somehow developed from the stimulus input. . . . Cognitive processes surely exist, so it can hardly be unscientific to study them. (pp. 4–5)

Similarly, in discussing the processing operations he postulates to explain sentence perception, Fodor (1968) asserts:

> We posit such operations simply because they are required for the construction of an adequate theory of speech perception. . . .
>
> It has been recognized since Helmholtz that such cases [of constancies] provide the best argument for unconscious mental operations, for there appears to be no alternative to invoking such operations if we are to explain the disparity between input and percept. (pp. 84–85)

The force of this cognitivist "must" can be summarized in the following schematic argument:

(1) Behavior is typically not in one-to-one correspondence with the environment.
(2) Therefore, there must be something else to which behavior corresponds, namely, an internal representation of the world.
(3) Therefore, there must be internal operations by which the organism transforms its input from the external world into the internal representation.
(4) Therefore, an adequate theory of behavior must postulate internal representations and processing operations.

The cognitive "must" thus rests on an empirical finding, statement (1), and three logical deductions.

Evidence for the empirical assertion appears to be persuasive and pervasive. Even in the simple case of a psychophysical experiment, the subject's judgments of the brightness of a light do not correspond linearly to the intensity of the light. In a more complex example, the reactions of a hydrophobic patient to water have more to do with the patient's thoughts and feelings about water than the physical properties of the water. With so much support, the empirical premise must be granted and scrutiny shifted to the logical deductions.

Statement (4) is the most relevant for behaviorism. Even if statements (2) and (3) be granted so that internal representations and internal operations are admitted to exist, statement (4) does not necessarily follow. The mere existence of an event or process does not logically entail that it must be included in a particular scientific theory. Recall the discussion of molar behaviorism in chapter 3. Obviously, molar behaviorism does not deny the existence of neurophysiological events mediating between the environment and behavior. Nor does it deny that these events may eventually provide an explanation of behavior. Nevertheless, molar behaviorism adopts the strategic decision to bypass the mediating physiology. It attempts to establish a behavioral science with a domain limited to the relationship between behavior and the environment and theories limited to summarizing concepts and basic behavioral laws, both at the molar level. The viability of molar behaviorism thus demonstrates that the existence of events mediating between behavior and environment does not necessitate that those events be included in a theory of behavior. The question for behaviorism, then, is twofold: Do internal representations and processing operations exist; and even if so, should they be included in behavioral theories?

Part of the problem in answering these questions lies in the vagueness of the concept "internal representation." It has, at least, three interpretations. It may refer to the fact that in interacting with the organism, the environment causes certain enduring changes inside the organism which affect later behavior. Since these changes represent the effects of the environment, they may be termed an "internal representation." In this sense, internal representations surely exist. Second, the concept of internal representation may be related to the fact that behavior is not solely a function of the stimulus energy impinging on the organism. Instead, behavior is brought about by a number of interacting factors including the present stimulus, sensory states, the organism's previous experience, and its motivational states. All these factors effect changes inside the organism where they interact to yield the final link in the causal chain producing behavior. Since this final state does not correspond precisely to the effects of the stimulus but is rather the effects of the stimulus in interaction with other factors, it may be said to be the organism's "internal representation" of the stimulus as opposed to the stimulus itself. If this is all that is meant by the assertion that internal representations exist, then, again, the assertion is a truism.

However, the term "representation" has connotations beyond this truism. "Representation" implies a certain sort of relationship between the environment and its internal representation. Under this third interpretation, the representation must somehow symbolize or act as a substitute for the environment. It is as if in addition to the external environment, the internal representation is yet another object which the organism can react to, know, or scan. For example, Mahoney (1977a) contends that: "The human organism responds primarily to cognitive representations of its environments rather than to those environments per se" (p. 7). It is this internalization of the environment that many behaviorists find objectionable. The problems of how the organism comes to know and adapt to the world are transferred to the internal problems of how the organism comes to know and adapt to its inner representations. Internal representation is thus a modern version of the Copy Theory.[37]

Although behaviorists reject this third interpretation of representations, there is no more reason to deny their existence in their two unproblematic senses than there is to deny internal neurophysiology. Even granting this, however, the question still remains as to whether internal representations and transformations, in their acceptable senses, "must" be postulated in a theory of behavior. In answering this question, it will prove helpful to start with the simplest cases.

Behaviorist Alternatives

Psychophysics. Consider the psychophysical experiment in which the subject judges the brightness of lights of various intensities.[38] Typically it is found that the subject's judgments do not correspond to the light intensities but are rather some function, F, of intensity, I. Thus, $B = F(I)$, where B is the subject's behavior, in this case a verbal judgment. Extrapolating the cognitivist "must" to this simple situation, the claim is that since the subject's judgments do not correspond to the light, there must be an internal representation directly judged by the subject, and F must be the transformation operation the subject applies to the incoming light energy to create this internal representation of the light. If we call this internal representation a "sensation," then it is clear that the notion of an internal representation is a version of the Copy Theory. Since the sensation, S, is a product of the transformation F, it follows that $S = F(I)$ and $B = S$. The subject's judgments are now in one-to-one correspondence with what supposedly the subject is directly judging, namely, the representation of the light rather than the light itself.

The first thing to note about the cognitivist "must" in this simple case is that F, the processing operation which "must" be postulated, is relative to the physical measurements used. If values of light intensity are measured on a log scale then F will be different. In the extreme case, imagine a primitive physics in which lights are measured by having a standard observer judge the relative effects of various lights. In this primitive scientific community, behavior in the psychophysical experiment would correspond directly to the environment as measured by "physics." No internal transformations would be necessary.

The second important feature about the cognitivist argument is that it explains less than it appears to. Even after the processing operations, F, transform I into S, it is still necessary to get from S to B. All that is accomplished by the multiplicity of internal processing is that behavior is now related to S by an identity function rather than to stimulus intensity by the more complicated function F. To be sure, the identity function is mathematically simpler than F, but why should B = S be preferred to B = F(I)? Both are lawful relationships, and both are equally useful for the prediction and control of behavior.

The F empirically derived from the psychophysical experiment can be interpreted in three ways: (1) a set of processing operations transforming I into S; (2) a mathematical function describing the relationship between I and behavior; (3) a mathematical description of the functional stimulus for a response B.[39] The cognitive "must" declares that the first interpretation is the only legitimate one, but it is not clear why this is so. When the velocity of a falling body is given as $\frac{1}{2} gt^2$, we do not demand that the falling body "must" contain internal operations to transform the physical quantities into an internal representation that corresponds directly to its velocity.

Pattern Recognition. Consider a second type of case, pattern recognition, in which representations are postulated. Humans can, for example, recognize a face even though it may change in a variety of ways including size, orientation, distance, and background. An information-processing theory of this phenomenon would be a program describing the operations needed to process the information arriving from the stimuli so that they are all recognized as the same face—i.e., responded to in the same way. A cognitivist interprets this program as an abstract description of events actually occurring inside the organism. In contrast, a behaviorist can interpret it as a complex mathematical equation describing the relationship between behavior and the environment, in this case a mathematical description of a functional stimulus class.[40] For the cognitivist, however, only the former interpretation is acceptable. Again, however, it is not clear why.

Meaning. Consider a third case in which behavior is a function neither of the current environment nor of a mathematical transformation of the current environment. Frequently people's reactions to the events taking place about them are heavily dependent on their beliefs, thoughts, and feelings about those events, even when objectively unfounded. A hydrophobic patient, for example, finds water threatening. Here there seems to be a more compelling argument in favor of internal representations. The patient's behavior seems unrelated to properties of the environment.

This argument for representations is based on a rather narrow construal of environmental properties. It ignores properties of the environment based on past interactions with organisms. Consider the property of being a war veteran. One is a war veteran not because of any current activity or bodily feature. Rather, one is *now* a veteran because of one's previous actions. Similarly, a stimulus like water may now be threatening to a person due to its past interaction with the person. The quality of being threatening to a person can be viewed as a current dispositional property of the *stimulus* acquired through its membership in a stimulus class which previously interacted with that person. Just as the property of being a war veteran does not require an internal representation to explain how a person can be a war veteran in the absence of any current activity or bodily features, so being a threatening stimulus does not require a representation of the stimulus inside the threatened person to explain why only this person is threatened by the stimulus. Thus, for the behaviorist, the behavior of the hydrophobic is a function of a number of *environmental* variables, and one of these is the environment's history of interaction with this person.[41]

In all three cases reviewed—psychophysical judgments, pattern recognition, and phobias—behavior does not correspond to the environment as described by the standard properties of physics. For each, the cognitive "must" requires an internal representation to which behavior can correspond, as well as operations to create the representation. Behaviorists, on the other hand, can deal with these cases by seeking the function which relates behavior to the environment, even though this function may not be the identity function and may refer to the past. Thus, if behavior is seen as a complex function of the environment, and a history of interaction with an organism is accepted as a property of an environment, then the cognitive "must" loses most of its force.

Cognitivist Internalism

Although the cognitivist "must" lacks the *a priori* force that information-processing theorists often attribute to it, it is nevertheless a logical consequence of certain underlying assumptions accepted by cognitivists but rejected by behaviorists. One set of these fundamental assumptions concerns the nature of causality and scientific explanation. The arguments cognitivists offer in support of internal representations suggest what was earlier termed the "bead theory of causality" (chapter 4). Whereas most behaviorists are willing to conceptualize behavior as being a function of its remote conditioning history, many cognitivists seem unwilling to tolerate temporal gaps. A conditioning history may precede the behavior being explained by a considerable time. Therefore, cognitivists prefer to conceive of the organism's experiences as creating an internal representation stored inside. Later, when behavior occurs, it may be conceptualized as caused, in part, by a contemporaneous representation, fashioned in the past but held in store to act in the present. In this respect, cognitivists are similar to field theorists who conceptualize behavior as a response to a contemporaneous psychological field gradually created through the organism's experiences. Both fields and representations are theoretical entities constructed to fill a causal gap by theorists who require temporal contiguity for causation and eschew action at a temporal distance.[42]

Cognitivists extend the bead theory of causality yet further. Not only is it necessary that cause and effect be temporally contiguous, but it is also required, as seen above, that they be related by the identity function. If behavior is found to be some complex function, F, of the environment, then it is necessary, according to implicit cognitivist doctrine, that the stimulation arriving from the environment be transformed to create a representation to which behavior can directly correspond.

In contrast, most behaviorists in the empiricist tradition recognize that there is no observable causal necessity, even in temporally and spatially contiguous causation, and therefore, for them, causation at a temporal or spatial distance is acceptable. Nor does a lack of an identity relationship between cause and effect disturb them.

Underlying these divergent views of causation are more fundamental differences concerning standards of adequacy in explanation. When a behavioral change occurs as a result of an interaction between organism and environment, at least three changes may be said to have occurred. First, there is a change in the organism, for its behavior is now changed. Second, there is a change in the relationship between behavior and the environment. Third, there is a change in the environment in that the environment now has different effects on behavior although it may remain constant in all other respects. Cognitivists prefer to view behavioral changes in terms of changes in the organism.[43] For example, an interaction is said to change the organism's internal representation or its beliefs. The other two changes, changes in the environment and changes in the organism-environment relationship, are explained in terms of changes in the organism. Jones avoids water because of changes in his representation of water.

In contrast, behaviorists tend to emphasize changes in the environment and to explain the other changes in terms of the former. Thus, as a result of conditioning, a neutral stimulus is said to become a "conditioned stimulus," or a "controlling stimulus," or a "secondary reinforcement." Changes in behavior are explained as due to these changes in features of the environment. Jones avoids water because it has become a conditioned aversive stimulus.[44]

These differences in emphasis give rise to disagreements over standards of adequacy in explanation. Cognitivists insist that an adequate explanation must refer to internal features of the *organism*, features which furthermore are contemporaneous and in correspondence with behavior. Cognitivists thus manifest an "internalism" in counterpoint to behaviorist "externalism" described in the next chapter. Behaviorists prefer to explain behavior in terms of the environment, including dispositional properties the environment possesses only by virtue of its previous interactions with the organism. To achieve adequacy for behaviorists, an explanation must ultimately relate behavior to these features of the external environment.

Because of these disagreements over standards of explanatory adequacy, the difference between behaviorists and information-processing theorists, like all debates between behaviorists and cognitivists, extends throughout all behavior.[45] Explanations within behaviorist molar theories rest ultimately upon a few fundamental behavioral principles, such as the Law of Effect, or the principles of classical and operant conditioning. They refer to relationships among stimuli and responses, and they are "primitives" in that the system offers no further principles to account for them. For cognitivist internalism, such explanations are inadequate because they do not refer to changes in the organism. Therefore, neomentalist theories explain the behaviorist primitive principles as the result of information-processing operations occurring within the organism. Because the information-processing theory accounts for what is left unexplained in molar behaviorist theories, cognitivists claim that the former achieves greater explanatory adequacy.

This criticism of molar behaviorist explanations is analogous to the arguments, reviewed in chapter 4, that "black-box theories" which do not refer to the physiological events mediating between the environment and behavior are not truly explanatory. The replies offered in that chapter in defense of molar behaviorism are sufficient to rebut the criticisms from information-processing theorists. In addition, there are two comments especially relevant to the present discussion.

First, although the primitive behavioral principles can be decomposed into even more primitive processes, be they characterized physiologically or cybernetically, this does not imply that a science of behavior "must" perform this analysis. Each science defines its own domain of discourse, depending on its own interests and goals, and, as shown in chapters 3 and 9, the interests and goals of molar behaviorism justify its strategic choice in limiting its scope to behavior. The events characterized by information-processing theories lie outside this domain, and therefore need not appear in behaviorist theories, despite the cognitive "must."[46]

Second, it is not clear that information-processing theories are not themselves black-box theories. For one thing, they are formulated in the mathematical terms of automata theory, not in physiological terms. Furthermore, their theoretical terms are inferred from behavior and involve no observations inside the "black box," i.e. inside the organism.[47]

Because of this black-box nature of information-processing theories, they can always be given an instrumentalist interpretation. That is, any well-formulated description of internal computational processing postulated to mediate input and output can also be described as a Turing machine. In turn, the Turing machine can be described mathematically, and the postulated processing can thus be viewed as a complex mathematical function relating behavior to the environment. An information-processing program can be viewed as nothing more than an elaborate equation relating observables, or else as an intervening variable serving the same purpose.[48]

Cognitivist internalism, however, suggests that the program be seen as an abstract characterization of a set of events taking place inside the organism.[49] These events take place over time, and their sequence parallels the sequence of processing operations in the program. In an instrumentalist interpretation, in contrast, the sequence of steps used to solve the equation is arbitrary. There are many orders in which to solve the equation as well as many ways to write it, and each is equally valid. The equation is merely a device used by a scientist to calculate the values of certain behavioral dependent variables, and the computational operations do not represent events with their own spatial and temporal location. This realist-versus-instrumentalist analysis of information-processing theories thus parallels the discussion in the preceding chapter as to whether the transformations described by a grammar represent operations inside the organism or are merely structural descriptions of stimulus and response classes.

The Behaviorist Rejection of Information-Processing Theories

Although cognitivists fail to prove that information-processing constructs "must" be postulated, they may still claim that such constructs are desirable. In defense of their constructs, cognitivists argue that a realist interpretation of information-processing programs is heuristically fertile. For example, in postulating that the operations occur in parallel rather than sequential processing they are led to hypotheses about behavior which would never have occurred to them if programs were viewed as mere equations. Similarly, hypotheses concerning latencies of responses would not be as easily arrived at if information processing were not conceived of as occurring over time.

Despite these arguments in favor of information-processing constructs, behaviorists generally reject these concepts for a variety of reasons. Some of these reasons are reviewed in chapter 4 in which the objections of many behaviorists to hypothetical constructs are discussed. In addition to these objections are several criticisms specific to the hypothetical constructs of information-processing theories, criticisms held even by behaviorists who favor hypothetical constructs. Basically, these criticisms contend that the constructs of information-processing theories are not well formulated and have been misused.

First and foremost, behaviorists complain that the information-processing constructs become the center of attention for cognitive psychology while behavior and the environment are ignored.[50] In Skinner's (1977a) words: "Cognitive psychologists study [the] relations between organism and environment, but they seldom deal with them directly. Instead they invent internal surrogates which become the subject matter of their science" (p. 1). In ignoring behavior, important questions are also ignored. Skinner (1977a) continues:

> The [computer] metaphor gains power from the way in which it disposes of troublesome problems. By speaking of input one can forget all the travail of sensory psychology and physiology; by speaking of output one can forget all the problems of reporting and analyzing action; and by speaking of the storage and retrieval of information one can avoid all the difficult problems of how organisms are indeed changed by contact with their environments and how those changes survive. (p. 7)

Information-processing models are thus accused of providing spurious explanations for behavior.[51] A behavior can be explained by postulating internal processing which is functionally characterized in an *ad hoc* fashion as having precisely the properties needed to produce the observed behavior.

Behaviorists also contend that an emphasis on internal information processing obstructs attempts to modify important behavior. For example, it is less appealing to teach effective thinking and problem solving when they are conceived as unconscious information processing operations than when they are interpreted as precurrent behaviors.[52] The latter can be directly taught through explicit instruction, but not the former. Even precurrent behavior which eventually recedes to the covert level can initially be taught in overt form.

Indeed, cognitive theories are often not concerned with the acquisition of behavior. Information-processing theories typically model the behavior of adult humans who have already acquired complex behavioral repertoires along with underlying information-processing operations. Cognitive theories thus often ignore the long history of interaction with the environment necessary for the acquisition of complex behavior.

Information-processing theories are particularly vulnerable to this sort of omission because they postulate contemporaneous internal processes to represent the effects of past experience. Therefore, the theories can appear to refer exclusively to current processes while ignoring the history by which these processes were acquired. In addition, history is often circumvented by using the subject's verbal reports,[53] a method unacceptable to behaviorists for the reasons discussed in chapters 2 and 11.

Ironically, then, both behaviorists and cognitivists accuse one another of not advancing their analysis far enough. As seen above, cognitivists criticize molar behaviorists for stopping at behavioral primitives and not explaining them in terms of more primitive information processing. For their part, behaviorists accuse cognitivists of presupposing complex processes and thereby failing to account for them in terms of a complex history of conditioning.

Intensionality. As seen in chapter 3, behaviorists object to the use of intensional language in science. Not surprisingly, therefore, behaviorists are critical of information-processing theories which not only make extensive use of intensionality but also extend it to new domains. The processing operations themselves are described in terms of intentional actions such as "storing," "computing," "comparing," "encoding," and "retrieving." From some cognitivist writings it appears as if these processes are unconscious activities of the organism. Katz (1964/1967), for example, in describing the processes underlying the production of speech says:

> The speaker . . . uses the sentence production procedure to obtain an abstract syntactic structure having the proper conceptualization. . . . After he has a suitable syntactic structure, the speaker utilizes the phonological component of his linguistic description to produce a phonetic shape for it. (p. 80)

It is not at all clear, however, in what sense information-processing operations are actions of a person.[54] Not only are they unconscious, but unlike the Freudian unconscious, most of the processing of cognitivist theory can never enter awareness. Furthermore, if the processing operations are the actions of the person, then the theory in effect explains behavior as the result of the activities of an agent. For the reasons discussed in the next chapter, behaviorists reject the concept of agency in explaining behavior. The notion of an agent who "stores," "computes," and "retrieves" information is too suggestive of a self-initiating, free-willed, and immaterial cause of behavior.

In other contexts it appears that the storing, coding, computing, and so forth are actions, not of the person, but of the processing systems themselves. That is, for example, a "long-term memory" is postulated, and it is this system which is said to do the storing and retrieving. This practice not only raises all the problems of intensionality in science, but it compounds them with the difficulties of applying intensional language at the subpersonal level.[55] We have some general understanding of what it is for a person to store, compute, compare, etc., but what is it for a neurophysiological structure, as the realization of some information-processing theory, to compare, store, and compute?

Moreover, information-processing theories also attribute propositional content to certain internal events. For example, a process may be said to represent a belief, or rule, or computational result. Thus, in addition to the problems associated with the attribution of propositional attitudes to nonverbal organisms, information-processing theories raise the problem of attributing propositional content at the subpersonal level.[56] The intensional idiom is not readily escaped. Processing systems are based on primitive operations which are also intensionally characterized.[57]

One particular piece of subpersonal intensionality especially irksome to behaviorists is the cognitivist concept of rules. If all behavior is explained by information-processing operations, and given that these operations are expressed by a program of rules, then, according to the information-processing paradigm, *all* behavior involves rules. Aside from the problems associated with applying the concept of rule-following at the subpersonal level, behaviorists argue that the concept of rules as used by cognitivists blurs an important distinction. Consider a paradigm case of rule-governed behavior: A cook prepares a meal using a cookbook. Before each step, the cook consults the recipe, a set of rules, and then carries out the next command. Compare this to a cook who adds salt to a soup until it tastes right. In the latter case there is no rule that the cook consults. Because the behavior is controlled by stimuli other than a written or spoken rule, it is what Skinner calls "contingency shaped" rather than rule governed (chapter 7). Nevertheless, an information-processing explanation of contingency-shaped behavior would refer to rules describing internal operations of which the cook is unaware.

Similarly, in the former case, i.e., the rule-governed cook, information-processing theories insert rules where behaviorally there are none. When the cook reads a rule, it is not necessary for the cook to consult another rule in order to know how to carry out the first rule.[58] However, according to an information-processing account, the cook's ability to read a rule and carry it out is explained by reference to a program of rules which characterize operations inside the cook. Thus cognitivists find intensional rule-following in all behavior, both contingency shaped and rule governed, and they thereby ignore an important distinction.[59]

CONCLUSION

"Thinking" is a concept from everyday language, not a technical term within psychology. Therefore, behaviorist theories are under no obligation to define, interpret, or explain it. Behaviorists who do undertake this task are engaged in behavioral interpretation, discussed in chapter 10. However, behaviorist theories *are* obliged to explain the behavioral phenomena to which the term "thinking" refers. As is the case with purposive behavior, behaviorists at this point can offer only theoretical sketches of such explanations with the hope that further research and theorizing will fill them in. Sketches which simply transform everyday accounts of thinking into the terms of S-R psychology (e.g., the equation of thinking with subvocal speech) do not advance the analysis of behavior. More promising are those which develop theoretical concepts when needed to account for complex behavior rather than when needed as behaviorist counterparts for everyday concepts. In the final analysis, it may be that the cognitive concepts of everyday speech, such as "thinking" and "belief," will not prove useful in a science of behavior.

Cognitivists appear to retain more everyday concepts along with the intensional idiom in which they are couched. However, as information-processing theories develop, their relationship to the everyday concepts becomes increasingly attenuated although the names remain the same. Cognitivist claims that these concepts "must" be included in a psychological theory are far from conclusive, as indicated in this chapter. They do, however, follow from an underlying cognitivist internalism. The opposing behaviorist externalism will be explicated in the next chapter. Because the differences between behaviorism and cognitivism stem from these opposing underlying ideas about causation, explanation, and theoretical adequacy, very little of the disagreement is based on strictly empirical questions. The important differences are not over whether certain theories can explain certain interesting experimental results but rather how *all* behavior, from the simplest to the most complex, is to be conceptualized.

PART III

MIND

CHAPTER 9

Exorcising the Agent

Behaviorists adopt the thesis that an epistemically satisfactory explanation of behavior must relate behavior to the external environment. This "externalism" is assumed as a strategy to promote the behaviorist goals of prediction and control not readily acheived when behavior is explained in terms of internal causes such as a self-initiating agent. Externalism also protects the objectivity of the behavioral science by locating the causes of behavior in the observable environment.

Because R-R psychology explains behavior as a function of other behavior, it violates externalism, and behaviorists therefore reject R-R theories of traits, psychological fields, and instincts. Externalism also implies that even though behavior and the environment may be related by reciprocal determinism, explanations should interrupt the causal sequence so that behavior is seen as a function of enviromental variables.

Within reflexology, externalism suggests a neural model based on complete arcs and peripheralism. However, in more highly developed behavioral theories, neither principle is necessary, although the latter is often preserved for tactical reasons.

The rejection of inner causes leads to the criticism that behaviorism is a "mechanistic" approach. Of nine senses of "mechanistic" considered, only a few apply to behaviorism. A related question is whether the effects of reward are "automatic" or are mediated by cognition and selective attention. This disagreement is partly a reflection of the differences between cognitivist internalism and behaviorist externalism. Behaviorists attempt to explain the cognitive and attentional factors of reinforcement with a number of externalist theories.

Having rejected the popular concept of the self, behaviorists offer a variety of substitutes. In a contextual theory of agency, all behavior is ultimately explained in terms of "automaticisms"—i.e., acts which occur without any intervening actions on the part of the agent. An automaticism is the act of an agent when it occurs in a particular behavioral context involving the person's history of learning and current dispositions. Thus, action language embeds a response in a system of relationships with its current and historical context and is therefore of a higher order than response language. Mixing the two languages leads to conceptual confusions, including those underlying the charge that behaviorism portrays the organism as "passive" and "helpless."

The conception emerging from part II is that of behavior under the strict control of environmental independent variables. When these variables take on particular values, behavior of a specific character necessarily ensues. What appears to be missing from this framework is any role for the organism, or person, in bringing about its own behavior. Chein (1972) summarizes this point in remarking that:

> The . . . prevailing image among psychologists . . . is that of Man as an impotent reactor. . . . Response is at all times and at every moment an automatic consequence of the interaction of body and environment. Man, as such, plays no role in determining the outcome of [this] interplay. . . . He is implicitly viewed as a robot. (p. 6)

The behaviorist conception thus differs from the popular notion of persons as active agents who are responsible for their own acts.[1] This agent, or self, although basic to our everyday understanding of the world, finds no place in the behaviorist conceptual framework. Indeed, the exclusion of an initiating self from the behavioral science is a family trait of behaviorism.[2] Skinner (1947) states the point precisely:

> A proper theory must be able to represent the multiplicity of response systems. It must do something more: it must abolish the conception of the individual as a doer, as an originator of action. This is a difficult task. The simple fact is that psychologists have never made a thoroughgoing renunciation of the inner man. (p. 40)

This rejection of the agent as "an originator of action," and its reinterpretation within the behavioral science form a basic component of the behaviorist philosophy of mind, and they constitute the subject of the present chapter.

OBJECTIONS TO AGENCY

Determinism

One fundamental problem with the concept of agency is that it implies free will. As an initiator of action rather than a link in a causal chain, the self appears free to act on its own choice, unconstrained by antecedent causes. Indeed, if a bodily movement is caused by an external force, as when a person is pushed by the wind, then that movement is not viewed as the agent's action. Agency seems to be reserved for those cases in which behavior is the result of the actor's volition and not the effect of some cause external to the doer.

To some extent, behaviorist objections to this picture of the agent are philosophical. The notion of a free agent seems counter to the deterministic conception of the universe underlying the physical sciences. If agents and therefore behavior are truly free, then there exist physical systems, namely the bodies of living organisms, not subject to the deterministic natural laws of the physical sciences. The causal chains of physics appear to break down when agency enters the sequence. Because behaviorists generally subscribe to the world view of the natural sciences, they profess grave philosophical doubts about the possibility of a free agent operating in behavior.[3]

More important than these philosophical objections, however, is the strategic, or methodological, behaviorist critique of agency. For the behaviorist program to succeed in establishing a science, lawfulness in behavior is necessary. Without it, not only are the behavioral laws sought by S-R psychology impossible, but so are the prediction and control of behavior, the twin goals of behaviorism.[4] It is precisely this lawfulness that the concept of agency seems to deny. Therefore, for the behaviorist enterprise to make any sense, the absence of a free self must be assumed. Determinism, thus, is a methodological working assumption for the behaviorist, rather than a metaphysical commitment.[5] It is a hypothesis adopted both to permit research to escape the philosophical thickets surrounding the question free will and to encourage the search for causes of behavior.

Agent Causation

A second source of behaviorist dissatisfaction with the concept of agency concerns the nature of agent causation. If the self is ultimately responsible for behavior, then bodily movements are brought about by causes qualitatively different from those investigated by the natural sciences. The self is generally understood as the seat of conscious awareness which directs behavior and is distinct from the material processes by which behavior is manifested. This immediately suggests a dualism of mind and matter, threatening to return consciousness to psychology. Hence, behaviorist philosophical opposition to dualism and consciousness partially underlies the rejection of agent causation.[6]

Again, however, the strategic considerations are more salient than the metaphysical. As shown in chapters 2, 3, and 4, behaviorist criteria of empiricalness and objectivity are strongly related to observability. The concept of agent causation tends to undermine these canons. If the choices of the agent are not determinately linked to observable external causes, then the only secure bond is between the private volitions of the agent and subsequent behavior. In this case, the causes of behavior cannot be known by public observation but only by the introspections of the agent. Thus, if the concept of agent causation is correct, then the causes of behavior can be studied only by a methodology rejected by behaviorism as unscientific and nonobjective.

Agent Explanation

Third, behaviorists object to the kind of explanation offered by the concept of agency. They argue that explanations in terms of a self-initiating agent are spurious in that such explanations merely assign to a mysterious entity, the self, whatever properties are required to account for an otherwise inexplicable action.[7] *Ad hoc* explanations of this sort simply attribute the unexplained activities of an organism to an equally unexplained inner agent. Behaviorists also see this type of explanation as a reversion to, or as a later form of, animistic thinking in which human actions are understood as the outward manifestation of the internal workings of a spirit, soul, or homonculus. This mysticism diverts attention away from the scientific study of behavior and discourages attempts to control behavior through the modification of the conditions under which it occurs.

In conclusion, although the concept of agency is foreign to the philosophical predilections of behaviorism, strategic considerations are more important in the behaviorist rejection of agency. As it is popularly understood, the concept of the agent stands in the way of the objective behavioral science conceived by behaviorism. Lawfulness, objectivity, observability, and scientific explanation, the hallmarks of behaviorist science, as well as prediction and control, the goals of that science, can be achieved only if, as a working assumption, agency is abandoned.

EXTERNALISM

While the foregoing arguments may justify the behaviorist rejection of agency, they do not, on their own, establish the S-R contention that behavior is a function of *environmental* independent variables (chapter 6). It is possible that behavior should be studied and understood as a function of deterministic physical *internal* causes. Such causes are not subject to all the objections reviewed above.

There are two types of internal causes to consider. The first is the organism's genetic endowment. A functional relationship holds between the environment and behavior only by virtue of the structure of the organism, which is partly genetically determined. Internal causes of this type do not necessarily upset the S-R formula. On the one hand, behaviorists can study the *environmental* contingencies of survival ultimately responsible for the organism's genetic endowment through the process of natural selection.[8] Or, on the other hand, behaviorists can assume the genetically determined structure of the organism as an initial condition and seek to explain behavior as a function of environmental variables, given this structure.

The second type of internal cause consists of inner events, physiological, mental, or behavioral, which directly affect behavior. Causes of this sort may undermine the S-R premise that behavior can be fully understood in terms of environmental variables. There are three possibilities:

Alternative A. Behavior is fully determined by internal causes, which are fully determined by environmental causes. In this case, lawfulness can be found both in the relation between behavior and the environment as well as between behavior and its internal causes. The internal causes can be conceived as physiological, but they can also be thought of as constituting an agent responsible for behavior but under the control of external factors.[9]

Alternative B. Behavior is fully determined by internal causes, but they are totally independent of the environment. Examples of this are free will or a behavior genetically determined and entirely insensitive to the environment in which it occurs.

Alternative C. Behavior is jointly determined by internal and by environmental causes, but the internal causes are not fully determined by the environment.

In all three alternatives, internal events play an important role in the causation of behavior. Yet many behaviorists tend to negate the importance of internal causes and to emphasize the primacy of the external environment in the understanding of behavior. Sechenov expresses this "externalism" in his insistence that "the real cause of every human activity lies outside man."[10] Likewise, Skinner (1953a) argues:

We cannot account for the behavior of any system while staying wholly inside it; eventually we must turn to forces operating upon the organism from without. (p. 35)

The practice of looking inside the organism for an explanation of behavior has tended to obscure the variables which are immediately available for scientific analysis. These variables lie outside the organism, in its immediate environment and in its environmental history. (p. 31)

Behaviorist externalism can be analyzed into two theses, one empirical and one conceptual:

(1) Virtually no behavior can be described by Alternative B. That is, practically no behavior is brought about by internal events not causally related to the current or previous environment. On occasion, Alternative C may be the case, but only rarely. Most typical is Alternative A, or something closely approaching it. That is, the internal causes of most behavior are determined primarily by environmental causes, including the organism's conditioning history.

(2) Although under the remaining Alternatives A and C, the relationship between behavior and its inner causes is lawful, an epistemically satisfactory explanation of behavior must not restrict itself to these relationships; it must relate behavior to the external environment.[11] This means that even on those occasions in which Alternative C is the case, explanations should invoke laws which: (a) relate behavior to environmental variables; and (b) represent internal causes as either parameters or inferred theoretical terms constructed by the methods described in chapter 4. Because this thesis concerns criteria of explanatory adequacy, it is conceptual rather than empirical.

As is the case with many behaviorist positions reviewed in previous chapters, externalism must be understood as a working assumption believed to further behaviorist goals of prediction and control. Explanations that stop at internal causes do not provide useful methods for predicting or controlling behavior because we have little access to, or control over, the internal causes of behavior. In discussing these internal causes, or what he calls the "second link," Skinner (1953a) states:

> The second link is useless in the *control* of behavior unless we can manipulate it. At the moment, we have no way of directly altering neural processes at appropriate moments in the life of a behaving organism, nor has any way been discovered to alter a psychic process. (p. 34)

> The objection to inner states is not that they do not exist, but that they are not relevant in a functional analysis. (p. 35)

The conceptual thesis requiring that explanations get outside the organism ensures that behavioral explanation will prove useful for behavioral prediction and control.[12] The empirical thesis that internal causes have, in turn, external causes encourages the search for environmental, and therefore observable and manipulable, causes. Externalism thus promotes the aims of the behaviorist program.

Externalism is also adopted to protect the behaviorist program against what behaviorists perceive as the failings of other approaches. As compared to environmental variables, internal causes are not easily accessible. Observability is a serious problem, even when the internal causes are conceived to be physiological processes. The temptation, therefore, is to speculate about internal causes or to derive them from introspection. Inevitably, in the behaviorist reading of the history of psychology, such speculation leads to unscientific explanations of behavior in terms of consciousness, mentalism, agency, and the soul. To prevent such thinking, behaviorists adopt externalism as a strategy to ensure concentration on the accessible, observable environment about which there is little room for speculation. The behaviorist critique of internal causes thus parallels behaviorist objections to hypothetical constructs (chapter 4), cognitive processes (chapter 8), and agency (above).

Implications for S-R Psychology

One implication of externalism is that there is no spontaneous behavior; all behavior can be causally traced to the environment.[13] If environmental causes are restricted to the discrete and relatively brief impinging of energy on a receptor immediately before a response, then externalism collapses into the simple reflexological model discussed and dismissed in chapter 6. If external causes are conceived more broadly as environmental independent variables specified in abstract terms and integrated over time, then the causes of behavior may be functionally defined variables, temporally and spatially distant from the response.

If the externalist empirical thesis is then simply that every response can be functionally related to some environmental event, no matter how remote or how insignificant, then the thesis amounts to nothing more than the truism that organisms are not closed systems. Obviously, food, water, and oxygen must be supplied from the outside. What saves the externalist empirical thesis from vacuity are two additional corollaries. The first is that the environmental variables causally implicated in the occurrence of a response are related to that response by *behavioral* laws rather than those of some other science. The second is that the environmental variables are *relevant and important* for an adequate explanation of the response. Thus the empirical theses of externalism converge with the conceptual into the single behaviorist strategy of looking to the environment for the causes and explanations of behavior.

Rejection of R-R Psychology

Another important consequence of externalism is the behaviorist distrust of psychological explanations which account for one bit of behavior by relating it to other behavior rather than to the environment. Because such explanations explain one response by reference to another response, they constitute what is known as "R-R psychology." A number of methods and theories are subsumed under the rubric of R-R psychology, and in each case, the behaviorist rejection can be seen as a version of externalism.[14]

Traits. Often a bit of behavior is explained by showing it to be an instance of a class of behaviors known to be characteristic of the organism. This class is referred to as a "trait," "factor," or "disposition." For example, a particular friendly response by Smith is explained by saying that Smith is gregarious, that is, the response is subsumed under a pattern of behavior generally displayed by Smith. Similarly, certain patterns of psychopathological behavior can be discovered by factor analysis, and the behavior of a particular patient can be predicted on the basis of other behavior which classifies the patient in a specific category. Thus, R-R laws allow for the prediction and explanation of behavior.

Behaviorists tend to be deeply suspicious of such laws and explanations.[15] Part of this distrust is based on the fact that traits are often constructed without sufficient research to show that the behaviors classified by the trait really do correlate in the way required. The more fundamental objection is that trait-explanations, by failing to relate behavior to the environment, do not meet the standards of externalism. Because traits are not mainpulable, trait-explanations are not useful in the control of behavior. Furthermore, traits tend to be reified and placed inside the organism where they assume the properties of mental causes known by introspection and attributed on an *ad hoc* basis.

Field Theory. Field theories view behavior as a function of the "psychological field," rather than the external environment. The organism is said to react to the world as perceived rather than the physical world. This psychological field is constructed by the theorist on the basis of the subject's introspective reports and other behavior. It is therefore inferred from the subject's responses, both verbal and nonverbal. Laws relating behavior to the psychological field are therefore R-R laws and do not meet externalist criteria.[16]

Instinct. Behaviorists tend to line up on the nurture side of the nature-nurture debate. This is due in part to behaviorism's empiricist heritage, of course, but externalism plays a part as well. First, in an extreme nativism, behavior is seen as the result of the maturation of innate factors and independent of the environment. For example, the concept of instinct suggests a reified inner cause which springs forth a complex sequence of behavior independent of the environment.[17] It is therefore contrary to the empirical thesis of externalism. Second, when a response is explained as being a manifestation of an instinct, the account is an R-R explanation since the internal physiology of the instinct is unknown, and the instinct must be inferred from behavior. Thus, environmentalism follows directly from externalism.

Reciprocal Determinism

As discussed in chapter 6, some critics of S-R psychology claim that it is incorrect to view behavior as caused by the environment. Instead, they argue, the environment is just as much an effect of behavior as behavior is an effect of the environment. They therefore contend that behavior and the environment participate in a system of reciprocal determinism rather than the unidirectional causation implied by the S-R formula. Although there is much in behaviorist thought to support the notion of reciprocal determination (chapter 6), the debate continues. While acknowledging that behavior affects the environment, opponents of reciprocal determinism argue that these effects are themselves ultimately due to environmental causes. This controversy resembles the chicken-and-egg question and is sometimes framed as if it could be answered by careful observation of a neonate at the moment of birth to see if it affects its environment before the environment affects it.

The debate continues unresolved because there are two fundamental issues underlying the manifest disagreement. First is the issue of image, to be discussed below, as to whether humans are to be viewed as "passive reactors" or "active agents." Externalism is the second issue. In a feedback system, the causal sequence can be interrupted at any point: Behavior can be seen as a cause of the environment, and the environment can be seen as a cause of behavior. Both sides of the debate recognize this. They differ, however, on where the sequence should be interrupted for an adequate explanation of behavior.

Opponents of reciprocal determinism, adhering to the conceptual thesis of externalism, prefer explanations which interrupt the reciprocal system in such a way as to produce laws portraying behavior as a function of the environment. It is for this reason that the behavior-independent laws of chapter 6 are preferred over behavior-dependent laws even in theories which explicitly acknowledge the reciprocity of behavior and the environment. In contrast, supporters of reciprocal determinism prefer explanations which interrupt the causal sequence in such a way as to emphasize the role of the organism in affecting the environment and its own behavior. Thus, both sides of the debate can agree on the facts of behavior; they disagree in their preferred form of explanation.

Neural Models

The theses of externalism also have implications for the behaviorist conception of the nervous system. If no behavior is spontaneous, then there are no autonomous processes in the nervous system that initiate behavior.[18] To allow such processes would be to reinstate an autonomous initiating self operating via the nervous system. Externalism therefore requires that neural processes be related to environmental factors. Behaviorist views of the nervous system depend heavily on how these environmental factors are conceived.

Reflexological Model. In the simple reflexological model of chapter 6, the environmental factors are stimuli in the form of discrete and brief energy impinging on a receptor immediately before a response. Since the nervous system cannot add any autonomous processes to the sensory event, it can serve only as a conduit for linking afferent impulses to efferent channels, that is, a passive conductor and integrator of incoming and outgoing signals.[19] A common analogy is to a telephone exchange serving to establish and switch connections but never supplementing or changing the messages flowing through the lines.[20]

In the reflexological model, the mode of neural operation is always in "complete arcs," a fixed sequence consisting of: sensory stimulation, afferent impulse, connector, efferent impulse, motor response.[21] The first two steps are never lacking.[22] Otherwise, response would be attributable to an autonomously acting central nervous system. Another requirement of complete arcs is that afferent impulses are immediately switched to the efferent system and do not remain to travel around freely within the central nervous system as autonomous sensory processes.[23] For many behaviorists, an autonomous sensory process suggests a return to dualism since many parallelists, including the introspectionists, view the contents of consciousness (images, sensations, thoughts) as the mental manifestations of centrally aroused impulses traveling around the sensory areas of the brain. Perhaps this reluctance to permit sensory impulses to travel partly explains why some behaviorists prefer S-R connections over S-S connections (chapter 6).[24]

A third requirement of complete arcs is that the neural impulses are not stored for efferent exit at some later time.[25] If they were, then the later production of a response by the stored impulse would seem to be determined by some inner agent which decides when to release the impulse. Also the concept of stored impulses gives rise to notions of stored memory images which can be called up at will. Thus, the three requirements of the doctrine of complete arcs entail the reflexological maxim: No response without an immediately preceding stimulus, and no stimulus without an immediately following response.

Peripheralism. In viewing the central nervous system as a passive switching system, the reflexological model assigns only a minimal role to that system in the causation of behavior. Similarly, in those instances in which inner events are postulated to explain behavior, as in the case of covert stimuli and responses (chapters 4, 6, 7 and 8), these events tend to be conceived as muscular or efferent events rather than central ones. There is thus a strong tendency to deemphasize the central nervous system and to view it as under sensory control rather than as an autonomous system.[26] This "peripheralism" is expressed by Hunter (1930b):

> It is an excellent scientific maxim not to appeal to central processes so long as there remains the *possibility* of explaining the given phenomenon in peripheral terms. . . . However, such a position is not equivalent to the denial of central neural processes. The insistence is merely that such processes should not be appealed to until peripheral possibilities of explanation are excluded. We know that behavior can be controlled by receptor processes, whereas we still seek to prove a similar possibility for central processes. To be sure, data on behavior justify the assumption of neural changes as a result of training, but they do not justify the assumption that such changes can somehow occur *in the absence of stimulation*. (p. 462, emphases added)

Behaviorist peripheralism is based partly on the cautious attitude of restricting theorizing to the known rather than guessing about the unknown, but it also derives from a fear of the central nervous system. There is a long tradition of locating the seat of the soul, or agent, in the brain, or nearby it. Descartes, for one, suggests that the interaction of mind and corporeal substance takes place at the pineal gland. Even as physiologists gradually came to understand the reflex at the time of the behaviorist revolution, they thought that since the peripheral nervous system could mediate only reflexive action, volitional, or conscious, action must originate in the central nervous system. It is not surprising, therefore, that behaviorists tend to see the unknown territory of the central nervous system as the last refuge of the agent they seek to exorcise.[27] Peripheralism is thus best understood as an attempt to block the reentry of agency into behaviorist psychology.

Although decades of neurophysiological research have elapsed since the formulation of the reflexological model, the dangers of speculation about the central nervous system have not abated. The writings of two prominent later neurophysiologists bear out the point. Eccles (1973, p. 107) poses the question, "How can your willing of a muscle movement set in train neural events that lead to the discharge of pyramidal cells?" His answer involves the "liaison brain," which is the "special area of the brain in liaison with consciousness" (p. 214). He suggests that there is "an incessant interplay in the interaction between World 2 [i.e., the world of consciousness] and the liaison brain, but we know nothing about its nature" (p. 218). Volitional activity can take place because "brain actions . . . give experiences and these experiences can result in thoughts that lead to a disposition to do something and so to the operation of free will—of thought taking expression in action" (p. 192).

Whereas Eccles appears as a modern version of Cartesian interactionism, Granit (1977) asserts that "encephalization has left the cortex in supreme control of purpose. In men and monkeys the cortex is possessed of every bit of information that is needed for posture and movement" (p. 158). He continues:

> During the drawn-out processing of the voluntary movement, the cortex has had time to explore a large amount of stored and incoming information from skin, joints, muscles, and balance organs. . . .
>
> The finding implies that during processing of a demanded act the cortex takes in and uses information. . . . the motor cortex must be cognizant of the peripheral conditions for the movement. (pp. 165-166)

For Eccles, the brain is the locus for contact between the body and the agent, while Granit seems to treat the cortex as if it *is* the agent controlling the body. Even if it be argued that Eccles and Granit do not mean to be taken literally and that they are determinists and materialists at heart, their choice of language certainly rouses in behaviorists latent fears about the damage inflicted on psychology by loose neurophysiological theories of behavior. Although the agent does not dwell in the brain, it lurks within many theories of the brain.[28]

Relaxation of the Complete-Arc Requirement. The conception of the nervous system as a passive switching exchange follows from the reflexological model. However, as discussed in chapter 6, this model proves inadequate for most well developed behaviorist theories. If the environmental variables controlling behavior are abstract features of the world, integrated over time and temporally distant from the response, then a different conception of the nervous system is required. Furthermore, current knowledge of brain function, with its descending control over afferent input, reverberating circuits, and spontaneous firing, also demands a more complex model.[29] However, since molar behaviorism is not interested in theories of the brain, its brain model can best be expressed as a denial of the reflexological model.

The first feature to be rejected is that environmental causes must have immediate effects on behavior. In highly developed behaviorist theories, the requirement of temporal contiguity between dependent and independent variable is dropped. For example, in Skinnerian operant theory, a reinforcement may affect a response occuring in the distant future. Similarly, Hullian $_sH_r$ may be changed by environmental variables but not eventuate in a response until drive conditions are appropriate at some later time.[30] Thus, the effects of the environment on the nervous system are long-lasting and do not simply travel through to complete an arc immediately.

Second, because the environmental independent variables are complex, abstract, relational, and integrated over time, the nervous system must be more than a mere passive switching station. It must be sensitive to the environmental properties found to be functionally related to behavior. The molar behaviorist need not be concerned with the exact location of the mechanism, central or peripheral, nor with the form in which environmental events modify the nervous system, nor with the description of this mechanism, be it in information-processing terms or physiochemical operations.

Relaxing the peripheralist doctrine also permits behaviorists to entertain the possibility that covert stimuli and responses may be central neural events.[31] As discussed in chapter 3, this means that behaviorists may hypothesize that certain events in the central nervous system are subsumed by the laws, or the theories, found applicable to overt behavior and therefore qualify as "behavior" under empirical or theoretical definitions of that term. Still, this more liberal attitude is reflected mostly in behaviorist metapsychological statements rather than in behaviorist theory or research. Behaviorist fears of the agent lurking in the central nervous system are obviously deep and long lasting.

MECHANISM

One consequence of the behaviorist exorcism of the agent is that behaviorism is accused of harboring a "mechanistic" view. It is often charged that behaviorism conceives of the environment as operating "mechanically" on behavior, or that it tries to give a "mechanical explanation" of action, or that it considers organisms to be "mechanisms."[32] The term "mechanical" as used in this context has been given many different meanings including:

1. Often the "mechanical" objection means that behaviorists regard behavior as occurring without the causal intervention of consciousness, spirit, or a soul.[33] In this sense, the allegation is correct.
2. By "mechanical," some mean that behaviorists claim that all behavior consists of individual movements elicited by punctate stimuli.[34] The charge applies only to the simple reflexological model discussed in chapter 6, but for the reasons reviewed there, this model is generally dismissed by most behaviorists.

3. "Mechanical" can also be used to mean that behavior is unintelligent, blind, and without forethought.[35] This charge is unfounded because, as shown in chapter 8, behaviorist theory is devoted to the explanation of intelligent behavior. Several behaviorists postulate, for example, that intelligent behavior is preceded by chains of covert mediating responses which constitute thought. A separate question, to be discussed below, is whether the primitive learning operations from which behaviorist theories derive intelligent behavior are themselves unintelligent, thoughtless, and therefore "mechanical."
4. A "mechanical" explanation may also be one which accounts for behavior in terms of the material structure of the organism. It provides for an unbroken causal sequence of physiological processes which eventuate in an overt response.[36] Although most behaviorists believe that such a causal sequence exists and may someday be found, molar behaviorism is not concerned with it. Molar behaviorism leaves temporal gaps between environmental variables and behavior, and in this sense does not provide mechanical explanations.[37]
5. "Mechanical" may sometimes refer to explanations which deal exclusively with the movements of bodies in space.[38] Behavior would in this sense appear in the subject matter of the science of mechanics. Since most behaviorist theories define behavior in terms of achievement response classes (chapter 3) rather than movement classes, the "mechanical" criticism in this sense is irrelevant.[39]
6. In contrast to Gestalt dynamic and holistic explanations, behaviorist theories are sometimes called "mechanical" because they analyze the causes of behavior into components.[40] However, as shown in chapter 6, well developed behaviorist theories do include the interaction of variables as well as composition laws.
7. Probably the most common sense of "mechanical" used in criticims of behaviorism is "nonteleological."[41] As the discussion in chapter 7 makes clear, behaviorists admit that behavior has purposive qualities. Thus, the ciritics are off the mark if they claim that behaviorists deny behavior is purposive. The basic difference is whether the *explanation* of purposive behavior must be teleological. Chapter 7 reviews some of the major behaviorist attempts to explain purposive behavior with nonteleological principles. As shown there, some of these principles are nearly teleological themselves. Whether or not behaviorist nonteleological explanations can account for purposive behavior is still an open question.
8. Some critics claim that behaviorism is "mechanistic" because it considers organisms to be "machines."[42] However, the meaning of "machine" is often as unclear as "mechanistic." A common meaning is that it is a device, consisting of parts, whose functioning can be explained in terms of these parts and their interactions among themselves and with the external world. Although most behaviorists would subscribe to this view, it is irrelevant to molar behaviorist theories which are not concerned with the "parts" of the organismic "machine."
9. A final sense in which behaviorist theory is "mechanical" is that it assumes behavior is an invariable, lawful, and therefore "automatic" consequence of antecedent environmental causes.[43] This is perhaps the broadest sense of all, for it says nothing about the nature of these antecedents. "Mechanical" in this sense excludes future goals, free will, self-initiating agents, or supernatural mind, as interfering with the lawful relation between behavior and its antecedents. Under this interpretation, "mechanical" is an apt description of behaviorist psychology.

Clearly, the term "mechanical" has manifold meanings, only a few of which apply to behaviorism. Some apply to the conception of behavior underlying behaviorist molar theories but not to the theories themselves. All too often when the term is used to attack behaviorism, no clear meaning is attached to it, and the criticism is impossible to evaluate. In many cases, no precise meaning is intended, and the term serves merely as a blunt weapon to disparage behaviorism, not so much for specific features of its program but for the attitudes it is alleged to foster.[44] Many critics believe that the behaviorist image engenders a disrespect for human beings and a willingness to control and even to coerce them.[45]

Are the Effects of Reward "Automatic"?

The question of mechanism and agency underlies much of the controversy over the Law of Effect that has marked the history of behaviorist psychology. According to the Law of Effect, a reward or reinforcement strengthens either the response it follows or the connection between that response and a stimulus. In simple versions of the Law of Effect, the reward, the response, and the antecedent stimulus are conceptualized in the simple reflexological model described in chapter 6 as brief, discrete, and topographically specified. Therefore, the response, or connection, can be said to be "stamped in" by the reward. In better developed versions, reinforcements, responses, and stimuli are described in more abstract terms, and the "stamping-in" metaphor is inappropriate (chapter 6).[46] Nevertheless, an underlying issue remains: Does reward "automatically" change behavior through the mere temporal associations of behavior, stimuli, and rewards?[47]

The two sides of the question are well illustrated by Thorndike and Tolman. In discussing the "strengthening of a rewarded connection by its sequent reward," Thorndike (1949) remarks:

> The satisfier acts upon it unconsciously and directly, much as sunlight acts upon plants . . . or the earth upon the moon. . . .
>
> Beneath all deliberate choice, prior to all conscious selection, is the fundamental fact in nature that a satisfier strengthens tendencies which are "at hand," as it were, when the satisfier happens. From it issues a strengthening force, which they absorb. Which of them will absorb it depends upon laws of nature, not of logic or teleology. (pp. 30–32)

Tolman (1932) disagrees:

> Our final criticism of the trial and error doctrine is that it is its fundamental notion of stimulus-response bonds, which is wrong. Stimuli do not, as such, call out responses willy nilly. Correct stimulus-response connections do not get "stamped in," and incorrect ones do not get "stamped out." Rather learning consists in the organisms' "discovering" or "refining" what all the respective alternative responses lead to. And

then . . . the organism will tend, after such learning, to select and to perform the response leading to the more "demanded-for" consequences. (p. 364)

As framed by Tolman and Thorndike, and by numerous successors, the question is whether the effects of reward depend on the volitional processes of the agent in "discovering" information and "selecting" a response or whether rewards act "willy nilly," that is, "automatically," independent of the agent.[48]

Selective Attention. One sub-issue in the debate arises from the finding that not all stimuli present at the time of a reward acquire control over the reinforced response. One way to interpret this fact is to state that the organism actively attends to its environment and selects those stimuli to which it will associate the response.[49] Under this view, an agent which attends and selects is reintroduced into conditioning theory. Because these volitional processes intervene between reward and its effects on behavior, the Law of Effect cannot be said to operate "automatically."

Behaviorist attempts to exorcise the agent of selective attention take various forms. One common strategy is to formulate laws that determine which stimuli are attached to responses.[50] Because these laws refer only to properties of the stimuli, they leave no room for the volitional choices of a selective agent. For example, some S-R theorists suggest that among the stimuli present at the time of a reward, those that are "salient," or "impressive," or have a "belongingness" with the responses are most likely to become attached to the response. Because these properties of stimuli are inferred from the effects of reward, there is often a dose of circularity in explanations of this type. However, if the class of effective stimuli is specified independent of behavior, then the explanation is not circular. Stimulus selection is "automatically" determined by the properties of stimuli, and the selective agent drops out. Again, the explanation of behavior shifts from the internal self to the external environment.

A second behaviorist approach is to construe selective attention as the automatic consequence of a set of attentional responses prior to the rewarded response. A common example is the receptor-orienting response. When an organism is confronted by a variety of stimuli, due to the orientation of its body, head, and eyes, light from only a small subset of these stimuli actually falls on its retinae. Only stimuli from this small subset will gain control over the subsequently rewarded response. "Selective attention" is thus the result of orienting responses which are, in turn, fully determined by environmental variables.[51] They are presumably learned through conditioning principles, including the Law of Effect. Hence, orienting responses that lead to the connection of relevant stimuli to the rewarded response will themselves be rewarded and thereby strengthened. Thus, the process of learning to respond only to appropriate stimuli comes about without the intervention of a selective agent and is therefore automatic.

Yet a third way of understanding selective attention is to regard it as a covert mediating response.[52] Consider an adult human confronted by a stimulus with an array of properties: square, red, large, and distant. If the person emits a covert verbal response "red," the overt response reinforced in the presence of the external stimulus is connected to the mediating covert response "red." Therefore, when the person later encounters a stimulus that is square but not red, the overt response will not be emitted since the stimulus does not elicit the mediating response "red." Only a red stimulus will elicit the overt response because it alone elicits the mediating "red" response. The mediating response is commonly assumed to obey the same laws as overt behavior, and the person eventually learns to emit the mediating responses that lead to reward. The mediating response constituting selective attention is not a volitional act of a selective agent but is a response ultimately under the control of environmental variables.

One other way of interpreting selective attention is to maintain it as a behavioral primitive.[53] That is, a theory defines the behavioral conditions under which certain features of the environment acquire control over a response without explaining why this occurs. Under this interpretation, attention is conceived as a relation between the environment and behavior which results from a primitive learning operation rather than as an episodic response. For example, according to Skinner, if the reinforcement of a particular response is contingent upon the presence of a particular stimulus, then that stimulus will gain more control over the response than a concurrent stimulus not part of the contingency. This control is not due to an inherent property of the stimulus or to a second response, either covert or receptor-orienting, but is simply a primitive relation demonstrated by a functional relationship between stimulus and response. Again, the selective control is a lawful result of contingencies of reinforcement and not the volitional choice of a free agent.

Cognitive Mediation. A second sub-issue in the debate concerns whether rewards operate "automatically" or whether they depend on the subject's being aware of and understanding the connection between the response and the reward. Numerous experiments have been performed with human subjects to see if behavior can be changed by reward when the subjects are unaware that they are being rewarded for a particular response.[54] Many other experiments have been carried out to determine whether all stimulus-response connections are strengthened by reward or if the effects of reward are limited to only those relationships that the subject has insight into or forms hypotheses about.[55] With cognitive mediation of the effects of reward, agency reappears in the Law of Effect. It is the agent that is aware of the reward, has the insight, formulates the hypotheses, and develops the expectations.

Although the debate over the cognitive mediation of reward has raged for over half a century, it remains unresolved. For one thing, the question is plagued by methodological pitfalls. Awareness and cognitive hypotheses are often measured by using the subject's reports. These reports, however, are just further behavior under the influence of their own controlling variables and not necessarily a reliable guide to internal cognitions. Furthermore, since the reports are only additional behavior, the experiments can establish only R-R correlations. Although causal connections may be postualated to hold in addition to the observed R-R correlations, the linkage between first-person reports and cognitive theoretical constructs, such as awareness and hypotheses, is itself open to debate, as discussed in chapters 4, 8, and 11.

Instances in which the effects of reinforcement do appear to depend on the subject's cognitive state can nearly always be interpreted either in terms of the mediational behavior or the control of behavior by abstract properties described in chapters 7 and 8. Consider, for example, rule-governed behavior in which verbal responses, in the form of rules, function as discriminative stimuli controlling subsequent behavior. If this latter behavior is reinforced, the behavior strengthened is the particular response class described in the rule. Thus, mediating verbalized rules, whether covert or overt, serve many of the same functions as cognitive hypotheses.[56] Similarly, when through a long history of conditioning, a functional stimulus or response class becomes extremely complex and abstract, the effects of a reinforcement will be determined by the boundaries of the functional class. Thus, a history of conditioning substitutes for an episodic cognitive event and serves the same function as a hypothesis.

The Basic Conflicts. Given these behaviorist theories of attention and cognition, the differences between behaviorists and their cognitivist critics with regard to the human adult are attenuated. Both agree that as a result of some learning operation, behavior at some later time is changed. They also agree that the effects of the learning operation depend on other accompanying conditions, termed "attention and cognition" by cognitivists and "orienting and mediating responses" by behaviorists. One major difference between the two is whether these accompanying conditions are under the control of the external environment, as behaviorists contend, or are relatively autonomous, as some cognitivists imply.

Another important difference between the two is whether *all* instances of reward are mediated. The behaviorist generally assumes that the mediating behavior found in the adult human must itself be acquired by learning operations which are not mediated. Cognitivist critics of behaviorism often appear to claim that *all* reward is cognitively mediated (chapter 8), but this position is difficult to defend. For one thing, reinforcement is effective with lower animals to which the concepts of awareness or cognitive hypotheses do not clearly apply.

Second, the claim that all rewards are cognitively mediated falls prey to an infinite regress.[57] The effects of a reward are claimed to be the confirmation of a hypothesis. The next time the person is in a relevant situation, the confirmed hypothesis is recalled, and the appropriate behavior ensues. Why does the relevant situation rearouse the correct hypothesis? Either it does so directly without further mediation, and the effect of reward on hypotheses is unmediated, or additional mediation is required. If the former is the case, then some effects of reward are unmediated. If the latter, then an infinite regress is generated as each mediational process requires an additional mediational process. A similar argument can be made over the question of why the appropriate behavior follows from the correct hypothesis.

Thus, it appears that some learning operations must be unmediated, and in this sense they operate "automatically."[58] Behaviorists and their critics tend to disagree over the importance of these unmediated operations. The behaviorist is likely to deemphasize the role and frequency of mediation even in adult humans. As discussed in chapter 8, abstract discriminations, a paradigm of intelligent behavior, can occur without intervening mediation. Cognitivist opponents of behaviorism place great emphasis on cognitive mediation and tacitly contend that unmediated learning operations occur, if at all, only in very early childhood and are irrelevant to adult human behavior in which cognitive mediation prevails.

At a deeper level, the difference between the two sides involve the kinds of explanations considered satisfactory. Behaviorists, with their leanings toward externalism, prefer explanations that refer to the unmediated primitive operations no matter how temporally far removed from the complex mediated behavior being explained. Such explanations highlight the role of the environment in adult human behavior. Critics of behaviorism lean toward the internalism discussed in chapter 8 and are often satisfied with explanations which begin with the mediational processes already in place. Reinforcement effects can then be seen as under the control of the subject's attentional, cognitive, and volitional processes which are themselves left unexplained. Such cognitivist accounts emphasize the role of the organism in affecting the environment and its own behavior.[59] Just as with the debate over reciprocal determination, the two kinds of explanations interrupt the causal sequence at different places, depending on which image of human nature is preferred.

BEHAVIORIST ACCOUNTS OF AGENCY

Although behaviorists reject the notion of an agent as an initiator of behavior, many of them attempt to explain why we have a concept of agency and how we distinguish acts which are "voluntary," and attributed to the agent, from those which are "involuntary." These accounts are sketches at best, but they do point in the direction of a behaviorist interpretation of agency.[60]

Self as Locus

In the behaviorist framework, human action is a function of a variety of variables, environmental and genetic. The point at which these variables converge is a locus which some behaviorists identify with the self.[61] The self thus represents the interaction of independent variables and the integration of responses. In particular, the self can be identified with functional response systems whose members covary. The Freudian id, for example, can be interpreted as a functional response class whose members covary with changes in levels of basic drives.[62]

The Volitional

Another approach to the problem of agency is to find objective features of behavior which define the class of actions called "voluntary." One possibility is that behavior caused in part by chains of covert mediating behavior is "voluntary" because it is the result of thought and deliberation.[63] The relationship between the environment and behavior is mediated by intervening responses so that behavior does not appear as "automatically" imposed by external stimuli. Although this feature may distinguish voluntary from involuntary, it does not imply free will. The mediating behavior on which the distinction is based is neither uncaused nor free.

Another possibility is that the voluntary-involuntary distinction corresponds roughly to the operant-respondent distinction.[64] Reflexes, both innate and conditioned, are not conceived of as actions of the agent but are rather imposed from without and are therefore involuntary. Operant behavior, on the other hand, seems to flow from the wishes and desires of the actor and thus appears voluntary. Discriminative stimuli are said to "set the occasion" for the response rather than to elicit it.[65] Again, although the operant-respondent distinction provides an objective basis for the voluntary-involuntary distinction, it does not suggest free will since operant behavior is also subject to behavioral laws.

The Internalization of the Other

In interpreting the self, several behaviorists note the importance of treating oneself as an other.[66] Humans learn to discriminate their own behavior in the way they discriminate the behavior of others. When these discriminations take the form of verbal tacts, people can come to describe their own behavior. Later they learn to report their own dispositions, feelings, thoughts, and other private events in the ways described in chapter 11. These verbal discriminations along with the correct usage of "I," "me," and "mine," gradually establish a self-concept.[67] These self-descriptions not only report, but the roles and capacities people ascribe to themselves also influence later behavior to conform to the verbal labels.[68]

At the same time, people gradually learn to modify their own behavior in the way they modify the behavior of others. Smith can change Jones' behavior by altering the variables of which Jones' behavior is a function. But Smith can modify his own behavior in the same way. Smith can emit response, R_1, which changes the environment in such a way that the probability of another of his responses, R_2, is altered. If this change in R_2 results in a reinforcement for Smith, then both R_1 and R_2 will be strengthened. Thus, Smith learns "self-control," that is, he learns precurrent behavior which changes the environment in such a way as to modify his other behavior. Self-control is thus conceptualized as behavior, exemplified by R_1, subject to behavioral laws, and therefore compatible with determinism.[69] Behaviorists tend to emphasize the role of the external environment in the original acquisition and maintenance of self-control behavior, even though, in the adult human, the self-control response, R_1, and its immediate reinforcement may be covert.

A most important step in learning to treat the self as other is when speakers become their own listeners. Humans can then use verbal responses as stimuli to control their subsequent behavior. Indeed, some behaviorists suggest that voluntary acts are those brought about by the actor's verbalizations functioning as controlling stimuli.[70] This suggestion may have merit in some cases, but it cannot serve as the sole criterion of the voluntary. First, many voluntary acts are not preceded by verbalizations. Second, a verbalization is a voluntary act, and if verbalizations also require prior verbalizations, then the entire scheme is threatened by the familiar infinite regress.

A Contextual Theory of Agency

In yet another behaviorist theory of the self, agency is interpreted in terms of the context of a response rather than the inherent properties of the response. Critics argue that in the behaviorist scheme, when the environmental independent variables assume certain values, specific behaviors result "automatically," independent of the agent. To analyze this argument a definition of "automatic" will prove useful. Let us say that a response that follows from an event without any intervening actions on the part of the agent is "automatic" and will be termed an "automaticism."[71] The contextual theory of agency maintains that an automaticism can be the act of an agent, depending on the behavioral context.

It is clear from the familiar infinite regress argument that human behavior must involve some automaticisms.[72] When Smith uses a map to find a street in a "nonautomatic" way, mental acts of understanding, thinking, and recalling are said to occur. What is the relationship between the map and these acts? If they follow directly from Smith's looking at the map, without the intervention of further acts on Smith's part, then they are automaticisms. For example, he looks at the map, and an image of his destination forms in his mind, without his having to do anything to bring it about. If the mental acts are not automaticisms, then further acts by Smith must intervene to bring them about. For example, in order to recall the image of his destination, Smith must first free associate to an image of his point of departure. These prior mental acts must either be automaticisms, or they too would require prior intervening acts. Obviously, the infinite regress of intervening acts would end only if an automaticism is admitted into the sequence.

A similar argument can be made for the link between the intervening mental acts and Smith's response of turning right. Why is it that an image of his destination results in Smith's turning right? Either the behavior follows without any further actions on Smith's part, in which case it is an automaticism, or Smith must do something else to get from the image to the response. In the latter case, an infinite regress would be generated unless an automaticism were admitted.

Thus, automaticisms are a necessary element in behavior. As Wittgenstein frequently remarks, the chain of reasons must have an end.[73] One important class of automaticisms is the primitive learning operations of S-R theory. These operations state how behavior to a stimulus is acquired as the result of a particular configuration of stimuli and responses, but no further explanation is offered to account for this result. Following the operation, the behavior occurs to the stimulus without the intervention of further behavioral events. This is not to say that in either primitive learning operations or in other automaticisms there are no physiological events intervening between environment and behavior. The claim is only that there are no further intervening *behavioral* events nor actions of the agent.

The exorcism of agency in behaviorist psychology means that the fundamental explanatory principles of the behavioral science must involve automaticisms. The basic building blocks on which all behavior, even the most intelligent, ultimately rests are direct responses to the environment without the interventions of thoughts, insight, acts of perception and understanding, or volitions.[74] The occurrence of these intervening events is not ruled out from the science, but they too must be explained by the primitive learning operations involving automaticisms.

Automaticisms and Agency. If all behavior is ultimately based on automaticisms, then it might be supposed that all behavior is indeed "mechanical," "blind," "unconscious," and "agentless." However, this is not the case. Automaticisms are unintelligent and agentless only if it is assumed that something is an intelligent act of an agent only when it is preceded by special prior mental acts. Once this assumption is refuted by the infinite regress argument, it is clear that agency and intelligence depend on other criteria.

To say that a response is an intelligent act of an agent is not to say something about the hidden mental events that precede it but rather to say something about the broad context of that response.[75] When Smith merely looks at his map and then "automatically" proceeds to turn right without any images, rules, thoughts, or memories popping into his mind, that right turn may still be the intelligent act of an agent. If the right turn is the result of a long history of learning to read maps, that is, a history of discrimination training to behave differentially with respect to marks on maps, then this fact counts toward considering the automaticism to be the intelligent act of an agent.

Another important factor is whether Smith is currently using the map for a purpose, where "purpose" is given one of the behaviorist interpretations of chapter 7. For example, does Smith have a history of reinforcement for using maps in certain situations, and is he currently in such a situation? The context of the response also includes Smith's dispositions to behave. If the right turn is the intelligent action of an agent, then Smith should be prepared to give some explanation for the use of the map, if asked; he should be able to correct a mistake if he misreads the map and ends up on the wrong street; and he should be able to use the map in other situations, should they arise.

In contrast, imagine that the map triggers a muscle spasm in Smith's legs that causes him to turn right. This, too, is an automaticism, but it is not an agent's action. It is something that happens to Smith; not something he does. The difference between the two cases does not lie in any hidden mental actions Smith performs between his looking at the map and the right turn. The critical distinction is in the type of functional relationship between the stimulus and the response in the two cases. In the first case, the functional relationship developed as the result of a history of learning to use maps, and the right turn is just one manifestation of a disposition acquired through that history. The relationship between the map and the muscle spasm has an entirely different origin, and the right turn is not a manifestation of a more general disposition for using maps. The muscle spasm is also insensitive to other aspects of the environment, and Smith, for example, would turn right even if he were facing the opposite direction.

Two Languages

Thus, to speak of an organism's response as an agent-act is to say something about the context of that movement. It is to embed that response in a system of relationships with the current and historical context. Only when these relationships are of a special type does the response represent an agent-act. Specifying that type precisely is not yet possible, but it is obvious that humans can recognize it, and perhaps the behaviorist sketches of agency described above point in the right direction. Thus, agency concepts provide rather high order descriptions of behavior in that they implicitly refer to relationships between behavior and the environment.[76]

In contrast, to say that a *response* has occurred is to say very little about the context. Indeed, as discussed in chapter 3, behaviorists try to avoid action language and prefer a behavioral data language which is action-neutral. For example, a report that a bar-press has occurred says nothing about whether the occurrence was an agent-act (i.e., the rat pressed the bar down) or a non-action (e.g., the rat was passively dropped onto the bar). Furthermore, whereas an action description of behavior implicitly says something about the provenance of that behavior, a response description is specified independent of the causes of behavior. In short, action language and response language are on two different levels of discourse. Action language is of a higher order level than response language in the sense that the basic concepts of action language implicitly refer to relationships between behavior and the environment of a greater complexity than those of response language.

Mixing these two levels of discourse leads to conceptual confusions. For instance, the environmental independent variables of S-R theories are described on the level of response language. Responses are specified independent of their controlling variables, and it is therefore appropriate to say that responses are caused by, or are a function of, certain environmental variables. However, these independent variables are not on the same level of discourse as agents and agent-acts. It is therefore illegitimate to say that the environmental independent variables caused an agent-act or caused an agent to act.[77] The difference between "Smith's arm rose" (response description) and "Smith raised his arm" (action description) is that the latter already implicitly says something about the relationship between the movement and its environmental context. The relevant environmental events and Smith's raising his arm are not two distinct sets of events which can be causally related.

The situation is analogous to the relationship between Jones' shooting of Smith and Smith's murder. Jones' shooting of Smith may be a cause of Smith's *death*, but it cannot be said to have caused Smith's *murder* since Jones' shooting Smith under those circumstances *is* Smith's murder. Likewise, environmental independent variables may cause Smith's arm to rise (a response), but they cannot be said to cause Smith to raise his arm (an agent-act). Under the proper conditions, the rising of Smith's arm caused by certain independent variables *is* Smith's raising his arm. The agent is not a link in the causal chain between environment and behavior.

Similarly, the explanations for agent-acts must be given at the level of action language, not response language.[78] The former involves the reasons, desires, and beliefs of the agent. These concepts are also of a higher order level of discourse than response language, and there is no simple one-to-one correspondence between them. The two languages categorize the world in different ways, and the two resulting systems are not easily related.[79]

The Passive-Reactive Image

The illegitimate conflating of action language and response language is also partly responsible for certain misconceptions about the behaviorist image of the organism. Behaviorists are often accused of maintaining that organisms are "passive," merely "*re*active" (rather than "active"), "helpless," and "coerced" by stimuli.[80] Mischel (1969) states the criticism this way: "Both [behaviorism and associationism] regarded man as passive and sought to explain the responses he "learns" to make in terms of external inputs. . . . man never acts, he only reacts (p. 28)." Similarly, Bandura (1977a) complains: "In theories that recognize only the role of external consequences and contend that they shape behavior automatically, people are viewed mainly as reactors to environmental influences" (p. 97).

Part of this objection to the "passive-reactive image" stems from differences between behaviorists and their critics over preferences for certain kinds of explanations, as shown above. Explanations satisfying externalist standards tend to emphasize the role of the environment while internalist explanations tend to emphasize the role of the organism. The two sides do not differ on the facts, but they see the facts in different lights.

On the other hand, much of the objection to the behaviorist image arises from conceptual confusions. At the level of action language, there is a clear sense for expressions such as "Smith was coerced into raising his arm," or "Smith helplessly watched his arm rise." An example of the former is that Jones holds a gun on Smith and threatens to shoot unless Smith raises his arm. The latter expression might be used in a situation in which a strong gust of wind forces Smith's arm to rise while he struggles to keep it down. Thus, there are instances in which an agent may appropriately be said to be "passive," "helpless," or "coerced." These expressions are useful only because they demarcate a class distinguishable from situations in which the agent is not "helpless," "passive," or "coerced."

One common conceptual error is to draw an analogy between the gust of wind forcing Smith's arm to rise and the functional relationship between the environment and behavior. It is erroneously believed that according to behaviorism, Smith is "coerced" into his actions by the environment, leaving him "helpless." However, as argued above, this criticism illegitimately conflates action language and response language. Environmental variables control responses, not agent-actions, and agents are not links in this causal chain.

Another serious conceptual error is to force inappropriately the active-passive distinction of action language onto the conceptual grid of response language. The active-passive, volitional-coerced, voluntary-involuntary distinctions within action language map in a very complex way onto the distinctions of response language. Specifying this mapping would consist of defining in response language two classes of environment-behavior relationships.

One, class A, projects into action language as agent-acts, while the other, class N, represents nonaction language. The behaviorist interpretations of agency, reviewed above, are attempts to accomplish this task.

At least one member of class N is already known, namely behavior brought about by respondent reflex action. A tap to the patellar tendon elicits a knee jerk. This kind of environment-behavior relationship projects into action language as an example of a nonaction, not under the control of the agent who may resist the movement but remain helpless to prevent it. The conceptual error is to assimilate all behavior caused by, or under the functional control of, environmental variables to the model of the patellar reflex.[81] If the only relationship between environment and behavior is that represented by the patellar reflex, then all behavior belongs in class N, and class A is the null set, given the behaviorist assumption of lawfulness in behavior. The behaviorist is then accused of portraying the organism as "passive," "helpless," and "coerced" into acting.

This erroneous assimilation ignores the variety of relationships reviewed in the preceding chapters on S-R psychology. Its roots are to be found in the simple reflexological model which similarly assimilates all behavior to a stimulus-elicitation-response picture. With the rejection of this model arises the possibility of discovering a distinction within response language corresponding to class A. This distinction would then characterize those features of environment-behavior interaction which define agent-acts. That humans can reliably discriminate between actions and nonactions indicates that such features exist. Whether these features also correspond to the properties of behavior singled out as important in the behavioral science is a question yet to be answered.[82]

CONCLUSION

S-R psychology thus leaves organisms as it found them. All behavior is assumed to be lawfully related to the environment, but some of this behavior is related to the environment in such a way as to be categorized in action language as an agent-act, volitional, active, and brought about by a person. S-R psychology can thus be seen as compatible with the concept of agency understood in this way.[83] Whether this concept of agency will prove useful in the behavioral science is as yet unknown.

S-R psychology is not, however, compatible with the notion of a free-willed self-initiating agent. Indeed, *any* deterministic psychology, behavioristic or not, must reject this type of agency. Determinism is a critical working assumption not readily abandoned by any scientific psychology, even if the former is restricted to the macro-level and to statistical laws.

Behaviorism's externalism, on the other hand, with its concentration on external environmental causes of behavior, does not follow necessarily from determinism. Deterministic internal causes, relatively autonomous of the environment, are surely conceivable. If, as I have argued, externalism is adopted primarily on strategic grounds, then it is possible that some of its usefulness will dissipate with the growth in our knowledge about internal causes. With significant increases in our ability to observe and modify inner causes, the behaviorist aims of prediction and control might be well served by laws and explanations relating behavior to inner causes. On the other hand, the history of psychology gives every indication that once attention is focused on inner causes, they tend to take over: The environment is ignored, behavior is relegated to a minor position, agency is reinstated, and loose speculation abounds. It thus appears that behaviorist externalism will be appropriate for some time to come.

CHAPTER 10

Behavioral Interpretation

The mentalistic conceptual framework implicit in everyday speech about human action competes with behaviorism. Behaviorists treat this mentalistic language in a variety of ways:

1. Eliminative behaviorism hypothesizes that as scientific accounts of behavior develop, mentalistic accounts will simply be abandoned as were prescientific beliefs in demons.

2. According to methodological behaviorism, mentalistic language applies only to the private phenomenal world beyond the scope of science.

3. The verificationist theory of meaning proposed by logical behaviorism translates mentalistic statements in terms of the publicly observable conditions used to test their truth.

4. Operational behaviorism defines a mental concept by the operations used to measure or detect that concept.

5. Tolman suggests that mental concepts can be identified with certain intervening variables in behavioral theories.

6. In analytic behaviorism mental concepts refer to behavior and dispositions which serve as the criteria for the application of mental terms.

7. An empirical reduction first determines the features of behavior referred to by a mental term and then explains these features with a behavioral theory.

8. An empirical translation of a mental term provides the independent variables controlling its emission as a verbal response.

9. Mental terms can also be identified with certain hypothetical constructs in behavioral theories.

Interpretations which identify mental concepts with behavioral concepts (i.e., 3, 4, 5, 6) are challenged by neomentalism, which equates mental processes with internal functional states of the organism. This objection, however, is inconclusive in the absence of an agreed-upon theory of meaning.

Interpretations which attempt behavioral explanations of complex behavior (ie., 7, 8) are criticized for illegitimately extrapolating from simple contexts in which behav-

ioral concepts clearly apply to complex situations in which they apply only "metaphorically." However, this objection ignores the conditions under which the analogical extension of a scientific theory is not only justified but is actually an essential aspect of scientific progress.

The agent, or self, discussed in the preceding chapter, is but one concept in the rich and complex conceptual framework of everyday psychological speech. In popular discourse, human action is accounted for by wishes, desires, and motives. Conscious contents such as feelings, images, and sensations are matters of everyday conversation. This mentalistic framework is a rival to behaviorism. Therefore, behaviorists attempt to come to terms with it, and they propose a variety of resolutions to this issue, an important node in the behaviorist tree diagram. Some are conceptual in that they derive primarily from a philosphical analysis of mental concepts. Others are empirical because they make use of scientific discoveries. Both of these types of behavioral interpretation of mentalistic language, in third-party application, are the topic of this chapter. The next chapter will deal with mentalistic language when applied to oneself.

CONCEPTUAL TREATMENTS

Eliminative Behaviorism

One approach is simply to deny the legitimacy of mentalist language. Mental concepts, it can be argued, are merely the residue of prescientific animistic notions of souls and spirits.[1] Just as the development of natural science eliminated many erroneous popular concepts about the world, so behavioral psychology will provide suitable scientific concepts to supplant mental ones. A completed behavioral science will leave nothing for which the descriptive or explanatory concepts of mental language are required.[2] Weiss (1929a) looks in that direction in stating:

> Behaviorism claims to render a *more* complete and a *more* scientific account of the totality of human achievement *without* the concept of consciousness, than traditional psychology is able to render *with* it. The factors which traditional psychology vaguely classifies as conscious or mental elements merely *vanish* without a remainder into the biological and social components of the behavioristic analysis. (p. vii)

This approach is intuitively difficult to accept. In rejecting mental language as false, this "eliminative behaviorism" in effect asserts that, contrary to what we have always believed, people do not act on their ideas, they do not have beliefs, and they are not swayed by emotions. Perhaps these notions are so hard to accept because the elimination of mental language is envisioned as abrupt, and no conceptual scheme stands ready to replace it. Probably there was a time when it was equally incomprehensible that falling objects do not strive to return to the ground, or that demons do not possess the bodies of the ill. Nevertheless, these concepts were gradually replaced by scientific ones that proved more useful. Similarly, it is conceivable that with the growth of a behavioral science, mental concepts will slowly give way to behavioral ones, and the loss will not be acutely felt.

If eliminative behaviorism proves correct and mental concepts "vanish without a remainder," it will not be through the empirical discovery that mental phenomena do not exist but rather through the development of more effective ways of describing and explaining behavior. The gradual replacement of an entire conceptual framework is quite different from the discovery that a particular event does not occur as previously thought. Behavior will come to be seen in a new light, and the dismissal of mental concepts will no longer seem incomprehensible.[3] On the other hand, it is possible that even with a completed theory of behavior, mentalistic language will be retained for its convenience, just as we still speak of the sun "setting." Thus, eliminative behaviorism depends not only on the success of the behaviorist program but also on the practical utility of its creation.

Methodological Behaviorism

A second interpretation is that the two conceptual schemes apply to different domains. According to this second approach, psychology must limit itself to the observable facts of behavior while the language of consciousness finds application in the private phenomenal world of the mind, beyond the scope of science. In discussing their experiments with a cat in a puzzle box, Guthrie and Horton (1946) suggest this resolution:

> We do not at all deny that the cat undoubtedly has experience analogous to ours. But it appears to us highly desirable to find an adequate description of the cat's behavior without recourse to such conscious experience. . . . the unobservable and unverifiable supposititious mental life of the cat is of no use in a theory of learning. That should be confined to observable antecedents and observable results. . . . If we lean too heavily on conscious ideas in explaining behavior we may find ourselves predicting what the cat will think, but not what we can observe it to do. (p. 7)

Thus, in its decision to exclude the realm of consciousness from scientific scrutiny, methodological behaviorism offers an area in which mental concepts are appropriate. However, methodological behaviorism can succeed in establishing a science of behavior, with laws of behavior, only if the realm of consciousness does not intrude into the behavioral domain. Yet, in the mentalist conceptual framework, events in consciousness determine behavior and cannot be ignored in explaining behavior. Therefore, in so far as mentalist language implies the interaction of consciousness and behavior, it is incompatible with even methodological behaviorism, and the latter offers only a limited resolution of the contradiction between the popular conception of behavior and the behavioristic one.[4]

Logical Behaviorism[5]

Logical behaviorism offers a verificationist treatment of mental language. According to the verificationist theory, the meaning of a *sentence* is determined by the conditions for testing the truth of that sentence, and the meaning of a *term* is given by the conditions under which the term can be correctly applied. Any proposition that, in principle, cannot be observationally verified, or a term whose application cannot be empirically determined, is meaningless. Since language is an interpersonal means of communication, the conditions of verification and correct application must be publicly observable; otherwise the meanings of language could not shared, and communication would be impossible. Therefore, meaning cannot include the contents of introspection.[6]

Instead, according to logical behaviorism, the meaning of mental concepts is given by other concepts referring to observables which are the conditions of application and verification.[7] Thus, the meaning of "Mr. Jones is angry" is given by the observable conditions by which one tests to determine if Jones is angry. Since Jones' state of consciousness is, in principle, not accessible to others, the correct application of the term "angry" and the verification of the sentence cannot depend on assessing Jones' private experience. Rather, the conditions of application and verification are observable conditions of Jones' body, especially his behavior, including verbal behavior. For example, the conditions for the application of "angry" can be formulated with terms such as "pounds the table," "turns red in the face," and "screams 'I hate you.' " With this method, the mental concept "angry" is said to be "reducible" to the behavioral terms.

An obvious problem for this analysis is that Jones may be angry but may not be manifesting any of the behavioral symptoms because he is, for example, suppressing them. One solution would be to include internal physiological states, which are in principle observable, as conditions of verification and application. This is of limited value, however, because current knowledge is insufficient for determining emotional states by physiological observation, yet we readily apply the term "angry" in cases of this sort.

Another solution is to construe "anger" and other mental terms as dispositional concepts.[8] In this case the reduction of "Mr. Jones is angry" is formulated as "under conditions a, b, c, . . . , Jones shows the behaviors x, y, z, . . ." The conditions mentioned in the antecedent can include things such as asking Jones how he feels or placing Jones in a private room where he has no need to suppress his anger. The reduction assumes the form of bilateral reductive sentences discussed in chapter 4. As shown there, reductive chains provide only a partial definition of a dispositional concept, rather than a translation.

Thus, for logical behaviorism, mental language is maintained, but it is shorn of its dualistic interpretation. Its sole meaning is given by its intersubjectively verifiable implications while any alleged dualistic connotations are dismissed as meaningless because unverifiable. However there are several problems with this doctrine which call into question the logical behaviorist program.[9]

First, verificationism is inappropriate for the analysis of the meaning of many theoretical terms. As discussed in chapter 4, the meaning of certain theoretical terms is not exhausted by their observational implications. Second, there are many arguments, reviewed in chapter 2, against limiting verification to intersubjective observation. If private observation is accepted as a method of verification, then the reduction of mental concepts need not be limited to the publicly observable.

Yet a third problem with verificationism is that it does not justify its basic assertion that meaning is given by conditions of verification. This principle does not correspond to common intuitive or psychological notions of meaning. Verificationism is therefore best viewed as a proposal as to how terms *should* be understood in order to facilitate communication and scientific progress.[10] It is a purely methodological decision to use the predicates of the public "physical thing language" as primitives rather than phenomenalistic predicates. Thus, logical behaviorism resolves the contradiction between the mentalist conceptual framework and that of behaviorism only by fiat. It legislates a theory of meaning, and then, using this theory as a pruning hook, it eliminates all the features of mentalist language that are problematic for behaviorism. To be sure, the legislation is not purely arbitrary. It does promote intersubjective agreement; it establishes the unity of science through its physicalism; and it ensures that the terms of science have empirical meaning. However, unless the verificationist theory of meaning is justified, logical behaviorism is eliminative behaviorism in disguise: It keeps the terms of mentalism, but it eliminates what was thought to be their meaning.

Operationism

In psychology, the verificationism of logical behaviorism appears as operationism, discussed in chapter 4.[11] According to operationism, the meaning of a concept, and mental concepts in particular, is to be found in the operations used to measure or detect the presence of that concept.[12] For example, Jones' anger is operationally equivalent to the force with which he pounds on the table, or the intensity of his shouting, or the number he circles when asked to rate his anger on a questionnaire.

Thus, for operational behaviorism, a behavioral interpretation is an operational definition. Operationism permits behaviorists to study traditional psychological phenomena such as images, sensations, and emotions. They are operationally equated with various behavioral measures, and the latter are experimentally investigated.

Although mental and behavioral languages are thereby rendered compatible, mental concepts do not retain their causal force. "Jones kicked the door because he was angry" attributes a causal role to Jones' anger. However, if anger is operationally defined by some behavioral index, such as galvanic skin response, then the relationship between the anger and the kicking is one of correlation between two response measures rather than cause and effect. If operationism is regarded as a valid theory of meaning, then the fact that mental concepts lose causal functions when given operational definitions would indicate merely that it was a mistake to have ascribed such causal roles to them in the first place.[13] On the other hand, if operationism is merely a recommendation on how science ought to treat its concepts, then operational meaning does not coincide with the traditional meaning.[14]

This lack of congruence lies at the root of two of the unresolved controversies between behaviorists and cognitivists discussed in chapter 9. The first is the continuity-noncontinuity controversy over whether a reinforcement can strengthen a correct response before the subject adopts a correct hypothesis. The second is the reinforcement-without-awareness controversy over whether reinforcement strengthens behavior if the subject is unaware of the contingency of reinforcement. Both debates feature mental concepts, "hypothesis" and "awareness." In both cases, behaviorists operationally define the mental concepts in terms of behavioral measures. "Hypothesis" is defined as systematic response tendencies, "awareness" as the subject's verbal report of being aware. By these operational definitions, an awareness or hypothesis cannot be said to have occurred until the appropriate behavior occurs. On the other hand, for cognitivists implicitly using a definition closer to the traditional concept, hypotheses and awareness can occur prior to behavior and can be causally related to subsequent behavior. The result of this discrepancy is that the two sides agree on the data but disagree on interpretation. In both controversies, behaviorists argue that the mental process, whether hypothesis or awareness, is absent because the behavioral index does not appear, while their opponents implicitly argue that the mental event has occurred in the absence of the behavioral measure.[15]

The Mental as Intervening Variable

Tolman is responsible for a version of operationism which provides yet another form of behavioral interpretation. In Tolman's system, mental concepts are identified with intervening variables (chapters 4 and 8). These variables are neither stimuli nor responses but rather represent relationships among them.

Mental concepts identified with intervening variables therefore refer to states of the organism which determine the relationship of behavior to the environment.[16] As Tolman (1932) expresses it:

> The behaviorism here to be presented will contend that mental processes are most usefully to be conceived as but dynamic aspects, or determinants, of behavior. They are functional variables which intermediate in the causal equations between environmental stimuli and initiating physiological states . . . on the one side, and final overt behavior, on the other. (p. 2)

On the intervening-variable account of mental concepts, to say that Jones is angry is not to state anything about his private conscious experience. Rather it is to say something about the value of an intervening variable which summarizes the correlation between a particular set of independent variables and a particular set of behavioral variables.[17] The intervening variable can be identified as "anger" because the variables chosen are those commonly associated with the everyday use of the term. Of course, the intervening variable is more precise and formal than the term used conversationally. Nevertheless, in an important sense, the intervening variable is merely a natural extension of the everyday term as scientific psychology gradually discovers more about behavior.

It is important to note that on the intervening-variable account of mental concepts, to attribute a mental term to an organism is not to imply anything definite about its current or future behavior. In order for an intervening variable to be reflected directly in behavior, test conditions must obtain and many other intervening variables have to assume appropriate values.[18] Therefore it is possible for Jones to be angry—i.e., to have a high value on the anger-intervening-variable—but for him to fail ever to act in an angry way because test conditions do not obtain or the other intervening variables never, in fact, take on the necessary values. This accords well with the everyday use of mental terms in which people are often said to be in a particular psychological state even though they may never act in the ways most typically associated with that state. In the absence of any anger-behavior, the anger-intervening-variable may be derived from the values of the independent variables of which the intervening variable is a function.[19] When anger-behavior does occur, the anger, as an intervening variable, cannot be said to cause it because as a purely conceptual relationship, an intervening variable is generally conceived of as having no causal status.[20]

Analytic Behaviorism

Analytic behaviorism represents an approach to mental concepts as they occur in natural language rather than a prescription as to how these concepts are to be incorporated into scientific discourse.[21] Its aims are twofold. One purpose, the negative one, is to show that everyday talk about the mind does not entail dualism. Through painstaking philosophical analysis of traditional mental concepts, analytic behaviorists demonstrate that dualistic interpretations of mental language are founded on logical errors. Ryle (1949) describes his method this way:

> To determine the logical geography of concepts is to reveal the logic of the propositions in which they are wielded, that is to say, to show with what other propositions they are consistent and inconsistent, what propositions follow from them and from what propositions they follow. The logical type or category to which a concept belongs is the set of ways in which it is logically legitimate to operate with it. The key arguments employed . . . are intended to show why certain sorts of operations with the concepts of mental powers and processes are breaches of logical rules. (p. 8)

An illustration of the methods of analytic behaviorism is Wittgenstein's treatment of the mental concept of "understanding." A possible mentalistic interpretation is that to understand the meaning of a word like "red" one must have a mental image when one hears the word. Wittgenstein constructs a case in which one is ordered to fetch a red flower. On the mentalist interpretation, carrying out this order with understanding means comparing various flowers with the mental image and finding the one that matches. In considering this interpretation, Wittgenstein (1958) notes:

> But this is not the only way of searching and it isn't the usual way. We go, look about us, walk up to a flower and pick it, without comparing it to anything. To see that the process of obeying the order can be of this kind, consider the order "*imagine* a red patch." You are not tempted in this case to think that *before* obeying you must have imagined a red patch to serve you as a pattern for the red patch which you were ordered to imagine. (p. 3)

Through Wittgenstein's simple example, one is disabused of the notion that understanding always involves mental images.[22] After a number of philosophical arguments of this sort, one is finally freed from Cartesian dualism, or what Ryle calls the "myth of the ghost in the machine." Because analytic behaviorism aims at removing misconceptions, its first goal can be said to be a therapeutic one.[23]

Analytic behaviorism maintains, in addition, a positive thesis, as well. This position is that everyday mental concepts refer to aspects of behavior rather than private consciousness.[24] As Ryle (1949) expresses this thesis: "when we describe people as exercising qualities of mind, we are not referring to occult episodes of which their overt acts and utterances are effects; we are referring to those overt acts and utterances themselves" (p. 25). This thesis is similar to the relational theory of mind which maintains that consciousness is not a substance but is rather a particular kind of relationship between an organism's action and the environment.[25]

According to analytic behaviorism, statements about Jones' emotions are statements about Jones' behavior and dispositions to behave.[26] The problem of other minds is dissolved because others do not require access to Jones' private experience to know about his states of mind.[27] Furthermore, a statement like "Jones pounded the table because he was angry" does not attribute a nonphysical unobservable cause to Jones' observed behavior. Instead, it explains the behavior as a manifestation of Jones' disposition to act angry.

Analytic behaviorism differs from logical behaviorism over the relationship between the mental concept, on the one hand, and the behavior and dispositions, on the other. For logical behaviorism, the mental concept *means* the associated behavior and disposition. For Wittgensteinian analytic behaviorism, the relationship is more complicated and less clear. The behavior is said to be the "criterion" for the application of the mental concept, but the connection between the concept and the criterion is conceptualized as neither logical entailment nor inductive inference. Instead, the criterion is assumed to constitute noninductive evidence for the mental concept and to adequately justify its application.[28]

This criteriological account shares features with intervening-variable interpretations of mental concepts. A dispositional mental concept, like an intervening variable, neither entails nor is entailed by any particular behavior. The specific behavior that actualizes a disposition or intervening variable depends entirely on the circumstances.[29] In this sense, mental dispositions are "indefinitely heterogeneous," in Ryle's phrase,[30] and the behaviors that realize them share a family resemblance rather than identical common features. No behavior is either necessary or sufficient for the ascription of a mental state to Jones. His pounding the table may be a result of his pretending to be angry, and when he is angry it is possible that a reaction formation leads him to act with extreme politeness. Thus the difference between his pounding the table out of anger and his pounding the table in order to attract attention does not lie in unobserved conscious events in his mind but rather in the observable environmental causes of his behavior and in his future behavior.

OBJECTIONS TO CONCEPTUAL TREATMENTS

The Irreducibility of the Mental

In most of the forms of behavioral interpretation reviewed thus far, mental concepts are explicated in terms of behavior, thereby eliminating mental language. A common objection to this enterprise is that the meaning of a mental concept cannot be formulated solely in terms of nonmental concepts and therefore mental terms cannot be totally eliminated.[31] For example, it is argued that the interpretation of "Jones is angry" in terms of Jones' dispositions to behave must include the qualifier that Jones is not trying to deceive. If Jones is dissembling, his behavior will not correspond to the behavioral interpretation of anger. Therefore, Jones' intentions must be mentioned in the behavioral interpretation, and the mental is not eliminated.

In replying to this objection, it is important to recall that on an intervening-variable, or dispositional, account of mental terms, the specified behavior ensues only under certain circumstances. Jones' attempts at deception would not be one of these circumstances. The question is whether these circumstances can be specified without the use of other mental terms. Under an intervening-variable interpretation this should be possible, at least in theory. Jones' attempts at deception are behaviors under the control of independent variables, including his conditioning history. These independent variables interact with the independent variables of the anger-intervening-variable to produce the behavior of an angry man who is pretending not to be angry rather than the typically angry behavior of an angry man. In this way, the intervening-variable account eliminates all mental concepts by including the values of all the other relevant independent variables when specifying the conditions under which a behavior ensues from one intervening variable.

It is not clear, however, that a similar elimination is always possible under a dispositional interpretation. Such an elimination would entail that not only Jones' attempts at deception but also every conceivable interfering mental factor can be given a dispositional analysis. An intervening-variable interpretation is successful at this elimination because it assumes that every aspect of behavior is a function of environmental variables, and therefore, every interfering mental factor can be replaced by a set of independent variables. Since a dispositional analysis does not make this assumption, it cannot prove that in principle no mental terms need appear in its interpretations. On the other hand, there is no argument that shows that in principle mental terms cannot be eliminated entirely in a dispositional analysis.

Another version of the argument that the mental is irreducible is the claim that intensional language, discussed in chapter 3, cannot be eliminated.[32] The force of this objection depends on the definition of a behavioral interpretation. Most analytic behaviorists accept intensional language in their interpretations of mental language and do not feel the need to eliminate it. Similarly, as discussed in chapter 3, Tolman may be understood to allow intensional language in his behavioral data language in that he "propositionalizes" the organism's demands and expectations.[33] For those behaviorists who do not admit intensional language into the behavioral data language another solution is required. One possibility is to interpret intensional language as characterizing the dispositional determinants of behavior in terms of the propositions that the actor *would* assert.[34] Thus, to say that Jones is searching for a unicorn is not to say that a unicorn "inexists," as Brentano expresses it, but rather to say that if asked what he is doing, Jones would assert something about a one-horned horse with a lion's tail.

Neomentalism

A second major challenge to conceptual behavioral interpretations arises from neomentalism.[35] Neomentalism rejects the thesis of analytic behaviorism that the mental can be identified with behavior.[36] Instead, it claims, behavior is merely an external symptom while mental events, in the form of functional states, are the internal cause of the observed behavior.[37] However, neomentalism is uncommitted as to how the functional state is in fact actualized in living organisms. Thus, neomentalism is neutral as to the ontological status of mental events and differs from the dualism of traditional mentalism.[38]

Support for neomentalism derives from a variety of philosophical arguments. A common one is to construct situations in which mental concepts apply although the tie between a mental state and its behavioral symptom is severed. For example, imagine that a living brain is removed from its body but kept alive and provided with all the incoming electrical impulses that would occur if it were still connected to its body. Here it seems natural to say that this "bodyless person" can think and experience feelings even though no behavior is occurring.[39] Another example is Putnam's "X-world" populated by "super-super-spartans" who have pains which they do not admit to, never show pain behavior, and pretend not to know either the word "pain" or the phenomenon to which it refers.[40] Again, the mental concept applies in the absence of any behavior.

Replies to Neomentalism

One line of defense against neomentalism is in response to its counter-examples. It can be argued in the counter-examples of the "bodyless person" and the "super-super-spartans" that it is not at all obvious that our linguistic intuitions call for the application of mental concepts.[41] Furthermore, even if mental concepts are to be extended to cover these cases, cannot the concepts of behavior and behavioral disposition be similarly extended? As noted above, intervening variables and dispositions do not necessarily eventuate in behavior. Outcomes depend on circumstances. Jones' anger, as an intervening variable or disposition, will not be realized as behavior if Jones is tied up so tightly that he cannot move. Therefore, it can be said in response to neomentalism that the bodyless brain also has dispositions to behave, and under the right circumstances—i.e., connection to a body—behavior would ensue. In a like manner, it could be argued that the super-super-spartan has a disposition to show pain behavior, and under the right circumstances—e.g., transfer to a different society, administration of an anti-stoicism drug—will show this behavior. Thus the presence of behavioral dispositions can justify for the analytic behaviorist the application of mental terms in these borderline cases.

Alternatively, the concept of behavior can be extended to cover these cases.

Effector impulses in the bodyless brain that would have produced behavior had the brain been connected to a body can be counted as behavior. Similarly, the concept of "behavior" can be extended to include the super-super-spartans' "V-waves" (by which Putnam supposes his hypothesis about pain in the X-world can be tested) since they can be decoded into English messages.

A second line of defense against neomentalism involves its contention that mental states are functional states. The identification of the mental with functional states is proposed as a scientific hypothesis to be confirmed or disconfirmed by empirical research.[42] Analytic behaviorism, on the other hand, concerns concepts in natural language. People currently use mental concepts even though they are unaware of the functional states of a neomentalist theory that has not yet even been formulated. Thus, in reply to neomentalism, analytic behaviorism can argue that the current everyday meaning of mental concepts is given by the behavioral interpretation while the functional state interpretation, as a proposed empirical hypothesis for the theoretical reduction of a mental concept, constitutes a new technical meaning.

Putnam, however, argues vigorously against this reply.[43] He argues, for example, that before the discovery of the cause of polio, the term "polio" meant "the disease normally responsible for symptoms a, b, c, etc." rather than "the simultaneous presence of symptoms a, b, c, etc." Consequently, advancing scientific knowledge that came to identify the disease with certain viral causes did not change the meaning of the term. Similarly, he claims, a mental concept such as "pain" *currently* means the presence of a condition which normally causes certain kinds of behavior. Therefore, the theoretical identification of a mental concept with a functional state, if empirically confirmed, would not change the meaning of the concept.

In reply to Putnam, it can be argued that our concept of meaning is not precise enough to permit a definitive judgment of his claim that the identification of mental concepts with functional states would not constitute a change in meaning. For the same reason it is not clear whether analytic behaviorism provides the current meaning of mental terms, or merely states the grounds on which mental terms are justifiably applied. What is certain is that the functional states of an as yet unformulated psychological theory are neither the current meaning of mental terms nor the inferred grounds for the application of those terms. To the query "What do you mean by saying that Jones is angry?" one does not reply with a description of functional states of Jones' nervous system. A more likely reply is in terms of Jones' behavior.

A third line of defense is against the neomentalist attack on the analytic behaviorist rejection of mentalistic "paramechanical" explanations of behavior. Analytic behaviorism denies that when we give an explantion of behavior in terms of the person's beliefs or desires we are referring to internal events which cause the external behavior. In contrast, neomentalists claim that such explanations do refer to inner causes, namely the internal functional states of the person. In response to this neomentalist attack, it can be argued that the neomentalist's functional states are not the "mental" events analytic behaviorism seeks to exorcise. For the most part, neomentalist functional states are neither actions of the person nor processes the person is conscious of.[44] The mental causes to which analytic behaviorism objects are generally conceived as covert acts the person consciously performs in the mind. Although analytic behaviorism aims at the dissolution of the "paramechanical hypothesis," it does not deny either that behavior has a neurophysiological cause or that events which are neither conscious nor acts occur in the person's body. The tasks of neomentalism and analytic behaviorism can be seen as complementary rather than contradictory. The latter provides the behavior which is the meaning or the criteria of application for mental terms, and the former supplies a causal explanation of that behavior.[45]

The conceptual analysis offered by analytic behaviorism is in terms of behavior and behavioral dispositions, but the functional psychological theory formulated by neomentalism may make reference to states or information-processing operations which are not behavioral dispositions. However, this fact does not point to a contradiction between the two. A conceptual analysis is not a causal explanation, and there is no reason why the two should have the same logical form.

Furthermore, in behaviorist psychological theory, as opposed to conceptual analysis, theoretical terms appear which, like the theoretical entities of neomentalism, are neither behavior nor behavioral dispositions. Hypothetical constructs, for example, need not be defined in terms of behavior. Moreover, the intervening variables of both Hullian and Tolmanian theory can interact in ways analogous to functional states. For example, the intervening variable, reaction potential, ${}_SE_R$, is a function of the intervening variable habit strength, ${}_SH_R$. Therefore ${}_SH_R$ is not only a behavioral disposition, but also a disposition for changing another disposition, ${}_SE_R$.

Symptom and Cause in Behavioral Disorders

Just as neomentalism criticizes analytic behaviorism for providing merely the behavioral symptoms of mental concepts rather than the meaning of those concepts, so a common objection to behavioral analysis in behavior therapy is that it addresses only the behavioral symptoms of an emotional disorder rather than the disorder itself. Typically, a client enters behavior therapy with psychological complaints, such as "depression," stated in mentalistic language. In the first stage of therapy, the client's mental problem is defined in terms of an array of behavioral measures. Depression, for example, might be measured by frequency of crying and number of hours per day spent alone. Treatment then consists of a set of methods designed to change these "target" behaviors.[46] The most common objection to this approach to clinical disorders is that it treats only the symptoms without curing the underlying problem.[47] In this objection, the mental term is identified with the underlying problem and the target behaviors are regarded as mere manifestations.

This criticism of behavioral interpretation for clinical terms is often a confusion of several distinct objections. First, the criticism may be understood to be asserting that behavior therapy ignores the client's feelings, thoughts, and emotions. This objection is misguided. Because most behavior therapists subscribe to one of the forms of behavioral interpretation reviewed in this chapter, behavior therapy may be said to deal with feelings, thoughts, and emotions *as behaviorally interpreted.*

A second possible meaning of the criticism is that behavior therapy treats behavior but not its causes. For example, alcoholism may be treated by punishing drinking behavior with electric shocks. However, the original causes responsible for the drinking behavior are not changed and may therefore produce other forms of undesired behavior (e.g., drug addiction).[48]

The force of this criticism depends on whether the other undesired behaviors do in fact appear. If the alcoholism is cured and no new undesired behaviors replace it, then the treatment has been successful, and the objection carries little weight. If new undesired behaviors do appear ("symptom substitution"), it may indeed be necessary to modify the independent variables responsible. In this case, a good behavior therapist would implement the necessary steps. There is nothing in the principles of behavior therapy that require it to ignore the behavioral variables controlling a response. Therefore, the criticism is directed at behavior therapy improperly carried out rather than at the principles of behavior therapy.

A third version of the criticism is that in focusing on target behaviors, behavior therapy treats symptoms and not the "unconscious conflict" or the "repressed wish" that is the cause of the target behaviors. These psychodynamic "underlying causes," however, are clearly explanatory theoretical concepts, and there is no reason why one theory must explain (or cure!) the theoretical concepts of a rival theory. Or the criticism might be that behavioral theory does not adequately account for the clinical observations from which psychodynamic theoretical constructs are inferred, nor do behavioral treatments affect them appropriately. This criticism of behavior therapy shifts the issue to the question of behaviorist views of psychodynamic method and theory.

Psychoanalysis. Behaviorist attitudes toward psychoanalysis are at best ambivalent. Behaviorists generally agree that psychoanalytic methods of observation and theory construction do not meet behaviorist standards of objectivity and empiricalness.[49] However, there is disagreement on what to do with psychoanalytic theory. On the one hand, many of the classic behaviorists, including Watson, Guthrie, Tolman, Dollard and Miller, and Skinner offer behavioral interpretations of psychoanalytic concepts.[50] These interpretations are unusual because they involve theoretical concepts rather than everyday mental concepts. Therefore the interpretation must proceed at two levels. First, it is necessary to assess legitimacy of the clinical observations the theoretical concept is postulated to explain. Second, if these observations are found acceptable, then theoretical concepts meeting behaviorist criteria must be substituted for the psychoanalytic explanation.

On the first level, behavioral interpretations of psychoanalytic concepts incorporate a good deal of psychoanalytic clinical observations. The influence of childhood family events on adult behavior, the importance of the sex drive, the effects of factors of which the client is unaware (and may even deny), and conflict are accepted as facts to be explained in many of these interpretations. On the second level, behaviorists, for the most part, choose concepts from learning theory as substitutes for psychoanalytic constructs. For example, Skinner reinterprets "repression" as occurring when a response of some strength is punished and is displaced by an incompatible response maintained by negative reinforcement. The displaced response maintains its strength but does not occur, and in this sense is "repressed." The notion of a strong response which does not occur is clearly a theoretical concept as described in chapter 3. Skinner thus replaces one theoretical concept with another which he finds more acceptable but which plays a theoretical role similar to that of the original. In this first approach to psychoanalysis, the claim that behaviorists ignore psychodynamic clinical observations is refuted.

On the other hand, many other behaviorists, especially behavior therapists, deny that psychoanalytic concepts have any use whatsoever. They reject psychoanalytic clinical observations as unsubstantiated, and they therefore believe that behavioral reinterpretation of psychoanalytic concepts is pointless.[51] This *a priori* rejection of data which may yet be confirmed, is not clearly justified. It most likely represents the methodological decision that the methods and constructs of psychoanalysis are so deficient that to formulate a behavioral reinterpretation or to use them as heuristics to guide research is simply not worth the effort.[52]

EMPIRICAL TREATMENTS

Empirical Reduction

Whereas analytic behaviorism accepts both the descriptive and explanatory functions of mental language, some behaviorists accept only the former while rejecting the latter. As in analytic behaviorism, this approach views mentalist descriptions as denoting aspects of behavior. The first step, therefore, in this type of behavioral interpretation is to determine what features of behavior correspond to descriptive terms such as "purposeful," "insightful," and "intentional."[53] The second step is to explain these features of behavior with an empirical behavioral theory that incorporates no mental concepts. Alternate mentalist explanations in terms of inner conscious processes are discarded as misleading, unhelpful, or simply false.[54]

Hull illustrates this type of "empirical reduction." He first notes that behavior is called "purposeful" when it shows persistence and variation in achieving a goal. Using a simple trial-and-error learning situation as his paradigm, he then shows how this characteristic of behavior can be deduced from a "miniature" theory consisting of postulates and theorems.[55] Although he grants that the resulting behavior may be accurately *described* in mentalist terms such as "intelligent," he denies that it must be *explained* as resulting from inner mental events since his theory makes no reference to them.[56] In Hull's (1930a) words:

> The behavior deduced . . . is one of the most commonly remarked differences between behavior, usually called psychic or mental, and that of ordinary automatic machines. . . . these . . . terms represent extremely important aspects of mammalian behavior, but . . . instead of being ultimate entities, all may be derived from certain combinations of more basic principles. . . . the account sketched above . . . deduces a type of behavior which, if observed in an animal, would be called purposive by most psychologists. (pp. 255–256)

Because Hull thus accepts the descriptive function of mentalist concepts he is led to a somewhat misleading statement:

> What, then, shall we say about consciousness? Is its existence denied? By no means. But to recognize the existence of a phenomenon is not the same thing as insisting upon its basic, i.e., logical, priority. Instead of furnishing a means for the solution of problems, consciousness appears to be itself a problem needing solution. (1937, p. 30)

This statement can easily be misinterpreted to indicate Hull's acceptance of consciousness into the science of behavior. However, the two senses in which he accepts consciousness are extremely limited. First, mental concepts may be used as mere descriptions of behavior as discussed above. Second, mental concepts may appear as theoretical constructs in the postulates of a scientific theory of behavior. To be sure, Hull denies that any truly scientific deductive theory using mental concepts has ever been developed, but he grants the logical possibility. Nevertheless, even if such a theory were to be developed, consciousness would appear merely as an inferred construct, not as an immediately given experiential reality. Thus, whether consciousness is taken as a description of behavior or as a hypothesized construct, it is neither the phenomenal nor the ontologically distinct substance of Cartesian dualism, and Hull accepts "consciousness" only in a Pickwickian sense.[57]

For Hull, explanation consists of deduction of a theorem from a system of postulates (chapter 5), and an empirical reduction would therefore include a deduction of this type. However, not all behaviorists subscribe to this form of explanation, and each view of explanation generates a different type of empirical reduction. Skinner, for example, sees the determination of the environmental variables controlling a behavior as critical for explaining that behavior. Therefore, Skinner maintains that many mentalistic descriptions and explanations of behavior are really oblique references to the variables controlling behavior.[58]

Empirical Translations

Whether explicit or not, the task of behavioral interpretation often involves elucidating the meaning of mental concepts. However, the concept of "meaning" itself is not well defined, nor is it one in which behaviorists place much trust.[59] Therefore, a number of behaviorists offer empirical conceptions of meaning as precise and scientific substitutes for the traditional concept. Skinner (1945a) suggests that the meaning of a verbal response consists of the variables controlling it:[60]

> A considerable advantage is gained from dealing with terms, concepts, constructs . . . as verbal responses. Meanings, contents, and references are to be found among the determiners . . . of response. The question "What is length?" would appear to be satisfactorily answered by listing the circumstances under which the response "length" is emitted. . . . What we want to know in the case of many traditional psychological terms is, first, the specific stimulating conditions under which they are emitted . . . and, second . . . why each response is controlled by its corresponding condition. (pp. 271–272)

Weiss (1929a) extends this approach to metaphysical discourse:

> All metaphysical discussions, no matter how profound and involved they may be, are in the *last* analysis nothing but language responses and linguistic habits. . . .
>
> In other words, for the behaviorist the metaphysical problem is merely that of trying to understand the conditions under which the language habits of the metaphysician have been acquired. (pp. 46, 48)

Thus, the meaning of mental concepts with dualistic connotations is given by the independent variables controlling the emission of certain verbal responses. A verbal description of these variables provides a "translation" of a mental concept. For Skinner, a translation is defined as a verbal stimulus which has the same effect as the original on a different verbal community.[61] Applying this definition to a behavioral interpretation, the "different language community" is the community of behavioral scientists, and the translation is from a natural language containing mental concepts to a behavioral language, rather than from, say, English to French.[62]

Chief among the independent variables constituting the empirical translation of a mental concept is the discriminative stimulus. In most instances, the discriminative stimulus consists of certain features of behavior. The speaker A is stimulated by these features in the behavior of another organism, B, and given that certain other conditions are appropriate, A emits a verbal response from the class known as "mental terms." In this respect, the empirical translation is similar to the other forms of behavioral interpretation discussed above—the meaning of a mental term is identified with aspects of behavior. However, an empirical translation carries the analysis a step further. Whereas an empirical reduction explains the behavior of the organism B, whose activities are the discriminative stimulus for A, the speaker of the mental term, an empirical translation explains the behavior of A, and this involves more than just the discriminative stimulus.

In addition to the discriminative stimulus, the verbal behavior of A is under the control of a number of other variables, each of which is part of the meaning of the term. Some of these variables are in A's conditioning history in acquiring the mental term. In learning to use mental terms to describe certain aspects of behavior, people also learn to discriminate the variables controlling that behavior. Therefore, much of A's explanatory mental language can be empirically translated into statements about variables controlling B's behavior although these variables are not immediately present in the discriminative stimulus for A's current verbal response.[63] Thus, while Hull rejects the explanatory role of mental concepts, Skinner uses it as a suggestion pointing toward controlling variables that may prove scientifically acceptable.

Another set of variables controlling A's verbal response but not included among stimulus features of B's behavior are contingencies of reinforcement for A's verbal responses. Some of A's verbal responses are maintained partly by the reinforcements that accrue to A by the changes in B's behavior brought about by A's using certain verbal responses.[64] Skinner contends that many concepts associated with the notions of freedom and dignity are maintained because members of society are reinforced by the consequences of the use of these concepts. These contingencies, then, represent another difference between empirical reduction and empirical translation.

The validity of empirical translation rests on the adequacy of its notion of meaning. This notion cannot, of course, be defended by an empirical translation of "meaning" without begging the question. Nor do intuitive notions of meaning support empirical translations. A list of the variables controlling the emission of the verbal response "table" is not what is usually meant by the word "table." Perhaps, therefore, the empirical concept of meaning ought to be regarded as an "explication" of the traditional concept of meaning rather than a definition.[65] In an explication, a more precise and more useful concept is substituted for a vague but important traditional concept. The explication tries to capture the significant features of the traditional concept while discarding those aspects which interfere with clarity of communication. Given a behaviorist explication of meaning, empirical translations purge mentalistic language of dualistic connotations.

Problems of Extrapolation

Empirical treatments of mentalistic language, both empirical reductions and empirical translations, face the formidable task of explaining rather complex behavior. For empirical reduction, the behavior is that of the person described by the mentalistic language, while for empirical translation it is the verbal behavior of the person using the mentalistic language. In both cases, the behavior is far too complex to be fully explained by any current or immediately foreseeable psychological theory.

Plausibility Claims. One way to deal with this problem is to analyze samples of the behavior in situations so simple that explanations are currently possible. Insightful behavior may be too complex to explain in an adult human faced with real life problems, but it may be tractable in a rat running toward food in a maze. If the "insightful" behavior of the rat can be successfully explained, then an empirical interpretation of "insight" is achieved.

However, this approach is not without difficulties of its own. First, it is often not clear whether the behavior in the simple situation truly exemplifies the mental concept. Does the rat's behavior deserve to be called "insightful"? Second, even if this be granted, there is still no guarantee that the variables responsible for the behavior in the simple case are also those responsible for the behavior in the prototype complex case. Since this cannot be shown without already having an explanation of the complex case, this strategy of using simple cases rests ultimately on a plausibility claim. Explicitly stated, this argument is that although no conclusive evidence currently proves the relevance of the simple case to the complex one, nothing in our present knowledge rules it out, and our everyday experience with other human beings makes it appear reasonable.[66]

Since plausibility must be appealed to in any event, it is not a formidable intellectual leap to dispense entirely with the simple case and suggest plausible accounts of the complex case directly. Proposals of this sort fall into what Skinner calls the "field of interpretation,"[67] in which principles derived from rigorous experimental research are used to explain behavior in the everyday world. The research is designed to elucidate fundamental behavioral principles rather than to create simple simulated versions of complex cases. In discussing his books *Beyond Freedom and Dignity* and *Verbal Behavior*, Skinner (1973b) describes his notion of interpretation:

Beyond Freedom and Dignity does not use a scientific analysis of behavior for purposes of prediction or control. The science lies behind the book rather than in it. It is used merely for purposes of interpretation. . . . Interpretation is a substantial part of many fields of science, including geology, astronomy, subatomic physics, and evolution. When phenomena are out of reach in time or space or too large or small to be directly manipulated, we must talk about them with less than a complete account of relevant conditions. What has been learned under more favorable conditions is then invaluable. . . .

My *Verbal Behavior* was an exercise in interpretation. In it, I pointed to similarities between the contingencies of reinforcement which generate verbal behavior and the contingencies which have been analyzed with much greater precision in the laboratory. The account is, I believe, more plausible than those proposed, without benefit of laboratory experience, by linguists. (pp. 260–261)

Plausibility is appealed to on two different levels. First, the interpretation assumes that the principles derived from laboratory research, usually with lower animals, hold in the outside world with adult humans. Second, it also hypothesizes which particular behavioral variables are responsible for the observed complex behavior. Although neither of these assumptions is claimed to be conclusively established, an interpretation can nevertheless serve important functions as a scientific hypothesis to guide research and to facilitate society's transition to a behaviorist conception of human action.

Extrapolation and Metaphorical Extension. In extrapolating behavioral principles to the world outside the laboratory, empirical interpretations extend concepts fairly well defined in the controlled experimental situation to areas in which application of these concepts is not as definitive. The application of terms such as "stimulus," "response," and "conditioning" to complex human behavior has been variously attacked as "metaphorical," "allegorical," and "verbal magic."[68] Behaviorists are charged with formulating spurious "explanations by translation" into their own "specious" terminology. This issue is most sharply drawn in the area of behavior therapy in which behavioral concepts are directly applied to complex human behavior outside the laboratory.[69]

In considering the issue of what constitutes an "application" of a theory or when an extrapolation is justified, it is useful to consider two extremes. Imagine on the one hand a clear case of legitimate application. Assume a formalized theory of learning in conjunction with initial conditions from which is deduced an observed behavioral disorder or the observed treatment results. In this case, the application is clearly justified.

In reality, of course, no such formalized theory exists. Instead, we have only an unsystematized body of knowledge, Q, consisting of informal theories, empirical generalizations, and paradigmatic situations in which the behavioral concepts clearly apply. Derivations are necessarily nondeductive. Now consider the other extreme case. Imagine that a scientist reads statements from Q and then goes on to make a statement, D, but no one else can see how D was derived from Q. The scientist claims that knowledge of Q was necessary for the derivation of D, but for the rest of the scientific community the derivation is as mysterious as the reading of tea leaves. In this case, despite the scientist's protestations and the confirmation of D, his conclusion cannot be said to be an application of Q.

The clear-cut extremes leave a vast array of intermediate cases in which a statement is nondeductively derived from Q. Suppose that after a scientist derives D from Q, other members of the scientific community also come to see the appropriateness of the derivation. They come to perceive a domain of behavior in a new light through the concepts and principles of Q. The derivation is regarded as a "brilliant insight" and as a demonstration of the heuristic fertility of Q. Extensions of this sort are extremely important to science and are surely justified. What then distinguishes this case from the "tea leaves case," where the extrapolation is invalid? In both cases the scientist may be supposed to provide a defense of the derivation by pointing to specific alleged similarities between the domains of Q and D. The difference is that in the one case others see the similarity and in the latter case they do not.

Theoretical terms are assigned their initial applications through demonstrations in paradigmatic situations. "Stimulus" and "response" are used unproblematically in relation to a rat pressing a lever. Extension of theoretical terms to new situations requires the ability to see the novel circumstances as instantiating the theoretical concept.[70] In some cases, a kind of perceptual learning is needed in order to achieve the necessary "seeing-as."[71] Thus, similarity justifies the derivation of D from Q, and the validity of the extrapolation rests ultimately on human pattern recognition. The legitimacy of the extension depends on the degree of the similarity, but because there is no metric to measure similarity in this situation, a precise distinction between acceptable and unacceptable applications of a theory cannot be established. Even if such a metric were available, a degree of required similarity could be chosen only arbitrarily.[72]

More fundamentally, what would be the purpose of declaring that certain explanations or treatment procedures are not "true" applications of a particular theory because the required degree of similarity is lacking? A proposed extension of a theory has the status of a scientific hypothesis, and it should be judged by the same canons of evidence and clarity as any other hypothesis rather than by the degree of similarity between the new and old domains. If the extension meets these criteria, if it brings an increased degree of prediction and control to the phenomena of the new domain, and if the concepts can be applied with intersubjective agreement to the new domain, then the extrapolation is a success.

Indeed, extension to a new domain is one of the hallmarks of a great scientific theory, and it occurs because gifted scientists make use of the models, analogies, and metaphors accompanying the formal parts of a theory. Far from being pejorative, the adjectives "metaphorical" and "analogical" are at the very core of the best scientific thought.[73] A heuristically fertile theoretical concept is open in the sense that its meaning develops as it is applied to new domains. Thus the extrapolations involved in behaviorist empirical interpretations ought not to be rejected on *a priori* grounds as "metaphorical" but should be empirically evaluated as scientific hypotheses.[74]

The Mental as Hypothetical Construct

Another behaviorist approach to mental language is the view that mental concepts are theoretically reducible to covert events which are hypothetical constructs in a behavioral theory.[75] Because hypothetical constructs are conceived as physical events and are generally subject to the conditions discussed in chapter 4, the dualist connotations of mental language are eliminated. An advantage to this kind of behavioral interpretation is that it is consistent with everyday intuitions. "Jones is angry" is interpreted to refer to something currently occurring in Jones which is responsible for his behavior.[76] Statements about Jones' thoughts are interpreted in a similar way as statements about events inside Jones.[77] Furthermore, mental explanations may be regarded as causal explanations. "Jones pounded the table because he was angry" is understood as explaining Jones' outward behavior as the effect of prior covert events. On this type of behavioral interpretation, the differences between behaviorism and neomentalism are attenuated. The major remaining difference is that in the former, the internal causes of behavior are usually conceived as having the properties of overt behavior while in the latter, they are functional states not restricted in this way.

Although the use of hypothetical constructs in behavioral interpretation offers several advantages, it is open to problems of its own. First, it undermines the common behaviorist solution to the problem of other minds. If mental concepts refer to aspects of behavior, then "other minds" are observable, and the problem is solved.[78] However, if mental concepts refer to internal events, then the ascription of mental terms is an inference that must be justified.

Nevertheless, the behaviorist inference is on stronger ground than the dualist's. For the latter, internal process can be known only by the person in whose mind the process is taking place. Others can know of it only by analogy from their own consciousness, and the weaknesses of this "argument from analogy" are well known.[79] In contrast, the hypothetical constructs of the behaviorist are presumed to be physical events inside the body which are in principle publicly observable under the right circumstances. The inference is not from the consciousness of the observer to the consciousness of the observed actor, but from observed behavior to potentially observable internal events which can explain the behavior.

A second problem with identifying the mental with hypothetical covert stimuli and responses is that such behavioral interpretations tend to confuse dispositions with episodes. Stimuli and responses are generally conceived as episodic, and occurrences such as "sharp pain in the elbow" or "mentally calculating a sum" might therefore plausibly refer to covert stimuli or responses. However, to say that Jones has certain beliefs, interests, or qualities of character is not to say anything about current episodes in Jones' behavior, covert or overt. Instead these are dispositional concepts reporting about tendencies, potentialities, and patterns in Jones' behavior. Nevertheless, some behaviorists interpret dispositional concepts, including urges, opinions, beliefs, intentions, and determination (as a quality of character), as episodic covert responses.[80]

This type of behavioral interpretation is an example of what Ryle calls a "category mistake."[81] Ryle's attack on this logical error of treating dispositional mental concepts as episodes in his exorcising the "myth of the ghost in the machine" applies equally well to what might be termed the "myth of covert response in the machine." Beliefs, desires, and interests are things individuals possess continuously, even while engaged in unrelated activities or while sleeping. Covert responses, however, are not conceptualized as functioning this way. Furthermore, covert responses may themselves express a belief, occur intentionally, or be motivated, and an infinite regress is generated if additional covert processes must be postulated to explain these characteristics. Of course, dispositions may be theoretically identified with physiological *states* of the organism, but state variables are distinct from stimulus and response.[82]

For all its problems, the theoretical identification of the mental with covert hypothetical constructs has one great asset. Thus far, the analysis of behavioral interpretation has treated the application of mental concepts to others, or what is termed "third-person reports." With a third-person report it is plausible to interpret "Jones is angry" in terms of Jones' behavior, for that is all the speaker really has direct access to. Covert responses or processes of consciousness are unobserved by the speaker. However, what of the first-person report? If *Jones* says "I am angry" it is less plausible to say he is referring to his behavior, but it makes sense to say he is referring to covert events he has access to. Thus, first-person reports seem to support the identification of the mental with covert events while posing difficulties for other behavioral interpretations. This question of first-person reports will be addressed in the next chapter.

CONCLUSION

Behaviorist conceptual treatments of mentalistic language facilitate the acceptance of behaviorism. In their therapeutic role, they cure us of dualism and make behaviorism appear more plausible by showing that it is compatible with our everyday speech. However, these conceptual behavioral interpretations are not unassailable. As proposals about the meaning of mental concepts, they are basically philosophical theses. They are therefore open to philosophical attack not only with regard to their proposed interpretations but also their presupposed theories of meaning. For example, critics reject the theories of meaning assumed by logical, operational, and analytic behaviorism.

Because the philosophical question of the meaning of meaning will not readily be resolved, it is unlikely that conceptual behavioral interpretations will soon be firmly established. Fortunately, the validity of behaviorism as an approach to psychology is not dependent on the success of conceptual interpretations of natural language. A completed behaviorist theory will be validated by its own success in the prediction and control of behavior. The relationship of this theory to everyday mentalistic schema may not be of critical interest. Indeed, it may be so complicated that it will be deemed not worth determining.[83]

Empirical treatments of everyday mental concepts are not vulnerable to the same philosophical objections. Their weakness lies in their questionable extrapolations from the simple to the complex, from the known to the unknown. However, these extrapolations are not inherent features of empirical behavioral interpretations. As a science of behavior develops, the gap traversed by the extrapolations should shrink, and their legitimacy will be less open to doubt. At present, empirical behavioral interpretations, even with their dubious extrapolations, serve an important function. They help transform the rich and complex psychology of everyday speech into a heuristic to guide research and application into new areas.

CHAPTER 11

First-Person Reports

First-person reports seem to refer to conscious contents and pose a problem for behaviorism. According to logical behaviorism, the meaning of a first-person report consists only of the publicly observable conditions for verifying it, even though the speaker may not have to observe those conditions in order to make the report. According to operationism, first-person reports are merely verbal responses, and "sensation" is operationally defined as that which is measured by a set of publicly observable procedures.

Many behaviorists interpret first-person reports as verbal responses to discriminative stimuli. These stimuli may consist of overt behavior, environmental variables responsible for behavior, or covert events. Even under this interpretation, first-person reports are not scientific observations but are rather verbal behavior from which theoretical concepts such as intervening variables and hypothetical constructs can be inferred. One reason for not including first-person reports as scientific observations is that they are unreliably linked to their stimuli.

Behaviorists also interpret the first-person reports of "psychological measurement" which purports to measure "psychological," or "subjective" magnitudes. Under an intervening-variable interpretation, psychophysical experiments are like defining experiments in which the experimenter, not the subject, assigns a value to an intervening variable. The behavior of the subject can be explained as the transfer of verbal behavior from situations in which intersubjective rules are defined to a situation in which they are not. Under a hypothetical-construct interpretation, psychophysical judgments can be construed as responses to covert events. Nevertheless, it is an error to view the subject, rather than the experimenter, as measuring these covert events.

These interpretations of psychophysical scaling can be extended to cover a large body of research on "subjective experience." In general, these experiments can be understood as studying how subjects follow their "inclinations" in transferring intersubjec-

tive rules to new situations. These inclinations may constitute the quale of experience. Because these behaviorist interpretations account for subjective experience in terms of the relationship between behavior and the environment, they eliminate much of the rationale for the Copy Theory which says that we respond not to the world but to an internal copy of the world.

The preceding chapter reviewed a variety of behavioral interpretations of mentalistic language when it is used to describe the actions of others. This chapter will explore behaviorist treatments of mentalistic language when it is ascribed to oneself in first-person reports. The first problem for behaviorism is that in a first-person report such as "I am in pain," one appears to be referring to an aspect of one's conscious experience rather than to one's behavior or behavioral dispositions. Second, even if the implied dualism of first-person reports can be avoided, they must still be explained in ways that meet behaviorist standards of objectivity and empiricalness. First-person reports, after all, are behavior in the form of verbal responses and therefore fall in the domain the behaviorist is committed to explaining. Both these questions constitute the node of the behaviorist conceptual tree diagram to be examined in this chapter.

In discussing first-person reports it is important to distinguish between first-person reports in everyday conversation and those of classical introspectionism. Classical, or "analytic," introspectionism was a dominant school within psychology until the early part of this century. The behaviorist revolution was primarily a reaction to introspectionism, and therefore much behaviorist discussion of first-person reports is directed against analytic introspectionism rather than everyday first-person reports.[1]

Because analytic introspectionism was a highly developed methodology, its terms must be understood in their technical rather than their popular senses. Classical "introspection" is a special procedure designed to enable introspectors, after a great deal of training, to "inspect" the contents of their minds, namely, the elements of consciousness.[2] Titchener (1912), the leading American proponent of analytic introspectionism, explains his method in this way:

> In introspection we are describing a conscious process at first hand, or describing at first hand the representative memory of a past process. . . .
> The categories of description . . . are the last terms of analysis, the elementary processes and their attributes; and consciousness has been described when analysis is, qualitatively and quantitatively, complete. (pp. 494–495)

Thus, analytic introspection differs from everyday first-person reports in three important respects. First, it is considered a highly specialized form of scientific observation. Second, its objects are thought to be conscious elements described in a technical vocabulary different from conversational speech. Third, these elements are assumed to be the basic data of psychology. Behaviorists reject all three of these contentions. Note, however, that the rejection of analytic introspectionism has no logical bearing on everyday first-person reports.[3]

VERIFICATIONIST TREATMENTS

Logical Behaviorism

As described in the preceding chapter, for logical behaviorism, the meaning of a statement is to be found in the conditions for verifying it. Therefore, there is a distinction between the method of arriving at first-person reports and the meaning of those reports. Logical behaviorists admit that people can make statements about themselves intuitively without observing their own behavior, but the *meaning* of these statements involves only the publicly observable conditions constituting the verification of the statement. Therefore, the meaning of first-person statements consists of statements about the observable behavior (including verbal behavior) and physiological states of the subject who makes the statement, even though the subject need not have observed either of these in order to have made the statement. Carnap (1932–1933/1959) states the position:

> The meaning of a sentence, no matter how obtained, can unequivocally be determined by a logical analysis of the way in which it is derived and tested. A psychologist who adopts the method of . . . "introspection". . . . admits sentences of the form "I have experienced such and such events of consciousness" into his experiment-protocol. . . . But . . . we must conclude . . . that the . . . sentences must be interpreted physically. . . . If A's protocol sentence . . . were not subject to a physical interpretation, it could not be tested by B, and would, thus, be meaningless to B. (pp. 192–194)

Thus, logical behaviorism permits introspection as a method of observation for psychology but denies that this method provides scientific knowledge about private events. Instead, it furnishes science with the same information about publicly available events that can in principle be supplied by other forms of observation.[4]

Malcolm presents an application of the verificationist argument, from an analytic behaviorist perspective, that is of interest because it is so counterintuitive.[5] He notes that it is logically impossible to verify the occurrence of a dream other than by a first-person report. Therefore, the telling of a dream is the "criterion" of having dreamed. However, Jones' report about his dream experiences is not a criterion for his actually having had those experiences because the latter event cannot be distinguished from his simply having the *impression* that he had those experiences. Therefore, his having had certain experiences during the dream cannot logically be verified, and the statement that a dream consists of certain experiences is meaningless. The same is true for statements about the duration, contents, or time of occurrence of a dream. Hence, a first-person report about a dream is not a report about private experiences that occurred during sleep. For Malcolm, it has the same meaning as Jones' reporting that he awoke with certain convictions which proved false and he readily concluded that he was only dreaming.[6] According to Malcolm, sleep researchers who use rapid-eye-movements and brain electrical recordings to detect the time and duration of dreams are not measuring what is normally meant by "dreaming." Rather by proposing physiological measures as new criteria for "dreaming" they have established a new concept.[7]

Operationism

The verificationism of logical behaviorism is the operationism of psychological behaviorism. Operationist analyses of first-person reports are most clearly illustrated in the treatment of psychophysics. In a psychophysical experiment, a subject is typically asked to judge the psychological attributes of stimuli—e.g., the loudness of a tone. On the operationist interpretation of psychophysics, private observation must be excluded since all operations must be intersubjectively observable. Therefore, the first-person report in the psychophysical experiment is conceived as nothing more than discriminatory behavior—that is, behavior which is differential with respect to physical stimuli. "Sensations" are not private events reported by the subject but are rather concepts operationally defined as that which is measured in psychophysical experiments by means of the observable operations of instructions, stimuli presentation, and the subject's verbal behavior.[8] Stevens (1935b) develops the operationist interpretation of psychophysics in these terms:

> Since sensation cannot refer to any private or inner aspect of consciousness which does not show itself in any overt manner, it must exhibit itself to an experimenter as a differential reaction on the part of the organism. . . .
>
> from the point of view of science we never find *red* as such; we find only such situations as *man sees red, i.e.*, an organism discriminates. Thus the *sensation red* is a term used to denote an "objective" *process* or event which is public and which is observable. . . .
>
> We find operationally that when we present a given stimulus to an observer we may get a discriminatory reaction in terms of any one of several aspects of the stimulus. . . .
>
> Therefore, we apply a different name to each of these several classes of reaction. (p. 524)

Thus, operationism solves the problem posed by first-person reports by treating them as mere verbal responses, to be explained, just as any other bit of behavior, and not as indicants of private experience.

First-Person Report as Artifact

If first-person reports are regarded as mere verbal behavior then it is questionable whether they are to be considered as reports altogether. Some behaviorists suggest that the behavior constituting a first-person report does not, in fact, reflect the occurrence of other events, whether internal or external. Instead, it is argued, this verbal behavior is often an artifact of certain unusual situations. For example, in the analytic introspectionist experiment, the verbal behavior may be a product solely of the long and intensive training undergone by the subject prior to the experiment. During this training, the subject is taught what is and what is not valid introspection (cf. the "stimulus error") and learns a technical and rather esoteric terminology. The verbal behavior of the subject is thus molded in the desired direction, so that under the instructions and stimuli peculiar to the introspective experiment, verbalizations such as "sensation," "image," and "impalpable awareness" emerge.[9] Similarly, it is claimed that in psychoanalysis, the analyst implicitly shapes the verbal behavior of the patient, and as a result responses about the patient's unconscious are supposedly emitted.[10] However, neither the responses of the analytic introspector nor those of the psychoanalytic patient are reports about unobserved processes. Instead, they are behaviors shaped by observable environmental conditions.[11]

Although this approach solves the problem of first-person reports, it is clearly only a partial solution at best. Although undoubtedly explicit and implicit rewards greatly influence the verbal behavior of the introspector and the patient, it is unlikely that these are the *only* important variables. Furthermore, even if it could be shown that in *some* cases a first-person report can be explained solely in terms of the shaping of verbal behavior, it is unlikely that *no* first-person report ever depends on the object it reports about.

FIRST-PERSON REPORTS AS DISCRIMINATIONS

If first-person reports are not pure artifacts, then they may correspond in some way to the objects or events they appear to report. Many behaviorists interpret this relationship between first-person report and the object of the report as the relationship between a verbal discriminative response and the discriminative stimulus for that response. The exact nature of the discriminative stimulus depends on the circumstances, and behaviorists propose a variety of theories to account for the range.

Aspects of Behavior as Discriminative Stimuli

For some first-person reports, the discriminative stimuli may be the reporter's own overt behavior.[12] Statements such as "I did not realize how hungry

I was until I started eating," or "I was unaware of how anxious I was until it was pointed out to me that I was clenching my jaw," are evidence that we sometimes come to self knowledge by discriminating our own behavior. Often when people report on their interests, motives, and character, they are reporting on what they have learned about themselves from their own behavior. In all these cases, the first-person report can be understood as based on the same facts as a third-person report. Because people have better access to their own behavior than do others, first-person reports may have some advantage over third-person reports, but this difference is not of any systematic importance.

Skinner suggests that first-person reports of images may also be understood as discriminations of behavior.[13] He argues that perceiving is a kind of learned behavior. Normally it occurs in the presence of the distal object perceived. However, because that behavior is a function of a number of other independent variables, it may occur in the absence of the distal object, and the person is said to be having an "image." As Skinner (1963a) explains:

> The heart of the behaviorist position on conscious experience may be summed up in this way: seeing does not imply something seen. We acquire the behavior of seeing under stimulation from actual objects, but it may occur in the absence of these objects under the control of other variables. . . . We also acquire the behavior of seeing-that-we-are-seeing when we are seeing actual objects, but it may also occur in their absence. (p. 955)

Thus a first-person report of a visual image may be construed as a discrimination of seeing-behavior rather than of a mental picture. If the seeing-behavior is covert, then the report is a discriminative response to a private event of the sort to be discussed below.

Other first-person reports seem to resist such an interpretation. Reports of thoughts and intentions, for example, do not appear to be discriminations of behavior. In these cases, some behaviorists suggest, the discriminative stimuli are subtle features of overt behavior, including the behavior of the report itself. For example, the first-person report "I think that is Smith standing by the pool" need not be understood as a report about an internal event, the thought. Instead it can be interpreted as a discrimination of the strength of the response "That is Smith standing by the pool." The autoclitic frame "I think . . ." represents a discrimination of the weakness of the response.[14] Similarly, the first-person response "I remember Smith was at the pool yesterday" need not be construed as a report of an internal memory image. Instead it can be interpreted as an autoclitic discrimination that the response "Smith was at the pool yesterday" is being emitted under the control of a stimulus no longer present.[15]

Discriminations of independent variables can also account for first-person reports which appear to concern behavior not yet emitted. For example, statements of intention such as "I intend to leave" may be explained as discriminations of the independent variables that are about to produce the behavior. Similarly, statements of purpose may be discriminations of the history of reinforcement responsible for the present behavior. In both these examples, the statements do not report internal mental processes of intention or purpose but are rather responses to environmental stimuli.[16]

In other situations, certain first-person reports are interpreted as functioning as independent variables themselves rather than reports of independent variables. People learn, for example, that by stating an intention, they make it more likely that the intended action will be carried out.[17] Under this interpretation the first-person report serves as a discriminative stimulus rather than a discriminative response, and there is no need to find a stimulus referent for it.

Covert Events as Discriminative Stimuli

A common behaviorist interpretation of first-person reports is to construe them as verbal discriminative responses to covert stimuli.[18] As noted above in chapter 4, many behaviorist theories postulate hypothetical constructs in the form of covert events. These covert events may serve as stimuli for the verbal responses that constitute first-person reports. For example, "I am hungry" can be interpreted as a verbal response to covert stimuli arising from stomach contractions, and "I am in pain" as a response to internal stimuli associated with tissue damage.[19]

First-person reports may also come under the control of the stimulus consequences of covert responses. Thus, if thinking is postulated to consist of implicit responses as described in chapter 8, then a first-person report of an episodic thought can be viewed as a verbal response to an implicit response series.[20] Similarly, if perception is postulated to involve a covert perceptual response, then "I see the apple" may be understood as a discrimination of this internal response.

The postulation of covert perceptual responses suggests an explanation for first-person reports of images. Under normal circumstances, a first-person perceptual report involves three events: (1) a distal stimulus (e.g., the apple) which produces (2) the covert perceptual response which evokes (3) the verbal response "I see the apple." Ordinarily, the distal stimulus is the primary determinant of the covert perceptual response. However, this response is a function of other variables as well, and it can therefore occur in the absence of the distal stimulus. When it does, it may evoke the verbal response "I see the apple," and we can say the person is having an image. If the person also discriminates the absence of the distal stimulus when the covert perceptual response occurs, then the first-person report may be "I have an image of the apple." Dreams, hallucinations, and memory images can similarly be explained as due to perceptual responses in the absence of external stimuli.[21]

Acquisition. A major problem for these theories is to explain how humans can acquire verbal responses to stimuli hidden from their language teachers. Skinner proposes one theory, according to which language is acquired when verbal communities establish contingencies of reinforcement for verbal responses.[22] When reinforcement for a verbal response is made contingent on the presence of a particular overt stimulus, that stimulus eventually comes to exert fairly precise discriminative control over the response, and the occurrence of the verbal response, or "tact," is a reliable indicator of the stimulus. In establishing reinforcement contingencies, the verbal community must by necessity use public stimuli, the only ones it has access to. Therefore, in teaching verbal responses (e.g., "I am in pain") to private stimuli, the verbal community must make reinforcement contingent on public accompaniments of the covert stimulation. These include both environmental events (e.g., a pin stuck in the finger) and the subject's own behavior (e.g., crying) which correlate with the private stimuli. Through this method, the verbal response comes under the control of both the private stimuli and the concurrent public stimuli. Eventually the private stimuli alone are sufficient to evoke the verbal response. Alternatively, a verbal response under the control of public stimuli may transfer to control by covert stimulation, either because the covert stimuli share common components with the overt (e.g., the private stimulus is produced by a small-scale version of an overt response) or the two are similar.

Thus, Skinner's analysis begins with behavior in response to the external world, and responses to the internal world of private stimuli are a later product of social training. This contrasts sharply with traditional epistemological approaches which begin with knowledge of the self from which knowledge of the external world is constructed. For Skinner, self knowledge—knowledge of one's own feelings, motives, intentions, etc.—is the result of a long history of discrimination training carried out by a verbal community.[23]

In most complex cases, self knowledge is not the simple discrimination of a covert event. Whether a covert stimulus is reported as a pang of remorse or a twinge of jealousy may depend on a discrimination of the context in which that covert event occurs. The most important aspects of that context consist of the independent variables controlling the covert event, as well as the overt behavior and behavioral dispositions ensuing from it. Thus, the functional role of a covert event may determine how that event is described and known.[24]

Analytic Introspection. Behaviorists also interpret the first-person reports of analytic introspectionism as verbal responses to obscure internal stimuli arising chiefly in the muscles and tendons.[25] Weiss is illustrative of this approach.[26] He notes that the subject in analytic introspection is usually given two tasks. The first task, the "major reaction," involves an overt response.

For example, the subject is asked to name objects as they are presented. The second task is to "introspect" during the first task. Weiss suggests that the original learning of the major reaction (the subject's previous learning of the names of the objects) is accompanied by what he terms "auxiliary processes," consisting of obscure internal effector processes that play only a minor role in the learning process. During the introspection experiment, when the major reaction occurs, it reinstates, by association, "residuals" of these auxiliary processes, and these constitute the "minor reaction." In introspecting, the subject is responding to this set of reinstated residuals. Thus, rather than analyzing the conscious content of the major reaction, introspection merely reveals a group of unimportant effector reactions that accompany the major reaction.

Report Versus Discriminative Response

For those theories which construe first-person reports as discriminations of stimuli, it would seem natural to view the verbal responses as reports which convey information about the stimuli. In particular, verbal responses to covert stimuli should qualify as observational reports about those inner events. However, as discussed in chapter 2, behaviorists do not accept verbal reports about inner events as valid data reports for science. What then is their status for a science of behavior?

For most behaviorists, the first-person report is treated as a datum rather than as a report of a datum. The subject's first-person report, R_1, e.g., "I am in pain," is of a lower logical order of discourse than the experimenter's third-person report, R_2, "Smith said, 'I am in pain.' " A description of the object of R_2 (i.e., Smith's behavior) enters the behavioral data language, while the putative object of R_1 (i.e., a covert stimulus inside Smith) does not. Talk of the covert stimulus can enter scientific discourse only via the theoretical language. That is, the experimenter can use R_2 of the behavioral data language to infer, or postulate, a hypothetical construct. Thus, the first-person report functions as a datum from which covert events are *inferred* rather than an observational report of those events.[27] Spence concisely summarizes the logical status of first-person reports:

> [The behavior scientist] accepts verbal response as just one more form of behavior and he proposes to use this type of data in exactly the same manner as he does other types of behavior variables. Thus he attempts to discover laws relating verbal responses to environmental events of the past or present. . . . He also makes use of them as a basis for making inferences as to certain hypothetical or theoretical constructs. . . . which presumably represent internal or covert activities. (1948, p. 70; also 1956, p. 15)

This distinction is not without pragmatic import. Were first-person reports construed as observational reports, then scientific statements about the covert events would have to conform to those reports. However, since R_1 is merely a datum, from whose description, R_2, an inference, R_3, is drawn, R_3 does not have to correspond to R_1. That is, in attributing properties to the hypothetical construct, the experimenter is not constrained by what the subject has to say in the first-person report.[28] In fact, R_1 may be just one of a number of data from which R_3 is inferred. First-person reports are not incorrigible guides to covert events, and inferences are drawn by the experimenter, not the subject.

The Unreliability of First-Person Reports. Skinner, on the other hand, can be interpreted as maintaining that covert events, or "private events," are observed stimuli rather than inferred hypothetical constructs.[29] Nevertheless, he, in fact, does not make use of first-person reports as observational reports for a science of behavior because he considers them to be unreliable discriminations of private events. As noted above, Skinner hypothesizes that the verbal community establishes first-person reports by contingencies of reinforcement that rely on public correlates of private stimuli. However, in the absence of the public correlates, the verbal community cannot be certain that the private discriminative stimulus for the first-person report is consistent. With no public stimuli to serve as guides, the verbal community cannot maintain precise contingencies to ensure a rigid discriminative relationship between the verbal response and the private stimuli.[30] Therefore, the association between the verbal response and the private stimulus cannot be considered a reliable one, and first-person reports are not to be used as observational reports of private stimuli.

Distrust of first-person reports stems also from the fact that, like all responses, first-person reports are affected by variables other than the discriminative stimulus. For example, a person who reports having a headache may gain certain benefits in the form of attention and escape from responsibilities. Hence reports of headaches may come under the control of these conditions of reward rather than the private event that is assumed to be the discriminative stimulus for these reports. In the absence of public criteria, the verbal community has only limited control over these distortions in discriminative control of first-person reports.[31]

Yet another reason for behaviorist distrust of first-person reports is that they often misrepresent the causal role of private events. To the reporter, the private events responded to in first-person reports seem to be the major cause of overt behavior. In everyday conversation one might say, "I stammered because I felt so anxious," thus explaining overt behavior as the effect of certain feelings. However, many behaviorists deny that the private events acting as the discriminative stimuli for first-person reports are the causes of overt behavior. They contend that these private events are mere accompaniments of the overt behavior. Both the covert events and the overt behavior are the effects of the same environmental independent variables, and are thus "collateral byproducts" of those variables rather than causally related to one another.[32] In contrast, the physiological processes which truly mediate behavior do not function as discriminative stimuli for first-person reports.[33]

The Role of First-Person Reports in Research. Because first-person reports are unreliably related to private events, are usually given a dualistic interpretation, and do not reflect the true determinants of overt behavior, behaviorists generally make little use of them in their science of behavior. Indeed, the study of private events through first-person reports is usually regarded as a worthless diversion from the study of overt behavior, the proper subject matter of the behaviorist science.[34]

This orientation expresses itself in many aspects of behaviorist research methodology. Whenever possible, behaviorists prefer to supply subjects with an experimentally controlled learning history rather than to ask subjects to report their pre-experimental history. Similarly, behaviorist methodology opposes asking subjects how they think they would respond to certain situations rather than exposing them to those conditions and observing the actual results. In a like manner, behavior therapists ascribe more value to observations of change in a client's overt target behavior than to the client's verbal report about changes. Thus, although first-person reports are given a behavioral interpretation and, for some behaviorists, are linked to private events, first-person reports play only a minor role in behaviorist research.[35] Distrust of first-person reports and their deemphasis in research are family traits of behaviorism.

Although behaviorists generally tend to exclude first-person reports from their finished theories, or what Reichenbach calls the "context of justification,"[36] some use such reports as a heuristic in the "context of discovery." That is, they find first-person reports (including those of the theorist) to be suggestive of fruitful hypotheses that can be tested without further recourse to the reports.[37] Within the context of discovery, or theorizing, these reports and scientific hypotheses are related neither by formal inference nor as evidence to hypothesis. Rather they are related psychologically. A first-person report somehow inspires a creative mind to formulate a hypothesis which proves useful.

Objections

Interpretations under which a first-person report is construed as a discriminative response are congenial to S-R psychology. They suggest that the discriminative stimuli for first-person reports are physical, conform to behavioral laws, and are not the conscious contents of the experiential world. Nevertheless, these interpretations are subject to a number of criticisms.

Knowledge without Observation. A common objection to the discrimination interpretation of first-person reports is that it seems to base first-person reports on observation. That is, it appears to imply that in order for one to say "I am in pain," or "I intend to go" one must first observe stimuli, either overt or covert. This, however, is contrary to the normal use of such expressions. People issue first-person reports with neither observation nor inference, and anyone who based such reports on observational evidence ("From the moans I am emitting, I gather that I am in pain") would be regarded as not understanding the basic concepts involved.[38]

Although this objection is correct in asserting that first-person reports are rarely based on observation, it is mistaken in equating discrimination with observation. As noted in chapter 3, not every response to a stimulus is an observation of that stimulus, nor is every verbal response to a stimulus a report of that stimulus. Only when a response plays a certain role in a particular context is it either an observation or a report. Therefore, a first-person report may be a response to a stimulus, overt or covert, even though the person cannot be said either to be observing the stimulus, or to be reporting it.[39]

An illustration makes this point clear. It is well known that our ability to report the location of a sound source depends on our discriminating differences in sound waves between the two ears in phase, arrival time, and intensity. Yet, in no sense do we "observe" those differences and infer a sound's location. Nor is our report on the sound's location a report about those differences. What we may be said to observe and report is the location of the sound. In fact, few people can report anything about the acoustical properties of the sound wave which determine the report. Thus, just as verbal reports of sound location are responses to stimuli which are neither observed nor reported, so first-person reports may be responses to stimuli which are neither observed nor reported.[40]

Meaning in the Object Language. A second objection arises over whether first-person reports are meaningful statements. As noted above, in the typical behaviorist paradigm, the first-person report is treated as a verbal response, R_1, rather than an observational report. The experimenter's observational report, R_2, which describes R_1 as well as the experimenter's statement, R_3, about a hypothetical construct inferred from R_2, are in what Bergmann and Spence call the "pragmatic meta-language" while the subject's R_1 is in the "object language."[41] Critics of the behaviorist position charge that if R_1 is to be regarded as just behavior rather than a report of inner events, then it should be treated as mere noises and movements of facial muscles rather than meaningful discourse. Yet, in practice, behaviorists do not regard R_1 as mere movements since they base their inferences, R_3, on the *meaning* of R_1.[42]

The sense in which behaviorists treat R_1 as meaningful is that the responses constituting the first-person report are classified not on the basis of their topography or acoustical properties but on their meaning. Thus, the verbal responses "I am in great pain" and "It hurts a lot" are likely to be classified in the same response class although acoustically and topographically they may be less similar than "It hurts a lot" and "It hurts a little," which are likely to be classified in different response classes. The objection is to this sort of response classification of the object language.

To reply to this objection, the classification must be defended on two levels. First, an important justification for a response class criterion is that it results in more orderly functional relationships in the behavioral data (chapter 3). Clearly this justification is applicable here. In psychophysics, for example, some of the most orderly and comprehensive laws in psychology are derived by classifying responses by meaning. Psychophysical laws are based on experiments in which subjects emit a variety of responses such as pressing a telegraph key, saying "yes" or "no," turning a knob, matching a comparison stimulus to a standard stimulus, stating "more" and "less," and so forth. All these responses are classified on the basis of meaning, not similarity of movement, and the results are elegant and orderly scientific laws. Therefore, on this level, classification by meaning is methodologically justified by its consequences.

On a second level, the behaviorist must justify this practice by appeal to plausibility argument, described in chapter 10. A subject entering an experiment involving first-person reports arrives with a long history of verbal behavior that is neither known nor capable of being reconstructed. Nevertheless, the behaviorist argues that it is plausible that the American who says "yes" in a psychophysical experiment has had a history of verbal behavior that is similar enough in relevant respects to the German who says "ja" so that "yes" and "ja" are functionally equivalent in that they play similar roles in functional laws.

In the same way, the behaviorist must appeal to a plausibility argument in assuming that instructions can make pressing a telegraph key and saying "yes" functionally equivalent because of the subject's unknown history in learning to follow instructions. In effect, the plausibility argument claims that were the verbal behavior history of the subject known completely, first-person responses could be treated as mere responses and classified on the basis of their functional relationship to environmental independent and dependent variables. Such a classification would result in roughly the same categories as those based on meaning. In the absence of such thorough knowledge of the subject's history, classification by meaning is the only practical alternative, although it is eliminable in principle.[43]

Awareness. Behaviorist interpretations of first-person reports as response-to-stimulus are often criticized for failing to fully capture the notion of self knowledge. When we report our thoughts, feelings, and intentions, it seems as if more is involved than a conditioned response to a stimulus. A rat's lever press to the presentation of a light is also a discrimination of a stimulus, yet we do not attribute to the rat an awareness of the light. In short, conscious awareness seems to be missing from behaviorist accounts of first-person reports.

To remedy this situation, some behaviorists have suggested a more complex sort of discrimination to accommodate instances of conscious awareness. Consider a simple discrimination without conscious awareness. In the presence of a particular distal stimulus, an apple for example, a subject emits a discriminative response, R. This R might be the verbal response, or tact, "apple." Now assume that the simple discriminative response, R, itself becomes the stimulus for yet a second discriminative response R*. The subject now says "I am aware of an apple." According to some behaviorists, this discrimination of a discrimination, or "second-order discrimination," constitutes awareness.[44] If R consists of perceptual behavior, then R* might be, "I see an apple." If R is a response to a covert autonomic event, then R* might be "I feel anger."

Although the distinction between first-order and second-order discriminations may be an important one for understanding how certain discriminations are acquired and maintained, it does not adequately solve the problem of awareness. Whether a discrimination is first-order or second-order, it is still a response-to-stimulus. If a first-order discrimination can be made automatically without conscious awareness, there is no reason why a second-order discrimination cannot also be made automatically and without awareness. The only difference between the two types of discrimination is that in the second-order discrimination, the discriminative stimulus is the person's own behavior. Why should this difference in the nature of the discriminative stimulus ensure that the discriminative response is made with awareness? There are many instances, such as sleepwalking or absentminded car driving, in which we react to our own behavior, but without awareness of having done so. It appears that conscious awareness cannot be identified solely with second-order discriminations.[45]

Another possibility is that awareness is a dispositional state. We say the sleepwalker and the absentminded driver are unaware of their behavior because when asked about their actions, they are unable to report anything about them. Answers to questions are relevant to awareness because these answers are a manifestation of a disposition—i.e., the ability to answer a variety of questions about activities and to take other actions with respect to those activities. Hence to do X with awareness is to do X while prepared to do a, b, c, . . . should certain circumstances arise.[46] Similarly, to discriminate Y with awareness is to discriminate Y while in a dispositional state to take a variety of actions with respect to Y and the discriminative response to Y, should the occasion arise.

Neural Identity Theory

The hypothetical-construct interpretation of first-person reports maintains, as described above, that they are discriminations of covert events. According to the neural identity theory, states of consciousness are identical to certain brain states.[47] Thus the brain states of neural identity theory and the covert events of the hypothetical-construct interpretation appear to have much in common. Nevertheless, there are important conceptual differences between the two.

First, the brain states of neural identity theory are introduced to explain states of consciousness while the covert stimuli of the hypothetical-construct interpretation are postulated to explain the behavior of first-person reports. States of consciousness do not enter the latter account. (Ironically, by ignoring states of consciousness in this way, the hypothetical-construct interpretation leaves itself open to the dualist argument that the discrimination of covert events is mediated by conscious awareness just as is the discrimination of overt stimuli.)[48]

Second, covert stimuli are assumed to function as do overt stimuli. Just as an overt stimulus can occur and fail to be discriminated, so a covert stimulus may occur without its being discriminated. Therefore, for the occurrence of a sensation or an awareness of a feeling, it is necessary that a discriminative response occur in addition to the covert stimulus. In contrast, according to the neural identity theory, the occurrence of the brain state is sufficient for the occurrence of the sensation or feeling. The remaining relationship between the brain state and the first-person report is left unclear.

From this second difference between the two views, a third immediately follows. Since under the hypothetical-construct interpretation a discriminative response is necessary for the having of a sensation and yet can take any number of forms, depending on the subject's learning history, the physiological processes which mediate the having of a sensation or feeling can be identified only functionally—that is, by the role they play—rather than anatomically.[49] Therefore, the hypothetical-construct interpretation is incompatible with any token-identity theory which identifies the having of a sensation with particular brain events anatomically described.

The Discrimination of Dispositions

As discussed in chapter 4, not all behaviorists are willing to admit hypothetical constructs into the behaviorist science. The alternative is to treat mental terms as referring to behavioral dispositions or intervening variables. Hence, a first-person report such as "I am hungry" is a report of a disposition to behave or an intervening variable. Problems arise, however, in explaining the occurrence of this report. If dispositions and intervening variables are strictly conceptual in nature then how can they serve as discriminative stimuli for first-person reports?[50]

One possibility is that in reporting one's own dispositional state, one is discriminating the environmental independent variables which determine the value of the intervening variable. For example, to state "I am hungry" is to respond discriminatively to features of the environment such as number of hours of deprivation. Alternatively, the report may be a discriminative response to the dependent variables of the intervening variable—i.e., the overt behaviors which are the "realization" of the intervening variable. For example, "I am hungry" is possibly a discriminative response to the overt behaviors which change as the value of the hunger-intervening-variable changes.

An Alternative to Discrimination Interpretations

A third answer is to abandon the model of response-to-stimulus for first-person reports and to construct a different schema for the relationship between first-person report and intervening variable. Consider a nonverbal response such as a rat's pressing a lever for food. This response is a function of the hunger-intervening-variable. Increasing the hours of food deprivation, for example, increases the value of the hunger-intervening-variable and the rate of lever pressing. Thus, rate of lever pressing is one of the dependent variables that manifest the hunger-intervening-variable, and it joins this set through learning.

Although rate of lever pressing is a function of the hunger-intervening-variable, it is not conceptualized as a discrimination of that intervening variable, nor is it regarded as a discrimination of the independent variables such as hours of food deprivation. Not every feature of the environment controlling the lever press is considered a discriminative stimulus for that response. Only when the control is acquired in a particular way and when it conforms to certain behavioral laws is the control "discriminative."

This nondiscriminative relationship between lever pressing on the one side and the hunger-intervening-variable and the independent variables on the other side can serve as a model for first-person reports. Consider the report "I am angry" as analogous to lever pressing and the anger-intervening-variable as analogous to the hunger-intervening-variable. The preverbal child is said to be "angry"—i.e., have a high value on the anger-intervening-variable—on the basis of its nonverbal overt behavior and the environmental independent variables present. The anger-independent-variable is a concept that represents the relationship among these observations, and in teaching the child to say "I am angry" the verbal community must rely on these public stimuli. As a result of this training, the verbal response "I am angry" joins the set of behaviors which manifest the anger-intervening-variable. Just as it is not necessary for the rat to discriminate hours of food deprivation or the hunger-intervening-variable in order to determine its rate of lever pressing, so the child does not have to discriminate the anger-intervening-variable (or the independent variables of which it is a function) in order to emit the verbal response "I am angry." That verbal response is simply one of the behaviors which covaries with the anger-intervening-variable in the same way that screaming and kicking do.[51] Just as screaming and kicking are functions of the anger-intervening-variable but are not discriminations of it, so is "I am angry."

Incorrigibility. This analysis has interesting implications for the logical status of a first-person report. If "I am angry" is viewed as one of the dependent variables for the anger-intervening-variable then it is a manifestation of a disposition as well as a report of it. In their first-person reports people are not only describing their dispositions, they are also expressing them.[52] This first-person case contrasts with the third-person use of "Smith is angry." On a dispositional analysis, the latter statement is a report about Smith's behavioral dispositions but cannot be an expression of it. Therefore, the first-person object language in which the first-person report, R_1, occurs must be distinguished from the third-person pragmatic meta-language in which the experimenter reports the subject's intervening variable. The latter is based on an observation while the former involves neither inference nor observation.

This distinction helps clarify the "incorrigibility" of first-person reports. In the pragmatic meta-language, it is always possible for the experimenter to err in measuring the value of the subject's intervening variable. In contrast, there is a sense in which the subject cannot logically be mistaken in first-person reports expressed in the object language. Recall the defining experiment discussed in chapter 4. Under the appropriate experimental conditions, a particular measure of a behavioral variable is taken as defining the value of the intervening variable. Logically there can be no question as to the validity of the measurement because the assumed relationship between the value of the intervening variable and the value of the dependent variable is true by stipulation rather than empirical discovery. For example, a rat's rate of lever pressing (or a mathematical transformation of it) under the appropriate conditions might *by definition* be taken as a measure of the hunger-intervening-variable. The rat's response rate is thus an "incorrigible" measure of hunger.

In a like manner, one of the dependent variables of the anger-intervening-variable might be taken as the defining measure and thereby become incorrigible in the same sense. If first-person reports, or avowals, are given the greatest weight, as they usually are in human affairs, then they cannot be mistaken in the same way as third-person reports of intervening variables. Under the appropriate circumstances a first-person report logically defines the person's psychological state. This incorrigibility is not the result of the person's excellent ability to discriminate psychological states. Rather it is a consequence of the logic of the intervening variable.

Nor does this incorrigibility mean that the report is infallible. The first-person report incorrigibly determines the intervening variable only under the appropriate circumstances. If the conditions are not appropriate then the report is not incorrigible. For example, if the first-person report "I am angry" is a function of variables other than those belonging to the anger-intervening-variable (e.g., the person is pretending to be angry), then the first-person report is not an infallible reflection of the anger-intervening-variable. In this sense, the first-person report can be true or false.[53]

PSYCHOLOGICAL MAGNITUDES

This review of behaviorist interpretations of first-person reports has dealt primarily with the first-person reports of everyday speech in which people converse about their feelings, thoughts, and emotions. Some of these interpretations can be extended to cover the first-person reports found in the large body of research on "psychological measurement" in which subjects are asked to judge their impressions of certain objects or events under controlled experimental conditions. From the results of these experiments, "psychological scales" are derived which are viewed as measurements of "subjective," or "psychological," magnitudes, often contrasted with the "physical" magnitudes measured by the natural sciences. The dualism implicit in this traditional interpretation of psychological scaling poses a problem for behaviorism.

Psychophysical Scaling

One important kind of psychological measurement is psychophysical scaling, in which first-person reports are used to measure "sensations" or "sensory magnitudes." On a traditional interpretation, it is assumed that a distal stimulus such as a tone produces certain sensations in the subject who then judges the sensation and reports its magnitude. From judgments of this sort, psychological scales such as "loudness" are derived. Loudness does not correspond to the physical dimensions of the tone, such as its intensity and frequency, and is often conceptualized as a dimension of the sensation rather than of the tone.[54] The equations relating a dimension of the sensation to the physical dimensions of the stimulus are known as "psychophysical functions."

An Intervening-Variable Interpretation. On an intervening-variable analysis the interpretation is quite different. The measurement of sensory magnitude and the construction of a psychological scale are performed by the experimenter in the pragmatic meta-language, not by the subject. The measurement procedure used by the experimenter consists of the conditions of the standard psychophysical scaling experiment, the responses (both verbal and nonverbal) of the subject, and certain transformations applied to the resulting data.[55] From the outcome of this measurement procedure a psychological scale is constructed and psychophysical functions are derived. That this procedure constitutes the measurement of sensory magnitudes is a stipulation.[56] It is the experimenter who decides what the conditions of the experiment shall be, what instructions to give the subject, and how to transform the subject's responses into a psychological scale.

The correlation between the subject's responses and the psychological scale is not an empirical finding or the result of the subject's incorrigible knowledge of sensations. It is rather a stipulation of the measurement procedure. The choice of stipulation is constrained only by theoretical considerations, such as the simplicity of the resulting theoretical structure, or what Stevens calls the "nomothetic imperative."[57] Under this interpretation, the psychophysical scaling procedure is a kind of defining experiment (chapter 4) stipulated to assign values to an intervening variable.

If the subject is not performing a measurement, then what *is* the subject doing? One explanation of the experiment is that the subject is engaged in a transfer of training experiment.[58] The subject's verbal responses were presumably acquired in the context of publicly observable stimuli in which the subject could learn of the correctness or incorrectness of reporting "more," "ten," "double," etc. Having learned these verbal responses in a context in which precise rules are enforced, the subject in the psychophysical experiment is transferring this training to another public context, one in which no rules have been defined. For example, a subject with a long training history in emitting the word "double" (e.g., saying when the number of books in one pile is "double" the number of books in another pile or when the distance to one tree is "double" the distance to another tree), must now transfer this training and say when one sound is "double" another sound without any instruction on what is a correct judgment. Under the psychophysicists's stipulation, the results of this transfer experiment are designated to be a critical step in a measurement procedure and are transformed into a psychological scale.

Under this interpretation, what is measured by the experimenter can be viewed either as an intervening variable or as an aspect of physical stimuli, namely their effect on an organism in a transfer experiment. This aspect is "psychological," or "subjective," only in that it involves the behavior of living subjects as an instrument for its measurement. Sensation as an inner experience measured by the subject is dispensed with.

A Hypothetical-Construct Interpretation. A second possible interpretation of psychophysical scaling is that the subject is responding to a covert stimulus produced by the distal stimulus. There are two ways to conceptualize the relationship between the subject's first-person reports and the covert stimuli.

The first is to apply the intervening-variable analysis reviewed above. Thus, the psychological magnitude measured by the experimenter can be construed either as an intervening variable relating verbal responses to covert stimuli or as an aspect of covert stimuli.

The second is to conceptualize the *subject* as performing the measurement of the covert stimulus. One common version of this view is that the subject is measuring the output of neural transducers. That is, energy from the distal stimulus impinges on neural receptors which then transform the input into neural impulses. The magnitude of these neural impulses is then judged and reported by the subject, and the resulting psychophysical function is therefore a direct reflection of the operating characteristic of the sensory transducer.[59]

In its substitution of covert physical events for traditional mental sensations, this interpretation would seem more in accordance with behaviorist leanings. However, this interpretation commits the same logical error as the mentalist theory. Both assume that measurement is possible in the absence of rules of measurement.[60]

Whether the stimuli judged are overt or covert, no rules of measurement are defined for the subjects of a psychophysical experiment. They are expected to follow their inclinations as to what is correct when they transfer their training from contexts in which rules do exist. In this respect they are like the speaker of a "private language," discussed in chapter 2. This speaker cannot logically be mistaken in applying a word because the "correct" application depends solely on the speaker's impression. Therefore, there is no rule and no language. Similarly, in a psychophysical experiment, subjects follow their impression and, under the proper test conditions, logically cannot be mistaken. Without notions of correct and incorrect, there is no rule, and therefore no measurement.

It is, of course, possible that lawful relationships can be found between the subject's judgments and certain aspects of covert stimuli, or neural firing, for which rules of measurement are defined. For example, the subject's judgments may be related to the frequency of neural firing, a dimension for which rules of measurement are defined. However, these relationships are psychophysical functions, not rules of measurement. They define functional stimulus classes (chapter 3) for the subject's verbal responses, but they are not rules followed by the subject.

The logical error is not in the search for such functions but in the assumption that the subject in psychophysical experiments is performing a measurement. Note that the logical error stems from the absence of a selected measurement rule and not from the covert nature of the assumed stimulus. Thus, even on the hypothetical-construct interpretation of first-person reports, psychophysical scaling must be construed as performed by the experimenter in the pragmatic meta-language, not by the subject.

Experience

This analysis of psychophysical scaling can be generalized to a large class of reports traditionally conceived as reports of "subjective experience." It is first necessary to distinguish between two kinds of reports. On the one hand are what will here be termed "objective reports." These are characterized by the fact that the reports can logically be described as "right" or "wrong," and correction by a third-person observer is possible in principle. Hence, the report may be said to be governed by a "public rule." Typically the ability to make reports of this sort is acquired through discrimination training with differential consequences for correct and incorrect responses. They are the kind of report one makes about the external environment, such as "The table is brown." For third-person correction of these reports to be possible, it is necessary that some of the discriminative stimuli for these reports have intersubjective meaning—that is, their referents are publicly observable, and the contents of the report can be understood by others.

"Subjective reports" are the second type to be distinguished. In order for these reports to function in human communication, it is necessary that they, too, use terms with intersubjective ties. If a person were to use a word that is in no way tied to public observables, the word would convey no information to others. What distinguishes subjective from objective reports is that the former consist of the transfer of verbal responses from contexts in which there are public rules for their use to contexts where there are no such rules. The speaker generalizes from the situations in which the terms were learned with public discriminative stimuli and correction to situations in which "right" and "wrong" have not been defined. Reporters respond in the way that they deem appropriate on the basis of their previous experience, and in this sense they may be said to be following "inclinations" rather than rules. Under the appropriate conditions, the report is taken as the result of the transfer, and there is no question of the report being "correct" or "incorrect," just as there is none when a pigeon's generalization gradient is tested along a wavelength continuum.

Examples of subjective reports can include an individual's description of private stimuli. For example, reports about afterimages, pains, feelings, and phenomenological experience are often subjective, because the reporter is transferring verbal responses acquired in one contest with a public rule to another context in which no public rule exists. Therefore, talk about internal events is often metaphorical.

However, subjective reports are not limited to private stimuli. The critical distinguishing feature of such reports is the absence of a public rule. Therefore, reports about public stimuli may also be subjective if they are based on the reporter's inclinations rather than public rules. For example, if someone is asked to report on how a round plate "appears" or "looks" when it is tilted, this too may be a subjective report. A report that the round plate "looks" elliptical is a response transferred from the context in which the subject is presented with an elliptical object and is taught to say that the object is elliptical. A similar analysis applies when the subject is asked to judge the brightness of a light or the seriousness of a crime. These magnitudes are said to be "subjective" because the subject is following inclinations to generalize, not because the subject is judging an internal subjective realm.

To the third-person experimenter in a transfer study, the subject's responses signify lines of similarity. In transferring a particular verbal response from a situation, S_1, in which a public rule is defined, to situation S_2, lacking a public rule, the subject's behavior indicates that under the experimental conditions, S_2 is similar to S_1. Likewise, the subject may match S_2 to S_3, another situation in which no public rule is defined. Yet, the description of S_3 retains intersubjective meaning because of its link to S_1 via S_2. Using numerous judgments of this sort the experimenter can map lines of similarity among a multiplicity of situations. The resulting map may be said to represent the subject's "quality space" or "structure of experience."[61] The entire relational structure is anchored only at certain points by lines of similarity which extend to situations governed by public rules.

Quale. The experimenter's knowledge of what the subject is reporting about in subjective reports is represented by the quality space constructed from the subject's behavior. It seems, however, that this knowledge is deficient in that it is knowledge only about relationships among situations. It does not concern itself with their inherent nature, which accounts for their relating in the ways described by the quality space. The subject, on the other hand, seems to possess more adequate knowledge. In addition to knowing how situations are related, the subject also knows by direct acquaintance the quale of a particular experience.[62] This difference between the knowledge of the subject and that of the experimenter can be captured by considering the knowledge of a blind psychologist who knows how all the colors are related but who does not know the experience of redness. Thus, it appears that on the analysis under consideration, the qualia of experience are forever inaccessible to a behaviorist science which must remain "blind."

This objection distinguishes between knowledge as absolute acquaintence and knowledge of relations. It is questionable, however, whether knowledge can assume the absolute form required by the criticism. Suppose a person could experience only one color. By hypothesis, this person could not discriminate on the basis of color. Would such a person have knowledge of this one color? If not, then knowledge, even knowledge of simple qualia, seems to depend on relationships.[63] Furthermore, is the "having" of a stream of conscious experiences to be considered knowledge? If so, then do animals and infants also have knowledge of their experiences? The passing of a sequence of unconceptualized experiences does not, in itself, constitute knowledge. In knowing their experience, human adults do not merely experience; they also conceptualize.[64] To conceptualize, in turn, is to classify and categorize on the basis of similarities and differences. Thus, even the subject's knowledge of experience is the knowledge of relationships among those experiences.

How then does the knowledge of the blind psychologist differ from that of the sighted subject? Both have knowledge of the structure of visual experience in that both can construct the subject's visual quality space. The difference between them is that the blind experimenter knows of the quality space only by observing the subject's behavior. Subjects in a transfer experiment, on the other hand, do not have to observe their own behavior to know when things are similar. Their inclination, or disposition, to transfer is sufficient for them to know lines of similarity. As discussed above, knowledge of dispositions does not require observation. Thus although the blind experimenter and the sighted subject can both know that S_1 and S_2 are similar, only the subject has, in addition, a disposition to transfer behavior from S_1 to S_2, and this inclination may be the quale of S_2.[65]

Copy Theory Undone

The above analysis of first-person reports undermines much of the rationale for what behaviorists call the "Copy Theory," more generally known as the "Sense-Datum Theory."[66] This theory, rejected by behaviorists, asserts that what we directly know, or what we respond to, is not the external world but rather an inexact copy of that world. From our immediate knowledge of our sense data we construct our mediate knowledge of the external world.

Much of the justification of the Copy Theory derives from the observation that our perception of the world frequently does not conform to the world. For example, round plates often do appear elliptical, the loudness of a tone does not correspond exactly to its intensity, and a stick partially under water looks bent. To explain these phenomena, the Copy Theory suggests that we directly perceive a realm of subjective experience in which elliptical plates, loudness, and bent sticks exist as sense data. Our perception thus conforms to inner sense data if not to the external world.

This justification of the Copy Theory is based on the premise that if we perceive X then there must be an X. If X cannot be found in the external world, then it must exist as a sense datum. The present analysis of subjective reports denies this premise. A stimulus may be responded to in a variety of ways depending on what learning is being transferred to the stimulus, but the responses are all to the same stimulus. For example, a tilted plate can be responded to with "round" or with "elliptical," depending on what kind of learning is being transferred to the plate. Both responses, however, are to the same plate.[67] There is no need to postulate two sense data for the two reactions. Although it may be possible to determine empirically which response is more likely to occur early in life, there is no determinant way to decide which response is "perception" and which is "interpretation." Both are responses to the plate without the intervention of copies, and both provide knowledge about the plate.

The analysis need not change if the stimulus is covert. Consider a piece of hot metal. Just as with the plate, there are many ways to respond to this stimulus, and none of them requires the mediation of copies. Now suppose that someone swallows the piece of metal. The person can still respond to this stimulus although the response is likely to be different since different receptors are now stimulated. Nevertheless, the relocation of the metal to the other side of the skin is not a sufficient reason to postulate copies to explain the response.

With secondary qualities, sensations, illusions, quale, and phenomonological experience all finding a place in behaviorist theory, the Copy Theory holds no advantage. Behaviorists can maintain an epistemology in which human reaction, and therefore knowledge, is directly in response to the environment rather than to copies of the environment. Although humans may come to know and respond to events within their bodies, this knowledge, too, is not mediate by copies of these events. Knowledge of the self and the inner world of experience arises as a social product with ties to the external world.

CONCLUSION

Behaviorist interpretations of first-person reports are attempts at exorcising conscious contents from psychology. In chapter 2 this was accomplished by excluding introspection from scientific psychology on epistemological and methodological grounds. In this chapter it is accomplished by giving plausible accounts of first-person reports without appealing to conscious contents. These accounts do not disprove the existence of conscious contents. They do, however, eliminate some of the motivation for postulating conscious contents in psychology. In the final analysis, it can always be argued that certain aspects of one's own phenomenal experience are not captured by behaviorist accounts.

If the alleged unexplained contents of consciousness entail no implications for the prediction and control of behavior, they can be safely ignored by behaviorism. Indeed, in this case, the disagreement over consciousness would not be empirically resolvable by behaviorist standards of empiricalness. If, on the other hand, conscious contents are implicated in behavior, then they would have to appear in some form within the theoretical concepts of the behavioral science. They could not appear in the behavioral data language because of behaviorist strictures against introspection and because the limits of molar behaviorism exclude even their neurophysiological correlates from the behavioral data language.

The theory that first-person reports are verbal discriminative responses, although subject to a number of criticisms, survives these attacks quite well, given certain adjustments and additions to the basic theory. This theory accomplishes the two major objectives of a behaviorist interpretation of first-person reports. First, it suggests an S-R theory to explain the verbal responses involved in first-person reports. Second, it suggests an alternative to dualism by hypothesizing how the "contents" of first-person reports can be construed as discriminative stimuli in S-R theory.

Even though the discrimination theory interprets first-person reports as responses to stimuli, behaviorists for the most part do not use them as data reports about these stimuli. Instead, they are regarded as data from which theoretical concepts can be inferred. One type of inference is to a hypothetical construct in the form of covert stimuli and responses. A second type is the construction of an intervening variable. If psychological measurement is interpreted as this kind of inferential construction, then a large body of research on psychological scaling can be integrated within the behaviorist framework.

Thus, contrary to popular misconceptions, behaviorists do not ignore first-person reports. To be sure, behaviorists disagree with the interpretations of first-person reports offered by everyday mentalistic language and by certain other schools of psychology. But behaviorists offer alternative interpretations which they claim are superior for their avowed goals of prediction and control of behavior.

CHAPTER 12

Behavioral Epistemology

Behaviorists suggest a variety of behavioral epistemologies (i.e., theories of knowledge based on theories of behavior) which analyze science as the behavior of the scientist. The psychologism of these theories implies that knowing, including scientific knowing, can be seen as an instrument in the human organism's adaptation to the world. This notion associates behaviorism with pragmatism, the philosophy that knowledge is an implement to satisfy human needs. For behaviorism these needs are best satisfied through the prediction and control of natural events. Therefore, in psychology, only those methods which promote the prediction and control of behavior possess pragmatic validity.

This behaviorist pragmatism can be understood as a version of positivism, the intellectual tradition characterized by its varied attempts to distinguish between positive knowledge and metaphysics (i.e., questions which do not lend themselves to progress and resolution). For behaviorism, positive knowledge is science. Science is defined in behaviorism as those methods which the behavioral science determine to be the most effective in enhancing the knower's ability to predict, control, and therefore adapt to the environment.

The positivist emphasis on direct experience underlies molar behaviorism, peripheralism, externalism, and behaviorist attitudes toward theoretical concepts, causation, and explanation. The positivist search for positive methods is expressed in Hull's hypothetico-deductive method, Skinner's experimental analysis of behavior, and the behaviorist insistence on precision and intersubjective consistency in verbal behavior. Positivist nominalism appears in behaviorist opposition to hypostatization and in behaviorist relational theories of mind. Behaviorism also shares positivism's rejection of metaphysics and defends its positions on consciousness on pragmatic rather than ontological grounds. Along with positivists, behaviorists reject the distinction between reality and appearance. They view the laws of nature as human inventions serving human purposes.

Because behaviorist positivism is based on an advancing science, it may retain more flexibility than other forms of positivism. This flexibility derives, in part, from the

view that scientific activity is underdetermined both by the rules of scientific method and by the natural world. It is relative to the psychological nature of the scientist.

In the preceding chapters, I have constructed a behaviorist conceptual tree diagram. In this final chapter I attempt to explain the resulting behaviorist conceptual framework by outlining a coherent pattern to characterize it. This family resemblance derives from behaviorist theories of knowing. These theories underlie behaviorist pragmatism which is, in turn, part of a larger pattern of positivism. This thesis, that behaviorism can be understood as a psychological pragmatic positivism, makes intelligible the behaviorist assumptions about science, empiricalness, and objectivity reconstructed in this book.

KNOWING

A science of behavior inevitably turns inward on itself. Scientists are organisms, and science, as a human activity, falls into the domain of a behavioral science. Eventually psychology is drawn into the description and explanation of scientific activity. Beyond this, a scientific analysis of science promises the possibility of justifying scientific methodology, and ultimately, perhaps, improving scientific practice. This endeavor is necessarily what Skinner describes as a "bootstrap" operation in that a scientific methodology is used to generate principles and theories which, in turn, are used to explain, justify, and improve that methodology. This enterprise generates an empirical epistemology—a theory of knowledge derived from a scientific investigation of the psychology of the knower.[1]

Knowledge and Behavior

In behaviorist epistemology, knowing is intimately linked with behaving. Indeed, for Skinner (1969), knowledge *is* behavior:[2]

> The world which establishes contingencies of reinforcement of the sort studied in an operant analysis is presumably "what knowledge is about." A person comes to know that world and how to behave in it in the sense that he acquires behavior which satisfies the contingencies it maintains. (p. 156)

As discussed in chapter 8, much cognitive and epistemic behavior can be interpreted as behavior in relation to the environment. Contemplative knowledge, the passive absorption of the world, is therefore a parasitic concept, derivative from a more fundamental active knowing involving behavioral interactions.[3]

In Hullian theory, knowledge of the world is composed of internal pure stimulus acts which mirror the external world. These inner replicas of the environment result from the conditioning of internal responses during the organism's interaction with the world (chapter 8). They also mediate the habit-family hierarchies through which the organism adapts to the environment (chapter 6). Knowledge is thus a habit mechanism developed in accordance with behavioral principles.[4]

Even for those behaviorists like Tolman, for whom a response is not necessary for learning to occur, knowledge cannot be separated from behavior. For Tolman, knowledge is represented by cognitive intervening variables defined solely in terms of the relationship of behavior to the environment (chapter 8). Knowledge is thus a disposition to behave, a potential for action, a response repertoire.[5] Knowledge may be acquired without action, but it possesses significance only as an ingredient in a formula contributing ultimately to performance.

Scientific Knowing

In a behavioral epistemology, scientific knowledge is acquired and maintained in qualitatively much the same way as everyday knowledge. No sharp demarcation differentiates scientific activity from other forms of epistemic behavior. Science is seen as a gradual development from more simple forms of knowing. What differentiates science as a subspecies of general knowledge is its claim to a special validity, a claim granted by behaviorism and for which a behavioral epistemology must account.

Skinner. For Skinner, the scientific verbal community is a social grouping especially concerned with that verbal behavior which contributes to successful action.[6] Since successful action depends on the accuracy of verbal behavior, the community takes special steps to ensure that the verbal behavior of its members is under precise stimulus control. It establishes strict contingencies of reinforcement so that irrelevant controlling variables do not distort the relationship between verbal behavior and the stimuli described or reported upon. The community may also construct novel verbal responses, in the form of precisely defined technical terms, equations, and symbols.

As the community evolves it tends to codify its practices in the form of verbal rules. Therefore, much scientific behavior becomes rule governed behavior in the sense of chapter 7. Since the rules selected are those the community has found to be successful in the past, the rule governed behavior of its members is more likely to be effective. These rules may include directions on conducting research as well as regulations on how verbal responses, such as those in an equation or theory, can be manipulated to produce further verbal behavior.

In addition, the verbal community establishes strict standards of confirmation for a statement to be accepted into the community's verbal repertoire. Confirmation, in behavioral epistemology, is a behavioral process. A scientific statement is a verbal response, and it is confirmed, as is any verbal response, by the generation of supplementary variables which increase the strength of that response.[7] Of course, not all methods for strengthening a verbal response count as methods of confirmation, and the scientific community must construct rules of evidence to characterize those methods which qualify. An example will illustrate the confirmation process.

Suppose a scientist derives a conclusion from a set of equations. The conclusion, in the form of a verbal response "R," is an "intraverbal" response in the sense that "R" is evoked by other verbal behavior embodied in the equations and in verbal rules for manipulating them. To confirm the verbal response, the scientist attempts to modify the environment so that the verbal response "R" is strengthened. One way to achieve this is to perform an experiment to test the conclusion. If the results of the experiment are stimuli which strengthen the verbal response "R," then the confirmation of "R" increases because it now has two sources of strength: It is an intraverbal evoked by other verbal behavior, and it is a tact evoked by the stimulus results of the experiment. In everyday terms, the conclusion is confirmed by observation.

Thus, for Skinner, scientific behavior is merely one subcategory of the intellectual self-management behavior discussed in chapter 8. Scientists manipulate their own behavior by manipulating the environmental variables of which their behavior is a function. By performing experiments, rearranging symbols, and using instruments, they change their immediate environments so that their verbal behavior is altered. This precurrent intellectual self-management behavior is itself maintained by the reinforcement contingencies established by the scientific community. The behavior of the community in establishing and maintaining these contingencies is explained, in turn, by the resulting reinforcement which accrues to the community in the form of successful nonverbal behavior made possible by the verbal behavior of scientists.

Hull. In Hullian epistemology, the paradigm of scientific knowing is the hypothetico-deductive technique described in chapter 5. Although this methodology can be given a purely formal analysis, Hullians also provide a behavioral interpretation which conceptualizes the activity of the theoretician within Hullian principles of behavior.[8] The deduction of theorems from postulates is viewed as a behavior mediated by the interaction of pure stimulus acts within the scientist. As Hull (1930a) describes it:

> The deductive process is a true generative activity. The known principles give rise to new knowledge as a result of a causal sequence in a high-class redintegrative organism. According to one plausible hypothesis, principles are symbolic habits which, as a result of their functional interaction within the organism possessing them, give rise to new and distinct habits. These latter constitute the new knowledge. (p. 242)

Similarly, the testing and experimental confirmation of a theoretical deduction are behavioral phenomena, and within the Hullian scheme they are seen as forming a habit-family hierarchy (chapters 6 and 7). The scientist, as a behaving organism, is confronted by a scientific problem, serving as an initiating stimulus. Solving the problem is a goal because a solution meets certain human needs and is therefore drive reducing. Eventually scientific truth becomes a secondary reinforcer. Just as the habit-family hierarchy possessed by the rat in the maze enables it to get from the starting box to the goal box by a variety of routes, so the hypothetico-deductive habit-family hierarchy supplies the scientist with alternate methods for arriving at a scientific solution to a specific problem. One method is the deduction of the solution as a theorem from a postulate set, and a second is the direct empirical observation of the solution.[9] Therefore, for Hull (1943b),

> The critical characteristic of scientific theoretical explanation is that it reaches independently through a process of reasoning the same outcome with respect to . . . principles as is attained through the process of empirical generalization. (p. 5)

This convergence of the habit-family on a single solution confirms this solution. In Hull's (1943b) words:

> The fact that . . . the same statements . . . can be attained quite independently by empirical methods as by theoretical procedures. . . . makes possible the checking of results obtained by one method against those obtained by the other. It is a general assumption in scientific methodology that if everything entering into both procedures is correct, the statements yielded by them will never be in genuine conflict. (p. 5)

Although Hull and Skinner propose different theories and advocate different scientific methodologies, the parallels between them with regard to confirmation are striking. For both, a scientific proposition is a verbal response, and for both, it is confirmed by evoking that response in multiple ways. Within a Skinnerian operant analysis, confirmation occurs when supplementary variables are brought to bear to strengthen the response, while according to the Hullian interpretation, the response is confirmed along with a verbal theory when it occurs as the result of several sequences within a habit-family hierarchy.

Tolman. Because Tolman uses relatively high level cognitive concepts in the description and explanation of even the elementary behavior of lower organisms (chapter 8), his behavioral theories are readily extended to the behavior of the scientist. The cognitive maps attributed to rats in a maze (chapter 6) are also attributable to the scientist. Just as the rat's cognitive map represents the rat's expectations of what leads to what, or S-S connections, so the scientist's theory is a cognitive map in verbal form, symbolizing the scientist's expectations concerning the interrelation of events in the world. Both cognitive maps are acquired by the same principles.[10]

According to Tolman, all behavior, including that of the rat as well as that of the scientist, can be viewed as the organism operating upon its environment. These operations both contribute to the further elaboration of the map and are guided by it. In particular, the behavior of scientists in developing their concepts and theories is to be understood in terms of the operations they perform in applying and testing their scientific maps. Thus, Tolman subscribes to a peculiar form of operationism (chapter 4) in which concepts are defined by operations, but the operations are broadly conceived as the response-terms in a general theory of behavior. In this "operational behaviorism" the behavior of the psychologist and the behavior of the experimental subject, be it rat or human, are both conceptualized via the map (i.e., theory) produced by a behavioral science.[11]

For Tolman, the maps of science are not to be divorced from the scientific behavior that produced them. According to him, the intervening variable is not a purely formal logical construct. Rather it mirrors the actual behavior of careful scientists. Tolman argues that good scientists investigate the same relationships among variables that are the essence of the intervening variable. They develop a cognitive map, in the form of an intervening variable which tells us what to expect of behavior given certain environmental circumstances, or what leads to what. Tolman's operational behaviorism merely makes explicit the practices of the competent scientist.[12]

Behaviorist Psychologism

The three behavioral epistemologies reviewed, those of Skinner, Hull, and Tolman, as well as those developed by other behaviorists,[13] demonstrate a common characteristic, despite their differences in terminology and conditioning theory. Each views knowledge in terms of the behavior of the knower, and science, in particular, in terms of the behavior of the scientist. Therefore, knowledge can be analyzed and explained by theories developed by a science of behavior, and epistemology becomes the psychology of knowing.

In contrast to this psychologistic approach, in a purely formal analysis of knowledge, the structure and contents of knowledge are considered independent of the behavior that generated them and are detached from their organismic origins. The formal analysis tries to construct formal rules for the manipulation and interpretation of the products of epistemic behavior, rules which may differ considerably from the laws and principles of a behavioral theory. In doing so, the formal analysis ignores not only the epistemic behavior responsible for the products but also the rule governed behavior of the formal analyst.[14]

Logic. These differences between a formal epistemology and an empirical, or behavioral, epistemology appear mostly clearly with regard to theories of logic. In a purely formal analysis, logic is conceptualized as independent of human activity. Either it is considered a set of transcendental truths, not at all dependent on human experience for their validity, or it is viewed as one vast tautology, a set of conventions with no empirical contents. Rules of logic can be constructed in various ways, all of which are equally valid since logic is unrelated to the empirical realm.

In a behavioral epistemology, logic is a property of verbal behavior. It is a set of rules describing certain relationships extracted from the speech of human organisms. Just like all other aspects of behavior, these special relationships appear because of certain laws of behavior.[15] Similarly, the behavior of the logician in explicating the rules of logic must also be explained by a behavioral theory. At a more advanced level, the theory must, in addition, account for the behavior of the logician in constructing and following rules for nonstandard logics.

According to Hull, for example, the rules of standard logic are acquired as verbal behavior in much the same way as scientific postulates are.[16] As explained above, theoretical postulates are acquired as verbal behavior, or are confirmed, when a theorem is both deduced from a postulate set and is also a description of an experimental observation. Similarly, Hull argues, the rules of logical deduction used in deriving the theorem are also confirmed by the correspondence between an empirical observation and the deduced theorem. Therefore, Hull concludes:

> Despite much belief to the contrary, it seems likely that logical (mathematical) principles are essentially the same in their mode of validation [as scientific systems]; they appear to be merely rules of symbolic manipulation which have been found by trial in a great variety of situations to mediate the deduction of existential sequels verified by observation. . . . each observationally confirmed theorem increases the justified confidence in the logical rules which mediated the deduction, as well as in the "empirical" postulates themselves. (Hull et al., 1940, p. 7)

Thus, according to Hull, the principles of logic, as aspects of verbal behavior, are acquired because they are reinforced by the deduction of experimentally confirmed observations.

Hull's interpretation seems deficient on two counts. First, it does not account for the behavior of logicians who invent and use nonstandard logics which have never mediated the deduction of observationally confirmed theorems. Second, it also fails to explain the logic of confirmation itself. Consider how a logic, L, is tested under the Hullian scheme. Using L, an observational theorem, T, is deduced from a postulate set. To test T, observational results, R, are compared to T. According to Hull, both L and the postulate set gain in confirmation if R = T. But this presupposes standard logic. Consider a nonstandard logic, L*, in which the finding R = T would *dis*confirm the postulate set. Therefore, a logic is confirmed in Hull's account only by presupposing standard logic, which is itself not confirmed by the hypothetico-deductive method. In general, for any logic L tested by Hull's method, and any set of observations, there is always a logic of confirmation by which the observations confirm L and another logic of confirmation by which the obsevations disconfirm L.

If every form of logic needed to be confirmed in the way Hull prescribes, an infinite regress would be generated since every test presupposes a logic of confirmation itself in need of confirmation. The infinite regress is avoided only because certain forms of logic are adopted without confirmation. These forms are the formal analog of the primitive behavioral operations (chapters 6 and 7) which state the conditions under which behavior is changed. These primitive principles can be reformulated as the primitive rules governing the organism's behavior although the behavior is not rule governed in the sense of chapter 7. The primitive behavior principle, "Under conditions C, behavior D occurs," can be interpreted as, "From a set of statements describing C, the organism comes to believe B as expressed in behavior D" (chapter 8). Thus, primitive behavioral principles can be reformulated as a primitive logic which holds because of the nature of the organism, not because it is formally confirmed. The only sense in which it may be said to be confirmed is that it presumably evolved through natural selection.

BEHAVIORIST PRAGMATISM

If knowledge in a behavioral epistemology is viewed as intimately tied to aspects of behavior, then knowledge, like behavior, must be understood in relation to its function. Within the behaviorist tradition, the central role of behavior is the adaptation of the organism to its environment. Although behaviorists disagree as to the mechanisms mediating this adaptation (e.g., reinforcement, association, drive reduction), they share the belief that these mechanisms evolved through a process selective of behavioral features that enhanced adaptation and ultimately survival. Therefore, epistemic behavior, too, can be seen as part of the overall adaptation of the organism to the natural world, and it can be evaluated with regard to how well it executes this function.[17]

This association of knowledge with adaptation is closely related to the philosophy of American pragmatism as developed by Peirce and James.[18] Pragmatism regards knowledge and belief as instruments to satisfy human needs and to further human interests. Epistemology is thus biologically grounded. Just as the "validity" of an instrument depends on its effectiveness so the truth of a statement and the meaning of a concept are matters of their usefulness rather than abstract and transcendent properties of words. As James (1907/1975) describes it:

> The possession of true thoughts means everywhere the possession of invaluable instruments of action. . . .
>
> You can say of it then either that "it is useful because it is true" or that "it is true because it is useful." Both these phrases mean exactly the same thing. . . .

> From this simple cue pragmatism gets her general notion of truth as something essentially bound up with the way in which one moment in our experience may lead us towards other moments which it will be worth while to have been led to. (pp. 97–98)

An important implication of this pragmatic approach is the provisional nature of human knowledge. Just as an instrument is useful at one time but not at another, for one purpose but not for another, so human knowledge bears no claim on absolute validity. Its validity is relative to its usefulness, and it is to be discarded when it no longer serves its purpose or when better instruments come along.

Science and Adaptation

Strains of this pragmatism can be found throughout behaviorist epistemology. Behavioral analysis suggests that knowledge best mediates human adaptation when it enhances human prediction and control of the environment. Scientific knowledge, in particular, develops because of its extraordinary effectiveness in enabling humans to achieve these two functions. Thus, the behaviorist belief that the goals of a scientific psychology are prediction and control is not dogmatic doctrine but is rather an implication of the psychologism derived from that very science of psychology. Hence, the bootstrap nature of the argument. A behavioral science, in its analysis of scientific behavior, notes the adaptive qualities of certain kinds of behavior. It then declares, on pragmatic grounds, that these behaviors of predicting and controlling ought to be the goals of science. This conclusion is mediated by the pragmatist maxim: " 'The true' . . . is only the expedient in the way of our thinking, just as 'the right' is only the expedient in the way of our behaving," (James, 1907/1975, p. 106). The "right" aims of science, then are the "expedient" goals of prediction and control.

Explicit statements of these themes of behaviorist pragmatism can be found, for example, in Guthrie (1936):

> A scientific understanding of the world is an equipment of verbal rules which assist a man to prepare for what is about to happen when he notices the advance signs; to make him able . . . to interfere with a situation and avoid trouble or gain advantage. . . .
>
> Principles . . . are then like tools. We use them as long as they are useful or until we have better tools. (pp. 104, 106)

In this brief passage Guthrie expresses several pragmatic motifs: the instrumental nature of science as "equipment" and "tools" in serving human purposes of prediction and control, its provisional character, and its grounding as concrete verbal behavior.

Although he uses different metaphors, Tolman shares the pragmatic spirit. In characterizing science, Tolman (1935) says:

> Physics is a set of logical constructs—a set of rules and equations whereby we are aided in finding our way about from one moment of immediate experience to another. Further . . . psychology is . . . but another such set of logical constructs . . . which . . . will give us still further aid in finding our way about from one moment of experience to the next. (p. 359)

Tolman (1932) identifies these "constructs," used to get about our world, with the cognitive "maps" of his learning theory:

> That "map" knowledge is "true" which "works," given the particular behavior-needs and the particular behavior-capacities of the type of organism gathering such knowledge. Physics and purposive behaviorism are both, therefore, but humanly conditioned, "behavioral" maps. In conclusion, it seems . . . that we are asserting, are we not, a pragmatism? For we are asserting that all human knowledge, including physics . . [is] but a resultant of, and limited by, human behavioral needs . . . and capacities. (p. 430)

The pragmatism is evident. Scientific knowledge is an instrument, in this case a "map," whose function it is to enable us to adjust our world and whose truth depends on its usefulness in satisfying our needs. Just as maps of different forms may be equally useful, so scientific theories may differ and yet possess equal pragmatic validity.[19]

Although Hull does not share this instrumentalist approach to scientific theory, he nevertheless shows certain pragmatic themes. He acknowledges that the hypothetico-deductive method can never establish the absolute truth of a scientific theory. The method confirms a theory only by committing the logical fallacy of affirming the consequent. That is, if the theory is true then certain observational consequences should follow. However, the observation of those consequences does not logically entail the truth of the theory. They may have come about for many other reasons. Therefore, Hull admits, the hypothetico-deductive method can, at best, build up a "favorable presumption or probability" for a given theory.[20]

Second, Hull recognizes that experimental observations can be deduced from more than one theory. His procedure is to select that theory which yields the greatest number of theorems.[21] Thus, in a sense, he regards theories as theorem generators, and the theory that accomplishes its task most effectively is the one chosen. Third, Hull recognizes that the hypothetico-deductive method is used because of its consequences. Scientific truth is sought because it is a means to need reduction and eventually because it is a secondary reinforcement in and of itself.[22] Thus, like the pragmatists, Hull sees scientific knowledge as biologically based.

Skinner adopts an extreme form of pragmatism. He rejects the possibility that knowledge, even scientific knowledge, can claim absolute truth. Instead, he substitutes a pragmatic theory of truth which states that a verbal response can be said to be "true" only in the sense that it produces effective or successful behavior.[23] Skinner thus subscribes to James' maxim that the "true" is the "expedient." In Skinner's own words:

> Scientific knowledge . . . is a corpus of rules for effective action, and there is a special sense in which it could be "true" if it yields the most effective action possible. (1974, p. 235)
>
> Empirical research . . . is a set of practices which are productive of useful behavior. . . . An important part of scientific practice is the evaluation of the probability that a verbal response is "right" or "true"—that it may be acted upon successfully. (1957a, p. 428)

Success and effectiveness are presumably related to the reinforcing consequences of the behavior evoked by the verbal response. The reinforcement mechanism, in turn, has evolved by natural selection through phylogenic contingencies of survival and adaptation. Similarly, Skinner's identification of the ethical "good" with the "reinforcing" and ultimately with that which promotes survival[24] parallels the other half of James' maxim, "The 'right' is only the expedient in the way of our behaving."

Knowing by Interaction

In pragmatist epistemology, objects are known not by passive sensing but rather through the consequences of our interaction with them. Thus, this knowledge can be analyzed into three terms: the object, our behavior with respect to the object, and the practical results of that behavior.[25] This three-term analysis reappears throughout behaviorist theories. It can be found in Tolman's conceptualization of our knowledge of objects only in their guises as behavior supports and discrimination manipulanda.[26] It is echoed in Skinner's three-term contingency (discriminative stimulus, response, reinforcement) by which operant behavior (and knowing behavior) is acquired (chapter 6).

It is similarly expressed in various behaviorist theories as to how concepts are known. Operationism and Carnap's reductive chains (chapter 4) both make use of the three terms in the form of test conditions, operation (behavior), and outcome (results). Tolman's intervening variables (chapter 4) and the dispositional analysis of mental concepts (chapter 10) also explicate concepts in terms of the consequences of certain interactions.

Beliefs and assumptions are also to be judged by usefulness in furthering human goals, and behaviorists adopt this pragmatist spirit liberally. A number of behaviorist working assumptions are incorporated because they are viewed as enhancing the progress of behaviorist science. One of the most basic behaviorist assumptions is that there is lawfulness in behavior. This premise has not been proven by the behavioral science, but it is accepted as a working assumption by behaviorist on pragmatic grounds (chapter 9). Without it, the science of human behavior cannot get started.

The rejection of agency and the acceptance of determinism are thus not metaphysical doctrines but are rather pragmatic instruments serving important human purposes. Ironically, James appeals to the same pragmatic spirit to justify the assumption of free will because of its important consequences in everyday life. This irony points to one of the difficulties of pragmatism—deciding what is useful. There is no agreed upon metric for usefulness, and what is useful in one context, e.g., scientific research, may not be useful in another, e.g., interpersonal relations.

BEHAVIORIST POSITIVISM

Behaviorist pragmatism is woven into the more comprehensive intellectual tradition of positivism, especially the positivist empiriocriticism of Mach and Avenarius.[27] In many ways, behaviorism can usefully be understood as a psychological version of positivism. This thesis is supported by a review of the characteristics of positivism and how they underlie the behaviorist conceptual framework.

Positive Knowledge

In its essence, positivism, throughout its many manifestations, is characterized by its repeated attempts to demarcate "positive knowledge" and to describe what sorts of beliefs properly deserve the designation "knowledge" and what sorts do not.[28] The aim of these attempts is not only to characterize knowledge but also to direct human intellectual pursuits. By defining knowledge, positivists hope to distinguish those issues, questions, and methods which can profitably be pursued with benefit to the human community, and those which do not merit our attention. In particular, positivists aspire to isolate those questions which are "metaphysical" and therefore give rise to endless disputes with no possibility of resolution. Positivists hope to promote intellectual progress by eliminating this futile controversy and directing a convergence toward positive knowledge. Applied to social problems, positive knowledge will result in social harmony and cooperation.

In this fundamental sense, behaviorism is a version of positivism. Behaviorism begins with the basic premise that psychology is a science. The remaining conceptual development of behaviorism concerns the characterization of what is scientific (chapter 1). Thus, for behaviorist positivism, "positive" is equivalent to "scientific," and behaviorism can be characterized as a positivism devoted to the demarcation of scientifically acceptable psychological methods, questions, and concepts. Behaviorism, too, was struck at its outset by the seemingly endless and futile disputes raging among its predecessors in introspective and faculty psychologies. It, too, hopes that by putting psychology on an objective and empirical footing worthless controversies can be eliminated and valuable research pursued. It, too, aspires to an applied scientific psychology to solve social problems and to create social harmony.

Justification. A major problem encountered by all forms of positivism is in justifying the various criteria proposed to distinguish between positive knowledge and worthless inquiry. If these criteria are defended on positivist grounds, then the argument is circular in that appeal is made to positivist standards to justify positivist standards. On the other hand, if the criteria do not follow from positivist analysis, then what is their source? They appear as the sort of unsubstantiated metaphysics that positivism is designed to eliminate.

Behaviorism may be seen as proposing its own unique solution to this traditional positivist dilemma. Behaviorist pragmatism suggests that knowledge, as epistemic behavior, can be evaluated by its effectiveness in promoting the adaptation of the human organism to its environment, as measured by prediction and control. Therefore, the evaluation of knowledge is best performed by a behavioral science which can competently judge the effectiveness of various forms of epistemic behavior and prescribe methods for improving it. This, then, is the behaviorist solution to the positivist dilemma: The criteria delineating positive knowledge, or science, are those which psychology determines best enhance the knower's ability to predict, control, and therefore adapt to the environment.

To be sure, this solution is no less circular than others, for the psychology used to determine the criteria is a positivist psychology based on positivist methods and concepts. What behaviorism adds are two elements to make the circularity a bit less vicious. First, by injecting a dose of pragmatism, behaviorism shifts the argument over positivist criteria from the question of what is philosophically true to the question of what is biologically useful. Second, by developing a science of science, behaviorism may someday provide an empirical theory of how science progresses.

Of course, no behavioral theory is currently advanced enough to state precisely what sort of epistemic behavior best enhances the knower's ability to predict and control. Therefore, no current theory can demarcate sharply the kinds of behavior that are to be considered scientific on behaviorist positivist grounds. Instead, behaviorists attempt to extrapolate from what is known to the more complex problems of scientific behavior. In some cases this is an extrapolation from a theory formulated for simple behavior.[29] In others, it is merely an informed guess, based on a deep appreciation of the behavioral roots of science. In all cases it is heavily influenced by acute observation of the history of science, psychology in particular, with its various successes and failures. Because behaviorists differ in their behavioral theories, extrapolations, and readings of history, it is not surprising that they differ in their prescriptions for positive knowledge, or science. What they share, however, is that their prescriptions are influenced by their conception of human psychology.

Because of the pragmatism woven throughout much of behaviorism, these prescriptions are not merely tactical suggestions. If "the true is the expedient," then criteria for expedient science are also the criteria for *valid* science. If the philosophically legitimate is that which is practically effective, then methodological decisions based on pragmatic considerations are *philosophical* decisions as well. In short, for a pragmatic behaviorist positivism, the distinction between the strategic and the philosophical collapses. Since the distinction rests on the distinction between organismic behavior and formal knowledge, a behavioral epistemology which rejects the latter distinction also undermines support for the former. The strategic *is* the philosophical.

Importance of Science

Along with positivism, behaviorism emphasizes the leading role of science in human affairs. Science is viewed as the paradigm of knowledge. Both also share a fundamental belief in the unity of scientific method (chapter 1).

Behaviorism, pragmatism, and positivism all place importance on the biological foundations of knowledge, and science in particular. All three see scientific knowledge as ultimately serving human needs and therefore relative to its organismic context. Just as behaviorists construe scientific knowing as a subcategory of behavior and therefore continuous with other forms of behavior, so empiriocriticism conceives of science as a gradual development from human craft which evolved, in turn, from more "instinctive" forms of knowing. Therefore, there is a reluctance to dissociate knowledge from its behavioral origins or to treat it as a product independent of individual organisms in a formal analysis. As in behaviorism, epistemology becomes the psychology of knowing.[30]

In the psychologism of both behaviorism and empiriocriticism, the human needs served by scientific knowledge are directly related to the prediction and control of nature. Antedating behaviorism by more than half a century, Bernard (1865/1927) writes:

> Experimental reasoning . . . sets itself the same goal in all the sciences. Experimenters try to reach determinism; . . . they try to connect natural phenomena with their necessary conditions or, . . . with their immediate causes. . . . The whole experimental problem may be reduced to foreseeing and directing phenomena. (p. 57)

In agreement with behaviorism, Bernard thus argues for the unity of scientific method, and his "foreseeing and directing" correspond to the behaviorist "prediction and control."[31] Along with behaviorism, empiriocriticism also deduces the relative and provisional character of scientific knowledge from its instrumental and adaptive role in the prediction and control of the environment.

Experience

Traditionally, positivists establish positive knowledge on direct experience. In behaviorism, this feature of positivism is expressed in the great emphasis on experiment and direct observation, and, in general, in behaviorism's deep commitment to scientific empiricism.[32] Psychologically, this means that the scientist's verbal behavior is to be linked as closely as possible to environmental stimuli. When this link is attenuated and verbal behavior comes under the control of the scientist's internal stimuli or of other verbal stimuli, distortions tend to occur, and action based on that verbal behavior is less effective. In particular, as psychologists move away from direct observation, they turn to speculation about the unobserved, and this cannot yield positive knowledge. Furthermore, since the unobserved objects of this speculation cannot be manipulated or scientifically meaured, they are useless for prediction and control.

This positivist emphasis on direct experience underlies the assumptions of molar behaviorism, peripheralism, and externalism. The decision of molar behaviorism to exclude internal physiology from the behavioral science is based partly on the fear that theorizing about unobserved processes leads to idle speculation, the invention of fictions, and an excessive concern with internal mechanisms which, for practical reasons, cannot be used for the prediction and control of behavior (chapter 3). Similarly, peripheralism was popular within behaviorism when very little was known about the central nervous system. It was an attempt to guard against talk about a transempirical soul lurking in the unobserved recesses of the brain and to keep the behavioral science focused on parts of the nervous system more readily observed and better understood (chapter 9). A third example is externalism, which encourages the search for environmental, and therefore observable, causes of behavior (chapter 9). It ensures that the causes discovered will be useful for prediction and control and that scientists will not be tempted to speculate about events inside the organism. Thus, molar behaviorism, peripheralism, and externalism are based, in part, on empirical hypotheses about how various strategies affect the scientist's behavior.

Concepts. The emphasis on experience also underlies the attitudes toward theoretical concepts reviewed in chapters 4 and 5. Theoretical terms admitted to the behavioral science retain strong links with observations. Wherever possible, theoretical concepts are defined or translated into observational terms. Operational concepts, intervening variables, and bilateral reduction chains all effect a strict connection between theory and observation. In the case of hypothetical constructs, behaviorists generally impose limitations so that they are securely anchored to observables.

Much of the rationale for these behaviorist attitudes toward theoretical terms derives from judgements about the effects of excessive theorizing on the behavior of scientists. Behaviorists fear that unbridled theorizing leads to useless and even harmful speculation. Scientists are diverted from their true subject matter and talk instead about fictions that are useless for prediction and control. Such verbal behavior provides only spurious explanations which do not enhance the verbal community's ability to act effectively. Behaviorists point to cognitive psychology and theories of agency as examples of how ineffective theoretical verbal behavioral interferes with the practical behavior of the scientist (chapters 7, 8, and 9).

Explanation. To the extent that behaviorists avoid the unobserved insides of the organism they must also relinquish the search for immediate causes. Many of the psychological cases of behavior precede it by a considerable time. Those behaviorists who do not admit hypothetical constructs must limit themselves to causal relationships which span temporal gaps. Therefore, many behaviorists find congenial certain positivist conceptions of casual explanation. With its emphasis on direct experience, positivism must deny that we have positive knowledge of any necessary casual connection beyond the observation of the invariable succession of events. From this premise, Mach draws the conclusion that casuation is to be identified with functional dependence, for that is all that can be observed. This Machian identification of causation with functional dependence is adopted by a number of behaviorists, especially those who are most interested in the environmental, as opposed to the physiological, causes of behavior (chapter 4 and 8).

By the same token, a positivism which sticks closely to direct experience must insist that a positive explanation not make reference to a realm beyond experience. Therefore, Mach concludes, a valid explanation is nothing more than an economical abstract description of experience. It does not go beyond experiential phenomena and therefore does not exceed positive knowledge. It is a useful expedient, nevertheless, because in its economical form it can efficiently aid its user, and because as an abstraction it can be used in a variety of practical situations.[33] This identification of explanation with description is adopted by many behaviorists including Skinner (chapter 5). For these behaviorists, the policy of limiting explanation to description is also psychologically sound. It protects the scientist from the dangers of theorizing, which interfere with prediction and control.

Positive Method

Behaviorism and positivism also share a commitment to the development of objective methods that ensure positive knowledge. In behaviorist positivism, the choice of these methods is dictated, in part, by psychological considerations. A behavioral epistemology views scientific methods as descriptions of the behavior of the scientist and evaluates them in terms of their ultimate biological effectiveness in enhancing adaptation.

Hull's advocacy of the hypothetico-deductive method (chapter 5) conforms to positivist tradition. Hull argues that his procedure guarantees valid knowledge because both its aspects are objective. On the one hand is the deduction of theorems from the postulates. This is objective because the deductive logic used is a chain of responses with high $_{S}H_{R}$, built up through the many times that logic works to bring about reinforcement. Therefore, all who examine the deduction will agree to the conclusion, and the deduction is no longer the subjective possession of the theorist. On the other hand is the experimental observation to test the theory. The observation is direct experience, the core of positive knowledge, and if the description is precise enough, the test of the theory is a simple comparison of the theorem with the observational report. The method is thus an algorithm to ensure that no invalid postulates are accepted. Although different theorists may begin with differing postulates, according to Hull, the continued use of the hypothetico-deductive method guarantees that all theories will converge to the point at which they are isomorphic, differing only in terminology. In a positivist spirit, Hull argues that the continuing disagreements and controversy in psychology are due to the refusal of theorists to cast their theories in the hypothetico-deductive mold and their continued use of unacceptable methods such as intuition.

Skinner also bases his methodology (chapter 5) on a psychological analysis of scientific behavior. He argues that the most effective way of doing research is the attempt to gain greater control over behavior. Experiments designed merely to test hypotheses are a diversion from this more effective pursuit. In true positivist fashion, Skinner claims that postulates themselves are "fictions" because they can never become facts, that is, directly observed. The hypothetico-deductive method, with its logical and statistical accompaniments, imposes too long a delay between the scientist's behavior in performing the research and the reinforcement, the result of the experiment. Thus, the research behavior of the scientist is weakened. Instead, Skinner promotes an experimental approach in which the discovery and manipulation of variables controlling behavior are the guiding principles. Control of behavior is quickly and clearly seen so the behavior of the scientist is immediately reinforced.

Although Skinner and Hull thus disagree sharply about scientific methodology, they both base their recommendations on a psychological analysis of science as the behavior of the scientist. Both aim at a positive methodology producing relatively indisputable knowledge either because it is derived by logic and observation (Hull) or because of the conspicuousness of the behavioral control (Skinner). Finally, both seek an objective methodology to promote the prediction and control of behavior either by generating a large number of theorems to be used for this purpose (Hull) or by directing research toward the systematic investigation of important environmental variables (Skinner).[34]

Social Consistency. Positivist recognition of the psychological origins of knowledge draws in its wake an emphasis on the social character of science. Because of the critical importance of language and symbols in scientific behavior, science requires a verbal community for its fullest development. Furthermore, science is a cumulative enterprise dependent on cooperation and communication within an organized social group. If science is to implement its function in the adaptation of the human species, it must communicate its findings to the community at large in useful ways. Therefore, scientific behavior is seen as a social enterprise mediated by a scientific verbal community.[35] In discussing the validity of knowledge, de Laguna (1927/1963) captures many of these notions:

> No procedure could grow up, and no standard be adopted, which did not to some degree represent and correspond to the objective order of nature. But such correspondence is acquired only through the medium of cooperation, as a result of the indirect dealing with nature through the group. The individual's contact with reality is measured by the extent and adequacy of the social organization through which he operates. (p. 355)

Given the central importance of communication for the development and adaptive functioning of science, clarity of language assumes a paramount significance for the objectivity of positive method. Indeed, as noted above, Skinner maintains that the sharpening of stimulus control over verbal behavior is one of the major features of a scientific community. Nevertheless, this precise stimulus control would be useless if each member of the community displayed it for a particular verbal response but it differed from person to person. Thus, social consistency, in which the precise stimulus control over a verbal response is consistent across members of a scientific community, is also necessary for objectivity. In fact, sharp stimulus control over a verbal response may be impossible to achieve in the absence of at least one other person to train the verbal response.

This emphasis on the precision and consistency of verbal behavior for communicability and cooperation finds expression throughout behaviorist methodology.[36] In selecting criteria for acceptability into the behavioral data language (chapter 3) behaviorists tend to reject terms lacking precision and intersubjective consistency. Intensional language and action language are excluded partly on the grounds that they fail to meet these standards. Similarly, descriptions involving a high degree of interpretation are banned because they are subjective, differing from observer to observer. Even though these descriptions are related to direct experience, they do not contribute to positive method because they lack the objectivity necessary for communication and cooperation.

Terms and symbols from the physical sciences generally possess high degrees of precision and intersubjective consistency. Behaviorists, therefore, prefer to use them whenever possible. However, because in practice a behavioral science cannot be limited to these terms and symbols, behaviorists must add vocabulary the clarity of which is less than that of the physical sciences (chapter 3). Nevertheless, behaviorists strive for a system of terms with as much precision and consistency as possible. Behavioral interpretation (chapter 10) is an attempt to reformulate mentalistic terms so that they acquire the precision and consistency necessary for positive knowledge.

First-person reports and introspection are not considered positive methods for a number of reasons (chapters 2 and 11). One important reason is that they are deficient in both precision and intersubjective consistency. The lack of objectivity is evident in the inability of introspectors to agree on their observations. Positivist rejection of introspection for this reason appears in Comte (1855/1974):

> After two thousand years of psychological pursuit, no one proposition is established to the satisfaction of its followers. They are divided, to this day, into a multitude of schools, still disputing about the very elements of their doctrine. This interior observation gives birth to almost as many theories as there are observers. (p. 33)

and is echoed by Watson (1913a):

> I firmly believe that two hundred years from now, unless the introspective method is discarded, psychology will still be divided on the question as to whether auditory sensations have the quality of "extension," whether intensity is an attribute which can be applied to color . . . and upon many hundreds of others of like character. (p. 164)

Some behaviorists also reject introspective reports on theoretical grounds. Various theories of the development of first-person reports explain why the relationship between verbal responses of this sort and the stimuli they report is not an exact one (chapter 11). Rejecting introspection on these grounds nicely demonstrates the bootstrap nature of behavioral epistemology. A behavioral science developed along positivist lines and excluding introspection eventually formulates a theory to explain the deficiencies of introspection and thereby justifies its exclusion from the science.

Behaviorist insistence on precision and intersubjectivity is not a mere exercise in pedantry. It is a natural consequence of behaviorist pragmatic positivism. A behavioral analysis of science points to the social character of scientific knowledge and the importance of communicability and cooperation. Pragmatic considerations indicate that science achieves its role as an instrument for adaption, and therefore its pragmatic validity, only when it adopts practices to ensure clarity in verbal behavior. Positivist impulses then seek to regulate epistemic behavior by legislating that positive method, i.e., science, be limited to those practices which achieve the necessary precision and intersubjective agreement.

Nominalism

Behaviorist positivism attributes a central role to direct experience—i.e., observation—in positive knowledge. Much of our knowledge, however, is in the form of abstract concepts which seem to provide us with access to a realm beyond observation. To assign an epistemic function to these abstractions while not forfeiting the primacy of experience, behaviorists and positivists alike assume a nominalist stance with regard to concepts. This means that abstractions are not taken to refer to transcendents, such as Platonic forms, but are related to the concrete and the particular as well as to relationships among them.

Behavioral epistemology sees great dangers in the practice of reification, or hypostatization, in which an abstract term is treated as the name of substantial entity with an independent existence of its own.[37] Reification misleads the scientist into asking fruitless questions, pursuing futile lines of investigation, and formulating specious explanations. Much behaviorist opposition to mentalism is based on this criticism of reification as ineffective scientific behavior.

For example, in his attack on dualism, Ryle attributes many of the errors underlying the "myth of the ghost in the machine" to the practice of reification. Ryle argues that followers of the myth misconstrue dispositions to be episodes (chapters 4 and 10). They ask questions about the duration, location, and casual effects of these fictitious episodes, and the resulting "paramechanical theory," Ryle claims, is both a logical error and a detriment to the understanding of human psychology.

Similarly, one common behaviorist objection to cognitivist theory (chapters 7 and 8) is that it takes properties of behavior such as grammar and remembering, hypostatizes them into entities or processes, and then locates them inside the organism as unobservables.[38] Research is then diverted toward investigating these hypostatizations which are useless in prediction and control. Properties are often assigned to the hypostatizations to explain the very features of behavior from which the unobservables are inferred. Circular theories of this sort can supply only spurious explanations and do not promote the adaptive functions of science.

In a similar vein behaviorists object to the reification of R-R correlations (chapter 9). Traits, instincts, faculties, and fields are examples of behavioral correlations which tend to be hypostatized as internal causes of behavior. Behaviorist externalism rejects explanations based on reifications of this sort because they reduce the effectiveness of scientific behavior. The reified internal causes cannot be observed or manipulated, and therefore they cannot aid in prediction, control, or positive knowing. They, too, lead to spurious explanations that retard scientific progress.[39]

The errors of hypostatization can be seen as the result of a formalistic epistemology. If verbal responses are analyzed independent of their behavioral context, it is easy to develop a theory of meaning in which meanings are transcendental properties of words.[40] Abstract words, therefore, can represent transempirical entities and events. Grammar, for example, can be derived from sentences created by linguists independent of normal verbal behavior in use. A behavioral epistemology, on the other hand, in conceptualizing words and sentences as verbal responses, is less likely to hypostatize. It is more likely to formulate a theory of meaning more closely related to the ways in which verbal behavior actually functions for an individual and in a verbal community.

The debate between realists and nominalists cannot be resolved on empirical grounds. Whether, for example, a dispositional concept is to be given a realist or nominalist interpretation (chapter 4) cannot be decided by observation. Possibly this is one of those "metaphysical" questions positivists and pragmatists hope to avoid. If the question is to have any solution, perhaps it can be resolved on pragmatic grounds. Behaviorist positivism argues that because the realist position with its reification of abstractions leads to ineffective behavior, nominalism is pragmatically more valid for positive knowledge.

Relational Theories. Having rejected the hypostatization of abstractions, behaviorism is left with the task of providing nominalist interpretations. Behaviorists often accomplish this by interpreting abstractions in terms of relationships among observables. For example, Skinner interprets meaning by an analysis of the controlling relations between environmental variables and verbal behavior (chapter 10). Controlling relations are similarly implicated in Skinner's interpretation of purpose (chapter 7). The theory of grammar proposed in chapter 7 and the theory of agency suggested in chapter 9 are both relational theories. A grammar is interpreted not as an internal mechanism but rather as a description of a functional class defined by empirical relationships. Likewise, agency is not conceptualized as a causal entity behind behavior, but rather as a higher-order description of a special relationship between behavior and certain aspects of the environment.

Another example of a relational theory is the intervening-variable, or dispositional, analysis of mental concepts (chapters 8 and 10). Mental terms are said to refer not to unseen processes in consciousness, but rather to dispositions to behave in certain ways under certain conditions. These, and many other examples scattered throughout the preceding chapters, add up to what early behaviorists called a "relational theory of mind." Mind in its various manifestations is not a hidden entity or process but rather is behavior in a special relationship to the world.[41]

Nominalist strands are also apparent in the arguments of those behaviorists who prefer dispositional concepts, operationally defined terms, and intervening variables over hypothetical constructs (chapter 4).[42] The first three are exhaustively defined by relations among observables while the last is not. Arguments advanced against hypothetical constructs are for the most part versions of the arguments against reification. The suggestion in chapter 8 that the information processing operations of cognitive theories can be interpreted as mathematical equations relating behavior to the environment is an example of an attempt to transform a hypothetical construct into an intervening variable.

Anti-Metaphysicalism

Because metaphysics transcends experience and refers to a realm inaccessible to empirical means of investigation, positivism rejects metaphysical discussion. Such discourse cannot lead to positive knowledge and is more likely to generate endless disputes that thwart the purposes of intellectual inquiry. Therefore, ontological issues, such as whether the universe consists only of matter or whether there are two fundamental substances, are avoided as metaphysical.

Behaviorists share this anti-metaphysicalism but in a peculiar way. For the most part, behaviorists do adopt an ontological stand. They generally maintain a materialist monism in which matter is considered the sole constituent of the universe and the existence of consciousness as an independent substance is denied. Nevertheless, in their case against consciousness, they set forth methodological arguments rather than ontological ones. Therefore, their position is more pragmatic and positivist than metaphysical.

Weiss, for one, is quite explicit about his physical monism. Yet he recognizes that this position is not empirical and therefore not scientifically supportable. He contends, however, that the premises of physical monism are the most useful for the development of a behavioral science. He therefore adopts materialism as a working assumption justified by its beneficial practical consequences for scientific progress.[43] Weiss' approach is thus pragmatic rather than metaphysical.

In an analogous fashion, Hull's materialism is subordinated to his positivist methodological concerns. He is willing, for example, to grant that consciousness may appear as a term in a theoretical postulate system (chapters 5 and 10). The existence of consciousness can then be accepted if the theoretical system meets the standards of the hypothetico-deductive method. Hull's contention is merely that no such system has in fact been properly formulated and tested. Hull's rejection of consciousness is thus based on the contingent fact that this concept does not yet meet his positivist methodological requirements.

Skinner represents another example of the methodological treatment of consciousness. In discussing conscious processes Skinner (1963a) asserts:

> No entity or process which has any useful explanatory force is to be rejected on the ground that it is subjective or mental. (p. 958)

> The objection is not that these things are mental but that they offer no real explanation and stand in the way of a more effective analysis. (p. 951)

Skinner's claim is pragmatic, not metaphysical: Psychic theories impede the behavior of the scientist, are therefore ineffective, and hence, by behaviorist positivist standards, do not constitite positive knowledge.

In contrast to Weiss, Hull, and Skinner, Tolman's metaphysical position borders on a dualism, or what he calls a "naturalism plus." This naturalism acknowledges that something, namely "raw feels," are left out of the account. In describing this "naturalism plus" Tolman (1932) says:

> Naturalism is the type of metaphysics which takes the features of prediction and controls as all important. (p. 425)

> "Raw feels" are our naturalistic "map-name" for a side of mind which our map then ignores, or reduces to impotency. (p.426)

The reason for ignoring raw feels is not their ontological illegitimacy but rather their ineffability:

> Our behaviorism will reply that whether or not there is such a private something or other present in the conscious behavior situation and lacking in the unconscious one, the private something or other never "gets across," as such, from one individual to another. All the things that do "get across" are merely *behavior* phenomena or the objective possibilities of such phenomena. (1922a, p. 47)

Thus, raw feelings are useless for a "map" (i.e., a science) the function of which is prediction and control. If they cannot be communicated to other members of the community then they are tools without a purpose. They may be of use to poetry, esthetics, and religion, but for science they are mere "will-of-the-wisps." Thus, Tolman's rejection of consciousness in science, just as that of the other three behaviorists reviewed, flows from his pragmatic behavioral epistemology rather than from metaphysical argument.[44]

Another way of excluding consciousness from psychology is through the behaviorist rejection of introspection (chapter 2). The arguments against introspection are, for the most part, methodological in nature. Public confirmation, verifiability, and intersubjective agreement are all methodological canons which introspection is said to violate. These canons, in turn, are justified on pragmatic grounds as increasing the effectiveness of scientific behavior. Because introspection fails to meet behaviorist standards, the conscious phenomenal world investigated by introspection is excluded from positive knowledge.

Apparent knowledge of consciousness must then be analyzed behaviorally. People talk about the consciousness of others and readily offer first-person reports of their own phenomenal world. In a formal theory of meaning, questions arise concerning the referents of such statement, and metaphysical debates concerning the existence of mind inevitably ensue. In contrast, for a behavioral epistemology, meaning is closely associated with verbal behavior. Both first-person and third-person reports of consciousness are dealt with in terms of the verbal behavior of the speaker rather than by searching for the fixed meanings of static words (chapters 10 and 11).

Reality

Positivism, and behaviorist positivism in particular, avoids the issue of whether there is a transcendent reality underlying our experience and beyond scientific investigation. The question is metaphysical and cannot be settled by the positive knowledge of experience. Therefore, behaviorist positivism rejects the Copy Theory (chapters 2, 6, 8, and 11), with its metaphysical thesis that we directly experience only copies of a reality lying beyond our immediate experience.[45] For behaviorist positivism, the distinction between appearance and reality must be replaced by a worldview that draws its distinctions *within* positive knowledge.

One distinction of this sort is among various kinds of behavior. Consider, for example, a stick partially submerged in water and appearing bent. According to the Copy Theory, we are immediately aware of a sense datum of a bent stick which is a mere copy of an external straight stick. In contrast, Skinner, for example, argues that there is but one stick and two ways to respond to it (chapter 11). One way, exemplified by the verbal response "That is a straight stick," simply will prove a more effective way of acting than the other, exemplified by the verbal response "That is a bent stick." People who behave in the former way improve their chances of reinforcement and adaptation, but otherwise there is no sense in which their behavior is closer to reality.[46] For the distinction between appearance and reality Skinner thus substitutes the distinction between effective and ineffective behavior.

Effectiveness is a property of behavior rather than a feature of the world to which that behavior is a reaction. In a similar fashion, some behaviorists conclude that scientific laws, the "laws of nature," are not descriptions of how the universe operates but instead are rules for effective human behavior with respect to nature.[47] Guthrie (1936), for one, asserts:

> Eighteenth century scientists . . . confused [the] human need for simplicity in the verbal description of the world with the ways of the cosmos itself, and there was . . . the impression that nature obeyed simple and absolute laws. It is not nature but men that are simple. The complexity of natural events will always evade exact description. (p. 105)

Along the same lines Skinner (1969) argues:

> Scientific laws . . . specify or imply responses and their consequences. They are not . . . obeyed by nature but by men who deal effectively with nature. The formula $s = \frac{1}{2}gt^2$ does not govern the behavior of falling bodies, it governs those who correctly predict the position of falling bodies at given times. (p. 141)

Both behaviorists echo Mach's (1905/1976) earlier formulation:[48]

In origin, the "laws of nature" are restrictions that under the guidance of our experience we prescribe to our expectations. (p. 351)

Natural laws may be viewed as a kind of collection of instruments for the intellectual completion of any partially given facts or for the restriction . . . of expectations in future cases. (pp. 355-356)

An important implication of this positivist attitude toward science and nature is that there is no unique set of descriptions and properties for portraying nature.[49] Those we in fact use are the ones which have proved useful in adaptation and which harmonize with human dimensions of generalization and quality spaces (chapters 3 and 11). Behaviorist criteria for acceptability into the behavioral data language (chapter 3) represent attempts to formulate rules for choosing the most effective properties and descriptions.

Behaviorist Solipsism. A behavioral epistemology restricts knowledge of the world to our behavior with respect to the world. No means are provided for making epistemic contact with reality other than by reacting to it in some fashion. In a sense, we cannot transcend the stream of behavior to gain access to the world in a more direct way.[50] We are subject to what Weiss calls a "behaviorist solipsism," in which each of us cannot step outside our own behavior.[51]

We nevertheless do, in fact, establish a body of knowledge about the natural world, including the behavior of others. How? A behavioral science suggests one possible resolution of behaviorist solipsism. Given the principles of behavior and the contingencies of reward and punishment presented by the world, the particular effective action that we call "science" inevitably develops. A component of this scientific behavior is verbal behavior about the external world. The principles that bring about this type of behavior are explained, in turn, by phylogenic contingencies which select genetic predispositions for effective, adaptive behavior.[52]

An obvious problem with this solution to behaviorist solipsism is that it begins with a science of behavior which already presupposes a resolution to behaviorist solipsism. Again the bootstrap nature of behavioral epistemology is evident. The entire epistemological structure is like Neurath's boat which we rebuild, plank by plank, while staying afloat in it.[53] Before humans first became self-reflective and developed verbal behavior about their own verbal behavior, they were already engaged in a crude kind of science. Much of this primitive science was contingency shaped rather than rule governed and evolved out of manual skills and what Mach calls "instinctive knowledge." This is the boat of science that humans found themselves in and must keep afloat as they rebuild it. We begin with primitive knowledge about behavior from which a science of behavior develops. Out of this science evolves a behavioral epistemology which both gives rise to the problem of behaviorist solipsism and suggests how it is to be resolved without sinking the boat that keeps us afloat.[54]

Positivism and the Practice of Science

A common criticism of positivism, one leveled at behaviorist positivism as well, is that in its attempt to regulate human knowledge, positivism may become overly restrictive. By imposing *a priori* strictures on intellectual pursuits, positivism runs the risk of curbing the creative imagination of the scientist. How can positivists know in advance the paths that innovative minds will pursue in investigating entirely new areas of science? In fact, by some positivist standards of the last century, much of modern physics would have to be eliminated as metaphysical and excluded from positive science.

Behaviorist positivism is in a particularly favorable position with regard to this criticism. First, the historical record for psychology is far different from that of physics. For the most part, psychological approaches antithetical to behaviorist positivism have not proven to be overwhelming successes. Second, because of its behavioral epistemology, behaviorist positivism is not a fixed *a priori* doctrine. Its criteria for positive knowledge are derived from the empirical study of the behavior of scientists and the scientific community. If certain procedures prove restrictive and therefore ineffective, then this fact should eventually be discovered by the behavioral science of science. The procedures in question should then be modified or even abandoned. Ideally, therefore, the positivist criteria of a behavioral epistemology are inherently flexible.

This flexibility assumes, of course, that a conceptual framework like behaviorism is capable of discovering evidence which contradicts its fundamental presuppositions. If to the contrary, a scientific framework determines its own canons of evidence and even the nature of observations performed within it (chapters 3 and 5), then behaviorism cannot be self-correcting in the ways described. If, for example, behaviorist prohibitions against introspective observation (chapter 2) make it impossible ever to discover evidence contrary to behaviorist empirical claims concerning introspection, then those claims are immune to correction.[55] Hence, behavioral epistemology must contend that observations are sufficiently theory-neutral to permit the disconfirmation of a theory as well as the comprehensive scientific conceptual framework in which it is developed (chapter 3).

Underdetermination. A third reason why behaviorist positivism need not excessively fear being overly restrictive is that behavioral epistemology implies that science is underdetermined by rules of scientific methodology.[56] Since in a behavioral epistemology science is the behavior of scientists, the underdetermination of science by rules follows from the general underdetermination of behavior by explicit rules (chapter 5). This general undetermination results from the fact that a rule does not logically determine behavior uniquely. Given a particular rule, it is always logically possible to carry out this rule in more than one way. All these ways are consistent with the rule, yet different from one another. Conversely, given a set of behaviors there is always more than one rule which can describe the set. Although all the rules are consistent with the set of behaviors, they are inconsistent with one another.

Despite these logical truths about the underdetermination of behavior by rules, rules are nevertheless useful in directing behavior. This is because the underdetermination in question is a *logical* underdetermination. Psychologically, and in practice, rules do determine behavior within useful limits. Given the psychological nature of an organism and given its particular training history, rules can be used to direct its behavior. It is thus rules in conjunction with the psychology of the organism that direct behavior. Behavior can be rule governed only because the behavior of following rules is itself contingency shaped by primitive learning operations rather than rule governed (chapter 8). The primitive learning operations and the lines of primitive generalization, or quality space, are not given by rules but by our biology.

As a type of behavior, science shares this underdetermination. Rules for scientific procedures logically do not determine scientific behavior uniquely. It is only in combination with the psychology and experience of a community of scientists that rules are useful. Even proponents of operationism (chapter 4) and the hypothetico-deductive method (chapter 5) have come to recognize that these methods are not sufficient to guarantee the advancement of science. Within operationism, there are many ways to define a concept consistent with operationist standards, and within the hypothetico-deductive procedure there are many ways to modify a theory given an observational disconfirmation. Not all of these ways are scientifically productive, and the creation and selection of fruitful theories and concepts are not covered by the rules of operationism or hypothetico-deductivism. In general, the rules of scientific methodology are useful only because they are supplemented by the psychology of the scientist and the history of a scientific community.[57]

Another aspect of this underdetermination is that science is also underdetermined by the world it studies. If science is a kind of behavior, mostly verbal, which is particularly effective for human adaptation to the environment, then science is relative to human nature. Given the natural world as it now exists but a different species of organism as scientists, presumably needs and interests would be different, adaptation would be different, and therefore scientific behavior and science would be different. If, in Machian and Skinnerian terms, scientific laws are rules for effective action, then they are relative to the organism for whom "effectiveness" is measured. If, in Tolman's metaphor, science is a "map," then the nature of that map depends on the goals and cognitive abilities of its user. In Tolman's (1932) own words:

In the case of physics human knowledge of the external object is still limited and conditioned by a sort of distillation from all human behavioral needs and capacities. Even physics' account of the external world is . . . an ultimately, though very abstracted, behavioral account. For all knowledge of the universe is always strained through the behavior-needs and the behavior-possibilities of the particular organisms who are gathering that knowledge. (p. 430)

If the verbal form of scientific knowledge must satisfy the curiosity and understanding of Guthrie's proverbial "freshman," then science is relative to the discriminative capacities of those being trained as scientists.

In short, there are no "raw facts," and the nature of science is not uniquely determined by the world. It is to some unknown extent also dependent on psychological characteristics of the scientist which determine the categories invented by humans to portray the world.[58] In the absence of a completed psychology of the scientist, it is not known what sorts of classifications are most suited to human nature, and we are often forced to rely on intersubjective agreement as an indirect index of suitability (chapter 3).

CONCLUSION

Science and Values

A behavioral science suggests the methods most effective for scientific behavior. Behaviorist positivism then establishes standards of objectivity and empiricalness based on these methods. This derivation begins with matters of fact concerning behavior and concludes with prescriptions for scientific propriety. It thus appears to violate the traditional positivist distinction between value and fact. It seems to deduce statements about what *ought* to be the case from statements about what *is* the case. Can science dictate values?

One way to avoid this problem is to reinterpret the behaviorist imperative. Behaviorist prescriptions of the form "Scientific practices x, y, and z *ought* to be adopted" can be transformed into conditionals of the form "If practices x, y, and z are adopted then scientific behavior will be more effective in prediction and control." This revision leaves the question of values outside science. The decision as to whether to adopt effective procedures is arrived at on nonscientific grounds. Or the gap between "is" and "ought" can be bridged by a pragmatism which identifies the "right" with the "expedient in the way of our behaving."

A third way to resolve the issue is to interpret behaviorist prescriptions as verbal behavior on the part of behaviorists and then to explain that behavior. Behaviorists are themselves behaving organisms, subject to the laws of behavior. A basic law is that organisms tend to learn and maintain behavior that is rewarded. If it is assumed that success in predicting and controlling the environment is rewarding, then the behavioral science predicts that eventually humans will come to discriminate and acquire methods to improve their prediction and control. Behaviorists are the humans who have come to do so. Their espousing certain values is thus explained by the behavioral science although the values are not prescribed by that science.

The behavioral science furthermore predicts that behaviorist methodology will be adopted by most, if not all, scientists because scientists find prediction and control particularly rewarding. Thus, in the competition among various rival scientific methodologies, behaviorism is expected to succeed for two reasons. First, it provides greater rewards in the form of prediction and control than the others and therefore will be chosen by scientists. Second, a community which uses a methodology that is most effective for its adaptation will, by definition, have the greatest probability of adapting and surviving. Other communities, not possessing equally effective methodologies, will not survive as well in this cultural form of competition and natural selection.[59] Thus, behaviorist standards of scientific acceptability can be viewed as a scientifically based explanation and prediction of what *will* eventually become scientific practice rather than a prescription of what it *ought* to be.[60]

Agon[61]

Of course, this prediction is far from being fulfilled, and it is not obvious which premise from the above argument is at fault. Perhaps the contingencies of survival have not had enough time to operate. Perhaps prediction and control are not the most powerful reinforcers controlling the behavior of scientists. Perhaps current behaviorist dictates about science do not in fact maximize prediction and control.

In any case, the received wisdom of today is that behaviorism has been refuted, its methods have failed, and it has little to offer modern psychology. Attacks against behaviorism have reached the frequency and vehemence that marked behaviorism's assaults against its own predecessors. Polemics, intemperate invective, *ad hominem* argument, and caricature prevade discussions of behaviorism by those who seek its demise. Such is the nature of Oedipal conflict. Factors other than effectiveness hold sway, and the search for truth is lost in the battles between movements. Clearly, this is not useful to psychology, or to society. What is needed rather is an accurate portrait of behaviorism and an honest search for what is still valuable in it.

Notes

1. GENERAL OVERVIEW

1. For the use of "praxiology," see Moore (1923) and Harrell and Harrison (1938), for "behavioristics," see Roback (1923, p. 200), Hebb (1958, pp. 3–4), Price (1961), and Hempel (1969), and for "anthroponomy," see Hunter (1930a).

2. This distinction between behaviorism and the science of behavior is discussed by Roback (1923, pp. 200–201), Watson (1930, pp. 18–19), Hunter (1930a), Spence (1948), Skinner (1963a; 1967; 1974, pp. 3–8), and Hebb (1980, pp. 8–10).

3. This aspect of behaviorism is criticized by Newbury (1953), Spielberger and DeNike (1966), Kessell (1969), Bowers (1973), and Brewer (1974).

4. "Conceptual framework" avoids the question as to whether behaviorism constitutes a "scientific paradigm," or "disciplinary matrix," in Kuhn's (1962/1970; 1974) sense. Those suggesting that it does include Katahn and Koplin (1968), Burnham (1968), Palermo (1970; 1971), Kendler and Spence (1971), Segal and Lachman (1972), Brewer (1974), Dulany (1974), and Lachman, Lachman, and Butterfield (1979, pp. 27–28, 39–46). Watson (1967) and Turner (1971, pp. 7–11) describe it as "pre-paradigmatic," while D. L. Krantz (1972), Berlyne (1975), and Robinson (1979, ch. 3) conceptualize it in other ways. Briskman (1972) and Mackenzie (1972; 1977, ch. 1) argue that behaviorism is not a scientific paradigm. Eysenck (1970), Krasner (1971), and Dunlap and Lieberman (1973) claim that behavior therapy represents a Kuhnian paradigm, and for further discussion see Wilson (1978) and Kazdin (1978, ch. 1). The controversy is difficult to resolve partly because the concept of a "scientific paradigm" is vague, as Masterman (1970) and Shapere (1971) note, and partly because there is no universally accepted characterization of behaviorism.

5. Already in 1924, Woodworth (1924) distinguishes four varieties of behaviorism, while a bit later, Williams (1931) distinguishes five.

6. See McLeish (1981) for example. Cohen (1974) discusses the distinction between the critical philosophy of science and the history of scientific ideas.

7. See also Woodworth (1924) and Suppes (1969c).

8. There have been many attempts to characterize behaviorism. These include proposals by Lashley (1923a), de Laguna (1927/1963, pp. 123–131), Kuo (1928), Maltzman (1966), Brody and Oppenheim (1966), Day (1976a; 1980), and Ledwidge (1978).

9. Wittgenstein (1953, pp. 31–36, 1958; pp. 17–20), Bambrough (1960–1961), Achinstein (1969), Rosch and Mervis (1975). Harzem and Miles (1978, pp. 34–35) also use the concept of family resemblance to characterize behaviorism, and Erwin (1978, pp. 37–46) uses it to describe behavior therapy.

10. See Roback (1937, pp. 152–163) for a "who's who" of behaviorism in its first 25 years.

11. See Roback (1923) and review by Harrell and Harrison (1938).
12. See, for example, Weiss (1928a; 1930).
13. Analytic behaviorism is discussed by Mace (1948–1949), Whiteley (1961), Beloff (1962, pp. 36–44), and Fodor (1968, ch. 2). Also see chapter 10.
14. For discussions of the relationship between behaviorism and logical positivism see Bergmann (1940a), Weber (1942), Koch (1959; 1964), Turner (1967, chs. 1, 5, 6), Hempel (1969), Scriven (1969), Day (1969b), Mackenzie (1977, ch. 4), and Smith (1983). Also see chapters 10 and 11.
15. Locke (1971) and Erwin (1978, ch. 2) argue that behavior therapy is not behavioristic while Eysenck (1972) and Waters and McCallum (1973) disagree. Also see Craighead, Kazdin, and Mahoney (1976, ch. 3) and Kalish (1981).
16. The centrality of this premise is echoed by Dashiell (1928, pp. 8–18), Weiss (1929a, pp. v–vi), Guthrie (1960, chs. 1, 2), Kantor (1968), and Wolpe (1978a). Also see historical reviews by Tait (1932), Herrnstein (1967; 1969b), Koch (1959; 1974), and Mackenzie (1977, ch. 1) as well as analysis by Schwartz and Lacey (1982, ch. 1).
17. Turner (1967, ch. 2) and Broadbent (1973, pp. 187–207) discuss the relationship between empiricism and psychology.
18. For discussions of the relationship between behaviorism and objectivism see Carr (1915), Woodworth (1924), Diserens (1925), Dashiell (1928, pp. v, 8–18; 1937, p. v), and Bergmann (1953). Also see survey by Fuchs and Kawash (1974).

2. OBSERVATION

1. See Spence (1957) on empathic projection (but cf. Scriven, 1969), Hull (1934) and Wasserman (1981) on anthropomorphism, and Wolpe and Rachman (1960) on psychoanalytic interpretation.
2. Calkins (1913), Broad (1925, ch. 6), McDougall (1926), Farrow (1927), Lieberman (1979).
3. Woodworth (1931, ch. 3), Williams (1934), McTeer (1953).
4. Boring (1953), Turner (1967, ch. 1), and Herrnstein (1969b) review pre-behaviorist objections to introspection.
5. Holt (1915b, p. 88; 1937), Hebb (1980, pp. 8–9).
6. Boring (1953).
7. Watson (1913a; 1924a, ch. 1), Weiss (1925a), Broadbent (1961, pp. 40–41).
8. Otis (1920), Bentley (1926), Waters and Pennington (1938), Pennington and Finan (1940).
9. Carr (1938).
10. Pavlov (1928, p. 192), for example, equates "objective" with "existing in space and time." See also Heidbreder's (1933, ch. 7) and Harrell and Harrison's (1938) critiques of Watson.
11. Bode (1914), Weiss (1928a).
12. Bawden (1919a), Kantor (1942).
13. Watson (1913a; 1924a, ch. 1), Pepper (1923), Weiss (1929a, pp. 43–55).
14. This is discussed at length in chapter 11.
15. Dashiell (1928, pp. 10–12), Heidbreder (1933, p. 282), Pratt (1939, pp. 48–51), Spence (1948).
16. This circularity is noted by Pratt (1922), Weber (1942), and Mackenzie (1977, pp. 9–13).
17. Pratt (1939, pp. 50–54), Köhler (1947, pp. 25–33), Zaner (1967), Radford (1974). Also see replies by Weiss (1929a, pp. 68–72) and Brody and Oppenheim (1967). The metaphysical assumptions in behaviorist views on observation are discussed by Heidbreder (1933, ch. 7), Williams (1934), Harrell and Harrison (1938), Crissman (1944), and Mackenzie (1977, ch. 1).
18. Titchener (1914), Thomson (1920), Prince (1926), Muenzinger (1927).
19. Fernberger (1922), Moore (1923). Smith and Guthrie's (1921) behaviorist introduction to psychology has an appendix devoted to introspected consciousness.

20. Dodge (1912), Wheeler (1925), Titchener (1929, ch. 2), Pratt (1939, ch. 1).
21. See below.
22. Thorndike (1915), Hull (1943b, p. 30; 1952, p. 353), Guthrie (1950), Staats and Staats (1964, pp. 2, 10), Brody and Oppenheim (1966).
23. Meyer (1911, p. 229), Weiss (1918), Hull (1943b, p. 30), Guthrie and Edwards (1949, pp. 23–25).
24. Bode (1914), de Laguna (1919b; 1927/1963, pp. 126–129), Watson (1924a, pp. 1–2), Singer (1925), Weiss (1929a, p. 49), Guthrie and Horton (1946, p. 7), Broadbent (1961, pp. 37, 44), Treisman (1962). Verificationism is extremely important in operationism (discussed in chapter 4) and logical behaviorism (discussed in chapters 10 and 11). Note, however, that behaviorist leanings to verificationism precede logical positivism and operationism.
25. Bawden (1918), de Laguna (1918; 1930), Weiss (1917a; b), Tolman (1932, p. 426; 1935), Tolman and Horowitz (1933), Guthrie and Horton (1946, p. 7), Guthrie (1959), Treisman (1962). Also see discussion of methodological behaviorism in chapter 10.
26. See discussion of logical behaviorism in chapters 10 and 11.
27. Robinson (1920), Washburn (1922), Zener (1958), Burt (1962), Zaner (1967), Alston (1972), Lieberman (1979).
28. Crissman (1944), Whiteley (1961).
29. Wheeler (1923), Zener (1958), Whiteley (1961), Zaner (1967), Newbury (1972), Lieberman (1979).
30. The issue of how to treat contradictory introspective reports underlies the controversy between Baldwin (1896) and Titchener (1895). See Krantz (1969) for a review.
31. Pratt (1939, pp. 14, 99; 1945), Burt (1962), Henle and Baltimore (1967), Dulany (1968). Goodson (1976) traces the history of this position. Also see Köhler's (1947, pp. 19–33; 1966) distinction between "objective experience" and "subjective experience."
32. Kantor (1938; 1942).
33. The Copy Theory is discussed in chapters 8, 11, and 12.
34. Ryle (1949, ch. 7). Also see chapters 8 and 11.
35. Watson (1913a), Tolman (1935), Spence (1956, pp. 13–15; 1957), Kendler and Spence (1971), Kendler (1981, ch. 2). Also see related remarks by Bridgman (1927; 1945) and by Stevens (1935a; b; 1939).
36. Calverton (1924), Weiss (1925a; 1929a, pp. 21–22; 1929b), Ritchie (1944), Guthrie (1946; 1959; 1960, pp. 276–277), Spence (1948; 1956, p. 14; 1957), Guthrie and Edwards (1949, pp. 23–29), Kendler and Spence (1971), Marx (1976a), Kendler (1981, ch. 2). Intersubjective agreement and public observation are criteria for the data base but not for theoretical concepts (see chapter 4). Therefore, criticisms of the intersubjective agreement criterion which argue that the natural sciences commonly admit theoretical entities not open to public observation, e.g., Erwin (1978, p. 70), miss the mark. Among logical behaviorists, intersubjective agreement is emphasized by Carnap (1937; 1955) and Hempel (1958, 1960; 1969). Also see Quine (1960, ch. 1; 1969a) who identifies behaviorism with the use of intersubjective observational terms.
37. Crissman (1944).
38. See discussion by Kendler (1968; 1970; 1981, pp. 45–65, 69–77, 94–99). Boring (1953) and Palermo (1971) assume that the fall of introspectionism was due largely to its failure to reach agreement on basic observations. However, this traditional view is questioned by Briskman (1972) and Mackenzie (1977, ch. 1) who interpret introspectionism's decline as due to a scientific revolution.
39. Ellson (1963) addresses some of these questions.
40. Otis (1920), Wheeler (1923).
41. The argument against the possibility of a private language appears in de Laguna (1918; 1919b), Wittgenstein (1953), Hampshire (1959, ch. 1), Treisman (1962), Turner (1967, pp. 207–209), and Zuriff (1979a). Jones (1971) presents a selection of the arguments for and against the Wittgensteinian position. See also Kripke (1982).

42. Köhler's (1947, pp. 19–33; 1966) distinction between subjective and objective experience is relevant here.

43. de Laguna (1927/1963, pp. 136–139), and Goodson (1976) explain this fact in terms of its selective adaptive value.

44. Wittgenstein (1953, p. 100).

45. Dollard and Miller (1950, pp. 119, 180–181) and see Crissman (1944).

46. See Carnap (1932–1933/1959), Ryle (1949, pp. 201–210), Hampshire (1959, ch. 1), Quine (1960, ch. 1), Aune (1966), and Fodor (1968, pp. 71–74).

47. Tolman (1923).

48. Skinner (1945a) and see chapter 11.

49. Wittgenstein (1953) and see chapter 10.

50. Skinner (1945a; 1953a, p. 280; 1957a, p. 140) argues that it is not possible to establish a discriminative response to privacy as such. Day (1969b) notes the similarity between Skinner and Wittgenstein on the implausibility of a private language.

51. See Broadbent (1961, pp. 37–41) and the distinctions drawn by Holborow (1967) among various types of private language.

52. See chapter 12 for an examination of Skinner's truth criteria, and chapters 4, 5, and 11 for a discussion of private events.

53. See chapter 11.

54. This position is found most commonly among behavior therapists. Homme (1965) advances the strongest statement of the position. Mahoney (1970; 1974, pp. 4, 51; 1977a) and Craighead, Kazdin, and Mahoney (1976, pp. 45–46) seem sympathetic to it, while Eysenck (1964) objects to it. See Kazdin (1978, pp. 209, 320–321) for a review. Also see Skinner (1969, p. 242), Day (1969a; 1976a), Kendler (1970), Radford (1974), and Leiberman (1979).

3. BEHAVIORAL DATA LANGUAGE

1. For an unsympathetic review see Koch (1959; 1964).

2. Bentley (1941).

3. Attempts to define an *a prioiri* distinction between behavior and physiology appear in Watson (1917a), Meyer (1921, pp. 8–10), Hunter (1932), Hunter and Hudgins (1934), Tolman (1938d), Bentley (1941), and Broadbent (1961, pp. 42–43).

4. See, for example, the definition of "response" in Miller and Dollard (1941, p. 59, fn. 5) and Miller (1959). Also see discussion of functional definition below.

5. Kitchener (1977). Also see chapter 10 for a discussion of the theoretical extension of the terms "stimulus" and "response."

6. Lashley (1923b), Pratt (1939, chs. 5, 6), Hebb (1949, introduction; 1958, pp. 259–266), Davis (1953), Joynson (1970), Maltzman (1971).

7. The classic statement of molar behaviorism is by Skinner (1938, ch. 12), discussed by Pratt (1939, pp. 132–134), Sidman (1960, pp. 183–185), and Teitelbaum (1977). Other versions can be found in Tolman (1922a; 1932, ch. 1, pp. 415–417; 1936; 1959), Watson (1917a; 1924a, p. 215, fn. 1, pp. 39–41; 1930, pp. 15, 209–210), Weiss (1919b), Skinner (1931; 1932; 1972c), Tolman and Horowitz (1933), Kantor (1942), Woodrow (1942), Hull (1943a), Spence (1947), Silverstein (1966), MacCorquodale (1970), and Day (1980).

8. Skinner (1931).

9. Meyer (1921, pp. 173–174), Johnson (1963), Schoenfeld (1970), MacCorquodale (1970), and see Aronson (1976) for objections. The explanatory adequacy of "black-box models" in molar behaviorism is discussed in chapter 4.

10. Guthrie (1933a; 1934), Skinner (1938, ch. 12; 1947; 1953a, pp. 28–29), Johnson (1963).

11. Skinner (1938, p. 4; 1974, pp. 217–218), Bergmann (1953). Also see chapter 9.

12. Weiss (1919b; 1924b), Holt (1931, p. 213). Also see the debate between Kantor (1922; 1923b) and Warren (1923a; b), as well as chapter 9.

13. Cf. Bergmann (1956) and Miller (1959).

14. Watson (1913a; 1914, pp. 53–54), Tolman (1925b), Hull (1937; 1943b, pp. 167–169), Skinner (1947; 1953a, p. 28; 1969, pp. 281–284), Feigl (1951), Carnap (1956), but cf. Putnam (1973).

15. Watson (1914, pp. 53–54), Skinner (1935a; 1938, ch. 12; 1969, pp. 282–283), Tolman (1936), Broadbent (1961, p. 43), Kendler and Spence (1971).

16. Hull (1943b, p. 20), Hebb (1958, pp. 262–265), Schwartz (1967).

17. See chapter 12.

18. See the discussion of attention in chapter 9.

19. See, for example, Weiss (1924b; 1929a, ch. 9), Guthrie (1938, pp. 301, 317–318), Bentley (1940), and Skinner (1957a, pp. 415–417).

20. See Rozeboom (1974) for a review. Covert responses are discussed in the next chapter.

21. Carnap (1937), Guthrie (1959).

22. Day (1969a; 1976c), Bennett (1964). Also see Wittgenstein's (1953) "form of life."

23. Skinner (1957a, pp. 84–86, 224–226), Lacey (1974).

24. Cf. Pylyshyn (1973; 1978). The propositional nature of human knowledge is emphasized by Guthrie (1950; 1960, pp. 276–277), Guthrie and Edwards (1949, pp. 24–25), and it is discussed by Hebb (1951) and Brody and Oppenheim (1966). See also Goodman (1960).

25. In addition to the behaviorists mentioned in the preceding footnote, Mach (1905/1976, p. 99) and Hampshire (1959, ch. 1) elaborate on this point. Also see chapter 12.

26. Hanson (1958), Kuhn (1962/1970), Feyerabend (1965). See discussions by Hesse (1966; 1969), Lakatos (1970), and Tuomela (1973). Suppe (1974) provides a comprehensive review. Kessel (1969) and Turner (1967, pp. 190–205; 1971, ch. 1) examine the implications for behaviorist psychology. The distinction is defended by Nagel (1979, ch. 2), and the thesis of the incommensurability of competing theories is criticized by Scheffler (1967) and Shapere (1971). Quine (1969b, ch. 3), Hempel (1970; 1974), and Feigl (1970) attempt to accommodate the changing views on the observation-theory distinction in ways that make them more palatable to traditional behaviorist philosophy of science. Also see discussion of theory and observation in chapter 5.

27. See, for example, Rozeboom (1970) and Kendler (1981, pp. 48–64).

28. One possible example of the theory-ladeness of data can be found in Guthrie and Horton (1946, p. 38) who report relabeling a photograph to read "Cat G" because it had earlier been mislabeled. The only evidence for the "error" was that the posture shown by the cat in the photograph was one shown only by Cat G. Thus their theory that only stereotyped movements are learned dictated a particular datum.

29. Guthrie (1946), Guthrie and Edwards (1949, pp. 24–25), Quine (1969a), but cf. Mahoney (1977b). Intersubjective agreement is discussed in chapters 2 and 12.

30. Nagel (1979, ch. 2), Kendler (1981, pp. 48–64).

31. Watson (1917a), Hull (1943b, p. 25), Guthrie and Horton (1946), Guthrie and Edwards (1949), Voeks (1950), Guthrie (1960), Schoenfeld and Cumming (1963). Among the logical behaviorists, Carnap (1932–1933/1959; 1937) insists that behavior be given a "physical" description, and see Bergmann (1940b) and Hempel (1969) for a discussion of Carnap's views. The requirement that stimuli be described using the properties of physics is stated by Skinner (1931; 1935b; 1953a, p. 36; 1957a, p. 117; 1966b), Hull (1939), Spence (1956, pp. 2, 39), Guthrie (1960, pp. 25–26), and Schoenfeld and Cumming (1963). It has its origin in the use of the term "stimulus" in physiology (e.g., Sherrington, 1906, pp. 5–6). Gibson (1960) reviews the various uses of the term in psychology.

32. Rozeboom (1960; 1961; 1974), Brodbeck (1963), Lawrence (1963), but cf. Gray (1931).

33. Meehl (1945). See below for a discussion of the empirical psychological question.

34. Rosenow (1923), Malcolm (1971b, section 26). For behaviorist views see Weiss (1924b; 1925b; 1928a; 1929a, pp. 49–51; 1930), de Laguna (1930), Hebb (1946) and Guthrie (1959). For further discussion see Koch (1954; 1964), Bergmann (1956), Rozeboom (1974), and Herrnstein (1982a).

35. Guthrie (1960, p. 276), Guttman (1963), Stenius (1969).

36. Tolman (1951; 1959), Ferster and Skinner (1957, pp. 10, 733), Kimble (1967b), Staats (1968, p. 90). Also see discussions by Hull (1939; 1943b, pp. 32–33), Spence (1956, pp. 39–42), and Gibson (1960).

37. Thorndike (1913, pp. 49, 358–359), Orata (1928).

38. The following three paragraphs are based on Zuriff (1976).

39. Hampshire (1959, ch. 1), Goodman (1960), Koch (1964), Quine (1969b, ch. 5), Dodwell (1970), Kuhn (1974), Weimer (1976), Tuomela (1977, ch. 3), Herrnstein (1982a).

40. Weiss (1924a; 1929a, pp. 59–60).

41. Kantor (1923b; 1942), Weiss (1924a), Guthrie (1946; 1960, pp. 5–6; 1959), Graham (1950), Bergmann (1953), Kendler and Spence (1971), Herrnstein (1977a).

42. Similar formulations are endorsed by Skinner (1938, pp. 6–7) and Harzem and Miles (1978, ch. 6). Skinner's formulation is discussed by Verplanck (1954) and Scriven (1956).

43. The distinction is not the same as the movement-achievement distinction examined below. An achievement (e.g., lever press) can be brought about by a movement that is not an action, and a description of a movement can be in action language.

44. For more on the concept of an action see Shaffer (1968, ch. 5), Mischel (1969), Borger (1974), Zuriff (1975), Davis (1979), and ch. 9.

45. Zuriff (1975). Also see chapter 9.

46. Hamlyn (1962), Taylor (1966), Toulmin (1969), Davidson (1974).

47. Zuriff (1975). Guthrie and Horton (1946) are a good example, and see Kitchener's (1977) discussion.

48. Dewey (1918), Brodbeck (1963), Shwayder (1965), Zuriff (1975), Kendler (1981, pp. 26–27), and see review by Davis (1979). Guthrie and Edwards (1949, p. 29) suggest limiting "behavior" to only those movements that result from nerve impulses activating muscles or glands so as to exclude passive movement. However, reflexes fit their definition but are not actions.

49. Rosenow (1923; 1925), Taylor (1964, pp. 90–95).

50. See Shuford (1966) and Place (1981). Intensionality is also discussed in chapters 7, 8, and 10.

51. Dewey (1914), Rosenow (1925), Davies (1926), Taylor (1964), and Hamlyn (1970).

52. Guthrie and Horton (1946, p. 40), Guthrie (1946; 1959), Suppes (1969c), Harzem and Miles (1978, ch. 6), Day (1980), Place (1981).

53. Behavioral interpretations of intensional language are reviewed in chapter 10. Taylor (1964, ch. 4) argues that they all fail.

54. Mowrer (1960a, p. 310), Dennett (1971; 1975; 1978b; 1978d), Skinner (1972i; 1977a).

55. Quine (1960, pp. 220–221). An analogous indeterminacy holds for the expectancy construct of MacCorquodale and Meehl (1953; 1954) which is not uniquely related to a belief proposition (Rozeboom, 1970).

56. Dewey (1914), Davies (1926), McDougall (1926), Taylor (1964; 1970), Dennett (1969; 1971), Alston (1974). See chapter 10 for a discussion of this point.

57. Tolman (1925b; 1926a; b; 1927b; 1933). See MacCorquodale and Meehl (1954) and Newbury (1972).

58. Part of the confusion stems from the fact that, as he himself notes (Tolman, 1959), the distinction between data language and construct language is not one that interests him. See Tolman (1937; 1951).

59. Guthrie (1936; 1940; 1944), Guthrie and Horton (1946, p. 7), Guthrie and Edwards (1949, pp. 67–68), Spence (1956, pp. 42–43), Kitchener (1977), Kendler (1981, pp. 28–30).

60. Davis (1953), Mueller and Schoenfeld (1954), Salzinger (1973b). Also see Skinner (1969, pp. 130–131). Replies are set forth by Schick (1971), Kitchener (1977), and Kendler (1981, p. 29, fn. 4).

61. See Carnap (1932–1933/1959), Mueller and Schoenfeld (1954), Guthrie (1959), and Zuriff (1975). The practical application of this notion is discussed by Baer, Wolf and Risley (1968), O'Leary, Kent, and Kanowitz (1975), and Wolf (1978). See also the distinction drawn by Weiss

(1922; 1924a; b; 1929a, pp. 84–88; 1930) between biophysical descriptions (those in the units of the physical sciences) and biosocial descriptions (those based on the reactions of human observers). Also relevant are the discussions by Mackenzie (1977, pp. 166–169) and Day (1980).

62. Hunter (1930a), Kantor (1938), Guthrie (1960, p. 276; 1959) but cf. Skinner (1935a; 1966b), Guttman (1963), and Köhler (1966). In practice, however, Skinner uses perceptual stimuli as is noted by Verplanck (1954).

63. Versions of "purposive behaviorism" appear in Holt (1915b), Perry (1918; 1921a; b), Wallis (1924), and Tolman (1925a; 1926b; 1932). They are reviewed by Herrnstein (1967), Boden (1972), and Kitchener (1977). The term comes from McDougall (1926).

64. Holt (1915a), Tolman (1932, pp. 7–8), Tolman and Horowitz (1933).

65. See discussions by Varvel (1934) and Kitchener (1977).

66. Kuo (1928), Weiss (1929b), Guthrie (1960, pp. 140–141), but cf. Wright (1976, ch. 1).

67. Tolman (1932, pp. 11–16), Kitchener (1977), but cf. Woodfield (1976, ch. 6).

68. On occasion (e.g., Tolman, 1928b) Tolman implies that purpose is an inference. Taylor (1970), on the other hand, argues that teleological descriptions are directly observable. See also Wright (1976, chs. 1, 2).

69. The terms "molar" and "molecular" and the distinction between them have so many meanings, as reviewed by Littman and Rosen (1950), Herrnstein (1967), Kitchener (1977), and Place (1981), that psychology would probably do well to drop them entirely. As first introduced by Broad (1925, pp. 616–617), "molar" referred to observable behavior and "molecular" to unobserved internal events. This is basically the same sense intended by Hull (1943a; b, pp. 19–21; 1951, pp. 5–6). However, Hull (1943b, p. 31) claims to have adopted Tolman's usage even though Tolman (1932, pp. 1–12; 1935) uses the distinction to differentiate between behavior described in terms of movements versus behavior described in purposive terms. For Spence (1956, p. 42) the distinction corresponds to the difference between movement and achievement definitions of a response. However, Spence (1948; 1960b) also uses level of analysis as the basis for the distinction as does Watson (1917a). In their "micro-molar" theories, Hull (1952, ch. 7) and Logan (1959; 1960) attempt to explain phenomena at one level of analysis by appeal to a more elemental level. Another version of this issue arises in the debate between "molar" and "molecular" explanations of response rate (Shimp, 1974; Rachlin, 1976, pp. 176–184; Heyman, 1979). See also the debate between Shimp (1976) and Branch (1977) on the choice of behavioral units.

70. The individuation of actions is discussed by Pepper (1934), Walker (1942), Skinner (1969, pp. 127–131), and Davis (1979).

71. Holt (1915b, pp. 77–91), Wallis (1924), Naess (1965), Mischel (1969). Also see Hamlyn (1964) and Madell (1967).

72. Both Weiss (1917b) and Watson (1924a, pp. 11–12, 40), despite their popular images as "muscle-twitch" psychologists, emphasize that their psychologies are to analyze molar behavior at a level of interest to society.

73. The classic statement of the functional approach is by Skinner (1935a), and the concept is developed by de Laguna (1919a; b; 1927/1963, pp. 141–155, 168–177), Kantor (1933), Skinner (1938, pp. 33–43; 1957a, pp. 19–22), Miller (1959), Guttman (1963), Lawrence (1963), Staddon (1967), Shimp (1976), and Gewirtz (1978). The functional stimulus is discussed by Gibson (1950; 1960), Tighe and Tighe (1966), and Zuriff (1976). The notion of "functional class" is formally defined by Moore and Lewis (1953). Illustrations of how functional classes are constructed in the context of experimental research are provided by Spence and Ross (1959), Sidman (1960), Killeen (1968), Salzinger (1973b), and Honig and Urcuioli (1981). Skinner generally defines an operant class as an achievement class, but the latter is not necessarily a functional class. Therefore, Catania (1973) distinguishes between the "descriptive operant" (defined by the achievement or movement that reinforcement is contingent upon) and the "functional operant" (defined as the class of responses empirically found to be strengthened by a reinforcement). On this point see Verplanck (1954), Ferster and Skinner (1957, p. 724), Skinner (1969, pp. 131–132), and Kitchener (1977).

74. Israel and Goldstein (1944), Chomsky (1959/1967), Breger and McGaugh (1965), Tuomela (1971), Bowers (1973), Erwin (1978, pp. 99–101). Replies are offered by Skinner (1938, pp. 9–10), Meehl (1950), Miller (1959), Hocutt (1967), whose formulation is adopted here, Schick (1971), Dunham (1977), and Schnaitter (1978a).

75. See chapter 11 for a discussion of psychological properties.

76. Spence (1937a; b; 1941b), Zeiler (1963), Hebert and Krantz (1965). Goldstein, Krantz, and Rains (1965) present a selection of papers on this controversy. Many behaviorists, including Meyer (1911, ch. 14), Weiss (1924b; 1929a, pp. 218–221), Dashiell (1928, pp. 420–422), Lashley (1929, pp. 158–159; 1938), Guthrie (1930; 1960, p. 165), Dunlap (1930), Hebb (1949, chs. 3, 5), Guthrie and Edwards (1949, pp. 246–249), Dollard and Miller (1950, p. 34), Spence (1952b), Skinner (1953a, pp. 137–138; 1957a, pp. 107–113), Miller (1959), and Rozeboom (1972; 1974), admit that a relationship or pattern among stimuli can serve as a functional stimulus. Also see reviews by Reese (1968), Carter and Werner (1978), Schrier and Thompson (1980), and Kehoe and Gormezano (1980). Briskman (1972) is therefore incorrect in asserting that the finding of relational stimuli is a fundamental challenge to behaviorism.

77. Chapter 10 examines the charge that stimuli and responses specified in this way are "stimuli" and "responses" only in a "metaphorical" sense. Among those who advocate specifications of this sort are Tolman (1926b), de Laguna (1927/1963, pp. 157–159, 171, 197–200), Thorndike (1949, chs. 5, 7), Miller (1959), Lawrence (1963), Staddon (1967), Salzinger (1975), Zuriff (1976), Herrnstein (1977a; 1982a), and Eysenck (1979). Such specifications are universally used in the practice of behavior therapy (e.g., Wolpe, 1969), and examples in experimental research include the "thematic class" of Holz and Azrin (1966), the work of Premack (1970), "group norms" as used by Gewirtz (1971) to define kinds of self-regulatory behavior, the "filial response" of Hoffman and Ratner (1973), Bandura's (1977a, pp. 41–48) abstract modeling, and "prestigiousness" as a stimulus dimension defined by Howard (1979). See also Premack's (1978) cautionary critique.

78. The problem is most compelling with regard to Skinner's (1957a) analysis of verbal behavior. For example, in this analysis Skinner uses the following to describe functional stimulus classes: "Frenchness" (p. 183), "singularity," "activity," and "currency" (p. 332) and "action-in-the-past" (p. 121). Skinner (1938, p. 168; 1957a, pp. 114, 128) is aware of the problem and attempts to justify the "bootstrap" (1957a, p. 115) nature of the practice of verbally specifying the stimuli for verbal behavior, but Chomsky (1959/1967) and Lacey (1974) object while MacCorquodale (1969; 1970) tries to defend Skinner's analysis. See Wells (1919) for an earlier version of this issue.

79. Holt (1915b).

80. Tolman and Brunswik (1935), Brunswik (1937). Also see Alston (1974).

81. Bijou (1979).

82. The controversy over what is learned can be traced in Honzik and Tolman (1936), Spence (1936; 1960c), Tolman, Ritchie, and Kalish (1946a; b; 1947a; b), Tolman and Gleitman (1949), Nissen (1950; 1952), Smedslund (1953), Campbell (1954), Tolman (1955b), and Mowrer (1960b, pp. 24–26). The controversy over transposition, discussed above, is the "stimulus" version of the what-is-learned question. This question, as defined here, is at times conflated with the independent question of how best to portray learning in a theoretical model (cf. Kendler, 1952; Smedslund, 1953). The conventional wisdom (e.g., Goldstein, Krantz, and Rains, 1965, pp. 228–229) is that the what-is-learned question was settled by Restle (1957). However, Restle shows only that the experimental circumstances determine which cues control the behavior but leaves unanswered the question of what description best characterizes the response associated with the controlling cue. As Segal and Lachman (1972) note, a supposed empirical question floated away in a "cloud of obscurity." Wasserman (1981) indicates the question may be the subject of renewed interest.

83. Campbell (1954).

84. MacCorquodale and Meehl (1954, pp. 218–231) present an excellent discussion of the relationship between response specification and the what-is-learned issue.

85. See MacCorquodale and Meehl (1954).

4. THEORETICAL CONCEPTS

1. See Koch (1959; 1964) and Mackenzie (1977) for unsympathetic historical reviews. Kurtz (1968) discusses neo-behaviorist theory in social sciences other than psychology.

2. Cf. Turner (1967, pp. 92–94), Shimp (1976), and Branch (1977).

3. See Tolman (1920) and Mursell (1922b) on "adjustments," Skinner (1932; 1936; 1938, pp. 23–28, ch. 9; 1969, pp. 27–28; 1978, pp. 116–118) on "third variables," Thorndike (1932, ch. 15), Spence (1944), Burns (1960), Herrnstein (1977b), and Mahoney (1974, ch. 3).

4. See debate among Arbib (1969), Nelson (1969; 1975) and Suppes (1969a; 1975).

5. Singer (1924, pp. 40, 91–93) speaks of "virtual behavior," while Tolman (1922b; 1923; 1926a) often refers to a "readiness," or a "recurring tendency." Although generally opposed to state variables, Skinner (1953a, pp. 168–169, 246) describes an unemitted response of high probability as well as mood in terms of dispositions, and his concept of "response repertoire" (1957a, p. 22) is dispositional.

6. Stevens (1935a; b; 1939), McGregor (1935), Janus (1940), Boring (1945), Hempel (1965, ch. 5), but cf. Newbury (1953).

7. Israel and Goldstein (1944), Bridgman (1945), Skinner (1963a), Taylor (1964, pp. 76–82), Mackenzie (1977, ch. 4), but cf. McGregor (1935). Boring (1945), Garner, Hake, and Eriksen (1956), and Maltzman (1968) provide examples of operationism in psychology.

8. Crissman (1939), Koch (1941), Skinner (1945a; b), Hempel (1960).

9. Koch (1941), Carnap (1956), Hempel (1960), Suppe (1974).

10. Carnap (1936), and see Suppe (1974), Mackenzie (1977, pp. 131–133), Erwin (1978, pp. 56–57), and Quine (1982, pp. 21–26).

11. Carnap (1936).

12. Carnap (1936), Hempell (1958; 1960; 1965, ch. 5; 1974), Suppe (1974). Scheffler (1963, pp. 169–178) raises objections to the use of reduction chains. Miller (1959), Dulany (1968), Tuomela (1971), and Olshewsky (1975) discuss the relevance of reduction chains to psychological theoretical terms. Examples of concrete attempts to introduce psychological concepts through reduction chains include Koch (1941), Maltzman (1955), and Cotton (1963). Tolman, Ritchie, and Kalish's (1946a) classic attempt to introduce the concept of "expectation" via a bilateral reduction sentence is criticized by MacCorquodale and Meehl (1954) and Taylor (1964, pp. 79–82). MacCorquodale and Meehl's objection can be answered by substituting an open reduction chain for Tolman, Ritchie, and Kalish's closed bilateral reduction sentence. Taylor's objection is answered below.

13. In practice, behaviorists often are not strict in their use of operational definitions and therefore equate operational definitions with open reductive chains. See, for example, Koch (1941) and Miller (1959), and discussion below.

14. This is a criticism raised by Waters and Pennington (1938), Kantor (1938), Crissman (1939), Weber (1942), Ginsberg (1955), and Erwin (1978, p. 57), and anticipated by Miller (1911).

15. Waters and Pennington (1938), Pennington and Finan (1940), Suppe (1974). Also note that Bridgman (1927) maintains that as physics progresses, more fundamental concepts, fewer in number, replace the older concepts, thereby reducing the number of operations.

16. Stevens (1939), Bergmann and Spence (1941), Weber (1942), Boring (1945), Suppe (1974).

17. Israel (1945), Hempel (1960).

18. Stevens (1939), Boring (1945).

19. Pennington and Finan (1940), Ginsberg (1955), Scriven (1969), Mackenzie (1977, ch. 4).

For the common criticism that the concept of "operation" is vague, see McGeoch (1937), Crissman (1939), Israel (1945), and Newbury (1958).

20. Pennington and Finan (1940), Bergmann and Spence (1941), Hull (1944), Feigl (1951), Miller (1959).

21. See Spence and Ross (1959) for an example of the judgment required for the operational definition of the eyelid response.

22. Stevens (1939), Israel and Goldstein (1944), Bridgman (1954), Koch (1959), Kendler (1967; 1981, pp. 93–94), Seligman (1969), Kendler and Spence (1971), Staddon (1971), D. H. Krantz (1972), and Shepard (1978).

23. The implication is that when the theory is not put to formal tests, concepts need not be given operational definition during the process of theorizing. See Pratt (1945), George (1953b), Maatsch and Behan (1953), Kendler and Spence (1971), Marx (1976b), and Kendler (1981, pp. 87–94).

24. See Feigl (1945), Pratt (1945), Kendler and Spence (1971), Scriven (1956), and Kendler (1981, pp. 87–94) for a further discussion of operationism in the development of scientific theory. As it became clear that operationism is not a substitute for human ingenuity and that strict operational definitions are both impossible to state and unduly restrictive, "operationism" came to mean simply the practice of good scientific method as well as clarity and precision in stating scientific theory. See, for example, the way the word "operational" is used by Seashore and Katz (1937), Ullmann and Krasner (1965), and Gewirtz (1978). For loose definitions of operationism see McGeoch (1937), Pratt (1939, chs. 3, 4), Feigl (1959), Broadbent (1961, p. 41), Turner (1967, p. 304), Marx (1976a), and Staats and Staats (1964, pp. 11–13).

25. For the development of Tolman's concept of the intervening variable see Tolman (1928b; 1932; 1935; 1936; 1938d), Koch (1959), and Smith (1983, ch. 4). Brown and Farber (1951) illustrate the use of the intervening variable.

26. Hull (1943a; 1943b, pp. 22, 118; 1951, p. 105). Koch (1944; 1959) notes that the anchoring is actually to "systematic variables."

27. Tolman (1936; 1937; 1938a).

28. Marx (1958), Miller (1959).

29. The dispositional aspects of an intervening variable make it akin to Mackenzie's (1977, ch. 3) "objective inference," and see Zuriff (1979c), Wasserman (1981; 1982), and Malone (1982).

30. In practice, as noted above, operational definitions are also open. Israel and Goldstein (1944) discuss additional differences between operationally defined concepts and concepts like intervening variables. Ginsberg (1954b), Koch (1954), and Pap (1962, pp. 387–388) deny that intervening variables are open concepts.

31. Nevertheless, MacCorquodale and Meehl (1948), Carnap (1956), and Nelson (1975) identify intervening variables with Carnapian dispositions. In addition, Tolman, Ritchie, and Kalish (1946a) attempt to introduce Tolman's concept of "expectation," an intervening variable, by a Carnapian reduction sentence. Also Hull (1943a) notes a similarity between his intervening variables and Carnap's physicalistic reduction of psychological predicates, but note Smith's (1983, ch. 7) discussion of Hull's confusion. On the other hand, Cotton (1963) emphasizes the stimulus-side anchoring, and Rozeboom (1956) notes that this anchoring means that the ontological referent for the intervening variable is the same as that of the independent variables. Pap (1962, p. 387, fn. 8) recognizes that the stimulus-side anchoring distinguishes the intervening variable from the disposition, but he dismisses the distinction on the grounds that the independent variables are only "historical."

32. Tolman and Krechevsky (1933), Keller and Schoenfeld (1950, pp. 265–271). See chapter 12.

33. Rozeboom (1956), Pap (1962, pp. 387–388). But cf. Tolman (1932; 1935) who appears to assign a causal role to intervening variables, and Hull's opinion that intervening variables mediate causal gaps, as discussed below. Also see Maze (1954), and Pap (1962, pp. 384–385).

34. See discussion by Goodman (1965, ch. 1).

35. Woodrow (1942). This argument is a version of the "paradox of theorizing" discussed below.

36. Among those who fear the reification and internalization of these concepts are Kuo (1928), Skinner (1932; 1953b), Kendler (1952), Cotton (1963), and Branch (1977). The dangers of mentalism in the use of theoretical concepts are discussed by Guthrie (1937), Guthrie and Horton (1946, pp. 16–17), Cotton (1963), Skinner (1972i; 1978, ch. 6), Ledwidge (1979), and Malone (1982). Replies to these objections can be found in Bergmann (1953), Scriven (1956), Mahoney (1974, ch. 3), and Shimp (1976).

37. Guthrie and Edwards (1949, pp. 162–163), Skinner (1953a, ch. 3; 1954), Johnson (1963), Salzinger (1973a), Branch (1977). Replies appear in Scriven (1956), Keat (1972), Mahoney (1974), Wasserman (1981; 1982), and Wessells (1981; 1982).

38. See chapter 9.

39. Kendler (1968), Wasserman (1981; 1982).

40. Hull (1943a; 1943b, p. 109), Hempel (1958), Cotton (1963). Also see Chapman (1928).

41. O'Neil (1953), Maze (1954), Deutsch (1960, pp. 2–5), Pap (1962, pp. 388–389), Kitchener (1977).

42. See for example Hull's (1952, ch. 4) introduction of the stimulus trace to make stimulus and response contemporaneous. Holt (1915a) names and attacks the "bead theory." Pap (1962, p. 389) calls it the "postulate of contiguous causation." See objections to it by Skinner (1966a; 1972i) and Rachlin (1977a; b; c; 1978a).

43. Holt (1915a), Skinner (1931; 1953a, p. 23), Staats and Staats (1964, p. 18), Rachlin (1978a). Also see chapters 8 and 12.

44. Scriven (1956) and Bowers (1973) argue against this approach. See reply by Johnson (1963).

45. Feigl (1945), Miller (1959), and Cotton (1963) note the savings in equations afforded by the use of an intervening variable. Skinner (1932), MacCorquodale and Meehl (1948), and Seward (1955) are careful to point out that this savings is only in number of equations and *not in number of experiments* needed to establish the equations. Rozeboom (1956; 1970), however, claims that the intervening variable actually *increases* the number of equations since the $m+n$ equations are added to the original $m \times n$ equations. However, in a formal expression, the $m+n$ equations contain everything covered by the $m \times n$ equations, and therefore the latter are superfluous.

46. Tolman (1938a), Bergmann and Spence (1941), Hull (1943a; b, pp. 110–111), Spence (1944; 1957), Seward (1954; 1955), Hempel (1958).

47. Carnap (1936), MacCorquodale and Meehl (1948), Kessen and Kimble (1952), Bergmann (1953), Seward (1955), Spence (1957), Shimp (1976), but cf. Beck (1950). Hempel (1958) and Tuomela (1971) reject Craigian substitutes for theoretical concepts partly on the grounds that they do not allow for inductive systematization. Tolman (1959) abandons intervening variables in part because he doubts that values of intervening variables can be predicted for nonstandard conditions. However, in this he misconstrues the heuristic role of intervening variables to be more than a source of hypotheses to be tested.

48. Kolakowski (1968, ch. 6) traces conventionalism in positivism. Mursel (1922b) and Meyer (1921, pp. 365–369) are early examples of it in behaviorism. Kendler (1952) makes use of conventionalism to resolve the S-S vs. S-R controversy. See discussion of instrumentalism in chapter 12. Hull (1952, p. 133) is, in effect, doubting the stipulative nature of his intervening variables when he wonders whether it is possible to determine how the delay of reinforcement gradient affects his basic function for the gradient of reaction potential, or whether the question is a false one. Seward (1954) asserts that it is not a false question and offers a method for answering it. However, Seward's method works only because all the stipulations necessary to define the intervening variables have already been legislated.

49. See Spence (1952c; 1956, ch. 4) on the stipulative nature of Hull's definition of habit strength and cf. Ginsberg (1954b).

50. Tolman (1933; 1937; 1938a; 1949b; 1952a; 1955a; b). See also Tolman's (1939; 1941b) "sowbug" and Boring's (1946) "robot."

51. Armstrong (1968, pp. 85–88), Tuomela (1977). Within the psychological literature, Chapman (1928), Maze (1954), Ginsberg (1954b), Locke (1972), and perhaps Boring (1950) appear to lean toward realism.

52. Armstrong (1968, pp. 82–88).

53. Debate concerning the distinction constitutes one of the most tortuous chapters in behaviorist metatheory. The distinction itself is clearly stated by MacCorquodale and Meehl in their classic 1948 paper and is further clarified by Rozeboom (1956). Part of the confusion stems from the fact that what MacCorquodale and Meehl call a "hypothetical construct," B. Russell (1917) had already termed an "inferred entity;" while the latter's "logical construction" is the former's "intervening variable." Also see Beck (1950). Much confusion also arises because the distinction launched a debate over which sort of concept is superior (see below) although this question is irrelevant to the validity of the distinction. Another irrelevant question that is enmeshed is whether any concepts in psychology actually correspond to the intervening variable as defined by MacCorquodale and Meehl. For example, Hebb (1951), Bergmann (1953), Maze (1954), Tolman (1959), and Mackenzie (1977, pp. 143–148) maintain that, in practice, intervening variables have excess meaning, contrary to the original definition of the intervening variable. These irrelevant issues so cloud the distinction that many psychologists simply deny the distinction and substitute their own, e.g., Marx (1951), O'Neil (1953), Ginsberg (1954b), Hochberg (1961), and Deutsch (1960, ch. 1). See outline by Turner (1967, p. 259).

Consequently, the original distinction has become confused with other possible ways of drawing the differentiation between two kinds of theoretical concepts. One alternate distinction is between terms which refer to internal events which are observable, in principle, given the right conditions and those which are purely conceptual because they refer to relationships rather than things (Deutsch, 1960, p. 5; Mahoney, 1974, pp. 19–20). Under this distinction, hypothetical constructs are observables (although unobserv*ed*) and intervening variables are unobservables, reversing the usual characterization. A second kind of distinction often confused with the original one is between unobserved *hypothesized* events thought to occur inside the organism and *hypothetical* events conceived as mere convenient fictions for the purpose of extending a theory to a new domain but not as actually occurring (see Lachman, 1960; Gough and Jenkins, 1963; Goldstein, Krantz, and Rains, 1965, p. 37). Finally Meissner (1958) and Mackenzie (1977, p. 186, n. 67) distinguish between theoretical terms which are required to have their theory-relevant meaning specified entirely within the theory and those which are not. According to this distinction, both hypothetical constructs and intervening variables belong to the former. Mackenzie is forced into this position because his central thesis is that behaviorists adopt an instrumentalist attitude toward theoretical concepts. The inclusion of hypothetical constructs in most behaviorist theories (see below) seems to contradict this conclusion. To escape this contradiction, Mackenzie misconstrues hypothetical constructs as having no surplus meaning beyond the postulates of the theory. However, this interpretation is contrary to the bulk of behaviorist writings on the nature of hypothetical constructs (see below) and to the fact that few hypothetical constructs are introduced by a postulate set.

The tangle of issues surrounding MacCorquodale and Meehl's original distinction are reviewed by Meissner (1960) who only adds to the confusion. It is not surprising that the terms "hypothetical construct" and "intervening variable" are commonly misused. Many of the inconsistencies in Hull's and Tolman's use of the intervening variable as noted in this and the next chapter stem from the fact that Meehl and MacCorquodale's characterization of the intervening variable is not fully congruent with those of Tolman, Hull, and Spence.

54. MacCorquodale and Meehl (1948), Ginsberg (1955), Scriven (1956), Hempel (1960), Mahoney (1974, ch. 3), Erwin (1978, p. 55).

55. The "model" presented here is actually a synthesis of a number of similar models developed by logical empiricists including Carnap (1956), Hempel (1958; 1960; 1965; 1969), Feigl (1955; 1959; 1970) and Nagel (1961, ch. 5). Criticisms of these models leading to their revision and, in some cases, rejection are presented in Radner and Winokur (1970), Suppe (1974), and Brown

(1977). The relevance of these models for psychology is discussed by McGuigan (1953) and Ginsberg (1954b; 1955). Applications of the model to psychological theories are carried out by MacCorquodale and Meehl (1954) for expectancy, Gough and Jenkins (1963) for the mediating response, and Dulany (1962; 1968) for his theory of awareness. Verplanck (1954) tries unsuccessfully to fit Skinner's (1938) theory into the model.

56. Cf. Quine's (1960, pp. 13–17) notion of contextual meaning, and Skinner's (1957a, pp. 71–80) "intraverbal."

57. See Hochberg (1961) and Naess (1965) for related points.

58. Koch (1964), Fodor (1968, pp. xiv–xv), Mackenzie (1977, chapter 4).

59. Versions of this argument can be found in Waters and Pennington (1938), Carnap (1956), Hempel (1958; 1969), Feigl (1959), Pap (1962, p. 387, fn. 9), Taylor (1964, pp. 82–87), Mischel (1969), Mackenzie (1977, pp. 130–133), and Erwin (1978, pp. 58–59). See discussion in MacCorquodale and Meehl (1954, pp. 233–234).

60. Cf. Polanyi's (1968) "tacit knowledge." Even Bridgman (1927, p. 10) is aware that it is futile to try to fully explicate the *ceteris paribus* clause in an operational definition.

61. See Krech (1950; 1955), Feigl (1951), and Davis (1953). Hebb (1951; 1958) is a behaviorist proponent of this position, but Amsel (1965) claims that Hebb's constructs are psychological not physiological. Part of the confusion is related to a common error (e.g., Kimble, 1967b) of supposing that just because a construct is inferred from behavioral data, the construct itself must therefore be behavioral rather than physiological. Pratt (1938; 1939, pp. 138–143) distinguishes between the "formal properties" of a hypothetical construct which are inferred from behavioral data and the "material properties" which are hypothesized physiological features (see also Melton, 1941).

62. Tolman (1938d), Marx (1951), Kessen and Kimble (1952), Maatsch and Behan (1953). See also the discussions by Pratt (1938; 1939, ch. 5) and Turner (1967, pp. 338–339).

63. Tolman (1932, pp. 415–416), Tolman and Horowitz (1933), Spence (1941a; 1947), Bergmann (1954).

64. See reviews by Turner (1967, pp. 239–242; 1971, pp. 34–35, 69–71) and Kendler (1981, pp. 119–129). See Bunge (1963) for a formalization of black-box theory. Cognitivist objections to black-box theories are reviewed in chapter 8. Also see debate between Chomsky (1959/1967) and MacCorquodale (1970).

65. Guthrie (1933a), Goodson and Morgan (1976), and Kendler (1981, ch. 5) discuss the concept of "understanding."

66. Chapman (1928) Cronbach and Meehl (1955), Rozeboom (1956), Carnap (1956), Koch (1959), Feigl (1955; 1959), Broadbent (1961, pp. 141–142), Tolman (1952b), Johnson (1970), Tuomela (1971; 1973), Mahoney (1974; 1977a). Also see the debate between Maxwell (1962) and Schnaitter (1975).

67. Krech (1950), Tolman (1950), Beck (1950), Hebb (1951), Ginsberg (1955), Turner (1967; 1971), Tuomela (1973).

68. Strategic arguments against hypothetical constructs appear throughout the history of behaviorist thought. A representative sampling includes Honzik and Tolman (1936), Tolman (1937), Skinner (1938, ch. 12; 1953a, ch. 3), Kantor (1942), Keller and Schoenfeld (1950, pp. 269–271), Maatsch and Behan (1953), Kanfer (1968), Salzinger (1973a), Rachlin (1976; 1977a; b; c; 1978a), Ledwidge (1979), and Bijou (1979). For examples of arguments against particular hypothetical constructs see Azrin and Holz's (1966) objections to the competing response theory of punishment and Herrnstein's (1969a) criticisms of inferred stimuli used to explain avoidance conditioning. Compare the preference for intervening variables over hypothetical constructs to B. Russell's (1917) maxim that whenever possible, logical constructions are to be substituted for inferred entities. Hochberg (1961) and Maxwell (1961) suggest possible metaphysical biases underlying the opposition to hypothetical constructs. Replies to the strategic arguments against hypothetical constructs are offered by Hebb (1949, pp. xiv–xvi), Feigl (1951), Ginsberg (1954b). Wessells (1981; 1982), and Kendler (1981, pp. 313–321).

69. The paradox of theorizing, or the "theoretician's dilemma" is best stated by Skinner (1953a, ch. 3) who, along with Woodrow (1942) and Schoenfeld (1970), concludes from it that theories are unnecessary. In contrast, Hempel (1958) and Tuomela (1971; 1973) resolve the dilemma in favor of theory. Craig (1956) presents a theorem which formally demonstrates the dispensibility of theoretical terms. However, his method of replacement has a number of practical drawbacks, as pointed out by Hempel (1958), Nagel (1961, pp. 134–137), and Tuomela (1971), in addition to Craig (1956) himself, which make it unworkable. Also see the debate between Suppes (1969a; b; 1975) and Nelson (1969; 1975).

70. Watson (1913b; 1914; 1917a; 1919; 1920; 1924c; 1930). Unobserved responses, variously known as "covert," "virtual," "incipient," "implicit," "internal," "minimal," "visceral," and "subvocal" are quite common in behaviorist theory. A representative sampling includes Bawden (1919b), Kantor (1920; 1921a; b; 1923a), Meyer (1921, p. 361), Smith and Guthrie (1921, pp. 162–166), Weiss (1924b; 1929a, pp. 280–286), Dashiell (1925; 1928, pp. 480–485, 528–535), Tolman (1927a; 1932, pp. 210–214) who terms them "behavioral feints," de Laguna (1927/1963, pp. 307–310), Dunlap (1930), Dollard and Miller (1950, pp. 68–69, 99), Keller and Schoenfeld (1950, pp. 212–221), Spence (1951), Hull (1952, pp. 151–152), Staats and Staats (1964, pp. 91–94), and Berlyne (1965, p. 309; 1966). In the field of behavior therapy, private events play a major role as noted by Mahoney (1970), Yates (1970), Waters and McCallum (1973), Wolpe (1978a), and Heppner (1978).

71. Hull (1931; 1934), Spence (1956, p. 176), Mowrer (1960a; b). Although Mowrer (1960a, p. 163) introduces hope and fear as intervening variables, it is clear from their role in his theory that they have surplus meaning and are hypothetical constructs (cf. Mowrer, 1960b, pp. 68–69). Other examples in this category include the concepts of fear and anxiety in Dollard and Miller (1950, pp. 68–69) and Wolpe (1969, p. 96).

72. Lawrence (1963), Schoenfeld and Cumming (1963), Cohen (1969), Kamil and Sacks (1972). See Carter and Werner (1978) for a review. The coding response is a later version of the perceptual response as discussed, for example, by Dashiell (1928, ch. 13) and Dollard and Miller (1950, p. 179), and see review by Rozeboom (1974).

73. Hull (1939), Keller and Schoenfeld (1950, p. 160), Mowrer (1954), Goss (1955; 1961a), and see Goss (1961b) for a review. The most extensive theoretical use of the mediating response is by Osgood (1953; 1957; 1966), Osgood, Suci and Tannenbaum (1957), and Kendler and Kendler (1962; 1966; 1968). However, their metatheoretical statements on the nature of the mediating response leaves some ambiguity as to whether it is a hypothetical construct as defined here. Gough and Jenkins (1963) and Maltzman (1968) argue that it is not, while Tuomela (1971; 1977, pp. 99–100) argues that it is (and see Marx, 1958).

74. Guthrie (1946). See also Weiss (1917a) and Spence (1956, p. 41). Skinner (1950) and Guthrie (1959; 1960, p. 26) offer the disingenuous suggestion that postulated movement-produced stimuli are not unobservable because they can be observed by observing the subject's movements.

75. Hull (1930b).

76. Sherrington (1906, pp. 338–344). See Fearing (1930, ch. 13). For examples of the use of "postural adjustments," "tonus," and "motor readiness" to explain psychological states see Holt (1915b), Perry (1918; 1921a), de Laguna (1919a), Dashiell (1928, pp. 279–293, 540), Rexroad (1933a), Guthrie (1938, pp. 85–86, 186; 1960, pp. 168–170), Berlyne (1951), and Pribram (1971, pp. 225–231).

77. Other examples include Estes' (1950) "stimulus elements," Dinsmoor's (1954) interfering responses during punishment, Guthrie's (1959) "total response" (see Mueller and Schoenfeld, 1954), Perkins' (1968) "preparatory responses," Herrnstein's (1970) "r_0," and the "background stimuli" of Rescorla and Wagner (1972).

78. Watson (1924a, p. 361), Dollard and Miller (1950, p. 99, fn. 1), Miller (1959), Kendler and Kendler (1962), Staats and Staats (1964, p. 94), Salzinger (1973a). In behavior therapy, this assumption is known as the "continuity" or "homogeneity" assumption. Meichenbaum (1973)

and Cautela and Baron (1977) argue in favor of the assumption while Mahoney (1974, pp. 118–120) and Kazdin (1977; 1978, pp. 225–226) oppose it. See the discussion in Kazdin and Wilson (1978, pp. 3–6). Rachlin (1975; 1977c) and Schnaitter (1978b) point out some of the methodological difficulties in empirically testing the assumption. Fodor, Bever, and Garrett (1974, pp. 66–77) and Paivio (1975) note that this assumption is one of the main differentiations between behaviorism on the one hand and cognitivism and neomentalism on the other. Also see chapter 8.

79. See the discussion of peripheralism in chapter 9.

80. See chapters 6, 8, and 9. Also relevant is the debate between Fodor (1965) and Osgood (1966).

81. See for example Schoenfeld and Cumming (1963), Skinner (1974, p. 103), and Gough and Jenkins' (1963) comment on Skinner.

82. See chapter 9.

5. THEORIZING

1. MacCorquodale and Meehl (1948). But cf. Goldstein, Krantz, and Rains (1965, p. 3).

2. Hull (1943a; 1943b, pp. 21–22, 31), Spence (1944; 1948; 1957), Bergmann and Spence (1941), but cf. Turner (1967, pp. 313–314).

3. O'Neil (1953) and Maze (1954) note ambiguities in Hull's treatment of his constructs. Another problem with construing Hull's concepts as intervening variables is that, as noted by Skinner (1944; 1969, p. 28), Ritchie (1944), Koch (1954; 1964), and Cotton (1963), many of his constructs, notably $_sO_r$, $_sL_r$, and neural interaction, are not anchored on both sides. Some of these objections can be met if the concepts are viewed merely as mathematical transformations of anchored constructs. For example behavioral oscillation, $_sO_r$, can be viewed as merely the transformation of a determinate response value into a probability distribution. Compare this suggestion with Hull's (1951, p. 6) comment that he speaks of "stimulus traces" merely as a means of applying a logarithmic transformation to the stimulus value. Also see Hilgard and Bower (1975, p. 168).

4. Bergmann and Spence (1941), Spence (1944; 1947; 1948; 1950; 1951; 1957), Kendler (1952; 1981, pp. 120–121), Seward (1954).

5. Hull (1943b, p. 277).

6. MacCorquodale and Meehl (1954).

7. See Hull (1943b, pp. 235–236). Similar considerations apply to Brown and Farber's (1951) Hullian analysis of emotion.

8. Problems concerning the causal status of Hull's intervening variables are discussed in the preceding chapter. Hull frequently speaks of constructs as internal conditions indirectly observable, e.g., Hull (1943a; 1944; 1952, p. 344), and he compares them to atoms, as constructs (Hull, 1943b, p. 29; Hull et al., 1947). One source for the ambiguity derives from understanding Hull through Spence's commentary. Spence convinced Hull that the latter's constructs are intervening variables, and although Hull explicitly accepted Spence's interpretation, Hull's writings are not always consistent with it. For further discussion, see Koch (1954).

9. Hull (1935b; 1937), Hull et al. (1940).

10. See Koch (1941), Kattsoff (1939), and chapter 4.

11. Hull et al. (1940, pp. 2–3).

12. Marx (1976a).

13. This is essentially how Hull (1950; 1951, pp. 119–120) and Spence (1944; 1948; 1952c; 1953; 1956, pp. 18–19, 54–55, 88–92; 1957) eventually came to understand the Hullian postulates. See also Bergmann and Spence (1941) and Amsel (1965). Koch (1941) calls Hull's procedure "telescopic" because it skips the uninterpreted formal calculus stage. Also see Koch (1954) for a full discussion.

14. Hull (1951, p. 1; 1952, p. 1).

15. Hull (1943b, pp. 10–12), Hull et al. (1940, p. 11).

16. Hull (1930a; 1934; 1943b, ch. 1; 1944), Spence (1936; 1956; 1960a), Miller (1959). Miller and Dollard (1941) illustrate a classic extension of the hypothetico-deductive method to human social learning. Koch (1959), Marx (1976a; b), and Kendler (1981, pp. 104–110), distinguish various senses of "hypothetico-deductive method." It might mean a research strategy in which experiments are dictated by the theorems derived from the theory. Or it might represent a method for testing a theory. In this latter sense, a theory evolving from a research program is formalized at various stages into a deductive system in order to determine whether empirical findings are consistent with and explained by the theory. In this case the method is really a *post hoc* reconstruction of a research program that may have developed in a variety of ways. Koch (1959) and Mackenzie (1977, ch. 4) fault behaviorism for using the hypothetico-deductive method in the first sense. Broadbent (1961, pp. 138–140; 1973, pp. 32–34) criticizes the hypothetico-deductive method because it works with only one theory at a time. Many of these objections directed at the first sense of "hypothetico-deductive" are irrelevant to the second.

17. Hull (1943b, pp. 30–31), Kendler (1981, pp. 210–216).

18. Hull (1937; 1951), Spence (1952a; c; 1953; 1954; 1956), Logan (1959).

19. These intervening variables are introduced in Skinner (1931; 1932; 1935b; 1938, pp. 24–28) although he sometimes appears to be claiming that they are not intervening variables, e.g. Skinner (1938, p. 26). Also see discussion by Verplanck (1954). "Reflex reserve" is bid farewell in Skinner (1950) and the others in Skinner (1953a, e.g., p. 144). See Skinner (1956a; 1977b) for his own account.

20. Blanshard and Skinner (1967), Skinner (1969, pp. 255–262; 1974, pp. 17, 158; 1977a).

21. Zuriff (1979b).

22. Skinner (1945b; 1953a, pp. 258, 282). However, in a personal communication (1980) Skinner writes, "A person directly observes private events but . . . the behaviorist must infer them in explaining behavior under their control. . . . My wife may directly perceive a telephone call and I *infer* from the note she leaves that she perceived it, corroborating it by contacting the caller. I do not then say that telephone calls are '*theoretical* entities.' " Skinner implies here that private events are not "theoretical" in the sense of "theoretical" to which he objects (see below), but they are, nevertheless, inferred entities. Also see Skinner (1969, p. 242), Day (1976a; b), Zuriff (1980), and Malone (1982).

23. Meyer (1921).

24. Zuriff (1979a).

25. Skinner (1957a, p. 371).

26. Skinner (1945a; 1953a, ch. 17; 1957a, pp. 130–138; 1963a; 1969, p. 242; 1974, ch. 2).

27. Indeed, Skinner (1950) claims that his concept of "reflex reserve" is not theoretical, but it is not clear whether he considers it to be an intervening variable. Seward (1955) argues that the intervening variables of Hull and Tolman are not "theoretical" in Skinner's sense.

28. Skinner (1947; 1969, pp. ix–xi; 1972i).

29. Skinner (1956a; 1969, p. x), Moore (1975).

30. Skinner (1938, p. 437; 1956a; 1967; 1969, pp. x–xi), Sidman (1960, pp. 4–16), Boakes and Halliday (1970).

31. Skinner (1950; 1966b).

32. Skinner (1944; 1950; 1953b; 1963b; 1969, p. xi; 1972i), Kanfer (1968), and see criticism of Skinner's claim in Broadbent (1961, pp. 132–137) and Spence (1956, pp. 199–200).

33. Skinner (1944; 1950; 1956b).

34. Skinner (1956a; 1969, p. xi).

35. See discussions by Hebb (1949, pp. xiv–xvi), Ginsberg (1955), Scriven (1956), Johnson (1963), Kendler and Spence (1971), Keat (1972), Noble (1974), Lacey (1974) and Schnaitter (1975).

36. See Koch (1951).

37. See, for example, Sidman (1960, ch. 1), and de Villiers and Herrnstein (1976).

38. See Mach, who describes hypotheses which cannot become facts as an "evil" (Nagel, 1961, p. 126, fn. 17).

39. MacCorquodale and Meehl (1948), Seward (1954).

40. See for example the editorial in the Skinnerian *Journal of the Experimental Analysis of Behavior* (Nevin, 1980) in which contributors are forewarned that papers should address issues of *systematic* significance and not merely report factual information about a determiner of behavior, however clear the results.

41. This picture is pieced together from Skinner (1938; 1947; 1950; 1956a; 1957a; 1963c; 1966b; 1967; 1969), Gough and Jenkins (1963), Boakes and Halliday (1970), Moore (1975), and Teitelbaum (1977). Sidman (1960) gives the most complete account of the kinds of scientific tactics not governed by theory.

42. Verplanck (1954), Scriven (1956), Boakes and Halliday (1970), Staddon (1971), Noble (1974). See also Skinner (1931) on the "reflex" as an experimentally derived concept.

43. This conception of theory is developed in Skinner (1931; 1938, pp. 44–47, ch. 13; 1947; 1950; 1956a; 1957a, chs. 1, 18; 1966b), and Ferster and Skinner (1957, ch. 1). Its relationship to positivism is discussed in chapter 12. Since this form of descriptivism is open to the same charges of explanatory inadequacy (see, e.g., Miller, 1946; Scriven, 1956; Wolman, 1965) as are leveled at black-box theories, the discussion of the latter in the preceding chapter is also relevant to Skinner's theorizing.

Skinner also speaks of an acceptable theory in two other senses. First, there is the analysis of the methods and concepts of a science of behavior, and second, the "interpretation" of the everyday facts of behavior in ways consistent with that science. Both are discussed in chapter 10, and see MacCorquodale (1969; 1970). That Skinner finds certain kinds of theory acceptable makes irrelevant his image as a scientist without a theory as well as the many attempts to show that in fact there is a theory lurking behind his behavioral system.

44. An example is the theory of matching. In its initial formulation (Herrnstein, 1961) it was a simple description of the results of a single operant conditioning experiment carried out under a very restricted set of conditions. This description, the "matching law," was eventually generalized into a form which subsumed the original data as well as data from a variety of other conditions (Herrnstein, 1970). Later the matching law was itself subsumed under a more comprehensive formulation, "melioration," covering the matching law as well as several other phenomena (Herrnstein and Vaughan, 1980; Herrnstein, 1982b).

45. Skinner (1945a; 1947; 1956a; 1957a, ch. 18), Staats and Staats (1964, pp. 245–258). See chapter 12.

46. Skinner (1953a, section 6; 1971c).

47. Ferster and Skinner (1957).

48. Similarities between Hullian deductivism and Skinnerian inductivism are discussed by Amsel (1965) and Noble (1974), but cf. Day (1969b) and Moore (1975).

49. Reviews of objections to linear models appear in Achinstein (1969), Suppe (1974), Lakatos (1970), and Kuhn (1962/1970). These objections are applied to psychology by Koch (1964) and Kessel (1969).

50. See chapter 3.

51. See discussions by Ginsberg (1955), Logan (1959), and Rozeboom (1970).

52. Polanyi (1968), Kuhn (1962/1970), Mackenzie (1977, ch. 2). A good illustration is Miller (1959, pp. 256–257) who uses drive-reduction theory to guide research because it is the best theory available for this purpose even though he does not believe it likely that the theory is true.

53. This is true, although to a lesser degree, even of Hull as indicated by Hull et al. (1940, pp. 5–6) and Hull (1950).

54. Maltzman (1966; 1968) and Kendler (1981, pp. 18–19) following Reichenbach (1938, pp. 9–10) call decisions of this sort "volitional." See also Suppe (1974).

55. See chapter 3.

56. Compare, for example, Tolman (1949a) with Sidman (1960, chs. 1, 2).
57. Kuhn (1962/1970).
58. Rozeboom (1970), Zuriff (1971).
59. Fitch and Barry (1950) attempt the beginnings of a formalization of Hull's theory, and Voeks (1950) attempts the same for Guthrie's theory. Cronbach and Meehl (1955) argue that a mere sketch of nomological net is sufficient.
60. See Koch (1959), Achinstein (1969), Hempel (1970), and Suppe (1974).
61. Tolman (1950; 1951; 1952b; 1959).
62. See note 3.
63. The possibility of an infinite regress is noted by McGeoch (1937), Ginsberg (1955), and Scriven (1969). Solutions to it are suggested by Stevens (1935a), Kantor (1938), Koch (1941), Boring (1945), and Bridgman (1945).
64. Wittgenstein (1953; 1958), Hampshire (1959, ch. 1), Koch (1964), Turner (1967, pp. 95–97). George (1953a) also notes the ambiguity of pointing, and see Dauer (1972). Skinner (1957a, pp. 359–360) suggests that pointing, or ostensive definition, is not a simple act but is rather the result of a long history of conditioning. This conditioning would not be possible unless humans generalized as they in fact do. Thus, pointing works effectively because of psychological factors rather than logical ones, and this is precisely Wittgenstein's claim.
65. See chapter 3.
66. See Kuhn (1974) and Hebb (1980, pp. 121–128). That perceptual training is necessary even in Skinner's descriptivism in order to apply descriptive concepts like "contingency of reinforcement" and "knee in a cumulative record" is noted by Verplanck (1954), Koch (1964), Boakes and Halliday (1970), and Mackenzie (1977, pp. 166–169).
67. See Lachman (1960) and Hesse (1966) on theoretical models.
68. See chapter 12 for a discussion of pragmatism in behaviorism.

6. S-R

1. Discussions can be found in Kendler and Kendler (1962), Kendler (1968), Maltzman (1968), Kendler and Spence (1971), Koch (1959; 1964), Wilcoxon (1969), and Robinson (1979, ch. 3).
2. Kimble (1967b). Also see Lashley (1931).
3. See Fearing (1930), Kimble (1967a), Lowry (1970), and the selections in Herrnstein and Boring (1965, ch. 9).
4. Sherrington (1906, pp. 5–8), Pavlov (1928, pp. 73–74, 116–117).
5. Skinner (1931; 1935a), Peak (1933).
6. See Fearing (1930, pp. 286–311), Skinner (1931), Thorndike (1932, p. 19), Boring (1950, pp. 35–39, 46–47), Tuomela (1971), and Collier, Hirsch, and Kanarek (1977).
7. Watson (1913a; 1917a; 1930, p. 18), Mursell (1922b), Fearing (1930), Guthrie and Edwards (1949, pp. 68, 228), Guthrie (1960, p. 25), Mackenzie (1977, pp. 94–95).
8. The term is from Bechterev (1917/1931), but the ideas were initially formulated by Sechenov (1863/1935). Also see Watson (1914), Woolbert (1920), and Kazdin (1978, pp. 50–71).
9. Watson (1917a; 1924c; 1926), Skinner (1938, pp. 32, 52–55, 102–108).
10. See Guthrie (1930; 1938; 1940; 1944; 1960, ch. 13).
11. Watson (1916a), Pavlov (1928).
12. Watson (1914, pp. 206–209; 1924c), Smith and Guthrie (1921, pp. 54–60), Pavlov (1928, pp. 167, 257), Dashiell (1928, p. 44), Hull (1930b), Holt (1931, ch. 11), Skinner (1938, pp. 52–55, 300), Guthrie (1938, p. 67; 1940; 1944; 1960, pp. 107–108), Guthrie and Edwards (1949, pp. 117–118).
13. Hull (1930b), Guthrie (1938, ch. 8).
14. Sherrington (1906), Meyer (1911; 1921), Kuo (1921), Lashley (1923b), Reiser (1924), Pavlov (1928, ch. 25), Dashiell (1928, ch. 7), Watson (1930, pp. 90–91), Holt (1931, chs. 17–20),

Guthrie and Edwards (1949, pp. 62–64), Guthrie (1960, pp. 268–269). See also the criticism by Kantor (1922) and Crosland (1922), and Kitchener's (1977) review.

15. Cf. Sherrington's (1906, p. 185) "immediate induction," Holt's (1915b) "motor attitude" (and see Watson [1917b]), and Lashley's (1923b) "tonic innervation." See also discussion of state variables in chapter 4 and section on purpose in chapter 7.

16. Sherrington (1906, p. 114), Watson (1924a, p. 254), Skinner (1931), Rexroad (1933b), Sloane (1945).

17. Holt (1915a; b; but cf. 1931, ch. 22), and see review by Kitchener (1977).

18. Holt (1915a; b), but cf. Robinson (1917–1918). See discussion of the receded stimulus in chapter 3.

19. Spence (1959), Kitchener (1977).

20. See discussion of covert events in chapter 4. Examples of mediational constructs include the implicit response of Watson (1924a, pp. 343–356) and Dashiell (1925), Hull's (1930b) pure stimulus acts, and Kendler and Kendler's (1962) mediation mechanism. Contrary to Palermo's (1971) claim that mediation is an *ad hoc* attempt to deal with anomalies in S-R theory, mediation has been a prominent feature of S-R theories since their beginnings.

21. See chapter 8.

22. de Laguna (1927/1963, ch. 17), Hull (1934), Guthrie (1940), Miller and Dollard (1941), Maltzman (1955), Spence (1956), Staats (1961; 1968), Berlyne (1965).

23. Hull (1935c), Spence (1956, pp. 36–37; 1959).

24. Weiss (1924a), Lashley (1929, p. 163).

25. Skinner (1938, pp. 20–21, 51, 234–236, 241; 1957a, p. 36; 1963c), Teitelbaum (1964), Wilcoxon (1969), Boakes and Halliday (1970), Hamlyn (1970).

26. Skinner (1966b; 1969, p. 7).

27. Skinner (1931; 1953a, p. 23).

28. Skinner (1957b; 1966a; 1973b), Rozeboom (1970).

29. Skinner (1979, pp. 201–203) discusses his change from Skinner (1931).

30. Morse and Kelleher (1977).

31. See Staddon and Motheral (1978), Rachlin, et al (1981), and Hinson and Staddon (1981) for maximization theory, Herrnstein and Vaughan (1980) and Herrnstein (1982b) for melioration theory, and de Villiers (1977) and Herrnstein (1979) for matching theory. Comparisons among the various theories can be found in Baum (1981) and Vaughan (1981).

32. Herrnstein (1970), Baum (1973), Rachlin (1976, pp. 174–184; 1977b). As Fetterman and Stubbs (1982) note, even "molecular" theories of reinforcement, such as that of Shimp (1969), make use of molar properties of response and reinforcement.

33. See chapter 3 for a discussion of achievement-descriptions. Even Guthrie (1938, pp. 36–37), who prefers to define response classes in terms of movements, denies that behavior consists of well defined stereotyped reflexes. Similarly, Thorndike (1949, ch. 5) does not limit S-R connections to discrete stimuli and isolated movements. Rozeboom (1960; 1961; 1972; 1974) argues that responses are caused by environmental facts with propositional structure rather than by stimuli.

34. The classic formulation of this argument is by Dewey (1896), and it recurs in various versions in Bode (1914; 1917; 1922), Tawney (1915), Davies (1926), Bentley (1941), Miller, Galanter, and Pribram (1960, p. 30), Bowers (1973), Bandura (1977a, ch. 1; 1978), and Bijou (1979). It is also closely related to the criticism that S-R theories must incorporate a principle of negative feedback (Slack, 1955; Mowrer, 1960a, pp. 309–312; 1960b, pp. 178–180, ch. 7; Powers, 1973). Also see chapter 9.

35. Kantor (1920; 1933; 1942; 1968).

36. Skinner (1953a, ch. 15; 1974, pp. 176–180), and see discussion of self-control in chapter 9.

37. Skinner (1953a, ch. 16; 1968, ch. 6; 1974, ch. 7).

38. Skinner (1953a, pp. 321–322; 1974, pp. 190–196).

39. For example, obtained relative rate of reinforcement (matching theory), obtained local rate of reinforcement (melioration theory), and obtained marginal rate of reinforcement (maximization theory).

40. Baum (1973), Rachlin (1978b), Nevin and Baum (1980).

41. These ideas are implicit in Ferster and Skinner (1957) and Skinner (1958) and are made explicit by Baum (1973; 1981). But cf. Heyman (1982).

42. Prelec and Herrnstein (1978), Baum (1981).

43. The behaviorist preference for behavior-independent laws is discussed in chapter 9.

44. Wheeler (1940), Tolman (1948).

45. For example, in the theories of reinforcement discussed above, the effect of a reinforcement depends on its value relative to other reinforcements. Similarly, for Rescorla and Wagner (1972), the effect of a reinforcement depends on the existing associative strengths of the other stimuli concurrently present.

46. Koch (1944), Spence (1948).

47. See chapters 4 and 9.

48. See Kantor (1921a), Spence (1944), Dulany (1968), and Bowers (1973).

49. See chapter 4 for hypothetical constructs and chapter 8 for a discussion of cognitivism.

50. Tolman (1938b; c), Spence (1951; 1953) but cf. Tolman (1952b; 1955b; 1959). Also see Guthrie (1933b), Estes (1969), Kimble and Perlmuter (1970), Carroll (1971), Brewer (1974), Bandura (1977a), Wasserman (1981), and chapter 9.

51. Guthrie (1937; 1960, pp. 198–199), MacCorquodale and Meehl (1953), Skinner (1977a). Compare this criticism with Ryle's (1949, ch. 2) attack on the "intellectualist legend." Also see Tolman's (1955b) reply.

52. Guthrie (1960, p. 143).

53. See Hull's views on objective derivations as discussed in chapter 5, Spence (1937b), and Spence and Lippitt (1946).

54. Tolman (1948), MacCorquodale and Meehl (1954), Amsel (1965).

55. MacCorquodale and Meehl (1954).

56. Jones (1924), Bandura (1969, chapter 3).

57. Bandura (1974, p. 864; 1977a, pp. 22, 35).

58. See Gewirtz (1971) and Whitehurst (1978). See related discussion by Bem (1972).

59. See MacCorquodale and Meehl (1954), Bolles (1972), and Bindra (1978).

60. Spence (1950), Kendler (1952), but cf. Rozeboom (1958).

61. Tolman (1948), Spence (1950; 1951; 1953).

62. Loucks (1935), Spence (1950), Maltzman (1968). Other aspects of this physiological question are presented by Hebb (1949), MacCorquodale and Meehl (1954), and Gyr (1972).

63. Leeper (1944), Breger and McGaugh (1965; 1966), Chomsky (1972, p. 72), Kazdin (1978, pp. 308–316). See the discussion of the psycholinguist's version of this objection in chapter 7.

64. For attempts to derive expectancy phenomena from Hullian learning principles see Behan (1953), Cotton (1963), and Rozeboom (1970), and for illustrations of how learning by contiguity is derivable from Hullian postulates see Hilgard (1954) and Koch (1954).

65. Tolman, Ritchie, and Kalish (1946a), Thistlethwaite (1951), and see selections in Goldstein, Krantz, and Rains (1965).

66. Smith and Guthrie (1921, pp. 201–203), Thorndike (1932, chs. 3, 4, esp. p. 79), Guthrie (1933b; 1960, pp. 48 ff; 1959), Osgood (1953, pp. 460–462).

67. Hull (1952). See Miller (1935), Skinner (1957a, pp. 357–367; 1974, pp. 138–141), and Wolpe (1978a) for similar derivations.

68. Gewirtz and Stingle (1968), Gewirtz (1971; 1978). See Miller and Dollard (1941) for an earlier attempt.

69. See also Whitehurst (1978).

70. Bandura (1969; 1977a).

71. Bandura (1977a, p. 41).
72. Spence and Lippitt (1944), Thorndike (1946), Silverstein (1966).

7. ORGANIZATION OF BEHAVIOR

1. See Hebb (1949) for a discussion of what is meant by the organization of behavior.
2. Dewey (1914), Thurstone (1923), Tolman (1925a; 1927b; 1949a), Davies (1926), McDougall (1928, ch. 1), Bartley and Perkins (1931), Allport (1943), Granit (1977, pp. 186–187, 212–214).
3. See review by Woodfield (1976, ch. 3) replies by Malcolm (1967), Taylor (1970), and Wright (1976).
4. Kuo (1929b), Hull (1943b, pp. 22–27).
5. Weiss (1925b; 1929a; b), Hull (1943b, pp. 22–27), Guthrie (1960, pp. 140–141).
6. Objections to intensional descriptions are discussed in chapter 3.
7. Taylor (1964, p. 62), Malcolm (1967).
8. Hull (1937; 1943b, pp. 25–26, 28), Guthrie (1938, p. 43), Feigl (1955).
9. Perry (1921a), Weiss (1925b; 1928b), Hull (1943b, p. 26), Guthrie and Edwards (1949, p. 103), Guthrie (1960, p. 140).
10. Note Mach (1886/1959, p. 97).
11. Perry (1921a), Kuo (1929a), Guthrie (1933a; 1960, ch. 13), Herrnstein (1967). Examples can be found in Herrick (1925) and Locke (1969).
12. Guthrie (1924; 1933a; 1936; 1960, pp. 292–295), Singer (1925), Weiss (1925b).
13. See discussion of purposive behaviorism in chapter 3.
14. Tolman (1925a; b; 1932), Hull (1937). Also see objections by Kuo (1928) and historical reviews by Herrnstein (1967) and Kitchener (1977). Discussions on the compatibility of teleological and nontelelogical explanation appear in Taylor (1964; 1970), Malcolm (1967), Locke (1969), Turner (1971, pp. 158–176), and Boden (1972), and are reviewed by Wright (1976), Woodfield (1976), and Nagel (1979, ch. 12).
15. Holt (1915a; b), Perry (1918; 1921a), Thorndike (1932, ch. 15), Rexroad (1933a), Tolman (1920; 1926b; 1928b; 1938d), Hebb (1949, pp. 140–146), Guthrie (1960, pp. 168–170). Also see objections by Pratt (1922) and Woodbridge (1925).
16. Hull (1930a; b; 1931), Guthrie (1938, chapter 8; 1940; 1960, chapter 8), Guthrie and Edwards (1949, p. 85).
17. Skinner (1938, pp. 373–376; 1953a, pp. 87–90; 1963c; 1974, pp. 55–57; 1977a), Herrnstein (1964; 1967; 1972), Staats (1968, pp. 435–440), Ringen (1976), Day (1976a).
18. Wright (1976, pp. 35–39). Woodfield (1976, ch. 12) suggests an alternate formulation for teleological explanation: S does B because B characteristically and normally contributes to G, and G is good, either intrinsically or because it leads to a further good. This formulation is also closely related to reinforcement because of Skinner's (1971c, pp. 98–99, 122; 1972g) identification of the good with what is reinforcing.
19. de Laguna (1927/1963, pp. 296–310), Hull (1930b; 1937; 1952, p. 152), Miller (1935), Miller and Dollard (1941, pp. 49–53), Spence, Bergmann, and Lippitt (1950). But see objections by Deutsch (1960, ch. 8).
20. Hull (1931).
21. Mowrer (1960a; b). See the preceding chapter for a discussion of covert mediating chains.
22. S. B. Russell (1917), Bawden (1918), Kantor (1923a), Watson (1924a, pp. 342–356), Weiss (1929a, pp. 382–391), Mowrer (1960b, pp. 65–66, 212–214), Broadbent (1961, pp. 108–115), Staats (1968, pp. 108–109).
23. Perry (1918; 1921a), Mowrer (1960a; b). Tolman (1939; 1959) discusses vicarious trial and error, and Spence (1960c) introduces the "orienting response." Also see Hilgard and Bower (1975, pp. 178–182, 189–192, 403–406) for a discussion of scanning and incentive motivation.

24. See, for example, Guthrie (1960, pp. 284, 295–296; 1959), Miller (1959), and Broadbent (1973), but cf. Powers (1973). The relationship between cybernetics and purpose is discussed by Rosenblueth, Wiener, and Bigelow (1943) and Woodfield (1976, ch. 11).

25. See discussion in Skinner (1966a).

26. Skinner (1963c).

27. de Laguna (1927/1963, pp. 296–310), Hull (1952, p. 152).

28. Hunter (1924b), Gray (1932), Guthrie (1938, pp. 174–179).

29. Skinner (1953a, p. 237; 1957a, p. 44; 1969, p. 153; 1972g), Blanshard and Skinner (1967), Kanfer and Karoly (1972). But cf. Pears (1975, ch. 1).

30. Weiss (1925b), Guthrie (1933a), Skinner (1966a; 1969, p. 147; 1974, pp. 55–57). See chapter 11.

31. Skinner (1963c; 1969, pp. 146–171; 1974, pp. 125–128).

32. See similar arguments by Ryle (1949, ch. 2), Kuhn (1962/1970, pp. 194–195), Skinner (1969, pp. 146–152; 1974, pp. 127–128), Malcolm (1971a), and Schwartz (1978).

33. Skinner (1963c; 1969, p. 147), and see chapter 9.

34. See chapter 3.

35. de Laguna (1927/1963, pp. 305–307) and see Rice (1946) and the concept of "role" in Ullmann and Krasner (1965).

36. The "Skinner-Chomsky debate" is the centerpiece in this controversy between behaviorists and psycholinguists. The basic documents are Skinner's (1957a) *Verbal Behavior* and Chomsky's (1959/1967) review. Chomsky is supported by Breger and McGaugh (1965; 1966) and Erwin (1978, pp. 87–97) and answered by Wiest (1967), MacCorquodale (1970), Salzinger (1970; 1973a; b; 1975; 1978), Skinner (1972e), and McLeish (1981, ch. 7). See review by Lachman, et al. (1979, pp. 76–85). In order to conform to the traditional polemical tone of this controversy, the terms "nonsense," "vacuous," "utterly worthless," and "trivial" are hereby mentioned and dispensed with.

37. Chomsky (1959/1967; 1965, pp. 57–58).

38. See similar objections by Hebb (1972, pp. 259–261), and Fodor, Bever, and Garrett (1974, pp. 24–27).

39. See Meyer (1911, pp. 168–175) for an example.

40. See the discussion by Catania (1972).

41. Lashley (1951), Mowrer (1960a, pp. 493–494), Kimble and Perlmuter (1970), Robinson (1979, ch. 3).

42. Bever, Fodor, and Garrett (1968), Horton and Dixon (1968), Staats (1971). The inadequacies of Markov models in animal behavior are discussed by Hunter (1930b), Straub, et al. (1979), and Richardson and Warzak (1981). The general issues are reviewed by Miller, Galanter, and Pribram (1960, pp. 144–148) and Root (1975).

43. Lashley (1923b; 1929; 1938; 1951).

44. See Perry's (1921a) "determining tendency," Rachlin's (1976, p. 231) "molar appreciation" of verbal behavior, and Pribram (1971, pp. 221–237).

45. Salzinger (1973a; b), Shimp (1976).

46. See Tolman (1938d), Staats (1961; 1968, pp. 133–147), Millenson (1967), Segal (1977), and Robinson (1977).

47. The debate over how much of the structure of verbal behavior can be explained by mediation can be traced through Osgood (1957; 1963; 1968), Mowrer (1960b, ch. 4), Jenkins and Palermo (1964), Berlyne (1965, pp. 165–174), Bever (1968), McNeill (1968), Bever, Fodor, and Garrett (1968), and Fodor, Bever, and Garrett (1974, pp. 66–77).

48. Skinner (1957a, pp. 336 ff), Zimmerman (1969), Broadbent (1973, pp. 201–204), Lacey (1974), Salzinger (1975), Winokur (1976, pp. 138–139).

49. Skinner (1957a, chs. 12 and 13), MacCorquodale (1969), Segal (1975; 1977), Winokur (1976, ch. 11). Also see criticisms by Chomsky (1959/1967).

50. Skinner (1957a, chs. 14 and 15), and see Skinner (1973a).

51. MacCorquodale (1970), Segal (1975; 1977).
52. Miller, Galanter, and Pribram (1960, pp. 139–148), Miller (1965), Bandura (1977a, pp. 173–180).
53. Chomsky (1957, p. 44).
54. See Segal's (1977) analogy between this distinction and Skinner's distinction between primary verbal responses and autoclitic processes.
55. See also Tolman (1932, ch. 1).
56. This interpretation is developed by Catania (1972), Salzinger (1973a), and Zuriff (1976). It also appears in Horton and Dixon (1968) and Stich (1971). It is rejected by Chomsky (1959/1967, p. 169, fn. 46; 1972, p. 92, fn. 21; 1975, p. 245, fn. 5) in several footnotes, Miller (1965), and Katz (1964/1967).
57. Wiest (1967), Catania (1972).
58. See chapters 3 and 6.
59. The open frame, discussed above, is also relevant to this question.
60. Black (1970), Cowan (1970), Stich (1972), Schwartz (1978).
61. See the discussion of stimulus and response properties in chapter 3 and psychological properties in chapter 11. Miller (1965) and Garrett and Fodor (1968) unnecessarily limit D_F to the simple properties of physics and thereby justify their rejection of S-R psychology.
62. Staats (1968, pp. 154–158; 1971), Cowan (1970), MacCorquodale (1970), Black (1970), Catania (1972), Stich (1972), Broadbent (1973, pp. 192–194), Skinner (1974, pp. 98–99), Richelle (1976).
63. Catania (1972), Zuriff (1976).
64. See Brown (1916), Rice (1946), Thorndike (1949, ch. 5), and Herrnstein (1982a). The case against limiting a science of behavior to "physical descriptions" is presented in chapter 3.
65. Pylyshyn (1972), Broadbent (1973, pp. 192–194).
66. Chomsky (1959/1967, pp. 170–171; 1965, pp. 4–5, 8, 25, 58, 59; 1972, pp. 26–27, 30, 31, 38).
67. See Wiest (1967), Root (1975), and Skinner (1977a).
68. Braine (1963; 1965), Bever, et al. (1965a; b). For more, see Bever (1968), McNeill (1968), and Segal (1977).
69. Also see Cowan (1970), Pylyshyn (1972), Broadbent (1973, pp. 208–209), Fodor, Bever, and Garrett (1974, pp. 510–513), and Ringen (1975), but cf. Chomsky (1975, pp. 169–172; 1980, pp. 104–109).
70. Cowan (1970), Salzinger (1973a), Ringen (1975), Lachman, et al. (1979, p. 85), Juliá (1982).
71. The issue of what is learned is discussed in chapter 3.
72. Salzinger (1975), McLeish (1981, ch. 7).
73. Wiest (1967), Malcolm (1971a).
74. Skinner (1969, pp. 89–90), Black (1970), Salzinger (1975), McLeish (1981, p. 131), and see Chomsky (1965, pp. 18–21).
75. Staddon (1967).
76. Skinner (1974, pp. 11–12, 64–68, 97–100), Salzinger (1978), Juliá (1982).
77. Primitive learning operations are discussed in the preceding chapter.
78. Quine (1969a), Herrnstein (1982a).
79. Chomsky (1975, p. 13).
80. This question is debated by Skinner (1963c; 1969, p. 162; 1977a), Shwayder (1965, pp. 233–247), Osgood (1968), Zimmerman (1969), Stich (1971), Malcolm (1971a), Chomsky (1975, pp. 164–166; 1980, pp. 69–70, 89–103), Root (1975), Salzinger (1978), and McLeish (1981, p. 132).
81. See discussion in Herrnstein (1977a; b; 1982a).
82. See Premack (1970) and Rumbaugh (1977) for some empirical data, and see discussion in Braine (1971), Salzinger (1975; 1978), and Skinner (1957a, pp. 357–367).
83. See Herrnstein (1977a).

8. COMPLEX PROCESSES

1. See chapter 10.
2. White (1967, ch. 4) reviews the various senses of "think."
3. Perry (1918), Singer (1924, pp. 40, 91–93), de Laguna (1927/1963, p. 332–333), Tolman (1932, ch. 4; 1951), Ryle (1949), Skinner (1974, p. 138). Also see chapters 4 and 10 for a further discussion of dispositions.
4. Tolman (1935; 1937). Also see Marx (1958) and Wasserman (1981).
5. Rachlin (1977a; b), but cf. Mahoney (1977b) and Ellis (1977). Under the hypothetical-construct interpretation (see below), thoughts *can* be rewarded or punished.
6. Meichenbaum (1973), Heppner (1978).
7. For the cognitive side see Breger and McGaugh (1965), Wilkins (1971; 1972), Bandura (1974; 1977a, pp. 78–85; b), Mahoney (1974; 1977a; c), and Mahoney and Kazdin (1979). Opponents include Rachman and Eysenck (1966), Davison and Wilson (1972), Wolpe (1976b; 1978a; c), Ledwidge (1978; 1979), and Eysenck (1979).
8. Similar arguments appear in Davison and Wilson (1972), Waters and McCallum (1973), Wolpe (1976b; 1978a; c), and Ledwidge (1979).
9. Woolbert (1924), Norris (1928).
10. Bartlett and Smith (1920), Gray (1932), Thorndike (1949, pp. 120–123).
11. Hebb (1949), Maltzman (1955), Mandler (1962), Estes (1971), Shimp (1976). See also chapters 6 and 7.
12. de Laguna (1927/1963, pp. 185–188), Dashiell (1928, pp. 333, 491–495), Thorndike (1932, pp. 347–352), but cf. Guthrie (1930).
13. The question as to whether the effects of reward are cognitively mediated is discussed in the next chapter. One persistent problem in this area is the ambiguity of the term "cognitive" (Moroz, 1972).
14. Gewirtz and Stingle (1968), Gewirtz (1978).
15. Hull (1935c), Spence (1936; 1937b; 1938; 1940; 1951), Hebb (1949, pp. 162–163), Staats and Staats (1964, pp. 199–200), Skinner (1968, p. 134–138).
16. Spence and Lippitt (1946), Guthrie and Horton (1946, p. 7), Guthrie (1960, p. 143), Nawas (1970), Bem (1972), Rachlin (1977c), Ledwidge (1978).
17. Goss (1961a), Homme (1965), Kendler and Kendler (1968), Kendler (1968), Mahoney (1970), Ullmann (1970). See discussion of mediation in chapters 6 and 7.
18. Hull (1930b; 1931; 1933; 1937; 1952, pp. 151–152), Miller (1935), Spence, Bergmann, and Lippitt (1950), Dollard and Miller (1950, pp. 100–103), Berlyne (1954; 1965), Maltzman (1955).
19. Hunter (1924a), Mowrer (1960a, pp. 61–62), Berlyne (1965), Osgood (1968).
20. See Mowrer (1960b, p. 167), Kendler (1971), and Berlyne (1975).
21. This is illustrated by the mediational theories of Osgood (1957; 1963; 1968) and Berlyne (1965). The point is further discussed by Bourne (1968), Kendler (1971; 1981, pp. 359–361), Levine (1971), and Paivio (1975).
22. Tolman (1927a; 1928a; 1932, ch. 13; 1951), Dashiell (1928, pp. 521–530), Norris (1929a; b), Langfeld (1931), Dollard and Miller (1950, p. 110), Spence (1951), Mowrer (1960b, pp. 212–218), Bandura (1977a, pp. 172–173), but cf. Miller (1959).
23. Watson (1913a; b; 1914, ch. 1; 1917a; 1920; 1924a, pp. 343–356; c; 1926; 1928, pp. 82–92; 1930, pp. 238–251), Brown (1916), S. Russell (1917), Weiss (1918), Bawden (1919b), Smith and Guthrie (1921, pp. 163–164), Mead (1922), Hunter (1924b), de Laguna (1927/1963, pp. 341–343), Guthrie (1938, p. 164), Miller and Dollard (1941, pp. 84–90), Guthrie and Edwards (1949, ch. 18), Dollard and Miller (1950, ch. 8), Schoenfeld and Cumming (1963), Staats (1968, p. 103). Also see reviews by Harrell and Harrison (1938) and Goss (1961b).
24. Muscio (1921), Lovejoy (1922), Roback (1937, pp. 51–53), Blanshard (1940, ch. 9), Hartnack (1972).
25. McComas (1916), Otis (1920), Pear (1920), Bartlett and Smith (1920), Weber (1920), War-

ren (1921), Farrow (1927), Woodworth (1931, ch. 3), Blanshard (1940, ch. 9), Shaffer (1968, p. 16).

26. Calkins (1921).

27. Otis (1920), Skinner (1961; 1968, p. 119).

28. Skinner (1953a, ch. 16; 1957a, chs. 17, 19; 1961; 1968, chs. 6, 8; 1972d; 1974, ch. 7). Also see Gray (1932) and Staats and Staats (1964, pp. 210–212).

29. See Hartnack (1972).

30. Versions of a contextual theory of thinking can be found in Holt (1915a; b, pp. 96–99), Bawden (1918), Weiss (1922; 1924b; 1929a, pp. 345–357), de Laguna (1927/1963, pp. 337–355), Brewster (1936), White (1967, ch. 4), and Malcolm (1971a).

31. In this sense, thinking is a polymorphous concept (Ryle, 1949, ch. 2; White, 1967, ch. 4).

32. See also Skinner (1968, p. 119–120; 1974, p. 117) and Skinner and Vaughan (1983, p. 157).

33. For a general discussion of the information processing paradigm see Hilgard and Bower (1975, ch. 13) and Lachman, Lachman, and Butterfield (1979, ch. 4). Some of the historical background for this paradigm is provided by Segal and Lachman (1972) and Hilgard (1977). Critiques appear in Dreyfus (1972), Dreyfus and Haugeland (1974), and Kendler (1981, pp. 358–370).

34. See Pylyshyn (1980) for a discussion of the relationship between cognition and computation, and Rorty (1972), Putnam (1973), and Block (1978) for criticism of functional theories of mind. Meyer (1911), Deutsch (1960), and Gregory (1961) represent early versions of a functional approach.

35. Neomentalism is further discussed in chapter 10. Also see Chomsky (1965, p. 4) and Paivio (1975).

36. Miller, Galanter, and Pribram (1960, p. 7), Reitman (1965, p. 106), Locke (1972), Mahoney (1974, p. 5), Fodor (1975, pp. 30–31), Bandura (1977a, ch. 5). See criticism by Harman (1978).

37. Skinner (1963a; 1977a) and see discussion of Copy Theory in chapters 2, 6, 11, and 12.

38. Psychophysical experiments are discussed in chapter 11.

39. Zuriff (1976).

40. See Gibson's (1950) approach and Ullman's (1980) criticisms.

41. Rachlin (1977c).

42. See discussions in Hull (1943a; b, p. 109), Burns (1960), Skinner (1972i), and Rachlin (1977c). Also see comments on causation in chapter 4.

43. Segal (1977).

44. See Mowrer's (1960a, pp. 49–50) and Bandura's (1977a, p. 11; b) criticism of behaviorists who explain avoidance in terms of a "conditioned aversive stimulus" rather than the subject's anticipation of pain.

45. In this sense the debate might be described as a "paradigm clash" in Kuhn's (1962/1970) sense (Katahn and Koplin, 1968; Palermo, 1970; 1971; Lachman, Lachman, and Butterfield, 1979, p. 46).

46. But cf. Ullman's (1980) argument against this point with respect to Gibson's direct theory of perception.

47. Joynson (1970), Kendler (1981, pp. 368–370), but cf. Turner (1967, pp. 240–242; 1971, pp. 70–71).

48. Spence (1950; 1951), Kendler (1952), Millenson (1967), Suppes (1969a; b; 1975), Zuriff (1976), Harzem and Miles (1978, p. 46).

49. Since the information-processing paradigm represents a number of positions, it is not clear that the paradigm necessarily assumes a realist position. See, for example, Anderson (1978), Palmer (1978), and Lachman, Lachman, and Butterfield (1979, p. 117). Although Fodor (1975, pp. 51–52) and Chomsky (1980, pp. 48–51) recognize instrumentalism as a logically possible alternative to their positions, they dismiss it as not meriting serious consideration. Also see Berlyne (1975) and Shimp (1976).

50. Skinner (1963a; 1968, p. 205; 1969, pp. 273–280; 1972g; i; 1974, chapter 13), Holz and Azrin (1966), Gewirtz and Stingle (1968), Salzinger (1970), Nawas (1970), Ullmann (1970), Gewirtz (1971; 1978), Branch (1977), Kantor (1978), Ledwidge (1979), Kendler (1981, pp. 361–362). But also see critique of this objection by Wessells (1981; 1982).

51. Skinner (1953a, ch. 3; 1957a, pp. 5–10; 1964; 1973a; 1974, chapter 7), Maltzman (1966), Wiest (1967), Staats (1968, pp. 154–158), Salzinger (1973a; 1975; 1978). Also see reply by Fodor (1981).

52. Skinner (1961; 1968, ch. 6; 1977a).

53. Examples include Ausubel (1965), Neisser (1967, p. 20), Deese (1969), and Honig (1978), but cf. Pylyshyn (1973), Paivio (1975), and Anderson (1978). See Osgood (1968), Kanfer (1968), and Kendler (1970) for behaviorist criticisms.

54. See Fodor (1975, pp. 52–53) and Nisbett and Wilson (1977).

55. Dennett (1969; 1971; 1975; 1978a; d), Boden (1972, ch. 4). and Nagel (1979, ch. 12) suggest solutions, and see criticism of this practice by Bennett (1964), Gibson (1973), and Skinner (1974, p. 77; 1977a)

56. This is defended by Dennett (1969) and Fodor (1975, ch. 2; 1978).

57. Fodor (1981).

58. Farber (1963), Malcolm (1971a), Schwartz (1978). Also see ch. 7.

59. Skinner (1963c; 1966b; 1969, pp. 146–171; 1974, p. 125–128; 1977a).

9. EXORCISING THE AGENT

1. The concept of agency is discussed by Taylor (1966), Shaffer (1968, chapter 5), and Davis (1979).

2. Watson (1924a, p. 426), Weiss (1929a, pp. 273, 300–304, 380–387), Thorndike (1932, p. 400), Skinner (1938, pp. 3–6; 1971a; 1971c; 1974, p. 168), Kantor (1942), Hebb (1949, p. 158), Rogers and Skinner (1956), Schwartz and Lacey (1982, ch. 1).

3. Weiss (1929a, pp. 427–433), but cf. Keat (1972).

4. See chapter 3.

5. Skinner (1947; 1953a, p. 6; 1968, p. 171; 1974, p. 189), Erwin (1978, p. 80).

6. See discussion in Warren (1916).

7. Weiss (1919a), Skinner (1953a, pp. 29–31; 1963a; 1964; 1969, ch. 9; 1972c).

8. Skinner (1966a; 1977a; 1981).

9. The latter alternative would be akin to Calkins' (1913; 1917; 1921; 1922) "behavioristic self-psychology."

10. Sechenov (1863/1935, p. 334). Expressions of behaviorist externalism can be found in Skinner (1953a, ch. 3; 1971c; 1972i; 1977a), Herrnstein (1964), Deitz (1978), and Schwartz and Lacey (1982, chs. 1, 2), and see Zuriff (1979b). Objections are raised by Broadbent (1973, pp. 125–132), Bowers (1973), and Mahoney (1977a).

11. Johnson (1963). See criticisms by Dulany (1968), Keat (1972), Mahoney (1974, pp. 28–29), Bandura (1978), and Erwin (1978, p. 68).

12. Skinner (1972f), Schnaitter (1975). Schwartz and Lacey (1982, chs. 1, 2) reverse the argument.

13. See Fearing (1930, chapter 11) and the S–R reflex thesis in chapter 6, but also note Hull's (1943b, chapter 17) "behavioral oscillation" and Baum's (1981) "intrinsic modulating factors."

14. Kantor (1921a), Hull (1935c), Guthrie (1938, ch. 12), Burns (1960), Skinner (1966b), Staats (1971), Gewirtz (1978), Harzem and Miles (1978, pp. 75–76). See criticism by Dulany (1968), Bowers (1973), and Bandura (1977a, pp. 5–10).

15. Tolman (1938a), Guthrie (1938, ch. 12), Spence (1944), Skinner (1947; 1953a, ch. 13; 1963b; 1969, p. 88), Burns (1960).

16. See Spence (1944), and chapter 6.

17. Kuo (1921; 1929a), Kantor (1921b), Weiss (1924b), Wallis (1924), Dunlap (1927), Holt (1931,

pp. 4–5), Guthrie (1933a), Lashley (1938), Koch (1941), Hebb (1949, pp. 166–168), Skinner (1953a, p. 157; 1974, p. 35). Also see reviews by Diamond (1971) and Kitchener (1977).

18. See, for example, Watson's (1913a; b) rejection of "centrally initiated" processes, along with Bergmann's (1956) comments, and Salzinger's (1973b) criticism of cognitivists for postulating spontaneous processes. The behaviorist position is attacked by Ginsberg (1954a), Deese (1969), and Hebb (1949, ch. 1; 1951; 1954; 1963) who argues for "semi-autonomous" processes in the nervous system. See Fearing (1930, ch. 11) for historical background.

19. This passive model is implicit in Watson (1914, ch. 1; 1924a, ch. 4; 1930, pp. 48–50), Meyer (1921, pp. 171–172), Dashiell (1925), Pavlov (1928), and Weiss (1929a, pp. 201–203), and note reviews by Broadbent (1961, ch. 6) and Lowry (1970), and criticism by McDougall (1923), Lashley (1929), Sperry (1969), and Oatley (1978, ch. 4).

20. Sherrington (1906, p. 233), Meyer (1911, p. 5).

21. Dashiell (1925; 1928, pp. 34–36, 531–534), Langfeld (1927), and see McComas (1916) and Woodworth (1931, pp. 58–59).

22. Watson (1913a; b), Hunter (1930b), and see criticisms by Thorndike (1915), Weber (1920), and Hebb (1980, pp. 32–35). Also cf. Guthrie (1959).

23. Dashiell (1928, pp. 131, 533), Norris (1928).

24. Kantor (1921a).

25. Watson (1914, p. 20; 1930, pp. 15–16), Smith and Guthrie (1921, pp. 201–202), Guthrie (1960, p. 50).

26. Watson (1914, pp. 19–20; 1924a, pp. 170, 355–356), Woolbert (1920), Smith and Guthrie (1921, p. 130), Lashley (1923a), Weiss (1924b; 1929a, p. 203), Hull (1930b), Guthrie and Powers (1950, pp. 123–124), Guthrie (1960, pp. 24, 91, 95, 184–185). The implication for theoretical concepts is discussed by MacCorquodale and Meehl (1954) and Cotton (1963). See Koch (1954), Bergmann (1956), Kendler and Kendler (1966), and Kendler (1968) for a general discussion, and Titchener (1914), Crosland (1922), Lashley (1938), Leeper (1944), and Breger and McGaugh (1965) for criticisms of peripheralism.

27. Watson (1913b; 1930, pp. 49–50), Weiss (1922; 1924b), de Laguna (1927/1963, p. 242), Guthrie (1930), Fearing (1930, p. 66), Holt (1931, p. 213), Heidbreder (1933, pp. 254–255), Bergmann (1953; 1956), Kendler and Kendler (1966), Maltzman (1968).

28. Oatley (1978) is another example.

29. See Pribram (1971).

30. Also, as noted in chapter 6, the operant is emitted rather than elicited. See Rozeboom (1970) and Boakes and Halliday (1970). Also see discussion of causality in chapters 4 and 8.

31. Meyer (1911, p. 231), Lashley (1931; 1951), Miller and Dollard (1941, p. 59), Dollard and Miller (1950, p. 69), Berlyne (1951), Mowrer (1954), Spence (1956, p. 189), Osgood (1957; 1968), Miller (1959), Wolpe (1978a), Carter and Werner (1978). Also see Koch (1959).

32. For an early version see Calkins (1913). Willis and Giles (1978) review the history of this criticism. Fearing (1930, pp. 141–145) and Lowry (1970) provide some of the pre-behaviorist background. General discussions of "mechanical explanation" can be found in Broad (1918–1919), Deutsch (1960, ch. 1), Nagel (1961, ch. 7), and Gregory (1981, ch. 3). For a discussion of behaviorism and mechanism, see Wallis (1924) and Boring (1964).

33. Warren (1923b; 1925), Calverton (1924), Cason (1924), Dulany (1974).

34. McDougall (1926), Kuo (1928), Herrnstein (1964).

35. Köhler (1927, ch. 7), McDougall (1928, pp. 21–34, 177–182), Hull (1929), Spence (1936), Guthrie (1938, pp. 43–44), Mowrer (1960b, p. 210), Bandura (1974), Harzem and Miles (1978, p. 91).

36. Warren (1916), Heidbreder (1933, ch. 7), Sepnce (1941a; 1951), Hebb (1958, p. 3), Turner (1971, pp. 23–26).

37. See chapter 3.

38. Kuo (1928), Pepper (1934), Moore and Lewis (1953), Nagel (1961, ch. 7), Broadbeck (1963), Breger and McGaugh (1965).

39. Moore and Lewis (1953).

40. Wheeler (1940, pp. 15–18), Allport (1943), Sloane (1945), Rice (1946), Burns (1960).

41. McDougall (1923), Singer (1924, pp. 109–112), Davies (1926), Weiss (1928b), Hull (1952, pp. 347–350), Bergmann (1953), Taylor (1970), Boden (1972, pp. 32–39), Ringen (1976).

42. Behaviorists who say organisms are machines include S.B. Russell (1917), Bode (1918), Smith and Guthrie (1921, p. 1), Holt (1931, p. 252), Gray (1932), Guthrie and Edwards (1949, p. 36), and Skinner (1969, p. 294). Also see discussions by Meyer (1913), McDougall (1926), Gregory (1961; 1981, ch. 3), and Gray (1968).

43. Guthrie (1942), Weiss (1928b; 1931), Skinner (1938, p. 433), Hull (1943b, p. 384), Hebb (1949, p. xi), Moore and Lewis (1953), Dreyfus and Haugeland (1974), Wright (1976, pp. 57–60), Wolpe (1978a).

44. Pratt (1939, pp. 130–131).

45. E.g., Chomsky (1975, pp. 132–133).

46. Herrnstein (1970), Baum (1973), Rachlin, et al. (1981).

47. See reviews by Postman (1947), Wilcoxon (1969), and Estes (1971).

48. See also Tolman (1949a; 1951; 1952b) and Mahoney (1974, p. 119).

49. Bartley and Perkins (1931), Tolman and Krechevsky (1933), Tolman (1948), Mackintosh (1965), Sutherland and Mackintosh (1971), Broadbent (1973, pp. 126–129). Also see discussion in Skinner (1966b) and Rozeboom (1974).

50. Meyer (1921, ch. 5), Weiss (1928a), Kuo (1929b), Watson (1930, pp. 276–278), Thorndike (1932, chs. 5, 13; 1949, ch. 7).

51. Holt (1915a), Smith and Guthrie (1921, pp. 204–205), de Laguna (1927/1963, pp. 163–165), Spence (1937a; 1945; 1950; 1952b; 1956, pp. 40–41, 100; 1960c), Miller and Dollard (1941, p. 23), Guthrie and Edwards (1949, pp. 220–224), Skinner (1950; 1957a, pp. 415–416; b; 1961; 1968, p. 122), Dollard and Miller (1950, p. 103), Guthrie and Powers (1950, pp. 48–50), Tolman (1959), Staats (1968, pp. 408–414), Zuriff (1979b). Dashiell (1928, pp. 279–289), Fearing (1930, p. 231), and Guthrie (1940) discuss attention as a state of motor readiness.

52. Dollard and Miller (1950, p. 103), Berlyne (1951), Miller (1959), Lawrence (1963), Schoenfeld and Cumming (1963), Kendler and Kendler (1966), Kendler (1968; 1971), Maltzman (1968; 1971), Zuriff (1979b). The "motor theory" of attention is presented in Washburn (1914), Langfeld (1931), and Holt (1931, pp. 216–221).

53. Kantor (1920), Spence (1950), Skinner (1953a, pp. 123–124, 134–136; 1973b; 1974, p. 105), Carter and Werner (1978), Honig and Urcuioli (1981). Also see Tighe and Tighe (1966) and Zuriff (1979b).

54. Eriksen (1962), Spielberger (1962), Verplanck (1962), Farber (1963), Holz and Azrin (1966), Maltzman (1966), Bandura (1974), Salzinger (1975), Eysenck (1979). Also see chapter 10.

55. Köhler (1927, ch. 7), Spence (1936), Spielberger and DeNike (1966), Bourne (1968), Estes (1969), Levine (1971), Mahoney (1974, ch. 10), Brewer (1974), Dulany (1974), Bandura (1974; 1977a, chs. 2, 5; 1978). Also see the discussion of the continuity-noncontinuity debate in chapter 10.

56. Bourne (1968), Levine (1971), and see chapter 7.

57. Versions of this argument appear in Miller and Dollard (1941, p. 32), Ryle (1949, ch. 2), Farber (1963), Malcolm (1971a), and Zuriff (1975). Also see parallels to the argument in chapter 7 that not all behavior can be rule governed.

58. See Thorndike (1946), Dollard and Miller (1950, pp. 43–44), Skinner (1968, pp. 134–144), Premack (1970), and Dennett (1975).

59. See Bourne (1968), Estes (1971), Kendler (1971), Suppes (1975), and Lachman, Lachman, and Butterfield (1979, p. 118).

60. See Kimble (1967a), Kimble and Perlmuter (1970), and Natsoulas (1978) for reviews. Also note parallels with behaviorist interpretations of intentional behavior in chapter 7.

61. Weiss (1925a; 1929a, pp. 61–66, 429–430), Skinner (1947; 1972e; g; 1974, p. 168), Guthrie (1960, pp. 289–295), Smith (1983, ch. 9).

62. Skinner (1953a, ch. 18).

63. Kantor (1923a), Hebb (1949, p. 144; 1974), Mowrer (1960b, pp. 208–214).

64. Skinner (1953a, p. 112; 1974, p. 54), Ringen (1976), Day (1977).

65. See chapter 6.

66. See Mead (1922), Markey (1925), Weiss (1929a, pp. 221–223), Skinner (1954; 1957a, pp. 138–139; 1972g), Sellars (1956), Bem (1972), Hebb (1980, pp. 24–27). Objections are considered in chapter 11.

67. Weiss (1924b; 1929a, pp. 221–223).

68. Guthrie (1938, pp. 138–146), Guthrie and Edwards (1949, pp. 120–123), Guthrie and Powers (1950, pp. 378–379).

69. For behaviorist views of self-control see Skinner (1953a, ch. 15; 1974, pp. 176–180), Gewirtz (1971), Kanfer and Karoly (1972), Waters and McCallum (1973), Ainslie (1975), Mahoney (1976), Goldiamond (1976), Rachlin (1974; 1978a), Brigham (1978), Wolpe (1978a), and Grosch and Neuringer (1981). Objections are raised by Secord (1977).

70. Watson (1924b; 1928, p. 82), Hunter and Hudgins (1934), Guthrie (1938, ch. 13), Guthrie and Edwards (1949, pp. 156–159), Goss (1961b), Staats (1968, pp. 40, 65). For other behaviorist accounts of the self and volition see Meyer (1921, pp. 146–149), Lashley (1923a; b), Weiss (1929a, pp. 380–391), and Holt (1937). Also see chapter 7.

71. See Fearing (1930, pp. 244–246) for earlier senses of "automatism."

72. This argument is elaborated in Zuriff (1975) based on Wittgenstein (1953; 1958).

73. Wittgenstein (1953, pp. 84, 106, 135). Also see Skinner's (1972e) discussion of "having" a poem.

74. Cf. the use of "automatic" by Hull (1937; 1943b, p. 69).

75. de Laguna (1919b), Ryle (1949, ch. 2), Brodbeck (1963), Borger (1974), Zuriff (1975).

76. For discussions of the relationship between action language and response language see Strawson (1958), Hamlyn (1964), Madell (1967), Mischel (1969), Toulmin (1970), and Alston (1974).

77. See Hamlyn (1962), Fodor (1968, pp. 32–48), Toulmin (1969), Suppes (1969c), and Zuriff (1975).

78. See Hamlyn (1970) and Davidson (1974).

79. Brodbeck (1963), Mischel (1969), Borger (1974), Zuriff (1975).

80. The debate over the passive-reactive image includes Crosland (1922), Thurstone (1923), Bentley (1926), Kuo (1929a), Hull (1930b), Tolman (1948), MacCorquodale and Meehl (1954), Burt (1962), Blanshard and Skinner (1967), Hunt (1969), Mischel (1969), Palermo (1970; 1971), Nawas (1970), Rozeboom (1970), Copeland (1971), Pribram (1971, pp. 95–96), Briskman (1972), Mahoney (1974, ch. 10), Segal (1975), Day (1976c), Bandura (1977a, pp. 19–22, 68–72, 96–97), Gewirtz (1978), and Wolpe (1978a; b).

81. Skinner (1973b) and Ringen (1976) argue against this error.

82. Suppes (1969c).

83. But cf. Taylor (1964; 1970). See also Malcolm (1967) and Zuriff (1975).

10. BEHAVIORAL INTERPRETATION

1. Holt (1915b, pp. 85–86), Hull (1937), Skinner (1953a, pp. 27–31), Kantor (1968).

2. The term "eliminative" comes from Rorty (1965) who speaks of an "eliminative materialism". For versions of eliminative behaviorism see Watson (1920), Weiss (1918; 1930), Verplanck (1962), Treisman (1962), and Herrnstein (1964).

3. See Perry (1921a) and Putnam (1969; 1975b). Wimsatt (1976) describes this process as "intralevel reduction."

4. Geissler (1929).

5. Logical behaviorism is discussed by Carnap (1932–1933/1959), Bergmann (1940a;b), and Hempel (1949; 1969). Also see Singer (1912; 1924, p. 53) and chapter 1.

6. See chapter 2 for a discussion of verification and introspection.

7. Carnap (1932–1933/1959; 1955), Hempel (1949).

8. Carnap (1955), Hempel (1969). See Tolman, Ritchie, and Kalish (1946a) for an illustration.

9. See Putnam (1962; 1969).

10. See Carnap (1937), Maatsch and Behan (1953), Hanna (1968), and Achinstein (1969).

11. If it is assumed that verification must consist of the performance of some operation, then operationism is easily identified with verificationism (Stevens, 1939).

12. Bergmann and Spence (1944), Boring (1945), Maatsch and Behan (1953), Waters and McCallum (1973).

13. Bridgman (1945). Also see Brodbeck (1966) on "model identity."

14. See Erwin (1978, pp. 54–60) for a review.

15. In the continuity vs. noncontinuity controversy, the critical comment is by Krechevsky (1938) who suggests, without behavioral evidence, that a particular experimental reversal occurred after the end of the pre-solution period. However, as Spence (1940; 1945) notes, if the solution period is operationally defined as the observation of systematic responding on the part of the rat, then Krechevsky's suggestion is operationally illegitimate. Of course, Krechevsky can reply that the rat's solution is to be conceived as a hypothetical construct which can occur before the systematic behavior. However, Krechevsky (1932) is himself committed to operational definitions of his mental concepts. See Prentice (1946) and Hebb (1949, p. 163). In the reinforcement-without-awareness controversy, the problem is best illustrated by Spielberger (1962) who gives both an operational definition of "awareness" as well as a "pre-scientific" meaning in terms of conscious experience. Therefore, he can suggest that conditioning without awareness can erroneously appear to be found if an insensitive interviewing procedure fails to detect the subject's awareness. Note that it is only the "pre-scientific" concept of awareness which can be said to exist although defining operations fail to detect it. See also Spielberger and DeNike (1966).

16. Tolman (1932, ch. 1; 1935; 1936; 1937; 1959), Tolman and Horowitz (1933). See also the discussions in Boring (1953), Koch (1959), Locke (1969; 1972), and Kitchener (1977).

17. For attempts to construe emotions as intervening variables see Skinner (1938, pp. 406–409; 1957a, pp. 215–216), Brown and Farber (1951), and Marx (1958). Guttman (1963; 1964) and Taylor (1962) do the same for perception.

18. See chapter 4.

19. See Shaffer's (1968, pp. 20–21) objection to this approach and Carrier's (1973) reply.

20. See chapter 4.

21. The term "analytic behaviorism" is from Mace (1948–1949), but the view is also known as "philosophical behaviorism" and "logical behaviorism." See chapter 1. Analytic behaviorism is often lumped together with the logical behaviorism of Carnap and Hempel. For similarities between the two, see Malcolm (1964), Chihara and Fodor (1965), and Hempel (1969).

22. Note the parallels with the arguments for automaticisms in chapter 9.

23. Wittgenstein (1953, pp. 49–51), Ziff (1962).

24. Early behaviorists argued for this thesis prior to analytic behaviorism. See Singer (1911), Holt (1915b, pp. 98–99), Weiss (1917a), de Laguna (1918), Perry (1921b), and Wallis (1924). Tolman (1922b; 1925a; b; 1926b) provides good examples. Spence (1950) and Skinner (1968, ch. 6) offer behavioral analyses of cognitive terms, and see Guthrie (1960, p. 3). Among behavior therapists, Eysenck (1972), Waters and McCallum (1973), and Wolpe (1976b), endorse analytic behaviorism. See also Erwin (1978, pp. 60–66) on the relationship between analytic behaviorism and behavior therapy.

25. Holt (1915b), Bawden (1918), Williams (1934), Brewster (1936). Also see contextual theories in chapters 8 and 9.

26. Attempts to describe the aspects of behavior referred to by emotion concepts include: de Laguna (1919a; b; 1930), Meyer (1921, pp. 212–215), Kantor (1921c; 1966), Tolman (1922a; 1923; 1932, pp. 263–268), Hunter (1924a), Woolbert (1924), Dashiell (1928, pp. 426–433); Kuo (1929a),

Watson (1930, chs. 7, 8), Guthrie and Edwards (1949, ch. 7), and Skinner (1953a; ch. 10; 1957a, pp. 214–218). Also see Hebb (1946).

27. Singer (1924, ch. 3), Ryle 1949, pp. 60–61).

28. Wittgenstein (1953), Strawson (1958), Malcolm (1959, ch. 12). See Albritton (1959), Lycan (1971), and criticisms by Chihara and Fodor (1965), and Ayer (1968). Criteria are thought to be acquired as a result of training which must be based on publicly observable stimuli. In this respect they resemble the discriminative stimulus for the "tact" of Skinner's (1957a) theory of verbal behavior. Both the criterion and the discriminative stimulus "justify" the emission of the verbal response (or mental concept) in that the "chain of reasons has an end" in Wittgenstein's (1953) phrase, and we are left with the automatic results of drill and training.

29. Nevertheless, the fact that no particular behavior is either a necessary or sufficient condition for a mental concept is used as an objection to behaviorism by Washburn (1919), Roback (1923, pp. 92–93), Broad (1925, pp. 612–624), Putnam (1963), Burt (1968), Shaffer (1968, p. 42), Locke (1969; 1972), and Alston (1972).

30. Ryle (1949, p. 44).

31. Pratt (1922), Gundlach (1927), Putnam (1963; 1967b; 1975c), Dennett (1969), Erwin (1978, pp. 65–66), Fodor (1981).

32. Lovejoy (1922), Taylor (1964; 1970), Malcolm (1967), Armstrong (1968, p. 57), Dennett (1969, ch. 2; 1971), Alston (1974), Davidson (1974), Pritchard (1976), Fodor (1978).

33. Tolman (1933; 1935; 1949b). See discussions by MacCorquodale and Meehl (1954) and Newbury (1972).

34. Place (1981). Other suggestions are offered by Perry (1918), Brewster (1936), Turner (1967, pp. 346–347; 1971, pp. 158–161, 179–188), Rozeboom (1972), and Kendler (1981, pp. 133–135). Ringen (1976) and Day (1980) claim that, in Skinner's system, intensionality is covered by descriptions of contingencies of reinforcement. McCorquodale and Meehl (1954), Quine (1960, ch. 5; 1970, pp. 32–33), and Brodbeck (1963) suggest fusing propositional attitudes into unanalyzable complexes. Brunswik (1937) describes an empirical method for determining a subject's intensional world. Also see Shuford (1966), Suppes (1969c), and Dennett (1971; 1975; 1978b; d).

35. For versions of neomentalism see Katz (1964/1967), Chomsky (1965), Garrett and Fodor (1968), Fodor, Bever, and Garrett (1974), and Fodor (1981). Turner (1971, ch. 7) and Paivio (1975) present overviews. Neomentalism in cognitive psychology is discussed in chapter 8.

36. Fodor (1968, pp. 55–60, 86–89; 1981).

37. Putnam (1963; 1967a; b; 1975a), Fodor (1968; 1981), Block (1978). See Armstrong (1968, ch. 6) for a materialist version.

38. Fodor (1968, pp. 57–59).

39. Warren (1921), Putnam (1967b), Armstrong (1968, pp. 71–72). See Shaffer (1968, p. 16) for other examples.

40. Putnam (1963).

41. Gibbs (1969–1970), Finn (1971), and Lycan (1974) present objections to the conclusions Putnam (1963) draws from his imagined X-world.

42. Putnam (1967b; 1969).

43. Putnam (1961; 1962; 1963). Malcolm (1959, ch. 3) argues for it.

44. See Block (1978) and reply by Fodor (1968, pp. 86–89; 1975, pp. 52–53). Also see Nisbett and Wilson (1977).

45. Fodor (1975, pp. 8–9).

46. For example see Craighead, Kazdin, and Mahoney (1976, ch. 12).

47. Breger and McGaugh (1965). Also see review by Yates (1975, ch. 19).

48. For a while it appeared that the issue of "symptom substitution" might provide empirical content to this controversy. See Meyer (1921, pp. 387–389), Yates (1958), Costello (1963), and Cahoon (1968). However, it soon became clear that psychoanalytic theory does not invariably predict symptom substitution and that learning theory does predict what might be called "symp-

tom substitution" when the variables controlling a problem behavior are not modified along with the target behavior.

49. Watson (1924a, p. 426), Guthrie (1936; 1944), Skinner (1954), Nagel (1959).

50. Watson (1916b; 1924b; 1936), Guthrie (1938), Tolman (1932; 1941a; 1942), Dollard and Miller (1950), Skinner (1953a, ch. 24; 1974). Also see Bergmann (1943; 1956), and Hovland (1952). Other behaviorist interpretations of psychoanalysis include Stogdill (1934), Shaw (1946), Shoben (1949), and Seeman (1951a; b).

51. Eysenck (1960; 1970), Wolpe (1963; 1976a), Rachman (1970).

52. See Eysenck (1970) and Wolberg (1970). However, Wachtel (1977) and Marmor and Woods (1980) may indicate a renewed rapprochement between behaviorism and psychoanalysis.

53. See Wolf (1978) and Shwayder's (1965, ch. 2) "conceptual epiphenominalism."

54. See discussions by Weiss (1924b; 1925b), Spence (1951), and Ringen (1976).

55. See chapter 7 and Hull (1933).

56. Hull (1943b, pp. 25–26).

57. See Koch (1954), Mackenzie (1977, pp. 108–111), and Zuriff (1979c).

58. Skinner (1953a, p. 285).

59. See Skinner (1957a) and Quine (1960).

60. See also Skinner (1957a, p. 14; 1973a; 1977a), Day (1969a), MacCorquodale (1970), and Erwin (1978, pp. 63–64).

61. Skinner (1957a, pp. 41, 77–78, 195–198, 311–312; 1974, pp. 95, 241), Segal (1977).

62. Skinner (1953a; 1957a) presents numerous examples of translations although he questions their usefulness (Skinner, 1938, pp. 7–8; 1945a; 1957a, pp. 9–10, 115; 1972i; 1974, pp. 19–20). Also note the "glossary" in Skinner and Vaughan (1983, pp. 155–157). The relationship between translation and interpretation is discussed by Day (1976a) and Harzem and Miles (1978, ch. 5). Note that in an empirical translation *four* parties must be taken into consideration. First, there is the speaker, A, who uses the mental term in talking about a second organism, B. The behavior analyst, C, then explains A's verbal behavior by providing further verbal behavior directed at D, the community of behavioral scientists.

63. Skinner (1953a, pp. 87–90; 1953b; 1969, pp. 125–126).

64. Rogers and Skinner (1956), Skinner (1971c). Also see Skinner (1963a) on the role of covert stimuli.

65. Verplanck (1954), MacCorquodale (1970). Also see Hanna (1968). Johnson (1963) describes Skinner's interpretations as "explanation analyses" rather than "meaning analyses," while Malcolm (1964) suggests that they are philosophical analyses. Criticisms can be found in Scriven (1956) and Dennett (1978b), and see replies to Scriven by Skinner (1963a) and Johnson (1963).

66. Epstein, Lanza, and Skinner (1980; 1981), Epstein (1981). Hull (1945; 1952, p. 4), Dollard and Miller (1950, p. 63), Miller (1959), and Salzinger (1978) discuss extrapolation across species, and Kazdin and Wilson (1978, pp. 158–166) discuss extrapolation from "analog" studies to clinical populations. Also see Schwartz (1974).

67. Verplanck (1954), Skinner (1957a, pp. 11–12; 1958; 1963b; 1969, pp. 100–103; 1972i; 1973b; 1974, pp. 19, 226–232), MacCorquodale (1970), Schnaitter (1975), Day (1976a). For examples of interpretations guiding research see Miller and Dollard (1941), Grosch and Neuringer (1981), and Baer's (1978) discussion of the relationships between basic and applied research.

68. McDougall (1926), Bentley (1926), Dunlap (1927), Gundlach (1927), Heibreder (1933), Ginsberg (1954a), Chomsky (1959/1967), Metzner (1963), Breger and McGaugh (1965), Fodor (1965), Weitzman (1967), Lacey (1974), Mahoney (1974, pp. 118–119), Mackenzie (1977, pp. 156–158). Also see replies by Wiest (1967), Staddon (1967), and MacCorquodale (1970).

69. Eysenck (1964; 1970), Ullmann and Krasner (1965), and Wolpe (1976a) define behavior therapy as an application of learning theory. However, current opinion is that it must be defined more broadly. See, for example, Craighead, Kazdin, and Mahoney (1976, pp. 5–6), Kazdin and Wilson (1978, pp. 1–8), Erwin (1978, ch. 1), and Kazdin (1979a). Critics who deny conditioning theory is applicable to human behavior therapy include Breger and McGaugh (1965; 1966), re-

plied to by Wiest (1967); Costello (1970), reply by Wolpe (1971); Wilkins (1971; 1972); London (1972), replies by Dunlap and Lieberman (1973), Wolpe (1976a), and Eaglen (1978); Kazdin (1979b), and Schwartz and Lacey (1982, ch. 8). See Kalish (1981) for an overview.

70. See Kuhn (1970; 1974), Kitchener (1977), and Hebb (1980, pp. 121–128).

71. Mackenzie (1977, pp. 166–169).

72. Similarly, the question as to whether the "principles of learning" are "universal," e.g., MacCorquodale (1969), Seligman and Hager (1972), may be unanswerable without criteria as to when equations with slightly different forms instantiate the "same" principle. For example, Hull (1945) suggests that equations exemplify the same behavioral law if they differ only in their constants, but Logue (1979) argues that this is an arbitrary criterion. A similar problem arises in Estes' (1971) discussion of whether conditioning principles are the same for humans and lower animals. Therefore, to characterize behaviorism as "anti-emergent" in maintaining that humans differ from lower animals only in "complexity" but not "underlying mechanisms" (Palermo, 1971) may be to assert an empty claim in the absence of a theoretical context. See Nagel's (1961, pp. 366–380) discussion of emergence.

73. See Hesse (1966) and Kuhn (1970; 1974) on the role of models and analogies in science, Lachman (1960) on their role in psychology, and Lorenz (1974) for one example.

74. MacCorquodale (1970) and Richelle (1976) argue along these lines in reply to Chomsky's (1959/1967) attack against Skinner's (1957a) extension of learning theory to verbal behavior.

75. See chapters 4, 8, and 11.

76. Meyer (1911, pp. 201–204), Watson (1913b; 1914; 1919; 1924a; c; 1928, chapter 3), Smith and Guthrie (1921, pp. 36–39), Weiss (1929a, pp. 400–403), Dollard and Miller (1950, pp. 68–69), Spence (1956, pp. 179–180; 1958; 1964), Mowrer (1960a), Wolpe (1978a). For the philosophical issues involved see Sellars (1956) and Chihara and Fodor (1965).

77. See chapter 8 for a discussion of cognitive events as covert behavior.

78. Singer's (1911) classic article is entitled "Mind as an Observable Object."

79. Carnap (1932–1933/1959), Ryle (1949, pp. 51–60), Malcolm (1958). It is defended by Carr (1927), Adams (1928), and Ayer (1968).

80. Examples include Schoenfeld and Cumming (1963, pp. 238–239), Staats (1968, p. 76), Ullmann (1970), Hebb (1972, p. 288), Ackerman (1973), Meichenbaum (1975), Mapel (1977), Wolpe (1978a), and Holland (1978). See Olshewsky (1975) and Rachlin (1977a; b) for criticisms. Keat (1972) and Day (1976a) carefully distinguish dispositions from episodes. See also Skinner (1974, p. 69).

81. Ryle (1949, chs. 1, 5).

82. See chapter 4.

83. Kuo (1928), Weiss (1918; 1924b), Meyer (1933), Skinner (1938, pp. 7–8; 1945a; 1957a, pp. 9–10, 115; 1972i; 1974, pp. 19–20).

11. FIRST-PERSON REPORTS

1. See reviews by Williams (1931) and Boring (1953).

2. For a critical history of introspectionism see Dodge (1912).

3. Locke (1971) ignores the distinction.

4. Bergmann (1940b), Carnap (1955), Hempel (1969).

5. Malcolm (1959). Also see criticisms by Beloff (1962, pp. 42–43) and Armstrong (1968, pp. 70–71).

6. Cf. Dennett (1978c).

7. Putnam's (1961; 1962; 1963) arguments against this claim are presented in chapter 10. Also see discussion by Stoyva and Kamiya (1968).

8. Stevens (1935a; b; 1939; 1971a), Graham (1950; 1958). The "converging operations" of Garner, Hake, and Eriksen (1956) are used to infer a hypothetical construct rather than a strictly opera-

tionally defined concept. Roback (1937, p. 110), Pratt (1939, pp. 102–109), and Zener (1958) criticize operationists for identifying sensation with verbal behavior.

9. Weiss (1929a, p. 256), Schoenfeld and Cumming (1963), Skinner (1972h).

10. Skinner (1972h).

11. See Verplanck (1962) for experimental data.

12. Singer (1911), Holt (1915a) de Laguna (1918), Hebb (1946), Ryle (1949, pp. 167–185), Skinner (1957a, pp. 138–140), Bem (1972). See Weiss (1929a, pp. 420–421) and Keller and Schoenfeld (1950, p. 256) on feelings of pleasantness.

13. Skinner (1953a, pp. 264–275; 1974, ch. 5).

14. Skinner (1957a, pp. 315–316; 1974, p. 103). See also Sellars (1956) and Collins (1969). The autoclitic is discussed in chapter 7.

15. Skinner (1957a, p. 315). For the view that memory is a behavioral skill rather than the reading of memory images, see Watson (1924b; 1926; 1928, ch. 4; 1930, pp. 220–223), Guthrie and Edwards (1949, ch. 17), Skinner (1957a, pp. 142–143; 1968, pp. 203–205), Guthrie (1960, pp. 285–287), and Holland (1978).

16. Weiss (1929a, pp. 384–385), Skinner (1953a, pp. 88–90, 263; 1957a, pp. 144–145; 1969, pp. 126–127; 1974, p. 28), Blanshard and Skinner (1967), Bem (1972), Hebb (1980, pp. 27–30). Also see the discussion of reinforcement theories of purpose in chapter 7.

17. Skinner (1957a, p. 444; 1963c; 1969, p. 126), but cf. Pears (1975, ch. 1). Also see the discussion of intention in chapter 7.

18. See Zuriff (1980) for a review.

19. Meyer (1911, p. 218; 1921, p. 360), Hunter (1925), Dollard and Miller (1950, p. 33), Keller and Schoenfeld (1950, p. 287), Hebb (1980, p. 27). A similar analysis of first-person reports of emotions appears in Watson (1914), Gray (1935), and Eysenck (1972). Other examples are suggested by S.B. Russell (1917), Holt (1937), Hull (1944; 1952, pp. 152, 344–345), Staats and Staats (1964, pp. 129–134), and Staats (1968, pp. 74–78).

20. But cf. Armstrong (1968, pp. 69–71).

21. Watson (1914; 1924a, pp. 127, 352), Weiss (1918; 1924b; 1929a, pp. 294–300), Meyer (1921, p. 290), Leuba (1940), Skinner (1945a; 1953a, pp. 266–275; 1963a; 1968, pp. 125–127), Dollard and Miller (1950, pp. 178–181), Berlyne (1951; 1965, pp. 130–144), Hebb (1954; 1958, p. 33), Schoenfeld and Cumming (1963), Staats (1968, ch. 3), Mahoney (1970), Kantor (1978). See objections to conditioned seeing by Hamlyn (1970).

22. Skinner (1945a; 1953a, ch. 17; 1957a, pp. 130–146; 1974, chapter 2). Also see Meyer (1921, p. 360).

23. Skinner (1945a; b; 1953a, ch. 18; 1957a, p. 140; 1963a; 1972g; 1974, pp. 168–171). Self knowledge as a social product is discussed also by Dewey (1918), Mead (1922), Rosenow (1923), Singer (1924, ch. 8), and Sellars (1956).

24. Dewey (1918), Singer (1924, pp. 47–49), Tolman (1932, pp. 264–268).

25. Dunlap (1912), Bode (1913), Bawden (1918), Watson (1924b; 1930, pp. 39, 265), Norris (1929a), Tolman (1932, p. 241), Holt (1937), Keller and Schoenfeld (1950, p. 220).

26. Weiss (1917a; b; 1918; 1924b; 1929a).

27. Thorndike (1915), de Laguna (1919b; 1927/1963, pp. 123–126), Watson (1924a, pp. 38–42), Hunter (1930a), Carnap (1932–1933/1959), Bergmann (1940a; b; 1953), Spence (1948; 1956, p. 15), Hebb (1958, p. 4), Marx (1958), Buchwald (1961), Buck (1961), Brody and Oppenheim (1967), Kendler (1968; 1981, ch. 3), Kendler and Spence (1971), Waters and McCallum (1973), Zuriff (1979a). Kanfer (1968) argues against using first-person reports for inferences of internal events. A common criticism of Watson is that he uses introspection to discover the implicit responses used to explain thought and emotion (Titchener, 1914; Carr, 1915; Pear, 1920; Heidbreder, 1933, ch. 7; Harrell and Harrison, 1938). However, as Watson (1924a, pp. 350–351) notes, these covert events are hypothesized as inferences from observed behavior rather than introspectively discovered.

28. Zuriff (1979a). Also see Pylyshyn (1973) and Anderson (1978).

29. See discussion in chapters 2 and 5.

30. Skinner (1945a; 1953a, pp. 259–261; 1957a, pp. 133–136; 1972h; 1972i), Blanshard and Skinner (1967). Also see Hunter (1925), Hull (1944), Hebb (1958, pp. 4–5), Buchwald (1961), Nisbett and Wilson (1977), and criticism by Begelman (1976).

31. Tolman (1936), Skinner (1945a), Marx (1958), Hebb (1958, pp. 30–32), Verplanck (1962), Kanfer (1968), Wolf (1978).

32. Watson (1913a), Holt (1915b, pp. 86–87; 1937), Weiss (1917b; 1924b; 1928a; 1929a, pp. 276, 420–421), Perrin (1921), Skinner (1972g; 1974, p. 17), Day (1976a), but cf. Zuriff (1979b).

33. Skinner (1974, p. 216; 1977a), Nisbett and Wilson (1977), Hebb (1980, p. 20).

34. Both Mahoney (1974, pp. 2–4) and Hilgard (1977) complain about this.

35. See Watson (1920; 1924a, ch. 1), Hunter (1930a), Guthrie (1936), Bergmann (1940a), Skinner (1963a; c; 1966b), Waters and McCallum (1973), and Rachlin (1980). See also objections by Woodworth (1931, ch. 3), Stephenson (1953), Hilgard (1977), and Lieberman (1979). Kurtz (1968) discusses the implications for social science.

36. Reichenbach (1938).

37. Tolman (1938a; 1959), Graham (1958), Spence (1966), Maltzman (1966), Kanfer (1968), Kendler and Spence (1971). A good illustration is Mowrer (1960a, p. 200).

38. Broad (1925, pp. 613–614), Malcolm (1958; 1964; 1971b, part 3), Collins (1969), Pritchard (1976). Malcolm (1971b, p. 83) misinterprets Carnap on this point, but as Carnap (1932–1933/1959, p. 193) makes clear, "rational support" is only one kind of test for "I am excited." The more usual test is the derivation of the system-sentence "I am excited" from the protocol-sentence "now excited" arrived at intuitively without observation of the body.

39. But see Malcolm (1964, p. 152).

40. Zuriff (1975; 1979a). See also Ziff (1962) and Day (1976b) for other solutions. The knowledge is "tacit" in Polanyi's (1968) term.

41. Bergmann and Spence (1944). Although the distinction is a logical one, it can also be given a psychological interpretation in terms of the conditioning history of the two classes of verbal responses.

42. Woodworth (1924), Watson and McDougall (1928, pp. 43–103), Roback (1937, p. 110), Locke (1971), Alston (1972), Lieberman (1979). See also Schoenfeld and Cumming (1963) on psychological scaling, and review by Bergmann (1956).

43. Watson (1913a; 1916a; 1924a, pp. 35–38).

44. Hunter (1924a), Skinner (1945a; 1953a, pp. 264–266; 1957a, pp. 139–140; 1969, pp. 244–247; 1972h), Boring (1946), Mace (1948–1949), Schoenfeld and Cumming (1963), Blanshard and Skinner (1967). Also see review by Natsoulas (1970).

45. Hunter (1924a; 1925) speaks of a "language response" (LR) becoming automatic.

46. Cf. Ryle (1949, pp. 174–181) and Tolman (1951).

47. For a statement of the neural identity theory see Place (1956) and Smart (1963, pp. 91–105). Weiss (1919b), Lashley (1923a; b), and Hebb (1980) seem to subscribe to the theory. Skinner (1974, p. 11) distinguishes his own approach from what he calls "physicalism," and see Keat (1972).

48. See for example Prince (1926) and Blanshard's argument in Blanshard and Skinner (1967).

49. Cf. de Laguna (1927/1963, p. 131) and Fodor (1981).

50. Although this is a problem primarily for Tolman it also poses difficulties for Skinner (1957a, pp. 145, 315–316; 1972g; 1974, p. 26) who speaks of people discriminating the probability of their behavior before it has occurred. Also see Wright (1976, p. 149, fn. 11).

51. One possibility is that the social consequences of saying "I am angry" become reinforcing to a person upon acquiring a high value on the anger-intervening-variable. In Michael's (1982) terminology, an anger-arousing event (e.g., an insult) is an "establishing stimulus" that makes those consequences reinforcing.

52. Compare Wittgenstein's (1953, p. 89) assertion that saying "I am in pain" is a natural kind of pain-behavior like crying or limping. See also Malcolm (1958) and Armstrong (1968, pp. 66–67).

53. Compare this analysis with criteriological analytic behaviorism discussed in the preceding chapter.

54. See Zuriff (1972) for a review.

55. Bergmann and Spence (1944), Graham (1958).

56. Treisman (1962; 1964a; b), Zuriff (1972).

57. Stevens (1971a).

58. Zuriff (1972). For other interpretations see Savage (1966; 1970) and Warren (1981).

59. Although Stevens (1970; 1971b) is very careful to avoid saying that in psychophysical experiments subjects are judging neural output, he has nevertheless been understood to be asserting this very theory, as can be seen in Warren (1981) and the peer commentary thereon. The sensory transducer theory remains conceptually murky in discussions by Marks (1974, pp. 278, 282–283), Scharf (1975), and Gescheider (1976, pp. 144–145).

60. See discussions by Kantor (1942), Treisman (1962; 1964a; b), and Shepard (1978).

61. See Tolman (1935; 1959), Brunswik (1937), and Quine (1960, pp. 80–85).

62. Zener (1958).

63. Lashley (1923a; b) identifies quality with unanalyzable quantitative diversity. Singer (1924, pp. 93–95) argues that quality exists only in contrast to other qualities. Weiss (1924b; 1929a, p. 292) and Skinner (1953a, p. 260) claim that nothing is perceived unless there is reason to behave discriminatively toward it. de Laguna (1927/1963, pp. 128–129) argues that science can know only relationships but not qualities. Also see Weimer (1976).

64. Singer (1924, ch. 9), Sellars (1956), Brody and Oppenheim (1967), Weimer (1976), and see chapter 3.

65. Compare Tolman (1922a; b; 1923; 1932, pp. 250–256; 1933), Tolman and Horowitz (1933). Also see Guttman (1964), Armstrong's (1968, chapter 10) analysis of perception as the acquisition of a belief, and Dennett's (1976) view of dreams.

66. The "Copy Theory" is described by Holt (1937) and generally is rejected by behaviorists, including Singer (1912; 1924, ch. 9), Woodbridge (1913), Weiss (1929a, pp. 212–216), Hunter (1930a), Ryle (1949, ch. 7), Skinner (1953a, pp. 276, 281; 1963a; 1969, pp. 247–251, 274; 1974, pp. 80–81; 1977a), Blanshard and Skinner (1967), and Hebb (1980, p. 19). Beloff (1962, pp. 36–41) and O'Neil (1968) provide some of the historical background. It is also discussed in chapters 2, 8, and 12.

67. See the discussion of "seeing-as" in Skinner (1953a, pp. 138–140; 1963a; 1974, chapter 5), Mach (1886/1959, pp. 10–12), and Blanshard and Skinner (1967).

12. BEHAVIORAL EPISTEMOLOGY

1. Skinner (1945a; 1957a, chapter 18; 1963a; 1968, p. 206), Naess (1965), Day (1969a), Rozeboom (1972).

2. Skinner (1953a, pp. 14, 140, 409; 1957a, p. 451; 1961; 1968, pp. 200–206; 1972h), Day (1969a; b; 1977), Skinner and Vaughan (1983, p. 157).

3. Skinner (1974, pp. 139–141).

4. Hull (1930b; 1934), Berlyne (1954), Smith (1983, ch. 8). For other S–R theories of knowing see Kantor (1923a), Dashiell (1928, pp. 301, 502–508), Thorndike (1949, chapter 12), Mowrer (1960a, pp. 61–62; 1960b, pp. 345–347). Also see objections by Blanshard (1928) and Ginsberg (1954a).

5. See also Hebb (1958, pp. 182–183; 1972, p. 33).

6. Skinner (1957a, chapter 18; 1969, pp. 254–255; 1972c; i). Also see Schnaitter (1975) and Day (1976a; b).

7. Skinner (1957a, pp. 425–428). Also see Chomsky's (1959/1967) objections.

8. Dollard and Miller (1950, part 3), Berlyne (1965).
9. Hull (1934; 1938; 1962, pp. 841–845), Smith (1983, ch. 8).
10. Tolman (1935; 1948).
11. Tolman (1936), Smith (1983, ch. 5).
12. Tolman (1936).
13. E.g., Meyer (1911, lecture 16; 1921, ch. 16), de Laguna (1927/1963), Hunter (1930a), Kantor (1938), Staats and Staats (1964, pp. 251–258), Mahoney (1974, chs. 15, 16), Hebb (1980, ch. 8).
14. See discussions by Stevens (1939), Feigl (1945), and Ginsberg (1954a).
15. Meyer (1911, pp. 221–226), Dollard and Miller (1950, ch. 9), Skinner (1957a, ch. 18; 1969, pp. 144–145), Guthrie (1959), Staats and Staats (1964, pp. 251–255), Berlyne (1965, ch. 7), Hebb (1980, pp. 121–128).
16. Hull et al. (1940, p. 7), Miller and Dollard (1941, pp. 84–90), Hull (1943b, pp. 13–14; 1952, p. 355), Berlyne (1954; 1965, ch. 7), Smith (1983, ch. 8).
17. Weiss (1918), Bawden (1919a; b), Lashley (1923b), de Laguna (1927/1963, pp. 136–139, 191–197).
18. For more on the relationship between pragmatism and behaviorism see Dewey (1922), Beloff (1962, p. 37), Day (1980), and Smith (1983).
19. See discussion of conventionalism in chapter 4. Instrumentalism is also suggested in statements by Meyer (1921, pp. 366–369), Spence (1948), Hebb (1958, pp. 259–260), and Waters and McCallum (1973). See also Guthrie (1936; 1946; 1950; 1959) who speaks of theory as a mere "mnemonic device" for teaching and research.
20. Hull et al. (1940, pp. 6–8), Hull (1943b, pp. 9–13).
21. Hull (1944).
22. Hull (1944; 1952, pp. 335–336, 355). Also see Smith (1983, ch. 8).
23. Skinner (1945a; 1953a, p. 139; 1957a, p. 428; 1974, p. 235), Zuriff (1980).
24. Skinner (1953a, p. 429; 1971b; c, pp. 98–99, 122; 1972b). See also Begelman (1975) and Graham (1977).
25. Lewis (1929, p. 140).
26. Tolman (1932, pp. 428–430; 1949b), Pepper (1934), Smith (1983, ch. 4).
27. Kolakowski (1968) presents an overall view of positivism. The influence of positivism on behaviorism is discussed by Roback (1923, pp. 202–204), Pratt (1945), George (1953b), Koch (1959), Beloff (1962, pp. 37–40), and Mackenzie (1972; 1977). Its effects on Skinner are discussed by Skinner (1931; 1967) and Day (1980), and on Thorndike, by Jonçich (1968).
28. Kolakowski (1968, ch. 1).
29. See discussion of behaviorist extrapolation in chapter 10.
30. Mach (1883/1974, pp. 89–106; 1886/1959, pp. 37, 316–319; 1905/1976, pp. 352–356), Skinner (1972a). The relationship between positivism and pragmatism is discussed by Kolakowski (1968, ch. 7).
31. In fact, this is how the passage is translated in Kolakowski (1968, p. 76).
32. The relationship between experience and observation is discussed in chapter 2. See especially the views of Tolman (1935) and Spence (1948; 1956, p. 12) concerning the "experiential matrix."
33. Mach (1883/1974, pp. 6–7, 89–90; 1905/1976, pp. 354–356). Also see von Mises (1951, pp. 6–8), and objections by Miller (1946).
34. Tolman's construction of intervening variables as a research procedure might also be considered a behaviorist "positive" method.
35. Weiss (1929a, pp. 323–325).
36. It is especially emphasized by Guthrie (1938, pp. 207–208; 1960, pp. 276–277; 1946; 1959), Guthrie and Edwards (1949, p. 302). See also Mach (1883/1974, pp. 1–9, 89–94).
37. Pratt (1939, pp. 110–116), Ginsberg (1954a; 1955), Eacker (1975, ch. 4). Examples include Meyer (1911, pp. xiii–xiv; 1921, pp. 324, 367–368), Bawden (1919a), Holt (1931, chapter 1),

Gray (1931), and Hull (1943b, p. 28). Within logical behaviorism see Carnap (1932–1933/1959) and Hempel (1969).

38. Ullmann (1970), Salzinger (1975), Skinner (1977a).

39. Skinner (1932; 1953a, ch. 13), Guthrie and Edwards (1949, pp. 210, 271–272), Davis (1953).

40. Mursell (1922a), Skinner (1957a, pp. 3–10; 1969, pp. 88–92; 1974, pp. 97–100).

41. Holt (1915b, pp. 95–99). Also see Kantor (1920; 1929), Mead (1922), and chapter 10.

42. See, for example, the arguments advanced by de Laguna (1930), Kessen and Kimble (1952), Kendler (1952), Maze (1954), and Cotton (1963). Also relevant are the discussion of conventionalism in Duhem (1906/1962, chs. 1, 2, 7), and Kolakowski (1968, chapter 6).

43. Weiss (1924a; b; 1925a; 1929a, pp. 68–72), and see criticism by Gundlach (1927). Hebb (1974) adopts a similar position.

44. Tolman (1922b; 1932, p. 426; 1935), de Laguna (1927/1963, pp. 123–129).

45. See discussions of the Copy Theory by Holt et al. (1912, pp. 1–11), Singer (1924, chs. 8 and 9), MacKinnon (1928), de Laguna (1930), Holt (1937), Quine (1960, pp. 1–5), Skinner (1963a; 1969, pp. 247–251; 1972g), Hebb (1980, pp. 35–38). Also relevant is Avenarius' rejection of "introjection" (Kolakowski, 1968, pp. 109–113).

46. Skinner (1953a, pp. 138–140, 275–280; 1969, pp. 247–251; 1974, pp. 77–80, 127), Blanshard and Skinner (1967).

47. Guthrie and Edwards (1949, pp. 25–26), Guthrie (1959), Skinner (1974, pp. 123–124, 144–145, 235).

48. Also see Mach (1883/1974, pp. 89–94, 582).

49. Guthrie (1950), Goodman (1960).

50. This aspect of behaviorism contrasts with the influence of neo-realism according to which the external world is directly known and perceived (Holt et al., 1912; Robinson, 1917–1918; Kantor, 1923b; Williams, 1934; Verplanck, 1954; O'Neil, 1968; Smith, 1983, ch. 3).

51. Davies (1926), Norris (1929a), Weiss (1931), Skinner (1974, p. 234), Zuriff (1980).

52. See Weiss (1931), Kantor (1938), Skinner (1963a), Eacker (1972), and Goodson (1976).

53. Quine (1960, p. 3).

54. Mach (1883/1974, p. 1), Singer (1911; 1912), and see Quine's (1969b) "epistemology naturalized."

55. Newbury (1953).

56. See Sidman (1960), Naess (1965), and Baer, Wolf, and Risley (1968). Also see discussions by Koch (1964), Polanyi (1968), Achinstein (1969), Kessel (1969), and Marx (1976b). Skinner's version is discussed in chapter 5.

57. See related discussions in Suppe (1974), Brown (1977, part 2), and chapters 3 and 5.

58. Also see Lashley (1923a), Hampshire (1959, chapter 1), Goodman (1960), and Brody and Oppenheim (1966).

59. Skinner (1953a, chs. 27, 28; 1971b).

60. Zuriff (1980).

61. This term refers to Bloom's (1982) theory of the human impulse to struggle with, overthrow, and revise accepted ideas.

References Cited

The numbers following each item indicate the chapter and note number in which the item is referred to and the page on which the item is quoted from. For example, (2:7; 9:1, 8) [pp. 62, 89] means that the item is referred to in note 7 of chapter 2 and in notes 1 and 8 of chapter 9 and that it is quoted from on pages 62 and 89.

Achinstein, P. 1969. Approaches to the philosophy of science. In P. Achinstein and S. F. Barker, eds. *The Legacy of Logical Positivism*, 259–291. Baltimore: Johns Hopkins. (1:9; 5:49, 60; 10:10; 12:56)

Ackerman, P. D. 1973. Formulations regarding an experimental analysis of covert impulse and depression responses as mediators of consummatory S-R sequences. *Psychological Record*, 23:477–486. (10:80)

Adams, D. K. 1928. The inference of mind. *Psychological Review*, 35:235–252. (10:79)

Ainslie, G. 1975. Specious reward: A behavioral theory of impulsiveness and impulse control. *Psychological Bulletin*, 82:463–496. (9:69)

Albritton, R. 1959. On Wittgenstein's use of the term "criterion." *Journal of Philosophy*, 56:845–857. (10:28)

Allport, G. W. 1943. The ego in contemporary psychology. *Psychological Review*, 50:451–478. (7:2; 9:40)

Alston, W. P. 1972. Can psychology do without private data? *Behaviorism*, 1:71–102. (2:27; 10:29; 11:42)

Alston, W. P. 1974. Conceptual prolegomena to a psychological theory of intentional action. In S. C. Brown, ed. *Philosophy of Psychology*, 71–101. London: Macmillan. (3:56, 80; 9:76; 10:32)

Amsel, A. 1965. On inductive versus deductive approaches and neo-Hullian behaviorism. In B. B. Wolman, ed. *Scientific Psychology: Principles and Approaches*, 187–206. New York: Basic. (4:61; 5:16, 48; 6:54)

Anderson, J. R. 1978. Arguments concerning representations for mental imagery. *Psychological Review*, 85:249–277. (8:49, 53; 11:28)

Arbib, M. A. 1969. Memory limitations of stimulus-response models. *Psychological Review*, 76:507–510. (4:4)

Armstrong, D. M. 1968. *A Materialist Theory of the Mind*. London: Routledge and Kegan Paul. (4:51, 52; 10:32, 37, 39; 11:5, 20, 52, 65)

Aronson, J. L. 1976. Some dubious neurological assumptions of radical behaviorism. *Journal for the Theory of Social Behaviour*, 6:49–60. (3:9)

Attneave, F. 1974. How do you know? *American Psychologist*, 29:493–499. [p. 161]

Aune, B. 1966. Feigl on the mind-body problem. In P. K. Feyerabend and G. Maxwell, eds.

Mind, Matter, and Method: Essays in Philosophy and Science in Honor of Herbert Feigl, 17–39. Minneapolis: University of Minnesota Press. (2:46)

Ausubel, D. P. 1965. Introduction. In R. C. Anderson and D. P. Ausubel, eds. *Readings in the Psychology of Cognition*, 3–17. New York: Holt Rinehart and Winston. (8:53)

Ayer, A. J. 1968. *The Concept of a Person*. New York: Macmillan. (10:28, 79)

Azrin, N. H. and W. C. Holz 1966. Punishment. In W. K. Honig, ed. *Operant Behavior: Areas of Research and Application*, 380–447. New York: Appleton-Century-Crofts. (4:68)

Baer, D. M. 1978. On the relation between basic and applied research. In A. C. Catania and T. A. Brigham, eds. *Handbook of Applied Behavior Analysis: Social and Instructional Processes*, 11–16. New York: Irvington. (10:67)

Baer, D. M., M. M. Wolf and T. R. Risley 1968. Some current dimensions of applied behavior analysis. *Journal of Applied Behavior Analysis*, 1:91–97. (3:61; 12:56)

Baldwin, J. M. 1896. The type theory of reactions. *Mind*, 5(ns):81–90. (2:30)

Bambrough, R. 1960–1961. Universals and family resemblances. *Proceedings of the Aristotelian Society*, 61:207–222. (1:9)

Bandura, A. 1969. *Principles of Behavior Modification*. New York: Holt, Rinehart, and Winston. (6:56, 70)

Bandura, A. 1974. Behavior theory and the models of man. *American Psychologist*, 29:859–869. (6:57; 8:7; 9:35, 54, 55) [p. 108]

Bandura, A. 1977a. *Social Learning Theory*. Englewood Cliffs, N.J.: Prentice-Hall. (3:77; 6:34, 50; 6:57, 70, 71; 7:52; 8:7, 22, 36, 44; 9:14, 55, 80) [pp. 113, 114, 153, 198]

Bandura, A. 1977b. Self-efficacy: Toward a unifying theory of behavioral change. *Psychological Review*, 84:191–215. (8:7, 44) [p. 153]

Bandura, A. 1978. The self system in reciprocal determinism. *American Psychologist*, 33:344–358. (6:34; 9:11, 55)

Bartlett, F. C. and E. M. Smith 1920. Is thinking merely the action of language mechanisms? (I) *British Journal of Psychology*, 11:55–62. (8:10, 25)

Bartley, S. H. and F. T. Perkins 1931. A consideration of Hunter's criticism of Lashley. *Psychological Review*, 38:27–41. (7:2; 9:49)

Baum, W. M. 1973. The correlation-based law of effect. *Journal of the Experimental Analysis of Behavior*, 20:137–153. (6:32, 40, 41; 9:46)

Baum, W. M. 1981. Optimization and the matching law as accounts of instrumental behavior. *Journal of the Experimental Analysis of Behavior*, 36:387–403. (6:31, 41, 42; 9:13)

Bawden, H. H. 1918. The presuppositions of a behaviorist psychology. *Psychological Review*, 25:171–190. (2:25; 7:22; 8:30; 10:25; 11:25)

Bawden, H. H. 1919a. Psychology and scientific method. *Journal of Philosophy, Psychology, and Scientific Methods*, 16:603–609. (2:12; 12:17, 37)

Bawden, H. H. 1919b. The evolution of behavior. *Psychological Review*, 26:247–276. (4:70; 8:23; 12:17)

Bechterev, V. M. 1917/1931. *General Principles of Human Reflexology*. Translated by Emma and William Murphy. New York: International. (6:8)

Beck, L. W. 1950. Constructions and inferred entities. *Philosophy of Science*, 17:74–86. (4:47, 53, 67)

Begelman, D. A. 1975. Ethical and legal issues in behavior modification. In R. M. Hersen, R. M. Eisler and P. M. Miller, eds. *Progress in Behavior Modification*, 1:159–189. New York: Academic. (12:24)

Begelman, D. A. 1976. Wittgenstein. *Behaviorism*, 4:201–207. (11:30)

Behan, R. A. 1953. Expectancies and Hullian theory. *Psychological Review*, 60:252–256. (6:64)

Beloff, J. 1962. *The Existence of Mind*. New York: Citadel. (1:13; 11:5, 66; 12:18, 27)

Bem, D. J. 1972. Self-perception theory. In L. Berkowitz, ed. *Advances in Experimental Social Psychology*, 6:1–62. New York: Academic. (6:58; 8:16; 9:66; 11:12, 16)

Bennett, J. 1964. *Rationality*. London: Routledge and Kegan Paul. (3:22; 8:55)

Bentley, A. F. 1940. Observable behaviors. *Psychological Review*, 47:230–253. (3:19)

Bentley, A. F. 1941. The behavioral superfice. *Psychological Review*, 48:39–59. (3:2, 3; 6:34)

Bentley, M. 1926. The major categories of psychology. *Psychological Review*, 33:71–105. (2:8; 9:80; 10:68)

Bergmann, G. 1940a. On some methodological problems of psychology. *Philosophy of Science*, 7:205–219. (1:14; 10:5; 11:27, 35)

Bergmann, G. 1940b. The subject matter of psychology. *Philosophy of Science*, 7:415–433. (3:31; 10:5; 11:4, 27)

Bergmann, G. 1943. Psychoanalysis and experimental psychology: A review from the standpoint of scientific empiricism. *Mind*, 52:122–140. (10:50)

Bergmann, G. 1953. Theoretical psychology. *Annual Review of Psychology*, 4:435–458. (1:18; 3:11, 41; 4:36, 47, 53; 9:27, 41; 11:27)

Bergmann, G. 1954. Reduction. In J. T. Wilson, ed. *Current Trends in Psychology and the Behavioral Sciences*, 59–81. Pittsburgh: University of Pittsburgh Press. (4:63)

Bergmann, G. 1956. The contribution of John B. Watson. *Psychological Review*, 63:265–276. (3:13, 34; 9:18, 26, 27; 10:50; 11:42)

Bergmann, G. and K. W. Spence 1941. Operationism and theory in psychology. *Psychological Review*, 48:1–14. (4:16, 20, 46; 5:2, 4, 13)

Bergmann, G. and K. W. Spence 1944. The logic of psychophysical measurement. *Psychological Review*, 51:1–24. (10:12; 11:41, 55)

Berlyne, D. E. 1951. Attention, perception, and behavior theory. *Psychological Review*, 58:137–146. (4:76; 9:31, 52; 11:21)

Berlyne, D. E. 1954. Knowledge and stimulus response psychology. *Psychological Review*, 61:245–254. (8:18; 12:4, 16)

Berlyne, D. E. 1965. *Structure and Direction in Thinking*. New York: Wiley. (4:70; 6:22; 7:47; 8:18, 19, 21; 11:21; 12:8, 15, 16)

Berlyne, D. E. 1966. Mediating responses: A note on Fodor's criticisms. *Journal of Verbal Learning and Verbal Behavior*, 5:408–411. (4:70)

Berlyne, D. E. 1975. Behaviourism? Cognitive theory? Humanistic psychology?—To Hull with them all! *Canadian Psychological Review*, 16:69–80. (1:4; 8:20, 49)

Bernard, C. 1865/1927. *An Introduction to the Study of Experimental Medicine*. Translated by H. C. Greene. New York: Macmillan. [p. 263]

Bever, T. G. 1968. Associations to stimulus-response theories of language. In T. R. Dixon and D. L. Horton, eds. *Verbal Behavior and General Behavior Theory*, 478–494. Englewood Cliffs, N.J.: Prentice-Hall. (7:47, 68)

Bever, T. G., J. A. Fodor and M. Garrett 1968. A formal limit of associationism. In T. R. Dixon and D. L. Horton, eds. *Verbal Behavior and General Behavior Theory*, 582–585. Englewood Cliffs, N.J.: Prentice-Hall. (7:42, 47)

Bever, T. G., J. A. Fodor and W. Weksel 1965a. On the acquisition of syntax: A critique of "contextual generalization." *Psychological Review*, 72:467–482. (7:68) [p. 143]

Bever, T. G., J. A. Fodor and W. Weksel 1965b. Is linguistics empirical? *Psychological Review*, 72:493–500. (7:68) [p. 143]

Bijou, S. W. 1979. Some clarifications on the meaning of a behavior analysis of child development. *Psychological Record*, 29:3–13. (3:81; 4:68; 6:34)

Bindra, D. 1978. How adaptive behavior is produced: A perceptual-motivational alternative to response-reinforcement. *Behavioral and Brain Sciences*, 1:41–91. (6:59)

Black, M. 1970. Comment. In R. Borger and F. Cioffi, eds. *Explanation in the Behavioural Sciences*, 452–461. Cambridge: Cambridge University Press. (7:60, 62, 74)

Blanshard, B. 1928. Behaviorism and the theory of knowledge. *Philosophical Review*, 37:328–352. (12:4)

Blanshard, B. 1940. *The Nature of Thought*. New York: Macmillan. (8:24, 25)

Blanshard, B. and B. F. Skinner 1967. The problem of consciousness—A debate. *Philosophical and Phenomenological Research*. 27:317–337. (5:20; 7:29; 9:80; 11:16, 30, 44, 48, 67, 68; 12:46)

Block, N. 1978. Troubles with functionalism. In C. W. Savage, ed. *Perception and Cognition: Issues in the Foundations of Psychology. Minnesota Studies in the Philosophy of Science*, 9:261–325. Minneapolis: University of Minnesota Press. (8:34; 10:37, 44)

Bloom, H. 1982. *Agon: Towards a Theory of Revisionism*. New York: Oxford University Press. (12:61)

Boakes, R. A. and M. S. Halliday 1970. The Skinnerian analysis of behaviour. In R. Borger and F. Cioffi, eds. *Explanation in the Behavioural Sciences*, 345–374. Cambridge: Cambridge University Press. (5:30, 41, 42, 66; 6:25; 9:30)

Bode, B. H. 1913. The method of introspection. *Journal of Philosophy, Psychology, and Scientific Methods*, 10:85–91. (11:25)

Bode, B. H. 1914. Psychology as a science of behavior. *Psychological Review*, 21:46–61. (2:11, 24; 6:34)

Bode, B. H. 1917. The nature of the psychical. *Journal of Philosophy, Psychology, and Scientific Methods*, 14:288–294. (6:34)

Bode, B. H. 1918. Consciousness as behavior. *Journal of Philosophy, Psychology, and Scientific Methods*, 15:449–453. (9:42)

Bode, B. H. 1922. What is psychology? *Psychological Review*, 29:250-258. (6:34)

Boden, M. A. 1972. *Purposive Explanation in Psychology*. Cambridge: Harvard University Press. (3:63; 7:14; 8:55; 9:41)

Bolles, R. C. 1972. Reinforcement, expectancy, and learning. *Psychological Review*, 79:394–409. (6:59)

Borger, R. 1974. Human action and psychological research. In S. C. Brown, ed. *Philosophy of Psychology*, 102–123. London: Macmillan. (3:44; 9:75, 79)

Boring, E. G. 1945. The use of operational definitions in science. *Psychological Review*, 52:243–245, 278–281. (4:6, 7, 16, 18; 5:63; 10:12)

Boring, E. G. 1946. Mind and mechanism. *American Journal of Psychology*, 59:173–192. (4:50; 11:44)

Boring, E. G. 1950. *A History of Experimental Psychology* (2d ed.)., New York: Appleton-Century-Crofts. (4:51; 6:6)

Boring, E. G. 1953. A history of introspection. *Psychological Bulletin*, 50:169–189. (2:4, 6, 38; 10:16; 11:1)

Boring, E. G. 1964. The trend toward mechanism. *Proceedings of the American Philosophical Society*, 108:451–454. (9:32)

Bourne, L. E. 1968. Concept attainment. In T. R. Dixon and D. L. Horton, eds. *Verbal Behavior and General Behavior Theory*, 230–253. Englewood Cliffs, N.J.: Prentice-Hall. (8:21; 9:55, 56, 59)

Bowers, K. S. 1973. Situationism in psychology: An analysis and a critique. *Psychological Review*, 80:307–336. (1:3; 3:74; 4:44; 6:34, 48; 9:10, 14)

Braine, M. D. S. 1963. On learning the grammatical order of words. *Psychological Review*, 70:323–348. (7:68)

Braine, M. D. S. 1965. On the basis of phrase structure: A reply to Bever, Fodor, and Weksel. *Psychological Review*, 72:483–492. (7:68)

Braine, M. D. S. 1971. On two types of models of the internalization of grammars. In D. I. Slobin, ed. *The Ontogenesis of Grammar: A Theoretical Symposium*, 153–186. New York: Academic. (7:82)

Branch, M. N. 1977. On the role of "memory" in the analysis of behavior. *Journal of the Experimental Analysis of Behavior*, 28:171–179. (3:69; 4:2, 36, 37; 8:50)

Breger, L. and J. L. McGaugh 1965. Critique and reformulation of "learning-theory" approaches to psychotherapy and neurosis. *Psychological Bulletin*, 63:338–358. (3:74; 6:63; 7:36; 8:7; 9:26, 38; 10:47, 68, 69)

Breger, L. and J. L. McGaugh 1966. Learning theory and behavior therapy: A reply to Rachman and Eysenck. *Psychological Bulletin*, 65:170–173. (6:63; 7:36; 10:69)

Brewer, W. F. 1974. There is no convincing evidence for operant or classical conditioning in adult humans. In W. B. Weimer and D. S. Palermo, eds. *Cognition and the Symbolic Processes*, 1–42. Hillsdale, N.J.: Erlbaum. (1:3, 4; 6:50; 9:55)

Brewster, J. M. 1936. A behavioristic account of the logical function of universals, I and II. *Journal of Philosophy*, 33:505–514, 533–547. (8:30; 10:25, 34)

Bridgman, P. W. 1927. *The Logic of Modern Physics*. New York: Macmillan. (2:35; 4:15, 60) [p. 58]

Bridgman, P. W. 1945. Some general principles of operational values. *Psychological Review*, 52:246–249, 281–284. (2:35; 4:7; 5:63; 10:13)

Bridgman, P. W. 1954. Remarks on the present state of operationalism. *Scientific Monthly*, 79:224–226. (4:22)

Brigham, T. A. 1978. Self-control. In A. C. Catania and T. A. Brigham, eds. *Handbook of Applied Behavior Analysis: Social and Instructional Processes*, 259–274. New York: Irvington. (9:69)

Briskman, L. B. 1972. Is a Kuhnian analysis applicable to psychology? *Science Studies*, 2:87–97. (1:4; 2:38; 3:76; 9:80)

Broad, C. D. 1918–1919. Mechanical explanation and its alternatives. *Proceedings of the Aristotelian Society*, 19:86–124. (9:32)

Broad, C. D. 1925. *The Mind and Its Place in Nature*. London: Routledge and Kegan Paul. (2:2; 3:69; 10:29; 11:38)

Broadbent, D. E. 1961. *Behaviour*. New York: Basic. (2:7, 24, 51; 3:3, 15; 4:24, 66; 5:16, 32; 7:22; 9:19)

Broadbent, D. E. 1973. *In Defense of Empirical Psychology*. London: Methuen. (1:17; 5:16; 7:24, 48, 62, 65, 69; 9:10, 49)

Brodbeck, M. 1963. Meaning and action. *Philosophy of Science*, 30:309–324. (3:32, 48; 9:38, 75, 79; 10:34)

Brodbeck, M. 1966. Mental and physical: Identity versus sameness. In P. K. Feyerabend and G. Maxwell, eds. *Mind, Matter, and Method: Essays in Philosophy and Science in Honor of Herbert Feigl*, 40–58. Minneapolis: University of Minnesota Press. (10:13)

Brody, N. and P. Oppenheim 1966. Tensions in psychology between the methods of behaviorism and phenomenology. *Psychological Review*, 73:295–305. (1:8; 2:17, 22; 3:24; 12:58)

Brody, N. and P. Oppenheim 1967. Methodological differences between behaviorism and phenomenology in psychology. *Psychological Review*, 74:330–334. (11:27, 64)

Brown, H. C. 1916. Language and the associative reflex. *Journal of Philosophy, Psychology, and Scientific Methods*, 13:645–649. (7:64; 8:23)

Brown, H. I. 1977. *Perception, Theory, and Commitment*. Chicago: Precedent. (4:55; 12:57)

Brown, J. S. and I. E. Farber 1951. Emotions conceptualized as intervening variables—With suggestions toward a theory of frustration. *Psychological Bulletin*, 48:465–495. (4:25; 5:7; 10:17)

Brunswik, E. 1937. Psychology as a science of objective relations. *Philosophy of Science*, 4:227–260. (3:80; 10:34; 11:61)

Buchwald, A. M. 1961. Verbal utterances as data. In H. Feigl and G. Maxwell, eds. *Current Issues in the Philosophy of Science*, 461–468. New York: Holt Rinehart and Winston. (11:27, 30)

Buck, R. 1961. Comments on Buchwald's "verbal utterances as data." In H. Feigl and G. Maxwell, eds. *Current Issues in the Philosophy of Science*, 468–472. New York: Holt Rinehart and Winston. (11:27)

Bunge, M. 1963. A general black box theory. *Philosophy of Science*, 30:346–358. (4:64)

Burnham, J. C. 1968. On the origins of behaviorism. *Journal of the History of the Behavioral Sciences*, 4:143–151. (1:4)

Burns, H. W. 1960. Pragmatism and the science of behavior. *Philosophy of Science*, 27:58–74. (4:3; 8:42; 9:14, 15, 40)
Burt C. 1962. The concept of consciousness. *British Journal of Psychology*, 53:229–242. (2:27, 31; 9:80)
Burt, C. 1968. Brain and consciousness. *British Journal of Psychology*, 59:55–69. (10:29)
Cahoon D. D. 1968. Symptom substitution and the behavior therapies: A reappraisal. *Psychological Bulletin*, 69:149–156. (10:48)
Calkins, M. W. 1913. Psychology and the behaviorist. *Psychological Bulletin*, 10:288–291. (2:2; 9:9, 32)
Calkins, M. W. 1917. Purposing self versus potent soul: A discussion of professor Warren's "study of purpose." *Journal of Philosophy, Psychology, and Scientific Methods*, 14:197–200. (9:9)
Calkins, M. W. 1921. The truly psychological behaviorism. *Psychological Review*, 28:1–18. (8:26; 9:9)
Calkins, M. W. 1922. The affiliations of behaviorism. *Psychological Review*, 29:490–492. (9:9)
Calverton, V. F. 1924. The rise of objective psychology. *Psychological Review*, 31:418–426. (2:36; 9:33)
Campbell, D. T. 1954. Operational delineation of "what is learned" via the transpositional experiment. *Psychological Review*, 61:167–174. (3:82, 83)
Carnap, R. 1932–1933/1959. Psychology in physical language. *Erkenntnis*, 3:107–142. Reprinted in A. J. Ayer, ed. *Logical Positivism*, 165–198. Translated by G. Schick. Glencoe: Free Press. (2:46; 3:31, 61; 10:5, 7, 79; 11:27, 38; 12:37) [p. 227]
Carnap, R. 1936. Testability and meaning. *Philosophy of Science*, 3:419–471. (4:10, 11, 12, 47)
Carnap, R. 1937. Testability and meaning—Continued. *Philosophy of Science*, 4:1–40. (2:36; 3:21, 31; 10:10)
Carnap, R. 1955. Logical foundations of the unity of science. *International Encyclopedia of Unified Science*, 1:42–62. Chicago: University of Chicago Press. (2:36; 10:7, 8; 11:4)
Carnap, R. 1956. The methodological character of theoretical concepts. In H. Feigl and M. Scriven, eds. *The Foundations of Science and the Concepts of Psychology and Psychoanalysis. Minnesota Studies in the Philosophy of Science*, 1:38–76. Minneapolis: University of Minnesota Press. (3:14; 4:9, 31, 55, 59, 66)
Carr, H. 1915. Review of Watson's *Behavior. Psychological Bulletin*, 12:308–312. (1:18; 11:27)
Carr, H. 1927. The interpretation of the animal mind. *Psychological Review*, 34:87–106. (10:79)
Carr, H. 1938. The law of effect. I. *Psychological Review*, 45:191–199. (2:9)
Carrier, L. S. 1973. Professor Shaffer's refutation of behaviourism. *Mind*, 82:249–252. (10:19)
Carroll, J. B. 1971. Reinforcement: Is it a basic principle and will it serve in the analysis of verbal behavior? In R. Glaser, ed. *The Nature of Reinforcement*, 334–342. New York: Academic. (6:50)
Carter, D. A. and T. J. Werner 1978. Complex learning and information processing by pigeons: A critical analysis. *Journal of the Experimental Analysis of Behavior*, 29:565–601. (3:76; 4:72; 9:31, 53)
Cason, H. 1924. Purposive psychology and the conditioned reflex. *Psychological Review*, 31:253–255. (9:33)
Catania, A. C. 1972. Chomsky's formal analysis of natural languages: A behavioral translation. *Behaviorism*, 1:1–15. (7:40, 56, 57, 62, 63)
Catania, A. C. 1973. The concept of the operant in the analysis of behavior. *Behaviorism*, 1:103–116. (3:73)
Cautela, J. R. and M. G. Baron 1977. Covert conditioning: A theoretical analysis. *Behavior Modification*, 1:351–368. (4:78)
Chapman, H. W. 1928. Behaviourism: A logical study. *Journal of Philosophical Studies*, 3:65–70. (4:40, 51, 66)
Chein, I. 1972. *The Science of Human Behavior and the Image of Man*. New York: Basic. [p. 176]
Chihara, C. S. and J. A. Fodor 1965. Operationalism and ordinary language: A critique of Wittgenstein. *American Philosophical Quarterly*, 2:281–295. (10:21, 28, 76)

Chomsky, N. 1957. *Syntactic Structures*. The Hague: Mouton. (7:53) [p. 132]
Chomsky, N. 1959/1967. A review of B. F. Skinner's *Verbal Behavior*. *Language*, 35:26–58. In L. A. Jakobovitz and M. S. Miron, eds. *Readings in the Psychology of Language*, 142–171. Englewood Cliffs, N.J.: Prentice-Hall. (3:74, 78; 4:64; 7:36, 37, 49, 56, 66; 10:68, 74; 12:7)
Chomsky, N. 1965. *Aspects of the Theory of Syntax*. Cambridge: MIT Press. (7:37, 66, 74; 8:35; 10:35) [pp. 137, 138, 141, 143, 147]
Chomsky, N. 1972. *Language and Mind* (enlarged edition). New York: Harcourt Brace Jovanovich. (6:63; 7:56, 66) [pp. 130, 131, 137, 139, 141, 145]
Chomsky, N. 1975. *Reflections on Language*. New York: Pantheon. (7:56, 69, 79, 80; 9:45) [p. 145]
Chomsky, N. 1980. *Rules and Representations*. New York: Columbia University Press. (7:69, 80; 8:49)
Cohen, I. B. 1974. History and the philosopher of science. In F. Suppe, ed. *The Structure of Scientific Theories*, 308–349. Urbana: University of Illinois Press. (1:6)
Cohen, L. 1969. Generalization during acquisition, extinction, and transfer of matching with an adjustable comparison. *Journal of the Experimental Analysis of Behavior*, 12:463–474. (4:72)
Collier, G., E. Hirsch and R. Kanarek 1977. The operant revisited. In W. K. Honig and J. E. R. Staddon, eds. *Handbook of Operant Behavior*, 28–52. Englewood Cliffs, N.J.: Prentice-Hall. (6:6)
Collins, A. W. 1969. Unconscious belief. *Journal of Philosophy*, 66:667–680. (11:14, 38)
Comte, A. 1855/1974. *The Positive Philosophy*. Translated by H. Martineau. New York: AMS Press. [p. 268]
Copeland, J. W. 1971. B. F. Skinner's skepticism about choices and future consequences. *Philosophy and Phenomenological Research*, 31:540–545. (9:80)
Costello, C. G. 1963. Behaviour therapy: Criticisms and confusions. *Behaviour Research and Therapy*, 1:159–161. (10:48)
Costello, C. G. 1970. Dissimilarities between conditioned avoidance responses and phobias. *Psychological Review*, 77:250–254. (10:69)
Cotton, J. W. 1963. Theory construction and instrumental learning. In M. H. Marx, ed. *Theories in Contemporary Psychology*, 526–551. New York: Macmillan. (4:12, 31, 36, 40, 45; 5:3; 6:64; 9:26; 12:42)
Cowan, J. L. 1970. The myth of mentalism in linguistics. In J. L. Cowan, ed. *Studies in Thought and Language*, 11–34. Tuscon: University of Arizona Press. (7:60, 62, 69, 70)
Craig, W. 1956. Replacement of auxiliary expressions. *Philosophical Review*, 65:38–55. (4:69)
Craighead, W. E., A. E. Kazdin and M. J. Mahoney 1976. *Behavior Modification: Principles, Issues, and Application*. Boston: Houghton Mifflin. (1:15; 2:54; 10:46, 69)
Crissman, P. 1939. The operational definition of concepts. *Psychological Review*, 46:309–317. (4:8, 14, 19)
Crissman, P. 1944. Are psychological data and methods subjective? *Psychological Review*, 51:162–176. (2:17, 28, 37, 45)
Cronbach, L. J. and P. E. Meehl 1955. Construct validity in psychological tests. *Psychological Bulletin*, 52:281–302. (4:55; 5:59)
Crosland, H. R. 1922. Conscious analysis in learning. *Psychological Review*, 29:75–87. (6:14; 9:26, 80)
Dashiell, J. F. 1925. A physiological-behavioristic description of thinking. *Psychological Review*, 32:54–73. (4:70; 6:20; 9:19, 21)
Dashiell, J. F. 1928. *Fundamentals of Objective Psychology*. Boston: Houghton Mifflin. (1:16, 18; 2:15; 3:76; 4:70, 72, 76; 6:12, 14; 8:12, 22; 9:21, 23, 51; 10:26; 12:4)
Dashiell, J. F. 1937. *Fundamentals of General Psychology*. Boston: Houghton Mifflin. (1:18)
Dauer, F. W. 1972. Empirical realists and Wittgensteinians. *Journal of Philosophy*, 69:128–147. (5:64)
Davidson, D. 1974. Psychology as philosophy. In S. C. Brown, ed. *Philosophy of Psychology*, 41–52. London: Macmillan. (3:46; 9:78; 10:32)

Davies, A. E. 1926. Mechanism, meaning, and teleology in behavior. *American Journal of Psychology*, 37:2–24. (3:51, 56; 6:34; 7:2; 9:41; 12:51)

Davis, L. H. 1979. *Theory of Action*. Englewood Cliffs, N.J.: Prentice-Hall. (3:44, 48, 70; 9:1)

Davis, R. C. 1953. Physical psychology. *Psychological Review*, 60:7–14. (3:6, 60; 4:61; 12:39)

Davison, G. C. and G. T. Wilson 1972. Critique of "Desensitization: Social and cognitive factors underlying the effectiveness of Wolpe's procedure." *Psychological Bulletin*, 78:28–31. (8:7, 8)

Day, W. F. 1969a. Radical behaviorism in reconciliation with phenomenology. *Journal of the Experimental Analysis of Behavior*, 12:315–328. (2:54; 3:22; 10:60; 12:1, 2)

Day, W. F. 1969b. On certain similarities between the *Philosophical Investigations* of Ludwig Wittgenstein and the operationism of B. F. Skinner. *Journal of the Experimental Analysis of Behavior*, 12:489–506. (1:14; 2:50; 5:48; 12:2)

Day, W. F. 1976a. Contemporary behaviorism and the concept of intention. In J. K. Cole and W. J. Arnold, eds. *Conceptual Foundations of Psychology. Nebraska Symposium on Motivation*, 23:65–131. Lincoln: University of Nebraska Press. (1:8; 2:54; 5:22; 7:17; 10:62, 67, 80; 11:32; 12:6)

Day, W. F. 1976b. Analyzing verbal behavior under the control of private events. *Behaviorism*, 4:195–200. (5:22; 11:40; 12:6)

Day, W. F. 1976c. The case for behaviorism. In M. H. Marx and F. E. Goodson, eds. *Theories in Contemporary Psychology* (2d ed.)., 534–545. New York: Macmillan. (3:22; 9:80)

Day, W. F. 1977. On the behavioral analysis of self-deception and self-development. In T. Mischel, ed. *The Self: Psychological and Philosophical Issues*, 224–249. Oxford, England: Basil Blackwell. (9:64; 12:2)

Day, W. F. 1980. The historical antecedents of contemporary behaviorism. In R. W. Rieber and K. Salzinger, eds. *Psychology: Theoretical-Historical Perspectives*, 203–262. New York: Academic. (1:8; 3:7, 52, 61; 10:34; 12:18, 27)

Deese, J. 1969. Behavior and fact. *American Psychologist*, 24:515–522. (8:53)

Deitz, S. M. 1978. Current status of applied behavior analysis: Science versus technology. *American Psychologist*, 33:805–814. (9:10, 18)

de Laguna, G. A. 1918. Dualism in animal psychology. *Journal of Philosophy, Psychology, and Scientific Methods*, 15:617–627. (2:25, 41; 10:24; 11:12)

de Laguna, G. A. 1919a. Emotion and perception from the behaviorist standpoint. *Psychological Review*, 26:409–427. (3:73; 4:76; 10:26)

de Laguna, G. A. 1919b. "Dualism and animal psychology": A rejoinder. *Journal of Philosophy, Psychology, and Scientific Methods*, 16:296–300. (2:24, 41; 3:73; 9:75; 10:26; 11:27) [p. 18]

de Laguna, G. A. 1927/1963. *Speech: Its Function and Development*. Bloomington: Indiana University Press. (1:8; 2:24, 43; 3:73, 77; 4:70; 6:22; 7:19, 27, 35; 8:3, 12, 23, 30; 9:27, 51; 11:27, 49, 63; 12:13, 17, 44) [p. 267]

de Laguna, G. A. 1930. Dualism and gestalt psychology. *Psychological Review*, 37:187–213. (2:25; 3:34; 10:26; 12:42, 45)

Dennett, D. C. 1969. *Content and Consciousness*. New York: Routledge and Kegan Paul. (3:56; 8:55, 56; 10:31, 32)

Dennett, D. C. 1971. Intentional systems. *Journal of Philosophy*, 68:87–106. (3:54, 56; 8:55; 10:32, 34)

Dennett, D. C. 1975. Why the law of effect will not go away. *Journal of the Theory of Social Behaviour*, 5:169–187. (3:54; 8:55; 9:58; 10:34)

Dennett, D. C. 1976. Are dreams experiences? *Philosophical Review*, 73:151–171. (11:65)

Dennett, D. C. 1978a. Toward a cognitive theory of consciousness. In C. W. Savage, ed. *Perception and Cognition: Issues in the Foundations of Psychology. Minnesota Studies in the Philosophy of Science*, 9:201–228. Minneapolis: University of Minnesota Press. (8:55)

Dennett, D. C. 1978b. Skinner skinned. *Brainstorms: Philosophical Essays on Mind and Psychology*, 53–70. Montgomery, Vermont: Bradford. (3:54; 10:34, 65)

Dennett, D. C. 1978c. Two approaches to mental images. *Brainstorms: Philosophical Essays on Mind and Psychology*, 174–189. Montgomery, Vermont: Bradford. (11:6)

Dennett, D. C. 1978d. Artificial intelligence as philosophy and as psychology. *Brainstorms: Philosophical Essays on Mind and Psychology*, 109–126. Montgomery, Vermont: Bradford. (3:54; 8:55; 10:34)

Deutsch, J. A. 1960. *The Structural Basis of Behavior*. Chicago: University of Chicago Press. (4:41, 53; 7:19; 8:34; 9:32)

de Villiers, P. A. 1977. Choice in concurrent schedules and a quantitative formulation of the law of effect. In W. K. Honig and J. E. R. Staddon, eds. *Handbook of Operant Behavior*, 233–287. Englewood Cliffs, N.J.: Prentice-Hall. (6:31)

de Villiers, P. A. and R. J. Herrnstein 1976. Toward a law of response strength. *Psychological Bulletin*, 83:1131–1153. (5:37)

Dewey, J. 1896. The reflex arc concept in psychology. *Psychological Review*, 3:357–370. (6:34)

Dewey, J. 1914. Psychological doctrine and philosophical teaching. *Journal of Philosophy, Psychology, and Scientific Methods*, 11:505–511. (3:51, 56; 7:2)

Dewey, J. 1918. Concerning alleged immediate knowledge of mind. *Journal of Philosophy, Psychology, and Scientific Methods*, 15:29–35. (3:48; 11:23, 24)

Dewey, J. 1922. Knowledge and speech reaction. *Journal of Philosophy*, 19:561–570. (12:18)

Diamond, S. 1971. Gestation of the instinct concept. *Journal of the History of the Behavioral Sciences*, 7:323–336. (9:17)

Dinsmoor, J. A. 1954. Punishment: I. The avoidance hypothesis. *Psychological Review*, 61:34–46. (4:77)

Diserens, C. M. 1925. Psychological objectivism. *Psychological Review*, 32:121–152. (1:18)

Dodge, R. 1912. The theory and limitations of introspection. *American Journal of Psychology*, 23:214–229. (2:20; 11:2)

Dodwell, P. C. 1970. *Visual Pattern Recognition*. New York: Holt, Rinehart and Winston. (3:39)

Dollard, J. and N. E. Miller 1950. *Personality and Psychotherapy: An Analysis in Terms of Learning, Thinking, and Culture*. New York: McGraw-Hill. (2:45; 3:76; 4:70, 71, 72, 78; 8:18, 22, 23; 9:31, 51, 52, 58; 10:50, 66, 76; 11:19, 21; 12:8, 15)

Dreyfus, H. L. 1972. *What Computers Can't Do: A Critique of Artificial Reason*. New York: Harper and Row. (8:33)

Dreyfus, H. and J. Haugeland 1974. The computer as a mistaken model of the mind. In S. C. Brown, ed. *Philosophy of Psychology*, 247–258. London: Macmillan. (8:33; 9:43)

Duhem, P. 1906/1962. *The Aim and Structure of Physical Theory*. New York: Atheneum. (12:42)

Dulany, D. E. 1962. The place of hypotheses and intentions: An analysis of verbal control in verbal conditioning. In C. W. Eriksen, ed. *Behavior and Awareness*, 102–129. Durham: Duke University Press. (4:55)

Dulany, D. E. 1968. Awareness, rules, and propositional control: A confrontation with S-R behavior theory. In T. R. Dixon and D. L. Horton, eds. *Verbal Behavior and General Behavior Theory*, 340–387. Englewood Cliffs, N.J.: Prentice-Hall. (2:31; 4:12, 55; 6:48; 9:11, 14)

Dulany, D. E. 1974. On the support of cognitive theory in opposition to behavior theory: A methodological problem. In W. B. Weimer and D. S. Palermo, eds. *Cognition and the Symbolic Processes*, 43–56. Hillsdale, N.J.: Erlbaum. (1:4; 9:33, 55)

Dunham, P. 1977. The nature of reinforcing stimuli. In W. K. Honig and J. E. R. Staddon, eds. *Handbook of Operant Behavior*, 98–124. Englewood Cliffs, N.J.: Prentice-Hall. (3:74)

Dunlap, J. T. and L. R. Lieberman 1973. On "The end of ideology in behavior modification." *American Psychologist*, 28:936–938. (1:4; 10:69)

Dunlap, K. 1912. The case against introspection. *Psychological Review*, 19:404–413. (11:25)

Dunlap, K. 1927. The use and abuse of abstraction in psychology. *Philosophical Review*, 36:462–487. (9:17; 10:68)

Dunlap, K. 1930. Response psychology. In C. Murchison, ed. *Psychologies of 1930*, 309–323. Worcester: Clark University Press. (3:76; 4:70)

Eacker, J. N. 1972. On some elementary philosophical problems of psychology. *American Psychologist*, 27:553–565. (12:52)

Eacker, J. N. 1975. *Problems of Philosophy and Psychology*. Chicago: Nelson-Hall. (12:37)

Eaglen, A. 1978. Learning theory versus paradigms as the basis for behaviour therapy. *Journal of Behavior Therapy and Experimental Psychiatry*, 9:215–218. (10:69)

Eccles, J. C. 1973. *The Understanding of the Brain*. New York: McGraw-Hill. [p. 185]

Ellis, A. 1977. Can we change thoughts by reinforcement? A reply to Howard Rachlin. *Behavior Therapy*, 8:666–672. (8:5)

Ellson, D. G. 1963. The scientists' criterion of true observation. *Philosophy of Science*, 30:41–52. (2:39)

Epstein, R. 1981. On pigeons and people: A preliminary look at the Columban simulation project. *The Behavior Analyst*, 4:43–55. (10:66)

Epstein, R., R. P. Lanza and B. F. Skinner 1980. Symbolic communication between two pigeons (*Columba livia domestic*). *Science*, 207:543–545. (10:66)

Epstein, R., R. P. Lanza and B. F. Skinner 1981. "Self-awareness" in the pigeon. *Science*, 212:695–696. (10:66)

Eriksen, C. W. 1962. Figments, fantasies, and follies: A search for the subconscious mind. In C. W. Eriksen, ed. *Behavior and Awareness*, 3–26. Durham: Duke University Press. (9:54)

Erwin, E. 1978. *Behavior Therapy: Scientific, Philosophical, and Moral Foundations*. Cambridge: Cambridge University Press. (1:9, 15; 2:36; 3:74; 4:10, 14, 54, 59; 7:36; 9:5, 11; 10:14, 24, 31, 60, 69)

Estes, W. K. 1950. Toward a statistical theory of learning. *Psychological Review*, 57:94–107. (4:77)

Estes, W. K. 1969. Reinforcement in human learning. In J. T. Tapp, ed. *Reinforcement and Behavior*, 63–94. New York: Academic. (6:50; 9:55)

Estes, W. K. 1971. Reward in human learning: Theoretical issues and strategic choice points. In R. Glaser, ed. *The Nature of Reinforcement*, 16–36. New York: Academic. (8:11; 9:47, 59; 10:72)

Eysenck, H. J. 1960. Learning theory and behaviour therapy. In H. J. Eysenck, ed. *Behaviour Therapy and the Neuroses*, 4–21. New York: Macmillan. (10:51)

Eysenck, H. J. 1964. The nature of behaviour therapy. In H. J. Eysenck, ed. *Experiments in Behaviour Therapy*, 1–15. New York: Macmillan. (2:54; 10:69)

Eysenck, H. J. 1970. Behavior therapy and its critics. *Journal of Behavior Therapy and Experimental Psychiatry*, 1:5–15. (1:4; 10:51, 52, 69)

Eysenck, H. J. 1972. Behavior therapy is behavioristic. *Behavior Therapy*, 3:609–613. (1:15; 10:24; 11:19)

Eysenck, H. J. 1979. Behaviour therapy and the philosophers. *Behaviour Research and Therapy*, 17:511–514. (3:77; 8:7; 9:54)

Farber, I. E. 1963. The things people say to themselves. *American Psychologist*, 18:185–197. (8:58; 9:54, 57)

Farrow, E. P. 1927. Some notes on behaviorism. *American Journal of Psychology*, 38:660–663. (2:2; 8:25)

Fearing, F. 1930. *Reflex Action: A Study in the History of Physiological Psychology*. Baltimore: Williams and Wilkins. (4:76; 6:3, 6, 7; 9:13, 18, 27, 32, 51, 71)

Feigel, H. 1945. Operationism and scientific method. *Psychological Review*, 52:250–259, 284–288. (4:24, 45; 12:14)

Feigl, H. 1951. Principles and problems of theory construction in psychology. In W. Dennis, ed. *Current Trends in Psychological Theory*, 179–213. Pittsburgh: University of Pittsburgh Press. (3:14; 4:20, 61, 68)

Feigl, H. 1955. Functionalism, psychological theory, and the uniting sciences: Some discussion remarks. *Psychological Review*, 62:232–235. (4:55, 66; 7:8)

Feigl, H. 1959. Philosophical embarrassments of psychology. *American Psychologist*, 14:115-128. (4:24, 55, 59, 66)

Feigl, H. 1970. The "orthodox" view of theories: Remarks in defense as well as critique. In M. Radner and S. Winokur, eds. *Analyses of Theories and Methods of Physics and Psychology*. *Minnesota Studies in the Philosophy of Science*, 4:3–16. Minneapolis: University of Minnesota Press. (3:26; 4:55)

Fernberger, S. W. 1922. Behavior versus introspective psychology. *Psychological Review*, 29:409–413. (2:19)

Ferster, C. B. and B. F. Skinner 1957. *Schedules of Reinforcement*. New York: Appleton-Century-Crofts. (3:36, 73; 5:43, 47; 6:41)

Fetterman, J. G. and D. A. Stubbs 1982. Matching, maximizing, and the behavioral unit: Concurrent reinforcement of response sequences. *Journal of the Experimental Analysis of Behavior*, 37:97–114. (6:32)

Feyerabend, P. 1965. Problems of empiricism. In R. Colodny, ed. *Frontiers of Science and Philosophy*, 145–260. Pittsburgh: University of Pittsburgh Press. (3:26)

Finn, D. R. 1971. Putnam and logical behaviourism. *Mind*, 80:432–436. (10:41)

Fitch, F. B. and G. Barry 1950. Toward a formalization of Hull's behavior theory. *Philosophy of Science*, 17:260–265. (5:59)

Fodor, J. A. 1965. Could meaning be an r_m? *Journal of Verbal Learning and Verbal Behavior*, 4:73–81. (4:80; 10:68)

Fodor, J. A. 1968. *Psychological Explanation: An Introduction to the Philosophy of Psychology*. New York: Random House. (1:13; 2:46; 4:58; 9:77; 10:36, 37, 38, 44) [p. 161]

Fodor, J. A. 1975. *The Language of Thought*. New York: Crowell. (8:36, 49, 54, 56; 10:44, 45)

Fodor, J. A. 1978. Computation and reduction. In C. W. Savage, ed. *Perception and Cognition: Issues in the Foundations of Psychology. Minnesota Studies in the Philosophy of Science*, 9:229–260. Minneapolis: University of Minnesota Press. (8:56; 10:32)

Fodor, J. A. 1981. Introduction. In *Representations: Philosophical Essays on the Foundations of Cognitive Science*, 1–31. Cambridge: MIT (8:51, 57; 10:31, 35, 36, 37; 11:49)

Fodor, J. A., T. G. Bever and M. F. Garrett 1974. *The Psychology of Language*. New York: McGraw-Hill. (4:78; 7:38, 47, 69; 9:35) [p. 161]

Fuchs, A. H. and G. F. Kawash 1974. Prescriptive dimensions for five schools of psychology. *Journal of the History of the Behavioral Sciences*, 10:352–366. (1:18)

Garner, W. R., H. W. Hake and C. W. Eriksen 1956. Operationism and the concept of perception. *Psychological Review*, 63:149–159. (4:7; 11:8)

Garrett, M. and J. A. Fodor 1968. Psychological theories and linguistic constructs. In T. R. Dixon and D. L. Horton, eds. *Verbal Behavior and General Behavior Theory*, 451–477. Englewood Cliffs, N.J.: Prentice-Hall. (7:61; 10:35)

Geissler, L. R. 1929. The objectives of objective psychology. *Psychological Review*, 36:353–374. (10:4)

George, F. H. 1953a. Logical constructs and psychological theory. *Psychological Review*, 60:1–6. (5:64)

George, F. H. 1953b. Formalization of language systems for behavior theory. *Psychological Review*, 60:232–240. (4:23; 12:27)

Gescheider, G. A. 1976. *Psychophysics: Method and Theory*. Hillsdale, N.J.: Erlbaum. (11:59)

Gewirtz, J. L. 1971. The roles of overt responding and extrinsic reinforcement in "self-" and "vicarious-reinforcement" phenomena and in "observational learning" and imitation. In R. Glaser, ed. *The Nature of Reinforcement*, 279–309. New York: Academic. (3:77; 6:58, 68; 8:50; 9:69)

Gewirtz, J. L. 1978. Social learning in early human development. In A. C. Catania and T. A. Brigham, eds. *Handbook of Applied Behavior Analysis: Social and Instructional Processes*, 105–141. New York: Irvington. (3:73; 4:24; 6:68; 8:14, 78; 9:14, 80)

Gewirtz, J. L. and K. G. Stingle 1968. Learning of generalized imitation as the basis for identification. *Psychological Review*, 75:374–397. (6:68; 8:14, 50)

Gibbs, B. 1969–1970. Putnam on brains and behavior. *Analysis*, 30:53–55. (10:41)

Gibson, J. J. 1950. *The Perception of the Visual World*. Boston: Houghton Mifflin. (3:73; 8:40)

Gibson, J. J. 1960. The concept of the stimulus in psychology. *American Psychologist*, 15:694–703. (3:31, 36, 73)

Gibson, J. J. 1973. Direct visual perception: A reply to Gyr. *Psychological Bulletin*, 79:396–397. (8:55)

Ginsberg, A. 1954a. Does Hullian theory provide the adequate foundations for a comprehensive theory of human behavior. *Journal of General Psychology*, 51:301–330. (9:18; 10:68; 12:4, 14, 37)

Ginsberg, A. 1954b. Hypothetical constructs and intervening variables. *Psychological Review*, 61:119–131. (4:30, 49, 51, 53, 55, 68)

Ginsberg, A. 1955. Operational definitions and theories. *Journal of General Psychology*, 52:223–245. (4:14, 19, 54, 55, 67; 5:35, 51, 63; 12:37)

Goldiamond, I. 1976. Self-reinforcement. *Journal of Applied Behavior Analysis*, 9:509–514. (9:69)

Goldstein, H., D. L. Krantz and J. D. Rains, eds. 1965. *Controversial Issues in Learning*. New York: Appleton-Century-Crofts. (3:76, 82; 4:53; 5:1; 6:65)

Goodman, N. 1960. The way the world is. *Review of Metaphysics*, 14:48–56. (3:24, 39; 12:49, 59)

Goodman, N. 1965. *Fact, Fiction, and Forecast*. Indianapolis: Bobbs-Merrill. (4:34)

Goodson, F. E. 1976. The problem of intercommunication. In M. H. Marx and F. E. Goodson, eds. *Theories in Contemporary Psychology* (2d ed.), 379–392. New York: Macmillan. (2:31, 43; 12:52)

Goodson, F. E. and G. A. Morgan 1976. Evaluation of theory. In M. H. Marx and F. E. Goodson, eds. *Theories in Contemporary Psychology* (2d ed.), 286–299. New York: Macmillan. (4:65)

Goss, A. E. 1955. A stimulus-response analysis of the interaction of cue-producing and instrumental responses. *Psychological Review*, 62:20–31. (4:73)

Goss, A. E. 1961a. Verbal mediating responses and concept formation. *Psychological Review*, 68:248–274. (4:73; 8:17)

Goss, A. E. 1961b. Early behaviorism and verbal mediating responses. *American Psychologist*, 16:285–298. (4:73; 8:23; 9:70)

Gough, P. B. and J. J. Jenkins 1963. Verbal learning and psycholinguistics. In M. H. Marx, ed. *Theories in Contemporary Psychology*, 456–474. New York: Macmillan. (4:53, 55, 73, 81; 5:41)

Graham, C. H. 1950. Behavior, perception, and the psychophysical methods. *Psychological Review*, 57:108–120. (3:41; 11:8)

Graham, C. H. 1958. Sensation and perception in an objective psychology. *Psychological Review*, 65:65–76. (11:8, 37, 55)

Graham, G. 1977. On what is good: A study of B. F. Skinner's operant behaviorist view. *Behaviorism*, 5:97–112. (12:24)

Granit, R. 1977. *The Purposive Brain*. Cambridge: MIT Press (7:2) [p. 185]

Gray, J. S. 1931. A behavioristic interpretation of concept formation. *Psychological Review*, 38:65–72. (3:32; 12:37)

Gray, J. S. 1932. A behaviorist interpretation of intelligence. *Psychological Review*, 39:271–278. (7:28; 8:10, 28; 9:42)

Gray, J. S. 1935. An objective theory of emotion. *Psychological Review*, 42:108–116. (11:19)

Gray, P. H. 1968. Prerequisite to an analysis of behaviorism: The conscious automaton theory from Spalding to William James. *Journal of the History of the Behavioral Sciences*, 4:365–376. (9:42)

Gregory, R. L. 1961. The brain as an engineering problem. In W. H. Thorpe and O. L. Zangwill, eds. *Current Problems in Animal Behaviour*, 307–330. Cambridge: Cambridge University Press. (8:34; 9:42)

Gregory, R. L. 1981. *Mind in Science: A History of Explanations in Psychology and Physics*. Cambridge: Cambridge University Press. (9:32, 42)

Grosch, J. and A. Neuringer 1981. Self-control in pigeons under the Mischel paradigm. *Journal of the Experimental Analysis of Behavior*, 35:3–21. (9:69; 10:67)

Gundlach, R. H. 1927. Some difficulties with Weiss's behavioristic postulates. *American Journal of Psychology*, 38:469–475. (10:31, 68; 12:43)

Guthrie, E. R. 1924. Purpose and mechanism in psychology. *Journal of Philosophy*, 21:673–681. (7:12; 9:43)

Guthrie, E. R. 1930. Conditioning as a principle of learning. *Psychological Review*, 37:412–428. (3:76; 6:10; 8:12; 9:27)

Guthrie, E. R. 1933a. On the nature of psychological explanations. *Psychological Review*, 40:124–137. (3:10; 4:65; 7:11, 12, 28; 9:17)

Guthrie, E. R. 1933b. Association as a function of time interval. *Psychological Review*, 40:355–367. (6:50, 66)

Guthrie, E. R. 1934. Pavlov's theory of conditioning. *Psychological Review*, 41:199–206. (3:10)

Guthrie, E. R. 1936. Psychological principles and scientific truth. In H. W. Hill, ed. *Proceedings of the 25th Anniversary Celebration of the Inauguration of Graduate Studies, the University of Southern California*, 104–115. Los Angeles: University of Southern California. (3:59; 7:12; 10:49; 11:35; 12:19) [pp. 258, 273]

Guthrie, E. R. 1937. Tolman on associative learning. *Psychological Review*, 44:525–528. (4:36; 6:51)

Guthrie, E. R. 1938. *The Psychology of Human Conflict*. New York: Harper. (3:19; 4:76; 6:10, 12, 13, 33; 7:8, 16, 28; 8:23; 9:14, 15, 35, 68, 70; 10:50; 12:36)

Guthrie, E. R. 1940. Association and the law of effect. *Psychological Review*, 47:127–148. (3:59; 6:10, 12, 22; 7:16; 9:51)

Guthrie, E. R. 1944. Personality in terms of associative learning. In J. McV. Hunt, ed. *Personality and the Behavior Disorders*, 1:49–68. New York: Ronald. (3:59; 6:10, 12; 10:49)

Guthrie, E. R. 1946. Psychological facts and psychological theory. *Psychological Bulletin*, 43:1–20. (2:36; 3:29, 41, 52; 4:74; 12:19, 36)

Guthrie, E. R. 1950. The status of systematic psychology. *American Psychologist*, 5:97–101. (2:22; 3:24; 12:19, 49) [p. 16]

Guthrie, E. R. 1959. Association by contiguity. In S. Koch, ed. *Psychology: A Study of a Science*, Vol. 2. *General Systematic Formulations, Learning and Special Processes*, 158–195. New York: McGraw-Hill. (2:25, 36: 3:21, 34, 41, 52, 61, 62; 4:74, 77; 6:66; 7:24; 9:22; 12:15, 19, 36, 47)

Guthrie, E. R. 1960. *The Psychology of Learning* (rev. ed.). Gloucester, Mass.: Peter Smith. (1:16; 2:36; 3:24, 31, 35, 41, 62, 66, 76; 4:74, 76; 6:7, 10, 12, 14, 51, 52, 66; 7:5, 9, 11, 12, 15, 16, 24; 8:16; 9:25, 26, 61; 10:24; 11:15; 12:36)

Guthrie, E. R. and A. L. Edwards 1949. *Psychology: A First Course in Human Behavior*. New York: Harper. (2:23, 36; 3:24, 29, 31, 48, 59, 76; 4:37; 6:7, 12, 14; 7:9, 16; 8:23; 9:42, 51, 68, 70; 10:26; 11:15; 12:36, 39, 47)

Guthrie, E. R. and G. P. Horton 1946. *Cats in a Puzzle Box*. New York: Rinehart. (2:24, 25; 3:28, 31, 47, 52, 59; 4:36; 8:16) [p. 203]

Guthrie, E. R. and F. F. Powers 1950. *Educational Psychology*. New York: Ronald. (9:26, 51, 68)

Guttman, N. 1963. Laws of behavior and facts of perception. In S. Koch, ed. *Psychology: A Study of a Science*, Vol. 5. *The Process Areas, the Person, and Some Fields: Their Place in Psychology and in Science*, 114–178. New York: McGraw-Hill. (3:35, 62, 73; 10:17)

Guttman, N. 1964. "Experience." *Proceedings of the American Philosophical Society*, 108:459–463. (10:17; 11:65)

Gyr, J. W. 1972. Is a theory of direct visual perception adequate? *Psychological Bulletin*, 77:246–261. (6:62)

Hamlyn, D. W. 1962. Behavior. In V. C. Chappel, ed. *The Philosophy of Mind*, 60–73. Englewood Cliffs, N.J.: Prentice-Hall. (3:46; 9:77)

Hamlyn, D. W. 1964. Causality and human behaviour. *Proceedings of the Aristotelian Society, Supplement*, 38:125–142. (3:71; 9:76)

Hamlyn, D. W. 1970. Conditioning and behaviour. In R. Borger and F. Cioffi, eds. *Explanation in the Behavioural Sciences*, 139–152. Cambridge: Cambridge University Press. (3:51; 6:25; 9:78; 11:21)

Hampshire, S. 1959. *Thought and Action*. London: Chatto and Windus. (2:41, 46; 3:25, 39; 5:64; 12:58)

Hanna, J. F. 1968. An explication of 'explication.' *Philosophy of Science*, 35:28–44. (10:10, 65)

Hanson, N. R. 1958. *Patterns of Discovery*. Cambridge: Cambridge University Press. (3:26)

Harman, G. 1978. Is there mental representation? In C. W. Savage, ed. *Perception and Cognition: Issues in the Foundations of Psychology. Minnesota Studies in the Philosophy of Science*, 9:57–64. Minneapolis: University of Minnesota Press. (8:36)

Harrell, W. and R. Harrison 1938. The rise and fall of behaviorism. *Journal of General Psychology*, 18:367–421. (1:1, 11; 2:10, 17; 8:23; 11:27)

Hartnack, J. 1972. On thinking. *Mind*, 81:543–552. (8:24, 29)

Harzem, P. and T. R. Miles 1978. *Conceptual Issues in Operant Psychology*. New York: Wiley. (1:9; 3:42, 52; 8:48; 9:14, 35; 10:62)

Hebb, D. O. 1946. Emotion in man and animal: An analysis of the intuitive process of recognition. *Psychological Review*, 53:88–106. (3:34; 10:26; 11:12)

Hebb, D. O. 1949. *The Organization of Behavior: A Neuropsychological Theory*. New York: Wiley. (3:6, 76; 4:68; 5:35; 6:62; 7:1, 15; 8:11, 15; 9:2, 17, 18, 43, 63; 10:15)

Hebb, D. O. 1951. The role of neurological ideas in psychology. *Journal of Personality*, 20:39–55. (3:24; 4:53, 61, 67; 9:18)

Hebb, D. O. 1954. The problem of consciousness and introspection. In J. F. Delafresnaye, ed. *Brain Mechanisms and Consciousness*, 402–421. Springfield: Charles C. Thomas. (9:18; 11:21)

Hebb, D. O. 1958. *A Textbook of Psychology*. Philadelphia: W. B. Saunders. (1:1; 3:6, 16; 4:61; 9:36; 11:21, 27, 30, 31; 12:5, 19) [p. 17]

Hebb, D. O. 1963. The semiautonomous process: Its nature and nurture. *American Psychologist*, 18:16–27. (9:18)

Hebb, D. O. 1972. *Textbook of Psychology* (3d ed.). Philadelphia: W. B. Saunders. (7:38; 10:80; 12:5)

Hebb, D. O. 1974. What psychology is about. *American Psychologist*, 29:71–79. (12:43)

Hebb, D. O. 1980. *Essay on Mind*. Hillsdale, N.J.: Erlbaum. (1:2; 2:5; 5:66; 9:22, 66; 10:70; 11:16, 19, 33, 47, 66; 12:13, 15, 45)

Hebert, J. A. and D. L. Krantz 1965. Transposition: A reevaluation. *Psychological Bulletin*, 63:244–257. (3:76)

Heidbreder, E. 1933. *Seven Psychologies*. New York: Century. (2:10, 15, 17; 9:27, 36; 10:68; 11:27)

Hempel, C. G. 1949. The logical analysis of psychology. In H. Feigl and W. Sellers, eds. *Readings in Philosophical Analysis*, 373–384. New York: Appleton-Century-Crofts. (10:5, 7)

Hempel, C. G. 1958. The theoretician's dilemma: A study in the logic of theory construction. In H . Feigl, et al., eds. *Concepts, Theories, and the Mind-Body Problem. Minnesota Studies in the Philosophy of Science*, 2:37–98. Minneapolis: University of Minnesota Press. (2:36; 4:12, 40, 46, 47, 55, 59, 69)

Hempel, C. G. 1960. Operationism, observation, and theoretical terms. In A. Danto and S. Morgenbesser, eds. *Philosophy of Science*, 101–120. Cleveland: Meridian. (2:36; 4:8, 9, 12, 17, 54, 55)

Hempel, C. G. 1965. *Aspects of Scientific Explanation*. New York: Free Press. (4:6, 12, 55)

Hempel, C. G. 1969. Logical positivism and the social sciences. In P. Achinstein and S. F. Barker, eds. *The Legacy of Logical Positivism*, 163–194. Baltimore: Johns Hopkins University Press. (1:1, 14; 2:36; 3:31; 4:55, 59; 10:5, 8, 21; 11:4; 12:37)

Hempel, C. G. 1970. On the "standard conception" of scientific theories. In M. Radner and S. Winokur, eds. *Analyses of Theories and Methods of Physics and Psychology Minnesota Studies in the Philosophy of Science*, 4:142–163. Minneapolis: University of Minnesota, Press. (3:26; 5:60)

Hempel, C. G. 1974. Formulation and formalization of scientific theories. In F. Suppe, ed. *The Structure of Scientific Theories*, 244–254. Urbana: University of Illinois Press. (3:26; 4:12)

Henle, M. and G. Baltimore 1967. Portraits in straw. *Psychological Review*, 74:325–329. (2:31)

Heppner, P. P. 1978. The clinical alteration of covert thoughts: A critical review. *Behavior Therapy*, 9:717–734. (4:70; 8:6)

Herrick, C. J. 1925. The natural history of purpose. *Psychological Review*, 32:417–430. (7:11)

Herrnstein, R. J. 1961. Relative and absolute strength of response as a function of frequency of reinforcement. *Journal of the Experimental Analysis of Behavior*, 4:267–272. (5:44)

Herrnstein, R. J. 1964. "Will." *Proceedings of the American Philosophical Society*, 108:455–458. (7:17; 9:10, 34; 10:2)

Herrnstein, R. J. 1967. Introduction. In J. B. Watson, *Behavior: An Introduction to Comparative Psychology*. New York: Holt Rinehart and Winston. (1:16; 3:63, 69; 7:11, 14, 17)

Herrnstein, R. J. 1969a. Method and theory in the study of avoidance. *Psychological Review*, 76:46–69. (4:68)

Herrnstein, R. J. 1969b. Behaviorism. In D. L. Krantz, ed. *Schools of Psychology*, 51–68. New York: Meredith. (1:16; 2:4)

Herrnstein, R. J. 1970. On the law of effect. *Journal of the Experimental Analysis of Behavior*, 13:243–266. (4:77; 5:44; 6:32; 9:46)

Herrnstein, R. J. 1972. Nature as nurture: Behaviorism and the instinct doctrine. *Behaviorism*, 1:23–52. (7:17)

Herrnstein, R. J. 1977a. The evolution of behaviorism. *American Psychologist*, 32:593–603. (3:41, 77; 7:81, 83)

Herrnstein, R. J. 1977b. Doing what comes naturally: A reply to Professor Skinner. *American Psychologist*, 32:1013–1016. (4:3; 7:81)

Herrnstein, R. J. 1979. Derivations of matching. *Psychological Review*, 86:486–495. (6:31)

Herrnstein, R. J. 1982a. Stimuli and the texture of experience. *Neuroscience and Biobehavioral Review*, 6:105–117. (3:34, 39, 77; 7:64, 78, 81)

Herrnstein, R. J. 1982b. Melioration as behavioral dynamism. In M. Commons, et al., eds. *Quantitative Analyses of Behavior*, Vol. 2: *Matching and Maximizing Accounts*, 433–458. Cambridge, Mass: Ballinger. (5:44; 6:31)

Herrnstein, R. J. and E. G. Boring, eds. 1965. *A Source Book in the History of Psychology*. Cambridge: Harvard University Press. (6:3)

Herrnstein, R. J. and W. Vaughan 1980. Melioration and behavioral allocation. In J. E. R. Staddon, ed. *Limits to Action: The Allocation of Individual Behavior*. 143–176. New York: Academic. (5:44; 6:31)

Hesse, M. B. 1966. *Models and Analogies in Science*. Notre Dame: University of Notre Dame Press. (3:26; 5:67; 10:73)

Hesse, M. B. 1969. Positivism and the logic of scientific theories. In P. Achinstein and S. F. Barker, eds. *The Legacy of Logical Positivism*, 85–114. Baltimore: Johns Hopkins University Press. (3:26)

Heyman, G. M. 1979. A Markov model description of changeover probabilities on concurrent variable-interval schedules. *Journal of the Experimental Analysis of Behavior*, 31:41–51. (3:69)

Heyman, G. M. 1982. Is time allocation unconditioned behavior? In M. Commons, et al., eds. *Quantitative Analyses of Behavior*, Vol. 2: *Matching and Maximizing Accounts*, 459–490. Cambridge, Mass.: Ballinger. (6:41)

Hilgard, E. R. 1954. Review of Hull's *A Behavior System*. *Psychological Bulletin*, 51:91–96. (6:64)

Hilgard, E. R. 1977. Controversies over consciousness and the rise of cognitive psychology. *Australian Psychologist*, 12:7–27. (8:33; 11:34, 35)

Hilgard, E. R. and G. H. Bower 1975. *Theories of Learning* (4th ed.). Englewood Cliffs, N.J.: Prentice-Hall. (5:3; 7:23; 8:33)

Hinson, J. M. and J. E. R. Staddon 1981. Maximizing on interval schedules. In C. M. Bradshaw, et al., eds. *Quantification of Steady-State Operant Behaviour*, 35–47. New York: Elsevier. (6:31)

Hochberg, H. 1961. Intervening variables, hypothetical constructs, and metaphysics. In H. Feigl and G. Maxwell, eds. *Current Issues in the Philosophy of Science*, 448–457. New York: Holt, Rinehart and Winston. (4:53, 57, 68)

Hocutt, M. 1967. On the alleged circularity of Skinner's concept of stimulus. *Psychological Review*, 74:530–532. (3:74)

Hoffman, H. S. and A. M. Ratner 1973. A reinforcement model of imprinting: Implications for socialization in monkeys and men. *Psychological Review*, 80:527–544. (3:77)

Holborow, L. C. 1967. Wittgenstein's kind of behaviourism? *Philosophical Quarterly*, 17:345–357. (2:51)

Holland, J. G. 1978. Radical behaviorism and consciousness. Paper presented at meeting of the American Psychological Association, as part of symposium entitled: "The Nature of Consciousness." (11:15)

Holt, E. B. 1915a. Response and cognition. *Journal of Philosophy, Psychology, and Scientific Methods*, 12:365–373, 393–409. (3:64; 4:42, 43; 6:17, 18; 7:15; 8:30; 9:51; 11:12)

Holt, E. B. 1915b. *The Freudian Wish and Its Place in Ethics*. New York: Holt. (2:5; 3:63, 71, 79; 4:76; 6:15, 17, 18; 7:15; 8:30; 10:1, 24, 25; 11:32; 12:41)

Holt, E. B. 1931. *Animal Drive and the Learning Process: An Essay Toward Radical Empiricism*, Vol. 1. New York: Holt. (3:12; 6:12, 14, 17; 9:17, 27, 42, 52; 12:37)

Holt, E. B. 1937. Materialism and the criterion of the psychic. *Psychological Review*, 44:33–53. (2:5; 9: 70; 11:19, 25, 32, 66; 12:45)

Holt, E. B., et al., eds. 1912. *The New Realism: Cooperative Studies in Philosophy*. New York: Macmillan. (12:45, 50)

Holz, W. C. and N. H. Azrin 1966. Conditioning human verbal behavior. In W. K. Honig, ed. *Operant Behavior: Areas of Research and Application*, 790–826. New York: Appleton-Century-Crofts. (3:77; 8:50; 9:54)

Homme, L. E. 1965. Perspectives in psychology: XXIV. Control of coverants, the operants of the mind. *Psychological Record*, 15:501–511. (2:54; 8:17)

Honig, W. K. 1978. On the conceptual nature of cognitive terms: An initial essay. In S. H. Hulse, et al., eds. *Cognitive Processes in Animal Behavior*, 1–14. Hillsdale, N.J.: Erlbaum. (8:53)

Honig, W. K. and P. J. Urcuioli 1981. The legacy of Guttman and Kalish (1956): 25 years of research on stimulus generalization. *Journal of the Experimental Analysis of Behavior*, 36:405–445. (3:73; 9:53)

Honzik, C. H. and E. C. Tolman 1936. The perception of spatial relations by the rat: A type of response not easily explained by conditioning. *Journal of Comparative Psychology*, 27:287–318. (3:82; 4:68)

Horton, D. L. and T. R. Dixon 1968. Traditions, trends, and innovations. In T. R. Dixon and D. L. Horton, eds. *Verbal Behavior and General Behavior Theory*, 572–580. Englewood Cliffs, N.J.: Prentice-Hall. (7:42, 56)

Hovland, C. I. 1952. Clark Leonard Hull 1884–1952. *Psychological Review*, 59:347–350. (10:50)

Howard, R. W. 1979. Stimulus generalization along a dimension based on a verbal concept. *Journal of the Experimental Analysis of Behavior*, 32:199–212. (3:77)

Hull, C. L. 1929. A functional interpretation of the conditioned reflex. *Psychological Review*, 36:498–511. (9:35)

Hull, C. L. 1930a. Simple trial and error learning: A study in psychological theory. *Psychological Review*, 37:241–256. (5:16; 7:16) [pp. 216, 253]

Hull, C. L. 1930b. Knowledge and purpose as habit mechanisms. *Psychological Review*, 37:511–525. (4:75; 6:12, 13,20; 7:16, 19; 8:18; 9:26, 80; 12:4) [p. 156]

Hull, C. L. 1931. Goal attraction and directing ideas conceived as habit phenomena. *Psychological Review*, 38:487–506. (4:71; 7:16, 20; 8:18)

Hull, C. L. 1933. *Hypnosis and Suggestibility*. New York: Appleton-Century. (8:18; 10:5)

Hull, C. L. 1934. The concept of the habit-family hierarchy and maze learning. I and II. *Psychological Review*, 41:33–54, 134–152. (2:1; 4:71; 5:16; 6:22; 12:4, 9)

Hull, C. L. 1935a. Review of Thorndike's *Fundamentals of Learning*. *Psychological Bulletin*, 32:807–823. [p. 124]

Hull, C. L. 1935b. The conflicting psychologies of learning—A way out. *Psychological Review*, 42:491–516. (5:9)

Hull, C. L. 1935c. The mechanism of the assembly of behavior segments in novel combinations suitable for problem solving. *Psychological Review*, 42:219–245. (6:23; 8:15; 9:14)

Hull, C. L. 1937. Mind, mechanism, and adaptive behavior. *Psychological Review*, 44:1–32. (3:14; 5:9, 18; 7:8, 14, 19; 8:18; 9:74; 10:1) [pp. 84, 216]
Hull, C. L. 1938. The goal-gradient hypothesis applied to some "field-force" problems in the behavior of young children. *Psychological Review*, 45:271–299. (12:9)
Hull, C. L. 1939. The problem of stimulus equivalence in behavior theory. *Psychological Review*, 46:9–30. (3:31, 36; 4:73)
Hull, C. L. 1943a. The problem of intervening variables in molar behavior theory. *Psychological Review*, 50:273–291. (3:7, 69; 4:26, 31, 40, 46; 5:2, 8; 8:42)
Hull, C. L. 1943b. *Principles of Behavior: An Introduction to Behavior Theory*. New York: Appleton-Century. (2:22, 23; 3:14, 16, 31, 36, 69; 4:26, 40, 46; 5:2, 5, 7, 8, 15, 16, 17; 7:4, 5, 8, 9; 8:42; 9:13, 43, 74; 10:56; 12:16, 20, 37) [pp. 82, 83, 254]
Hull, C. L. 1944. Value, valuation, and natural science methodology. *Philosophy of Science*, 11:125–141. (4:20; 5:8, 16; 11:19, 30; 12:21, 22)
Hull, C. L. 1945. The place of innate individual and species differences in a natural-science theory of behavior. *Psychological Review*, 52:55–60. (10:66, 72)
Hull, C. L. 1950. Behavior postulates and corollaries—1949. *Psychological Review*, 57:173–180. (5:13, 53)
Hull, C. L. 1951. *Essentials of Behavior*. New Haven: Yale University Press. (3:69; 4:26; 5:3, 13, 14, 18)
Hull, C. L. 1952. *A Behavior System: An Introduction to Behavior Theory Concerning the Individual Organism*. New Haven: Yale University Press. (2:22; 3:69; 4:42, 48, 70; 5:8, 14; 6:67; 7:19, 27; 8:18; 9:41; 10:66; 11:19; 12:16, 22)
Hull, C. L. 1962. Psychology of the scientist: IV. Passages from the "Idea Books" of Clark L. Hull. *Perceptual and Motor Skills*, 15:807–882. (12:9)
Hull, C. L., et al. 1940. *Mathematico-Deductive Theory of Rote Learning*. New Haven: Yale University Press. (5:9, 11, 15, 53; 12:16, 20) [p. 256]
Hull, C. L., et al. 1947. A proposed quantification of habit strength. *Psychological Review*, 54:237–254. (5:8)
Hunt, J. McV. 1969. The impact and limitations of the giant of developmental psychology. In D. Elkind and J. H. Flavell, eds. *Studies in Cognitive Development: Essays in Honor of Jean Piaget*, 3–66. New York: Oxford University Press. (9:80)
Hunter, W. S. 1924a. The problem of consciousness. *Psychological Review*, 31:1–31. (8:19; 10:26; 11:44, 45)
Hunter, W. S. 1924b. The symbolic process. *Psychological Review*, 31:478–497. (7:28; 8:23)
Hunter, W. S. 1925. The subject's report. *Psychological Review*, 32:153–170. (11:19, 30, 45)
Hunter, W. S. 1930a. Anthroponomy and psychology. In C. Murchison, ed. *Psychologies of 1930*, 281–300. Worcester, Mass.: Clark University Press. (1:1, 2; 3:62; 11:27, 35, 66; 12:13)
Hunter, W. S. 1930b. A consideration of Lashley's theory of the equipotentiality of cerebral action. *Journal of General Psychology*, 3:455–468. (7:42; 8:22) [p. 184]
Hunter, W. S. 1932. The psychological study of behavior. *Psychological Review*, 39:1–24. (3:3)
Hunter, W. S. and C. V. Hudgins 1934. Voluntary activity from the standpoint of behaviorism. *Journal of General Psychology*, 10:198–204. (3:3; 9:70)
Israel, H. E. 1945. Two difficulties in operational thinking. *Psychological Review*, 52:260–261. (4:17, 19)
Israel, H. and B. Goldstein 1944. Operationism in psychology. *Psychological Review*, 51:177–188. (3:74; 4:7, 22, 30)
James, W. 1907/1975. *Pragmatism*. Cambridge: Harvard University Press. [pp. 257, 258]
Janus, S. Q. 1940. The role of definition in psychology. *Psychological Review*, 47:149–154. (4:6)
Jenkins, J. J. and D. S. Palermo 1964. Mediation processes and the acquisition of linguistic structure. In U. Bellugi and R. Brown, eds. *The Acquisition of Language, Monographs of Social Research and Child Development*, 29:141–169. (7:47)
Johnson, R. J. 1963. A commentary on "radical behaviorism." *Philosophy of Science*, 30:274–285. (3:9, 10; 4:37, 44; 5:35; 9:11; 10:65)

Jonçich, G. 1968. *The Sane Positivist: A Biography of E. L. Thorndike*. Middletown, Conn.: Wesleyan University Press. (12:27)

Jones, M. C. 1924. The elimination of children's fears. *Journal of Experimental Psychology*, 7:382–390. (6:56)

Jones, O. R., ed. 1971. *The Private Language Argument*. New York: Macmillan. (2:41)

Joynson, R. B. 1970. The breakdown of modern psychology. *Bulletin of the British Psychological Society*, 23:261–269. (3:6; 4:66; 8:47)

Julià, P. 1982. Can linguistics contribute to the study of verbal behavior? *The Behavior Analyst*, 5:9–19. (7:70, 76)

Kalish, H. 1981. *From Behavioral Science to Behavior Modification*. New York: McGraw-Hill. (1:15; 10:69)

Kamil, A. C. and R. A. Sacks 1972. Three-configuration matching to sample in the pigeon. *Journal of the Experimental Analysis of Behavior*, 17:483–488. (4:72)

Kanfer, F. H. 1968. Verbal conditioning: A review of its current status. In T. R. Dixon and D. L. Horton, eds. *Verbal Behavior and General Behavior Theory*, 254–290. Englewood Cliffs, N.J.: Prentice-Hall. (4:68; 5:32; 9:53; 11:27, 31, 37)

Kanfer, F. H. and P. Karoly 1972. Self-control: A behavioristic excursion into the lion's den. *Behavior Therapy*, 3:398–416. (7:29; 9:69)

Kantor, J. R. 1920. Suggestions toward a scientific interpretation of perception. *Psychological Review*, 27:191–216. (4:70; 6:35; 9:53; 12:41)

Kantor, J. R. 1921a. Association as a fundamental process of objective psychology. *Psychological Review*, 28:385–424. (4:70; 6:48; 9:14, 24)

Kantor, J. R. 1921b. An objective interpretation of meanings. *American Journal of Psychology*, 32:231–248. (4:70; 9:17)

Kantor, J. R. 1921c. An attempt toward a naturalistic description of emotions. *Psychological Review*, 28:19–41, 120–140. (10:26)

Kantor, J. R. 1922. The nervous system, psychological fact or fiction. *Journal of Philosophy*, 19:38–49. (3:12; 6:14)

Kantor, J. R. 1923a. An objective analysis of volitional behavior. *Psychological Review*, 30:116–144. (4:70; 7:22; 9:63; 12:4)

Kantor, J. R. 1923b. The organismic vs. the mentalistic attitude toward the nervous system. *Psychological Bulletin*, 20:684–692. (3:12, 41; 12:50)

Kantor, J. R. 1929. Language as behavior and as symbolism. *Journal of Philosophy*, 26:150–159. (12:41)

Kantor, J. R. 1933. In defense of stimulus-response psychology. *Psychological Review*, 40:324–336. (3:73; 6:35)

Kantor, J. R. 1938. The operational principle in the physical and psychological sciences. *Psychological Record*, 2:3–32. (2:32; 3:62; 4:14; 5:63; 12:13, 52)

Kantor, J. R. 1942. Preface to interbehavioral psychology. *Psychological Record*, 5:173–193. (2:12, 32; 3:7, 41; 4:68; 6:35; 9:2; 11:60)

Kantor, J. R. 1966. Feelings and emotions as scientific events. *Psychological Record*, 16:377–404. (10:26)

Kantor, J. R. 1968. Behaviorism in the history of psychology. *Psychological Record*, 18:151–166. (1:16; 6:35; 10:1)

Kantor, J. R. 1970. An analysis of the experimental analysis of behavior (TEAB). *Journal of the Experimental Analysis of Behavior*, 13:101–108. [p. 108]

Kantor, J. R. 1978. Cognition as events and as psychic constructions. *Psychological Record*, 28:329–342. (8:50; 11:21)

Katahn, M. and J. H. Koplin 1968. Paradigm clash: Comment on "Some recent criticisms of behaviorism and learning theory with special reference to Breger and McGaugh and to Chomsky." *Psychological Bulletin*, 69:147–148. (1:4; 8:45)

Kattsoff, L. O. 1939. Philosophy, psychology, and postulational technique. *Psychological Review*, 46:62–74. (5:10)

Katz, J. J. 1964/1967. Mentalism in linguistics. *Language*, 40:124–137. In L. A. Jakobovitz and M. S. Miron, eds. *Readings in the Psychology of Language*, 73–84. Englewood Cliffs, N.J.: Prentice-Hall. (7:56; 10:35) [pp. 143, 170]

Kazdin, A. E. 1977. Research issues in covert conditioning. *Cognitive Therapy and Research*, 1:45–58. (4:78)

Kazin, A. E. 1978. *History of Behavior Modification: Experimental Foundations of Contemporary Research*. Baltimore: University Park. (1:4; 2:54; 4:78; 6:8, 63)

Kazdin, A. E. 1979a. The scope of *Behavior Therapy*. *Behavior Therapy*, 10:1–7. (10:69)

Kazdin, A. E. 1979b. Fictions, factions, and functions of behavior therapy. *Behavior Therapy*, 10:629–654. (10:69)

Kazdin, A. E. and G. T. Wilson 1978. *Evaluation of Behavior Therapy: Issues, Evidence, and Research Strategies*. Cambridge, Mass.: Ballinger. (4:78; 10:66, 69)

Keat, R. 1972. A critical examination of B. F. Skinner's objections to mentalism. *Behaviorism*, 1:53–70. (4:37; 5:35; 9:3, 11; 10:80; 11:47)

Kehoe, E. J. and I. Gormezano 1980. Configuration and combination laws in conditioning with compound stimuli. *Psychological Bulletin*, 87:351–378. (3:76)

Keller, F. S. and W. N. Schoenfeld 1950. *Principles of Psychology: A Systematic Text in the Science of Behavior*. New York: Appleton-Century-Crofts. (4:68, 70, 73; 11:12, 19, 25)

Kendler, H. H. 1952. "What is learned?"—A theoretical blind alley. *Psychological Review*, 59:269–277. (3:82; 4:36, 48; 5:4; 6:60; 8:48; 12:42)

Kendler, H. H. 1967. Kenneth W. Spence 1907–1967. *Psychological Review*, 74:335–341. (4:22)

Kendler, H. H. 1968. Some specific reactions to general S-R theory. In T. R. Dixon and D. L. Horton, eds. *Verbal Behavior and General Behavior Theory*, 388–403. Englewood Cliffs, N.J.: Prentice-Hall. (2:38; 4:39; 6:1; 8:17; 9:26, 52; 11:27)

Kendler, H. H. 1970. The unity of psychology. *Canadian Psychologist*, 11:30–47. (2:38, 54;8:53)

Kendler, H. H. 1971. Environmental and cognitive control of behavior. *American Psychologist*, 26:962–973. (8:20, 21; 9:52, 59)

Kendler, H. H. 1981. *Psychology: A Science in Conflict*. New York: Oxford University Press. (2:35, 36, 38; 3:27, 30, 48, 59, 60; 4:22, 23, 24, 64, 65, 68; 5:4, 16, 17, 54; 8:21, 33, 47, 50; 10:34; 11:27)

Kendler, H. H. and T. S. Kendler 1962. Vertical and horizontal processes in problem solving. *Psychological Review*, 69:1–16. (4:73, 78; 6:1, 20)

Kendler, H. H. and T. S. Kendler 1966. Selective attention versus mediation: Some comments on Mackintosh's analysis of discrimination learning. *Psychological Bulletin*, 66:282–288. (4:73; 9:26, 27, 52)

Kendler, H. H. and T. S. Kendler 1968. Mediation and conceptual behavior. *The Psychology of Learning and Motivation*, 2:197–244. (4:73; 8:17)

Kendler, H. H. and J. T. Spence 1971. Tenets of neobehaviorism. In H. H. Kendler and J. T. Spence, eds. *Essays in Neobehaviorism: A Memorial Volume to Kenneth W. Spence*, 11–40. New York: Appleton-Century-Crofts. (1:4; 2:35, 36; 3:15, 41; 4:22, 23, 24; 5:35; 6:1; 11:27, 37)

Kessel, F. S. 1969. The philosophy of science as proclaimed and science as practiced: "Identity" or "dualism"? *American Psychologist*, 24:999–1005. (1:3; 3:26; 5:49; 12:56)

Kessen, W. and G. A. Kimble 1952. "Dynamic systems" and theory construction. *Psychological Review*, 59:263–267. (4:47, 62; 12:42)

Killeen, P. 1968. On the measurement of reinforcement frequency in the study of preference. *Journal of the Experimental Analysis of Behavior*, 11:263–269. (3:73)

Kimble, G. A. 1967a. The concept of reflex and the problem of volition. In G. A. Kimble, ed. *Foundations of Conditioning and Learning*, 144–154. New York: Appleton-Century-Crofts. (6:3; 9:60)

Kimble, G. A. 1967b. The basic tenet of behaviorism. In G. A. Kimble, ed. *Foundations of Conditioning and Learning*, 73–81. New York: Appleton-Century-Crofts. (3:36; 4:61; 6:2)

Kimble, G. A. and L. C. Perlmuter 1970. The problem of volition. *Psychological Review*, 77:361–384. (6:50; 7:41; 9:60)

Kitchener, R. F. 1977. Behavior and behaviorism. *Behaviorism*, 5:11–71. (3:5, 47, 59, 60, 63, 65, 67, 69, 73; 4:41; 6:14, 17, 19; 7:14; 9:17; 10:16, 70)

Koch, S. 1941. The logical character of the motivation concept. I and II. *Psychological Review*, 48:15–38, 127–154. (4:8, 9, 12, 13; 5: 10, 13, 63; 9:17)

Koch, S. 1944. Hull's *Principles of Behavior*. *Psychological Bulletin*, 41:269–286. (4:26; 6:46)

Koch, S. 1951. Theoretical psychology, 1950: An overview. *Psychological Review*, 58:295–305. (5:36)

Koch, S. 1954. Clark L. Hull. In W. K. Estes, et al., eds. *Modern Learning Theory*, 1–176. New York: Appleton-Century-Crofts. (3:34; 4:30; 5:3, 8, 13; 6:64; 9:26; 10:57)

Koch, S. 1959. Epilogue. In S. Koch, ed. *Psychology: A Study of a Science*, Vol. 3. *Formulations of the Person and the Social Context*, 729–788. New York: McGraw-Hill. (1:14, 16; 3:1; 4:1, 22, 25, 26, 66; 5:16, 60; 6:1; 9:31; 10:16; 12:27)

Koch, S. 1964. Psychology and emerging conceptions of knowledge as unitary. In T. W. Wann, ed. *Behaviorism and Phenomenology: Contrasting Bases for Modern Psychology*, 1–41. Chicago: University of Chicago Press. (1:14; 3:16, 34, 39; 4:1, 58; 5:3, 49, 64, 66; 6:1; 12:56)

Koch, S. 1974. Psychology as science. In S. C. Brown, ed. *Philosophy of Psychology*, 3–40. London: Macmillan. (1:16)

Köhler, W. 1927. *The Mentality of Apes*. New York: Harcourt Brace. (9:35, 55)

Köhler, W. 1947. *Gestalt Psychology*. New York: Liveright. (2:17, 31, 42)

Köhler, W. 1966. A task for philosophers. In P. K. Feyerabend and G. Maxwell, eds. *Mind, Matter, and Method: Essays in Philosophy and Science in Honor of Herbert Feigl*, 70–91. Minneapolis: Unversity of Minnesota Press. (2:31, 42; 3:62)

Kolakowski, L. 1968. *The Alienation of Reason*. Translated by N. Guterman. Garden City, N.Y.: Doubleday. (4:48; 12:27, 28, 30, 42, 45)

Krantz, D. H. 1972. Measurement structures and psychological laws. *Science*, 175:1427–1435. (4:22)

Krantz, D. L. 1969. The Baldwin-Titchener controversy. In D. L. Krantz, ed. *Schools of Psychology*, 1–19. New York: Appleton-Century-Crofts. (2:30)

Krantz, D. L. 1972. Schools and systems: The mutual isolation of operant and non-operant psychology as a case study. *Journal of the History of the Behavioral Sciences*, 8:86–102. (1:4)

Krasner, L. 1971. Behavior therapy. *Annual Review of Psychology*, 22:483–532. (1:4)

Krech, D. 1950. Dynamic systems, psychological fields, and hypothetical constructs. *Psychological Review*, 57:283–290. (4:61, 67)

Krech, D. 1955. Discussion: Theory and reductionism. *Psychological Review*, 62:229–231. (4:61)

Krechevsky, I. 1932. "Hypotheses" in rats. *Psychological Review*, 39:516–532. (10:15)

Krechevsky, I. 1938. A study of the continuity of the problem-solving process. *Psychological Review*, 45:107–133. (10:15)

Kripke, S. A. 1982. *Wittgenstein on Rules and Private Language*. Cambridge: Harvard University Press. (2:41)

Kuhn, T. S. 1962/1970. *The Structure of Scientific Revolutions* (2d ed.) Chicago: University of Chicago Press. (1:4; 3:26; 5:49, 52, 57; 7:32; 8:45)

Kuhn, T. S. 1970. Logic of discovery or psychology of research? In I. Lakatos and A. Musgrave, eds. *Criticism and the Growth of Knowledge*, 1–23. Cambridge: Cambridge University Press. (10:70, 73)

Kuhn, T. S. 1974. Second thoughts on paradigms. In F. Suppe, ed. *The Structure of Scientific Theories*, 459–482. Urbana: University of Illinois Press. (1:4; 3:39; 5:66; 10:70, 73)

Kuo, Z. Y. 1921. Giving up instincts in psychology. *Journal of Philosophy*, 18:645–664. (6:14; 9:17)

Kuo, Z. Y. 1928. The fundamental error of the concept of purpose and the trial and error fallacy. *Psychological Review*, 35:414–433. (1:8; 3:66; 4:36; 7:14; 9:34, 38; 10:83) [p. 102]

Kuo, Z. Y. 1929a. The net result of the anti-heredity movement in psychology. *Psychological Review*, 36:181–199. (7:11; 9:17, 80; 10:26) [p. 102]

Kuo, Z. Y. 1929b. Purposive behavior and prepotent stimulus. *Psychological Review*, 36:547–550. (7:4; 9:50)

Kurtz, P. 1968. Neo-behaviorism and the behavioral sciences. In A. de Grazia, et al., eds. *The Behavioral Sciences: Essays in Honor of George A. Lundberg*, 63–85. Great Barrington, Mass.: Behavioral Research Council. (4:1; 11:35)

Lacey, H. M. 1974. The scientific study of linguistic behaviour: A perspective on the Skinner-Chomsky controversy. *Journal for the Theory of Social Behaviour*, 4:17–51. (3:23, 78; 5:35; 7:48; 10:68)

Lachman, R. 1960. The model in theory construction. *Psychological Review*, 67:113–129. (4:53; 5:67; 10:73)

Lachman, R., J. L. Lachman and E. C. Butterfield 1979. *Cognitive Psychology and Information Processing: An Introduction*. Hillsdale, N.J.: Erlbaum. (1:4; 7:36, 70; 8:33, 45, 49; 9:59)

Lakatos, I. 1970. Falsification and the methodology of scientific research programmes. In I. Lakatos and A. Musgrave, eds. *Criticism and the Growth of Knowledge*, 91–195. Cambridge: Cambridge University Press. (3:26; 5:49)

Langfeld, H. S. 1927. Consciousness and motor response. *Psychological Review*, 34:1–9. (9:21)

Langfeld, H. S. 1931. A response interpretation of consciousness. *Psychological Review*, 38:87–108. (8:22; 9:52)

Lashley, K. S. 1923a. The behaviorist interpretation of consciousness, I. *Psychological Review*, 30:237–272. (1:8; 9:26, 70; 11:47, 63; 12:58)

Lashley, K. S. 1923b. The behaviorist interpretation of consciousness, II. *Psychological Review*, 30:329–353. (3:6; 6:14, 15; 7:43, 70; 11:47, 63; 12:17)

Lashley, K. S. 1929. *Brain Mechanisms and Intelligence: A Quantitative Study of Injuries to the Brain*. Chicago: University of Chicago Press. (3:76; 6:24; 7:43; 9:19)

Lashley, K. S. 1931. Cerebral control versus reflexology: A reply to Professor Hunter. *Journal of General Psychology*, 5:3–20. (6:2; 9:31)

Lashley, K. S. 1938. Experimental analysis of instinctive behavior. *Psychological Review*, 45:445–471. (3:76; 7:43; 9:17, 26)

Lashley, K. S. 1951. The problem of serial order in behavior. In L. A. Jeffress, ed. *Cerebral Mechanisms in Behavior*, 112–146. New York: Wiley. (7:41, 43; 9:31) [pp. 132, 133]

Lawrence, D. H. 1963. The nature of a stimulus: Some relationships between learning and perception. In S. Koch, ed. *Psychology: A Study of a Science*, Vol. 5. *The Process Areas, the Person, and Some Fields: Their Place in Psychology and in Science*, 179–212. New York: McGraw-Hill. (3:32, 73, 77; 4:72; 9:52)

Ledwidge, B. 1978. Cognitive behavior modification: A step in the wrong direction? *Psychological Bulletin*, 85:353–375. (1:8; 8:7, 16)

Ledwidge, B. 1979. Cognitive behavior modification or new ways to change minds: Reply to Mahoney and Kazdin. *Psychological Bulletin*, 86:1050–1053. (4:36, 68; 8:7, 8, 50)

Leeper, R. 1944. Dr. Hull's *Principles of Behavior*. *Journal of Genetic Psychology*, 65:3–52. (6:63; 9:26)

Leuba, C. 1940. Images as conditioned sensations. *Journal of Experimental Psychology*, 26:345–351. (11:21)

Levine, M. 1971. Hypothesis theory and nonlearning despite ideal S-R reinforcement contingencies. *Psychological Review*, 78:130–140. (8:21; 9:55, 56)

Lewis, C. I. 1929. *Mind and the World Order*. New York: Dover. (12:25)

Lieberman, D. A. 1979. Behaviorism and the mind: A (limited) call for a return to introspection. *American Psychologist*, 34:319–333. (2:2, 27, 29, 54; 11:35, 42)

Littman, R. A. and E. Rosen 1950. Molar and molecular. *Psychological Review*, 57:58–65. (3:69)

Locke, E. A. 1969. Purpose without consciousness: A contradiction. *Psychological Reports*, 25:991–1009. (7:11,14; 10:16, 29)

Locke, E. A. 1971. Is "behavior therapy" behavioristic? (An analysis of Wolpe's psychotherapeutic methods). *Psychological Bulletin*, 76:318–327. (1:15; 11:3, 42)

Locke, E. A. 1972. Critical analysis of the concept of causality in behavioristic psychology. *Psychological Reports*, 31:175–197. (4:51; 8:36; 10:16, 29)

Logan, F. A. 1959. The Hull-Spence approach. In S. Koch, ed. *Psychology: A Study of a Science*, Vol. 2. *General Systematic Formulations, Learning and Special Processes*, 293–358. New York: McGraw-Hill. (3:69; 5:18, 51)

Logan, F. A. 1960. *Incentive: How the Conditions of Reinforcement Affect the Performance of Rats.* New Haven: Yale University Press. (3:69)

Logue, A. W. 1979. Taste aversion and the generality of the laws of learning. *Psychological Bulletin*, 86:276–296. (10:72)

London, P. 1972. The end of ideology in behavior modification. *American Psychologist*, 27:913–920. (10:69)

Lorenz, K. Z. 1974. Analogy as a source of knowledge. *Science*, 185:229–234. (10:73)

Loucks, R. B. 1935. The experimental delimitation of neural structures essential for learning; the attempt to condition striped muscle responses with faradization of the sygmoid gyri. *Journal of Psychology*, 1:5–44. (6:62)

Lovejoy, A. O. 1922. The paradox of the thinking behaviorist. *Philosophical Review*, 31:135–147. (8:24; 10:32)

Lowry, R. 1970. The reflex model in psychology: Origins and evolution. *Journal of the History of the Behavioral Sciences*, 6:64–69. (6:3; 9:19, 32)

Lycan, W. G. 1971. Noninductive evidence: Recent work on Wittgenstein's "criteria." *American Philosophical Quarterly*, 8:109–125. (10:28)

Lycan, W. G. 1974. Mental states and Putnam's functionalism hypothesis. *Australasian Journal of Philosophy*, 52:48–62. (10:41)

Maatsch, J. L. and R. A. Behan 1953. A more rigorous theoretical language. *Psychological Review*, 60:189–196. (4:23, 62, 68; 10:10, 12)

MacCorquodale, K. 1969. B. F. Skinner's *Verbal Behavior*: A retrospective appreciation. *Journal of the Experimental Analysis of Behavior*, 12:831–841. (3:78; 5:43; 7:49; 10:72)

MacCorquodale, K. 1970. On Chomsky's review of Skinner's *Verbal Behavior*. *Journal of the Experimental Analysis of Behavior*, 13:83–99. (3:7, 9, 78; 4:64; 5:43; 7:36, 51, 62; 10:60, 65, 67, 68, 74)

MacCorquodale, K. and P. E. Meehl 1948. On a distinction between hypothetical constructs and intervening variables. *Psychological Review*, 55:95–107. (4:31, 45, 47, 53, 54; 5:1, 39) [p. 72]

MacCorquodale, K. and P. E. Meehl 1953. Preliminary suggestions as to a formalization of expectancy theory. *Psychological Review*, 60:55–63. (3:55; 6:51)

MacCorquodale, K. and P. E. Meehl 1954. Edward C. Tolman. In W. K. Estes, et al., eds. *Modern Learning Theory*, 177–266. New York: Appleton-Century-Crofts. (3:55, 57, 84, 85; 4:12, 55, 59; 5:6; 6:54, 55, 59, 62; 9:26, 80; 10:33, 34) [p. 41]

Mace, C. A. 1948–1949. Some implications of analytical behaviourism. *Proceedings of the Aristotelian Society*, 49:1–16. (1:13; 10:21; 11:44)

Mach, E. 1883/1974. *The Science of Mechanics: A Critical and Historical Account of Its Development* (6th ed.). Translated by T. J. McCormack. LaSalle, Ill.: Open Court. (12:30, 33, 36, 48, 54)

Mach, E. 1886/1959. *The Analysis of Sensations: And the Relation of the Physical to the Psychical* (revised and supplemented by S. Waterlow). Translated by C. M. Williams. New York: Dover. (7:10; 11:67; 12:30)

Mach, E. 1905/1976. *Knowledge and Error: Sketches on the Psychology of Enquiry*. Translated by T. J. McCormack and P. Foulkes. Boston: D. Reidel. (3:25; 12:30, 33) [p. 274]

Mackenzie, B. D. 1972. Behaviourism and positivism. *Journal of the History of the Behavioral Sciences*, 8:222–231. (1:4; 12:27)

Mackenzie, B. D. 1977. *Behaviourism and the Limits of Scientific Method*. Atlantic Highlands, N.J.: Humanities Press. (1:4, 14, 16; 2:16, 17, 38; 3:61; 4:1, 7, 10, 19, 29, 53, 58, 59; 5:16, 52, 66; 6:7; 10:57, 68, 71; 12:27)

MacKinnon, F. I. 1928. Behaviorism and metaphysics. *Journal of Philosophy*, 25:353–356. (12:45)

Mackintosh, N. J. 1965. Selective attention in animal discrimination. *Psychological Bulletin*, 64:124–150. (9:49)

Madell, G. 1967. Action and causal explanation. *Mind*, 76:34–48. (3:71; 9:76)

Mahoney, M. J. 1970. Toward an experimental analysis of coverant control. *Behavior Therapy*, 1:510–521. (2:54; 4:70; 8:17; 11:21)

Mahoney, M. J. 1974. *Cognition and Behavior Modification*. Cambridge, Mass.: Ballinger. (2:54; 4:3, 36, 37, 53, 54, 66, 78; 8:7, 36; 9:11, 48, 55, 80; 10:68; 11:34; 12:13)

Mahoney, M. J. 1976. Terminal terminology: A self-regulated response to Goldiamond. *Journal of Applied Behavior Analysis*, 9:515–517. (9:69)

Mahoney, M. J. 1977a. Reflections on the cognitive-learning trend in psychotherapy. *American Psychologist*, 32:5–13. (2:54; 4:66; 8:7; 9:10) [p. 163]

Mahoney, M. J. 1977b. On the continuing resistance to thoughtful therapy. *Behavior Therapy*, 8:673–677. (3:29; 8:5)

Mahoney, M. J. 1977c. Cognitive therapy and research: A question of questions. *Cognitive Therapy and Research*, 1:5–16. (8:7) [p. 152]

Mahoney, M. J. and A. E. Kazdin 1979. Cognitive behavior modification: Misconceptions and premature evacuation. *Psychological Bulletin*, 86:1044–1049. (8:7)

Malcolm, N. 1958. Knowledge of other minds. *Journal of Philosophy*, 55:969–978. (10:79; 11:38, 52)

Malcolm, N. 1959. *Dreaming*. London: Routledge and Kegan Paul. (10:28, 43; 11:5)

Malcolm, N. 1964. Behaviorism as a philosophy of psychology. In T. W. Wann, ed. *Behaviorism and Phenomenology*, 141–155. Chicago: University of Chicago Press. (10:21, 65; 11:38, 39)

Malcolm, N. 1967. Explaining behavior. *Philosophical Review*, 76:97–104. (7:3, 7, 14; 9:83; 10:32)

Malcolm, N. 1971a. The myth of cognitive processes and structures. In T. Mischel, ed. *Cognitive Development and Epistemology*, 385–392. New York: Academic. (7:32, 73, 80; 8:30, 58; 9:57)

Malcolm, N. 1971b. *Problems of Mind*. New York: Harper and Row. (3:34; 11:38)

Malone, J. C. 1982. The second offspring of general process learning theory: Overt behavior as the ambassador of the mind. *Journal of the Experimental Analysis of Behavior*, 38:205–209. (4:29, 36; 5:22)

Maltzman, I. 1955. Thinking: From a behaviorist point of view. *Psychological Review*, 62:275–286. (4:12; 6:22; 8:11, 18)

Maltzman, I. 1966. Awareness: Cognitive psychology vs. behaviorism. *Journal of Experimental Research in Personality*, 1:161–165. (1:8; 5:54; 8:51; 9:54; 11:37)

Maltzman, I. 1968. Theoretical conceptions of semantic conditioning and generalization. In T. R. Dixon and D. L. Horton, eds. *Verbal Behavior and General Behavior Theory*, 291–339. Englewood Cliffs, N.J.: Prentice-Hall. (4:7, 73; 5:54; 6:1, 62; 9:27, 52)

Maltzman, I. 1971. The orienting reflex and thinking as determiners of conditioning and generalization to words. In H. H. Kendler and J. T. Spence, eds. *Essays in Neobehaviorism: A Memorial Volume to Kenneth W. Spence*, 89–111. New York: Appleton-Century-Crofts. (3:6; 9:52)

Mandler, G. 1962. From association to structure. *Psychological Review*, 69:415–427. (8:11)

Mapel, B. M. 1977. Philosophical criticisms of behaviorism: An analysis. *Behaviorism*, 5:17–32. (10:80)

Markey, J. F. 1925. The place of language habits in a behaviorist explanation of consciousness. *Psychological Review*, 32:384–401. (9:66)

Marks, L. E. 1974. *Sensory Processes: The New Psychophysics*. New York: Academic. (11:59)

Marmor, J. and S. M. Woods, eds. 1980. *The Interface Between Psychodynamic and Behavioral Therapies*. New York: Plenum. (10:52)

Marx, M. H. 1951. Intervening variable or hypothetical construct? *Psychological Review*, 58:235–247. (4:53, 62)

Marx, M. H. 1958. Some suggestions for the conceptual and theoretical analysis of complex intervening variables in problem-solving behavior. *Journal of General Psychology*, 58:115–128. (4:28, 73; 8:4; 10:17; 11:27, 31)

Marx, M. H. 1976a. Formal theory. In M. H. Marx and F. E. Goodson, eds. *Theories in Contemporary Psychology* (2d ed.), 234–260. New York: Macmillan. (2:36; 4:24; 5:12, 16)

Marx, M. H. 1976b. Theorizing. In Marx and Goodson, eds. (see 1976a), pp. 261–286. New York: Macmillan. (4:23; 5:16; 12:56)

Masterman, M. 1970. The nature of a paradigm. In I. Lakatos and A. Musgrave, eds. *Criticism and the Growth of Knowledge*, 59–89. Cambridge: Cambridge University Press. (1:4)

Maxwell, G. 1961. Comments on Hochberg's "Intervening variables, hypothetical constructs, and metaphysics." In H. Feigl and G. Maxwell. eds. *Current Issues in the Philosophy of Science*, 457–459. New York: Holt, Rinehart and Winston. (4:68)

Maxwell, G. 1962. The ontological status of theoretical terms. In H. Feigl and G. Maxwell, eds. *Formulations of the Person and the Social Context. Minnesota Studies in the Philosophy of Science*, 3:3–27. Minneapolis: University of Minnesota Press. (4:66)

Maze, J. R. 1954. Do intervening variables intervene? *Psychological Review*, 61:226–234. (4:33, 41, 51, 53; 5:3; 12:42)

McComas, H. C. 1916. Extravagances in the motor theories of consciousness. *Psychological Review*, 23:397–406. (8:25; 9:21)

McDougall, W. 1923. Purposive or mechanical psychology? *Psychological Review*, 30:273–288. (9:19, 41)

McDougall, W. 1926. Men or robots—I and II. In C. Murchison, ed. *Psychologies of 1925*, 273–305. Worcester, Mass.: Clark University Press. (2:2; 3:56, 63; 9:34, 42; 10:68) [p. 120]

McDougall, W. 1928. *Outline of Psychology*. New York: Scribner. (7:2; 9:35)

McGeoch, J. A. 1937. A critique of operational definition. *Psychological Bulletin*, 34:703–704. (4:19, 24; 5:63)

McGregor, D. 1935. Scientific measurement and psychology. *Psychological Review*, 42:246–266. (4:6, 7)

McGuigan, F. J. 1953. Formalization of psychological theory. *Psychological Review*, 60:377–382. (4:55)

McLeish, J. 1981. *The Development of Modern Behavioural Psychology*. Calgary, Alberta: Detselig. (1:6; 7:36, 72, 74, 80)

McNeill, D. 1968. On theories of language acquisition. In T. R. Dixon and D. L. Horton, eds. *Verbal Behavior and General Behavior Theory*, 406–420. Englewood Cliffs, N.J.: Prentice-Hall. (7:47, 68)

McTeer, W. 1953. Observational definitions of emotion. *Psychological Review*, 60:172–180. (2:3)

Mead, G. H. 1922. A behavioristic account of the significant symbol. *Journal of Philosophy*, 19:157–163. (8:23; 9:66; 11:23; 12:41)

Meehl, P. E. 1945. An examination of the treatment of stimulus patterning in Professor Hull's *Principles of Behavior, Psychological Review*, 52:324–332. (3:33)

Meehl, P. E. 1950. On the circularity of the law of effect. *Psychological Bulletin*, 47:52–75. (3:34)

Meichenbaum, D. H. 1973. Cognitive factors in behavior modification: Modifying what clients say to themselves. In C. M. Franks and G. T. Wilson, eds. *Annual Review of Behavior Therapy, Theory and Practice*, 416–431. New York: Brunner/Mazel. (4:78; 8:6)

Meichenbaum, D. H. 1975. Self-instructional methods. In F. H. Kanfer and A. P. Goldstein, eds. *Helping People Change: A Textbook of Methods*, 357–391. New York: Pergamon. (10:80)

Meissner, W. W. 1958. Nonconstructural aspects of psychological constructs. *Psychological Review*, 65:143–150. (4:53)

Meissner, W. W. 1960. Intervening constructs—Dimensions of controversy. *Psychological Review*, 67:51–72. (4:53)

Melton, A. W. 1941. Review of C. C. Pratt's *The Logic of Modern Psychology*. *Psychological Bulletin*, 38:227–236. (4:61)

Metzner, R. 1963. Re-evaluation of Wolpe and Dollard/Miller. *Behaviour Research and Therapy*, 1:213–215. (10:68)

Meyer, M. 1911. *The Fundamental Laws of Human Behavior*. Boston: Gorham. (2:23; 3:76; 6:14; 7:39; 8:34; 9:20, 31; 10:76; 11:19; 12:13, 15, 37)

Meyer, M. 1913. The comparative value of various conceptions of nervous function based on mechanical analogies. *American Journal of Psychology*, 24:555–563. (9:42)

Meyer, M. 1921. *The Psychology of the Other-One*. Columbia, Missouri: Missouri Book Co. (3:3, 9; 4:48, 70; 5:23; 6:14; 9:19, 50, 70; 10:26, 48; 11:19, 21, 22; 12:13, 19, 37)

Meyer, M. 1933. That whale among the fishes—The theory of emotions. *Psychological Review*, 40:292–300. (10:83)

Michael, J. 1982. Distinguishing between discriminative and motivational functions of stimuli. *Journal of the Experimental Analysis of Behavior*, 37:149–155. (11:51)

Millenson, J. R. 1967. An isomorphism between stimulus-response notation and information processing flow diagrams. *Psychological Record*, 17:305–319. (7:46; 8:48)

Miller, D. L. 1946. The meaning of explanation. *Psychological Review*, 53:241–246. (5:43; 12:33)

Miller, D. S. 1911. Is consciousness a "type of behavior"? *Journal of Philosophy, Psychology, and Scientific Methods*, 8:322–327. (4:14)

Miller, G. A. 1965. Some preliminaries to psycholinguistics. *American Psychologist*, 20:15–20. (7:52, 56, 61)

Miller, G. A., E. Galanter and K. H. Pribram 1960. *Plans and the Structure of Behavior*. New York: Holt. (6:34; 7:42, 52; 8:36)

Miller, N. E. 1935. A reply to "sign-gestalt or conditioned reflex?" *Psychological Review*, 42:280–292. (6:67; 7:19; 8:18)

Miller, N. E. 1959. Liberalization of basic S-R concepts: Extensions to conflict behavior, motivation, and social learning. In. S. Koch, ed. *Psychology: A Study of a Science*, Vol. 2. *General Systematic Formulations, Learning and Special Processes*, 196–292. New York: McGraw-Hill. (3:4, 74, 76, 77; 4:12, 13, 20, 28, 45, 78; 5:16, 52; 7:24; 8:22; 9:31, 52; 10:66)

Miller, N. E. and J. Dollard 1941. *Social Learning and Imitation*. New Haven: Yale University Press. (3:4, 13, 73; 5:16; 6:22, 68; 7:19; 8:23; 9:31, 51, 57; 10:67; 12:16)

Mischel, T. 1969. Scientific and philosophical psychology. In T. Mischel, ed. *Human Action: Conceptual and Empirical Issues*, 1–40. New York: Academic. (3:44, 71; 4:59; 9:76, 79, 80) [p. 198]

Moore, J. 1975. On the principle of operationism in a science of behavior. *Behaviorism*, 3:120–138. (5:29, 41, 48)

Moore, J. S. 1923. Behavior vs. introspective psychology. *Psychological Review*, 30:235. (1:1; 2:19)

Moore, O. K. and D. J. Lewis 1953. Purpose and learning theory. *Psychological Review*, 60:149–156. (3:73; 9:38, 39, 43)

Moroz, M. 1972. The concept of cognition in contemporary psychology. In J. R. Royce and W. W. Rozeboom, eds. *The Psychology of Knowing*, 177–205. New York: Gordon and Breach. (8:13)

Morse, W. H. and R. T. Kelleher 1977. Determinants of reinforcement and punishment. In W. K. Honig and J. E. R. Staddon, eds. *Handbook of Operant Behavior*, 174–200. Englewood Cliffs, N.J.: Prentice-Hall. (6:30)

Mowrer, O. H. 1954. The psychologist looks at language. *American Psychologist*, 9:660–694. (4:73; 9:31)

Mowrer, O. H. 1960a. *Learning Theory and Behavior*. New York: Wiley. (3:54; 4:71; 6:34; 7:21, 23, 41; 8:19, 44; 10:76; 11:37; 12:4)

Mowrer, O. H. 1960b. *Learning Theory and the Symbolic Processes*. New York: Wiley. (3:82; 4:71; 6:34; 7:21, 22, 23, 47; 8:20, 22; 9:35, 63; 12:4) [p. 127]

Mueller, C. G. and W. N. Schoenfeld 1954. Edwin R. Guthrie. In W. K. Estes, et al., eds. *Modern Learning Theory*, 345–379. New York: Appleton-Century-Crofts. (3:60, 61; 4:77)

Muenzinger, K. F. 1927. Physical and psychological reality. *Psychological Review*, 34:220–233. (2:18)

Mursell, J. L. 1922a. Behaviorism and the programme of philosophy. *Journal of Philosophy*, 19:549–553. (12:40)

Mursell, J. L. 1922b. The stimulus-response relation. *Psychological Review*, 29:146–162. (4:3, 48; 6:7)

Muscio, B. 1921. Psychology as behaviorism. *The Monist*, 31:182–202. (8:24)

Naess, A. 1965. Science as behavior: Prospects and limitations of a behavioral metascience. In B. B. Wolman and E. Nagel, eds. *Scientific Psychology: Principles and Approaches*, 50–67. New York: Basic. (3:71; 4:57; 12:1, 56)

Nagel, E. 1959. Methodological issues in psychoanalytic theory. In S. Hook, ed. *Psychoanalysis, Scientific Method, and Philosophy*, 38–56. New York: New York University Press. (10:49)

Nagel, E. 1961. *The Structure of Science: Problems in the Logic of Scientific Explanation*. New York: Harcourt Brace and World. (4:55, 69; 5:38; 9:32, 38; 10:72)

Nagel, E. 1979. *Teleology Revisited and other Essays in the Philosophy and History of Science*. New York: Columbia University Press. (3:26, 30; 7:14; 8:55)

Natsoulas, T. 1970. Concerning introspective "knowledge." *Psychological Bulletin*, 73:89–111. (11:44)

Natsoulas, T. 1978. Residual subjectivity. *American Psychologist*, 33:269–283. (9:60)

Nawas, M. M. 1970. Wherefore cognitive therapy?: A critical scrutiny of three papers by Beck, Bergin, and Ullmann. *Behavior Therapy*, 1:359–370. (8:16, 50; 9:80)

Neisser, U. 1967. *Cognitive Psychology*. New York: Appleton-Century-Crofts. (8:53) [p. 161]

Nelson, R. J. 1969. Behaviorism is false. *Journal of Philosophy*, 66:417–452. (4:4, 69)

Nelson, R. J. 1975. Behaviorism, finite automata, and stimulus-response theory. *Theory and Decision*, 6:249–267. (4:4, 31, 69)

Nevin, J. A. 1980. Editorial. *Journal of the Experimental Analysis of Behavior*, 33:i–ii. (5:40)

Nevin, J. A. and W. M. Baum 1980. Feedback functions for variable-interval reinforcement. *Journal of the Experimental Analysis of Behavior*, 34:207–217. (6:40)

Newbury, E. 1953. Philosophic assumptions in operational psychology. *Journal of Psychology*, 35:371–378. (1:3; 4:6; 12:55)

Newbury, E. 1958. The significance of assumptive and philosophic operations in psychological methodology. *Journal of General Psychology*, 59:185–199. (4:19)

Newbury, E. 1972. C. Lloyd Morgan, E. C. Tolman and comparative method. *Genetic Psychology Monographs*, 85:215–248. (2:29; 3:57; 10:33)

Nisbett, R. E. and T. D. Wilson 1977. Telling more than we can know: Verbal reports on mental processes. *Psychological Review*, 84:231–259. (8:54; 10:44; 11:30, 33)

Nissen, H. W. 1950. Description of the learned response in discrimination behavior. *Psychological Review*, 57:121–131. (3:82)

Nissen, H. W. 1952. Further comment on approach-avoidance as categories of response. *Psychological Review*, 59:161–167. (3:82)

Noble, C. E. 1974. Philosophy of science in contemporary psychology. *Psychological Reports*, 35:1239–1246. (5:35, 42, 48)

Norris, O. O. 1928. A behaviorist account of intelligence. *Journal of Philosophy*, 25:701–714. (8:9)

Norris, O. O. 1929a. A behaviorist account of consciousness, I. *Journal of Philosophy*, 26:29–42. (8:22; 11:25; 12:51)

Norris, O. O. 1929b. A behaviorist account of consciousness, II. *Journal of Philosophy*, 26:57–67. (8:22; 9:23)

Oatley, K. 1978. *Perceptions and Representations: The Theoretical Bases of Brain Research and Psychology*. New York: Free Press. (9:19, 28)

O'Leary, K. D., R. N. Kent and J. Kanowitz 1975. Shaping data collection congruent with experimental hypotheses. *Journal of Applied Behavior Analysis*, 8:43–51. (3:61)

Olshewsky, T. M. 1975. Dispositions and reductionism in psychology. *Journal for the Theory of Social Behaviour*, 5:129–144. (4:12; 10:80)

O'Neil, W. M. 1953. Hypothetical terms and relations in psychological theorizing. *British Journal of Psychology*, 44:211–220. (4:41, 53; 5:3)

O'Neil, W. M. 1968. Realism and behaviorism. *Journal of the History of the Behavioral Sciences*, 4:152–160. (11:66; 12:50)

Orata, P. T. 1928. *The Theory of Identical Elements*. Columbus: Ohio State University Press. (3:37)

Osgood, C. E. 1953. *Method and Theory in Experimental Psychology*. New York: Oxford University Press. (4:73; 6:66)

Osgood, C. E. 1957. A behavioristic analysis of perception and language as cognitive phenomena. In J. S. Bruner, et al., eds. *Contemporary Approaches to Cognition*, 75–118. Cambridge: Harvard University Press. (4:73; 7:47; 8:21; 9:31)

Osgood, C. E. 1963. On understanding and creating sentences. *American Psychologist*, 18:735–751. (7:47; 8:21)

Osgood, C. E. 1966. Meaning cannot be r_m? *Journal of Verbal Learning and Verbal Behavior*, 5:402–407. (4:73, 80)

Osgood, C. E. 1968. Toward a wedding of insufficiencies. In T. R. Dixon and D. L. Horton, eds. *Verbal Behavior and General Behavior Theory*, 495–519. Englewood Cliffs, N.J.: Prentice-Hall. (7:47, 80; 8:19, 21, 53; 9:31)

Osgood, C. E., G. J. Suci and P. H. Tannenbaum 1957. *The Measurement of Meaning*. Urbana: University of Illinois Press. (4:73)

Otis, A. S. 1920. Do we think in words? Behaviorist vs. introspective conceptions. *Psychological Review*, 27:399–419. (2:8, 40; 8:25, 27)

Paivio, A. 1975. Neomentalism. *Canadian Journal of Psychology*, 29:263–291. (4:78; 8:21, 35, 53; 10:35)

Palermo, D. S. 1970. Imagery in children's learning: Discussion. *Psychological Bulletin*, 73:415–421. (1:4; 8:45; 9:80)

Palermo, D. S. 1971. Is a scientific revolution taking place in psychology? *Science Studies*, 1:135–155. (1:4; 2:38; 6:20; 8:45; 9:80; 10:72)

Palmer, S. E. 1978. Fundamental aspects of cognitive representation. In E. Rosch and B. B. Lloyd, eds. *Cognition and Categorization*, 259–303. New York: Erlbaum. (8:49)

Pap, A. 1962. *An Introduction to the Philosophy of Science*. New York: Free Press. (4:30, 31, 33, 41, 42, 59)

Pavlov, I. P. 1928. *Lectures on Conditioned Reflexes*. Translated by W. H. Gantt. New York: International. (2:10; 6:4, 11, 12, 14; 9:19)

Peak, H. 1933. An evaluation of the concepts of reflex and voluntary action. *Psychological Review*, 40:71–89. (6:5)

Pear, T. 1920. Is thinking merely the action of language mechanisms? III. *British Journal of Psychology*, 11:71–80. (8:25; 11:27)

Pears, D. 1975. *Questions in the Philosophy of Mind*. London: Duckworth. (7:29; 11:17)

Pennington, L. A. and J. L. Finan 1940. Operational usage in psychology. *Psychological Review*, 47:254–266. (2:8; 4:15, 19, 20)

Pepper, S. C. 1923. Misconceptions regarding behaviorism. *Journal of Philosophy*, 20:242–244. (2:13)

Pepper, S. C. 1934. The conceptual framework of Tolman's purposive behaviorism. *Psychological Review*, 41:108–133. (3:70; 9:38; 12:26)

Perkins, C. C. 1968. An analysis of the concept of reinforcement. *Psychological Review*, 75:155–172. (4:77)

Perrin, F. A. C. 1921. Conscious analysis versus habit hierarchies in the learning process. *Journal of Comparative Psychology*, 1:287–308. (11:32)

Perry, R. B. 1918. Docility and purposiveness. *Psychological Review*, 25:1–20. (3:63; 4:76; 7:15, 23; 8:3; 10:34)

Perry, R. B. 1921a. A behavioristic view of purpose. *Journal of Philosophy*, 18:85–105. (3:63; 4:76; 7:9, 11, 15, 23, 44; 10:3)

Perry, R. B. 1921b. The independent variability of purpose and belief. *Journal of Philosophy*, 18:169–180. (3:63; 10:24)

Place, U. T. 1956. Is consciousness a brain process? *British Journal of Psychology*, 47:44–50. (11:47)

Place, U. T. 1981. Skinner's *Verbal Behavior*, I—Why we need it. *Behvaiorism*, 9:1–24. (3:50, 52, 69; 10:34)

Polanyi, M. 1968. Logic and psychology. *American Psychologist*, 23:27–43. (4:60; 5:52; 11:40; 12:56)

Postman, L. 1947. The history and present status of the law of effect. *Psychological Bulletin*, 44:489–563. (9:47)

Powers, W. T. 1973. Feedback: Beyond behaviorism. *Science*, 179:351–356. (6:34; 7:24)

Pratt, C. C. 1938. Psychological physiology. *Psychological Review*, 45:424–429. (4:61, 62)

Pratt, C. C. 1939. *The Logic of Modern Psychology*. New York: Macmillan. (2:15, 17, 20, 31; 3:6, 7; 4:24, 61, 62; 9:44; 11:8; 12:37)

Pratt, C. C. 1945. Operationism in psychology. *Psychological Review*, 52:262–269, 288–291. (2:31; 4:23, 24; 12:27)

Pratt, J. B. 1922. Behaviorism and consciousness. *Journal of Philosophy*, 19:596–604. (2:16; 7:15; 10:31)

Prelec, D. and R. J. Herrnstein 1978. Feedback functions for reinforcement: A paradigmatic experiment. *Animal Learning and Behavior*, 6:181–186. (6:42)

Premack, D. 1970. A functional analysis of language. *Journal of the Experimental Analysis of Behavior*, 14:107–125. (3:77; 7:82; 9:58)

Premack, D. 1978. On the abstractness of human concepts: Why it would be difficult to talk to a pigeon. In S. H. Hulse, et al., eds. *Cognitive Processes in Animal Behavior*, 423–451. Hillsdale, N.J.: Erlbaum. (3:77)

Prentice, W. C. H. 1946. Operationism and psychological theory: A note. *Psychological Review*, 53:247–249. (10:15)

Pribram, K. H. 1971. *Languages of the Brain: Experimental Paradoxes and Principles in Neuropsychology*. Englewood Cliffs, N.J.: Prentice-Hall. (4:76; 7:44; 9:29, 80)

Price, H. H. 1961. Some objections to behaviorism. In S. Hook, ed., *Dimensions of Mind*, 79–84. New York: Collier. (1:1)

Prince, M. 1926. Three fundamental errors of the behaviorists and the reconciliation of the purposive and mechanistic concepts. In C. Murchison, ed. *Psychologies of 1925*, 199–220. Worcester: Clark University. (2:18; 11:48)

Pritchard, M. S. 1976. On taking emotions seriously: A critique of B. F. Skinner. *Journal for the Theory of Social Behaviour*, 6:211–232. (10:32; 11:38)

Putnam, H. 1961. Minds and machines. In S. Hook, ed. *Dimensions of Mind*, 138–164. New York: Collier. (10:43; 11:7)

Putnam, H. 1962. Dreaming and "depth grammar." In R. Butler, ed. *Analytical Philosophy, First Series*. Oxford: Basil Blackwell and Mott. (10:9, 43; 11:7)

Putnam, H. 1963. Brains and behavior. In R. Butler, ed. *Analytical Philosophy, Second Series*. Oxford: Basil Blackwell and Mott. (10:29, 31, 37, 40, 41, 43; 11:7)

Putnam, H. 1967a. The "innateness hypothesis" and explanatory models in linguistics. *Synthese*, 17:17–22. (10:37)

Putnam, H. 1967b. Psychological predicates. In W. H. Capitan and D. D. Merrill, eds. *Art, Mind, and Religion*, 37–48. Pittsburgh: University of Pittsburgh Press. (10:31, 37, 39, 42)

Putnam, H. 1969. Logical positivism and the philosophy of mind. In P. Achinstein and S. F. Barker, eds. *The Legacy of Logical Positivism*, 211–225. Baltimore: Johns Hopkins University Press. (10:3, 9, 42)

Putnam, H. 1973. Reductionism and the nature of psychology. *Cognition*, 2:131–146. (3:14; 8:34)

Putnam, H. 1975a. Philosophy and our mental life. In *Mind, Language, and Reality: Philosophical Papers*, 2:291–303. Cambridge: Cambridge University Press. (10:37)

Putnam, H. 1975b. Other minds. In *Mind, Language, and Reality* (see Putnam 1975a), 342–361. (10:3)

Putnam, H. 1975c. The mental life of some machines. In *Mind, Language, and Reality* (see Putnam 1975a), 408–428. (10:31)

Pylyshyn, Z. W. 1972. Competence and psychological reality. *American Psychologist*, 27:546–552. (7:65, 69)

Pylyshyn, Z. W. 1973. What the mind's eye tells the mind's brain: A critique of mental imagery. *Psychological Bulletin*, 80:1–24. (3:24; 8:53; 11:28)

Pylyshyn, Z. W. 1978. Imagery and artificial intelligence. In C. W. Savage, ed. *Perception and Cognition: Issues in the Foundations of Psychology. Minnesota Studies in the Philosophy of Science,* 9:19–55. Minneapolis: University of Minnesota Press. (3:24)

Pylyshyn, Z. W. 1980. Computation and cognition: Issues in the foundations of cognitive science. *The Behavioral and Brain Sciences,* 3:111–169. (8:34)

Quine, W. V. O. 1960. *Word and Object.* Cambridge: MIT Press (2:36, 46; 4:56; 10:34, 59; 12:45, 53) [p. 43]

Quine, W. V. O. 1969a. Linguistics and philosophy. In S. Hook, ed. *Language and Philosophy,* 95–98. New York: New York University Press. (2:36; 3:29, 55; 7:78; 11:61)

Quine, W. V. O. 1969b. *Ontological Relativity and Other Essays.* New York: Columbia University Press. (3:26, 39; 12:54)

Quine, W. V. O. 1970. *Philosophy of Logic.* Englewood Cliffs, N.J.: Prentice-Hall. (10:34)

Quine, W. V. O. 1982. *Methods of Logic* (4th ed.). Cambridge: Harvard University Press. (4:10)

Rachlin, H. 1974. Self-control. *Behaviorism,* 2:94–107. (9:69)

Rachlin, H. 1975. Review of B. F. Skinner's *About Behaviorism. Behavior Therapy,* 6:437–440. (4:78)

Rachlin, H. 1976. *Introduction to Modern Behaviorism* (2d ed.). San Francisco: W. H. Freeman. (3:69; 4:68; 6:32; 7:44)

Rachlin, H. 1977a. Reinforcing and punishing thoughts. *Behavior Therapy,* 8:659–665. (4:42, 68; 8:5; 10:80)

Rachlin, H. 1977b. Reinforcing and punishing thoughts: A rejoinder to Ellis and Mahoney. *Behavior Therapy,* 8:678–681. (4:42, 68; 6:32; 8:5; 10:80)

Rachlin, H. 1977c. A review of M. J. Mahoney's *Cognition and Behavior Modification. Journal of Applied Behavior Analysis,* 10:369–374. (4:42, 68, 78; 8:16, 41, 42)

Rachlin, H. 1978a. Self-control. In A. C. Catania and T. A. Brigham, eds. *Handbook of Applied Behavior Analysis: Social and Instructional Processes,* 246–258. New York: Irvington. (4:42, 43, 68; 9:69)

Rachlin, H. 1978b. A molar theory of reinforcement schedules. *Journal of the Experimental Analysis of Behavior,* 30:345–360. (6:40)

Rachlin, H. 1980. A (stubborn) refusal to return to introspectionism. *American Psychologist,* 35:473. (11:35)

Rachlin, H., R. Battalio, J. Kagel and L. Green 1981. Maximization theory in behavioral psychology. *The Behavioral and Brain Sciences,* 4:371–417. (6:31; 9:46)

Rachman, S. 1970. Behavior therapy and psychodynamics. *Behavior Therapy,* 1:527–530. (10:51)

Rachman, S. and H. J. Eysenck 1966. Reply to a "critique and reformulation" of behavior therapy. *Psychological Bulletin,* 65:165–169. (8:7)

Radford, J. 1974. Reflections on introspection. *American Psychologist,* 29:245–250. (2:17, 54)

Radner, M. and S. Winokur, eds. 1970. *Analyses of Theories and Methods of Physics and Psychology. Minnesota Studies in the Philosophy of Science,* Vol. 4. Minneapolis: University of Minnesota Press. (4:55)

Reese, H. W. 1968. *The Perception of Stimulus Relations.* New York: Academic. (3:76)

Reichenbach, H. 1938. *Experience and Prediction.* Chicago: University of Chicago Press. (5:54; 11:36)

Reiser, O. L. 1924. Behaviorism as a monism of action. *American Journal of Psychology,* 35:545–558. (6:14)

Reitman, W. 1965. *Cognition and Thought.* New York: Wiley. (8:36)

Rescorla, R. A. and A. R. Wagner 1972. A theory of Pavlovian conditioning: Variations in the effectiveness of reinforcement and nonreinforcement. In A. H. Black and W. F. Prokasy, eds. *Classical Conditioning, II: Current Research and Theory,* 64–99. New York: Appleton-Century-Crofts. (4:77; 6:45)

Restle, F. 1957. Discrimination of cues in mazes: A resolution of the "place-vs.-response" question. *Psychological Review,* 64:217–228. (3:82)

Rexroad, C. N. 1933a. Goal-objects, purposes, and behavior. *Psychological Review*, 40:271–281. (4:76; 7:15)

Rexroad, C. N. 1933b. An examination of conditioned reflex theory. *Psychological Review*, 40:457–466. (6:16)

Rice, P. B. 1946. The ego and the law of effect. *Psychological Review*, 53:307–320. (7:35, 64; 9:40)

Richardson, W. K. and W. J. Warzak 1981. Stimulus stringing by pigeons. *Journal of the Experimental Analysis of Behavior*, 36:267–276. (7:42)

Richelle, M. 1976. Formal analysis and functional analysis of verbal behavior: Notes on the debate between Chomsky and Skinner. *Behaviorism*, 4:209–221. (7:62; 10:74)

Ringen, J. D. 1975. Linguistic facts: A study of the empirical scientific status of transformational generative grammars. In D. Cohen and J. R. Wirth, eds. *Testing Linguistic Hypotheses*, 1–41. Washington, D.C.: Hemisphere. (7:69, 70)

Ringen, J. D. 1976. Explanation, teleology, and operant behaviorism: A study of the experimental analysis of purposive behavior. *Philosophy of Science*, 43:223–253. (7:17; 9:41, 64, 81; 10:34, 54)

Ritchie, B. F. 1944. Hull's treatment of learning. *Psychological Bulletin*, 41:640–652. (3:36; 5:3)

Roback, A. A. 1923. *Behaviorism and Psychology*. Cambridge, Mass.: University Bookstore. (1:1, 2, 11; 10:29; 12:27)

Roback, A. A. 1937. *Behaviorism at Twenty-Five*. Cambridge, Mass.: Sci-Art. (1:10; 8:24; 11:8, 42)

Robinson, A. 1917–1918. Behaviour as a psychological concept. *Proceedings of the Aristotelian Society*, 18:271–285. (6:18; 12:50)

Robinson, A. 1920. Is thinking merely the action of language mechanisms? IV. *British Journal of Psychology*, 11:81–86. (2:27)

Robinson, D. N. 1979. *Systems of Modern Psychology: A Critical Sketch*. New York: Columbia University Press. (1:4; 5:1; 7:41)

Robinson, G. 1977. Procedures for the acquisition of syntax. In W. K. Honig and J. E. R. Staddon, eds. *Handbook of Operant Behavior*, 619–627. Englewood Cliffs, N.J.: Prentice-Hall. (7:46)

Rogers, C. R. and B. F. Skinner 1956. Some issues concerning the control of human behavior: A symposium. *Science*, 124:1057–1066. (9:2; 10:64)

Root, M. D. 1975. Language, rules, and complex behavior. In K. Gunderson, ed. *Language, Mind, and Knowledge. Minnesota Studies in the Philosophy of Science*, 7:321–343. Minneapolis: University of Minnesota Press. (7:42, 67, 80)

Rorty, R. 1965. Mind-body identity, privacy, and categories. *Review of Metaphysics*, 19:24–54. (10:2)

Rorty, R. 1972. Functionalism, machines, and incorrigibility. *Journal of Philosophy*, 69:203–220. (8:34)

Rosch, E. and C. B. Mervis 1975. Family resemblances: Studies in the internal structure of categories. *Cognitive Psychology*, 7:573–605. (1:9)

Rosenblueth, A., N. Wiener and J. Bigelow 1943. Behavior, purpose, and teleology. *Philosophy of Science*, 10:18–24. (7:24)

Rosenow, C. 1923. Behavior and conscious behavior. *Psychological Review*, 30:192–216. (3:34, 49; 11:23)

Rosenow, C. 1925. The problem of meaning in behaviorism. *American Journal of Psychology*, 36:233–248. (3:49, 51)

Rozeboom, W. W. 1956. Mediation variables in scientific theory. *Psychological Review*, 63:249–264. (4:31, 33, 45, 53, 66)

Rozeboom, W. W. 1958. "What is learned?"—An empirical enigma. *Psychological Review*, 65:22–33. (6:60)

Rozeboom, W. W. 1960. Do stimuli elicit behavior?—A study in the logical foundations of behavioristics. *Philosophy of Science*, 27:159–170. (3:32; 6:33)

Rozeboom, W. W. 1961. Formal analysis and the language of behavior theory. In H. Feigl and

G. Maxwell, eds. *Current Issues in the Philosophy of Science*, 473–483. New York: Holt, Rinehart and Winston. (3:32; 6:33)

Rozeboom, W. W. 1970. The art of metascience, or, what should a psychological theory be? In J. R. Royce, ed. *Toward Unification in Psychology: The First Banff Conference on Theoretical Psychology*, 53–160. Toronto: University of Toronto Press. (3:27, 55; 4:45; 5:51, 58; 6:28, 64; 9:30, 80)

Rozeboom, W. W. 1972. Problems in the psycho-philosophy of knowledge. In J. R. Royce and W. W. Rozeboom, eds. *The Psychology of Knowing*, 25–93. New York: Gordon and Breach. (3:76; 6:33; 10:34; 12:1)

Rozeboom, W. W. 1974. The learning tradition. In E. C. Carterette and M. P. Friedman, eds. *Handbook of Perception*, Vol 1. *Historical and Philosophical Roots of Perception*, 211–242. New York: Academic. (3:20, 32, 34, 76; 4:72; 6:33; 9:49)

Rumbaugh, D. M. 1977. *Language Learning by a Chimpanzee: The Lana Project*. New York: Academic. (7:82)

Russell, B. 1917. *Mysticism and Logic*. New York: Barnes and Noble. (4:53, 68)

Russell, S. B. 1917. Advance adaptation in behavior. *Psychological Review*, 24:413–425. (7:22; 8:23; 9:42; 11:19)

Ryle, G. 1949. *The Concept of Mind*. London: Hutchinson. (2:34, 46; 6:51; 7:32; 8:3, 31; 9:57, 75; 10:27, 30, 79, 81; 11:12, 46, 66) [p. 208]

Salzinger, K. 1970. Pleasing linguistics: A parable. *Journal of Verbal Learning and Verbal Behavior*, 9:725–727. (7:36; 8:50)

Salzinger, K. 1973a. Inside the black box, with apologies to Pandora: A review of Ulrich Neisser's *Cognitive Psychology*. *Journal of the Experimental Analysis of Behavior*, 19:369–378. (3:37; 4:68, 78; 7:36, 45, 56, 70; 8:51)

Salzinger, K. 1973b. Some problems of response measurement in verbal behavior: The response unit and intraresponse relations. In K. Salzinger and R. S. Feldman, eds. *Studies in Verbal Behavior: An Empirical Approach*, 5–15. New York: Pergamon. (3:60, 73; 7:36, 45; 9:18)

Salzinger, K. 1975. Are theories of competence necessary? *Annals of the New York Academy of Sciences*, 263:178–196. (3:77; 7:36, 48, 72, 74, 82; 8:51; 9:54; 12:38)

Salzinger, K. 1978. Language behavior. In A. C. Catania and T. A. Brigham, eds. *Handbook of Applied Behavior Analysis: Social and Instructional Processes*, 275–321. New York: Irvington. (7:36, 76, 80, 82; 8:51; 10:66)

Savage, C. W. 1966. Introspectionist and behaviorist interpretations of ratio scales of perceptual magnitudes. *Psychological Monographs*, 80(19, whole no. 627). (11:58)

Savage, C. W. 1970. *The Measurement of Sensation*. Berkeley: University of California Press. (11:58)

Scharf, B., ed. 1975. *Experimental Sensory Psychology*. Introduction. Glenview, Ill.: Scott Foresman. (11:59)

Scheffler, I. 1963. *The Anatomy of Inquiry*. New York: Knopf. (4:12)

Scheffler, I. 1967. *Science and Subjectivity*. Indianapolis: Bobbs-Merrill. (3:26)

Schick, K. 1971. Operants. *Journal of the Experimental Analysis of Behavior*, 15:413–423. (3:60, 74)

Schnaitter, R. 1975. Between organism and environment. A review of B. F. Skinner's *About Behaviorism*. *Journal of the Experimental Analysis of Behavior*, 23:297–307. (4:66; 5:35; 9:12; 10:67; 12:6)

Schnaitter, R. 1978a. Circularity, trans-situationality, and the law of effect. *Psychological Record*, 28:353–362. (3:74)

Schnaitter, R. 1978b. Private causes. *Behaviorism*, 6:1–12. (4:78)

Schoenfeld, W. N. 1970. *Oyepk* on mediating mechanisms of the conditional reflex. *Conditional Reflex*, 5:165–170. (3:9; 4:69)

Schoenfeld, W. N. and W. W. Cumming 1963. Behavior and perception. In S. Koch, ed. *Psychology: A Study of a Science*. Vol. 5. *The Process Areas, the Person, and Some Fields: Their Place in Psychology and in Science*, 213–252. New York: McGraw-Hill. (3:31; 4:72, 81; 8:23; 9:52; 10:80; 11:9, 21, 42, 44)

Schrier, A. M. and C. R. Thompson 1980. Conditional discrimination learning: A critique and amplification. *Journal of the Experimental Analysis of Behavior*, 33:291–298. (3:76)

Schwartz, B. 1974. On going back to nature: A review of Seligman and Hager's *Biological Boundaries of Learning*. *Journal of the Experimental Analysis of Behavior*, 21:183–198. (10:66)

Schwartz, B. and H. Lacey 1982. *Behaviorism, Science, and Human Nature*. New York: Norton, (1:16; 9:2, 10, 12; 10:69)

Schwartz, M. 1967. Physiological psychology: Or can a science over 95 afford to be "grubo"? *Psychological Bulletin*, 67:228–230. (3:16)

Schwartz, R. 1978. Infinite sets, unbounded competences, and models of mind. In C. W. Savage, ed. *Perception and Cognition: Issues in the Foundations of Psychology*. *Minnesota Studies in the Philosophy of Science*, 9:183–200. Minneapolis: University of Minnesota Press. (7:32, 60; 8:58)

Scriven, M. 1956. A study of radical behaviorism. In H. Feigl and M. Scriven, eds. *The Foundations of Science and the Concepts of Psychology and Psychoanalysis*. *Minnesota Studies in the Philosophy of Science*, 1:88–130. Minneapolis: University of Minnesota Press. (3:42; 4:24, 36, 37, 44, 54; 5:35, 42, 43; 10:65)

Scriven, M. 1969. Logical positivism and the behavioral sciences. In P. Achinstein and S. F. Barker, eds. *The Legacy of Logical Positivism*, 195–209. Baltimore: Johns Hopkins University Press. (1:14; 2:1; 4:19; 5:63)

Seashore, R. H. and B. Katz 1937. An operational definition and classification of mental mechanisms. *Psychological Record*, 1:1–24. (4:24)

Sechenov, I. M. 1863/1935. Reflexes of the brain. In *Selected Works*, 263–336. Translated by A. A. Subkov. Moscow: State Publishing House for Biological and Medical Literature. (6:8; 9:10) [p. 179]

Secord, P. 1977. Making oneself behave: A critique of the behavioral paradigm and an alternative conceptualization. In T. Mischel, ed. *The Self: Psychological and Philosophical Issues*, 250–273. Oxford, England: Basil Blackwell. (9:69)

Seeman, W. 1951a. On a stimulus-response analysis of insight in psychotherapy. *Psychological Review*, 58:302–305. (10:50)

Seeman, W. 1951b. The Freudian theory of daydreams: An operational analysis. *Psychological Bulletin*, 48:369–382. (10:50)

Segal, E. and R. Lachman 1972. Complex behavior or higher mental process. *American Psychologist*, 27:46–55. (1:4; 3:82; 8:33)

Segal, E. F. 1975. Psycholinguistics discovers the operant: A review of Roger Brown's *A First Language: The Early Stages*. *Journal of the Experimental Analysis of Behavior*, 23:149–158. (7:49, 51; 9:80)

Segal, E. F. 1977. Toward a coherent psychology of language. In W. K. Honig and J. E. R. Staddon, eds. *Handbook of Operant Behavior*, 628–653. Englewood Cliffs, N.J.: Prentice-Hall. (7:46, 49, 51, 54, 68; 8:43; 10:61)

Seligman, M. E. P. 1969. Control group and conditioning: A comment on operationism. *Psychological Review*, 76:484–491. (4:22)

Seligman, M. E. P. and J. L. Hager 1972. *Biological Boundaries of Learning*. New York: Appleton-Century-Crofts. (10:72)

Sellars, W. 1956. Empiricism and the philosophy of mind. In H. Feigl and M. Scriven, eds. *The Foundations of Science and the Concepts of Psychology and Psychoanalysis*. *Minnesota Studies in the Philosophy of Science*, 1:253–329. Minneapolis: University of Minnesota Press. (9:66; 10:76; 11:14, 23, 64)

Seward, J. P. 1954. Hull's system of behavior: An evaluation. *Psychological Review*, 61:145–159. (4:46, 48; 5:4, 39)

Seward, J. P. 1955. The constancy of the I-V: A critique of intervening variables. *Psychological Review*, 62:155–168. (4:45, 46, 47; 5:27)

Shaffer, J. A. 1968. *Philosophy of Mind*. Englewood Cliffs, N.J.: Prentice-Hall. (3:44; 8:25; 9:1; 10:19, 29, 39)

Shapere, D. 1971. The paradigm concept. *Science*, 172:706–709. (1:4; 3:26)

Shaw, F. J. 1946. A stimulus-response analysis of repression and insight in psychotherapy. *Psychological Review*, 53:36–42. (10:50)

Shepard, R. N. 1978. On the status of "direct" psychophysical measurement. In C. W. Savage, ed. *Perception and Cognition: Issues in the Foundations of Psychology. Minnesota Studies in the Philosophy of Science*, 9:441–490. Minneapolis: University of Minnesota Press. (4:22; 11:60)

Sherrington, C. S. 1906. *The Integrative Action of the Nervous System*. New York: Scribner. (3:31; 4:76; 6:4, 14, 15, 16; 9:20)

Shimp, C. P. 1969. Optimal behavior in free-operant experiments. *Psychological Review*, 76:97–112. (6:32)

Shimp, C. P. 1975. Perspectives on the behavioral unit: Choice behavior in animals. In W. K. Estes, ed. *Handbook of Learning and Cognitive Processes*, 2:225–268. Hillsdale, N.J.: Erlbaum. (3:69)

Shimp, C. P. 1976. Organization in memory and behavior. *Journal of the Experimental Analysis of Behavior*, 26:113–130. (3:69, 73; 4:2, 36, 47; 7:45; 8:11, 49)

Shoben, E. J. 1949. Psychotherapy as a problem in learning theory. *Psychological Bulletin*, 46:366–392. (10:50)

Shuford, H. R. 1966. Logical behaviorism and intentionality. *Theoria*, 32:246–251. (3:50; 10:34)

Shwayder, D. S. 1965. *The Stratification of Behaviour*. New York: Humanities. (3:48; 7:80; 10:53)

Sidman, M. 1960. *Tactics of Scientific Research: Evaluating Experimental Data in Psychology*. New York: Basic. (3:7, 73; 5:30, 37, 41, 56; 12:56)

Silverstein, A. 1966. The "grubo" psychology: Or can a science over 95 be happy without reductionism? *Psychological Bulletin*, 66:207–210. (3:7; 6:72)

Singer, E. A. 1911. Mind as an observable object. *Journal of Philosophy, Psychology, and Scientific Methods*, 8:180–186. (10:24, 78; 11:12; 12:54)

Singer, E. A. 1912. Consciousness and behavior. A reply. *Journal of Philosophy, Psychology, and Scientific Methods*, 9:15–19. (10:5; 11:66; 12:54)

Singer, E. A. 1924. *Mind as Behavior and Studies in Empirical Idealism*. Columbus, OH: R. G. Adams. (4:5; 8:3; 9:41; 10:5, 27; 11:23, 24, 63, 64, 66; 12:45)

Singer, E. A. 1925. Concerning introspection: A reply. *Journal of Philosophy*, 22:711–716. (2:24; 7:12)

Skinner, B. F. 1931. The concept of the reflex in the description of behavior. *Journal of General Psychology*, 5:427–458. (3:7, 8, 31, 43; 5:19, 42, 43; 6:5, 6, 16, 27, 29; 12:27)

Skinner, B. F. 1932. Drive and reflex strength: I. *Journal of General Psychology*, 6:22–37. (3:7; 4:3, 36, 45; 5:19; 12:39)

Skinner, B. F. 1935a. The generic nature of the concepts of stimulus and response. *Journal of General Psychology*, 12:40–65. (3:15, 62, 73; 6:5)

Skinner, B. F. 1935b. Two types of conditioned reflex and a pseudo-type. *Journal of General Psychology*, 12:66–77. (3:31; 5:19)

Skinner, B. F. 1936. Conditioning and extinction and their relation to drive. *Journal of General Psychology*, 14:296–317. (4:3)

Skinner, B. F. 1938. *The Behavior of Organisms: An Experimental Analysis*. New York: Appleton-Century-Crofts. (3:7, 10, 11, 15, 42, 73, 74, 78; 4:3, 55, 68; 5:19, 30, 41, 43; 6:9, 12, 25; 7:17; 9:2, 43; 10:17, 62, 83) [p. 106]

Skinner, B. F. 1944. *Principles of Behavior*, by Clark L. Hull. *American Journal of Psychology*, 57:276–281. (5:3, 32, 33)

Skinner, B. F. 1945a. The operational analysis of psychological terms. *Psychological Review*, 52:270–277. (2:48, 50; 4:8; 5:26, 45; 10:62, 83; 11:21, 22, 23, 30, 31, 44; 12:1, 23) [p. 217]

Skinner, B. F. 1945b. Rejoinders and second thoughts: Part V. *Psychological Review*, 52:291–294. (4:8; 5:22; 11:23)

Skinner, B. F. 1947. Experimental psychology. In W. Dennis, ed. *Current Trends in Psychology*, 16–49. Pittsburgh: University of Pittsburgh Press. (3:10, 14; 5:28, 41, 43, 45; 9:5, 15, 61) [p. 176]

Skinner, B. F. 1950. Are theories of learning necessary? *Psychological Review*, 57:193–216. (4:74; 5:19, 27, 31, 32, 33, 41, 43; 9:51) [p. 87]

Skinner, B. F. 1953a. *Science and Human Behavior* New York: Macmillan. (2:50; 3:10, 14, 31, 76; 4:5, 37, 43, 68, 69; 5:19, 22, 26, 46; 6:36, 37, 38; 7:17, 29; 8:28, 51; 9:5, 7, 10, 15, 17, 53, 62, 64, 69; 10:1, 26, 50, 58, 62, 63; 11:13, 16, 21, 22, 23, 30, 44, 63, 66, 67; 12:1, 23, 24, 39, 46, 59) [pp. 107, 180]

Skinner, B. F. 1953b. Some contributions of an experimental analysis of behavior to psychology as a whole. *American Psychologist*, 8:69–78. (4:36; 5:32; 10:63)

Skinner, B. F. 1954. A critique of psychoanalytic concepts and theories. *Scientific Monthly*, 79:300–305. (4:37; 5:34; 9:66; 10:49)

Skinner, B. F. 1956a. A case history in scientific method. *American Psychologist*, 11:221–233. (5:19, 29, 30, 41, 43, 45)

Skinner, B. F. 1956b. Another comment: Review of R. R. Bush and F. Mosteller *Stochastic Models for Learning*. *Contemporary Psychology*, 1:101–103. (5:33)

Skinner, B. F. 1957a. *Verbal Behavior*. New York: Appleton-Century-Crofts. (2:50; 3:19, 23, 31, 73, 76, 78; 4:5, 56; 5:25, 26, 41, 43, 45, 64; 6:25, 67; 7:29, 36, 48, 49, 50, 82; 8:28, 51; 9:51, 66; 10:17, 26, 28, 59, 60, 61, 62, 67, 74, 83; 11:12, 14, 15, 16, 17, 22, 23, 30, 44, 50; 12:1, 2, 6, 7, 15, 23, 40) [pp. 160, 260]

Skinner, B. F. 1957b. The experimental analysis of behavior. *American Scientist*, 45:343–371. (6:28; 9:51)

Skinner, B. F. 1958. Reinforcement today. *American Psychologist*, 13:94–99. (6:41; 10:67)

Skinner, B. F. 1961. Why we need teaching machines. *Harvard Educational Review*, 31:377–398. (8:27, 28, 52; 9:51; 12:2)

Skinner, B. F. 1963a. Behaviorism at fifty. *Science*, 140:951–958. (1:2; 4:7; 5:26; 8:37, 50; 9:7; 10:64, 65; 11:21, 23, 35, 66, 67; 12:1, 45, 52) [pp. 230, 271]

Skinner, B. F. 1963b. Reflections on a decade of teaching machines. *Teacher's College Record*, 65:168–177. (5:32; 9:15; 10:67)

Skinner, B. F. 1963c. Operant behavior. *American Psychologist*, 18:505–515. (5:41; 6:25; 7:17, 26, 31, 33, 80; 8:59; 11:17, 35)

Skinner, B. F. 1964. "Man." *Proceedings of the American Philosophical Society*, 108:482–485. (8:51; 9:7)

Skinner, B. F. 1966a. The phylogeny and ontogeny of behavior. *Science*, 153:1205–1213. (4:42; 6:28; 7:25, 30; 9:8)

Skinner, B. F. 1966b. What is the experimental analysis of behavior? *Journal of the Experimental Analysis of Behavior*, 9:213–218. (3:31, 62; 5:31, 41, 43; 6:26; 8:59; 9:14, 49; 11:35)

Skinner, B. F. 1967. B. F. Skinner. In E. G. Boring and G. Lindzey, eds. *A History of Psychology in Autobiography*, 5:387–413. New York: Appleton-Century-Crofts. (1:2; 5:30, 41; 12:27)

Skinner, B. F. 1968. *The Technology of Teaching*. Englewood Cliffs, N.J.: Prentice-Hall. (6:37; 8:15, 27, 28, 32, 50, 52; 9:5, 51, 58; 10:24; 11:15, 21; 12:1, 2) [p. 158]

Skinner, B. F. 1969. *Contingencies of Reinforcement: A Theoretical Analysis*. New York: Appleton-Century-Crofts. (2:54; 3:14, 15, 60, 70, 73; 4:3; 5:3, 20, 22, 26, 28, 29, 30, 32, 34, 41; 6:26; 7:29, 30, 31, 32, 33, 74, 80; 8:50, 59; 9:7, 15, 42; 10:63, 67; 11:16, 17, 44, 66; 12:6, 15, 40, 45, 46) [pp. 251, 273]

Skinner, B. F. 1971a. Humanistic behaviorism. *The Humanist*, 31:35. (9:2)

Skinner, B. F. 1971b. A behavioral analysis of value judgements. In E. Tobach, et al., eds. *The Biopsychology of Development*, 543–551. New York: Academic. (12:24, 59)

Skinner, B. F. 1971c. *Beyond Freedom and Dignity*. New York: Bantam/Vintage. (5:46; 7:18; 9:2, 10; 10:64; 12:24)

Skinner, B. F. 1972a. Some relations between behavior modification and basic research. In *Cumulative Record: A Selection of Papers* (3d ed.), 276–282. New York: Appleton-Century-Crofts. (12:30)

Skinner, B. F. 1972b. Compassion and ethics in the care of the retardate. In *Cumulative Record* (see Skinner 1972a), 283–291. (12:24)

Skinner, B. F. 1972c. The flight from the laboratory. In *Cumulative Record* (see Skinner 1972a), 314–330. (3:7; 9:7; 12:6)

Skinner, B. F. 1972d. Creating the creative artist. In *Cumulative Record* (see Skinner 1972a), 333–344. (8:28)

Skinner, B. F. 1972e. A lecture on "having" a poem. In *Cumulative Record* (see Skinner 1972a), 345–355. (7:36; 9:61, 73)

Skinner, B. F. 1972f. Why are the behavioral sciences not more effective? In *Cumulative Record* (see Skinner 1972a), 421–428. (9:12)

Skinner, B. F. 1972g. Humanism and behaviorism. *The Humanist*, 32:18–20. (7:18, 29; 8:50; 9:61, 66; 11:23, 32, 50; 12:45)

Skinner, B. F. 1972h. Psychology in the understanding of mental disease. In *Cumulative Record* (see Skinner 1972a), 249–256. (11:9, 10, 30, 44; 12:2)

Skinner, B. F. 1972i. What is psychotic behavior? In *Cumulative Record* (see Skinner 1972a), 257–275. (3:54; 4:36, 42; 5:28, 32; 8:42, 50; 9:10; 10:62, 67, 82; 11:30; 12:6)

Skinner, B. F. 1973a. Reflections on meaning and structure. In R. Brower, et al., eds. *I. A. Richards: Essays in His Honor*, 199–209. New York: Oxford University Press. (7:50; 8:51; 10:60)

Skinner, B. F. 1973b. Answers for my critics. In H. Wheeler, ed. *Beyond the Punitive Society*, 256–266. San Francisco: W. H. Freeman. (6:28; 9:53, 81; 10:67) [p. 219]

Skinner, B. F. 1974. *About Behaviorism*. New York: Knopf. (1:2; 3:11; 4:81; 5:20, 26; 6:36, 37, 38, 67; 7:17, 30, 31, 32, 62, 76; 8:3, 28, 32, 50, 51, 55, 59; 9:2, 5, 17, 53, 61, 64, 69; 10:50, 61, 62, 67, 80, 83; 11:13, 14, 16, 22, 23, 32, 33, 47, 50, 66, 67; 12:3, 23, 40, 46, 47, 51) [pp. 27, 124, 146, 260]

Skinner, B. F. 1977a. Why I am not a cognitive psychologist. *Behaviorism*, 5:1–10. (3:54; 5:20; 6:51; 7:17, 67, 80; 8:37, 52, 55, 59; 9:8, 10; 10:60; 11:33, 66; 12:38) [p. 169]

Skinner, B. F. 1977b. Herrnstein and the evolution of behaviorism. *American Psychologist*, 32:1006–1012. (5:19)

Skinner, B. F. 1978. *Reflections on Behaviorism and Society*. Englewood Cliffs, N.J.: Prentice-Hall. (4:3, 36)

Skinner, B. F. 1979. *The Shaping of a Behaviorist*. New York: Knopf. (6:29)

Skinner, B. F. 1981. Selection by consequences. *Science*, 213:501–504. (9:8)

Skinner, B. F. and M. E. Vaughan 1983. *Enjoy Old Age*. New York: Norton. (8:32; 10:62; 12:2)

Slack, C. W. 1955. Feedback theory and the reflex arc concept. *Psychological Review*, 62:263–267. (6:34)

Sloane, E. H. 1945. Reductionism. *Psychological Review*, 52:214–223. (6:16; 9:40)

Smart, J. J. C. 1963. *Philosophy and Scientific Realism*. London: Routledge. (11:47)

Smedslund, J. 1953. The problem of "what is learned?" *Psychological Review*, 60:157–158. (3:82)

Smith, L. D. 1983. Behaviorism and logical positivism: A revised account of the alliance. Dissertation, University of New Hampshire. (1:14; 4:25, 31; 9:61; 12:4, 9, 11, 16, 18, 22, 26, 50)

Smith, S. and E. R. Guthrie. 1921. *General Psychology in Terms of Behavior*. New York: Appleton-Century. (2:19; 4:70; 6:12, 66; 8:23; 9:25, 26, 42, 51; 10:76)

Spence, K. W. 1936. The nature of discrimination learning in animals. *Psychological Review*, 43:427–449. (3:82; 5:16; 8:15; 9:35, 55)

Spence, K. W. 1937a. The differential response in animals to stimuli varying within a single dimension. *Psychological Review*, 44:430–444. (3:76; 9:51)

Spence, K. W. 1937b. Experimental studies of learning and the higher mental processes in infrahuman primates. *Psychological Bulletin*, 34:806–850. (3:76; 6:53; 8:15)

Spence, K. W. 1938. Gradual versus sudden solution of discrimination problems by chimpanzees. *Journal of Comparative Psychology*, 25:213–224. (8:15)

Spence, K. W. 1940. Continuous versus non-continuous interpretations of discrimination learning. *Psychological Review*, 47:271–288. (8:15; 10:15)

Spence, K. W. 1941a. Köhler's *Dynamics in Psychology* (a review). *Psychological Bulletin*, 38:886–889. (4:63; 9:36)

Spence, K. W. 1941b. Failure of transposition in size discrimination of chimpanzees. *American Journal of Psychology*, 54:223–229. (3:76)

Spence, K. W. 1944. The nature of theory construction in contemporary psychology. *Psychological Review*, 51:47–68. (4:3, 46; 5:2, 4, 13; 6:48; 9:15, 16)

Spence, K. W. 1945. An experimental test of the continuity and non-continuity theories of discrimination learning. *Journal of Experimental Psychology*, 35:253–266. (9:51; 10:15)

Spence, K. W. 1947. The role of secondary reinforcement in delayed reward learning. *Psychological Review*, 54:1–8. (3:7; 4:63; 5:4)

Spence, K. W. 1948. The postulates and methods of "behaviorism." *Psychological Review*, 55:67–78. (1:2; 2:15, 36; 3:69; 5:2, 4, 13; 6:46; 11:27; 12:19, 32) [pp. 233]

Spence, K. W. 1950. Cognitive versus stimulus-response theories of learning. *Psychological Review*, 57:159–172. (5:4; 6:60, 61, 62; 8:48; 9:51, 53; 10:24)

Spence, K. W. 1951. Theoretical interpretations of learning. In S. S. Stevens, ed. *Handbook of Experimental Psychology*, 690–729. New York: Wiley. (4:70; 5:4; 6:50, 61; 8:15, 22, 48; 9:36; 10:54)

Spence, K. W. 1952a. Clark Leonard Hull: 1884–1952. *American Journal of Psychology*, 65:639–646. (5:18)

Spence, K. W. 1952b. The nature of the response in discrimination learning. *Psychological Review*, 59:89–93. (3:76; 9:51)

Spence, K. W. 1952c. Mathematical formulations of learning phenomena. *Psychological Review*, 59:152–160. (4:49; 5:13, 18)

Spence, K. W. 1953. Mathematical theories of learning. *Journal of General Psychology*, 49:283–291. (5:13, 18; 6:50, 61)

Spence, K. W. 1954. Current interpretations of learning data and some recent developments in stimulus-response theory. In *Learning Theory, Personality Theory, and Clinical Research: The Kentucky Symposium*, 1–21. New York: Wiley. (5:18)

Spence, K. W. 1956. *Behavior Theory and Conditioning*. New Haven: Yale University Press. (2:35, 36; 3:31, 36, 59, 69; 4:49, 71, 74; 5:13, 16, 18, 32; 6:22, 23; 9:31, 51; 10:76; 11:27; 12:32) [p. 233]

Spence, K. W. 1957. The empirical basis and theoretical structure of psychology. *Philosophy of Science*, 24:97–108. (2:1, 35, 36; 4:46, 47; 5:2, 4, 13) [p. 22]

Spence, K. W. 1958. A theory of emotionally based drive (D) and its relation to performance in simple learning situations. *American Psychologist*, 13:131–141. (10:76)

Spence, K. W. 1959. The relation of learning theory to the technology of education. *Harvard Educational Review*, 29:84–95. (6:19, 23)

Spence, K. W. 1960a. *Behavior Theory and Learning*. Englewood Cliffs, N.J.: Prentice-Hall. (5:16)

Spence, K. W. 1960b. The roles of reinforcement and non-reinforcement in simple learning. In Spence (1960a): 91–112. (3:69)

Spence, K. W. 1960c. Conceptual models of spatial and non-spatial selective learning. In Spence (1960a): 366–392. (3:82; 7:23; 9:51)

Spence, K. W. 1964. Anxiety (drive) level and performance in eyelid conditioning. *Psychological Bulletin*, 61:129–139. (10:76)

Spence, K. W. 1966. Cognitive and drive factors in the extinction of the conditioned eye blink in human subjects. *Psychological Review*, 73:445–458. (11:37)

Spence, K. W., G. Bergmann and R. Lippitt 1950. A study of simple learning under irrelevant motivational-reward conditions. *Journal of Experimental Psychology*, 40:539–551. (7:19; 8:18)

Spence, K. W. and R. Lippitt 1946. An experimental test of the sign-gestalt theory of trial and error learning. *Journal of Experimental Psychology*, 36:491–502. (6:53, 72; 8:16)

Spence, K. W. and L. E. Ross 1959. A methodological study of the form and latency of eyelid responses in conditioning. *Journal of Experimental Psychology*, 58:376–381. (3:73; 4:21)

Sperry, R. W. 1969. A modified concept of consciousness. *Psychological Review*, 76:532–536. (9:19)

Spielberger, C. D. 1962. The role of awareness in verbal conditioning. In C. W. Eriksen, ed. *Behavior and Awareness*, 73–101. Durham: Duke University Press. (9:54; 10:15)

Spielberger, C. D. and L. D. DeNike 1966. Descriptive behaviorism versus cognitive theory in verbal operant conditioning. *Psychological Review*, 73:303–326. (1:3; 9:55; 10:15)

Staats, A. W. 1961. Verbal habit-families, concepts, and the operant conditioning of word classes. *Psychological Review*, 68:190–204. (6:22; 7:46)

Staats, A. W. 1968. *Learning, Language, and Cognition*. New York: Holt, Rinehart and Winston. (3:36; 6:22; 7:17, 22, 46, 62; 8:23, 51; 9:51, 70; 10:80; 11:19, 21)

Staats, A. W. 1971. Linguistic-mentalistic theory versus an explanatory S-R learning theory of language development. In D. I. Slobin, ed. *The Ontogenesis of Grammar: A Theoretical Symposium*, 103–150. New York: Academic. (7:42, 62; 9:14)

Staats, A. W. and C. K. Staats 1964. *Complex Human Behavior: A Systematic Extension of Learning Principles*. New York: Holt, Rinehart and Winston. (2:22; 4:24, 43, 70, 78; 5:45; 8:15, 28; 11:19; 12:13, 15)

Staddon, J. E. R. 1967. Asymptotic behavior: The concept of the operant. *Psychological Review*, 74:377–391. (3:73, 77; 7:75; 10:68)

Staddon, J. E. R. 1971. Darwin explained: An object lesson in theory construction. *Contemporary Psychology*, 16:689–691. (4:22; 5:42)

Staddon, J. E. R. and S. Motheral 1978. On matching and maximizing in operant choice experiments. *Psychological Review*, 85:436–444. (6:31)

Stenius, E. 1969. Beginning with ordinary things. In D. Davidson and J. Hintikka, eds. *Words and Objections: Essays on the Work of W. V. Quine*, 27–52. Dordrecht, Holland: D. Reidel. (3:35)

Stephenson, W. 1953. Postulates of behaviorism. *Philosophy of Science*, 20:110–120. (11:35)

Stevens, S. S. 1935a. The operational basis of psychology. *American Journal of Psychology*, 47:323–330. (2:35; 4:6; 5:63; 11:8)

Stevens, S. S. 1935b. The operational definition of psychological concepts. *Psychological Review*, 42:517–527. (2:35; 4:6; 11:8) [p. 228]

Stevens, S. S. 1939. Psychology and the science of science. *Psychological Bulletin*, 36:221–263. (2:35; 4:6, 16, 18, 22; 10:11; 11:8; 12:14) [p. 58]

Stevens, S. S. 1970. Neural events and the psychophysical law. *Science*, 170:1043–1050. (11:59)

Stevens, S. S. 1971a. Issues in psychophysical measurement. *Psychological Review*, 75:426–450. (11:8, 57)

Stevens, S. S. 1971b. Sensory power functions and neural events. In W. R. Lowenstein, ed. *Handbook of Sensory Physiology*, 1:226–242. New York: Springer-Verlag. (11:59)

Stich, S. P. 1971. What every speaker knows. *Philosophical Review*, 80:476–496. (7:56, 80)

Stich, S. P. 1972. Grammar, psychology, and indeterminacy. *Journal of Philosophy*, 69:799–818. (7:60, 62)

Stogdill, R. M. 1934. Neurosis as learned behavior. *Psychological Review*, 41:497–507. (10:50)

Stoyva, J. and J. Kamiya 1968. Electrophysiological studies of dreaming as the prototype of a new strategy in the study of consciousness. *Psychological Review*, 75:192–205. (11:7)

Straub, R. O., M. S. Seidenberg, T. G. Bever and H. S. Terrace 1979. Serial learning in the pigeon. *Journal of the Experimental Analysis of Behavior*, 32:137–148. (7:42)

Strawson, P. F. 1958. Persons. In H. Feigl, et al., eds. *Concepts, Theories, and the Mind-Body Problem. Minnesota Studies in the Philosophy of Science*, 2:330–353. Minneapolis: University of Minnesota Press. (9:76; 10:28)

Suppe, F. 1974. The search for philosophic understanding of scientific theories. In F. Suppe, ed. *The Structure of Scientific Theories*, 3–241. Urbana: University of Illinois Press. (3:26; 4:9, 10, 12, 15, 16, 55; 5:49, 54, 60; 12:57)

Suppes, P. 1969a. Stimulus-response theory of finite automata. *Journal of Mathematical Psychology*, 6:327–355. (4:4, 69; 8:48)

Suppes, P. 1969b. Stimulus-response theory of automata and TOTE hierarchies: A reply to Arbib. *Psychological Review*, 76:511–514. (4:69; 8:48)

Suppes, P. 1969c. Behaviorism. In *Studies in the Methodology and Foundations of Science: Selected Papers from 1951–1969*, 294–311. Dordrecht, Holland: D. Reidel. (1:7; 3:52; 9:77, 82; 10:34)

Suppes, P. 1975. From behaviorism to neobehaviorism. *Theory and Decision*, 6:269–285. (4:4, 69; 8:48; 9:59)

Sutherland, N. S. and N. J. Mackintosh 1971. *Mechanisms of Animal Discrimination Learning*. New York: Academic. (9:49)

Tait, W. D. 1932. Behaviorism in science. *Science*, 75:462–463. (1:16)

Tawney, G. A. 1915. What is behavior? *Journal of Philosophy, Psychology, and Scientific Methods*, 12:29–32. (6:34)

Taylor, C. 1964. *The Explanation of Behaviour*. London: Routledge and Kegan Paul. (3:49, 51, 53, 56; 4:7, 12, 59; 7:7, 14; 9:83; 10:32)

Taylor, C. 1970. The explanation of purposive behaviour. In R. Borger and F. Cioffi, eds. *Explanation in the Behavioural Sciences*, 49–79. Cambridge: Cambridge University Press. (3:56, 68; 7:3, 14; 9:41, 83; 10:32)

Taylor, J. G. 1962. *The Behavioral Basis of Perception*. New Haven: Yale University Press. (10:17)

Taylor, R. 1966. *Action and Purpose*. Englewood Cliffs, N.J.: Prentice-Hall. (3:46; 9:1)

Teitelbaum, P. 1964. "Appetite." *Proceedings of the American Philosophical Society*, 108:464–472. (6:25)

Teitelbaum, P. 1977. Levels of integration of the operant. In W. K. Honig and J. E. R. Staddon, eds. *Handbook of Operant Behavior*, 7–27. Englewood Cliffs, N.J.: Prentice-Hall. (3:7; 5:41)

Thistlethwaite, D. 1951. A critical review of latent learning and related experiments. *Psychological Bulletin*, 48:97–129. (6:65)

Thomson, G. H. 1920. Is thinking merely the action of language mechanisms? II. *British Journal of Psychology*, 11:63–70. (2:18)

Thorndike, E. L. 1913. *The Psychology of Learning: Educational Psychology*, Vol. 2. New York: Teacher's College Press, Columbia University. (3:37)

Thorndike, E. L. 1915. Watson's "Behavior." *Journal of Animal Behavior*, 5:462–467. (2:22; 9:22; 11:27)

Thorndike, E. L. 1932. *The Fundamentals of Learning*. New York: Teacher's College Press, Columbia University. (4:3; 6:6, 66; 7:15; 8:12; 9:2, 50)

Thorndike, E. L. 1946. Expectation. *Psychological Review*, 53:277–281. (6:72; 9:58)

Thorndike, E. L. 1949. *Selected Writings from a Connectionist's Psychology*. New York: Appleton-Century-Crofts. (3:77; 6:33; 7:64; 8:10; 9:50; 12:4) [p. 188]

Thurstone, L. L. 1923. The stimulus-response fallacy in psychology. *Psychological Review*, 30:354–369. (7:2; 9:80)

Tighe, L. S. and T. J. Tighe 1966. Discrimination learning: Two views in historical perspective. *Psychological Bulletin*, 66:353–370. (3:73; 9:53)

Titchener, E. B. 1895. The type theory of simple reaction. *Mind*, 4(ns):506–514. (2:30)

Titchener, E. B. 1912. The schema of introspection. *American Journal of Psychology*, 23:485–508. [p. 226]

Titchener, E. B. 1914. On "Psychology as the behaviorist views it." *Proceedings of the American Philosophical Society*, 53:1–17. (2:18; 9:26; 11:27)

Titchener, E. B. 1929. *Systematic Psychology: Prolegomena*. New York: Macmillan. (2:20)

Tolman, E. C. 1920. Instinct and purpose. *Psychological Review*, 27:217–233. (4:3; 7:15)

Tolman, E. C. 1922a. A new formula for behaviorism. *Psychological Review*, 29:44–53. (3:7; 10:26; 11:65) [p. 272]

Tolman, E. C. 1922b. Concerning the sensation quality—A behavioristic account. *Psychological Review*, 29:140–145. (4:5; 10:24; 11:65; 12:44)

Tolman, E. C. 1923. A behavioristic account of the emotions. *Psychological Review*, 30:217–227. (2:47; 4:5; 10:26; 11:65)

Tolman, E. C. 1925a. Behaviorism and purpose. *Journal of Philosophy*, 22:36–41. (3:63; 7:2, 14; 10:24)

Tolman, E. C. 1925b. Purpose and cognition: The determiners of animal learning. *Psychological Review*, 32:285–297. (3:14, 57; 7:14; 10:24)

Tolman, E. C. 1926a. The nature of the fundamental drives. *Journal of Abnormal and Social Psychology*, 20:349–358. (3:57; 4:5)

Tolman, E. C. 1926b. A behaviorist theory of ideas. *Psychological Review*, 33:352–369. (3:57, 63, 77; 7:15; 10:24)

Tolman, E. C. 1927a. A behaviorist's definition of consciousness. *Psychological Review*, 34:433–439. (4:70; 8:22)

Tolman, E. C. 1927b. Habit formation and higher mental processes in animals. *Psychological Bulletin*, 24:1–35. (3:57; 7:2)

Tolman, E. C. 1928a. Habit formation and higher mental processes in animals. *Psychological Bulletin*, 25:24–53. (8:22)

Tolman, E. C. 1928b. Purposive behavior. *Psychological Review*, 35:524–530. (3:68; 4:25; 7:15)

Tolman, E. C. 1932. *Purposive Behavior in Animals and Men*. New York: Century. (2:25; 3:7, 63, 64, 67, 69; 4:25, 33, 63, 70; 7:14, 55; 8:3, 22; 10:16, 26, 50; 11:24, 25, 65; 12:26, 44) [pp. 45, 46, 188, 207, 259, 272, 277]

Tolman, E. C. 1933. Gestalt and sign gestalt. *Psychological Review*, 40:391–411. (3:57; 4:50; 10:33; 11:65)

Tolman, E. C. 1935. Psychology vs. immediate experience. *Philosophy of Science*, 2:356–380. (2:25, 35, 69; 4:25, 33; 8:4; 10:16, 33; 11:61; 12:10, 32, 44) [pp. 22, 259]

Tolman, E. C. 1936. Operational behaviorism and current trends in psychology. In H. W. Hill, ed. *Proceedings of the Twenty-Fifth Anniversay Celebration of the Inauguration of Graduate Studies, the University of Southern California*, 89–103. Los Angeles: University of Southern California. (3:7, 15; 4:25, 27; 10:16; 11:31; 12:11, 12)

Tolman, E. C. 1937. Demands and conflicts. *Psychological Review*, 44:158–169. (3:58; 4:27, 50, 68; 8:4; 10:16)

Tolman, E. C. 1938a. The determiners of behavior at a choice point. *Psychological Review*, 45:1–41. (4:27, 46, 50; 9:15; 11:37) [p. 63]

Tolman, E. C. 1938b. A reply to Professor Guthrie. *Psychological Review*, 45:163–164. (6:50)

Tolman, E. C. 1938c. The law of effect. *Psychological Review*, 45:200–203. (6:50)

Tolman, E. C. 1938d. Physiology, psychology, and sociology. *Psychological Review*, 45:228–241. (3:3; 4:25, 62; 7:15, 46)

Tolman, E. C. 1939. Prediction of vicarious trial and error by means of schematic sowbug. *Psychological Review*, 46:318–336. (4:50; 7:23)

Tolman, E. C. 1941a. Psychological man. *Journal of Social Psychology*, 13:205–218. (10:50)

Tolman, E. C. 1941b. Discrimination vs. learning and the schematic sowbug. *Psychological Review*, 48:367–382. (4:50)

Tolman, E. C. 1942. *Drives Toward War*. New York: Appleton-Century. (10:50)

Tolman, E. C. 1948. Cognitive maps in rats and men. *Psychological Review*, 55:189–208. (6:44, 54, 61; 9:49, 80; 12:10) [p. 112]

Tolman, E. C. 1949a. There is more than one kind of learning. *Psychological Review*, 56:144–155. (5:56; 7:2; 9:48)

Tolman, E. C. 1949b. The nature and functioning of wants. *Psychological Review*, 56:357–369. (4:50; 10:33; 12:26)

Tolman, E. C. 1950. Discussion. In J. S. Bruner and D. Krech, eds. *Perception and Personality*, 48–50. Durham: Duke University Press. (4:67; 5:61)

Tolman, E. C. 1951. A psychological model. In T. Parsons and A. Shils, eds. *Toward a Theory of Action*, 277–361. Cambridge: Harvard University Press. (3:36, 58; 5:61; 8:22; 9:48; 11:46)

Tolman, E. C. 1952a. A cognition motivation model. *Psychological Review*, 59:389–400. (4:50)

Tolman, E. C. 1952b. Edward Chase Tolman. In C. Murchison, ed. *History of Psychology in Autobiography*, 4:323–339. Worcester, Mass.: Clark University Press. (4:66; 5:61; 6:50; 9:48)

Tolman, E. C. 1955a. Performance vectors and the unconscious. *Acta Psychologica*, 11:31–40. (4:50)

Tolman, E. C. 1955b. Principles of performance. *Psychological Review*, 62:315–326. (3:82; 4:50; 6:50, 51)

Tolman, E. C. 1959. Principles of purposive behavior. In S. Koch, ed. *Psychology: A Study of a Science*. Vol. 2. *General Systematic Formulations, Learning and Special Processes*, 92–157. New York: McGraw-Hill. (3:7, 36, 58; 4:47, 53; 5:61; 6:50; 7:23; 9:51; 10:16; 11:37, 61)

Tolman, E. C. and E. Brunswik 1935. The organism and the causal texture of the environment. *Psychological Review*, 42:43–77. (3:80)

Tolman, E. C. and H. Gleitman 1949. Studies in spatial learning, VII. Place and response learning under different degrees of motivation. *Journal of Experimental Psychology*, 39:653–659. (3:82)

Tolman, E. C. and J. Horowitz 1933. A reply to Mr. Koffka. *Psychological Bulletin*, 30:459–465. (2:25; 3:7, 64; 4:63; 10:16; 11:65)

Tolman, E. C. and I. Krechevsky 1933. Means-end-readiness and hypothesis: A contribution to comparative psychology. *Psychological Review*, 40:60–70. (4:32; 9:49)

Tolman, E. C., B. F. Ritchie and D. Kalish 1946a. Studies in spatial learning, I. Orientation and the short cut. *Journal of Experimental Psychology*, 36:13–24. (3:82; 4:12, 31; 6:65; 10:8)

Tolman, E. C., B. F. Ritchie and D. Kalish 1946b. Studies in spatial learning, II. Place learning vs. response learning. *Journal of Experimental Psychology*, 36:221–229. (3:82)

Tolman, E. C., B. F. Ritchie and D. Kalish 1947a. Studies in spatial learning, IV. The transfer of place learning to other starting paths. *Journal of Experimental Psychology*, 37:39–47. (3:82)

Tolman, E. C., B. F. Ritchie and D. Kalish 1947b. Studies in spatial learning, V. Response learning vs. place learning by the non-correction method. *Journal of Experimental Psychology*, 37:285–292. (3:82)

Toulmin, S. 1969. Concepts and the explanation of human behavior. In. T. Mischel, ed. *Human Action: Conceptual and Empirical Issues*, 71–104. New York: Academic. (3:46; 9:77)

Toulmin, S. 1970. Reasons and causes. In R. Borger and F. Cioffi, eds. *Explanation in the Behavioural Sciences*, 1–26, 42–48. Cambridge: Cambridge University Press. (9:76)

Treisman, M. 1962. Psychological explanation: The "private data" hypothesis. *British Journal for the Philosophy of Science*, 13:130–143. (2:24, 25, 41; 10:2; 11:56, 60)

Treisman, M. 1964a. Sensory scaling and the psychophysical law. *Quarterly Journal of Experimental Psychology*, 16:11–22. (11:56, 60)

Treisman, M. 1964b. What do sensory scales measure? *Quarterly Journal of Experimental Psychology*, 16:387–391. (11:56, 60)

Tuomela, R. 1971. The role of theoretical concepts in neobehavioristic theories. *Reports from the Institute of Philosophy, University of Helsinki*, No. 1. (3:74; 4:12, 47, 66, 69, 73; 6:6)

Tuomela, R. 1973. *Theoretical Concepts*. New York: Springer-Verlag. (3:26; 4:66, 67, 69)

Tuomela, R. 1977. *Human Action and its Explanation: A Study of the Philosophical Foundations of Psychology*. Dordrecht, Holland: D. Reidel. (3:39; 4:51, 73)

Turner, M. B. 1967. *Philosophy and the Science of Behavior*. New York: Appleton-Century-Crofts. (1:14, 17; 2:4, 41; 3:26; 4:2, 24, 53, 62, 64, 67; 5:2, 64; 8:47; 10:34)

Turner, M. B. 1971. *Realism and the Explanation of Behavior*. New York: Appleton-Century-Crofts. (1:4; 3:26; 4:64, 67; 7:14; 8:47; 9:36; 10:34, 35)

Ullman, S. 1980. Against direct perception. *The Behavioral and Brain Sciences*, 3:373–415. (8:40, 46)

Ullmann, L. P. 1970. On cognitions and behavior therapy. *Behavior Therapy*, 1:201–204. (8:17, 50; 10:80; 12:38)

Ullmann, L. P. and L. Krasner, eds. 1965. *Case Studies in Behavior Modification*. Introduction. 1–63. New York: Holt Rinehart and Winston. (4:24; 7:35; 10:69)

Varvel, W. A. 1934. A gestalt critique of purposive behaviorism. *Psychological Review*, 41:381–399. (3:65)

Vaughan, W. 1981. Melioration, matching, and maximization. *Journal of the Experimental Analysis of Behavior*, 36:141–149. (6:31)

Verplanck, W. S. 1954. Burrhus F. Skinner. In W. K. Estes, et al., eds. *Modern Learning Theory*, 267–316. New York: Appleton-Century-Crofts. (3:42, 62, 73; 4:55; 5:19, 42, 66; 10:65, 67; 12:50)

Verplanck. W. S. 1962. Unaware of where's awareness: Some verbal operants—Notates, monents, and notants. In C. W. Eriksen, ed. *Behavior and Awareness*, 130–158. Durham: Duke University Press. (9:54; 10:2; 11:11, 31)

Voeks, V. W. 1950. Formalization and clarification of a theory of learning. *Journal of Psychology*, 30:341–362. (3:31; 5:59)

von Mises, R. 1951. *Positivism: A Study in Human Understanding*. Cambridge: Harvard University Press. (12:33)

Wachtel, P. L. 1977. *Psychoanalysis and Behavior Therapy*. New York: Basic. (10:52)

Walker, K. F. 1942. The nature and explanation of behavior. *Psychological Review*, 49:569–585. (3:70)

Wallis, W. D. 1924. Does behaviorism imply mechanism? *American Journal of Psychology*, 35:387–395. (3:63, 71; 9:17, 32; 10:24)

Warren, H . C. 1916. A study of purpose. I, II, III. *Journal of Philosophy, Psychology, and Scientific Methods*, 13:5–26, 29–48, 57–72. (9:6, 36)

Warren, H . C. 1921. Psychology and the central nervous system. *Psychological Review*, 28:249–269. (8:25; 10:39)

Warren, H . C. 1923a. Neurology: Mystical and magical. *Psychological Bulletin*, 20:438–443. (3:12)

Warren, H. C. 1923b. Reply to Dr. Kantor. *Psychological Bulletin*, 20:693–694. (3:12; 9:33)

Warren, H. C. 1925. Mechanism and teleology in psychology. *Psychological Review*, 32:266–284. (9:33)

Warren, R. M. 1981. Measurement of sensory intensity. *The Behavioral and Brain Sciences*, 4:175–223. (11:58, 59)

Washburn, M. F. 1914. The function of incipient motor processes. *Psychological Review*, 21:376–390. (9:52)

Washburn, M. F. 1919. "Dualism in animal psychology." *Journal of Philosophy, Psychology, and Scientific Methods*, 16:41–44. (10:29)

Washburn, M. F. 1922. Introspection as an objective method. *Psychological Review*, 29:89–112. (2:27)

Wasserman, E. A. 1981. Comparative psychology returns: A review of Hulse, Fowler, and Honig's *Cognitive Processes in Animal Behavior*. *Journal of the Experimental Analysis of Behavior*, 35:243–257. (2:1; 3:82; 4:29, 37, 39; 6:50; 8:4)

Wasserman, E. A. 1982. Further remarks on the role of cognition in the comparative analysis of behavior. *Journal of the Experimental Analysis of Behavior*, 38:211–216. (4:29, 37, 39)

Waters, R. H. and L. A. Pennington 1938. Operationism in psychology. *Psychological Review*, 45:414–423. (2:8; 4:14, 15, 59)

Waters, W. F. and R. N. McCallum 1973. The basis of behavior therapy, mentalistic or behavioristic? A reply to E. A. Locke. *Behaviour Research and Therapy*, 11:157–163. (1:15; 4:70; 8:8; 9:69; 10:12, 24; 11:27, 35; 12:19)

Watson, J. B. 1913a. Psychology as the behaviorist views it. *Psychological Review*, 20:158–177. (2:7, 13, 35; 3:14; 6:7; 8:23; 9:18, 22; 11:32, 43) [pp. 8, 268]

Watson, J. B. 1913b. Image and affection in behavior. *Journal of Philosophy, Psychology, and Scientific Methods*, 10:421–428. (4:70; 8:23; 9:18, 22, 27; 10:76)

Watson, J. B. 1914. *Behavior: An Introduction to Comparative Psychology*. New York: Holt. (3:14, 15; 4:70; 6:8, 12; 8:23; 9:19, 25, 26; 10:76; 11:19, 21)

Watson, J. B. 1916a. The place of the conditioned-reflex in psychology. *Psychological Review*, 23:89–116. (6:11)

Watson, J. B. 1916b. Behavior and the concept of mental disease. *Journal of Philosophy, Psychology, and Scientific Methods*, 13:589–597. (10:50; 11:43)

Watson, J. B. 1917a. An attempted formulation of the scope of behavior psychology. *Psychological Review*, 24:329–352. (3:3, 7, 31, 69; 4:70; 6:7, 9; 8:23)

Watson, J. B. 1917b. Does Holt follow Freud? *Journal of Philosophy, Psychology, and Scientific Methods*, 14:85–92. (6:15)

Watson, J. B. 1919. A shematic outline of the emotions. *Psychological Review*, 26:165–196. (4:70; 10:76)

Watson, J. B. 1920. Is thinking merely the action of the language mechanism? V. *British Journal of Psychology*, 11:87–104. (4:70; 8:23; 10:2; 11:35)

Watson, J. B. 1924a. *Psychology from the Standpoint of a Behaviorist* (2d ed). Philadelphia: J. B. Lippincott. (2:7, 13, 24; 3:7, 72; 4:78; 6:16, 20; 7:22; 8:23; 9:2, 19, 26; 10:49, 76;11:21,27,35,43)

Watson, J. B. 1924b. The unverbalized in human behavior. *Psychological Review*, 31:273–280. (9:70; 10:50; 11:15, 25)

Watson, J. B. 1924c. The place of kinaesthetic, visceral, and laryngeal organization in thinking. *Psychological Review*, 31:339–347. (4:70; 6:9, 12; 8:23; 10:76)

Watson, J. B. 1926. Behaviorism: A psychology based on reflex-action. *Journal of Philosophical Studies*, 1:454–466. (6:9; 8:23; 11:15)

Watson, J. B. 1928. *The Ways of Behaviorism*. New York: Harper. (8:23; 9:70; 10:76; 11:15)

Watson, J. B. 1930. *Behaviorism* (rev. ed.). New York: Norton. (1:2; 3:7; 4:70; 6:7, 14; 8:23; 9:19, 25, 27, 50; 10:26; 11:15, 25)

Watson, J. B. 1936. John Broadus Watson. In C. Murchison, ed. *History of Psychology in Autobiography*, 3:271–281. Worcester, Mass.: Clark University Press. (10:50)

Watson, J. B. and W. McDougall 1928. *The Battle of Behaviorism*. London: Kegan, Paul, Trench, Truber. (11:42)

Watson, R. I. 1967. Psychology: A prescriptive science. *American Psychologist*, 22:435–443. (1:4)

Weber, C. O. 1942. Valid and invalid conceptions of operationism in psychology. *Psychological Review*, 49:54–68. (1:14; 2:16; 4:14, 16)

Weber, P. H. 1920. Behaviorism and indirect responses. *Journal of Philosophy, Psychology, and Scientific Methods*, 17:663–667. (8:25; 9:22)

Weimer, W. B. 1976. Manifestations of mind: Some conceptual and empirical issues. In G. G. Globus, et al., ed. *Consciousness and the Brain: A Scientific and Philosophical inquiry*, 5–31. New York: Plenum. (3:39; 11:63, 64)

Weiss, A. P. 1917a. Relation between structural and behavior psychology. *Psychological Review*, 24:301–317. (2:25; 10:24; 11:26)

Weiss, A. P. 1917b. Relation between functional and behavior psychology. *Psychological Review*, 24:353–368. (2:25; 3:72; 11:26, 32)

Weiss, A. P. 1918. Conscious behavior. *Journal of Philosophy, Psychology, and Scientific Methods*, 15:631–641. (2:23; 8:23; 10:2, 83; 11:21, 26; 12:17)

Weiss, A. P. 1919a. The mind and the man-within. *Psychological Review*, 26:327–334. (9:7)

Weiss, A. P. 1919b. The relation between physiological psychology and behavior psychology. *Journal of Philosophy, Psychology, and Scientific Methods*, 16:626–634. (3:7, 12; 11:47)

Weiss, A. P. 1922. Behavior and the central nervous system. *Psychological Review*, 29:329–343. (3:61; 8:30; 9:27)

Weiss, A. P. 1924a. Behaviorism and behavior, I. *Psychological Review*, 31:32–50. (3:40, 41, 61; 6:24; 12:43)

Weiss, A. P. 1924b. Behaviorism and behavior, II. *Psychological Review*, 31:118–149. (3:12, 19, 34, 61, 76; 4:70; 8:30; 9:17, 26, 27, 67; 10:54, 83; 11:21, 32, 63; 12:43)

Weiss, A. P. 1925a. One set of postulates for a behaviorist psychology. *Psychological Review*, 32:83–87. (2:7, 36; 9:61; 12:43)

Weiss, A. P. 1925b. Purposive striving as a fundamental category of psychology. *Psychological Review*, 32:171–177. (3:34; 7:5, 9; 7:12, 30; 10:54)

Weiss, A. P. 1928a. Feeling and emotion as forms of behavior. In M. L. Reymert, ed. *Feelings and Emotions: The Wittenberg Symposium*, 170–190. Worcester, Mass.: Clark University Press. (1:12; 2:11; 3:34; 9:50; 11:32)

Weiss, A. P. 1928b. Behaviorism and ethics. *Journal of Abnormal and Social Psychology*, 22:388–397. (7:9; 9:41, 43)

Weiss, A. P. 1929a. *A Theoretical Basis of Human Behavior* (rev. ed.). Columbus, OH: R. G. Adams. (1:16; 2:13, 17, 24, 36; 3:19, 34, 40, 61, 76; 4:70; 7:5, 22; 8:30; 9:2, 3, 19, 26, 61, 66, 67, 70; 10:76; 11:9, 12, 16, 21, 26, 32, 63, 66; 12:35, 43) [pp. 202, 217]

Weiss, A. P. 1929b. Some succor for Professor Kuo. *Psychological Review*, 36:254–255. (2:36; 3:66; 7:5)

Weiss, A. P. 1930. The biosocial standpoint in psychology. In C. Murchison, ed. *Psychologies of 1930*, 301–306. Worcester, Mass.: Clark University Press. (1:12; 3:34, 61; 10:2)

Weiss, A. P. 1931. Solipsism in psychology. *Psychological Review*, 38:474–486. (9:43; 12:51, 52)

Weitzman, B. 1967. Behavior therapy and psychotherapy. *Psychological Review*, 74:300–317. (10:68)

Wells, W. R. 1919. Behaviorism and the definition of words. *Monist*, 29:133–140. (3:78)

Wessells, M. G. 1981. A critique of Skinner's views on the explanatory inadequacy of cognitive theories. *Behaviorism*, 9:153–170. (4:37, 68; 8:50)

Wessells, M. G. 1982. A critique of Skinner's views on the obstructive character of cognitive theories. *Behaviorism*, 10:65–84. (4:37, 68; 8:50)

Wheeler, R. H. 1923. Introspection and behavior. *Psychological Review*, 30:103–115. (2:29, 40)

Wheeler, R. H. 1925. Persistent problems in systematic psychology I. A philosophical heritage. *Psychological Review*, 32:179–191. (2:20)

Wheeler, R. H. 1940. *The Science of Psychology*. New York: Crowell. (6:44; 9:40)

White, A. R. 1967. *The Philosophy of Mind*. New York: Random House. (8:2, 30, 31)

Whitehurst, G. J. 1978. Observational learning. A. C. Catania and T. A. Brigham, eds. *Handbook of Applied Behavior Analysis: Social and Instructional Processes*, 142–178. New York: Irvington. (6:58, 69)

Whiteley, C. H. 1961. Behaviourism. *Mind*, 70:164–174. (1:13; 2:28, 29)

Wiest, W. M. 1967. Some recent criticisms of behaviorism and learning theory with special reference to Breger and McGaugh and to Chomsky. *Psychological Bulletin*, 67:214–225. (7:36, 57, 67, 73; 8:51; 10:68, 69)

Wilcoxon, H. C. 1969. Historical introduction to the problem of reinforcement. In J. T. Tapp, ed. *Reinforcement and Behavior*, 1–46. New York: Academic. (6:1, 25; 9:47)

Wilkins, W. 1971. Desensitization: Social and cognitive factors underlying the effectiveness of Wolpe's procedure. *Psychological Bulletin*, 76:311–317. (8:7; 10:69)

Wilkins, W. 1972. Desensitization: Getting it together with Davison and Wilson. *Psychological Bulletin*, 78:32–36. (8:7; 10:69)

Williams, D. C. 1934. Scientific method and the existence of consciousness. *Psychological Review*, 41:461–479. (2:3, 17; 10:25; 12:50)

Williams, K. A. 1931. Five behaviorisms. *American Journal of Psychology*, 43:337–360. (1:5; 11:1)

Willis, J. and D. Giles 1978. Behaviorism in the twentieth century: What we have here is a failure to communicate. *Behavior Therapy*, 9:15–27. (9:32)

Wilson, G. T. 1978. On the much discussed nature of the term "behavior therapy." *Behavior Therapy*, 9:89–98. (1:4)

Wimsatt, W. C. 1976. Reductionism, levels of organization, and the mind-body problem. In G. G. Globus, et al., eds. *Consciousness and the Brain: A Scientific and Philosophical Inquiry*, 205–267. New York: Plenum. (10:3)

Winokur, S. 1976. *A Primer of Verbal Behavior*. Englewood Cliffs, N.J.: Prentice-Hall. (7:48, 49)

Wittgenstein, L. 1953. *Philosophical Investigations*. Translated by G. E. M. Anscombe. New York: Macmillan. (1:9; 2:41, 44, 49; 3:22; 5:64; 9:72, 73; 10:23, 28; 11:52)

Wittgenstein, L. 1958. *The Blue and Brown Books*. New York: Harper and Row. (1:9; 5:64; 9:72) [p. 208]

Wolberg, L. R. 1970. The psychodynamic-behavioral polemic. *International Journal of Psychiatry*, 9:155–162. (10:52)

Wolf, M. M. 1978. Social validity: The case for subjective measurement or how applied behavior analysis is finding its heart. *Journal of Applied Behavior Analysis*, 11:203–214. (3:61; 10:53; 11:31)

Wolman, B. B. 1965. Toward a science of psychological science. In B. B. Wolman and E. Nagel, eds. *Scientific Psychology: Principles and Approaches*, 3–23. New York: Basic. (5:43)

Wolpe, J. 1963. Psychotherapy: The nonscientific heritage and the new science. *Behaviour Research and Therapy*, 1:23–28. (10:51)

Wolpe, J. 1969. *The Practice of Behavior Therapy*. New York: Pergamon. (3:77; 4:71)

Wolpe, J. 1971. The behavioristic conception of neurosis: A reply to two critics. *Psychological Review*, 78:341–343. (10:69)

Wolpe, J. 1976a. Behavior therapy and its malcontents, I. Denial of its bases and psychodynamic fusionism. *Journal of Behavior Therapy and Experimental Psychiatry*, 7:1–5. (10:51, 69)

Wolpe, J. 1976b. Behavior therapy and its malcontents, II. Multimodal eclecticism, cognitive exclusivism, and "exposure" empiricism. *Journal of Behavior Therapy and Experimental Psychiatry*, 7:109–116. (8:7, 8; 10:24)

Wolpe, J. 1978a. Cognition and causation in human behavior and its therapy. *American Psychologist*, 33:437–446. (1:16; 4:70; 6:67; 8:7, 8; 9:31, 43, 69, 80; 10:76, 80)

Wolpe, J. 1978b. The humanity of behavior therapy. *Journal of Behavior Therapy and Experimental Psychiatry*, 9:205–209. (9:80)

Wolpe, J. 1978c. Self-efficacy theory and psychotherapeutic change: A square peg for a round hole. *Advances in Behavior Research and Therapy*, 1:231–236. (8:7, 8)

Wolpe, J. and S. Rachman 1960. Psychoanalytic "evidence": A critique based on Freud's case of little Hans. *Journal of Nervous and Mental Diseases*, 130:135–148. (2:1)

Woodbridge, F. J. E. 1913. The belief in sensations. *Journal of Philosophy, Psychology, and Scientific Methods*, 10:599–608. (11:66)

Woodbridge, F. J. E. 1925. Behavior. *Journal of Philosophy*, 22:402–411. (7:15)

Woodfield, A. 1976. *Teleology*. Cambridge: Cambridge University Press. (3:67; 7:3, 14, 18, 24)

Woodrow, H. 1942. The problem of general quantitative laws in psychology. *Psychological Bulletin*, 39:1–27. (3:7; 4:35, 69)

Woodworth, R. S. 1924. Four varieties of behaviorism. *Psychological Review*, 31:257–264. (1:5, 7, 18; 11:42)

Woodworth, R. S. 1931. *Contemporary Schools of Psychology*. New York: Ronald. (2:3; 8:25; 9:21; 11:35)

Woolbert, C. H. 1920. A behaviorist account of sleep. *Psychological Review*, 27:420–428. (6:8; 8:9; 9:26)

Woolbert, C. H. 1924. A behavioristic account of intellect and emotions. *Psychological Review*, 31:265–272. (8:9; 10:26)

Wright, L. 1976. *Teleological Explanation: An Etiological Analysis of Goals and Functions*. Berkeley: University of California Press. (3:66, 68; 7:3, 14, 18; 9:43; 11:50)

Yates, A. J. 1958. Symptoms and symptom substitution. *Psychological Review*, 65:371–374. (10:48)

Yates, A. J. 1970. Misconceptions about behavior therapy: A point of view. *Behavior Therapy*, 1:92–107. (4:70)

Yates, A. J. 1975. *Theory and Practice in Behavior Therapy*. New York: Wiley. (10:47)

Zaner, R. M. 1967. Criticism of "Tensions in psychology between the methods of behaviorism and phenomenology." *Psychological Review*, 74:318–324. (2:17, 27, 29)

Zeiler, M. D. 1963. The ratio theory of intermediate size discrimination. *Psychological Review*, 70:516–533. (3:76)

Zener, K. 1958. The significance of experience of the individual for the science of psychology. H. Feigl, et al., eds. *Concepts, Theories, and the Mind-Body Problem. Minnesota Studies in the Philosophy of Science*, 2:354–369. Minneapolis: University of Minnesota Press. (2:29; 11:8, 62)

Ziff, P. 1962. About behaviorism. In V. C. Chappell, ed. *The Philosophy of Mind*, 147–150. Englewood Cliffs, N.J.: Prentice-Hall. (10:23; 11:40)

Zimmerman, M. 1969. Is linguistic rationalism a rational linguistics? In S. Hook, ed. *Language and Philosophy*, 198–207. New York: New York University Press. (7:48, 80)

Zuriff, G. E. 1971. Philosophy as epiphenomenon: A review of Radner and Winokur's *Analyses of Theories and Methods of Physics and Psychology. Minnesota Studies in the Philosophy of Science,* Vol. 4. *Contemporary Psychology,* 16:559–561. (5:58)

Zuriff, G. E. 1972. A behavioral interpretation of psychophysical scaling. *Behaviorism,* 1:118–133. (11:54, 56, 58)

Zuriff, G. E. 1975. Where is the agent in behavior? *Behaviorism,* 3:1–21. (3:44, 45, 47, 48, 61; 9:57, 72, 75, 77, 79, 83; 11:40)

Zuriff, G. E. 1976. Stimulus equivalence, grammar, and internal structure. *Behaviorism,* 4:43–52. (3:38, 73, 77; 7:56, 63; 8:39, 48)

Zuriff, G. E. 1979a. Covert events: The logical status of first-person reports. *Psychological Record,* 29:125–133. (2:41; 5:24; 11:27, 28, 40)

Zuriff, G. E. 1979b. Ten inner causes. *Behaviorism,* 7:1–8. (5:21; 9:10, 51, 52, 53; 11:32)

Zuriff, G. E. 1979c. The demise of behaviorism—Exaggerated rumor? A review of Mackenzie's *Behaviourism and the Limits of Scientific Method. Journal of the Experimental Analysis of Behavior,* 32:129–136. (4:29; 10:57)

Zuriff, G. E. 1980. Radical behaviorist epistemology. *Psychological Bulletin,* 87:337–350. (5:22; 11:18; 12:23, 51, 60)

Index

An index of all names cited in the Notes *is included in the* References Cited *beginning on p. 317.*

Bei Fragen zur Produktsicherheit wenden Sie sich bitte an:
If you have any questions regarding product safety,
please contact:

Walter de Gruyter GmbH
Genthiner Straße 13
10785 Berlin
productsafety@degruyterbrill.com